# The Illustrated Encyclopedia of the World's
# ROCKETS & MISSILES

# Bill Gunston
## A comprehensive technical directory and history
## of the military guided missile systems of the 20th Century

# The Illustrated Encyclopedia of the World's
# ROCKETS & MISSILES

a Salamander book

Published by
CRESCENT BOOKS
New York

# A SALAMANDER BOOK

**Library of Congress Cataloging in Publication Data**

Gunston, Bill.
    The illustrated encyclopedia of rockets and missiles.

    1. Guided missiles—Dictionaries. 2. Rockets
(Ordnance)—Dictionaries. I. Title.
UG1310.G86   1979   623.4'519   78-11174
ISBN 0-517-26870-1

Second impression 1979

This edition is published by
Crescent Books, a division of Crown
Publishers, Inc. by arrangement
with Salamander Books Ltd.
abcdefgh

Crescent Books, a division of Crown
Publishers, Inc. One Park Avenue,
New York, N.Y. 10016.

©Salamander Books Ltd. 1979
27 Old Gloucester Street,
London WC1N 3AF.

All correspondence concerning the
content of this volume should be
addressed to Salamander Books Ltd.

# CREDITS

**Editor:** Philip de Ste. Croix.
**Designer:** Nick Buzzard.

**Color and line drawings:**
Mike Badrocke, Terry Hadler and
Wilf Hardy.
© Salamander Books Ltd.
**Color fold-out artwork:**
Mike Badrocke
© Salamander Books Ltd.

**Filmset:** SX Composing Ltd.,
England.
**Color reproduction:**
Silverscan Ltd.,
Colourcraftsmen Ltd.,
Process Colour Centre and
Tenreck Ltd., England.

**Printed in Belgium:**
Henri Proost et Cie, Turnhout.

# PICTURE CREDITS

The publisher wishes to thank the following organisations and individuals who have supplied photographs for this book. Photographs have been credited by page number; for reasons of space some references have been abbreviated as follows:

British Aerospace: BA/Direction Technique des Constructions Navales: DTCN/Educational and Television Films Ltd: E and TV Films/Etablissement Cinématographique et Photographique des Armées: ECPA/General Dynamics: GD/Groupement Industrel des Armements Terrestres: GIAT/Imperial War Museum, London: IWM/McDonnell Douglas: McD/Messerschmitt-Bolkow-Blöhm: MBB/Ministry of Defence, London: MOD/Smithsonian Institution: SI/Soviet Studies Centre, Sandhurst: SSCS/US Air Force: USAF/US Army: USA/US Marine Corps: USMC/US Navy: USN

Endpapers: ECPA. 1: USA. 2–3: USAF. 4–5: Thomson-CSF/USN/Novosti. 6–7: RAE, Farnborough/IWM/Deutsches Museum, Munich/USAF. 8–9: Real Photos/Peter Grosz/ECPA/USAF. 20–21: Keystone Press/Aérospatiale. 22–23: Deutsches Museum, Munich/Oto-Melara/Kongsberg Vapenfabrikk/Matra/Saab-Scania. 24–25: Novosti. 26–27: Novosti. 28–29: Ron Pretty/Tass/SI/RAE, Farnborough. 30–31: Mark Hewish/SI. 32–33: USAF Museum/USAF. 34–35: SI/Jet Propulsion Laboratory/USAF. 36–37: USA. 38–39: USA/Mark Hewish/Vought. 40–41: Martin Marietta/Chris Foss/USA/GD. 44–45: SNIAS/CEL Photo/ECPA. 46–47: IWM. 48–49: USAF/Deutsches Museum, Munich/IWM/USN. 50–51: UPI/USAF/J. W. R. Taylor/Ken Gatland. 52–53: E and TV Films/Novosti/Associated Press. 54–55: Novosti/Flight International. 56–57: BA. 58–59: USAF/USA. 60–61: USAF/MOD. 62–63: USAF. 64–65: Martin Marietta/TRW/USAF. 66–67: USAF/TRW. 68–69: Boeing/USAF. 72–73: ECPA/SNIAS/Vosper Thornycroft/Aérospatiale. 74–75: Oto Melara/Associated Press/Israel Aircraft Industries. 76–77: Sistel/Kongsberg Vapenfabrikk/Sistel/Mark Hewish. 78–79: Saab-Scania/MOD/USN/Novosti. 80–81: USN/BA. 82–83: McD/USN. 86–87: ECPA/CEL Photo. 88–89: Keystone Press/Tass/MOD. 90–91: MOD/Grumman/USN. 92–3: MOD/USN. 94–95: USN. 96–97: GD. 100–101: Mark Hewish/BA/Aérospatiale. 102–103: MOD/Matra. 104–107: Aérospatiale/Peter

Grosz/Pilot Press. 106–107: Pilot Press. 108–109: Pilot Press(USAF/IWM. 110–111: MBB/BA/MOD/Marcel Dassault. 112–113: Sistel/Ron Pretty/Jet Propulsion. 114–115: Kongsberg Vapenfabrikk/Saab-Scania. 116–117: BA. 118–119: USAF/ SI. 120–121: SI/McD. 122–123: USN/USAF/Martin Marietta. 124–125: USN. 126–127: USN/Texas Instruments/Fairchild. 128–129: Hughes/USAF/USN. 130–131: Hughes/USN. 134–135: E and TV Films/Ron Pretty/Interinfo/Japanese Self Defence Force. 136–137: BA/MOD/USAF/McD. 138–139: USAF/Boeing. 140–141: Boeing. 142–143: GD/USAF. 146–147: SI/Thomson-CSF. 148–149: Thomson-CSF/USAF/SI/Mark Hewish. 150–151: SI. 152–153: Hughes/Boeing. 154–155: Contraves/Selenia/AB Bofors. 156–157: Mark Hewish/Contraves/Novosti/SSCS. 158–159: SSCS/SIPA Press/E and TV Films/Novosti. 160–161: SIPA Press/SSCS/USA. 162–163: SSCS/Novosti/E and TV Films. 164–165: Cossor Electronics/BA/MOD. 166–167: Flight International/MOD. 168–169: BA/MOD/Shorts. 170–171: USA. 172–173: USA/McD. 174–175: USAF/Raytheon. 176–177: USA/Ford Aerospace/GD. 178–179: USA. 182–183: Ron Pretty/DTCN/Thomson-CSF. 184–185: Deutsches Museum, Munich/GD. 186–187: Aldo Fraccaroli/Selenia/E and TV Films/USN/Novosti. 188–189: SI/USN/MOD/BA. 190–191: MOD/BA. 192–193: BA/MOD. 194–195: MOD/BA. 196–197: USN/SI/Bendix Aerospace. 198–199: USN. 200–201: USMC/USN/GD. 202–203: USN/RCA/GD. 204–205: USN/Raytheon. 208–209: Mark Hewish/Flight International/USAF. 210–211: Matra/BA. 212–213: MOD/Ron Pretty/Israel Aircraft Industries. 214–215: Mark Hewish/Ron Pretty/Saab-Scania/Selenia. 216–217: E and TV Films/Swedish Air Force/Flight International. 218–219: MOD. 220–221: Vickers (Mark Hewish)/MOD/BA/USN. 222–223: SI/USAF/McD. 224–225: Hughes/USAF. 226–227: MOD/USAF/Raytheon. 228–229: USN/GD. 230–231: MOD/BA/USN/Hughes. 232–233: Hughes/USN. 234–235: Mark Hewish/Hughes/Northrop/USAF/McD. 238–239: SI/MOD/ECPA/SNIAS. 240–241: SNIAS/GIAT/MBB/USA. 242–243: Euromissile/MBB. 244–245: Contraves/Ron Pretty/Kawasaki (Chris Foss)/J. W. R. Taylor/Swedish Army. 246–247: Novosti (Chris Foss)/Israel Sun/Novosti. 248–249: Mark Hewish/MOD/BA. 250–251: SI/USA/McD/J. W. R. Taylor. 252–253: USA/Vought Corporation/LTV Aerospace. 256–257: BA/ECPA/Kongsberg Vapenfabrikk/MOD/SI. 258–259: SI/USN/Goodyear Aerospace.

# EDITOR'S ACKNOWLEDGEMENTS

In the course of preparing this book for publication, both Bill Gunston and I have been fortunate in receiving assistance, information and pictures from a host of people and organizations. It is not possible to thank everyone individually here, but we would like to express our gratitude to all who contributed material for the book and who dealt patiently with persistent requests for information and illustrations. In particular I would like to thank Arthur Bowbeer, D. L. Brown, Jack Bruce and the staff of the RAF Museum Library, John Clemow, Aldo Fraccaroli, Chris Foss, Norman Friedman, Ken Gatland, Dennis Goode and the staff of the Main Library, RAE Farnborough, Bill Green, Peter Grosz, Mark Hewish, Philip Jarrett, Jay Miller, Dominick Pisano at the Smithsonian Institution, Ron Pretty and John W. R. Taylor.

The manufacturers of many of the weapon systems included have supplied excellent photographs of their products and I am grateful to them for their co-operation. I also received great assistance from the staffs of the picture libraries of the Ministry of Defence, London, ECPA in France and each of the US Services in Washington, and I take this opportunity of thanking them all.

Philip de Ste. Croix

# CONTENTS

# GENERAL INTRODUCTION

I believe this is the first book to include anything remotely approaching coverage of all the world's guided missiles. Inevitably there are difficulties in putting together such a work. Secrecy is responsible for a surprisingly small part of these difficulties. Admittedly I was unable to discover the span of the folding wings of one of the most important new American missiles, but this was because the manufacturer appeared not to have the figure on his engineering drawings or in the descriptive literature, and in the end I measured it on an actual missile with a ruler! To run into problems of secrecy one has to delve into matters quite outside the scope of this book.

There are, of course, areas where information is very hard to come by. The obvious example is weapons of the Soviet Union, where even hardware that has been around for 20 years is still full of annoying puzzles. Another concerns some of the early Western missiles of 26 or more years ago which at the time were protected by tight security classification and which never got into the public domain at all. In many cases all records, so far as they could be traced, were wilfully destroyed. Individuals who worked on these programmes are scattered, and often simply cannot remember the problems or the solutions. Modern offices, in manufacturers, the armed forces and research establishments, are staffed by small numbers of harassed and often overworked people who have never heard of these old weapons and have no idea where information might be stored. Even top management of several modern companies was intrigued to learn of its company's involvement in the early missile era.

But at the very start of any general treatment of missiles one has to decide what is meant by "missile". A dictionary is no help. A stone certainly qualifies, and in biblical times such missiles were instruments of judicial execution. Rocket-propelled missiles have been around for almost 1000 years, and are known to have been used in warfare in 1232. Self-propelled self-guided missiles arrived much later, and yet for various not very good reasons torpedoes are not considered to qualify for inclusion. In World War 2 the German army used baby tanks filled with explosives and guided towards Allied positions by trailing wires – a perfect example of a guided missile, and yet again not one most people would seriously consider for inclusion.

In the event there is no valid set of rules, and this book contains many weapons that occupy a grey area where there is room for argument. Honest John, one of the best-known Army

missiles, is merely a large rocket pointed at the enemy, and aimed by traditional artillery methods; so are the numerous Soviet "Frog" rockets. Durandal, a very recent air-launched weapon for cratering concrete airfield surfaces, likewise has no guidance and yet is so much more than an "iron bomb" (the derogatory term for a free-fall bomb) that it gets in. So too does Walleye, even though it has no propulsion and just falls from the launch aircraft; what it does have is pinpoint precision guidance. In recent years a new weapon has expanded the scope of the missile chronicler: the artillery shell has grown into a guided missile which can hit the target even if the gun is not pointing in quite the right direction, and these certainly qualify for inclusion. How a future edition of this book will cope with the year 2000, when guided missiles may spew from the muzzles of aircraft cannon and possibly even hand-guns is a problem we do not yet have to face.

There is another big grey area concerning

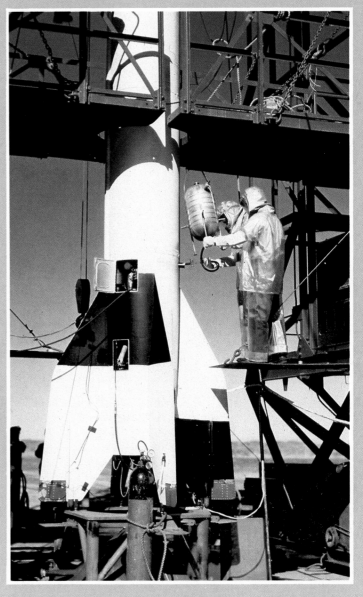

Above left: *Launch of a de Havilland Queen Bee target RPV in the 1930s. This Royal Navy radio-controlled derivative of the Tiger Moth could have led to a cruise missile.*

Left: *A German Goliath baby tank captured more or less intact in Italy in 1943. Was this wire-guided demolition device a missile?*

Top: *An aerodynamic-test A5, a scale model of A4 (V-2), before dropping from an He 111E at Karlshagen 1939.*

Above: *A Cook Skokie at Edwards AFB in 1957, one of many pure test vehicles.*

Right: *Topping up the lox in a Convair MX-774 at WSMR in 1948. This was the first gimballed-chamber vehicle.*

test vehicles. There are at least as many types of test vehicle as there are types of missile, and to the untrained eye there may not be much difference. This was a problem over 20 years ago when there were dozens of secret missile programmes, and it was difficult to sift the grain (missiles) from the chaff (test vehicles). In those days I used to prepare the annual review of missiles (the first ever published) by *Flight International*, and it often took years to discover that exciting "missiles" were in fact not missiles at all but programmes undertaken to solve problems. Today this difficulty hardly arises; Soviet test vehicles are not known at all, while the rest are on the public record as such.

A further important question to be covered here is the way the book is structured. Obviously there are points for and against each arrangement. We naturally gave the matter much thought and decided to divide the content into chapters by function, instead of treating missiles in rigid alphabetical order throughout,

or country by country, or in chronological order. Choosing the chapter titles was less simple than it appears. Some would argue for a separate section on anti-ship missiles, because today a large group of missiles have guidance systems tailored to this role alone, and almost useless for any other. But this would have raised more problems than it solved; for example, the SSM Sea Tactical section is full of anti-ship missiles but many can also be used against other targets, while the same can be said of the ASM Tactical family. Within each section missiles are grouped under the name of the country in which they were originally developed, these countries being in alphabetical order. Within each country the sequence is very broadly chronological, but it is deliberately modified when the occasion demands. The entire Nike family is treated consecutively, from Nike Ajax right through to the Nike-derived Safeguard ABM system. The Bumblebee-derived ship-to-air systems are also treated consecutively, right up to the versatile

# GENERAL INTRODUCTION

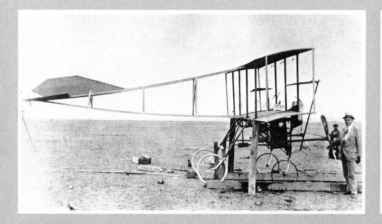

**Above left:** *One of the first true missiles, a twin-engined version of the Buck pilotless bomber of 1916, a period when design and construction were simultaneous.*

**Above:** *One of the last and best of the SSW cruise missiles hung under Zeppelin L.35, behind an Albatros D.V scout. Here again an effective air to surface missile only just missed seeing action.*

**Left:** *Splendid photograph taken in about 1958 showing launch of a Parca of the French Army. Today almost forgotten, this was one of many pioneer SAM systems with a short active life.*

**Right:** *Today missiles are usually just part of large and complex systems. Here a SAC launch officer oversees a distant training routine from the 44th SMW's underground HQ at Ellsworth AFB, S Dakota.*

Aegis system of today. Missiles derived from others presented problems, and it was decided to put Italy's Aspide (derived from the American Sparrow AAM) as a separate entry but to include Britain's Sky Flash along with Sparrow itself because Sky Flash actually uses most of the Sparrow airframe. It is especially important to note that many modern missiles exist in more or less different versions for totally different roles, and this book includes the same missile in every section in which it ought to appear. Exocet, Harpoon and Tomahawk are examples of versatile missiles which have multiple entries.

One rather valuable feature of a book which attempts to include all missiles is that it gives a better historical perspective. Most available sources do not include American air-to-surface missiles (ASMs) prior to Bullpup. The conclusion that might be drawn is that Bullpup was a pioneer programme that emerged from a vacuum, but such a belief is entirely erroneous: prior to Bullpup there was a long and fruitful history of

ASMs in the United States. Of course, there are plenty of discontinuities. Such truly pioneer programmes as the Siemens-Schuckert ASMs of World War 1, and the autopilot-controlled flying bombs flown in America and Britain at the same time, generated near-zero "spin-off" and little usable information for those that came after. In Britain the pioneer Brakemine SAM was foolishly allowed to fade away in 1948, so that when two years later the Red Shoes project was started its designers had to begin again from scratch; the design team trying to produce the ship-launched Seaslug SAM likewise had no benefit from Brakemine even though in many respects the guidance systems were identical. Then in Nazi Germany there was even greater inefficiency and lack of information being allowed to read across to assist parallel programmes.

So far as one can tell, the Germans were the first to use guided missiles in war. The Kaiser's navy came close to using ASMs from Zeppelins,

this book. When the USAAF and USN copied the flying bomb it subtly became a tactical weapon, and the JB series and Loon are discussed in the SSM Tactical sections. The distinction between tactical and strategic is often a fine one. Broadly, the terms are used in this book to denote the kind of target rather than its distance from missile launch. Strategic weapons are taken to be those that strike at enemy heartlands, either in "counterforce" attacks on his own strategic forces or in "countervalue" attacks on his society, which in essence means his cities. Tactical weapons are those that influence a battle, and the battle may be by land, sea, air or all together. Sometimes the category may appear nonsensical, as in the case of the USAF ground-launched Tomahawk which is to be used in a tactical role notwithstanding its range of some 2000 miles.

It will be seen that each entry is usually followed by three brief items of numerical data. The data section is brief because it is not possible to present stereotyped data applicable to all types of missile, and such basic information as the propulsion, guidance and warhead is best discussed in the text. It may be worth pointing out that the data apply only to the basic missile, the vehicle that flies the mission. In many cases this is only part of a much larger weapon system. Early attempts to deploy mobile missile systems emphasized the problem by putting the whole system on wheels or tracks, and in some cases the simple figure for "launch weight" ignores the fact that the whole system might weigh over 100 tons and present formidable logistic problems. Again, ship-to-air missiles that can be loaded on to their launchers by hand are often part of a weapon system that fills half a frigate and costs more than the basic ship. It is important not to forget such matters when trying to assign numerical values to missile systems.

Finally, some readers may doubt that in our discussion before starting the book it was agreed to keep the whole text simple and readily understandable to all. It was soon accepted that this starry-eyed good intention was not capable of fulfilment. To impart the information in a book of reasonable size and price it is not possible to escape from the shorthand jargon of modern defence and advanced technology, and I make no apologies for such sentences as "IOC was achieved aboard FPBs using an IIR seeker, with EO guidance predicted for 1982". The answer, of course, is the most comprehensive possible glossary which will be found at the end of the book. This book also has a thorough index.

and Hitler's Luftwaffe finally became operational with two types of radio-steered ASM in the summer of 1943. A year later the Luftwaffe at last – after prolonged delays for which Londoners can be thankful – began firing "V-1" flying bombs. It so happens that one of the first to come over passed at about 500 ft over the roof of my parents' house in the small hours of Tuesday 13 June 1944. The flak at so low a level was more frightening than the strange throbbing aircraft, and my comment to my mother was "I take my hat off to that pilot". Next day I went with a schoolfriend to see where the weapon had fallen, and soon found the site, in a field off Bury Street, Ruislip. Curiously, this bomb is not mentioned in histories of the flying bomb.

This missile, and the much less unpleasant "V-2" which began arriving a little later – one heard the bang first, followed by the long decreasing rumble of the shockwaves of its approach – were indisputably strategic weapons, and are accordingly included in that section of

# THE ICBM STORY

At the start of the story, at the left-hand end of the drawing, the concept of a true ICBM seemed far beyond the "state of the art". Even the German A4, today seemingly primitive, was actually not merely ahead of all other missiles but farther out in front than any single weapon has ever been in all history. It was a truly fantastic achievement, though ironically its chief effect on history was not to win a war but to assist its enemies after their victory to build similar weapons. One of the first of these post-war weapons was Redstone. Like A4 it was a single-stage weapon with one fixed thrust chamber and graphite vanes in the jet; it was not only larger

but it had a better mass ratio (ratio of mass at launch to mass at propulsion burnout) and many later features. It was designed by almost the same team as the A4, led by Von Braun, whose work for the US Army then produced the truly significant Jupiter, which was not only the first IRBM of 1,500 nautical miles range but was also designed for mobile deployment. Not pictured here, this valuable weapon system was handed to the US Air Force, who suffered from an NIH (not invented here) complex. The Air Force showed no interest in the ex-Army team, and instead developed its own IRBMs and ICBMs for installation in fixed

bases. There could have been no greater mistake.

While the Americans were ignoring the ICBM in 1947–54, and building winged cruise missiles instead (now hailed by President Carter as a marvellous new idea), the Russians predictably went ahead, tried to build one and found it could be done. Their "brute force and ignorance" approach, even with the important help of a

few German A4 workers and the experience of the very successful SS-4 and SS-5, resulted in a monstrosity which proved very useful as a space launcher—indeed, it launched the Space Age, on 4 October 1957—but as a weapon merely reaffirmed the Soviet belief that a temporary military advantage is worth unlimited expenditure. SS-6 had 32 rocket engines, all firing at lift-off, which is

Germany     USA     USSR     USSR     USSR     USA

A4 ("V-2")     Redstone     SS-4 Sandal     SS-5 Skean     SS-6 Sapwood     Thor

| Missile | Throw weight (lb/kg) | Warhead(s) yield (MT) | Range (st.m/km) | CEP (metres) | SSKP* | Remarks |
|---|---|---|---|---|---|---|
| A4 | 2,150/975 | 0·000001 | 200/300 | c8,000 | 0 | 6,000, 1944–5 |
| Redstone | 3,300/1500 | 0·04 | 249/400 | 1,000 | 0 | 1,000+, 1958–63 |
| SS-4 | 2,800?/1270? | c1 | 1,118/1800 | 1,000 | 0 | 500, 1959– |
| SS-5 | 6,600/3000 | c1 | 2,300/3700 | c2000 | 0 | 100+, 1962– |
| SS-6 | c15,000/6800 | c5 | c5,000/8000 | c2000 | 8% | Few, 1957– |
| Thor | 4,000/1800 | 3 | 1,976/3180 | c2000 | 4% | 60, 1959–65 |
| Atlas D | 4,000/1800 | 3 | 6,300/10,100 | c2000 | 4% | 30 (+32 E) 1960–5 |
| Atlas F | 4,000/1800 | 4 | 9,000/14,500 | c2000 | 6% | 80, 1962–5 |
| SS-7 | 8,800/3630 | c8 | 6,800/11,000 | c2500 | 9% | c200, 1961– |
| SS-N-4 | 1,500/680 | 1 | 373/600 | c5000 | 0 | 114, 1959–69? |
| SS-8 | 3,000/1360 | 5 | 6,200/10,000 | c2500 | 5% | Few, 1963– |
| Polaris A-1 | 1,400/635 | 0·5 | 1,380/2221 | 2000 | 0 | 80, 1960–62 |
| Blue Streak | 4,000?/1800? | 2? | 2,880/4635 | 2000? | 0·2% | Cancelled before flight |
| Titan I | 4,000/1800 | 4 | 7,500/12,000 | 2000 | 6% | 62,1962–5 |
| Titan II | 7,500/3400 | 10 | 9,300/15,000 | 1500 | 25% | 54, 1963– |
| SS-9 Mod 1, 2 | 12,000/5450 | 25 | 7,500/12,000 | 1300 | 40% | 238 (all Mods), 1965– |
| SS-9 Mod 4 | 12,000/5450 | 3 x 5 | 7,500/12,000 | 650 | 58% | Included in previous |
| Minuteman I | 1,400/635 | 1 | | 1000 | 15% | 800, 1962–9 |
| SS-11 Mod 1, 2 | 1,500/680 | 2 | 6,500/10,500 | 900 | 24% | 1,018 (all mods) 1968– |
| SS-13 | 1,200/545 | 1 | 5,000/8,000 | ? | ? | Few, 1968– |
| Minuteman III | 1,500/680 | 3 x 0·17 | 8,000/13,000 | 370 | 24% | 550,1970– |
| Poseidon | 1,500/680 | 10 x 0·05 | 2,850/4600 | 800 | low | 496, 1971– |
| SS-N-6 | 2,000?/900 | 2 | 1,864/3000 | 800 | 30% | 544, 1967– |
| SSBS S-2 | 1,500?/680? | 0·15 | 1,700/2750 | 1000? | c0·1% | 18 emplaced, 1971– |
| MSBS M-20 | 1,500?/680? | 1 | 1,864/3000 | 1000? | c12% | 16, 1976– (plus 48 earlier Mod., 1971–) |
| SS-16 | 2,000/900 | 1+ | 6,000/9650 | 500? | c30% | Many, but unknown, 1976–? |
| SS-17 Mod 1 | 4,500/1000 | 4 x 0·2 | 6,500/10,500 | 550 | 22% | 70 so far, 1975– |
| Trident D-4 | 2,500?/1135? | 8 x 0·1 | 4,350/7000 | 800? | c0·1% | 10C probably 1981 |
| SS-N-8 | 4,000/1800 | various | 5,717/9200 | 400 | high | 200+ so far |
| SS-18 Mod 1 | 15,000/6800 | 25 | 7,500/12,000 | 550 | 98% | c150 so far (All Mods), 1974– |
| SS-18 Mod 2 | 15,000/6800 | 10 x 2 | 5,750/9250 | 350 | 65% | Included in previous |
| SS-19 | 7,000/3175 | 6 x 0·34 | 8,000/13,000 | 350 | 25% | 240 so far, 1974– |

*Single-shot kill probability against target hardened to withstand 1000 lb/sq in of overpressure.

USSR

USSR

USSR

France

France

USA

USSR

USSR

USSR

S-N-6 Sawfly    SSBS S2    MSBS M1    SS-16    SS-17    Trident    SS-N-8    SS-18    SS-19

# CONTROL

Most winged missiles are controlled by aerodynamic surfaces driven by hydraulic, gas pressure, motor bleed, electric or other source of power. Future hypersonic types will steer by pointing the nose the way they want to go, eliminating wings and fins. In addition, all missiles have the option of steering by TVC, thrust-vector control, of which a selection of methods is explained here. Of course, TVC is ineffective once the motor has burned out or been cut off, and most of these schemes are used on ballistic missiles to guide the vehicle on to the precise trajectory at the moment of cutoff. Some in addition have a small vernier motor for fine adjustment, and a few have airbrakes in addition.

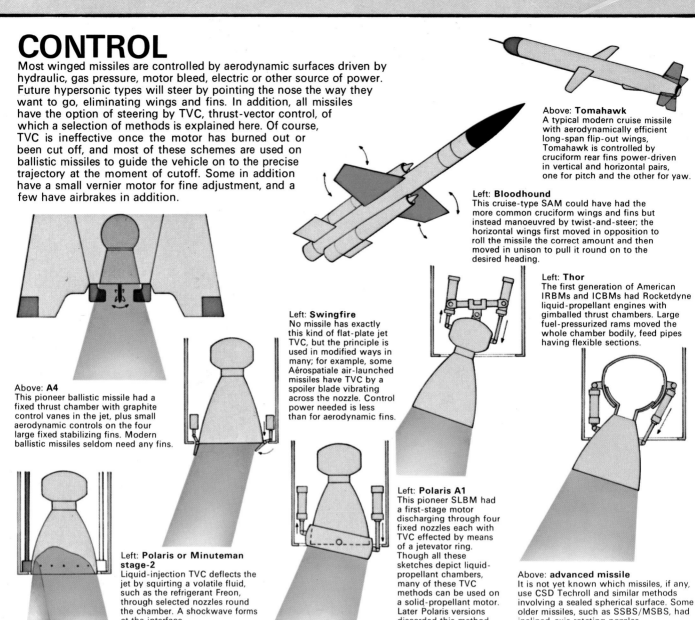

Above: **Tomahawk**
A typical modern cruise missile with aerodynamically efficient long-span flip-out wings, Tomahawk is controlled by cruciform rear fins power-driven in vertical and horizontal pairs, one for pitch and the other for yaw.

Left: **Bloodhound**
This cruise-type SAM could have had the more common cruciform wings and fins but instead manoeuvred by twist-and-steer; the horizontal wings first moved in opposition to roll the missile the correct amount and then moved in unison to pull it round on to the desired heading.

Left: **Thor**
The first generation of American IRBMs and ICBMs had Rocketdyne liquid-propellant engines with gimballed thrust chambers. Large fuel-pressurized rams moved the whole chamber bodily, feed pipes having flexible sections.

Above: **A4**
This pioneer ballistic missile had a fixed thrust chamber with graphite control vanes in the jet, plus small aerodynamic controls on the four large fixed stabilizing fins. Modern ballistic missiles seldom need any fins.

Left: **Swingfire**
No missile has exactly this kind of flat-plate jet TVC, but the principle is used in modified ways in many; for example, some Aérospatiale air-launched missiles have TVC by a spoiler blade vibrating across the nozzle. Control power needed is less than for aerodynamic fins.

Left: **Polaris or Minuteman stage-2**
Liquid-injection TVC deflects the jet by squirting a volatile fluid, such as the refrigerant Freon, through selected nozzles round the chamber. A shockwave forms at the interface.

Left: **Polaris A1**
This pioneer SLBM had a first-stage motor discharging through four fixed nozzles each with TVC effected by means of a jetevator ring. Though all these sketches depict liquid-propellant chambers, many of these TVC methods can be used on a solid-propellant motor. Later Polaris versions discarded this method.

Above: **advanced missile**
It is not yet known which missiles, if any, use CSD Techroll and similar methods involving a sealed spherical surface. Some older missiles, such as SSBS/MSBS, had inclined-axis rotating nozzles.

# MISSILE MISSIONS

This stylised drawing illustrates some of the missions flown by missiles in a full-scale modern conflict. It need hardly be pointed out that vertical and horizontal scales and relative sizes of items have been selected to present a clear picture, and that in general the targets do not represent any specific type or nationality.

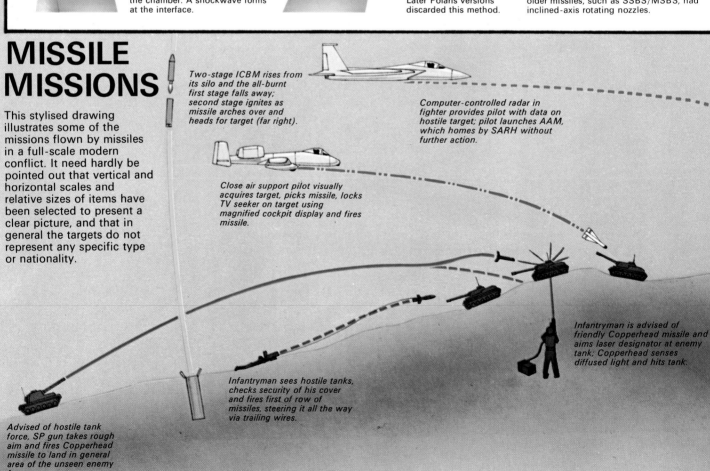

*Two-stage ICBM rises from its silo and the all-burnt first stage falls away; second stage ignites as missile arches over and heads for target (far right).*

*Computer-controlled radar in fighter provides pilot with data on hostile target; pilot launches AAM, which homes by SARH without further action.*

*Close air support pilot visually acquires target, picks missile, locks TV seeker on target using magnified cockpit display and fires missile.*

*Infantryman is advised of friendly Copperhead missile and aims laser designator at enemy tank; Copperhead senses diffused light and hits tank.*

*Infantryman sees hostile tanks, checks security of his cover and fires first of row of missiles, steering it all the way via trailing wires.*

*Advised of hostile tank force, SP gun takes rough aim and fires Copperhead missile to land in general area of the unseen enemy force.*

# LAUNCH TECHNIQUES

The first long-range ballistic missile, Germany's A4, was an army weapon treated as artillery and deployed in a mobile manner. But when the USAF took over all American strategic weapons it dropped the Army-developed mobile Jupiter and concentrated on fixed-base weapons such as Atlas and Thor. Realizing these were vulnerable to their own kind, it attempted to harden the sites, finally putting missiles in underground silos. Today it reluctantly realizes even these are vulnerable, and the only answer for future missiles appears to be a return to mobile deployment — by land, sea and air.

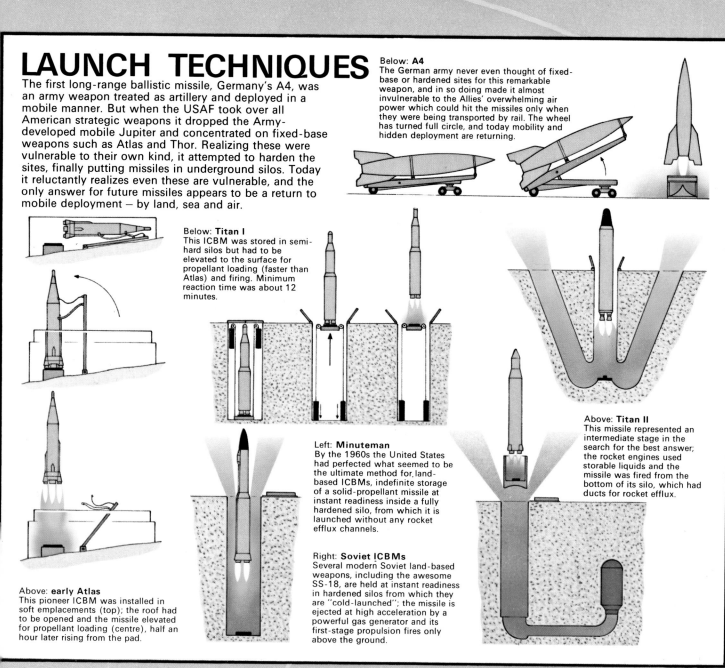

Below: **A4**
The German army never even thought of fixed-base or hardened sites for this remarkable weapon, and in so doing made it almost invulnerable to the Allies' overwhelming air power which could hit the missiles only when they were being transported by rail. The wheel has turned full circle, and today mobility and hidden deployment are returning.

Below: **Titan I**
This ICBM was stored in semi-hard silos but had to be elevated to the surface for propellant loading (faster than Atlas) and firing. Minimum reaction time was about 12 minutes.

Left: **Minuteman**
By the 1960s the United States had perfected what seemed to be the ultimate method for land-based ICBMs, indefinite storage of a solid-propellant missile at instant readiness inside a fully hardened silo, from which it is launched without any rocket efflux channels.

Right: **Soviet ICBMs**
Several modern Soviet land-based weapons, including the awesome SS-18, are held at instant readiness in hardened silos from which they are "cold-launched"; the missile is ejected at high acceleration by a powerful gas generator and its first-stage propulsion fires only above the ground.

Above: **Titan II**
This missile represented an intermediate stage in the search for the best answer; the rocket engines used storable liquids and the missile was fired from the bottom of its silo, which had ducts for rocket efflux.

Above: **early Atlas**
This pioneer ICBM was installed in soft emplacements (top); the roof had to be opened and the missile elevated for propellant loading (centre), half an hour later rising from the pad.

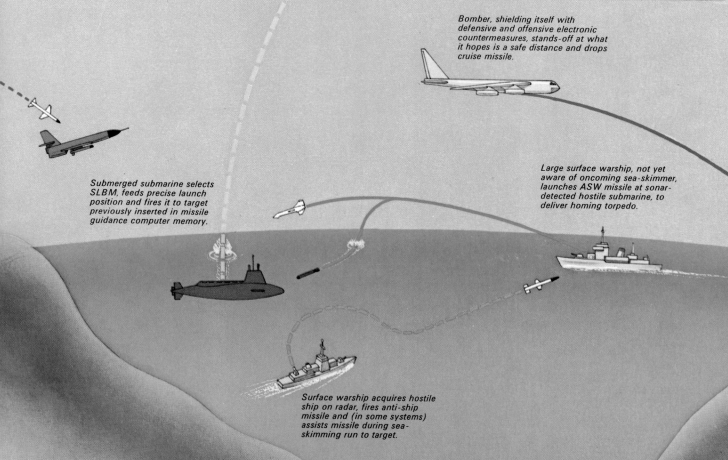

Bomber, shielding itself with defensive and offensive electronic countermeasures, stands-off at what it hopes is a safe distance and drops cruise missile.

Large surface warship, not yet aware of oncoming sea-skimmer, launches ASW missile at sonar-detected hostile submarine, to deliver homing torpedo.

Submerged submarine selects SLBM, feeds precise launch position and fires it to target previously inserted in missile guidance computer memory.

Surface warship acquires hostile ship on radar, fires anti-ship missile and (in some systems) assists missile during sea-skimming run to target.

54 far-from-young Titan IIs, could have been deployed aboard trains throughout the United States. Instead they are among the most immobile things on Earth, and are

increasingly vulnerable to the newer generations of Soviet land-based missiles, particularly SS-18. This monster ICBM is not merely cataclysmic in power; it is super-accurate, as many full-range firings monitored by American sensors have confirmed. Though deployed with a computer-controlled bus (Mirv-dispensing post-boost vehicle) it also continues to fly with giant single warheads, proof that its targets are Minuteman silos.

In response the US Air Force has become deeply concerned and tried to build a new ICBM. After years of planning for MX and wondering how to deploy it — naturally running foul of conservationists in the process — it now has ideas for a missile using at least

parts of the Trident SLBM, but is unlikely to get anything at all before 1985. Already the strategic deterrent is terrifyingly vulnerable, because of the extremely high and apparently unexpected kill probability of the latest Soviet missiles. These formidable weapons introduce many new features, chief of which is cold launch with first-stage ignition above ground. The contrast between the United States, where since 1963 new ICBMs have existed only on paper, and the relentless toil in the Soviet Union leads one to apprehend the situation in 1985 with less than equanimity. The table opposite lists the principal data, numbers and service life of all the missiles shown on these pages.

Titan I   Titan II   SS-9 Scarp   Minuteman I   SS-11 Sego   SS-13 Savage   Minuteman III   Poseid

probably 29 more than we shall ever see in future.

Thor, developed by Douglas, an aircraft manufacturer, in the fastest timescale of any major weapon system, had only one engine and would have been an excellent system had it not been linked to a fixed ground installation that filled most of the former RAF airfields where it was based. Atlas, the first non-Russian ICBM, was made like a thin stainless-steel balloon, inflated by gas pressure, first installed in highly vulnerable above-ground sites and carrying as payload a thermonuclear warhead of considerable bulk protected by a heavy "Chinaman's hat" of copper. Later Atlas went underground, at immense cost, and carried

much more compact warheads inside a slim ablative RV that improved accuracy, payload, range and impact velocity.

Here was the concept of global deterrence, the inter-continental "push-button" weapon; but it had the seeds of vulnerability in its fixed-base deployment. We know little about the installations for contemporary Soviet weapons, such as SS-7, but their size should have given an unmistakeable indication of Russian philosophy, at the very time the United States cut back on deterrence because of a morally justified rejection of

"overkill". It was at this time that the SLBM, such as Sark and Polaris, matured in both superpowers with remarkable speed, ever afterwards lurking in the depths of the oceans to menace cities. Contrary to many experts, the SLBM is today more difficult to destroy than the hardened land ICBM.

Britain wisely terminated Blue Streak but omitted to build a replacement. France, on the other hand, has sustained an on-going family of both IRBMs and SLBMs. Meanwhile, the scene has been increasingly dominated by the massive might of the Soviet Union, which has never ceased to build ever-bigger, more penetrating and more accurate ICBMs. Minuteman, the only ICBM in the West apart from

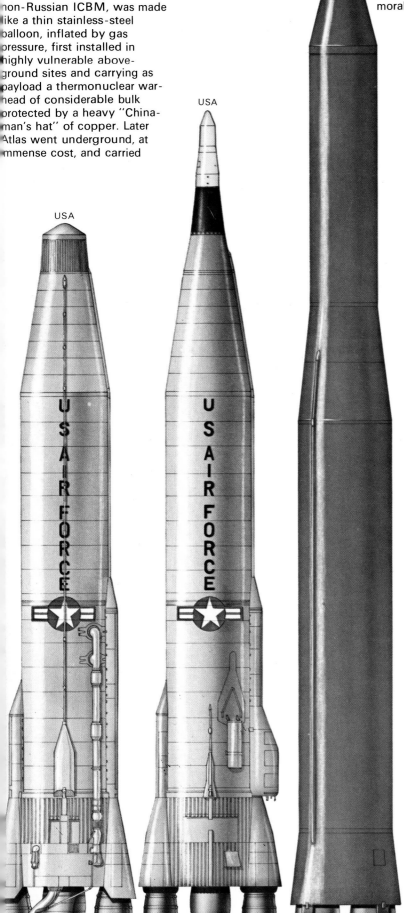

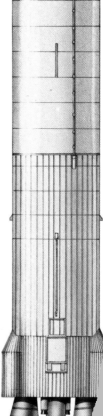

USA

USA

USSR

USSR

USSR

USA

United Kingdom

Atlas D     Atlas F     SS-7 Saddler     SS-N-4 Sark     SS-8 Sasin     Polaris A-1     Blue Streak

# PROPULSION

The whole concept of the ballistic missile rested upon the rocket. Today it might be interesting to consider a ballistic weapon with air-breathing propulsion, flying at hypersonic speed in the stratosphere with its trajectory controlled by aerodynamic forces on its body alone and with a range probably exceeding that of similar-size ballistic rockets. The latter are really more akin to long-range artillery, the only differences being that propulsion continues for a longer period, the trajectory can be corrected until propulsion cut-off, and a number of warheads can be delivered to different targets. But the use of staging – discarding spent rockets en route – took two decades to develop even to today's level.

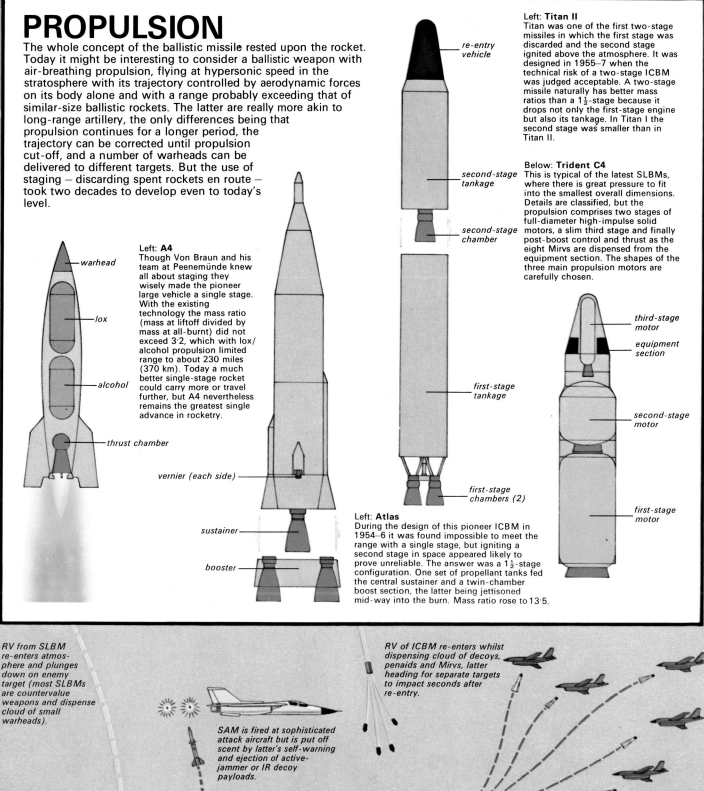

**Left: A4**
Though Von Braun and his team at Peenemünde knew all about staging they wisely made the pioneer large vehicle a single stage. With the existing technology the mass ratio (mass at liftoff divided by mass at all-burnt) did not exceed 3·2, which with lox/alcohol propulsion limited range to about 230 miles (370 km). Today a much better single-stage rocket could carry more or travel further, but A4 nevertheless remains the greatest single advance in rocketry.

warhead
lox
alcohol
thrust chamber
vernier (each side)
sustainer
booster

**Left: Atlas**
During the design of this pioneer ICBM in 1954–6 it was found impossible to meet the range with a single stage, but igniting a second stage in space appeared likely to prove unreliable. The answer was a 1½-stage configuration. One set of propellant tanks fed the central sustainer and a twin-chamber boost section, the latter being jettisoned mid-way into the burn. Mass ratio rose to 13·5.

re-entry vehicle
second-stage tankage
second-stage chamber
first-stage tankage
first-stage chambers (2)

**Left: Titan II**
Titan was one of the first two-stage missiles in which the first stage was discarded and the second stage ignited above the atmosphere. It was designed in 1955–7 when the technical risk of a two-stage ICBM was judged acceptable. A two-stage missile naturally has better mass ratios than a 1½-stage because it drops not only the first-stage engine but also its tankage. In Titan I the second stage was smaller than in Titan II.

**Below: Trident C4**
This is typical of the latest SLBMs, where there is great pressure to fit into the smallest overall dimensions. Details are classified, but the propulsion comprises two stages of full-diameter high-impulse solid motors, a slim third stage and finally post-boost control and thrust as the eight Mirvs are dispensed from the equipment section. The shapes of the three main propulsion motors are carefully chosen.

third-stage motor
equipment section
second-stage motor
first-stage motor

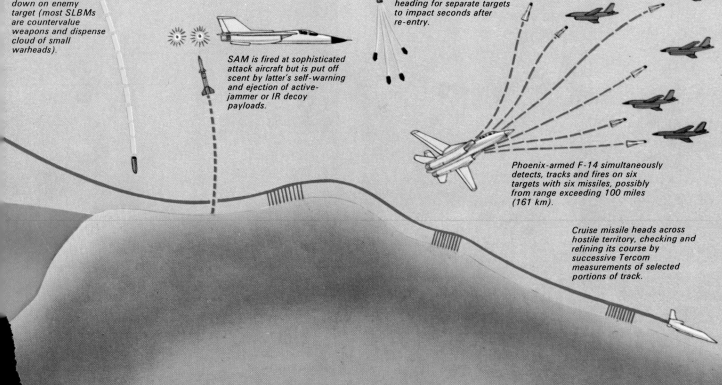

*RV from SLBM re-enters atmosphere and plunges down on enemy target (most SLBMs are countervalue weapons and dispense cloud of small warheads).*

*SAM is fired at sophisticated attack aircraft but is put off scent by latter's self-warning and ejection of active-jammer or IR decoy payloads.*

*RV of ICBM re-enters whilst dispensing cloud of decoys, penaids and Mirvs, latter heading for separate targets to impact seconds after re-entry.*

*Phoenix-armed F-14 simultaneously detects, tracks and fires on six targets with six missiles, possibly from range exceeding 100 miles (161 km).*

*Cruise missile heads across hostile territory, checking and refining its course by successive Tercom measurements of selected portions of track.*

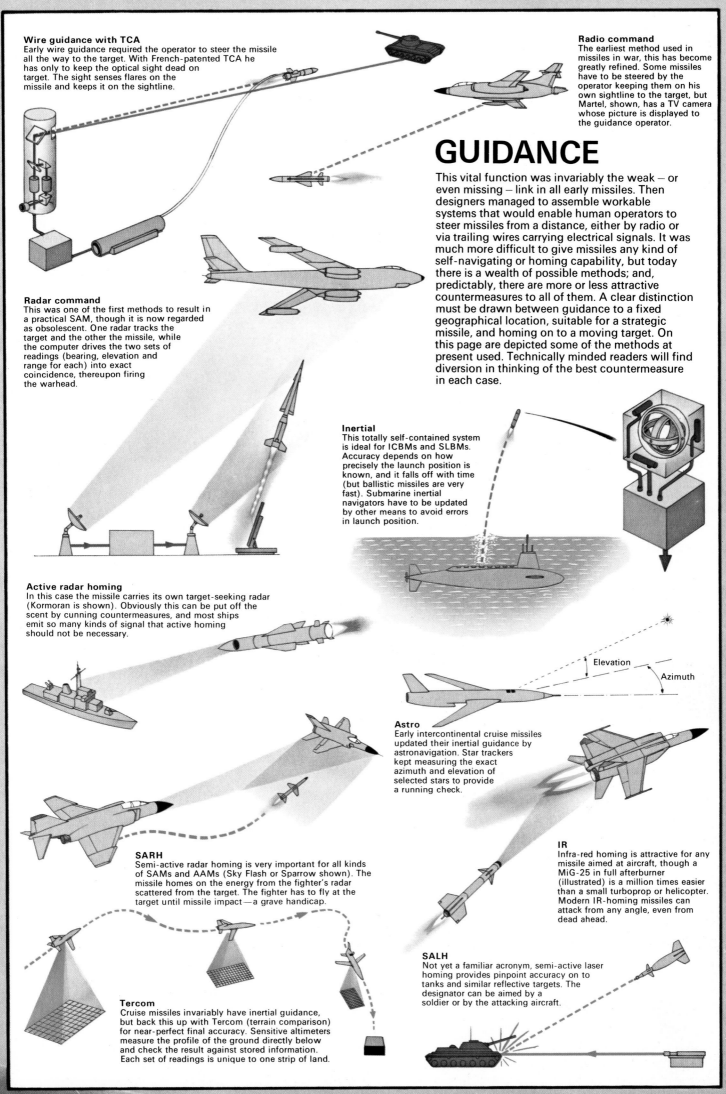

**Wire guidance with TCA**
Early wire guidance required the operator to steer the missile all the way to the target. With French-patented TCA he has only to keep the optical sight dead on target. The sight senses flares on the missile and keeps it on the sightline.

**Radio command**
The earliest method used in missiles in war, this has become greatly refined. Some missiles have to be steered by the operator keeping them on his own sightline to the target, but Martel, shown, has a TV camera whose picture is displayed to the guidance operator.

# GUIDANCE

This vital function was invariably the weak — or even missing — link in all early missiles. Then designers managed to assemble workable systems that would enable human operators to steer missiles from a distance, either by radio or via trailing wires carrying electrical signals. It was much more difficult to give missiles any kind of self-navigating or homing capability, but today there is a wealth of possible methods; and, predictably, there are more or less attractive countermeasures to all of them. A clear distinction must be drawn between guidance to a fixed geographical location, suitable for a strategic missile, and homing on to a moving target. On this page are depicted some of the methods at present used. Technically minded readers will find diversion in thinking of the best countermeasure in each case.

**Radar command**
This was one of the first methods to result in a practical SAM, though it is now regarded as obsolescent. One radar tracks the target and the other the missile, while the computer drives the two sets of readings (bearing, elevation and range for each) into exact coincidence, thereupon firing the warhead.

**Inertial**
This totally self-contained system is ideal for ICBMs and SLBMs. Accuracy depends on how precisely the launch position is known, and it falls off with time (but ballistic missiles are very fast). Submarine inertial navigators have to be updated by other means to avoid errors in launch position.

**Active radar homing**
In this case the missile carries its own target-seeking radar (Kormoran is shown). Obviously this can be put off the scent by cunning countermeasures, and most ships emit so many kinds of signal that active homing should not be necessary.

Elevation

Azimuth

**Astro**
Early intercontinental cruise missiles updated their inertial guidance by astronavigation. Star trackers kept measuring the exact azimuth and elevation of selected stars to provide a running check.

**IR**
Infra-red homing is attractive for any missile aimed at aircraft, though a MiG-25 in full afterburner (illustrated) is a million times easier than a small turboprop or helicopter. Modern IR-homing missiles can attack from any angle, even from dead ahead.

**SARH**
Semi-active radar homing is very important for all kinds of SAMs and AAMs (Sky Flash or Sparrow shown). The missile homes on the energy from the fighter's radar scattered from the target. The fighter has to fly at the target until missile impact — a grave handicap.

**SALH**
Not yet a familiar acronym, semi-active laser homing provides pinpoint accuracy on to tanks and similar reflective targets. The designator can be aimed by a soldier or by the attacking aircraft.

**Tercom**
Cruise missiles invariably have inertial guidance, but back this up with Tercom (terrain comparison) for near-perfect final accuracy. Sensitive altimeters measure the profile of the ground directly below and check the result against stored information. Each set of readings is unique to one strip of land.

# SURFACE TO SURFACE MISSILES

Included in this section are all the missiles that are launched from the land against tactical land targets, with the exception of those missiles explicitly for use against tanks and similar small hardened targets. In many cases the dividing line is almost impossible to draw. Though the earliest anti-tank missiles flew in a more or less straight line at low level, under the command guidance – essentially human steering – of an operator at or near the launcher, today's emergence of the gun-launched guided projectile opens up a fresh set of possibilities. Most of the guided projectiles home unerringly on to laser light diffused from wherever the designator is pointed. If the laser designator were to be pointed at a leaf on a tree, that leaf would be hit by the missile. Accordingly it could be argued that it is mistaken to include Copperhead, for example, in the Anti-tank section much later in this book. We have been guided by official terminology, with a grain of common sense.

In general the duty of the missiles in this section is relatively short-range bombardment of targets associated with land or sea warfare. This includes the coast-defence role, in which many missiles are used that have guidance systems specifically designed to home on surface ships. These missiles would find it as difficult to hit enemy forces approaching over land as did the big guns defending Singapore (and pointing out to sea) in February 1942. Nevertheless this is still the correct section in which to include them. What is more problematical is such long-range weapons as the GLCM Tomahawk, which is to be deployed in Europe by the USAF to replace fighter-bombers in the nuclear role in defending central areas. Unless the fuel tanks were only half-filled these missiles could hit targets beyond the Urals, and by any reasonable yardstick could perform a strategic role. Tomahawk is included here because of the announced intention of the USAF to use it in a tactical role.

This section includes many of the earliest aerial missiles, dating back to 1916. These were naturally like small-scale aeroplanes, similar in shape and construction and usually merely pointed towards a target and then left to fly on a primitive autopilot. None played much part in warfare until the mass-produced "V-1" which, because of the nature of its employment, is included in the next chapter. But long before World War 2 a slightly different category of air vehicle had emerged. This was variously called the aerial target, radio-controlled target or drone, and at first was usually a modified version of a manned aircraft. Today the RPV has emerged as a very important family of air vehicles which complement missiles and differ from them chiefly in that they are intended to return from their missions. It is instructive to note that there are hardly any examples of missiles and RPVs sharing the same airframe.

While the earliest SSM Tactical missiles were covered in fabric, those that were developed during and just after World War 2 were mostly made like the latest high-speed aircraft. Most missiles differ from aircraft in that they never have to fly slowly, and thus they can have relatively small wings much more highly loaded than those of aircraft. To hit surface targets may call for some guidance accuracy but not necessarily for violent manoeuvre because most surface targets are stationary or slow-moving. This is reflected in the style of missile adopted. Until 1945 virtually all missiles in this category had aeroplane-type configuration, with substantially horizontal wings and a tail. But the strategic "V-2", discussed in the next section, revolutionised thinking and since World War 2 an increasing proportion of tactical missiles have had no wings at all. Some fly ballistic trajectories, as explained in the introduction to the next section. A few rely on body lift at highly supersonic speeds to keep changing their trajectory to ensure that they will hit the target. Some have wings, but with four arranged round the body at 90°. This allows them to change direction up, down, left or right instantly, without first having to roll into a bank as do aeroplanes.

Early tactical-missile designers merely used an autopilot to stabilize the vehicle against flight disturbances as it flew into the general area of its target. Until after World War 2 it was not even possible reliably to send an SSM into a target area one mile square. This is unimpressive, and means were found to achieve precision guidance. Until well into the 1950s the only available methods all suffered from severe handicaps. Radio guidance required that the exact position of the target should be known in advance (impossible with a moving target) and that the enemy should make no attempt to interfere with the guidance signals transmitted to the missile far out over his territory. TV guidance seemed extremely attractive, with a camera in the nose or belly of the missile, but in practice it was discovered in Germany as early as 1943 that the difficulties are extremely severe. Even if the TV link can be made to work there is still the problem of enemy jamming of the guidance signals. An even more advanced method, pioneered in the United States, provided the missile with its own set of maps and a memory storing the route to the target, but this never overcame its inherent problems.

Today we have a wealth of choices of guidance method. Bearing in mind that a tactical missile sometimes has to hit mobile, fleeting targets, the most common methods are whittled down to a few. Inertial guidance is used in various simplified and relatively less-costly forms to make many tactical missiles hit a known point on the Earth's surface, the user having first translated the present or future position of the target into numerical co-ordinates acceptable to the guidance computer. A super-accurate refinement used as an add-on subsystem in one important missile is terminal radar; the missile flies most of its trajectory on inertial guidance but in the final seconds, as it plummets down on its target, it compares stored information – in effect it looks at detailed radar pictures of the target area, though these pictures are probably stored as digital information – with the scene its own active radar actually sees, and corrects its trajectory until the two scenes match exactly. Radio command is still a simple and useful method provided that means exist to relate the missile and target positions continuously and precisely and to defeat enemy interference. Of course, in any case where the target is itself an emitter – of radar or radio signals, visible light, heat or (in theory if not yet in practice) noise – it is relatively simple to make a missile home on to it automatically. Virtually any target that can be seen, by an infantryman or by a small RPV or other platform hovering or dodging about overhead, can quickly be turned into an emitter by pointing a laser at it. Laser designation has revolutionised the battlefield to as great an extent as radar or secure electronic communications. Merely by pointing a small laser exactly at a distant target it can be turned into an emitter of laser light, on to which a missile can home unerringly.

Most tactical missiles today are either fitted with very small wings or none at all, and they are usually supersonic. Aircraft-type weapons are judged to have poor survivability in a battle environment, though the remarkable longevity of small RPVs flying at very modest speeds whilst carrying laser designators has been amply demonstrated. One suspects that this is because missile designers had not, in 1979, produced low-cost SAMs tailored to the duty of eliminating them. As it is, baby model aeroplanes costing only a few pounds, dollars or roubles, appear to be able to roam over hostile armies sending

back useful information in real time and, when commanded to do so, directing a deadly laser at a choice target on which a missile can home a few seconds later.

It is this pinpoint accuracy that makes the tactical missile worthwhile. If an error of, say, 50 metres is of small consequence then it is probably more cost/effective to use conventional artillery or spin-stabilised rockets. The recent development of the TGSM – terminally guided sub-munition – has opened the way to a new family of relatively simple and cheap projectiles, delivered by guns or rockets over long ranges, which when nearing the target open to expel a cluster of individual small self-guided warheads which each unerringly plummet down on to whatever worthwhile targets they can find. There are limits to what the TGSM can achieve. They normally have no propulsion or wings, and so cannot make gross changes in trajectory. If they fail to lock-on to a target they will just hit the ground like a traditional artillery shell. But if there is a target in the neighbourhood, say within 200 metres, the seeker head will detect it, lock-on and steer the warhead towards it.

It is interesting to ponder the possibilities. Suppose the enemy has 40 tanks advancing in loose formation (it makes little difference whether they are visually hidden in a forest). It is possible to fire a missile or missiles that will dispense 40 TGSMs which will then detect the tanks by various means, such as electro-optical at a suitable wavelength or IIR on to the heat-emitting portions, and home on to them. We do not want all 40 TGSMs to choose the same tank, leaving the other 39 unscathed. So the problem is: can we teach the 40 warheads either how to share themselves evenly among all the targets, or even to choose individual targets, perhaps by picking out a number stencilled on it, while informing the other warheads of its choice so that they will eliminate that target from their own range of choices? Like the Copperhead and other cannon-launched guided projectiles, the TGSM tends to arrive from above and thus is making the designer of armoured vehicles think again about the thin sheet that used to suffice for upward-facing surfaces.

Similarly the vulnerability of today's warships has brought about the development of missiles able to shoot down other missiles with great reliability and rapidity. As is so often the case with warfare it is a case of weapon leading to counter-weapon, though mankind has not yet been able to recognise that the whole costly business is probably an open-ended exercise in futility.

# CHINA

The People's Republic of China (PRC) is today's name for the vast country that pioneered the rocket. As outlined briefly in the introduction, rockets had become reliable mass-produced military weapons as long ago as the Sung Dynasty, which began just over 1,000 years ago. But by 1960 the Chinese had to start again almost from scratch in a world of advanced technology, and all the first generation of tactical rockets were based on Soviet products, supplied in the 1950s. These included several versions of Frog rocket, and their launch vehicles. Scud and Scaleboard almost certainly were also known to the Chinese.

Published Western literature about PRC missiles concerns itself chiefly with strategic systems, and the known "MRBM" can be regarded as in that category. Current PRC effort is believed to have switched from cumbersome liquid-propellant rockets to solid propulsion, but little is positively known.

# EGYPT

For obvious political reasons Egypt has for 20 years had a strong incentive to deploy bombardment missiles. In the late 1950s large teams of German engineers and scientists were hired to further this and other objectives, and in July 1962 President Nasser witnessed "the firing of two larger and two smaller single-stage missiles" at a range some 50 miles (80 km) from Cairo. Subsequently both missiles were paraded through Cairo, followed in 1963 by a two-stage rocket.

## Al Kahir

The largest single stage, this had a cylindrical body, conical pointed nose, flared skirt, fixed fins and single fixed thrust chamber. Liquid propellants, refractory control vanes in the jet and initial wire guidance appeared likely. Nothing more has been heard of this unconvincing rocket.

**Dimensions:** (estimated) length 39 ft (12 m); diameter 47·2 in (1200 mm).
**Range:** (estimated) 373 miles (600 km).

## Al Zafir

This was the smaller rocket, said to be launchable from "a mobile platform". Main development effort might have been expected to be put into this weapon, which fitted in well with Egyptian requirements and might have posed least risk and cost burdens. The fact that nothing more has been heard is a clear indication that the available technology, in terms of skills and hardware, and probably both, were not equal to even this seemingly modest task.

**Range:** (estimated) 233 miles (375 km) with warhead of 1,102 lb (500 kg).

## Al Raid

This superficially impressive two-stage rocket had the same aura of mock-up status as its smaller brethren, and it has never been certain even that it was intended as a weapon (it was said to be able to carry a "2,205 lb (1000 kg) scientific payload", though its design would make little sense as an upper-atmosphere probe).

It is reasonable to conclude that none of these rockets ever reached the hands of Egyptian troops. In the 1973 Yom Kippur War President Sadat threatened to attack Israeli cities with long-range missiles said to be called Al Zafir. Most observers believe he was referring to Soviet Scud missiles then in Egypt. As noted in the description of Scud, several were then fired at Israeli targets.

*Below: Al Zafir drives past on 27 July 1962. The way this so-called missile was presented suggested that it was merely a rocket-shaped dummy.*

# FRANCE

# SE.4200 Caisseur

In the context of the 1950s the high-subsonic cruise missile had far more to commend it than it does today, yet France was one of only very few nations that built such a weapon for tactical use. The SNCASE aircraft group, later Sud-Aviation, flew the prototype SE.4200 in 1955. It comprised an integral ramjet body, delta wing with elevons and tip-mounted vertical surfaces, twin or quad solid boost rockets for launch from a mobile 25° ramp and underslung warhead. The weak feature was guidance, by radio command and visual tracking with bright flares. Later radar tracking was tried in the SE.4400 version, but line-of-sight limitations and poor accuracy were inherent. By 1958 small numbers had reached the operational stage after numerous test flights at Colomb-Béchar in north-west Algeria. Named Caisseur (Smasher) this primitive but effective flying bomb was not very relevant to the Algerian war and did not remain in service after the early 1960s. But, according to the Carter administration, it would have been ideal for the 1980s!

**Dimensions:** Length about 9 ft 10 in (3 m) (12 ft 6 in (3·8 m), with boosters); span 7 ft 1 in (2·19 m).
**Launch weight:** 661 lb (300 kg).
**Range:** Theoretical 124 miles (200 km); practical about 10 miles (16 km).
**Flight speed:** Mach 0·9: 685 mph (1100 km/h).

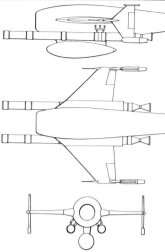

*Above: The production SE.4200 Caisseur complete with its long and slender boost motors. The large conventional warhead was housed in the underslung pod shown in the diagram.*

# Lutin

Designed by the BTZ (Bureau Technique Zborowski), Lutin (Imp, or Elf) was a battlefield bombardment weapon with tandem annular wings and four rear control fins, propelled by an 8 lb (3·6 kg) solid motor giving a long burn to sustain 280 mph (450 km/h). It had radio command guidance and delivered an 8·8 lb (4 kg) warhead. Small numbers were evaluated by troops in 1954–6.

**Dimensions:** Length 51·0 in (1·30 m); diameter of main wing 16·1 in (410 mm).
**Launch weight:** 33 lb (15 kg).
**Range:** 3 miles (5 km).

# Exocet MM.40

This important weapon family, the basic member of which is described on p. 72, includes various schemes for coast defence and land tactical use. The original coast-defence launcher was a Berliet 6 × 6 truck on which were mounted four standard shipboard box-type launchers, arranged 2 × 2. Subsequently Aérospatiale itself funded considerable development of the improved MM.40 Exocet with a new sustainer motor giving up to 100 sec longer burn (see data). Wings and control fins fold to fit a new glass-fibre tube launcher that greatly reduces weight and bulk and could lead to (for example) an eight-round 2 × 4 launch vehicle. Like the air-launched AM.39 this missile descends almost to the wave-tops in its final 984 ft (300 m) of flight when used against ships. The whole MM.40 system is carried in off-highway vehicles but the potential for general land tactical use, which would call for different forms of guidance, does not yet appear to have been explored. The basic MM.40 for shore-to-ship use is due to begin flight testing in 1979. The first customer is reported to be non-French, and deliveries are to begin by December 1979. The French Navy is expected also to place orders for this shore-based version of Exocet.

**Dimensions:** Length 18 ft 6 in (5·64 m); diameter 13·78 in (350 mm); span 39·37 in (1 m).
**Launch weight:** 1,819 lb (825 kg).
**Propulsion, guidance and warhead:** As MM.38 except steel-cased boost motor and 200/220 sec sustainer.
**Range:** Up to 43·5 miles (70 km) at Mach 0·93: 708 mph (1139 km/h).

*Below: The complete MM.40 coast-defence Exocet system rides on 6 × 6 cross-country trucks, apart from the radar which would be on a hill.*

# Pluton

This important all-French tactical bombardment weapon, in a class in which NATO has shown hardly any interest except to buy the American Corporal, Sergeant and Lance, is the only missile of its type ever successfully developed in Western Europe. First fired in 1969, it became operational with the French Army in 1974.

The missile body is supplied in a box container which is then lifted by the resupply vehicle and mounted on an AMX-30 chassis. Either of two nuclear warheads is then attached: the 25-kT AN-51 for use against rear areas or the 15-kT size for enemy forward troops. CEP is said to be 492–984 ft (150–300 m), depending on range, and air or ground burst can be selected. No conventional warhead has been announced. The system incorporates rigorous safety systems operative both before and after launch, to protect friendly troops. Aérospatiale claims "quick reaction time" despite the need to remove the spent container, load a new one and mate the warhead, and "a very high GO probability". Griffet supply the crane on the reloader, with Microturbo power.

Originally it was planned to deploy 120 Pluton systems, but this number was cut to 36 and finally to only 30 (though several times this number of missiles have been produced, to provide reloads). There are five Pluton regiments: 3rd, at Mailly; 25th, Suippes; 32nd, Haguenau; 60th, Laon-Couvron; and 74th, Belfort. Each is dispersed over an area of 10 000 km , with each launcher having a number of pre-surveyed firing locations and moving from one to another after each shot. The launch vehicle has a crew of four, but the complement of a regiment in vehicles and crews has not been disclosed.

*Below: The Pluton now in service rides on the AMX-30 chassis and is fed with target data (often from R.20/Cyclope RPVs) fed via an Iris 35M military computer of the Plan Calcul Militaire.*

*Inset: Development firing of a Pluton from the operational type launcher. This is the only West European army artillery missile in existence today.*

**Dimensions:** Length 25 ft 0¾ in (7·64 m); diameter 25·6 in (650 mm); span 55·7 in (1·415 m).
**Launch weight:** 5,342 lb (2423 kg).
**Propulsion:** SEP Styx dual-thrust motor with SNPE solid propellant (2,645 lb, 1200 kg mass) with 10·5 sec boost phase and 18 sec sustain.
**Guidance:** SFENA simplified strap-down inertial fed with target data (if necessary passed direct from R20/Cyclope reconnaissance RPV) processed by Iris 35M computer. Electrically driven control fins.
**Range:** Variable 6–75 miles (10–120 km).
**Flight speed:** Supersonic.

# Super Pluton

A weapon known by this name has been under study by the French Army for some years, for use in the 1980s. It would have greater range (one report says 112 miles (180 km) and another claims it would be doubled, to 150 miles (240 km)), greater accuracy and a wider range of warheads including non-nuclear charges, cluster dispensers and TGSMs.

# GERMANY

# Rheinbote

Almost certainly this was the first multi-stage missile to be used in warfare, though it was unguided and incapable of attacking targets smaller than a town. Rheinmetall-Borsig began work in 1942 to meet an Army (Heereswaffenamt) need for a bombardment rocket bridging the yawning gap between most artillery and the A-4 rocket. Following research with three-stage rockets using aircraft take-off boost charges, the final design was ready by 1944. Called RhZ 61/9 Rheinbote (Rhine Messenger) it had a powerful first stage giving 83,774 lb (38 000 kg) thrust for 1 sec to get it off a launcher of reasonable length (a converted 88 mm Flak 41 gun mount, or a modified A-4 Meillerwagen). This stage had one central and six surrounding nozzles, the diglycol propellant being in separated bars to give maximum burning area. Then followed three sustainer stages, each with a diglycol tube burning on inner and outer surfaces and discharging through a single nozzle which built up back-pressure to blow off the preceding spent stage. Guidance was by carefully aiming the launcher, each stage having six slightly canted fins which spun the missile to reduce inaccuracies. Velocity at burnout was a record not exceeded until the ICBM era. Just one of many problems was that the spent stages were scattered at distances of 2·17, 7·45 and 15·5 miles (3·5, 12 and 25 km) from the launcher. Many hundreds of Rheinbotes were made, and more than 200 were fired at Antwerp in the all-out bombardment of that city in November 1944.

**Dimensions:** Overall length 37 ft 5 in (11·4 m); diameter of final stage 7·5 in (190 mm); fin span of booster 58·5 in (1·49 m).
**Launch weight:** 3,781 lb (1715 kg).
**Range:** Up to 135 miles (218 km).
**Flight speed:** At 4th-stage burnout, Mach 5·55 (4,224 mph, 6800 km/h); also given as 3,663 mph (5900 km/h).

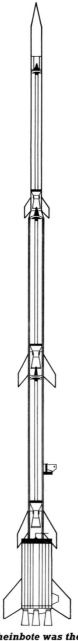

*Above: Rheinbote was the slimmest, most multi-staged missile in history. Second and third stages were identical. The airframe was mainly mild steel.*

*Right: These two photographs show the operational Rheinbote, on its specially designed trans-launcher. This was the first production launch vehicle.*

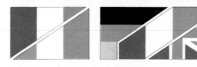

# Hydra

This 1973 proposal for a highly supersonic long-range anti-ship missile was a company project by MBB (Messerschmitt-Bölkow-Blohm), using one of the MBB ram-rockets on which work is continuing. It has been replaced by ASEM though even this may lead to something else.

# Mar

The Mittleres Artillerie Raketen system is a West German project for tactical rockets with terminal guidance.

# Bussard

Since 1977, and probably earlier, a German industrial consortium has been working on this guided projectile for firing from 120 mm mortars. Members of the team include AEG, Bodenseewerk and Diehl Elektronik. Martin Marietta of the United States is participating in "smart" guidance, almost certainly by laser designation. The missile has wings and control fins which flick open immediately it leaves the mortar barrel. Data not yet available but overall size is expected to be comparable to Copperhead.

# INTERNATIONAL

# Otomat

Though principally launched from ships and aircraft (p. 74) this Franco-Italian missile is also in production in a land system for coast defence. Originally a fixed-site installation was studied, but the present OCDS (Otomat Coastal Defence System) is fully mobile, though unwieldy and virtually impossible to conceal. The command and control group requires a column of large trucks, while the firing section needs even more; and it is doubt-

**Above: A demonstration land installation of Penguin, with twin missile boxes on a rotating mount. The missile is standard. Radar and support systems are out of the picture.**

ful that extended off-highway operation is possible. The basic missile remains similar to that launched from ships, with either sea-skimming or terminal zoom/dive guidance, and in the form known as Teseo having the ability to receive mid-course guidance from a helicopter or other target-sensing platform. Range of the OCDS is given as 124 miles (200 km), which is greater than for ship- or air-launched versions. This may be based on the premise that search and tracking radars could be on a mountain. System effectiveness is admitted to depend on topography, and in "favourable geography" one battery is said to be able to defend 186 miles (300 km) of coastline.

## ASEM

Sometimes written Asem, this Anti-ship Euromissile group is studying land-based applications of the weapon described on p. 74.

**Right: Test firing of the OCDS from the operational launch box. This version of Otomat is not yet believed to have been purchased.**

## ISRAEL

For at least eight years there have been persistent reports in the media describing Israeli battlefield missiles, invariably said to have nuclear warheads. One is called Jericho, and designated MD.620; another is a two-stage rocket designated MD.660. During the Yom Kippur war in 1973 Israel explicitly denied the existence of such programmes, and if the "MD" numbers have any meaning it is probably to identify Marcel Dassault studies in France on behalf of Israel, in the 1960s. The most recent story, equally unconfirmed, describes an artillery rocket called Ze'ev (Wolf), able to throw a 154 lb (70 kg) warhead 2·8 miles (4·5 km) or a 352·7 lb (160 kg) warhead 0·62 miles (1 km).

## NORWAY

### Penguin

In the early 1970s this shipboard system (p. 77) was redesigned for land use, primarily in the coast-defence role but also having potential in tactical battle-field scenarios. Fixed and mobile forms have been studied. The former includes a radar or optical sensor, computerized control system, power supply, firing panel and variable number of missiles in standard shipboard launch containers. Some or all items, especially the fire-control system, could be in deep hardened shelters. The chief mobile scheme is based on the IKV 91 amphibious tank chassis developed by Hägglund and Söner in Sweden. This carries three missile boxes transversely, with the crew of three, radar and fire-control system all packed in the front cab. The radar has a folding aerial, and the vehicle can use its tracks, dozer blade and lifting jacks to dig itself in. Other land Penguin systems are based on wheeled vehicles, mostly with two missiles, which drive to pre-surveyed sites. Full-scale demonstrations are expected to lead to production in 1979–80.

## SWEDEN

### RB 08A

Described on p. 78, this shipboard weapon is in service also in a coast-defence role. It was developed in fixed and mobile forms but it is not known which remain in use. Of 98 missiles delivered, more than half were assigned to land installations, where they have been in service since 1967.

**Below: Training shot of the Franco-Swedish RB 08 cruise missile. This land launcher can in fact be considered to be operational.**

# TAIWAN

In an hour-long parade through Taipei on 10 October 1978 two "home produced" missiles were proudly displayed, both said to be products of the Chung-Shan Institute of Research and Technology. One, called Worker Bee 4, was clearly the US Nike Hercules. The other, Hsiung Feng, meaning Hornet or Drone, appeared identical to the Gabriel missiles imported from Israel. The Nationalist Chinese insist they are local products.

# USSR

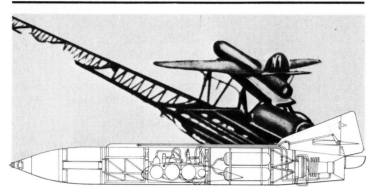

Top: **The only known photograph, heavily retouched, of the Korolev Type 212.**

Above: **Type 212A – this cross-section shows the propellant and gas-bottle feed system.**

## Type 212

Russia had many pioneers and visionaries interested in rocketry, and the tradition was maintained by the Soviet Union. N. I. Tikhomirov set up an official laboratory in 1921 which became the Gas Dynamics Laboratory (GDL) in 1928. Here work expanded in 1930 to include liquid-propellant engines, and by 1936 this branch of GDL under V. P. Glushko had fired the outstanding ORM-65 engine using nitric acid and kerosene and capable of making up to 50 firings with total burn-time of 30 minutes. Propellants were fed by gas pressure to a regeneratively cooled chamber, with electro-pyrotechnic igniter and excellent combustion at controllable thrusts up to 386 lb (175 kg). In 1933 a Reaction Propulsion Research Institute (RNII) had been set up, and the deputy chief, S. P. Korolev, headed the design of a winged rocket called Project 212. This was a research vehicle with military possibilities, with launch by GDL solid booster sled from a railed ramp and an ORM-65 sustainer engine in the cylindrical fuselage. Static-fired 13 times in 1937–8, it flew twice in 1939 under autopilot control. Though it carried 66 lb (30 kg) explosives and the same weight of propellants it did not receive a guidance system, and was not developed further.

**Dimensions:** Length 10 ft 4·4 in (3·16 m); span 10 ft 0½ in (3·06 m).
**Launch weight:** 463 lb (210 kg).
**Range:** 31 miles (50 km) at 311 mph (500 km/h).

## Type 212A

In 1937 this improved tactical missile was designed under Korolev, but apart from the drawing reproduced here few details are available, and official histories make no mention of flight trials. The airframe, entirely of light alloy and steel as was Project 212, was stressed for flight at 621 mph (1000 km/h), and there is little doubt that this was potentially the most formidable tactical missile in the world prior to World War 2.

# Frog

Though unguided, this family of artillery rockets has been so numerous over so long a period that it merits full treatment in this review. The name, believed to have stemmed from the United States in about 1959, is understood to be an acronym for Free Rocket Over Ground (or Free-flight Range Over Ground, or other variations on the same theme). Prior to this Western appellation they were dubbed by Western media T-5A, T-5C, etc, with no evidence that such nomenclature had any basis in fact.

# Frog-1

Like several other missiles this was disclosed to the public in the October Revolution parade through Red Square in November 1957. A somewhat basic single-stage spin-stabilized rocket, it was carried in a massive drum container mounted on surplus IS-3 (ex-Josef Stalin III) heavy tank chassis. This made a ponderous weapon system, but doubtless effective in a primitive war when used *en masse* to devastate large areas. The supposition that the casing incorporated heaters to prime the solid propellant has for some years been reported as fact. Often apparently called Luna in Warsaw Pact publications, these early rockets were in front-line service with most WP countries from 1957 until at least 1970, and large numbers have since been used for training, though not with the original nuclear or conventional warheads.

**Dimensions:** Length about 32 ft 9 in (10 m); diameter about 33·5 in (850 mm).
**Launch weight:** About 6,614 lb (3000 kg).
**Range:** Estimated at 20 miles (32 km).

Right: *Frog-2 was the smallest of the publicly displayed Frog rockets. It was light enough to ride on the amphibious PT-76 chassis, but by modern standards even this system was clumsy.*

Below: *Frog-3 is believed to be still in service. Likewise carried on the PT-76, it is thought to have been the first Frog with tandem stages of rocket propulsion.*

Bottom left: *Taken in 1964, this wintry scene shows the original Frog-1 still in use. Thousands of Frogs spurred no response by the West, other than Honest John.*

# Frog-2

This was the smallest of the family, and likewise was first seen in the 1957 parade. Though possibly still capable of having a nuclear warhead, this weapon's slim solid-propellant motor gives it a relatively short range, and the emphasis has been on light weight. It was the first missile to be mounted on the PT-76 light amphibious tank chassis, on which it rides on a hydraulically elevating cradle with limited azimuth movement for refining the aim.

**Dimensions:** Length about 29 ft 6½ in (9 m); diameter about 23·6 in (600 mm).
**Launch weight:** Estimated at 5,291 lb (2400 kg).
**Range:** Estimated at 15·5 miles (25 km); one estimate is only 7·5 miles (12 km).

# Frog-3

The oldest of the family believed to be still in service, this was first seen in the 1960 parade and was the first to have tandem two-stage propulsion, each motor having a central nozzle surrounded by a ring of 12 smaller nozzles. At launch, both front and rear motors fire together, the front efflux being canted out to avoid destruction of the rear. The whole rocket impacts on target. Around 1970, Western literature agreed on a nuclear or conventional warhead weighing 551 lb (250 kg) but by 1975 this estimate had changed to a figure of 992 lb (450 kg). Carrier remains the PT-76 chassis.

**Dimensions:** Length 34 ft 5½ in (10·5 m); diameter 15¾ in (400 mm); warhead diameter 21½ in (550 mm).
**Launch weight:** About 4,960 lb (2250 kg).
**Range:** About 25 miles (40 km).

# Frog-4

This weapon system appears to differ from Frog-3 only in that the rocket has a slim warhead the same diameter as the motor tube.

**Launch weight:** Estimated at 4,409 lb (2000 kg).
**Range:** About 31 miles (50 km).

# Frog-5

At first (1964) this was thought to be merely a Frog-4 with a conical nose. Later study showed that in fact the whole missile was increased in diameter to that of the Frog-3 warhead; in fact it is a fair guess that Frog-5 is a Frog-3 with a fatter but slightly shorter motor.

**Dimensions:** Length about 29 ft 10½ in (9·1 m); diameter 21½ in (550 mm).
**Launch weight:** Estimated at 6,614 lb (3000 kg).
**Range:** About 34 miles (55 km).

# Frog-7

NATO observers use "Frog-6" to identify a dummy rocket used in training, so Frog-7, first seen in 1967, is next and also the last in the family. Like all Frogs from —3 onwards it has a central sustainer and ring of peripheral boost nozzles (there are 20 of the latter), but there is only one stage of propulsion. The airframe is cleaner, the fins larger, motor performance higher and the launcher a plain girder rail with quicker elevation and limited traverse. There are thought to be speed brakes for range adjustment, but details of the necessary radar (doppler) tracking and radio command system are unknown. The carrier vehicle is the ZIL-135 wheeled prime mover, with an on-board crane for rapid reloading and cross-country performance as good as a PT-76 except for lack of amphibious capability. Large numbers of Frog-7 are in use with all WP members as well as Egypt, Iraq, N Korea, Syria and possibly other countries. Several smaller nations use earlier Frogs.

**Dimensions:** Length 29 ft 6½ in (9·0 m); diameter 23·6 in (600 mm).
**Launch weight:** About 5,511 lb (2500 kg).
**Range:** At least 37 miles (60 km).

# SS-1 Scunner

Designation applied to the supposed Soviet copy of the German A-4, never proved to exist.

# SS-2 Sibling

Little was ever discovered about this SRBM, beyond the assumption that it was an improved Scunner. Most reports speak of greater range and better reliability.

*Left: Frog-7 on the march on Soviet Army and Navy Day (23 February) in 1966.*

# SS-1 Scud

Soon after the original Scud-A was first seen in 1957 the author wrote: "So far as one can tell, it can be fired from an unprepared site with no more than one or two minutes' preparation time". This was a mistaken belief; after the IS-3 chassis rumbled up there followed a wait of about an hour before this guided ballistic missile could lift off. The time was spent in accurate site surveying, in kine-theodolite tracking of upper-atmosphere balloons and in pumping storable liquid propellants – calculated to be RFNA and UDMH – into the missile tanks. The original Scud-A version was thought to combine radio command of propulsion cutoff and gyro-stabilized guidance rather like A-4 and Corporal, and to have no trajectory control after motor cutoff. It remained in Soviet operational service until at least 1972.

Scud-B is estimated to be 1 ft 7½ in (0·5 m) longer and to have greater range (see data), and the propellant tanks appear to have been transposed. It was first seen in 1962 on the IS-3 chassis, with the steel-tube ladder round the tip of the missile suitably extended. In 1965 Scud-B made its appearance on the new MAZ-543 articulated eight-wheel prime mover, which is lighter and faster than the heavy tracked chassis. This carries a completely new erector/launcher much neater than that originally used. Soviet Ground Forces erector/launchers have numerous features not seen in the other Warsaw Pact Scud systems, probably betokening nuclear warheads which have not so far been permitted to other WP forces or export customers. The Scud-B erector/launcher is totally unlike that of Scud-A; there is extensive new equipment, large double calipers to grip the upper end of the missile, and redesigned structure, but the prominent ladder that extended up each side of the earlier weapon to meet above its nose is absent. Guidance of Scud-B is by simple strapdown inertial system, steering as before via refractory vanes in the motor efflux, the fins being fixed. There

does not seem to be any fine adjustment of cutoff velocity, and it is not known if the nuclear or conventional warhead separates before starting the free-fall ballistic trajectory. Resupply missiles are towed tail-first on an articulated trailer attached to a ZIL-157V, with a Ural-375 truck-mounted crane (Type 8T210) to swing the missile on to the lowered erector/launcher.

Certainly the time taken to set up and fire Scud-B is much less than the hour of Scud-A, and End Tray radar is used for radiosonde (radio-equipped balloon) tracking for upper-atmosphere data.

SS-1C Scud-B is widely deployed by all WP armies, and by Egypt, Iraq, Libya and Syria. The Syrian Army was reported to have flown a Scud 155 miles (250 km) in November 1975, but in the Yom Kippur war two years earlier three Scuds fired by Egypt all apparently missed their targets in Sinai. Persistent rumours of a Scud-C with range of 280 miles (450 km) have not been confirmed.

**Dimensions:** Length 36 ft 11 in (11·25 m); diameter 33·5 in (850 mm).
**Launch weight:** Scud-A, about 12,125 lb (5500 kg); Scud-B 13,888 lb (6300 kg).
**Range:** Scud-A, about 50–93 miles (80–150 km); Scud-B 100–175 miles (160–280 km).

Top: *The Soviet caption reads "daybreak on a training range of the Soviet missile forces". The Scud-A has been set on its launcher at a surveyed site.*

Facing page, top: *Scud-B missiles on an exercise in February 1971. That in the foreground is about half-way through the 60-second elevation.*

Left: *Scud-B on the march, on its superb transporter-erector of the MAZ-543 family. This example took part in the Red Square parade on 7 November 1965.*

# SS-12 Scaleboard

First reported in Western literature in 1967, this mobile ballistic missile almost comes into the strategic category, because it can menace Western Europe from WP soil and is universally agreed to have a warhead in the megaton range. Yet in many ways it is similar to Scud-B; it is little different in length, rides on an erector/launcher mounted on an MAZ-543, and almost certainly has similar strapdown simplified inertial guidance. One of the few obvious differences, apart from the much greater missile diameter, is that the erector/launcher is in the form of a ribbed container, split into upper and lower halves, which protects the weapon from the weather while it is travelling. It is possibly shock-mounted, and the container may even offer limited protection against nuclear attack.

Though there are clear illustrations of the complete weapon system on the march, or elevating for firing, the missile itself remains almost unknown, and the data are little more than the best guesses of Western intelligence. It is reasonable to assume that there is a single rocket engine burning storable RFNA/UDMH. Steering may be by refractory jet-deflector vanes, but a later method would be desirable for maximum range. The Soviet Ground Forces enjoy a wealth of superb purpose-designed vehicles, and the MAZ-543 transporter/launcher is one of the best. A beautiful exercise in packaging, it is powerful, highly mobile on rough ground, air-conditioned for extremes of heat or cold, and has automatic regulation of tyre pressure from the driver's cab on the left side. The right front cab is the launch-control station, as in the Scud-B system. The rest of the launch crew sit in the second row of seats in line with the rear doors on each side. Some related vehicles are amphibious.

Like all Soviet tactical missiles Scaleboard is intended for "shoot and scoot" operation. But it is too large for snappy reloading and in any case this needs the services of one, if not two, additional vehicles. Resupply missiles are carried in their own ribbed casings, with propellant tanks empty, and even with fast pressurized-gas transfer the fuelling process must take about a quarter of an hour. The likelihood is that the Soviet Ground Forces already have a detailed itinerary of pre-surveyed firing sites offering good concealment throughout Western Europe. So far as is known, this powerful thermonuclear weapon serves only with the Soviet Union.

**Dimensions:** Length 37 ft 9 in (11·5 m); diameter 43 in (1·1 m).
**Launch weight:** Probably about 17,636 lb (8000 kg).
**Range:** Estimated at up to 500 miles (800 km).

# SS-21

This is the US designation for the new battlefield rocket being introduced by Soviet Ground Forces. No NATO name has yet been published. Details are speculative, though a variety of types of warhead is a foregone conclusion. This may be the weapon often reported as "Frog 9", but this is a guess.

**Data:** none available.

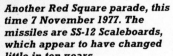

*Another Red Square parade, this time 7 November 1977. The missiles are SS-12 Scaleboards, which appear to have changed little in ten years.*

# SSC-1B Sepal

This is the land-based version of the large, formidable and widely deployed shipboard cruise missile called by NATO SS-N-3 Shaddock, described on p. 80. Sepal is thought to use an identical missile, though this assumption may be unjustified. As it rides inside a large cylindrical container, making the ZIL-135 family prime mover look for all the world like a tanker truck, little has been seen of it in Red Square parades; photographs with the rear lid raised reveal the expected Shaddock back-end with ventral fin, rocket boost motor on each side and large air-breathing cruise-engine nozzle covered by a plate. At each end the container has a full-diameter closure, swung open on to an upper ring by remote-control actuators on the left side. These could allow a cruise turbojet to be started prior to opening the rear lid for the launch, but this is speculation. The whole container is elevated to a suitable angle by two large jacks prior to launch in a forward direction across the prime-mover cab. Wings unfold in the first second or so of free flight.

Without too much to go on, Western observers have concluded that Sepal uses the same airframe as Shaddock but with rather more versatile guidance. IR-homing has often been associated with this land-based weapon, but not with Shaddock. Radio command, mid-course update and terminal radar homing seem to be common to both. So far as is known, Sepal serves only in the anti-ship role, not for overland missions. Each battalion is said to have 15 to 18 launchers, plus reloads.

**Data:** assumed as for SS-N-3.

# SSC-2A Salish

Derived from the pioneer long-range ASM known to NATO as AS-1 Kennel (p. 134), this and its close relative Samlet (below) are not fully understood. Both use the Kennel-based airframe, which is that of a miniature first-generation swept-wing jet fighter and clearly dates from the late 1940s at the time the MiG-15 was coming into production. The cruise engine is a simple small turbojet, of unknown type, fed from a plain nose inlet, and the wings fold upwards for easy ground handling. Launch is from an elevating ramp under the thrust of a single rocket booster with down-canted nozzle. Photographs showed both fixed and mobile launchers, as well as large quantities of ground-support equipment. Salish is obsolescent, and is believed to be withdrawn from combat duty with Soviet Ground Forces. Several observers believe it was an overland tactical missile, presumably with radio command guidance to a predetermined map location. If so, the small radome above the inlet remains an enigma.

**Data:** assumed similar to Samlet.

# SSC-2B Samlet

Compared with Salish, this missile has a larger nose radome, electronics pod above the fin and other smaller changes. The consensus of opinion is that it is a coast-defence missile, with active homing against ships. Semi-active homing has also been reported, and the Sheet Bend radar has been seen on vehicles at Samlet sites, but this could not give effective guidance against over-the-horizon targets which Samlet is capable of reaching. Of course, this weapon system may be associated with air- or ship-based mid-course guidance. In addition to the Soviet Union, Samlet has been seen in service with Polish coast-defence forces and in Cuba and Egypt, usually operated by naval personnel. It is believed still to be operational with all recipients.

**Dimensions:** Span about 23 ft (7 m); diameter 47 in (1·2 m).
**Launch weight:** Estimated at 6,614 lb (3000 kg).
**Range:** Estimated at 124 miles (200 km).

**Top:** *Transporter/launcher for SSC-1B Sepal erected to launch angle. The end-closures have been swung up on to their top rests.*

**Centre:** *Propaganda photograph of SSC-2A Salish on a most unconvincing launcher, which appears merely to be placed on the ground.*

**Left:** *April 1970 photograph showing a launch crew of the Red Banner Northern Fleet apparently eager to fire the SSC-2B Samlet seen waiting.*

# UNITED KINGDOM

**Below:** *Folland's neat little AT under construction at Farnborough. The man on the right is installing the radio receiver aerial wiring, wrapped round wings and fuselage.*

**Second below:** *The 1921 RAE Aerial Targets had a remarkable similarity to the Siemens-Schuckert Werke monoplane missiles built in Germany during World War I.*

## AT

Prior to the outbreak of World War 1 Professor A. M. Low had demonstrated an early form of television, and in late 1915 he was asked by the War Office if he could use this system to guide a pilotless aircraft carrying explosives. Under the cover-name AT, which it was hoped would be interpreted by the enemy as Aerial Target, a series of radio-controlled miniature aircraft were built and flown. The RFC Experimental Works where Low worked, first at Brooklands and then at an excellent plant in Feltham, built a high-wing monoplane using the lower wings of a Sopwith Pup and powered by a 50 hp Gnome-derived rotary. Sopwith Aviation built a biplane with four landing wheels arranged at the corners of a square, the fuselage being level on the ground. This was never finished, and a larger AT, the Sparrow, replaced it. One of the best types was a trim monoplane by Capt de Havilland, and another monoplane was designed under Harry Folland at the Royal Aircraft Factory at Farnborough. Both these monoplane types were powered by one of the more successful engines by Granville Bradshaw, an ABC flat-twin rated at 35 hp for a two-hour life and probably the first-ever expendable aero engine. Low sought flight stability without the use of a gyro, and most of his own team's effort was devoted to trying to perfect the radio control system, which required receiver wires to be wrapped round wings and fuselage. Work was hampered by various difficulties, and though impressive advances were made no AT ever saw active service. The intention was to launch production ATs as SAMs against Zeppelins and tactical SSMs against targets in the rear of the enemy on the ground. After the Armistice an enthusiast in Billericay modified a Farnborough-built AT into a sporting single-seater; he still has the engine.

## Low Rocket

In 1917 Professor Low designed, built and flew a radio-controlled rocket, with the help of Cdr Brock, RN. Brock was killed at Zeebrugge and this amazingly prophetic weapon system was never brought to the operational stage.

## RAE Target

In 1920 Farnborough, by now the Royal Aircraft Establishment, began work on a new series of radio-controlled monoplanes, powered by the 45 hp Armstrong Siddeley Ounce, for ship launching. Extensive trials took place from the carrier *Argus*, and

from the bow of a destroyer with takeoff boost by a falling bag of sea-water. Sea-skimming was demonstrated using no altitude guidance other than precision-aneroid control of the elevators, with steering by air-driven torpedo gyros precessed left or right by radio signals. Plans for an explosive-carrying version remained on paper, however.

## RAE Larynx

When the RAE Target was dropped in 1923 work continued on paper, and in 1925 an Air Ministry requirement was issued for an SSM to carry a 200 lb (91 kg) warhead 200 miles (322 km) in one hour. Only the RAE, a secure establishment, worked on this project, and it took shape in 1926. The name stemmed from the 220 hp Armstrong Siddeley Lynx radial engine (with a helmeted cowl representing hundreds of man-hours by the coppersmiths). The prototype made a fine 100 mile (160 km) flight down the Bristol Channel after hydraulic-catapult launch from a destroyer, with only autopilot guidance but using radio to plot progress by shore D/F and telemetry to transmit engine rpm. In 1928–30 many Larynx were flown on a desert range in Iraq, under George (later Sir George) Gardner. On some flights a 250 lb (114 kg) bomb was carried. These were the first missiles to be used by the RAF, and probably the first guided SSMs in the world to see active service.

*Right and below: Larynxes Nos 2 and 3 (numbers stencilled on packing cases) on the launcher aboard HMS Stronghold in 1927. There were no ailerons, and only autopilot guidance.*

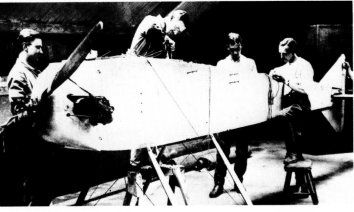

# Miles Hoop-la

In 1940, recognizing that circumstances called for unusual measures, Miles Aircraft at Woodley proposed to the Ministry of Aircraft Production (MAP) a pilotless flying bomb able to hit German cities. Possibly the idea was triggered by a well-argued feature in *The Aeroplane* by C. R. Tennant, pointing out the RAF's lack of success in finding point targets and insisting that future attacks should be aimed at whole cities (which is exactly what happened). The answer was clearly a flying machine that carried no gun turrets and large crews but just bombs. The Miles Hoop-la proposal was built round a 1,000 lb (454 kg) GP bomb, and a mock-up of 14 ft (4·3 m) span was quickly built, able to reach an estimated 300 mph (483 km/h) on a Gipsy Major engine. Miles suggested Hoop-las should be mass-produced and stored. The MAP showed not the slightest interest.

# Red/Blue Rapier UB.109T

In the heightened tension of the Korean war the British tried to make up for years of stagnation in defence procurement. One way of quickly acquiring deterrent capability appeared to be to deploy hundreds, or even thousands, of pilotless bombers – in the words of the C-in-C Bomber Command, Sir Hugh Pughe Lloyd, "just glorified V-1s". In the absence of any other form of guidance a radio area-coverage system was to be used, based on either Oboe (pulse) or Decca (CW), each bomb being programmed to dive at a particular point. This limited range to 461 miles (742 km) from the guidance transmitters. Flying at 600 mph (966 km/h) this meant targets could be hit in three-quarters of an hour, giving some capability

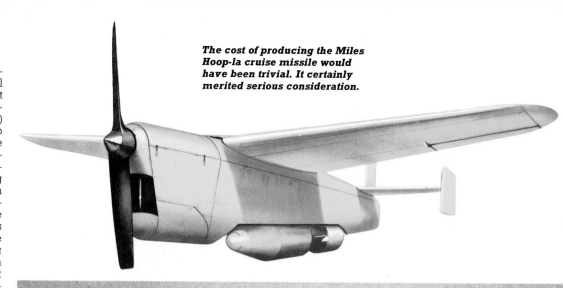

*The cost of producing the Miles Hoop-la cruise missile would have been trivial. It certainly merited serious consideration.*

*Blue Water was one of a long succession of British missiles and manned military aircraft of the late 1950s that were cancelled for reasons unconnected with design or performance.*

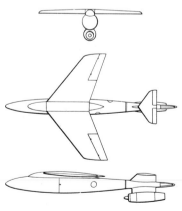

**Above:** *Three-view of the Blue Rapier, the Bristol 182 (in some publications incorrectly called Red Rapier). This again was cancelled before flight.*

**Right:** *Contrast between the clumsy unguided Honest John bought from the United States for the British Army and the neat precision-guided Blue Water which was cancelled.*

against moving targets with a conventional warhead weighing 5,000 lb (2268 kg); later it was hoped nuclear warheads could be made to fit these missiles, as certainly would have been the case. Contracts were let to specification UB.109T (UB, unmanned bomber), and the two accepted submissions, the Bristol 182 and Vickers 825, were respectively given the codenames Blue Rapier and Red Rapier. The latter was a sleek light-alloy missile with three Rolls-Royce Soar turbojets, each of 1,750 lb (794 kg) thrust, arranged ahead of a butterfly tail. The Bristol had a single BE.17 turbojet, of 3,000 lb (1361 kg) thrust, underslung at the back; it had a beautifully simple airframe of moulded Durestos, priced at £600 at a production rate of 500 per month. Both projects were well advanced when the programme was shortsightedly cancelled in July 1953.

## Blue Water

The pointless history of Red Rapier was to be repeated in the case of almost all the many British combat-aircraft and missile programmes of the 1950s. One of the later projects, and one that would have filled a vital niche in the NATO armoury, was Blue Water, despite the fact that its development was begun in 1958 to meet a War Office need for a Corps-Support Rocket (CSR) to replace the American Corporal, and the NATO Standing Group also announced a European need for such a weapon. Prime contractor was English Electric Aviation's GW Division at Stevenage, which had not only developed Thunderbird but also acted as foster-parent for Corporal in British Army service since 1956. Shortcomings of the US weapon were all too evident, and Blue Water could hardly have been more cost-effective. Though a six-round transporter/launcher was designed, the whole weapon system other than a self-testing digital computer could also be carried on a standard 3-ton Bedford truck. The missile had dual-thrust motor, inertial strapdown guidance, quick-change warheads and a reaction time of a few minutes. A theodolite set up the stable platform by looking through a hole in the missile at a mirror inside. Data on trajectory, cutoff time and (for nuclear heads) burst height were fed by the computer, and the firing countdown took less than 40 sec. Talks were held with West Germany on joint production, but the whole programme was killed by the existence of the American Sergeant which did the same job in a system weighing three times as much and costing five times as much. Cancellation was in 1962.

**Dimensions:** Length 25 ft (7·6 m); diameter 24 in (610 mm).
**Launch weight:** 3,000 lb (1361 kg).
**Range:** up to 55 miles (88·5 km).

**USA**

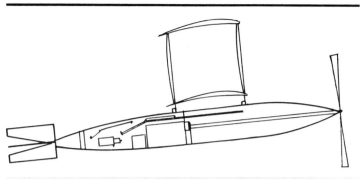

## Buck AT

In early 1916 Dr F. W. Buck, of Flagler, Colorado, designed and built a series of Aerial Torpedoes with biplane wings, flying the first in April. Launched by compressed-air catapult from an automobile, the flying bomb devices had different piston engines and timing mechanism to release the wings after covering the required distance on the launch heading. The drawing shows a later version.

**Left:** *A reconstruction of an American diagram showing the Aerial Torpedo by Dr Buck. Wing span was extremely short, but several examples flew.*

## Kettering and Sperry Bugs

With the support of the US Army (USA), Charles Kettering, of Delco Inc – a prolific engineer who also masterminded high-octane petrol – designed a tactical SSM system in the summer of 1917. The first tests were made with a modified trainer at Sperry Gyroscope's plant at Great Neck, Long Island, and at Wright Field, these eventually consistently demonstrating a 300 ft (91 m) accuracy after a 40 mile (64 km) flight. For operational use a smaller, purpose-designed missile was needed, and under "Ket" Delco and Sperry jointly produced a simple biplane powered by a 40 hp Ford two-stroke aircooled engine which also provided pressure and vacuum for the flight controls. Airframe was papier-maché reinforced with wood, with card skin. The "Bug" weighed 300 lb (136 kg) and carried the same weight of high explosive inside the circular-section fuselage. Height was governed by sensitive aneroid, and flight controls were driven by bellows taken from player-pianos (at first dihedral alone was used for lateral stability, proving inadequate). After taking off from a four-wheel railed trolley the Bug could fly up to 62 miles (100 km) with fair accuracy, a counter separating the wings when the calculated number of engine revolutions had been completed. The future Chief of Staff, "Hap" Arnold, went to France in October 1918 to set up Bug Squadrons to fire "thousands every day against German strong points, concentration areas, munition plants, etc"; then came the Armistice.

**Above left:** *The best photograph of the Kettering Bug, large numbers of which were tested in Ohio in 1917-18.*

**Middle:** *Four-cylinder Bugs in a Sperry inspection shop in the spring of 1918. Tails were fitted immediately before flight.*

**Left:** *This large autopilot-controlled recoverable aircraft was used by Sperry in the development of the Kettering Bug.*

# Modisette Hot Shot

Robert Modisette, perhaps ironically head of contract termination at Convair's Vultee Field Division in World War 2, built and flew pilotless bombers in 1917 when he was vice-president of Mullin Manufacturing of Salem, Ohio, a major car and aircraft subcontractor in World War 1. His Hot Shot was a spruce/fabric biplane with two "hotted up" Ford auto engines. A unique feature was lateral stabilization by air motors driven by fresh air pumped in by exhaust turbos,

the air supply being governed by a lateral pendulum. A clockwork drive caused the aircraft to level off at the desired altitude. The same mechanism put the elevators hard down when the correct air mileage had been covered, while air valves released the three 65 lb (29·5 kg) bombs and also disconnected the wings, causing the missile to follow its bombs. Four demonstrations for the Navy in July, August and September 1917 were impressive enough for negotiations to be opened for mass-production, and this SSM was actually in production at the Armistice.

**Dimensions:** Span 40 ft (12·2 m); length 19 ft 8 in (6·0 m).
**Launch weight:** 1,790 lb (812 kg).
**Range:** 160 miles (257 km).

**Below: *Contemporary sketch of the Modisette lateral-stability system. Inset: Hot Shots were built with both landing gear and a flying-boat hull.***

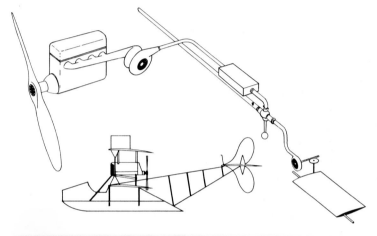

# BQ Series

This US Army category, introduced in 1942, was defined as Controllable Bomb, Ground Launched. It comprised a diversity of explosive-carrying versions of established aerial targets, converted piloted aeroplanes (including large bombers) and purpose-designed aircraft that were true SSMs. XBQ-1 was a completely new twin-engined design by Fleetwings, with Menasco or Ranger inline engines, and with fixed tricycle landing gear and cockpit added to the prototype. Flight testing by the manufacturer and USAAF in 1943 was soon backed up by the radial-engined XBQ-2A, with otherwise similar airframe. The XBQ-3 was a radio-controlled version of the Fairchild AT-21 Gunner twin-engined crew trainer, with a 4,000 lb (1814 kg) bomb payload, twice the load of XBQ-1 and -2. The next numbers were allotted to Interstate Aircraft & Engineering: XBQ-4 (Navy XTDR-1), -5, -6 and -6A were all low-cost single-engined flying bombs of low performance.

By far the largest of the BQ series were the BQ-7 and -8, respectively conversions of the B-17 Fortress and B-24 Liberator. In the summer of 1944 about 27 war-weary 8th Air Force B-17F and G Fortresses were taken off operations and completely gutted. A popular name for the project was Willie, from Weary Willie. Radio command equipment and autopilot/flight-control servos were then fitted, and the centre fuselage filled with 20,000 lb (9072 kg) of Torpex, a British explosive 50 per cent more powerful than amatol, with duplicated impact fuzes. The flight-deck roof was cut away, and the exterior sprayed white. The resulting ASM was designated BQ-7, officially named Aphrodite and used in a plan called Project Perilous. Assigned to the 562nd Bomb Squadron

**Left and below: *Two photographs of a BQ-7 Aphrodite, almost certainly taken at Fersfield in the summer of 1944. Warhead fuzes were set from the cockpit.***

of the 388th Bomb Group, operating from Fersfield, Norfolk, at least eight live missions were flown against extremely hard structures in the Pas de Calais. The BQ-7 was taken off by a human pilot and radio operator who set course, confirmed handover to radio control and activated the fuzes. Then, near the English coast, both men baled out by parachute. The BQ-7 was subsequently steered by a "mother" aircraft, invariably a DB-34 Ventura, with another B-17 to navigate and a P-38 ready to shoot down the missile should the command link be lost. Alternative schemes included guidance from the ground using an SCR-584 radar or a TV orthicon camera in the missile. Much argument centred on the missile's vulnerability and the inability of handling a mass attack. Results on operations were poor, and on at least two occasions control was lost while still over England, one aircraft hitting the ground with a devastating explosion at Sudbourne Park, Suffolk, on 4 August 1944. Data for BQ-7:

**Dimensions:** Length 74 ft 9 in (22·8 m); span 103 ft 9 in (31·6 m).
**Launch weight:** About 55,000 lb (24 948 kg).
**Range:** Several hundred miles, but only about 11 miles (17·7 km) from director aircraft.

There were not many BQ-8 Liberators, but two were converted in England under Project Anvil, and both had dramatic endings. Both were filled with 25,000 lb (11 340 kg) of Torpex, possibly the largest "warhead" of any conventional missile in history. The nose was rebuilt to house an RCA vidicon TV camera installation, with large transmitting aerials supplying the picture (looking down and ahead) to a monitor screen in an accompanying B-17 of the USAAF. Both the aircraft thus rebuilt belonged to the Navy, formerly being P4Y-1 Liberators of Bomb Squadron VB-110. Guidance was complex, because the B-17 crew had to watch the screen and pass guidance commands to a PV-1 Ventura director of the US Navy. On 12 August 1944 the first operational mission left Fersfield bound for a German secret-weapon installation in northern France. Over the Blyth estuary near Southwold the crew, one of whom was Lt Joseph P. Kennedy, brother of the future US President, set the fuzes and prepared to leave. The fuzes instantly detonated, causing damage over a 6-mile (10-km) radius on the ground far below. The second, with Lt Ralph Spaulding as pilot, was successfully set on course for an airfield in Heligoland on 3 September 1944. Just before the target heavy flak smashed the TV camera, but guidance remained and the B-17 and PV-1 saw the stupendous explosion on impact. This was the only successful mission of its kind by the Allies in World War 2.

# JB Series

In June 1944 the "V-1" appeared to exert a surprising influence on the US Army Air Force, which had known of the existence of this cruise missile for many months. Within three weeks a new JB – jet-powered bomb – category had been authorised, frantic studies launched at Wright Field, and contracts signed with several manufacturers. The first was with Northrop, whose JB-1 was one of that company's remarkable flying-wing aircraft. Trials began with the MX-543 "Bat" piloted model, which Harry Crosby found difficult to land because of its powerful ground-cushion effect. Then came the JB-1A proper, powered by two small GE turbojets and carrying two 2,000 lb (907 kg) bombs, with no landing gear and

launched from a sled acceler-ated by five JATO rockets. Range was to be 670 miles (1078 km) but too many technical difficulties supervened. The JB-2 was essentially an Americanized V-1, with Ford pulsejet of 800 lb (363 kg). About 330 were delivered to the AAF by a consortium of auto manufacturers for use against Japan but none saw action. Unlike the German original, acceleration along the ramp was by cordite rocket. Several flew nicely from Boeing B-17 Fortresses. JB-3 Tiamat was a 625 lb (283 kg) rocket with semi-active radar seeker and frag-mentation warhead for air-to-air use. JB-4 was a 3,000 lb (1361 kg) pulsejet of 75 miles (121 km) range cruising at 445 mph (716 km/h). JB-5 was an 850 lb (386 kg) wingless rocket of 4 mile (6½ km) range. JB-6 was a spin-

stabilized supersonic rocket. JB-7 was a 9,700 lb (4400 kg) turbojet pilotless bomber with 400 miles (644 km) range. JB-10 was the final Northrop flying-wing bomb, with integral Ford pulse-jet, which flew 200 miles (322 km) in half an hour with a 3,209 lb (1456 kg) warhead. The whole JB programme was halted in March 1946.

**Below left:** *A JB-3 Tiamat on an A-26 Invader in March 1945. Subsequently there were many other Tiamat versions for pure research purposes.*

**Below:** *JB-2 at Holloman Field in late 1944; most JB-2 flights were at Eglin Field in Florida.*

**Second below:** *A JB-2 before release from a B-29, over Santa Rosa island in April 1945.*

# Hellcat F6F

In the early 1950s the Grumman Hellcat was one of the most im-portant radio-controlled targets of the US Navy, used in at least 14 missile programmes. Not gener-ally known is the fact that several F6F-5K "targets" were convert-ed into powerful SSMs, with 2,000 lb (907 kg) warhead and in some cases with a TV camera, and embarked aboard USS *Boxer* in 1952 as equipment of a special unit, US Navy Guided Missile Unit 90, and used operationally in Korea. The first mission took place on 28 August 1952, and there were several subsequent operations. Director aircraft were AD-2D Skyraiders.

**Data:** As for F6F fighter, see companion volume *Combat Air-craft of World War 2* p. 230.

**Left:** *A Northrop JB-1 at Eglin Field on 25 November 1944. The heavy ordnance load of 4,000 lb (1814 kg) was carried in the two wing-root nacelles.*

**Below:** *On 6 April 1945 the same launch ramp received the first flight-cleared JB-10. This carried a single warhead surrounding a pulsejet.*

# Hermes

This was the first major US ballistic-rocket programme, the USA at Fort Bliss (with Von Braun's imported team from Germany) being backed by General Electric as prime industrial contractor. There were many subtypes, some being for research or the testing of hardware but A-3 being a ballistic missile to carry a 1,000 lb (454 kg) warhead 150 miles (242 km). In 1953–54 seven A-3A and six A-3B flew at White Sands, but accomplished little other than to provide an underpinning for later ballistic missiles.

# Corporal

The author was naturally impressed watching this slim ballistic rocket fly in 1955; but seen from nearly a quarter-century later it merely emphasizes how far missile technology has progressed. It was designed rather hastily in 1951 on the basis of the existing Corporal E research vehicle, with designation SSM-A-17. Prime contractor was JPL, the Jet Propulsion Laboratory of Caltech, and in the absence of any yardstick later than A-4 it was a creditable achievement. The fineness ratio (slenderness) of the vehicle was possibly a mistake, the weapon system weighed over 100 tons and rode on more than 15 vehicles, a battalion had 250 men, and once it had decided where to fire a missile it was seven hours before the button could be pressed. The guidance system was a complex combination of surveying, computing, doppler measurement and radio command, chiefly managed by Gilfillan. The 20,000 lb (9072 kg) thrust rocket chamber by Ryan was fed with monoethyl aniline and RFNA, and control was by refractory vanes and aerodynamic rudders. Though slim, this missile packed a punch; not many artillery shells have such a calibre, and this was the first weapon ever to put a kiloton warhead into the hands of a field army, in 1953. Production rounds, with Army designation M2, were assembled by Firestone, which made most of the airframe, and several hundred rounds were supplied to the USA and British army, the weapon remaining operational until 1966 with 47 GW Regt Royal Artillery. Subsequently M2 became MGM-5A and the refined M2A1 became MGM-5B. For most of their active life two USA battalions were based in Italy.

**Dimensions:** Length 46 ft (14 m); diameter 30 in (762 mm).
**Launch weight:** 12,000 lb (5443 kg).
**Range:** Up to 70 or 86 miles (113 or 138·4 km) depending on warhead.

*Right: A joint JPL/Army firing at White Sands of an early SSM-A-17 Corporal. At this stage one still needed hardened shelters for the launch crew and observers.*

**Above:** *This Hermes, an A-2, is seen at White Sands but never flew. General Electric tested engines at its Malta Test Station, Schenectady.*

# Matador and Mace

When the USAAF terminated its wartime BQ and JB programmes it already had much more advanced replacements. One was Snark (p. 58). The other was a pilotless bomber designated XB-61, less ambitious than Snark but still far in advance of previous concepts. The specification was drafted in August 1945, but the end of World War II took the pressure off and it was 1947 before the contract was let to Glenn L. Martin. Cutbacks stretched out the timescale, but the Korean war in July 1950 put the pressure on again and the production design of what had become B-61A (later TM-61A) Matador was approved in February 1951. Range was too great for inland desert ranges and flight testing took place at Patrick AFB, Cocoa Beach, nucleus of the future Cape Canaveral complex. Carrying a 3,000 lb (1361 kg) nuclear or conventional warhead, Matador was launched from a hardened shelter or mobile ramp under the 50,000 lb (22 680 kg) push of a boost motor under the T-tail, cruise propulsion being by a 4,600 lb (2087 kg) thrust Allison J33-A-37 centrifugal turbojet fed by a flush ventral inlet. The original MSQ guidance required line-of-sight radio links and limited usable range to much less than the design figure of 650 miles (1046 km); TM-61B added Shanicle hyperbolic guidance and could fly about 500 miles (800 km).

Over 1,000 Matadors served in the USAF inventory from 1955, subsequently being designated MGM-1C. By this time The Martin Company, as it had become, was testing much later versions that matured as TM-76 Mace. Powered by a 5,200 lb (2359 kg) thrust J33-A-41 expendable turbojet, Mace had a much bigger fuselage with double the fuel capacity and larger nuclear warhead. Full range was achieved by choice of either of two self-contained guidance systems: TM-76A (later MGM-13B and then MGM-13A) had Goodyear Atran terrain-comparison guidance and TM-76B (later CGM-13C and then CGM-13B) AC Spark Plug AChiever inertial guidance. Airframe was even more advanced metal sandwich than that of Matador, and Mace squadrons not only used harden-

**Above:** *Zero-length blast-off of an XB-61 Matador from Cape Canaveral on 19 November 1953. At this time neither the mobile vehicles nor hardened shelters had been designed.*

ed shelters (missile CGM-13B) but also cross-country mobile launchers (missile MGM-13A). The 38th Tac Missile Wing became operational in West Germany with Mace A in June 1959,

and the first Mace B wing became combat ready in 1961 and moved to Okinawa. Mace was withdrawn from combat service in 1966.

**Dimensions:** Span (Matador) 27 ft 10 in (8·5 m), (Mace) 22 ft 11 in (7 m); length (Matador) 39 ft 8·6 in (12·2 m), (Mace) 44 ft (13·4 m).
**Launch weight:** (Matador) 12,000 lb (5443 kg), (Mace) 18,000 lb (8165 kg).

**Below:** *Launch on 31 October 1962 of TM-76B from a hardened shelter at Cape Canaveral; inset, four TM-76A set for rapid fire at Holloman in 1960.*

**Above:** *Hangar A at Patrick AFB in July 1953 was full of test XB-61s (red) and unpainted B-61As of the 1st and 69th Pilotless Bomber Squadrons.*

# Honest John

This was the first post-war American missile to become operational, though it was a simple spin-stabilized rocket without guidance and posed few development or troop-training problems. USA Ordnance studies began in 1950, following which Douglas Aircraft submitted proposals and was appointed system prime contractor. Firing trials under what became the Army Rocket and Guided Missile Agency were completed at White Sands Missile Range in 1951, and the main contractor for production rounds was Emerson Electric who delivered over 20,000 of these formidable rockets. Each round was a 23 in (584 mm) solid motor to which was attached a nuclear, conventional, chemical or other 30 in (762 mm) warhead. The original designation for the two production rockets was M31 and M50, changed in 1962 to MGR-1A and -1B. At takeoff from a rail on a six-wheel truck the missile was spun by four canted spin motors, the rotation being sustained by the canted fins. Aiming was quick with a skilled launch crew, though the missile was no more accurate than conventional artillery rounds and more influenced by winds. Reloads of assembled rounds could be swung on by crane inside five minutes. At one time a lightweight launcher was used to permit the airlifting of complete systems slung under H-37 Mojave helicopters. In addition to the USA, Honest John was used by the armies of Belgium, Denmark, France, West Germany, Greece, Holland, Italy, South

**Above:** *South Korea, 1968, and an Honest John crew of the 2nd Inf Div receive target coordinates by field telephone.*

**Right:** *Test shot at White Sands.*

Korea, Taiwan, Turkey and the UK. Most have at least begun to phase out Honest John in favour of guided weapons.

**Dimensions:** Length 24 ft 10 in (7·57 m); fin span 54 in (1·37 m).
**Launch weight:** Typically 4,500 lb (2041 kg).
**Range:** $4\frac{1}{2}$–23 miles (7·25 to 37 km).

# Little John

The USA Rocket and Guided Missile Agency, predecessor of ABMA, developed this artillery rocket, much lighter and more mobile than ponderous Honest John, as an "in house" project at Redstone Arsenal in 1955–56. Industrial contractors were Emerson Electric (airframe), Hercules (motor) and Consolidated Western Steel (launcher). The original M47 missile and M32 launcher were replaced by the M51 carried on the M34 launcher designed at Rock Island Arsenal. The whole system was air- and helicopter-portable, and evaluation by the 101st Airborne Division took place in 1958. There were shortcomings, and Little John did not reach combat status until December 1961, thereafter having a short life. In the revised DoD scheme it became MGR-3A.

**Dimensions:** Length 14 ft 6 in (4·42 m); diameter $12\frac{1}{2}$ in (317 mm).
**Launch weight:** 780 lb (354 kg).
**Range:** Up to 10 miles (16 km).

**Left:** *Fort Knox, 1962, and men of the 101st Airborne persist with the Little John missile, despite the fact that by then major deployment was out.*

# Redstone

In 1950 Von Braun and his team of some 130 engineers were moved from Fort Bliss to Redstone Arsenal, Alabama, along with over 500 USA personnel, several hundred GE workers (ex-Hermes) and 120 government civilians. The Ordnance Guided Missile Center, which in 1956 became the chief part of ABMA, pioneered ballistic missiles in the Western world, and Redstone was its first product. Outbreak of the Korean war in June 1950 triggered and then accelerated first the study and then the engineering design of a missile more advanced than the A-4, with a range of 500 miles (805 km). In 1951 the Army reduced the range to 200 miles, which, while allowing the use of an engine derived directly from the Navaho (p. 59) cruise engine, permitted the missile to be mobile, used by combat troops in the field, and to carry a nuclear warhead (which in 1951 meant a 3-ton package).

Redstone, part of weapon system SSM-A-14 and designated M8, flew from Cape Canaveral on 20 August 1953. By May 1958 after 36 firings Redstone was launched by Battery A of the 40th Field Artillery Missile Group, and it became operational the following month with USA units in Germany. Each FAMG numbered about 600 men, with many large vehicles carrying among other things a lox plant producing 20 short tons per day. Over 1,000 missiles were delivered, prime contractor for most major parts of the whole system, including vehicles, being Chrysler.

Though naturally based on A-4 technology, Redstone was slightly fatter, much longer and heavier, and introduced a totally new pure-inertial guidance system by Ford Instrument division of Sperry Rand, using air-bearing gyros. North American Aviation's new rocket group, later Rocketdyne, produced the A-6 engine running on lox/alcohol supplied by a 780 hp turbopump and with refractory deflection vanes and precision cutoff system. The re-entry vehicle separated after cutoff, and was controlled by small wedge fins round the skirt. Redstone was the ultimate expression of the classic ballistic missile in which setting up a round and launching it was the outcome of hours of toil. By 1960 men of the USA were training with Pershing, which replaced Redstone completely by 1963. In the revised designation scheme Redstone became PGM-11A. The Redstone formed the basis of the Jupiter C vehicle that launched America's first satellite; and a Redstone launched America's first (sub-orbital) astronaut in May 1961.

**Dimensions:** Length (originally) 63 ft (19·2 m), (late production) 69 ft (21 m); diameter 70 in (1·78 m).
**Launch weight:** 61,000–62,000 lb (27 670–28 123 kg).
**Range:** Up to 249 miles (400 km) depending on payload (until July 1958 the USA was prohibited from deploying a weapon with range in excess of 200 miles).

**Right: *Launch of Redstone missile No 2011 at White Sands on 26 January 1960. The serial number does not mean over 2,000 M8 missiles were produced.***

**Above: *One of the superficially attractive weapon systems that failed to reach the hands of US Army troops was the M113 chassis carrying a multiple*** launcher for MGR-3A Little John. *Six rounds were carried on a trainable lattice launcher. Reloads had to be brought by a second M113 with a crane.*

# Sergeant

Before Corporal had progressed far it could be seen that with a fresh start a more attractive weapon system would be possible, but the Korean War pressure prevented this until in 1955 JPL was given a contract for the Sergeant system, the missile later being designated XM15 and subsequently MGM-29A. A year later Sperry Utah entered as associate for research, and not only handled production management but in July 1960 became (as Univac Salt Lake City) prime contractor for the system. Compared with Corporal, Sergeant is slightly fatter, much shorter and lighter. It has instantly ready solid propulsion by Thiokol, inertial guidance and far better performance and mobility. The whole battery travels in three semi-trailers and a standard truck, each missile is assembled prior to launch very quickly, and after a 30-minute count is launched at 75°. Control is by jet vanes and accurate timing of airbrakes which flick open around the rear of the guidance section. Sergeant became operational with the USA in April 1961. The only other user was West Germany, with the last being withdrawn in 1978.

**Dimensions:** Length 34 ft 10 in (10·6 m); diameter 31 in (785 mm).
**Launch weight:** 9,920 lb (4500 kg).
**Range:** 28–87 miles (45–140 km).

# Lacrosse

This fearsome battlefield missile, system SSM-A-12, was sponsored by the US Marine Corps, researched and engineered by Cornell Aeronautical Lab and JHU/APL, and finally put into production by the new Orlando (Florida) division of The Martin Company, the eventual customer being the USA, joined in 1958 by the Canadian Army. Each Lacrosse was assembled in the field from a high-impulse Thiokol solid motor, various conventional, nuclear or other warheads, four large swept wings and four small tail control fins. Launch from a 6 × 6 2½-ton truck was directed by a forward observer who could command the missile throughout its flight or hand over to a controller at another site or in a helicopter. Federal (IT&T) command guidance incorporated features giving night or bad-weather capability, though target position had to be known in advance. Once termed "the most accurate of all Army missiles" and by 1958 produced at the rate of nearly 280 per month, M4 Lacrosse was limited in value by its inability to resist countermeasures or hit a moving target. USA and Canadian battalions in Europe used Lacrosse until the early 1960s, the revised designation being MGM-18A.

**Dimensions:** Length 19 ft 2¼ in (5·83 m); diameter 20½ in (520 mm).
**Launch weight:** 2,300 lb (1043 kg).
**Range:** up to 19 miles (31 km).

Above: *White Sands, 14 October 1960, and troops of the 5th Bn, 30th Arty, from Ft Sill, have assembled their Sergeant missile ready for firing.*

Below left: *Grafenwöhr, Germany, 15 September 1961, and US artillerymen mate the warhead of a Lacrosse. Wings are on, but not yet the tail controls.*

Below: *Departure of a development Lacrosse (XSSM-A-12) from White Sands Navy blockhouse area on 23 May 1957. At this point Lacrosse looked great.*

Right: *Putting the wings on a Lance mounted on the air-portable lightweight launcher. This fits "Huey" helicopters and can be para-dropped.*

# Davy Crockett

This unguided spin-stabilized missile was by far the smallest in the world to have a nuclear warhead when introduced in 1962. A simple but frightening weapon, it comprised a solid motor (inserted into a tube aimed at the enemy) and fat warhead with fins. Titanium Metals gave a clue to the numbers involved when in 1960 it stated 5,000,000 lb (2,268,000 kg) of their alloys would be used in motor tubes alone by 1964. Little was heard of this missile in USA use, and it was not supplied to the British Army as had been planned.

# Lance

Whereas the 1957 plan by the USA was Missiles A, B, C and D (D becoming Pershing), the shorter-range weapons did not materialise as expected, and this excellent guided missile is far more powerful and effective than the original B or C. Vought Corporation's Michigan Division was selected as prime contractor in 1962, and the first test firing took place at WSMR in March 1965. By July missiles were being launched from the definitive launch vehicle, and a system was para-dropped the same year. Service testing in all climates and circumstances was complete by March 1972, and in the summer of that year Lance

was qualified as "standard".

Lance, MGM-52A, B and C, provides general fire support for a corps, replacing both Honest John and Sergeant and dramatically increasing effectiveness while reducing system personnel, weight, cost and problems. The missile itself has a Rocketdyne P8E-9 motor, burning hypergolic RFNA/UDMH, the first USA motor to use storable liquid propellants. The on-board gas generator pressurizes the

tanks, feeds propellants to the chamber and simultaneously discharges through four canted nozzles to spin the missile rapidly from launch. The USA developed the inertial guidance "in house", though production parts are by Bosch Arma and Systron-Donner. The motor has a 50,000 lb (22 680 kg) thrust boost nozzle and a sustainer whose thrust is variable from 5,000 lb (2268 kg) smoothly down to zero for near-perfect control of cutoff velocity.

*Left: 4 × 4 utility (Jeep) with Davy Crockett launcher, showing the recoil-cancelling rear nozzle. Missile container tubes are carried on the right.*

Various nuclear (M234, 10 kT) or conventional warheads (usually M251, with smaller fins on the missile) can be fitted, and the whole weapon system rides on two M113-type amphibious tracked vehicles, the M752 erector/launcher and the M688 resupply with two Lances and hoist. A different, light launcher by Hawker Siddeley Canada makes the system heli-portable or para-droppable from fixed-wing aircraft.

Vought has developed a Lance with DME precision guidance, and among many non-nuclear heads is a 1,000 lb (454 kg) Honeywell cluster head used by Lances serving with Israel, Belgium and Holland. (The only army to use nothing but the original M234 head is Britain's.) In 1977 the USA bought 360 non-nuclear heads and has extensively tested a TGSM system (p. 253) with six to nine hollow-charge heads individually fitted with IR seekers. An enhanced-radiation warhead – the so-called neutron bomb – exists for Lance but, despite its application to defence against oncoming armour, has been put on ice for political reasons. Other Lance operators include W Germany, Italy and, in 1978, two unnamed customers. Total cost of the Lance programme was $1,080 million. There is a possibility of reopened production for exports, and a range of proposals (which include the USN Sea-launched Cruise Missile) are being studied as replacements.

**Dimensions:** Length 20 ft 3 in (6·17 m); diameter 22 in (560 mm).
**Launch weight:** 3,373 lb (1530 kg); about 3,920 lb (1778 kg) with cluster head.
**Range:** Up to 75 miles (120 km); 45 miles (72 km) with cluster head.

*Left: Liftoff of Lance, spin-motors pouring smoke, from the M752 self-propelled erector/launcher.*

*Below: Lance elevated for firing from the M752 self-propelled erector/launcher.*

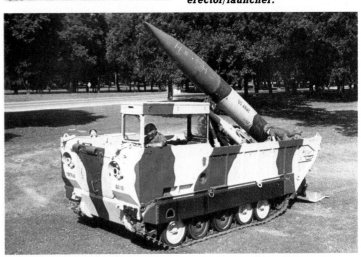

# Pershing

By 1957 the ABMA was conducting studies into future USA missiles, and Missile D was planned to cover the spread of ranges from 80 to 800 miles (129 to 1290 km). In 1958 the Wilson Memorandum forbidding USA missiles to exceed 200 miles (322 km) was rescinded, and the whole project was at once launched. Pershing, as it was named, was handed to The Martin Company (now Martin Marietta) Orlando Division, the first time the USA had followed the USAF in assigning a whole weapon system to an industrial prime contractor.

**Left:** *The white radar nose identifies the first Pershing II to be mated with the rest of the weapon system (1978). No Mk II missile had flown when this book went to press.*

In its original form Pershing 1 comprised a neat two-stage missile deployed as a Fire Unit on four FMC XM474 tracked vehicles. One carried the erector/launcher and missile body, another the programmer test station and power station, the third the radio terminal set and the fourth the nuclear warhead and azimuth laying equipment. Assembled, the missile was raised vertically, the erector arm lowered (leaving a reusable umbilical mast) and fired remotely. First-stage propulsion was a Thiokol TX-174, with average thrust of 26,290 lb (11 925 kg) for 38·3 sec. Second was a Thiokol TX-175, giving 19,220 lb (8718 kg) for 39 sec. The pre-launch programme inserted into the Eclipse-Pioneer inertial guidance controlled trajectory by three delta first-stage fins and three rectangular wedge fins on the second-stage skirt. The re-entry vehicle incorporated new technology in sharpcone ablation.

Flight testing down the AMR began on 24 February 1960, and in 1961 all shots were made using the full mobile weapon system, designated XM14. Initial operational capability with the USA was reached in July 1962, and in 1964 Pershing 1, by then designated MGM-31A, was in wide use in Germany with both the USA and Federal German Luftwaffe. In 1967 production switched to Pershing 1A, in which the same missile was matched with a completely new set of wheeled vehicles based on the M656 five-ton truck. Now transportable by C-130 aircraft, the system has cross-country performance, carries the whole missile on one vehicle, has better communications, and auto-countdown which reduces reaction time. In 1976 Europe-based units received the first of a further advance, Automatic Azimuth Reference System/Sequential Launch Adapter, which enables one commander to fire up to three missiles in succession and to shoot after only brief delay from a previously unsurveyed site (a task previously impossible).

Martin is now well advanced with Pershing II, which flies with Goodyear radar area-correlation guidance in the terminal phase. By comparing the oncoming target with stored images this gives such extreme accuracy that the unnecessarily powerful 400 kT warhead can be replaced by one of reduced yield. Various earth-penetrator heads are being studied, the terminal guidance is being tested in re-entry vehicles flown under the wing of an AF-1E Fury, and a modified Pershing II is being considered as the proposed Conventional Airfield Attack Missile to hit WP airbases.

**Dimensions:** Length 34 ft 9½ in (10·6 m); diameter 39½ in (1 m).
**Launch weight:** 10,141 lb (4600 kg).
**Range:** 100–460 miles (160–740 km).

# Longbow

In 1978 this name, previously used for a winged ASM (p. 122), was reported for a proposed "medium / intermediate - range ballistic missile" being studied by SAMSO and DARPA. Some $800,000 had then been allocated to conceptual studies for this weapon, which though having range of at least 1,000 miles (1600 km) would be used by the Air Force after 1985 in tactical roles.

# Tomahawk

The GLCM (Ground-launched Cruise Missile) version of Tomahawk emerged rather quietly in 1977 and in 1978 was expected to be designated BGM-109B. Surprisingly, it is to be used by USAF Tactical Air Command and the USAFE (USAF Europe) to cover targets in the European theatre worthy of a nuclear warhead, and release manned attack aircraft for other missions. GLCM will be launched by the same tandem boost motor as the Navy SLCM and, so far as is known in late 1978, will have maximum commonality. Data as for BGM-109 (p. 97).

*Left: Elements of the original Pershing I system ready for the march. The vehicles and loads are described in the text.*

*Below left: Launch of a Pershing from the Mk 1A system using cross-country wheeled vehicles. The canvas shelter at far right contains the Automatic Azimuth Reference System for the second missile.*

*Inset: The 56th Field Arty Bde, the only Pershing unit, on manoeuvres near Schwäbisch Gmund, Germany, in May 1976.*

*Below: Launch in 1978 of a dummy test vehicle from a land launcher being developed for the USAF Land Tomahawk.*

# SURFACE TO SURFACE MISSILES

This is the category of missiles that has most completely revolutionised warfare, and done most to deter it. When the first ICBMs towered balefully over a generally disinterested world in 1957 they were described as "the ultimate weapon". Most people, including the experts, believed this to be true. The few doubters based their arguments on the early ICBMs' poor reliability and accuracy; nobody publicly predicted until much later that what would actually happen would be that the ICBM would become so reliable and super-accurate as to be self-defeating, eliminating any weapon fired from a fixed base. Today the United States, at least, is scurrying around trying to find alternatives such as ICBMs whose location cannot be known to an enemy, and – a less likely concept – cruise missiles that can pierce modern defences.

The concept of the long-range rocket is ancient, and even the notion of push-button warfare was discussed in works of fiction well before World War 2. But the first strategic missile actually used was a baby pilotless aeroplane launched against London on 12 June 1944. Three months later came the utterly different A-4 ("V-2") rocket, probably the most futuristic weapon in history in that in structure, aerodynamics, propulsion, guidance, troop deployment, logistics and the problems posed to the defence, it reached out into totally uncharted regions and found workable answers. This is not to suggest that it was cost/effective or even of real value to Nazi Germany. It did not stave off that country's defeat; by diverting resources, it may even have hastened it. But it was the outstanding example of a weapon to which there was absolutely no answer.

After 1945 two super-powers, the United States and Soviet Union, had the resources and motivation to build an ICBM. The Russians predictably did so, though in an uninspired and plodding manner that by 1957 had put into service by far the biggest rocket the world had ever seen – or rather not seen, because it remained an enigma even after a derived vehicle had launched the world's first artificial satellite on 4 October 1957. Though a giant achievement, this pioneer ICBM, called Sapwood by the West, demonstrated the Soviet willingness to spend fantastic sums to achieve more offensive capability sooner. Subsequently much more efficient Soviet ICBMs replaced the 32-engined Sapwood, and year by year the Soviet ICBM capability has grown and grown until by 1979 it is frankly terrifying. All talk of a "strategic balance" has become sheer nonsense; in the series of missiles since SS-16 alone the Soviet RVSN has the capability of wiping out all the West's strategic missiles and all the West's cities, without even bothering to use the large numbers of earlier ICBMs.

In contrast, in 1947 the USAAF issued a contract to Convair to study the ICBM problem but then cancelled it (Convair flew three MX-774 vehicles partly with its own funds). Six years later, in 1953, it was mainly the USAF Assistant Secretary for R&D, Trevor Gardner, who gradually managed to convince people that an ICBM should at least be investigated. He convened the Teapot Committee under John Von Neumann, with a galaxy of scientific talent, and this reported that an ICBM was not only feasible but could be developed inside six years. One muses on the situation that would have existed in 1959 if Gardner had meekly accepted the prevailing view that an ICBM was either impossible or too far in the future to bother about. As it was, thanks to one or two dynamic managers such as Schriever in USAF uniform, Bossart at Convair and Drs Simon Ramo and Dean Wooldridge – both members of the Teapot Committee who went into business together as technical directors of the entire ICBM programme – and to the massive technical fallout from the Navaho cruise missile, including the complete propulsion system, the Atlas ICBM flew in mid-1957 and achieved IOC in September 1959. It was still woefully unreliable, and its CEP varied from a mile to many miles, from shot to shot – but it was infinitely better than nothing.

By 1959 the USAF had come a long way beyond Atlas. Spurred by the amazing success of a revitalised Navy in solving even newer problems with Polaris it asked Boeing to develop Minuteman, a much smaller ICBM whose limited throw-weight was more than compensated for by a CEP measured in metres. Fuelled by solid propellant, it could be stored out of reach of enemy ICBM attack in hardened silos, yet fired within a minute of the command being given – in contrast to the previous cryogenic ICBMs which had a reaction time of about an hour. Even more significant was the decision to deploy a proportion of the Minuteman force aboard special trains so that at any given moment they might be anywhere on the US railroad system. It is probably a grave mistake not to have built Mobile Minuteman. By 1959 it should have been possible to predict that inertial guidance systems were going to become more accurate year by year, so that it would eventually be possible to fire a single ICBM in order to destroy a hostile ICBM in a hardened silo more than 5000 miles (8000 km) distant. One suspects that, while this capability could indeed be foreseen, it was foolishly believed that it would be possessed only by the United States. Nowhere more than in strategic missiles has thinking about Soviet capability been more consistently under-rated.

During the 1960s the Soviet Union came from behind and overhauled the strategic missile strength of the USAF, and the submarine-based deterrence of the US Navy. In the 1970s American ICBM production wound down to a stop, but if anything Soviet RVSN installations grew even more rapidly than before. By this time the ICBM was as deadly a weapon as it is possible to imagine: a sledgehammer with the precision of a surgeon's scalpel. The previous targeting inaccuracy, which stemmed from such basic factors as the gaps between the reasonably accurate mapping of each of the Earth's land-masses, had been completely overcome, so that trajectories over the North Pole or any other remote region could be worked out with end-to-end accuracy in the order of ten metres. This was a prerequisite to increased accuracy of inertial guidance systems, and by combining many large and small advances the best ICBM guidance by 1975 had a CEP over full range of about 300 metres, or under 1000 ft. There is every reason to believe that in the latest Soviet ICBMs the CEP is considerably less. It is the recognition of this extremely unpalatable fact that makes the USAF wish it had not cancelled Mobile Minuteman, not cancelled the Skybolt ALBM, and not placed such 100% reliance on concrete silos which have rather suddenly become extremely vulnerable. Throughout the ICBM era it has been central to American defence policy that it should enjoy a second-strike capability; its own missiles could absorb the worst that hostile missiles could do in a first-strike, and still hit back with devastating force. This is no longer possible. In a surprise first-strike existing RVSN missiles could knock out almost all of the American land-based deterrent.

There is one vital matter still to be covered. An ICBM, like most missiles, has an effectiveness that depends mainly on its payload, a euphemistic term meaning (in the case of other categories of missile) the warhead. In the modern ICBM the payload is much more than a mere warhead. For one thing, the ICBM inevitably arches up far above the atmosphere and re-enters at speeds that would make any ordinary warhead burn up. The earliest ICBMs had a blunt RV (re-entry vehicle) faced with a thick slab of copper, but missiles are not built to throw thick slabs of copper; and the drag was so high the RV

slowed to subsonic speed before impact. Two powerful companies in the United States, GE and Avco, solved the problems of creating streamlined lightweight ablative RVs which not only put the payload back into the warhead but also increased terminal speed and accuracy. We do not know whether the Russian RVs were homegrown or whether the answers to the vital puzzles were obtained in the same way as those that led to Soviet nuclear weapons 30 years ago.

By the 1960s it was clear that a plain RV that merely stopped the warhead from burning up would soon not be enough.

Today the latest RVs are not only much lighter than the old copper heat-sinks but carry a warhead down to low levels with a terminal velocity ten times as fast. Inside the slim modern RV is a mass of penaids – penetration aids – which solve seemingly impossible problems. The basic penaid has always been chaff, clouds of fine aluminium foil cut to lengths to match the wavelengths of defending radars. Chaff must be ejected as early as possible to deny the enemy the clear radar picture from which he can plot the exact trajectory of the incoming RV; but as soon as it sinks into the upper atmosphere the light chaff slows, while the speeding RV emerges in what is called "atmospheric sifting". Today we have chaff that can do clever things. We have active ECM, that emit false signals or jam enemy defences. We have RVs which, despite incredible delicacy and complexity, are protected not only against the forces and temperatures of re-entry but also against all the manifold effects of nearby nuclear explosions. We have absolutely foolproof arming and fuzing systems so that it can be guaranteed that no warhead will ever fail to detonate at the correct place and time. By no means least, we have Mirvs that can eject a cloud of separate warheads, each in its own RV, and each with its own guidance towards a different target. Many trajectories, techniques and hardware designs have been investigated in great depth in arriving at the payload that, for reasons of cost, only rides on a few Minuteman III missiles, and the much later and better payloads that could ride on an MX missile if such were built.

In general terms, attack on a hard target such as a missile silo demands missiles of ever greater accuracy. Bigger warheads and even Mirved warheads are of relatively little use, but by cutting the size of the CEP – the circle within which the warhead has a 50/50 chance of impacting – the SSKP can be multiplied many times. In contrast, in attacks on cities and other soft targets it pays to Mirv to the maximum extent.

# CHINA

The difficulties of reporting on Chinese (PRC) missiles are self-evident. One has to rely largely on the statements of the US DoD, which leaves one in no doubt of the awesome scale of effort on all forms of weaponry, especially strategic systems. In late 1977 the DoD reaffirmed that no PRC solid-propellant ballistic missile had then been flown, but that the emphasis in rocket development had swung strongly from liquid to solid, as in other countries. The following designations are from the same source.

## CSS-1

The first Chinese long-range missile to be publicly announced by the West, this was in flight test in the 1960s and reached the IOC stage in 1971–2. Since then the number deployed has risen slowly and is today certainly in the order of several dozen. CSS-1 is an MRBM, with ultimate range given variously as 684 and 1,118 miles (1100 and 1800 km). In the 1977 Military Posture Statement by the Chairman of the JCS it was stated that it could menace targets in "the Eastern USSR, peripheral nations and some US bases in the Far East. It is an obsolescent and cumbersome missile system with slow reaction time". Most observers judge its basis to have been the Soviet SS-2, though this is just the most likely guess.

## CSS-2

This is an IRBM, estimated to have a range of up to 1,727 miles (2780 km). The apparent accuracy of this estimate is misleading: the figures correspond to 1,500 nautical miles (1,727 miles, 2780 km), the US unit for strategic-missile range. It is said to be a single-stage weapon reminiscent of Jupiter or Thor, and to be installed in large fixed sites. Unofficial sources reported in 1973 that 20 were in operation, and several reports emphasize that this number has not been increased.

## CSS-3

This "limited-range ICBM", which unofficial sources put in the 4,030 mile (6486 km) category, is described by DoD as "a major enigma". It could have reached IOC by the end of 1975 but in mid-1978 had not been deployed.

## CSSX-4

This is the full-range ICBM, described as "in the same class as the US Titan and the Soviet SS-9". The DoD posture statement continued, "Full flight testing of this missile will require launches to an open-ocean impact area, probably in the Pacific but possibly into the Indian Ocean." No missile had flown by mid-1978, but Soviet responses included rearranging the ABM defences around Moscow to counter attacks from Chinese territory. Showing a rather less-urgent outlook, the American 1977 Posture Statement said the Chinese had "no present capability to attack the Continental United States directly and are unlikely to obtain one for at least several years". It is universally concluded that the eventual CSS-4 will be deployed in hardened silos, but today such installations are no longer secure.

# FRANCE

## Arsenal 5501

This rudimentary cruise missile was based upon the wartime V-1, though developed entirely in France and with French detail features and components. SFECMAS developed the pulse-jet engine, and unlike the German missile the 5501 had radio command guidance as well as an autopilot. Another difference was that the launch was by two solid rocket boost motors. Testing began in 1948, and in 1949 an air-launch took place near St Raphaël from an LeO 45, the missile thereafter being guided from a Junkers Ju 88. In 1951 the 5501 was terminated as a missile, the original application as a target continuing and eventually leading to the Aérospatiale CT 10.

**Below: *Ars 5501 No 33 ready for launch. France never put this vehicle into service as an SSM but developed the basically similar Caisseur.***

## SSBS

The largest single weapon programmes ever undertaken in any West European country working alone are the French national deterrent delivery systems SSBS and MSBS. Both are wholly French, though to plug gaps in national technology some licensing was permitted provided there was absolute security of national supply. SSBS (Sol-Sol Balistique Stratégique) was begun as an IRBM in 1959, the original management being vested in SEREB, the ad hoc prime contractor interfacing with DTE, the state customer. The team that created the first-generation SSBS was: Nord-Aviation, airframe and (with SNECMA) motors; Direction des Poudres, propellant; Sud-Avia-

**Right: *Test launch of one of the current series of S-3 IRBMs from the CEL on the shore of the Bay of Biscay, with impact area near the Azores.***

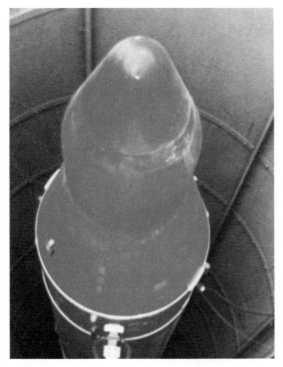

**Above:** *An SSBS Type S-2 photographed in its test silo at the CEL. The fission-type warhead has a nominal yield of 150 kT, and is not hardened.*

**Above:** *The CEL test silo is seen here occupied by an S-3 missile; this has a hardened thermonuclear warhead with a nominal yield of 1.2 MT.*

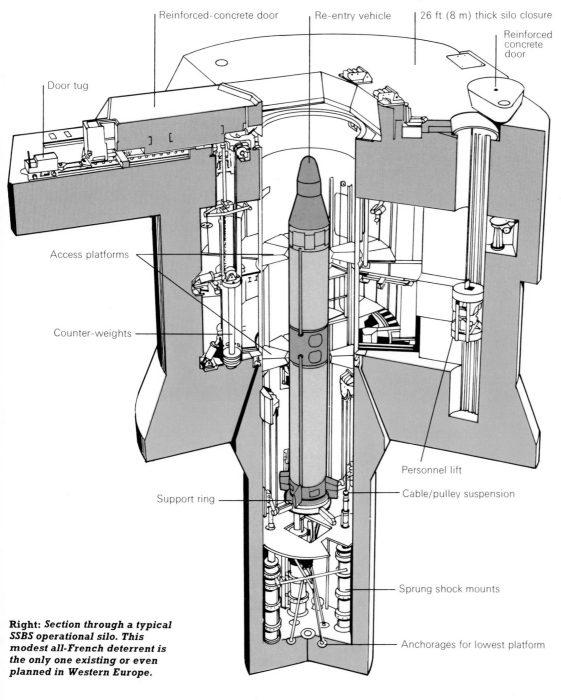

Reinforced-concrete door

Re-entry vehicle

26 ft (8 m) thick silo closure

Reinforced concrete door

Door tug

Access platforms

Counter-weights

Support ring

Personnel lift

Cable/pulley suspension

Sprung shock mounts

Anchorages for lowest platform

**Right:** *Section through a typical SSBS operational silo. This modest all-French deterrent is the only one existing or even planned in Western Europe.*

tion, RV and (with SEPR) gimballed nozzles. Later Aérospatiale was formed, absorbing Nord and Sud, and it assigned all the French ballistic systems to its Division Systèmes Balistiques et Spatiaux.

In the early 1960s a broad research programme included flight testing in Algeria of Agate, Topaze and Emeraude vehicles leading to a test missile combining all IRBM functions, Emeraude. In 1963 the go-ahead was given for the SSBS system for the Armée de l'Air. The first S-112 (dummy 2nd stage) was fired from a test silo in 1966. Tests of S-01 two-stage missiles followed, and the first SSBS prototype, of S-02 type, was launched in May 1969. The production S-2 reached IOC in the summer of 1971, and since then the full force of two groups each of nine silos has become combat-ready (a third group was cancelled in December 1974). The 1st GMS (Groupement des Missiles Stratégiques) is located in the Plateau d'Albion in Haute Provence. The area is officially St Christol airbase, with silos about 3 miles (5 km) apart; the group underground PCTs (fire-control posts) are at Rustrel and Reilhannette. Reaction time is about 200 sec.

S2 has a first stage, P-16/902, of maraging steel housing 35,273 lb (16 000 kg) of propellant giving 121,252 lb (55 000 kg) thrust for 76 sec through four gimballed nozzles. The second stage, P-10/903, has a flo-turned Vascojet casing, 22,046 lb (10 000 kg) of filling, and thrust of 99,206 lb (45 000 kg) for about 50 sec through four gimballed nozzles. The ablative RV houses a warhead of 150 kT. Guidance is inertial, SAGEM and SFENA being system leaders and incorporating licensed US technology.

In 1973 the go-ahead was received on the second-generation S-3 missile to replace S-2 in the same silos. This has the P-6 second stage developed for MSBS and a completely new Aérospatiale warhead with 1·2 MT yield and incorporating penaids. The whole missile is hardened against nuclear explosions at launch or from defending ABMs. An S-3 was first flown at CEL in December 1976, and IOC is planned for 1980.

**Dimensions:** Length (S2) 48 ft 7 in (14·8 m), (S3) 44 ft 11 in (13·7 m); diameter 59 in (1·5 m).
**Launch weight:** (S2) 70,547 lb (32 000 kg), (S3) 56,879 lb (25 800 kg).
**Range:** (S2) 1,709 miles (2750 km), (S3) 2,175 miles (3500 km).

# Cruise Missile

On 21 March 1977 the former Chief of the Defence Staff, Gen Gau Méry, announced that French industry had begun work on a cruise missile and a complementary satellite to provide precise guidance information. By mid-1978 there had been no further announcement on what surely ought to be a multinational programme.

# GERMANY

## Fieseler Fi 103 ("V-1")

Possibly the first guided missile to be used *en masse*, and one of the great weapon systems of history, this pioneer cruise missile stemmed from the pulsejet research begun by aerodynamicist Paul Schmidt in 1928. By 1939 the RLM had asked Argus to develop a "Schmidtrohr" engine, and this materialized as the As 109-014 rated at 660 lb (300 kg) at sea level. This engine had a grid of flap-valve springs in its inlet, which alternately admitted fresh air and then were blown shut against ram pressure by the ignition in the duct. Operating frequency was about 47 Hz, and noise and vibration were severe (though there were numerous aircraft applications as well as the missile).

After years of doubt the RLM finally gave the go-ahead for a Schmidtrohr-powered flying bomb on 19 June 1942 (not 1941 as often reported). The prime contract was placed with Gerhard Fieseler Werke, whose 1941 proposal had been planned under Dipl-Ing Robert Lusser. Walter were assigned the catapult with a slotted tube containing a free piston blown out by T/Z-stoff decomposition, and Siemens based the guidance on an Askania autopilot. Guidance was effected by compass heading, preset before launch, the autopilot, an aneroid for height, and an air-log propeller which, at the appropriate time, commanded a steep dive. Fieseler himself flew in an Fw 200C which in early December 1942 launched the first unpowered bomb; on 24 December a powered launch took place from Peenemünde-West. Frantic haste to beat the Army's A-4 rocket was hampered by initial failures, but the Ekdo Wachtel was beginning to work out the firing drill and train the first Luftwaffe launch units in July 1943.

As a cover the project was called FZG 76 (Flakzielgerät, flak aiming device), but the missile was the Fi 103 and the weapon was dubbed V-1 (Vergeltungswaffe, revenge weapon) by the Goebhels propaganda machine. To Londoners, first hit on 13 June 1944, it was the Doodlebug. Everyone ducked when the throbbing engine stopped, the cause being fuel starvation (despite pressurization of the tanks) at the start of the dive. Production of at least 29,000 missiles took place mainly at the gigantic slave mine called Mittelwerke near Nordhausen, with further production by Volkswagen at Fallersleben and Fieseler. The intended saturation attack never proved possible, and the best day's effort by "Flak Regiment 155(W)" was

316 launched from 38 catapults on 2 August 1944. By this time fighters and AA with prox-fuzes had gained the upper hand, and altogether only 2,419 bombs fell on London out of well over 8,000; another 2,448 fell on Antwerp. From July 1944 some 1,200 modified bombs were air-launched from Heinkel He 111H-22 bombers, some against northern England. An engineless Fi 103 was often towed at the Rechlin test centre behind an Arado Ar 234B jet to prove a scheme for jet air-launch at greater range. Reichenberg IV was the planned operational version of a piloted version extensively tested (initially by such famed people as Hanna Reitsch and Otto Skorzeny) but never used.

**Dimensions:** Span 17 ft 4¾ in (5·3 m) (tapered wing, 16 ft 0 in, 4·87 m); length 25 ft 11 in (7·9 m).
**Launch weight:** Typically 4,806 lb (2180 kg) (Reichenberg IV, 4,960 lb (2250 kg).
**Range:** With standard warhead up to 149 miles (240 km) at 400 mph (644 km/h) at 2,493 ft (760 m).

Above: *Probably taken on 23 June 1944, this authentic photograph shows a Spitfire IX on the point of tipping an Fi 103 over with its wing-tip.*

Above right: *Numerous shots exist of "Doodlebugs" falling on England. This one hit Drury Lane in London's west-central district, causing major damage.*

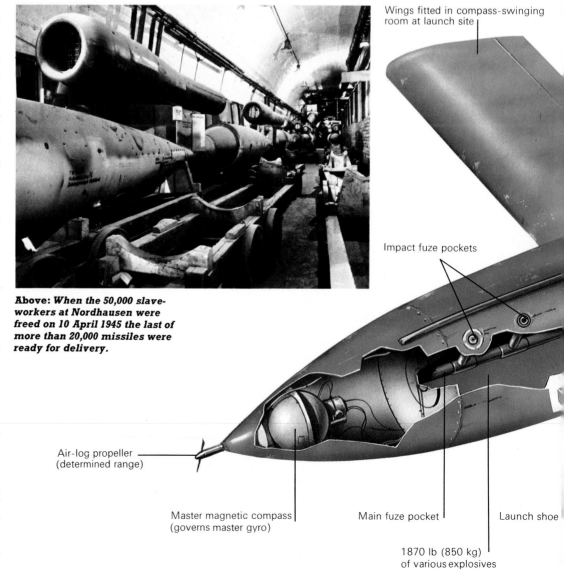

Above: *When the 50,000 slave-workers at Nordhausen were freed on 10 April 1945 the last of more than 20,000 missiles were ready for delivery.*

Wings fitted in compass-swinging room at launch site

Impact fuze pockets

Air-log propeller (determined range)

Master magnetic compass (governs master gyro)

Main fuze pocket

Launch shoe

1870 lb (850 kg) of various explosives

**Above right inset:** *A standard parallel-chord bomb leaving a "ski site" ramp in the Pas de Calais. Field commander was Oberst Max Wachtel.*

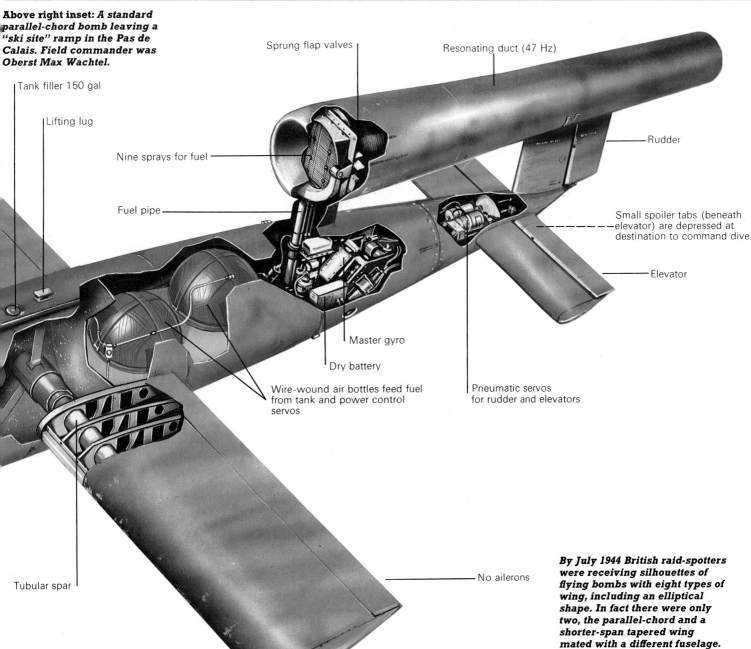

Tank filler 150 gal

Lifting lug

Sprung flap valves

Resonating duct (47 Hz)

Nine sprays for fuel

Fuel pipe

Rudder

Small spoiler tabs (beneath elevator) are depressed at destination to command dive

Elevator

Master gyro

Dry battery

Pneumatic servos for rudder and elevators

Wire-wound air bottles feed fuel from tank and power control servos

Tubular spar

No ailerons

*By July 1944 British raid-spotters were receiving silhouettes of flying bombs with eight types of wing, including an elliptical shape. In fact there were only two, the parallel-chord and a shorter-span tapered wing mated with a different fuselage. Many bombs were unpainted and a few had different colours.*

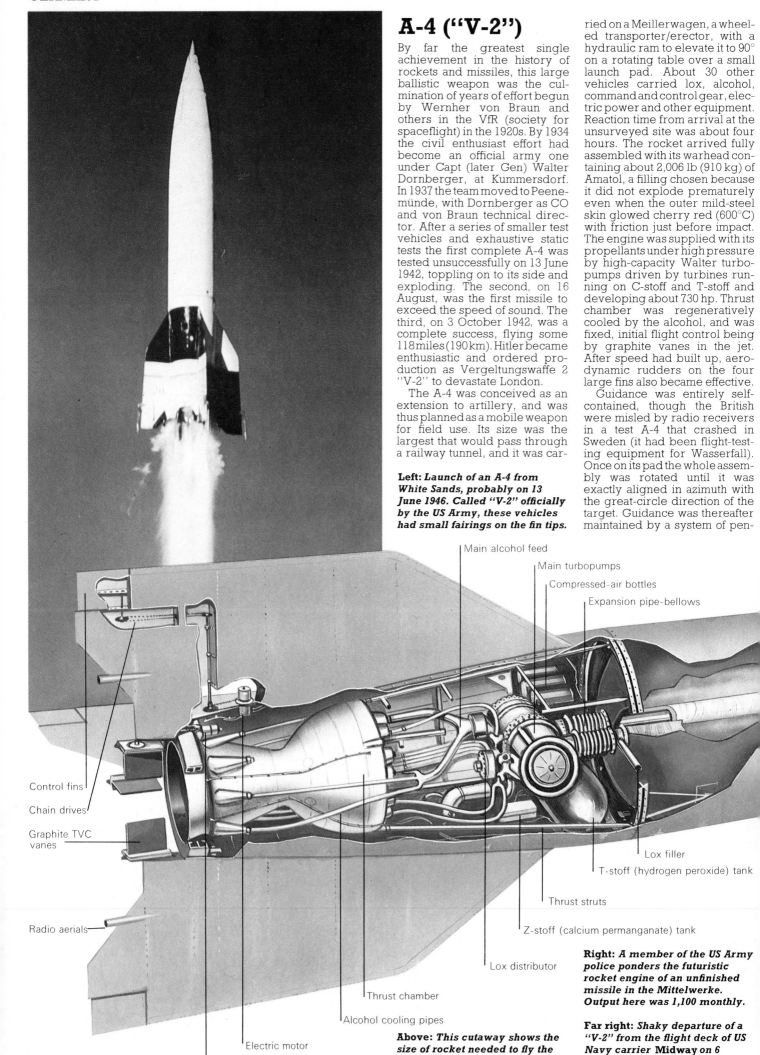

# A-4 ("V-2")

By far the greatest single achievement in the history of rockets and missiles, this large ballistic weapon was the culmination of years of effort begun by Wernher von Braun and others in the VfR (society for spaceflight) in the 1920s. By 1934 the civil enthusiast effort had become an official army one under Capt (later Gen) Walter Dornberger, at Kummersdorf. In 1937 the team moved to Peenemünde, with Dornberger as CO and von Braun technical director. After a series of smaller test vehicles and exhaustive static tests the first complete A-4 was tested unsuccessfully on 13 June 1942, toppling on to its side and exploding. The second, on 16 August, was the first missile to exceed the speed of sound. The third, on 3 October 1942, was a complete success, flying some 118 miles (190 km). Hitler became enthusiastic and ordered production as Vergeltungswaffe 2 "V-2" to devastate London.

The A-4 was conceived as an extension to artillery, and was thus planned as a mobile weapon for field use. Its size was the largest that would pass through a railway tunnel, and it was car-

*Left: Launch of an A-4 from White Sands, probably on 13 June 1946. Called "V-2" officially by the US Army, these vehicles had small fairings on the fin tips.*

ried on a Meillerwagen, a wheeled transporter/erector, with a hydraulic ram to elevate it to 90° on a rotating table over a small launch pad. About 30 other vehicles carried lox, alcohol, command and control gear, electric power and other equipment. Reaction time from arrival at the unsurveyed site was about four hours. The rocket arrived fully assembled with its warhead containing about 2,006 lb (910 kg) of Amatol, a filling chosen because it did not explode prematurely even when the outer mild-steel skin glowed cherry red (600°C) with friction just before impact. The engine was supplied with its propellants under high pressure by high-capacity Walter turbopumps driven by turbines running on C-stoff and T-stoff and developing about 730 hp. Thrust chamber was regeneratively cooled by the alcohol, and was fixed, initial flight control being by graphite vanes in the jet. After speed had built up, aerodynamic rudders on the four large fins also became effective.

Guidance was entirely self-contained, though the British were misled by radio receivers in a test A-4 that crashed in Sweden (it had been flight-testing equipment for Wasserfall). Once on its pad the whole assembly was rotated until it was exactly aligned in azimuth with the great-circle direction of the target. Guidance was thereafter maintained by a system of pen-

Control fins
Chain drives
Graphite TVC vanes
Radio aerials
Electro-hydraulic servos
Electric motor
Alcohol cooling pipes
Thrust chamber
Lox distributor
Thrust struts
Z-stoff (calcium permanganate) tank
T-stoff (hydrogen peroxide) tank
Lox filler
Expansion pipe-bellows
Compressed-air bottles
Main turbopumps
Main alcohol feed

*Above: This cutaway shows the size of rocket needed to fly the 200-mile (320-km) mission. A modern rocket would be much smaller and probably finless.*

*Right: A member of the US Army police ponders the futuristic rocket engine of an unfinished missile in the Mittelwerke. Output here was 1,100 monthly.*

*Far right: Shaky departure of a "V-2" from the flight deck of US Navy carrier Midway on 6 September 1947. This was the first ship launch of a large rocket.*

dulums giving a stable platform, two LEV-3 gyros and an integrating accelerometer. The guidance system commanded the electro-hydraulic actuators to turn the missile slowly over in the direction of the target until it was travelling – accelerating ever faster and faster, as weight reduced and thrust increased – at an angle about 40° to the vertical. Then the motor was cut off at the correct velocity for the ballistic trajectory to take it to the target. Apogee was usually about 60 miles (96 km), the greatest height of any man-made object at that time.

Preliminary production began in a new plant south of Peenemünde in late 1943, but mass-production was assigned to the gigantic underground Mittelwerke near Nordhausen, where 50,000 slave workers produced 300 of the rockets in the month of April 1944 and just over 1,000 in October, the final total being about 10,000. More than 1,800 had been stockpiled at army units when 836 Artillerie Abteilung opened the campaign on 6 September 1944 with two poor shots against Paris. Two days later a sustained barrage began from tree-camouflaged sites near Wassenaar, Holland, in which

**Right:** *Three A-4s ready for launch on 27 September 1944 by Mobile Artillery Section 485 near The Hague. Later rockets were green/grey camouflaged.*

1,120 were launched against England (1,050 hitting the ground in that country but others blowing up at various points in their trajectory or even impacting near Wiesbaden) and others being fired against continental targets, notably Antwerp. About 4,320 had been fired by 27 March 1945, and a further 600-odd were expended in troop training which took place mainly

near Blizna in Poland. Damage per "incident" was similar to that from the flying bomb, but casualties were rather higher because of lack of warning.

A-4b was a winged development with the objective of stretching the range to 466 miles (750 km); two were fired in 1944–5. The A-9 was a major second-generation rocket with lighter structure and the acid/hydro-

carbon fuel system of A-6, and A-10 was a futuristic two-stage vehicle for bombardment of the United States.

**Dimensions:** Length 45 ft 11¾ in (14·0 m); diameter 66 in (1·68 m); fin span 11 ft 9 in (3·57 m).
**Launch weight:** 28,373 lb (12 870 kg).
**Range:** 190–200 miles (306–320 km).

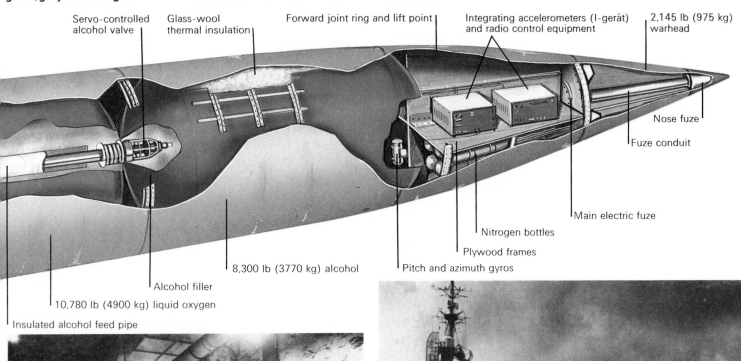

Servo-controlled alcohol valve · Glass-wool thermal insulation · Forward joint ring and lift point · Integrating accelerometers (I-gerät) and radio control equipment · 2,145 lb (975 kg) warhead · Nose fuze · Fuze conduit · Main electric fuze · Nitrogen bottles · Plywood frames · Pitch and azimuth gyros · 8,300 lb (3770 kg) alcohol · Alcohol filler · 10,780 lb (4900 kg) liquid oxygen · Insulated alcohol feed pipe

# USSR

## SS-3 Shyster

This MRBM represented the first major Russian advance beyond the A-4, and it was not only virtually all-Russian but it entered service as early as 1955. At first retaining lox/alcohol technology, but later, about 1959, switching from alcohol to kerosene, it had a single thrust chamber and jet vanes backed up by aerodynamic rudders. A nuclear or conventional warhead occupied the pointed nosecone, and the assembled missile was towed on an articulated trailer by a 415 hp AT-T half-track on which rode the launch crew of 16.

**Dimensions:** Length about 68 ft 10 in (21 m).
**Launch weight:** 57,300 lb (26 000 kg).
**Range:** Up to 750 miles (1200 km).

*Below: By 1961 the Soviet Union was ready to display "SS-4 Sandal", basically similar to Shyster but with longer tanks and storable propellants.*

*Bottom: SS-4 was at the heart of the Cuban crisis in November 1962. These containers were spotted on the deck of a ship, Bratsk, headed for Mariel port. Inside each was an MRBM.*

## SS-4 Sandal

This MRBM has often been seen in Red Square parades since 1961, but there is still argument over whether in its earliest forms it had radio command guidance like Shyster. At least the consensus of opinion is that by 1962 it was inertially guided. The missile itself has a simple monocoque light-alloy structure, with conical RV and flared rear skirt. It was the first operational Soviet weapon to use storable liquid propellants. The engine has four fixed thrust chambers fed by a common turbopump, and is a close relative of the GDL RD-214, the standard first-stage engine of Cosmos satellite launchers. This burns RFNA and kerosene, and has a vacuum thrust of 163,139 lb (74 000 kg). Vehicle control is by four jet vanes and four small aerodynamic rudders. The warhead is estimated at 1 MT, though a conventional head is also available. The whole weapon system includes about 12 vehicles, and some 20 men are

*Right: This photograph, taken at the 7 November 1957 Red Square parade, was the first to show SS-3 Shyster – or any other Soviet ballistic missile. The tug was the old AT-T tractor.*

in the erection/launch crew. Sandal entered service with the RVSN in 1959 and since 1963 about 500 systems have been deployed, mainly in Central Asia to menace China. Most are semi-mobile, though Sandals have been launched from silos. In 1962 Sandal was the missile at the heart of the Cuban crisis; emplaced on that island their range was sufficient certainly to have menaced the southern United States.

**Dimensions:** Length 73 ft 6 in (22·4 m); diameter 65 in (1·65 m).
**Launch weight:** About 61,728 lb (28 000 kg).
**Range:** Up to 1,118 miles (1800 km).

## SS-5 Skean

A logical geometrical scale of Sandal, this missile is longer and considerably fatter and moves into the IRBM class with a vengeance. First flown in the late 1950s and deployed with RVSN troops prior to 1964 (the year in which it was disclosed in a parade), Skean was one of the first Soviet missiles to dispense with aerodynamic fins. It also features a blunt nose on its RV, the radius being about 6 in (150 mm). The engine is the twin-chamber GDL RD-216, or a close relative, burning storable propellants (almost certainly RFNA and kerosene) and having a vacuum rating of 198,413 lb

90 000 kg). Vehicle control is by jet vanes in both effluxes. Guidance is inertial, and the warhead is estimated at 1 MT. Films show this missile in silos, and about 100 are still deployed, mainly in western IRBM complexes to menace Western Europe. With a restartable second stage SS-5 has launched some of the larger Cosmos military satellites, such as Nos 655 and 611. SS-20 is the replacement.

**Dimensions:** Length about 82 ft (25 m); diameter about 8 ft (2·44 m).
**Launch weight:** About 132,275 lb (60 000 kg).
**Range:** Estimated at 2,175 miles (3500 km).

# SS-6 Sapwood

One of the best-known yet least-publicised Soviet missiles, this was the original Russian ICBM, tested in August 1957 with complete success. It represented a quantum-jump in Russian rocketry, but was to some degree a manifestation of "brute force and ignorance" intended to provide a powerful launcher able to put the massive first-generation thermonuclear warhead into intercontinental trajectories. In the absence of large rocket engines the obvious answer was

**Below:** *Most SS-6 Sapwood ICBMs were refurbished and used as space launchers. It is unlikely that any vehicle will again lift off on 32 engines.*

more engines, and at liftoff SS-6 had 32 all firing together, and all burning lox/kerosene. The core was powered by an RD-107, with four fixed thrust chambers with a combined rating of 211,640 lb (96 000 kg), later raised to 224,868 lb (102 000 kg). Around this were disposed four tapered strap-on boosters, each with an RD-108 of 224,868 lb (102 000 kg). The other 12 chambers were groups of small gimbal-mounted verniers for fine control of trajectory. Structure weight was about 61,730 lb (28 000 kg). By the time Sapwood was at IOC in 1959 it was recognised as obsolescent as a weapon, and most served as space launchers. One put Sputnik 1 into orbit on 4 October 1957 and another put Yuri Gagarin into orbit on 12 April 1961; others have been the first stage of Sputnik, Vostok, Voskhod or Soyuz launchers.

**Dimensions:** Length 100 ft (30·5 m); diameter (max, each of five sections) 9 ft 9 in (2·95 m).
**Launch weight:** 650,353–661,376 lb (295 000 to 300 000 kg).
**Range:** At least 6,214 miles (10 000 km) with heavy warhead.

**Right:** *Basically a scale-up of SS-4 to more than double the launch weight, SS-5 Skean was the first Soviet missile to have global capabilities. The upper picture was taken at the 7 November 1964 parade through Red Square, and the picture at right on the 20th anniversary of victory in Europe (11 May 1965).*

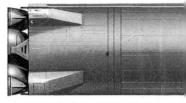

Above: *SS-9 Scarp was the first Soviet missile that really frightened the West. This was mainly because of its payload capability, but in the mid-1960s it also demonstrated accuracy.*

Left: *A frame from a Soviet propaganda film showing silo launch of an SS-7 Saddler. This was just another of the monster Soviet ICBMs.*

# SS-7 Saddler

In 1978 a few of these formidable ICBMs were still operational out of a force that two years earlier numbered about 190. It never appeared in a Moscow parade, but was exhaustively tested and put into service as the first standard ICBM, and backbone of the RVSN in its early years. A two-stage Titan-like missile, it uses storable liquid propellants, probably RFNA/kerosene, and is believed to have had radio-inertial guidance when it entered service in 1961. Later this may have been updated to pure inertial, just as the launch installations of the final three-quarters of the production run were not soft surface emplacements but hardened silos of impressive size (US reports identified "Mod 1", "Mod 2" and "Mod 3"). Yield of the large warhead was calculated to be no less than 20–25 MT. In accord with Salt I agreements the entire force of Saddlers is being deactivated, and replaced by SLBMs.

**Dimensions:** Length 104 ft 4 in (31·8 m); diameter about 9 ft 3 in (2·8 m).
**Launch weight:** Estimated at 224,868 lb (102 000 kg).
**Range:** about 6,835 miles (11 000 km).

Right: *The 1965 Red Square parade included the first public showing of the ICBM called by NATO SS-8 Sasin. The trailer on which this missile rides suggests that it has storable propellants (or solid propellant, but this is thought most unlikely). The inset shows a silo rim with what appears to be an SS-8 emplaced, (picture from a propaganda film).*

# SS-8 Sasin

For many years after this ICBM was first seen in a Moscow parade, in 1964, American official literature invariably linked it with SS-7 in such a way as to imply a technical similarity between the two systems. In fact the only links were geographical; the few SS-8s were apparently all emplaced at existing SS-7 sites. Technology is more akin to that of SS-5, though on a larger scale Sasin is very nearly of the same diameter as Saddler, though it is shorter. The storable liquid propellants are probably RFNA/kerosene, and control is almost certainly by four large jet vanes which were removed from the examples seen in 1964. These (two) missiles also had large circular covers over the base of the first stage, though it would be unwise to jump to the conclusion that this stage has one large thrust chamber. The second stage has prominent fairings over what are probably separation motors. Each stage has an external instrument conduit along the top of the tank sections. The warhead yield is estimated at 5 MT, and guidance is inertial. In the 1964 parade the transporter was of great interest, the new 8 × 8 tug of MAZ-537 ancestry pulling an articulated trailer with three axles, suggesting that the missile can travel with its tanks already filled. Number deployed is arguable: one US estimate of 209 SS-7 and -8 together was interpreted as 100 + 109, but the correct 1975 figure was apparently 190 + 19. The 19 have now been deactivated and replaced by SLBMs.

**Dimensions:** Length 80 ft (24·4 m); diameter 9 ft (2·74 m).
**Launch weight:** About 169,753 lb (77 000 kg).
**Range:** About 6,500 miles (10 460 km).

## SS-9 Scarp

On 7 November 1967 the Soviet Union struck a chill of fear into Western observers by trundling through Red Square some of the first of these mighty missiles, then easily the biggest and most capable of any mass-produced weapon in history. Development started as a far more capable successor to Sapwood around 1959, with two tandem stages, storable liquid propellants and a clean single-tube configuration. Probably RFNA/kerosene are used, and the first stage has a ring of six fixed thrust chambers, plus four gimbal-mounted verniers behind fairings around the skirt, which control the trajectory and trim the cutoff velocity at stage separation. The second stage has tankage of the same diameter but tapers to a very large blunt RV. The latter has its own post-boost propulsion, making three stages in all. Extremely long and accurate flights in 1963–65 disturbed the Americans, and when deployment in giant underground silos began in 1965 this missile was causing as much alarm as the Foxbat 2,000 mph aircraft. Subsequently five stages of development were identified by the DoD: Mod 1, the original ICBM, with the first-generation silo and warhead of about 20 MT; Mod 2, the main production SS-9 with 25 MT warhead, then the largest on any missile; Mod 3, flown over depressed-tra-

**Above:** *A most helpful photograph of an SS-9 being lowered into an operational silo.*

jectory missions, sacrificing range to reduce enemy radar warning time, and also over planned FOBS missions, the first being Cosmos 139 on 25 January 1967 and later followed by many others mostly at an orbital inclination of 49·5°; Mod 4, with three MRVs, used for tests in 1969–70 and 1973 with the three warheads impacting with the same spread as the three silos of a typical USAF Minuteman complex; and Mod 5, flown from Tyuratam with satellite-killing warheads against orbital targets put up from Plesetsk by a series of SS-5-derived launch vehicles. By 1975–6 there were 313 SS-9 silos operational with the RVSN, but, as the even bigger SS-18 takes over, these missiles are being withdrawn and used in trials and training programmes.

**Dimensions:** Length (Mod 2) about 118 ft (36 m); diameter about 10 ft 2 in (3·1 m).
**Launch weight:** About 418,871 lb (190 000 kg).
**Range:** (Mod 2) over 7,456 miles (12 000 km).

## SS-10 Scrag

Two of these large ICBMs took part in the 9 May 1965 Red Square parade, towed tail-first by MAZ-537 tugs on trailers similar to those used to carry SS-9. Compared with the latter SS-10 is less attractive because it uses cryogenic lox/kerosene propellants, prohibiting long silo storage with tanks filled at instant readiness. On its first appearance the Russian commentator described it as "a sister to the Vostok and Voskhod rockets", but this is hardly true. One claim to fame is that the first stage had gimballed nozzles, an innovation on large Soviet rockets at that time. The two upper stages had single nozzles, with unspecified means of TVC. The inter-stage trusses were fabricated from tubes arranged in Warren-girder rings, with no skinning over the gaps. SS-10 did not go into service, and may have assisted the development of SS-18.

**Dimensions:** Length about 124 ft 8 in (38 m); diameter 9 ft (2·74 m).
**Launch weight:** About 374,800 lb (170 000 kg).
**Range:** About 7,456 miles (12 000 km).

**Left:** *Two SS-10 Scrag ICBMs took part in the Red Square parade of 7 November 1968.*

# SS-11 Sego

Like SS-7 this missile has never been positively identified in any public parade, though in the 1973 October Revolution parade MAZ-537A 8 × 8 tugs drove past pulling a new articulated trailer carrying extremely plain drum-like containers of the appropriate size. To the public in Western nations neither "SS-11" nor "Sego" means anything, yet this is the ICBM that for 12 years has most greatly and universally menaced every Western capital and all other important industrial centres. The numbers deployed have been so great as to keep American photo-interpreters constantly busy watching the updating and other changes at silos all round the peripheries of the Soviet Union. The missile is a little longer than the USAF's Minuteman, but much fatter and carries a much greater payload. Study of the supposed SS-11 containers led to discussion of the cold-launch technique (see section introduction) and some reports imply or even announce that this is a feature of the SS-11 system; the author doubts this, and does not believe the container goes into the silo. There are two stages of storable-liquid propulsion, the first having four gimballed chambers. The so-called Mod 1 missile has a single RV with a reported choice of two warheads, one 500 kT and the other a thermonuclear device of 20–25 MT. After prolonged testing this achieved IOC in 1966, and by the 1972 SALT I agreement filled 970 silos, with 66 more being built. Mod 2 is: *(Jane's Weapon Systems)* Mod 1 plus penaids; *(Flight International)* "a more accurate re-entry vehicle...but not flight-tested recently"; and K. W. Gatland *(The Soviet War Machine)* "a non-operational test vehicle". Mod 3 is the first Soviet ICBM to have MRV, the first three-warhead test being detected in 1969. At least 60 of the Mod 3 were in silos in early 1978, the yield being put at 3 × 300 kT. In 1978 SS-11 was being replaced by SS-17 and -19.

**Dimensions:** Length about 62 ft 4 in (19 m); diameter about 8 ft (2·44 m).
**Launch weight:** In the neighbourhood of 105,820 lb (48 000 kg).
**Range:** Estimated at 6,525 miles (10 500 km).

**Above:** *Seen here in the Red Square parade of 7 November 1973, the SS-11 container is thought by some to be the pioneer cold-launch tube.*

# SS-13 Savage

This was almost certainly the first large Soviet missile to have solid propulsion; it has three stages linked by open Warren-girder trusses, each having four TVC nozzles. It was developed in parallel with SS-11, though it is smaller and more akin to Minuteman III. Shown in the 9 May 1965 parade, it reached IOC in 1968 and about 60 have since been in RVSN service around Plesetsk. SS-11 has much greater payload and accuracy, and SS-13 development appears to have ceased prior to 1970. No MRV version is known (despite some reports), yield of the single warhead being estimated at 1 MT. The two upper stages are thought to form SS-14, and there has been speculation that SS-13 itself has been deployed in a mobile role. Successor is SS-16.

**Dimensions:** Length about 65 ft 7 in (20 m); diameter of first stage 5 ft 7 in (1·7 m).
**Launch weight:** About 77,160 lb (35 000 kg).
**Range:** Over 5,000 miles (8000 km).

## SS-14 Scapegoat (Scamp)

For some unaccountable reason the NATO co-ordinating committee has seen fit to allocate two names to this weapon: Scapegoat for the missile itself and Scamp for the complete package inside its container riding on a rebuilt IS-3 tank chassis, with eight small road wheels on each side. All previous Soviet mobile missiles have a single code name, and the use of two causes needless confusion. To make things more involved, the missile is superficially identical to the two upper stages of SS-13 Savage, apart from small changes to the warhead which Western observers think may have lower yield. Classed as an IRBM, it in fact has greater range and can be regarded as a mobile land-based Polaris A3. Such a weapon can be driven to countless concealed sites all round the Soviet

Left: *Training deployment of the SS-14 system in a forest area, probably in 1970. US satellites cannot accurately count such mobile systems.*

Below: *The SS-13 is believed to have been the only Soviet solid-propellant strategic missile of its generation.*

frontier. There were many hundreds of IS-3 chassis available, some of them ex-Frog carriers, and the impossibility of satellite surveillance of so mobile a system results in "unknown" appearing beside Western estimates of the number deployed. Soviet films show the way the "Iron Maiden" container is elevated, opened and lowered back on the carrier which then drives off to control the launch.

**Dimensions:** Length about 35 ft 5 in (10·8 m); diameter of first stage 4 ft 7 in (1·4 m).
**Launch weight:** In the neighbourhood of 26,455 lb (12 000 kg).
**Range:** About 2,485 miles (4000 km).

## SS-15 (XZ) Scrooge

First seen in the November 1965 Red Square parade, this is the largest mobile weapon system in the world to have been seen publicly. The tracked chassis, of IS-3 ancestry with 16 road wheels, carries a very large tubular container which elevates vertically but cannot open to release the missile. It is sized to fit a shortened SS-13, and most observers agree that this missile is the most likely answer, but how it is launched is unknown.

Above: *SS-15 Scrooge vehicles on their way to Red Square for the parade of 7 November 1965. Exactly how this outsize mobile missile is launched is puzzling.*

Cold launch is not possible, and the assumption is that the tube is used to protect the still-attached carrier and is not recovered after firing. With the carrier driven to a distance the tube would stand on the supporting surface and the efflux would all pass up the interior. Neither answer seems satisfactory, neither is the gross vehicle weight of some 132,275 lb (60 000 kg) a happy situation. Another puzzle is why, after ten years as "SS-15", this system is now called "SS-XZ" in most American literature. Around 1970 it was accepted that this system was operational near the Chinese frontier around Buir Nor. Scrooges in the western Soviet Union could be targeted throughout Western Europe and the UK, even if (as has been suggested) the first stage is shorter than that of SS-13.

**Dimensions:** Length estimated at about 60 ft (18·3 m); diameter of first stage assumed 5 ft 7 in (1·7 m).
**Launch weight:** Probably about 61,828 lb (28 000 kg).
**Range:** Estimated at over 3,107 miles (5000 km).

# SS-16

Four new missile systems were in flight test in the early 1970s, all embodying completely new techniques and much more "unstoppable" than their predecessors, and all were timed to reach IOC in 1975. Of these SS-16 (then called SSX-16, because of its development status) is the only one with solid propulsion. It is universally regarded as a much superior replacement for SS-13, similar in size (the DoD said it is "slightly smaller" but the Pentagon artwork and desk-top models show it rather larger) but with such superior motor performance as to give greater range despite a considerably heavier warhead. Until mid-1978 all operational SS-16s were believed to carry a single warhead, with yield estimated at 1·5–2 MT, but from the early test period this missile was known to have a computer-controlled "dispensing bus" able to release MIRVs sequentially on to widely separated targets. A three-stage missile, SS-16 has multiple (probably quad) nozzles and uses the traditional hot launch technique. It is suitably configured for either silo or mobile deployment, and there is every reason for assuming that the Soviet Union long ago tested a new transport/erector suitable for such formidable missiles as SS-16 and possibly even larger weapons. In mid-1978 this missile was at last reported to have been deployed; previously the DoD view was that it had been manufactured in quantity and stored, possibly together with complete mobile weapon systems so that if politically desirable it could be put into large-scale service very rapidly. There were indications that all 60 SS-13 silos were receiving SS-16. Its two upper stages are used as the mobile SS-20, already in wide use. No NATO name has yet emerged.

**Dimensions:** Length about 65 ft 7 in (20 m); diameter about 5 ft 7 in (1·7 m).
**Launch weight:** Probably about 79,365 lb (36 000 kg).
**Range:** Over 5,592 miles (9000 km).

# SS-17

Again not yet associated with a NATO reporting name, this ICBM was first seen in flight test in 1972. Together with SS-19, which is almost certainly a competitive design to act as a spur and insurance, this extremely formidable missile is a successor for SS-11, and is now installed in many former SS-11 silos. Unlike all previous Soviet missiles known in the West, SS-17 has cold-launch ejection, with great advantage to the silo and also conferring an increase in ultimate range. Compared with SS-11 this missile has similar calibre but much increased length, the first stage being particularly long. Storable liquids are used, and an American

model shows fairing ducts past the tanks of both stages (this would not affect cold launching, which uses a piston or sabot to blow the missile out). Early testing featured three MIRV warheads, and this is the first Soviet MIRVed ICBM in service. The warhead is estimated to weigh twice as much as that of SS-11, and the Mod 1 missile in operation since 1975 has four heads estimated at over 200 kT each (the 1978 DoD Secretary's Report says 4 × 600 kT). Mod 2 has a single RV of very high yield which, in conjunction with reported outstanding accuracy, gives SS-17 the capability of backing up SS-18 as a counterforce weapon. Deployment has been slower than the Soviet Union could have achieved, but over 70 were operational by August 1978.

**Dimensions:** Length about 80 ft (24·4 m); diameter about 8 ft 3 in (2·5 m).
**Launch weight:** In the order of 143,300 lb (65 000 kg).
**Range:** Over 6,214 miles (10 000 km).

# SS-18

Again as yet devoid of a NATO reporting name, this is the missile that has demolished almost all the West's bargaining power and ability to deter aggression. The largest missile in the world, its appearance was not unexpected as a modern successor to SS-9; but nobody in the West was prepared for its frightening accuracy, which, in conjunction with by far the most formidable warhead(s) in history, renders

**Above: The five current Soviet ICBMs drawn to scale. Ignoring the awesome force of earlier weapons, these alone could in one strike destroy the West.**

any practical degree of hardening a waste of effort. The DoD view is that this chilling capability has been demonstrated "four to five years earlier than expected". SS-18 is cold-launched from a silo of new design, though this is often installed at existing SS-9 launch complexes. There are two stages of storable-liquid propulsion and separate computer-controlled post-boost propulsion for the RV or MIRVs. Throw-weight is estimated at 30 per cent greater than for SS-9, and this is multiplied in effectiveness dozens to hundreds of times by the truly remarkable guidance accuracy which in recent (1977–8 flights) has averaged about 180 m. According to DoD the Minuteman force is vulnerable as soon as large-warhead CEP is brought within 370 m. The Mod 1 SS-18, which reached IOC in 1974, has a single RV with a yield estimated at 25 to 50 MT, and most of the 80+ missiles deployed in mid-1978 are thought to be of this type. Probably any of them could be converted to Mod 2 standard, which has eight MIRVs with a yield put at 2 MT each (another estimate is eight to ten of 1 MT, but eight was the number invariably seen on the intensive Mod 2 test programme in 1975-6). Mod 2 entered service in 1976, but at a low rate of deployment. Mod 3 has a single RV, lighter and more accurate than Mod 1 and giving even longer

range. SALT I permits the Soviet Union to deploy 310 of these terrifying weapons.

**Dimensions:** Length about 121 ft 4 in (37 m); diameter about 10 ft 6 in (3·2 m).
**Launch weight:** About 485,000 lb (220 000 kg).
**Range:** Estimated at 7,456 miles (12 000 km); Mod 3, greater.

# SS-19

The competitive partner to SS-17, this ICBM again has no known NATO reporting name, despite the estimate of several hundred already deployed. One report suggests SS-19 is "less advanced technically" than SS-17, but one should not undervalue this missile. It gets results at least as impressive as SS-17, albeit by being fractionally larger. According to one report (Jane's Weapon Systems) SS-19 is hot-launched, but most DoD and other literature is agreed on cold launching. Again, the British annual, whose sources are excellent, refers to "a refinement of the traditional Soviet 'fly the wire' technique" (whatever that means), whereas other reports indicate pure inertial guidance in an advanced form. The DoD emphasize the complete success of SS-19 flight testing and in 1977 commented "We are convinced . . . that the SS-19 is clearly intended to achieve high accuracy; the Soviet designers have done everything right to attain that goal". The two stages, both with parallel tanks that fill the silo as completely as possible, use storable liquids; and the American plastic display model of this missile shows twin gimballed chambers projecting completely below the first-stage skirt, an unprecedented feature in a Russian ballistic missile and one that suggests the cold-launch sabot thrusts on the airframe above the chambers. Mod 1 SS-19, first deployed in 1974, has six MIRVs with an individual yield estimated in 1977 at 400–500 kT per head and in 1978 at 800 kT to 1 MT. Mod 2 has flown with a single super-accurate high-yield RV, but is not known to have reached IOC. In mid-1978 about 250 Mod 1 were in service, and it looks as if most of the 1,000-odd SS-11 silos are soon going to be occupied by this ICBM.

**Dimensions:** Length about 88 ft 6 in (27 m); diameter 8 ft 3 in (2·5 m).
**Launch weight:** Estimated at 171,958 lb (78 000 kg).
**Range:** Over 6,214 miles (10 000 km).

# SS-20

Based on the two upper stages of SS-16, this extremely useful mobile missile has much greater range, higher payload and greater accuracy than the DoD had predicted, and it is already being deployed at what could well be a considerable rate – though surveillance is next to impossible. In his annual Statement in 1977 the DoD Secretary said SSX-20, as it then was, had "a range of 2,000 n.m. (3700 km) but this could be extended to 3,000 n.m. (5560 km) either by the addition of a third stage or off-loading MIRVs". By 1978 the range estimates had jumped to the figures given in the data. Moreover, SS-20 poses other problems for SALT surveillance and negotiations because it falls outside the range provisions of such an agreement yet, by fitting an SS-16 first stage, it becomes an exceptionally powerful ICBM. Compared with the older weapons it replaces, such as SS-4 and -5, it is mobile, easily concealed, is fired from a tracked vehicle which can be rapidly reloaded, carries three MIRVs of 500–600 kT each and has accuracy of some 750 m CEP when firing from a pre-surveyed site. Initial deployment was in mid-1978 predicted at 300–400 launchers plus reloads.

**Dimensions:** Length about 34 ft 6 in (10·5 m); diameter 55 in (1·4 m).
**Launch weight:** Probably about 28,659 lb (13 000 kg).
**Range:** (3 × 600 kT) 3,542 miles (5700 km), (reduced payload) 4,660 miles (7500 km).

## SSX-22

This designation is probably applied to one of the "fifth generation" of Soviet long-range missiles which for several years have been under development (SS-21 being a tactical rocket). In his 1978 Statement the DoD Secretary announced "Flight testing of one or two of these missiles could begin at any time, with others following in the 1980s". With four known "fifth-generation" systems the DoD numbers thus probably extend to SSX-25. A sobering picture for the West, which has not deployed a single new ICBM system since 1963 and has no IRBM of any kind other than the 18 French SSBS.

# UNITED KINGDOM

# Blue Streak

Ordered in 1955, this so-called LRBM was based on Atlas technology, with a lox/RP-1 tank of pressurized stainless steel. Propulsion was by a Rolls-Royce RZ.12 engine based on Rocketdyne designs, with two RZ.2 gimballed chambers each rated at 137,000 lb (62 143 kg) at sea level, plus two Armstrong Siddeley PR.23 verniers each of 500 lb (227 kg) thrust. Prime contractor was de Havilland Propellers, with the airframe assigned to de Havilland Aircraft and inertial guidance to Sperry

*Above: A Blue Streak flight vehicle, having completed tests at Spadeadam, is given a pre-flight checkout at the Weapons Research Establishment at Woomera, S Australia, where all initial flights took place.*

Gyroscope Co. Blue Streak was designed for silo emplacement but for propellant loading and launching at the surface on an azimuth-aligned launch table by Morfax. Chief development centres were Hatfield (airframe and system integration), Spadeadam Waste (engine test) and Woomera (flight test). The warhead

*Above: Lift-off of a Blue Streak shortly after cancellation. The entire flight programme of Blue Streak was flawless. All work had ceased by 1973, leaving France with a large-rocket monopoly in Europe.*

was thermonuclear and all-British, and the operator RAF Bomber Command both within and outside the UK. Shortly before first flight the programme was cancelled in April 1960, and replaced by Skybolt, which itself was later cancelled. Blue Streak survived as a civil space launcher with European backing until

replaced by French Ariane.

**Dimensions:** Length 61 ft 6 in (18·75 m); diameter 10 ft 0 in (3·05 m).
**Launch weight:** About 199,000 lb (90 266 kg).
**Range:** 2,500 miles (assumed statute, not nautical) (4023 km).

## Cruise Missile

Much publicity has been accorded the fact that British Aerospace has a study contract for a cruise missile. The funding does not provide for any test hardware.

# USA

## Snark

This was probably the first intercontinental missile programme in the world, discounting the Peenemünde A-10. Snark was begun in January 1946 at a time of severe budget restraint, and progressed slowly and often unenthusiastically to the flight test stage with N-25 vehicles in 1951. By this time range and payload had been doubled, resulting in the N-69 first flown on 6 August 1953. Test vehicles were red, and production missiles grey. A clean pilotless bomber,

SM-62A Snark was devoid of a horizontal tail, but had a large fuselage housing the 26,000 lb (11 794 kg) of fuel, Nortronics stellar-inertial guidance and ventrally fed Pratt & Whitney J57-P-17 turbojet, rated at 10,500 lb (4763 kg) static thrust at sea level. The whole weapon system was intended to be air-transportable, though the transporter/launcher by Erco division of ACF Industries was a 15-ton monster with 16 wheels. A hydraulically elevated ramp provided zero-length pick-ups for the missile, which was hurled

bodily off in a diagonally upward direction by two solid boost motors each rated at 130,000 lb (58 968 kg) thrust. Despite the launch acceleration of over 5g the prime contractor, Northrop, learned the hard way that some positive flight control was necessary during the four-second boost phase, and each boost motor had a TVC ring worked by a system pressurized by gas from the rocket case. The subsequent trajectory was a smooth climb, an inlet at the base of the fin sensing ram air pressure which was held constant at the value reached after 50 sec of flight, this translating into a steep climb whose angle progressively levelled off into the high-altitude cruise at Mach 0·93 (about 614 mph, 988 km/h). The star tracker intermittently up-

dated the inertial system (the first to fly on an operational missile) and near the target commanded a pre-programmed zero-g dive on a ballistic trajectory. Ejectors separated the warhead, which fell at about Mach 1 on target, while the rest of the airframe violently pitched up and broke into several parts.

Snark's chief assets were large payload – which even in 1954 was equivalent to 5 MT and later reached 20 – and mission versatility. It had a small radar cross-section, could approach from any direction at any height, and could take evasive action without losing guidance accuracy. Launches were possible from small sites within "about an hour" of arrival. The first long-range astro-inertial flight (daytime) was on 14 November 1956,

Left and below: *Scarlet N-69 development Snarks at Cape Canaveral in 1955. Their many problems resulted in the quip: "Snark-infested waters".*

Above: *Training launch of an operational SM-62A Snark of SAC's 702nd Strategic Missile Squadron in 1959. This was the first intercontinental missile.*

and the first N-69E test with warhead delivery was on 31 October 1957. The first unit, authorised in April 1957, was the 556th Strategic Missile Squadron, USAF, activated at Patrick AFB and deployed at Presque Isle, Maine. It achieved numerous full-range 11-hr missions, and even out-and-return flights to recover the missile. In July 1959 it was redesignated the 702nd SMS, but was deactivated only two years later as Atlas became operational.

**Dimensions:** Length (with sensing probe) 75 ft 10½ in (23·1 m); span 42 ft 3 in (12·9 m).
**Launch weight:** (without boost motors) 60,000 lb (27 216 kg).
**Range:** 6,325 miles (10 180 km).

# Navaho

Though today almost forgotten, this cruise missile was one of the most significant in history, was one of the very few examples of a traumatic cancellation of a far-advanced American weapon system, and at the time was lambasted by the media as a waste of $691 million – which was no mean sum in 1957. In fact this programme paid for almost all the technical underpinning of the subsequent American ICBM programme, providing engines, cryogenic propellant technology, guidance systems, countless equipment items and also intangibles such as programme management.

In the decade after VJ-Day the DoD studied and re-studied the

cruise missile and the ICBM. The latter was clearly the better penetrator, but the technology did not exist to make a rocket fly the nominal intercontinental range of 5,500 n.m. (10 193 km) while carrying a multi-ton thermonuclear warhead. A classic Pentagon document on the subject launched Navaho in 1947 whilst cutting back on spending on studies for ICBMs. But even the winged Navaho was no pushover. It was the most advanced aerodynamic vehicle then considered, and even today would be a considerable challenge. Prime contractor North American Aviation, almost the only company able to tackle the project with some degree of assurance, first designed and built a series of test vehicles, the X-10 family, which proved the canard aerodynamics, flight-control system, inertial guidance, advanced honeycomb structure and new materials, and many equipment items. Powered by two J40 afterburning turbojets, the recoverable X-10s had retractable landing gear and were smaller than the missile itself.

Navaho was impressive indeed. The air vehicle was comparable in size to a bomber, flew at Mach 3·25 (2,150 mph, 3457 km/h) at over 60,000 ft (18 288 m) and at lift-off weighed twice as much as the biggest airliners then in use (Stratocruiser or DC-7). Moreover, on takeoff it was pointing up at 90°, and was launched riding piggyback on a giant booster filled with lox/RP-1 and thrust by three of the largest rocket engines ever built at that time. Together giving 415,000 lb (188 244 kg) thrust, these pump-fed engines led straight to the engines of Redstone, Atlas, Thor, Jupiter and Blue Streak. After the initial vertical climb the combined vehicles gradually arched over, accelerating fiercely as rocket propellants were consumed, until the missile's own twin Curtiss-Wright RJ47 ramjets – integral with the fuselage – could be turned on and lit. Then the boost package was jettisoned, itself as large as two V-2s, while the Navaho thundered on its way to Mach 3 and the target on the other side of the world.

By the time the whole of Weapon System 104 came together, and the combined vehicle flew (recoverable) in June 1958, the ICBM was known to be feasible and technically superior. On 11 July 1957 the system was cancelled, though the missile flew 11 times up to a perfect final mission on 18 November 1958.

**Dimensions:** Length (at liftoff) 95 ft 3 in (29·0 m), (without booster) 87 ft 4 in (26·6 m); span 40 ft 3 in (12·3 m); diameter 6 ft (1·83 m).
**Launch weight:** (SM-64A) 290,000 lb (131 540 kg).
**Range:** 6,325 miles (10 180 km).

**Right: *The fantastic Navaho provided much of the essential technology for the first generation of ICBMs. This XSM-64 left the Air Force Missile Test Center in June 1958.***

# Goose

In the financial cornucopia of the early 1950s, during the Korean war, it seemed a good idea to develop a missile as an ECM platform to confuse and dilute enemy defences and, during strategic attacks by SAC, work closely with the bombers to increase their chance of survival. The result was the Goose family, designated SM-73 though so far as is known none was to carry an offensive payload. Prime contractor was Fairchild, with GRP tailless-delta airframes subcontracted to the Omohundro company, and AMF being chief GSE contractor. Flight development did not begin until the winter 1957–8 with XSM-73 vehicles powered by imported Curtiss-Wright (Armstrong Siddeley) Viper turbojets. Development vehicles were styled Blue Goose or Bull Goose, and did not carry the comprehensive payload of passive sensors, jammers, relay communications and other ECM systems whose management was assigned to Ramo-Wooldridge. The definitive Goose would have been slightly larger, launched by a Thiokol boost rocket straight out of a fixed shelter with a roll-top front like a bread-box in shape, to cruise at up to Mach 1·5 on the 2,200 lb (907 kg) thrust Fairchild J83 turbojet. One of the unexplained puzzles is how Goose bases at Duluth Municipal Airport and Ethan Allen AFB in Vermont could have assisted bombers 4,000 miles (6437 km) away over the Soviet Union, because the Geese could not have flown further than Arctic Canada. A possible inference is that the real function of Goose was to enact the role of Soviet strategic bombers to test Norad's defences realistically. The programme was cancelled in 1959.

**Dimensions:** Length about 38 ft (11·6 m); span about 18 ft (5·5 m).
**Launch weight:** Up to 5,000 lb (2268 kg) without booster.
**Range:** Unlikely to exceed 1,500 miles (2414 km).

# Jupiter

In the first half of the 1950s the centre of ballistic-missile technology in the West was Redstone Arsenal, where the ex-German team under Von Braun strove for the USA which saw in their expertise a way to gain a new strategic significance previously enjoyed only by the USAF and USN. In 1954 the Redstone SRBM was followed by Jupiter, the first IRBM; and when the design of SM-78 was established the Sec-Def, Charles E. Wilson, decreed on 8 November 1955 that the Navy should collaborate with a view to a seagoing Jupiter as well. Then just over a year later the same SecDef issued a notorious memo that stripped the USA of weapons having range greater than 200 miles (322 km), and the Navy decided to go for a more attractive solid-propellant weapon. This made SM-78 Jupiter, an orphan given to the USAF.

Most of Jupiter comprised integral lox/RP-1 tankage fabricated by welding large extruded panels of light alloy. At the base was the Rocketdyne S-3 gimballed thrust chamber derived direct from Navaho, rated at 150,000 lb (68 040 kg), with vernier thrust and roll control effected solely by the gimballed turbopump exhaust. Above the tankage was a guidance bay with an inertial system developed in-house at ABMA and using air-bearing gyros and accelerometers, production being assigned to the Ford Instrument, Farragut and Sperry Gyroscope divisions of Sperry Rand. On top was the ablative RV, the first production example in the world, with multiple organic layers assigned to Goodyear for manufacture, shrouding a warhead of 1 MT. After departure of the spent main stage a small Thiokol solid motor provided final velocity trimming, the warhead and RV then separating from the guidance bay. Production missiles were assembled at the USA's Michigan Missile Plant operated by prime contractor Chrysler, where deliveries began at four per month in November 1957. Crane Fruehauf built the steel-tube transporter, towed by 6 × 6 truck, and Watertown Arsenal the launch table, on to which missiles were raised by a cable hoist and A-frame. Missiles thus remained upright, and for long periods were part-shrouded in a simple shelter of hinged petals.

Following component tests on modified Redstones called Jupiter A, of which 25 were fired in 1955–8, an ablative RV was tested on 20 September 1956 by a Jupiter C that reached a height of 682 miles (1098 km). A Jupiter IRBM was launched for the first time on 1 March 1957, and a full-range mission was flown on 31 May 1957. By July 1958 there had been 29 total successes and seven partials in 38 flights. On 15 January 1958 the 864th SMS was activated at Huntsville, followed by the 865th. Subsequently each squadron took 30 systems overseas, one to Italy and the other to Turkey, where they trained local units in 1960 which deployed the missile within a NATO context and with US supervision and custody of launch keys. Thanks to crass ineptitude at the political level the only mobile IRBM ever developed in the West was transferred to a service which suffered from the NIH (not invented here) syndrome and made no effort to do anything with it. Deployment in Europe, always in a

very low key indeed, was terminated prior to 1965. In the new scheme the system designation was PGM-19A.

**Dimensions:** Length 60 ft 1 in (18·3 m); diameter 8 ft 9 in (2·69 m).
**Launch weight:** 110,000 lb (49 896 kg).
**Range:** 1,976 miles (3180 km).

# Thor

Compared with the USA the USAF was late getting into the long-range ballistic business, because until 1953 it believed such missiles would take ten years to develop and not be cost-effective. Then, as outlined in the section introduction, policy changed dramatically. In November 1955 the USAF was authorized to develop an IRBM similar to Jupiter (there was nothing wrong with Jupiter, but the NIH factor made it unpalatable). Weapon System 315A was immediately given the highest national priority, previously enjoyed only by Atlas. On 27 December 1955 a complete system prime contract was signed with Douglas Aircraft. Under the most intense pressure the engineering team under J. L. Bromberg completed the SM-75 design in July 1956, by which time a production line of prototype missiles was visible at Santa Monica, using production tooling. The first SM-75 Thor was delivered to the USAF in October 1956. This timescale has never been equalled for any major weapon system.

Two-thirds of the airframe comprised tankage fabricated like Jupiter's from large chem-milled light-alloy panels. Lox/RP-1 were fed to a gimballed Rocketdyne LR79 rated at 150,000 lb (68 040 kg), almost identical to an Atlas booster and close relative of the Jupiter engine. On each side of the missile base was a small LR101 vernier to provide roll control and fine adjustment of velocity after propulsion cutoff. Guidance was by an improved AChiever inertial system by AC Spark Plug division of General Motors, already used in Mace, with liquid-floated gyros. Following a directive to

**Top:** *Pre-launch checkout of one of the Viper-powered XSM-73 Goose test vehicles at AFMTC on 27 June 1957. Note the instrumented nosecone.*

**Right:** *SM-78 Jupiter was an Army missile, designed for mobile deployment. This picture, taken on 12 May 1959 at Redstone Arsenal, shows how a cable truss was used to erect the missile over its petal shelter.*

use as much Atlas technology as possible, the RV was that of Atlas C, a copper heat-sink.

Unlike Jupiter, Thor was designed for fixed-base deployment. The GSE accounted for all but 13 per cent of the price of WS-315A and some of it can be seen in the drawing of an emplacement. After a flight-test programme which began with four failures the whole weapon system was declared operational in 1959. Operational deployment was assigned to the United Kingdom, and for three years C-124 and C-133 aircraft droned heavily from California to England with several thousand tons of WS-315A hardware. The first missile became operational at RAF Feltwell in December 1959, the first Bomber Command squadron on 22 April 1960 and the whole force of 20 three-missile squadrons was operational at bases from Yorkshire to Suffolk by 1961. They were withdrawn four years later, when they had US designation PGM-17A and (trainer) PTM-17A. Had mobile Jupiter been used they might still be operational.

**Dimensions:** Length 65 ft 0 in (19·8 m); diameter 8 ft 0 in (2·44 m).
**Launch weight:** 105,000 lb (47 630 kg).
**Range:** 1,976 miles (3180 km).

**Main picture right:** *Lift-off at The Cape of the very first XSM-75 after the world's fastest-ever missile-development programme.*

**Upper inset:** *Practice countdown by launch crew of 113 Sqn RAF Bomber Command at Mepal in late 1959. Note blow-off of lox vapour.*

**Lower inset:** *Arrival of the 60th and last Thor at RAF North Luffenham, brought by a C-124C Globemaster: the date, 10 March 1960.*

# Atlas

If Thor was the fastest development in history, Atlas was possibly the greatest; and had it not been for the gigantic prior work done in the Navaho programme it would have been much larger. Atlas was the West's original ICBM, started when the USAF discovered that its assessment of the ICBM was mistaken. As described in the section introduction, an ICBM was recognised as feasible in February 1954. Daunted by the magnitude of the task, the USAF set up a totally new management structure, creating a special company (Ramo-Wooldridge Inc, set up by two members of the original Teapot Committee) to direct the programme under a new USAF office called Western Development Division under a young brigadier-general, a dynamic and brilliant leader, Bernard A. Schriever (pronounced Skreever).

In 1954 these developments did not go unnoticed by Convair division of General Dynamics. Back in 1946 this company had been the one to go ahead on a USAAF proposal for a 5,000-mile (8047 km) ICBM, and under Belgian-born Karel J. Bossart the Vultee Field team built a test vehicle, MX-774, which flew three times in 1948 and tested such advanced features as a gimbal-mounted engine, separable nosecone and structure

made of stainless steel rolled so thin it had to be kept inflated like a balloon. In January 1955 Convair was awarded the prime contract for the giant Weapon System 107A, named Atlas, the missile becoming SM-65. It was a very important programme, given highest national priority the following June, and to create it Bossart's engineers were put into a vast new plant called Convair Astronautics built outside San Diego at Kearney Mesa. As far as possible the "principle of concurrency" was followed: all the 100,000-odd precision parts from over 3,500 suppliers were developed simultaneously, and making them all compatible was just one of the problems in a weapon that, even with Navaho's underpinning, broke new ground in every direction. Some of the decisions that had to be taken in 1955 were mistakes, part of the price of a truncated development cycle. None was allowed to delay or seriously degrade the final weapon system.

One of the decisions was to use thin-wall balloon-tankage and to fill it with lox/RP-1 to feed Rocketdyne engines of the kind already developed. Another was unique: because little was known about upper-atmosphere ignition of large thrust chambers, and an ICBM needs to be able to "stage" (drop off spent propulsion systems to save weight), Atlas was designed as a "1½-

stage" vehicle. At the conical base of the balloon tank was the gimbal mount for an LR89 sustainer rated at 57,000 lb (25 855 kg) at sea level. Around the base was a pick-up thrust ring for a boost unit, with corrugated structure (because it was not pressurized) carrying two gimballed LR105 engines each rated at 150,000 lb (68 040 kg), 165,000 lb (74 844 kg) in later versions. On each side of the base ring was a small LR101 vernier of 1,000 lb (454 kg) for final trimming of the trajectory. All five engines drew propellants from the main tanks and all ignited prior to liftoff. After about 140 seconds the boost assembly cut-off and separated. The sustainer and verniers then burnt for a further three minutes on a full-range flight.

The first launch, by Atlas 4A with only the boosters fitted, took place from Cape Canaveral on 11 June 1957 (one booster soon cut, the missile being destroyed by the range safety officer after its balloon tank had withstood violent loops and gyrations). 6A did slightly better on 25 September, 12A was completely successful, and the second B-series missile with operating sustainer flew 2,500 miles (4023 km) on 2 August 1958. Design range was achieved in November 1958, and a launch by a SAC crew from operational GSE came in September 1959. Early Atlas C mis-

siles used fascinating radio-inertial guidance, which precluded salvo firing yet was judged more accurate than early inertial systems. In 1958 it was decided to switch this GE/Burroughs system to Titan, and fit Atlas with the latter's Bosch Arma inertial guidance. Atlas C's payload was the GE Mk 2 RV with a blunt slab of thick copper serving as a heat-sink. Most of these C-models were used for troop-training at the first Atlas complex at Vandenberg AFB, manned by the 576th SMS. The first version deployed in numbers was Atlas D, SM-65D and later CGM-16D, with the greatly superior GE Mk 3 ablative RV with slim profile and flared skirt. This reached IOC in 1960 at Warren AFB, Wyoming. Here, the 564th SMS occupied six soft emplacements, entirely above ground and with end-sliding roofs to allow the missiles to be erected for propellant loading and launch. The 565th SMS had three triple sites, spaced further apart to give dispersion, with split side-opening roofs that cut precious minutes off the reaction time of some half-hour. The 549th SMS had nine semi-hard "coffin" installations recessed into the ground and widely separated. In October 1961 Fairchild AFB, Washington, and Forbes AFB, Kansas, both became operational with recessed missiles and a microwave communications system survivable

*Below: Atlas has a unique configuration, unlikely ever to be reapeated. This cutaway shows an Atlas D, but all versions have similar airframes.*

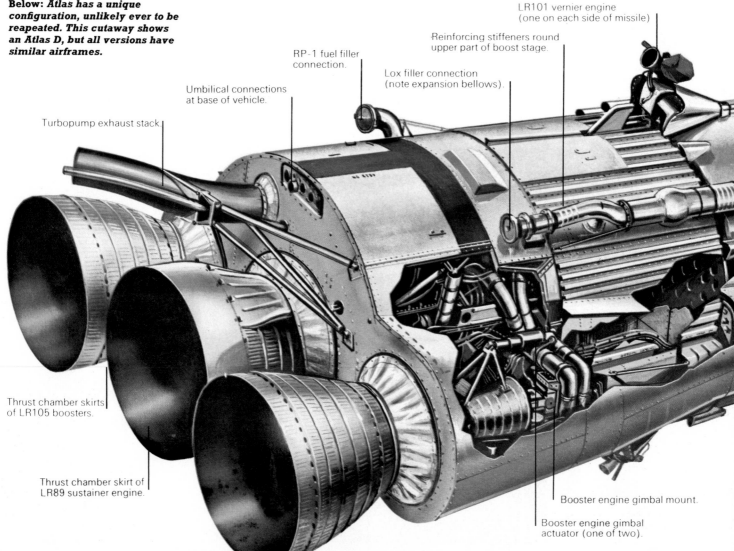

Turbopump exhaust stack.

Umbilical connections at base of vehicle.

RP-1 fuel filler connection.

Lox filler connection (note expansion bellows).

Reinforcing stiffeners round upper part of boost stage.

LR101 vernier engine (one on each side of missile)

Thrust chamber skirts of LR105 boosters.

Thrust chamber skirt of LR89 sustainer engine.

Booster engine gimbal mount.

Booster engine gimbal actuator (one of two).

in severe overpressure.

Owing to unexpected Soviet ICBM development the belated decision was taken in 1959 to put the rest of the Atlas force into hardened silos. Giant silos were needed, over 174 ft (53 m) deep and 52 ft (16 m) in diameter, with the missile upright on a mighty flame-deflector bucket on a shock-isolated crib, hydraulically elevated to the surface with all missile tanks filled, sprung against 150-ton counterweights. The next complex, at SAC headquarters at Offutt AFB, Nebraska, was already too far advanced for silos, but had three flights each of three of the Atlas E (CGM-16E) with up-rated boost engines and often the Avco Mk 4 RV. The Trainer Atlases, USM-65D and E, became CTM-16D and -16E. Silo emplacement demanded a substantially re-engineered missile, Atlas F, SM-65F and later HGM-16F. These were emplaced in 1961–3. Lincoln AFB, Nebraska, had nine, and there were 12 each at Walker AFB, New Mexico; Schilling AFB, Kansas; Dyess AFB, Texas; Altus AFB, Oklahoma; and Plattsburgh AFB, New York. The sites in the southern states were made possible by the achievement of almost double the design range.

Much was learned with this great ICBM. Perhaps unwisely the whole force was deactivated in 1965–7. Subsequently ex-SAC Atlas E and F missiles have been refurbished as launchers for

numerous space programmes. By mid-1978 Atlases had launched over 175 space payloads, and fewer than 30 remained.

**Dimensions:** Length (Mk 2 RV) 75 ft 1 in (22·9 m), (Mk 3) 82 ft 6 in (25·2 m); diameter 10 ft 0 in (3·05 m).
**Launch weight:** (D) 255,000 lb (115 668 kg), (E, F) 260,000 lb (117 936 kg).
**Range:** (D) 10,360 miles (16 673 km), (E, F) 11,500 miles (18 507 km).

**Above left:** *Launch of missile 134F on 1 March 1963 with the Chrysler ABRES re-entry vehicle, a pointed RV of minimal radar cross section (not used on Atlas).*

**Above:** *Dramatic scene at Cape Canaveral as Atlas 8-E departs on 24 January 1961. The RV is one of the Avco Mk 4 type also carried by Titan I.*

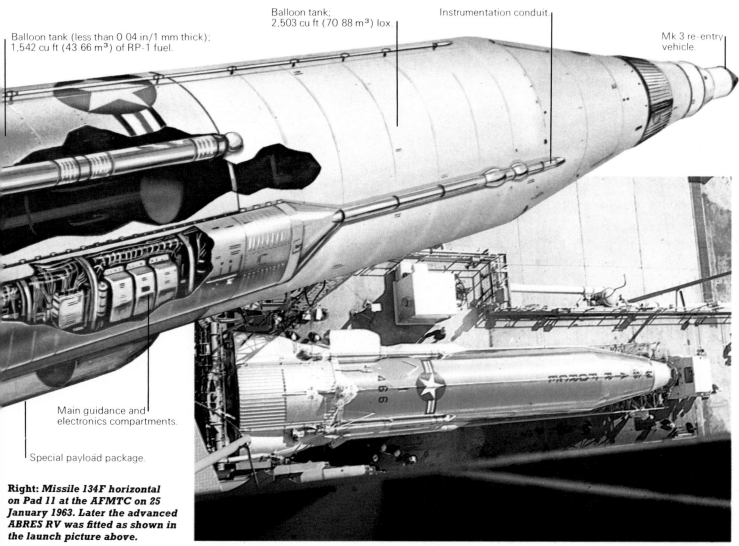

Balloon tank (less than 0·04 in/1 mm thick); 1,542 cu ft (43·66 m³) of RP-1 fuel.

Balloon tank; 2,503 cu ft (70·88 m³) lox.

Instrumentation conduit.

Mk 3 re-entry vehicle.

Main guidance and electronics compartments.

Special payload package.

**Right:** *Missile 134F horizontal on Pad 11 at the AFMTC on 25 January 1963. Later the advanced ABRES RV was fitted as shown in the launch picture above.*

# Titan I and II

In 1953, at the very start of the American ICBM effort, the Strategic Missiles Evaluation Committee had recommended that, in view of the high risk attending so great a technological leap, a second ICBM should also be ordered as insurance. This was not done at first, but by 1955 the picture looked different. Some of the basic features of Atlas, though valid, could be improved upon. A new ICBM would be more efficient if it had two tandem stages, the second ignited in near-vacuum conditions. Instead of thin balloon tankage it should have self-stabilized light-alloy structure so that the missile could be stored upright without pressurization, tanks empty or filled; and it was judged that such structure would allow higher acceleration at launch. By 1956 it was also appreciated that a new ICBM should have pure inertial guidance and be emplaced in an underground silo. So WS-107A-2, the same weapon-system as Atlas but with a "2" suffix, was specified in October 1955 and the prime contract placed with The Martin Company. Like Convair, Martin built a vast new facility on virgin soil, in this case outside Denver, Colorado, specifically to handle this ICBM, designated SM-68.

In 1958 Titan was robbed of its inertial guidance (see Atlas) and given the cumbersome but possibly more accurate radio system planned for Atlas; though, to spend more money, it was redesigned by different contractors, Western Electric becoming guidance prime and assigning the radar to Sperry and the new digital-technology computer to Remington Rand Univac. There were many problems, and no Titan flew until 6 February 1959, when only the first stage was live, with lox/RP-1 fed to an Aerojet LR87-1 with twin gimballed chambers each rated at 150,000 lb (68 040 kg). The second stage was ballasted with water. Over the following year there were many failures, but on 2 February 1960 Titan B-7A flew over 2,200 miles (3540 km), a distance limited by the quantity of propellants, with radio guidance operative. By late 1961 SAC crews had scored 31 out of 41 in test and training shots at Vandenberg. IOC was reached at Lowry AFB, near Denver, on 18 April 1962, with new designation HGM-25A. USM-68A Titan Trainer became HTM-25B.

Second-stage propulsion was an Aerojet LR91-1, rated at 80,000 lb (36 288 kg) in vacuum conditions, with nozzle expansion ratio of 25:1 matched to vacuum operation and with its turbopump exhausting through four nozzles providing roll control and vernier adjustment of cutoff velocity. The 4 MT warhead, largest then flown in the United States, was packaged in the Avco Mk 4 RV. As for the launch complex, this was almost an underground city. It was enormously enlarged and com-

**Above: *Titan I was designed to stand upright in its protective silo, but it still had to be hoisted to the surface prior to propellant loading and launch. This was a shot at the Cape.***

plicated by the large guidance radars and associated power station, which like every other part was hardened to the then-exceptional overpressure of 300 lb/sq in (21 kg/cm²). Reaction time was reduced to 20 minutes by super-rapid propellant loading and high-speed hoist prior to a surface launch. HGM-25A deployment was completed in early 1963: there were six SAC squadrons, each with nine missiles, two at Lowry and one each at Beale AFB, California; Mountain Home AFB, Idaho; Ellsworth AFB, S Dakota; and Larson AFB, Washington, all in the 15th Air Force. But by 1966 Titan I was no longer operational, for like Atlas it had been overtaken by galloping technology.

**Titan I data:**
**Dimensions:** Length 98 ft 0 in (29·9 m); diameter (1st stage) 10 ft (3·05 m), (2nd stage) 8 ft (2·44 m).
**Launch weight:** 220,000 lb (99 792 kg).
**Range:** Up to 8,000 miles (12 875 km).

**Above:** *Launch of Titan I from within the first W-deflector silo, built at Vandenberg, to prove that in-silo launch was possible. Date, 3 May 1961.*

It was only to be expected that, in a field as new as the ICBM, not everything could be got right first time. The launch of Sputnik 1 in October 1957 was a shock to the Americans, and immediately the vulnerability and long reaction time of SAC's ICBMs was recognised as a serious deficiency. In early 1958 Martin proposed an improved Titan using storable propellants and thus ready for immediate firing at any time. At the end of that year the company received a contract for an even more advanced design, SM-68B Titan II. Almost the only feature it shared with Titan I was the diameter of the first stage. In the new missile this stage was 7 ft (2·13 m) longer, and the second stage was the same diameter as the first. This enabled more missile to fit the same silo, and launch weight rose by 50 per cent.

Thanks to Aerojet-General the rocket engines, which were based on those of Titan I, burned Aerozine 50 and $N_2O_4$, which could be loaded into the missile and left for months without boil-off, evaporation, corrosion or other problem. The LR87-5 1st-stage engine had twin chambers each rated at 216,000 lb (97 978 kg); the LR91-5 2nd-stage engine had a chamber rated at 100,000 lb (45 360 kg), with nozzle area ratio of no less than 45:1. This gave Titan II double the payload/range of Titan I. A further very large advance was that Titan II was designed to be launched from the bottom of its silo, which had a mighty W-shaped flame deflector at the base leading to sloping exhaust ducts (see section introduction). These changes reduced the system reaction time to a mere 60 seconds. Naturally, a new pure-inertial guidance system was used, simplifying the launch complex dramatically and improving flight performance; prime contractors were AC Spark Plug and IBM. Not least, Titan II could fly a much bigger RV, the final model being the GE

Mk 6 with a warhead of 18 MT, much larger than on any other American missile.

Thanks to past experience Titan II developed swiftly. The first was launched in November 1961, the whole system met all its test objectives by 16 March 1962, and IOC was achieved in 1963, as system LGM-25C. A total of 54 were deployed, in

**Below:** *Biggest missile ever deployed by the West, the 54 Titan II missiles can be fired from within their silos.*

squadrons each having three widely dispersed triple complexes. Two squadrons were administered by Davis-Monthan AFB, Arizona, in SAC's 15th Air Force, and two each by Little Rock AFB, Arkansas, and Mc-Connell AFB, Kansas, both in the 2nd AF. Whereas all America's earlier ICBMs had short active lives, these 54 silos have been constantly on readiness for 15 years. They have been continually updated, and in 1978–79 new USGS (Universal Space Guidance Systems) were being

fitted to replace costly and obsolescent parts, such as the original computer logic modules. Although in 1970 the SecDef said "after Fiscal Year 1973 we can safely allow the Titan force to decline" this has fortunately not been allowed to happen.

**Dimensions:** Length 103 ft 0 in (31·4 m); diameter 10 ft 0 in (3·05 m).
**Launch weight:** 330,000 lb (149 688 kg).
**Range:** Up to 9,325 miles (15 000 km).

# Minuteman I, II and III

In 1955 the decision of the Navy to attempt a solid-propellant SLBM intensified USAF interest in such propulsion. Whilst accepting that the priority was to get the liquid-propellant ICBMs into service, these weapon systems increasingly appeared physically over-large, complicated, costly, hazardous, vulnerable and overlong in reaction time. In February 1956 WDD completed a proposal for an advanced solid IRBM called Project Q, in April the first contract for motor study was let to the ARDC Power Plant Lab, in March 1957 WDD began to refine details of Weapon System 133 and its flight vehicle, Strategic Missile 80, and in July 1957 the momentous decision was taken to upgrade the missile, by then named Minuteman, to ICBM status. In early 1958 RFPs were issued, and out of no fewer than 14 submissions that of The Boeing Company was accepted in October. Subsequently Boeing Aerospace has been prime for assembly and test, and has completed 20 years of outstanding performance in what became the chief, and virtually the only, land-based deterrent in the Western world.

At the start there were large areas of uncertainty. How to make rocket cases, how to achieve TVC, what propellant(s) to use, and even how to deploy the missile were significant. Spurred by the certainty that a second-generation solid ICBM would be smaller, simpler, cheaper, need one-tenth as many men and have near-zero reaction time – so that the "push-button missile" crept into the media – the AFBMD, successor to WDD, determined to make Weapon System 131, a model of good management. In its first five years, to 1960, the capabilities of the system were dramatically expanded by progressive reductions in warhead weight for given thermonuclear yields, by lighter ablative RVs, by better solid-propellant technology and by advanced airframe design. During this period, extending well into Boeing's fiercely swift engineering development and flight testing in 1958–60, there were two major possibilities that were eventually abandoned. Mobile Minuteman was to be deployed on the US railroads, SAC envisaging five squadrons each comprising ten trains, each made up of 12–14 vehicles including 3–5 launch cars housing single missiles elevated for firing through split roofs. Sidings were surveyed, and despite communications challenges the scheme was found wholly workable; indeed it would have been better than silos, in the author's opinion. The other non-starter was to use the three stages in different combinations, probably in mobile forms for global deployment, to produce MRBMs, IRBMs or ICBMs. In the event only the Russians did this.

To reduce risk each of the three stages was assigned to a different company: 1st, Thiokol Tu-122 (M55), 200,000 lb (90 720 kg) thrust; 2nd, Aerojet-General 60,000 lb (27 216 kg); 3rd, Hercules, 35,000 lb (15 876 kg). The chosen 1st-stage propellant was a mix of PBAA polymer binder

**Left:** *Launch of an unidentified Minuteman I in 1962. This gives a perfect indication of the geometry of the silo smoke-ring, efflux cloud and rising missile.*

**Below:** *The unique launch of two LGM-30F Minuteman II ICBMs from Vandenberg AFB in December 1969. Launches can be controlled from aircraft.*

with AP oxidant and aluminium powder additives; Aerojet chose Pu/AP. The first and second stages were fabricated from D6AC steel, and fitted with four small nozzles which, despite prior success with jetevator TVC, were boldly made to swivel – a breakthrough in solid rocketry. Hercules won the third stage after a protracted competition by demonstrating "superior performance" with another novelty, Nc/Ng/AP propellant in a case of filament-wound glass-fibre, again with four gimballed nozzles. By 1961 Aerojet had qualified a new 2nd-stage case of forged and machined titanium, which replaced steel on the production line. Autonetics handled the inertial guidance, which for the first time used solid-state technology and sub-miniature digital computers. Later (Minuteman II) systems were the first to use integrated-circuit microelectronics. Avco handled the Mk 5 RV, smaller and carrying a lower-yield (1·3 MT) warhead than the first-generation ICBMs.

On 15 September 1959, the day predicted when Boeing joined the programme, a cut-grain tethered missile roared out of a silo to prove that the latter could be a plain hole, with no efflux duct. (So every Minuteman to fly has been preceded out of the ground by a vivid smoke-ring which rapidly grows to 60 ft (18 m) diameter, followed by the flame and smoke from its own first stage through which the missile rises unscathed.) In November 1959 a great facility was planned at Hill AFB, Utah, for assembly and, later, the re-cycling, of all Minuteman mis-

siles. In March 1960 a flight-weight missile with guidance and control made a tethered launch. In June 1960 the first Mobile Minuteman train left Hill to test compatibility with the railroads and refine the communications system. On 1 February 1961 the first free flight scored a total success, flying 4,600 miles (7403 km). A little later came a spectacular failure: the first full silo launch cleared the silo rim but then blew up in "the biggest explosion ever seen at Cape Canaveral". This did not delay the programme.

Unlike previous ICBMs Minuteman was deployed in large wings with silos "filled like pouring cup-cakes" scattered over vast areas, and not only unmanned but with just two SAC officers in a distant underground LCC (launch control centre) for each flight of ten silos. The first base was Malmstrom AFB, Montana. Two flights of ten silos each were at IOC in December 1962, with HSM-80A, soon redesignated LGM-30A. By July 1963 the whole of Malmstrom was operational, with three squadrons each of five ten-missile flights.

**Top:** *Looking up inside a silo for a Minuteman II at Ellsworth AFB, home of the 44th Strategic Missile Wing. Ten silos make a flight, with one control centre.*

**Right:** *July 1975, and an LGM-30G Minuteman III is carefully lowered into a silo previously occupied by an LGM-30B. In turn, LGM-30G is updated.*

**Below:** *All Minuteman missiles were taken by air or road in special containers, which at the silo were elevated to 90° prior to lowering the missile.*

## USA

By this time production had switched to LGM-30B, fractionally longer and with the titanium 2nd-stage case giving longer range. This equipped the next four wings, at Ellsworth AFB, S Dakota; Minot AFB, N Dakota; Whiteman AFB, Missouri; and Warren, centred around the deactivated Atlas complexes. Wing 5 at Warren had 200 missiles and the others 150, making 800 silos at readiness by June 1965.

In September 1964 the first LGM-30F Minuteman .II flew at the Cape. This was a longer and heavier missile with a new 2nd-stage motor, the Aerojet SR19 of increased diameter and a submerged nozzle with liquid-injection TVC. Autonetics produced the largely new NS-11C guidance system with micro-electronic memory storing data for numerous targets, and offering improved accuracy over the greater range this missile flies, despite carrying a heavier payload. The Avco Mk 11B or 11C RV has a 2 MT warhead and Tracor Mk 1 or 1A penaids, the first on a US missile. IOC at Wing VI at Grand Forks, N Dakota, the first Minuteman II base, was achieved in 1966, and these later replaced Minuteman I entirely. At the time of writing it is planned to keep 450 Minuteman II missiles in the inventory for several years (see table), updating them with Mk 12 or 12A RVs, improved hardening and other changes. Fitting Minuteman III guidance was abandoned for lack of funds in 1977.

Minuteman III, LGM-30G, introduced a new third stage and RV. Aerojet and Thiokol jointly produced the glass-filament SR73, of 34,400 lb (15 604 kg) thrust, with diameter the same as the second stage and single fluid-injection nozzle. A new PBPS (post-boost propulsion system) by Bell Aerospace has a 300 lb (136 kg) motor for fore/aft thrusting, six 22 lb (10 kg) for pitch/yaw and four skin-mounted 18 lb (8 kg) motors for roll. At first this controlled a General Electric Mk 12 RV, with three MIRVs of 200 kT each, but since 1977 the Mk 12A has been in production for retro-fitting to about 60 of the 550 Minuteman III missiles in silos as well as a final batch of ten built to keep the line open until October 1977. Mk 12A carries three 350 kT W-78 heads, as well as improved chaff and decoys. CEP improved to 1,200 ft (366 m) with Mk 12 and has been roughly halved with 12A. There are no funds to re-head the bulk of the force, nor introduce the many other later RVs already tested such as Pave Pepper, LABRV or PGRV, but at least the NS-20 guidance will have improved software in 1979-80. The only other major improvement for which funds are available is a UHF line-of-sight link for instant retargeting from an E-4B airborne command post.

**Minuteman data:** A = LGM-30A etc.
**Dimensions:** Length (A) 53 ft 11¾ in (16·45 m), (B) 55 ft 9¼ in (17·00 m), (F, G) 59 ft 8½ in (18·20 m); diameter 72·4 in (1840 mm).
**Launch weight:** (A, B) 64,815 lb (29 400 kg), (F) 70,000 lb (31 750 kg), (G) 76,058 lb (34 500 kg) (modified F and G slightly heavier).

**Range:** (A, B) over 6,214 miles (10 000 km), (F) over 6,990 miles (11 250 km), (G) 8,078 miles (13 000 km).

# MMRBM

In 1962 three US companies studied the Mobile Medium-Range Ballistic Missile, with stellar-inertial guidance and range of 500–3,000 nautical miles (927–5560 km). The two-stage solid weapon was for European deployment but was abandoned in 1964.

**Left:** *An LGM-30G Minuteman III heads towards the Atlantic Missile Range after silo launch at AFMTC. The smoke-ring is high out of the picture.*

**Below:** *A Minuteman III silo, with a two-man launch-control centre (which would actually be remote from the ten silos it controls). Not much shows above ground, other than the LCC environmental stack and the silo surveillance system and concrete lid, shown open. Inside the silo the missile rides on shock-sprung mounts. To launch any missile the two officers in the flight's LCC must each open a safe, extract a key and together hold their keys open 2 seconds.*

### Present Minuteman Deployment

| Wing | Location | M II | M III |
|------|----------|------|-------|
| I | 341 SMW, Malmstrom | 150 | 50 |
| II | 44 SMW, Ellsworth | 150 | |
| III | 91 SMW, Minot | | 150 |
| IV | 351 SMW, Whiteman | 150 | |
| V | 90 SMW, Warren | | 200 |
| VI | 321 SMW, Grand Forks | | 150 |

# MX

The success of Minuteman and its capability of being progressively improved has for 20 years made it increasingly difficult to build a successor system. But by 1974 the alarming pace of Soviet hard-target-kill capability rather suddenly made Minuteman not only look obsolescent and puny but also dangerously vulnerable. Years earlier than expected, Soviet ICBMs have already gained the power and extreme accuracy to knock out virtually all Minuteman silos with only a fraction of the available Soviet force. This spurred urgent studies into a new MX (Missile X) ICBM system. Existing Minuteman missiles could be made mobile, as originally intended 20 years ago, but MX could be a vastly better delivery vehicle. Technology has advanced rapidly in the past 20 years, and some parts of Minuteman, such as the first stage, have scarcely changed at all in that time.

MX hardware testing has been considerable, most of the relevant propulsion, guidance and RV contractors being deeply involved. All the major solid-rocket companies have studied cases and TVC nozzles for the planned three stages, using high-energy Class 7 propellants, Kevlar cases and advanced wide-angle vectoring nozzles, the upper-stage nozzles having retractable extension skirts which deploy after stage separation. The Techroll nozzle, a likely choice for the first stage, is sketched on p. 14. Guidance research centres around AIRS (advanced inertial reference sphere), a single ball floated in low-viscosity fluid that has given encouraging results test-flown in various vehicles including a Minuteman III. The RV might be the Mk 12A, with about seven 400 kT warheads, or the Trident RV or, more probably, the more powerful ABRV carrying about 12 warheads.

How should MX be deployed? An ex-silo Minuteman I was successfully fired after air-drop from a C-5A Galaxy, but the air-mobile deployment concept suffers from many problems. The railroad scheme is in the author's view extremely attractive, but the two most likely options seem to be shelters and trenches. Shelters could assume various forms, from capsules buried in lakes to erector/launcher trucks parked in shallow concrete rooms with blastproof doors but still cheaper than a hardened silo. One idea is 8,500 shelters, between which about 300 missiles would continually be rotated, if possible by night, so that enemies could never pinpoint their location. Trenches would be much more costly, a 3,000-mile (4828-km) network costing about $10,200 million even on a mass-production basis. Tests at Luke AFB in late 1978 were exploring construction methods, the idea being to drive the missiles about in an underground tunnel system to keep their actual positions hidden. For firing, the missile in its capsule would be elevated by breaking clean through the trench roof. Total system price of a 300-missile force, including trenches, is put at about $32,700 million. On paper the proposed system has been refined for years, but already the Carter administration has slipped the schedule for possible IOC from 1984 to 1986. In the author's view the United States lacks the political will to build the MX system, and by the mid-1980s will no longer have even the semblance of a deterrent.

**Dimensions:** Length 70 ft 6 in

**Above:** *This full-scale MX is only a mock-up. In late 1978 it seemed likely that this ICBM will never be funded. Instead the USAF may get an ICBM based on Trident.*

(21·5 m); diameter 92 in (2337 mm).
**Launch weight:** 187,500 lb (85 000 kg).
**Range:** 7,500 miles (12 000 km).

**Below:** *The buried-trench concept is an alternative to rail flat-cars or barges as a way of making the proposed MX force viable in the face of overwhelming Soviet ICBM first-strike capability. A "break-out test" in September 1978 was successful.*

# Common Missile

In late 1978 budgetary problems were expected to force abandonment of the MX programme and its replacement by a so-called "common missile" based on the Navy Trident II – itself far from a fully funded project. The intention is that the USAF should deploy a new three-stage ICBM using the Trident II as second and third stages. It could not enter service until the late 1980s.

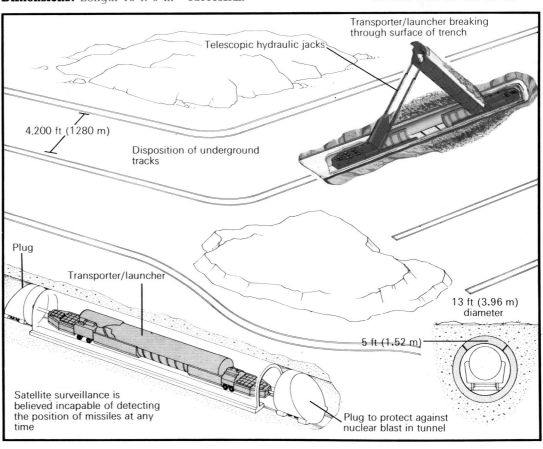

Transporter/launcher breaking through surface of trench

Telescopic hydraulic jacks

4,200 ft (1280 m)

Disposition of underground tracks

Plug

Transporter/launcher

13 ft (3.96 m) diameter

5 ft (1.52 m)

Satellite surveillance is believed incapable of detecting the position of missiles at any time

Plug to protect against nuclear blast in tunnel

# SURFACE TO SURFACE MISSILES

On 21 October 1967 the Israeli destroyer *Eilat* vanished in a cloud of smoke and the wreckage sank into the Mediterranean. She had been hit by three SS-N-2A Styx missiles fired by a small FPB that had boldly ventured out of Alexandria harbour. There was nothing remarkable about the achievement. It could have happened ten years earlier, and simple bombardment missiles had been played with ever since the US Navy fired Loons (copies of the German flying bomb) after World War 2. But this sinking of an Israeli destroyer suddenly jolted naval staffs all over the world into activity. At once designers in a dozen companies were hard at work on ship-to-ship missiles. Ship-based SAMs were converted to fire in the anti-ship role. New warships were built either to carry anti-ship missiles or to defend against them.

This section deals with more than just anti-ship missiles. Many ship-based SSMs can be used against land targets, and a few have such great range that they are hard to exclude from the strategic section which follows. But in general the mission is from ship-to-ship, and this can also be accomplished by many, if not most, of the ship-based surface-to-air missiles described in that section (pages 180–205).

Ships are the largest mobile targets in the world, the largest masses of metal and the only missile targets nicely positioned on a flat, level interface between dissimilar media. Most ships not only have radar cross-sections many times that of the proverbial "barn door" but also pump out an endless stream of radiation on many optical, microwave and IR wavelengths. The main problem facing the anti-ship missile designer has, in the past, been knowing how to pick the best guidance method from the wealth of possibilities. Power of manoeuvre did not in the past have to be very great; ships manoeuvre slowly. Nearly all today's anti-ship missiles are sea-skimmers, with a radio altimeter to keep them flying just above the tops of the waves (it is often possible to adjust the sea-skimming height just before launch, so that on a flat-calm day the missile can almost brush the sea and thus have the best possible chance of evading detection and defensive fire). Turning a missile into a sea-skimmer turns three-dimensional warfare into two-dimensional – like dodgem cars – so all the missile has to do is steer the right course. It can then hardly fail to strike its target, and in recent years a few clever missiles have learned how to go through the side of the target at the optimum height to do most damage, just above the level at which thick armour may be encountered. As in the anti-tank field, the anti-ship missile demands a rethink of the best disposition of armour on ships.

The earliest anti-ship missiles other than torpedoes were all air-launched. The German Blohm und Voss company concentrated on this category in World War 2, and the prolific Henschel firm also made several of its ASMs specifically for use against ships. Most of these missiles had long conical noses for diving into the sea and hitting the target hull below the waterline. No modern anti-ship missile attempts to do this. All aim to hit the target well above the water, and the main argument is what kind of terminal trajectory is best. Either the missile can carry straight on into the side of the ship or it can pop up high over the target and dive from above. Obviously if the target is not asleep the pop-up manoeuvre makes the oncoming missile conspicuous, but to kill it in the three or four seconds available is not easily accomplished.

Before describing actual trajectories it is important to look at the underlying basic problems. How does the missile-armed ship know it has a target available? How does it know the precise location of that target? If ship A can detect and precisely locate ship B, how does it know ship B is not a few jumps ahead of it in doing the same thing? These are pretty important questions, and one cannot avoid feeling cynical when reading the piles of brochures currently being printed describing anti-ship missiles at the way the enemy is always assumed to present a juicy ship target in an apparently passive state just waiting to be attacked. Warships do not behave like this. Most ship-to-ship missiles rely on the radar of their own launch platform to acquire targets and feed exact position information. This means the target must be above the horizon with a clear LOS (line of sight) to it, and it also means the launch ship must pump out radar at the enemy. It thus makes itself an ideal target. Shooting missiles at warships in full view does not seem to me a very attractive proposition, unless trading ships one-for-one is the deliberate intention. Far better to use different sources for target information.

This is what the supposedly backward Soviet Union did in the 1950s in designing the cruise missile we in the West call SS-N-3 Shaddock. For ten years this big and formidable missile has been deployed in substantial numbers aboard many submarines and surface warships, so we may confidently conclude that it works. But we do not (publicly, at least) know how it works. All we know publicly is that it has OTH (over the horizon) capability, which is just what most of the wealth of smaller Western anti-ship missiles lack. The AV-MF (Soviet naval air force) has in parallel with Shaddock deployed numerous radar-equipped ex-bombers whose role is known to include a targeting and guidance function in connection with ship-launched missiles, notably Shaddock. Some observers have even gone so far as to suggest that the aerial platform not only finds the target and passes its position to the missile ship but also uses its radar to illuminate the target so that the missile can home in semi-active fashion on the reflected radiation. If this were the case it is hard to see how there could be any doubt about the matter. Aircraft flooding ocean areas with powerful radar signals advertise the fact, and not only allow the other side to record every detail of the guidance signals but also make themselves extremely vulnerable, so that in actual warfare they might be on the receiving end before they could guide their first cruise missile.

What probably happens is that, like Western aircraft, the radar-equipped ocean patrol aircraft of the AV-MF are responsible for finding targets and quickly passing their co-ordinates to the missile ship or submarine. The missile is then fired on a course pointing at the future target position, which over a 500-mile (800-km) flight would be about 30 miles (48 km) ahead of that reported, in the hope (which the reconnaissance aircraft could probably verify) that the target was ignorant of the attention being paid to it. The missile would then have its own seeker, which would only have to search within a very small angular area, either using active radar or a passive method relying on the mass of emissions from most warships. An alternative which does not appear to have been explored is for the patrolling aircraft to release a small laser-carrying RPV – very hard to detect and even harder to shoot down – which could either use a laser designator to illuminate the target for the missile, or else could attract the ship's attention and result in the switching on of SAM radars on which the anti-ship missile could home.

Certainly it appears desirable to avoid relying on visual or radar contact with the target, to avoid any friendly emissions of any kind and to have OTH capability. It does not appear especially helpful to have in the West so many basically similar anti-ship missiles which fail to meet most or any of these criteria. All appear to be excellent at hitting ideal targets which foolishly may try to get out of the way but do not themselves have the capability of hitting back at a ship, helicopter or missile. Are there any ways of pinpointing hostile ships without the ship being aware of it? Satellites are obviously a near-ideal surveillance platform, against which few ships have any answer, but only two nations at present appear to use such high-flying spies. A modern reconnaissance satellite would have no difficulty in identifying all major surface warships, nor in relaying signatures of most of their emissions, and their precise position, heading and speed, all of which are capabilities accomplished only quite recently after prodigious effort. However, most satellites fly orbits which take them over any particular location only at infrequent intervals. Another possible covert source of target information is the shadowing submarine, but in this case a simpler answer would surely be to use a traditional torpedo.

It is instructive to note the paucity of naval missiles with TV guidance. TV and other EO methods usually are passive, and so ought to be able to hit the target without waking it up seconds or minutes beforehand. A self-contained TV guidance system would be very clever; however, most present systems of this type have to transmit the picture to a remote operator who then steers the missile, and this ruins the beauty of the system by adding noisy microwave links in both directions. Of course, old-fashioned primitive wire guidance is, in theory, not an emitter and so might not be detected by the target; but this restricts the missile to slow-flying short-ranged weapons.

Having amply belaboured the fact that glossy brochures extolling the virtues of missiles that need the parent ship or aircraft to illuminate the target with radar do not impress me in the slightest, I cannot avoid drawing attention to the staggering disparity between the naval missile performance of the major nations. By any yardstick the Soviet Union is way out in front in the sheer numbers, number of types and physical size of its ship-launched weapons. Tantalisingly little is known about most of these systems, though in many cases one can deduce at least basic information from the radar carried by the parent vessel. The missiles themselves are normally kept inside their launch containers, and the only one that is commonly known in the West, the redoubtable Styx, is not only older but likely to be quite different in character from the newer weapons. It is logical to assume that at least some of the longer-ranged Soviet weapons use ram-rocket propulsion, a field in which the United States and Sweden are trying to make up for an inexcusable amount of lost time by the West up to the present day.

# FRANCE

## SS.11M

This anti-tank missile exists in slightly modified forms for marine deployment. In all known cases SS.11M is guided by looking through a shipboard stabilized sight close to the launcher, and in some cases it is used as a training missile fired from a launcher normally occupied by an SS.12M. Users include Brunei (FPB, two quad launchers), Ethiopia (minesweepers), France (FPB), Greece (FPBs), Ivory Coast (FPB), Libya (FPBs), Senegal (small craft), and Tunisia (FPBs). Sweden uses the RB 52 in a coast-defence role.

**Right:** *Largest of the shipboard launchers for SS.11M is this rotatable 10-round installation.*

**Below:** *Standard two-missile FPB launcher with SS.11M (inboard) and the larger SS.12M in the outboard position.*

**Right:** *FPB Susa of the Libyan Navy firing SS.11M during contractors' trials by Vosper Thorneycroft. This class of 96 ft (29.3 m) boats has proved most successful.*

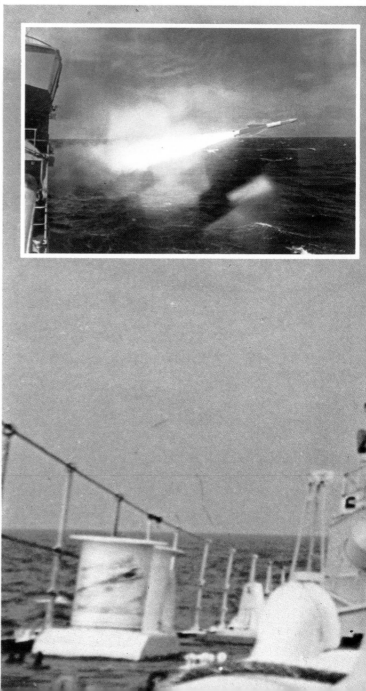

## SS.12M

Again similar to land and air-launched versions, this heavy wire-guided missile was developed in the early 1960s and convincingly demonstrated in 1966 aboard the French FPB *La Combattante*. Two SS.12Ms were fired against a moving target about 3.4 miles (5.5 km) away, both striking within about 3.3 ft (1 m) of the aiming mark. Typical FPB installations have a single gyro-stabilised high-magnification sight serving two twin launchers, one on each side of the vessel. All the navies listed above use SS.12M, as well as the *Perkasa* class boats of Malaysia.

## Malaface

This was a ship-to-ship bombardment missile using an airframe based on the Malafon (p. 000). The range was extended by an SEPR long-burn sustainer rocket, and the 2,205 lb (1000 kg) conventional warhead was built into a completely new forward fuselage with air-log propeller to arm the impact fuze.

## Exocet

By taking the proven aerodynamics, structure and propulsion of such weapons as AS.30, the motor of Martel and the guidance of Kormoran, Aérospatiale quickly developed the MM.38 Exocet in 1970–2 as the standard ship-to-ship weapon of the French Navy. Within months an export sale had been made to Greece, in a year Britain had been allowed to participate and buy missiles, and today sales exceed 1,500 rounds to 17 navies, and there are also land-based and air-launched versions, described separately. MM.38 is stored in and fired from a large light-alloy box which may be fixed or rotatable. The launch ship, or some other platform, feeds in target co-ordinates be-

**Right:** *Launch of MM.38 Exocet from a County class cruiser of the Royal Navy. The missile launcher replaced B turret.*

**Inset:** *Training launch from a French ship, probably a corvette with oblique launchers.*

fore launch. SNPE provide tandem boost/sustain motors, respectively the Epervier and Eole V with concentric nozzles, and mid-course guidance is inertial, height being held at about 8 ft (2·5 m) at Mach 0·93 by a TRT radio altimeter. At around 8½ miles (14 km) from the target the final homing phase begins using the EMD Adac X-band monopulse seeker. The 364 lb (165 kg) Hexolite/steel-block warhead penetrates up to 70° from normal (ie, a glancing shot at 20°) and has proximity and delay fuzing. This basic version is deployed aboard some 250 ships, ranging from the Royal Navy's *County* class cruisers to modest FPBs. First firing by Aérospatiale was in July 1970, and the French Navy began evaluation firings in November 1972. In late 1977 the score was claimed to be almost 90 out of 90, troubles having been very minor.

SM.38 for submarine launch was abandoned (Britain tried to replace it with Sub-Martel and bought Harpoon). Aérospatiale is trying to develop SM.39, derived from air-launched AM.39, to arm *Agosta* and other submarines. If this goes ahead MM.39 might also be reactivated as a second-generation Exocet for surface launch. Meanwhile MM.40 is being developed with Aérospatiale funds, though French Navy orders are likely. The lengthened boost motor has a steel case and the sustainer burns for more than twice as long (220 sec compared with 93) to give greater range. The launcher is a neat glass-fibre tube, much easier to handle or transfer between ships and able to fit four (in some cases eight) missiles in the space needed by one MM.38 box. The homing head has a wide-angle search and acquisition gate, and MM.40 descends below its normal sea-skimming height in the final 984 ft (300 m) to hit even the smallest target.

**Dimensions:** Length (MM.38) 17 ft 1 in (5·21 m), (MM.40) 18 ft 6 in (5·64 m); diameter 13·8 in (350 mm); span (MM.38) 39·5 in (1·004 m), ((MM.40) 39·37 in (1·000 m).
**Launch weight:** (MM.38) 1,620 lb (735 kg), (MM.40) 1,819 lb (825 kg).
**Range:** (MM.38) 2·5–26 miles (4–42 km), (MM.40) up to 43·5 miles (70 km).

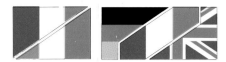

# INTERNATIONAL

## Otomat

This cruise missile was developed from 1969 under a fixed-price contract from the Italian Navy, the collaborators being Oto Melara of Italy and Matra of France (hence the name). Intended for launch from a wide variety of platforms including ships of FPB size upwards, aircraft and land mobile platforms, Otomat has cruciform wings and rear control fins and (except in air-launched form) is fired from its box container clipped to a fixed launch table. Target data are fed from any source such as a helicopter data-link, and launch direction can be up to 180° off-target. Twin boost rockets burn for 4 sec, and cruise propulsion is by a Turboméca TR281 Arbizon turbojet of 836 lb (379 kg) thrust, fed by ram inlets at each wing root. After cruising on radio-altimeter height-lock Otomat Mk 1 searches 20° on each side with a Thomson-CSF two-axis radar, locks-on target at about $7\frac{1}{2}$ miles (12 km) and finally swoops up to 574 ft (175 m) to dive on the lightly protected deck. Guided trials began in December 1971, and on 19 November 1975 a fully operational firing took place from the hydrofoil *Sparviero* when foilborne. Over 500 rounds are being supplied to *Lupo* class frigates of Italy, Peru, Venezuela and Egypt, and a wide range of other craft for Brazil, Taiwan, Nigeria and (unconfirmed) Ecuador. Otomat Mk 2, first fired in January 1974 and fired operationally from the Italian Navy test ship *Quarto* in January 1978, has SMA single-axis radar homing and is a sea-skimmer right to the target. The Téséo version incorporates a TG-2 radio link for mid-course guidance updating by an AB.212ASW or other airborne platform; this facilitates firings over the full design range. Otomat Mk 3, proposed to France, would have the EMD Adac (Exocet) head.

**Dimensions:** Length 15 ft $9\frac{3}{4}$ in (4·82 m); diameter 18·1 in (460 mm); span 47 in (1·19 m).
**Launch weight:** (with boost rockets) 1,697 lb (770 kg).
**Range:** (Mk 1) $3\frac{3}{4}$–37 miles (6–60 km), (Mk 2) up to over 62 miles (100 km).

**Top:** *Launch of Otomat from the Italian navy* Sparviero *whilst foilborne at full speed.*

**Right:** *Otomat launch from a Vosper Thorneycroft ship of the Venezuelan navy.*

**Inset:** *Otomat in flight, with controls commanding maximum nose-up attitude.*

## ASSM

Representing a glimmer of hope of NATO standardization, albeit in the 1990s, the Anti-Ship Supersonic Missile is being developed by ASEM (Anti-Ship Euromissile), a consortium embracing Aérospatiale, MBB and BAe, with about one-tenth of the funding allocated to Holland and Norway and with US monitoring of platform compatibility. All six NATO nations signed the Memorandum of Understanding in

April 1977, West Germany providing the contracting agency. The 1977 study ran for 14 months and in 1978 was to be succeeded by a contract for development of the system. ASSM originated in 1974, drawing upon experience gained with MM.100 (Aérospatiale), Hydra Fk 80 (MBB) and USGW/Sub-Martel (BAe). MBB's extensive work on ram-rockets is valuable, because this is the optimum propulsion for the specified range of some 112 miles (180 km), cruising at about Mach 2·2. Guidance is expected to involve strapdown inertial mid-course and dual active radar homing backed up by IR homing. Launch weight is not likely to be less than 2,140 lb (970 kg), or about 1,800 lb (816 kg) for an air-launched version without boosts. Of this, about 400 lb (180 kg) would be warhead.

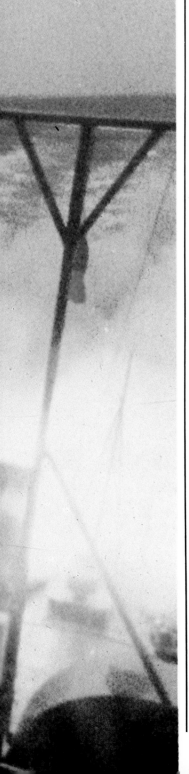

## ISRAEL

## Gabriel

Developed from scratch by MBT, a subsidiary of Israel Aircraft Industries, Gabriel gradually overcame its temperamental early nature in 1966–68, and by the October 1973 war was a mature shipboard weapon that played a major part in sinking nine Egyptian and Syrian vessels. Targets are acquired by ship's (or airborne) radar, and an optical sight and the glass-fibre launch box aligned with the target. The boost motor (solid rockets are almost the only bought-out parts) burns for 4 sec, taking the missile to 250 ft (76 m) at cruise speed of Mach 0·7; the slow-burning sustainer then takes over and holds the weapon at a height of 33 ft (10 m) using radio altimeter and twin-gyro platform. There is a facility for either direct azimuth control by radio command or slaving to an optical link. In any case terminal homing is provided, usually by semi-active radar. The usual Israeli radar is frequency-agile in the X-band. Gabriel can home on to a point source of jamming, but there are an unusual number of alternative choices, depending on hostile ECM. In the final phases the missile sinks close to the wave-tops, the height depending on sea-state. The 331 lb (150 kg) warhead has a delay-action fuze. By 1978 well over 300 launchers (readily re-usable) were deployed with Israel, Argentina, Singapore, Thailand, South Africa, Malaysia and (unconfirmed) Kenya. Gabriel 2 has a sustainer of higher specific impulse and greater diameter, which with other changes doubles the range. This is the chief current production version. A TV version is rumoured.

**Below:** *Close up of Gabriel box in one of the Saar class boats built in France to German design. Photographed at Ashdod, this is a fixed installation; many of the Gabriel launchers are trainable. Gabriel is too large and heavy for manual launch-box reloading.*

**Foot of page:** *Launch of Mk 1 Gabriel from one of the Israeli-built Reshef class missile boats which also have an Oto Melara 76 mm gun and other weapons. With this missile Israel has achieved considerable export business, sufficient to underpin further development.*

**Dimensions:** Length 11 ft 0 in (3·35 m); diameter (Mk 1) 12·8 in (325 mm), (Mk 2) 13·8 in (350 mm); span 54·5 in (1385 mm).
**Launch weight:** (Mk 1) 882 lb (400 kg), (Mk 2) 1,100 lb (499 kg).
**Range:** (Mk 1) 1¼–13½ miles (2–22 km); (Mk 2) 1¼–25½ miles (2–41 km).

# ITALY

## Sea Killer

This shipboard SSM system was developed by Contraves Italiana from 1963, and taken over by Sistel SpA when that large consortium was formed in 1969. It exists in two forms, Sea Killer Mk 1 (originally known inside Italy as Nettuno) and Mk 2 (originally known inside Italy as Vulcano). Sea Killer Mk 1 has a set of cruciform wings used as control surfaces and fixed tail fins. Sea Killer Mk 2 has wings of greater span and different shape and a tandem boost motor, but the systems are otherwise similar. Sea Killer Mk I was deployed only on the Italian FPB *Saetta*. Launched from a trainable five-box launcher, it rides a guidance beam from the ADT A40 Sea Hunter 2 radar fire-control system, with height governed by a radio altimeter whose setting can be changed by radio command from the launch station. In "interference conditions" the missile can be tracked by a TV subsystem and guided by direct radio command. Sea Killer Mk 2 fits into a virtually identical system. First flown in 1969, it equips Vosper Mk 5 frigates of the Imperial Iranian Navy, associated

with Sea Hunter 4 radars. It is the missile used in the Mariner and in the Marte ASM system (p. 113). A much more advanced Sea Killer Mk 3 system was abandoned.

**Dimensions:** Length (Mk 1) 138 in (3·5 m), (Mk 2) 185 in (4·7 m); diameter 8·1 in (206 mm).
**Launch weight:** (Mk 1) 375 lb (170 kg), (Mk 2) 661 lb (300 kg).
**Range:** (Mk 1) 6¼ miles (10 km), (Mk 2) 15½ miles (25 km).

## Mariner

This is not a separate missile but a weapon system based on Sea Killer Mk 2. It is essentially the

ASM Marte (p. 113) transferred to a ship platform. The SMA I/J-band radar, derived from the APQ-706 used in Marte, uses back-to-back aerials and is supplemented by an optical tracker and command joystick as in the existing Sea Killer Mk 2 system. Mariner is still under development. A two-missile installation for an FPB or similar ship is said to weigh about 3,527 lb (1600 kg). The possibility of Mariner ships and Marte helicopters collaborating against the same target is an obvious objective.

*Right: Launch of Sea Killer Mk 2 from an unidentified ship (probably a Vosper Mk 5 frigate of the Imperial Iranian Navy).*

*Right, inset: Frames from a cine film showing impact of Sea Killer Mk 2 just above the waterline of a target hull.*

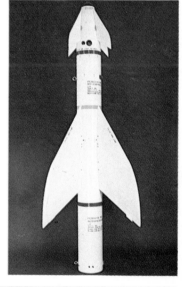

*Below: Flight profile of the Sea Killer Mk 2; Marte is the same but is dropped from aircraft. Sistel and SMA have jointly produced the Mariner shipboard weapon system of radars, computer, displays and controls to back up Sea Killer. Few sales have been achieved.*

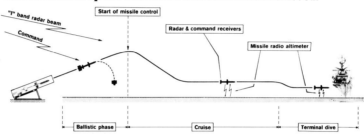

# NORWAY

## Penguin

Development of this ship-to-ship missile was begun in the early 1960s at the Norwegian Defence Research Establishment, and was completed in collaboration with Kongsberg Väpenfabrikk with some financial support from the US and West German governments and use of US Navy test support facilities. Penguin Mk 1 boldly discarded the possibility either of guidance from the parent vessel or emissions by the missile, either of which could be interfered with by the enemy. It is one of the very few missiles to use wholly passive guidance. The basic missile incorporates the warhead of Bullpup, the ASM (p. 123) which for many years was licence-built by a European consortium that included Kongsberg. It is delivered as a checked-out item of ordnance in a box launcher which is attached to a simple deck mount and an umbilical plugged in. The Norwegian *Storm* class FPBs have six missiles each. The vessel's radar or other data source is used to detect, acquire and designate a target, the data being fed to the Kongsberg SM-3 computer and the missile told the predicted point of impact.

The box launcher is opened and the round fired by Raufoss dual-thrust motor in the general direction of the target, while the parent ship turns away. Guidance is initially inertial, until an IR-seeker head scanning ahead detects heat from the target, whereupon homing is automatic. Passive D/F of hostile EM transmissions can also provide guidance information. Penguin Mk 2 carries a PEAB active radar homing head and is being adopted by missile boats of Norway, Sweden, Greece, Turkey and

at least one other country, with strong interest by the US Navy. Land and ASM versions are described separately.

**Dimensions:** Length 118 in (3·0 m); diameter 11·0 in (280 mm); wing span 55 in (1·4 m).
**Launch weight:** 750 lb (340 kg).
**Range:** (Mk 1) over 12½ miles (20 km), (Mk 2) 18½ miles (30 km).

*Right: Standard production Penguin with inertial midcourse guidance and passive IR homing.*

*Below: Launch of Penguin from P 967 Skud, of the Storm class missile boats of the Royal Norwegian Navy. There are 120 launchers on this class.*

# SWEDEN

## RB 315

The first Swedish-developed guided missile to enter service, this substantial ship-to-ship weapon stemmed from preliminary tests in 1949–50, at the very start of the Robotavdelningen, the original Swedish national guided-missile bureau. At that time the official organization carried out both development and manufacture, and RB 315 was produced mainly "in house", flight trials beginning in 1952. Eventually at least 100 production

*Left: RB 315 on its long rail launcher aboard Halland in the late 1950s.*

*Below: Launch of RB 315 from one of the two destroyers which were armed with this missile.*

missiles were built, to support launchers which in 1955–65 were operational aboard the destroyers *Halland* and *Småland*. Features included shallow-angle launch by four internal solid-motor nozzles between the cruciform wings, cruise propulsion by a resonant-duct engine with flush air inlets just ahead of the boost-motor nozzles, radio command guidance from the parent ship and an electro-pneumatic autopilot controlling cruciform nose fins. There was a large conventional warhead.

**Dimensions:** Length 24 ft (7·3 m); diameter 27 in (685 mm); span 84 in (2·13 m).
**Launch weight:** About 3,086 lb (1400 kg).
**Range:** 9⅓ miles (15 km) at 590 mph (950 km/h).

# RB 08A

Developed jointly by Nord-Aviation (later Aérospatiale) of France and Saab-Scania in Sweden, this cruise missile replaced the RB 315. Work began as a Royal Swedish Navy study in 1959, and using the Nord CT 20 RPV target as a basis the French and Swedish partners cleared the flight vehicle for production in 1966. Compared with the CT 20 the RB 08A is longer, heavier and has folding wings. First deliveries were made the same year to the destroyers *Halland* and *Småland*, and subsequently a coast-defence version was developed. Production of 98 missiles ceased in 1970. Launched by two solid boost motors which then drop free, RB 08A cruises under the 882 lb (400 kg) thrust of a Turboméca Marboré IID turbojet. Guidance is by launcher azimuth, autopilot and height-lock, followed when near the target by active-radar homing. This system enables the considerable theoretical range to be utilised in practice. The blast/frag warhead weighs 551 lb (250 kg).

**Dimensions:** Length 18 ft 9 in (5·72 m); diameter 26 in (660 mm); span 9 ft 10½ in (3·01 m).
**Launch weight:** 2,679 lb (1215 kg), including 694 lb (315 kg) boost unit.
**Range:** 155 miles (250 km).

*Below: Test launch of a SKA by Saab-Scania in 1974. Like many countries Sweden has been in severe trouble with defence budgets, and this promising anti-ship missile had to be abandoned. RB 04 Turbo is a much larger cruise weapon.*

# SKA

This third-generation missile was disclosed at the Paris Air Show in 1975 as a replacement SSM for Swedish torpedo boats and flotilla leaders. Saab-Scania, prime contractor, was developing SKA as a "fire and forget" missile, weighing about 1,411 lb (640 kg) to fly about 25 miles (40 km) at Mach 0·8 under solid-rocket propulsion. It would have had a homing head with ability to lock-on to both sea and land targets. Development was terminated in 1977.

# RB 04 Turbo

Derived from the RB 04 ASM, this proposed weapon for the *Spica II* class FPB mates the existing front end of the RB 04E with a new rear section with air-breathing engine and cruciform wings. The obvious propulsion would appear to be a ram-rocket, but an alternative would be boost rockets and a small turbojet. The Royal Swedish Navy was expected to decide whether to adopt this missile before this book is published but no decision had been made in late 1978.

*Above: Checkout and refurbishing of RB 08A missiles at Linköping.*

*Inset: Launch of RB 08A coast-defence version. Most launchers for this cruise missile are believed to be at land sites, only two being at sea.*

*Below: Artist's impression of RB 04 Turbo, drawn for this book.*

# USSR

## SS-N-1 Scrubber

Earliest of all cruise missiles of the Soviet Navy, this primitive bombardment weapon was developed in the early 1950s and entered service aboard destroyers of all the Soviet Fleets from 1957. By 1959 there was a single aft launcher in four *Kildin*-class ships and launchers both fore and aft in eight of the *Krupny* class. By 1974 these installations were being replaced by the much later SS-N-11. The chief problems with N-1 were, first, it was never publicly seen by the West, and second, it was a source of confusion because the designation was associated with two code-names, Scrubber by NATO and Strela by American agencies. It was concluded both names applied to the same missile, which required a rail launcher some 56 ft (17 m) long, trained through an arc of some 200° and with a presumably weather-proof enclosure over the missile at readiness. With the launcher aligned fore/aft reload missiles could be run out from an adjacent missile-preparation deck-house. The author inclines to the view that the missile was, in fact, no more than N-2 Styx, the long launcher being needed to ensure safe flying speed from a ship much slower than an FPB and possibly with the launcher trained down-wind. Other observers think N-1 was much larger, flying about 115 miles (185 km) with high-subsonic ramjet propulsion and IR homing, but this appears to be speculation on rather shaky evidence.

## SS-N-2 Styx

Whether or not this simple cruise missile is synonymous with N-1 Scrubber, it is certainly the most widely used and probably most numerous missile in its class at present. It has also seen action in three wars. Entering service with the Soviet Navy in 1958–9, it was subsequently supplied to many nations and was used in anger in the wars between Egypt and Israel in 1967 (when these missiles sank the destroyer *Eilat*) and 1973, and between India and Pakistan in 1971. N-2 has an aeroplane configuration, with stubby delta wings and tail and a fat bluff-nosed body. Despite this it appears to have rocket propulsion, take-off being under the thrust of a large ventral booster, jettisoned after burnout, and the small sustainer in the tail maintains a speed of around Mach 0·8. In the nose there appears to be a guidance radar, and the consensus of opinion is that the missile is either command guided or flies on autopilot and height lock until its seeker head detects and locks-on to the target. There is abundant evidence of

progressive updating of the missiles and launchers over the past 20 years, and most observers believe either or both radar or IR homing may be used by different models of this missile. Some sources use the designations SS-N-2A and -2B to differentiate the supposed original version and a later type with IR homing. The warhead is a linear or polygon charge weighing about 882 lb (400 kg). Soviet-built missile systems are still being built and over 1,200 are accounted for by the pioneer missile FPB classes, the two-

missile *Komar* (Mosquito) and four-missile *Osa* (Wasp), as used by the Soviet Union, Algeria, Bulgaria, Cuba, Egypt, Finland, East Germany, India, Indonesia, Iraq, Jugoslavia, North Korea, Libya, Morocco, Poland, Romania, Somalia, Sri Lanka, Syria, Vietnam and South Yemen. In addition China has its own production line of a derived missile deployed not only on FPBs but also on two destroyer classes and in coast-defence installations (Soviet pictures imply a coast-defence role for N-2, but not convincingly).

**Left:** *Taken from HMS* Ark Royal, *this photograph shows the SS-N-1 launcher on the foredeck of a shadowing* Krupny *class destroyer. These ships had one installation at each end.*

**Right:** *A fine picture by a US Navy aircraft of No 378, one of the Egyptian* Osa *class missile boats supplied by the Soviet Union in 1966. This example was under way off Port Said on 26 April 1974. N-2 launchers are prominent.*

**Below:** *Apparently taken from inside the awaiting launch bin, this photograph shows an SS-N-2 Styx being hoisted aboard a missile boat of the* Komar *class of the Soviet navy. These were the earliest Soviet missile boats, rebuilt from P-6 torpedo boats.*

**Dimensions:** Length about 20 ft 6 in (6·25 m); diameter 29½ in (750 mm); span 9 ft 2 in (2·8 m).
**Launch weight:** About 5,511 lb (2500 kg).
**Range:** Up to 26 miles (42 km).

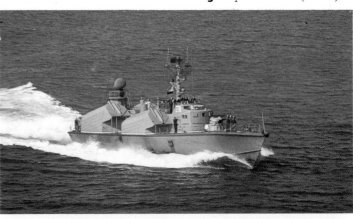

# SS-N-3 Shaddock

Though dating from the same time-frame as the N-1 and N-2 (design about 1951, development and flight-test 1954–57, operational 1958), N-3 Shaddock is vastly more formidable and even today could deliver crushing blows over very great distances. Unlike the US Navy Regulus (p. 91) this missile was put into the inventory in ever-increasing numbers and has greatly assisted development of a range of later weapons.

The missile itself is launched from a cylinder of various forms, normally sealed by a cover plate at both ends. Different launch tubes used by the land-based version (SSC-1, p. 28) have revealed basic information on the configuration. The large body has a pointed nose and internal turbojet or ramjet sustainer (details of the air inlet are unknown in the West); underneath are two solid boost motors which are jettisoned after burnout, when the short-span wings unfold. There is a ventral fin but no horizontal tail, and the inference is that there is either a foreplane as on Regulus II or elevons on long-chord wings. Cruising speed is certainly beyond Mach 1, a common guess being Mach 1·4; the author sees Mach 2·2 as more attractive. The warhead is either nuclear or conventional of 3,000 lb (1360 kg) or over.

Shaddock, quite apart from its Sepal relative, certainly exists in numerous sub-types with different guidance and other changes. Several of the earliest installations were on submarines, and in their haste to deploy this missile the Soviet planners, with total disregard for expenditure, quickly brought into service a succession of quite different installations. The first aboard the W-class submarine was dubbed Whisky Twin Cylinder by the West: two Shaddock tubes were installed in an elevating frame completely proud of the rear deck casing, making for an acoustically disastrous submarine. Then followed Whisky Long Bin: a batch of W-class were cut in two and given a long amidships section with new conning tower housing four fixed launch tubes. Then came the 16 diesel-engined J (Juliet) class, each with a much better installation of two twin launchers which could be elevated from a flush position in the decking. The final scheme was seen in the EI (Echo I) class nuclear boats, with three such twin launchers, and the 27 really impressive Echo II class with four twin launchers. None of these submarines carries suitable guidance equipment, and it has been assumed that mid-course guidance for their missiles is provided by aircraft. These submarines were all in operation by 1963, with 318 launchers in all.

In 1962 the Kynda class cruis-ers appeared, obviously designed around this missile system and carrying two quad launchers with an unknown number of reload rounds rammed in from adjacent deckhouses (how much credence can be placed on a Warsaw Pact illustration showing missiles like cartridge cases and shells is doubtful). Each launcher can train through about 25° and elevate to 30°. These ships bristle with radars, with Head Net A for surveillance and the distinctive Scoop Pair to guide the Shaddocks until they disappear over the horizon. In 1967 Kresta I cruisers appeared, with two twin launchers abeam the bridge and elevating but fixed in azimuth. Kresta I cruisers carry a Ka-25 Hormone A helicopter, but the use of this for target acquisition or missile guidance remains conjectural.

**Dimensions:** Length about 42 ft 8 in (13 m); diameter about 39 in (1 m); span possibly 6 ft 10 in (2·1 m).
**Launch weight:** About 9,920 lb (4500 kg).
**Range:** Up to 528 miles (850 km), though 124 miles (200 km) is thought optimum.

## SS-N-7 Siren

Called Siren by NATO, this puzzling missile is almost entirely unknown in the West. So far as is known, it is carried only by the C class (Charlie) submarines, first delivered from Gorki in 1968. Whilst equipped with eight ordinary torpedo tubes of full 21 in (533 mm) calibre, these vessels do not use these for the missiles which occupy a quite separate eight-round (4 ×2) launcher which can be elevated from the foredeck. Practically nothing is known of N-7 beyond the supposition that it needs a launcher larger than a 533 mm tube. (Suggestions that it is derived from N-2 Styx appear ridiculous.) One report (Flight International, 1978) suggests a length of 22 ft (6·7 m) and diameter of 20–21·5 in (500–550 mm), and while repeating various other estimates of range at around 34 miles (55 km) suggests a flight speed of Mach 1·5. One might have expected a speed of either Mach 0·9 or 2, but not in between? The important feature is that N-7 has a dived-launch capability, though at what depth is unknown. Taken in conjunction with the very high nuclear-driven performance of C class submarines, and the little-known P (Papa) class that probably also carries this missile, one is driven to conjecture on how these vessels find their targets and how the missiles are guided. It is universally assumed that no outside assistance is needed, in other words the submarines and the missile system form an organic complete system.

## SS-N-9

Though it is conceivable that the Papa class nuclear submarines carry this weapon, its only definite application is the outstanding Nanuchka class missile boat, sometimes classed as a corvette, which has been in production since 1969. Much larger and steadier than the N-2 boats, Nanuchkas carry a triple launch box for this missile on each side. Dominating these ships is the radome-enclosed surveillance radar code-named Band Stand (not Slim Net as first reported), which almost certainly serves a mid-course guidance function. Details of the missile are pure supposition, other than limits on size. Assumptions include flick-out wings, air-breathing or rocket propulsion with emphasis on the latter, radar or IR homing guidance and range of up to 68 miles (110 km) at Mach 0·8. It is noteworthy that Nanuchkas sold to India carry N-2 or N-11 missiles, not N-9.

**Dimensions:** Length less than 29 ft 6 in (9 m).

## SS-N-10

This weapon system was gradually recognised as having primarily an ASW role rather than surface-to-surface, and in 1978 was redesignated by the DoD as SS-N-14. It is described on p. 257.

Top: *Part of a Kynda class cruiser showing four SS-N-3 Shaddock tubes and (above bridge) Peel Group radar for SA-N-1 and (on mast) Scoop Pair for SS-N-3.*

Above: *Provisional sketch of SS-N-3 Shaddock.*

Below: *No 920 of Nanuchka class, deploying SS-N-9 missiles in two triple tubes. Largest of at least eight radars is Band Stand.*

## SS-N-11

Apparently developed from N-2 Styx, this is undoubtedly a much newer SSM of greatly enhanced performance, though similar in size. Jane's Weapon Systems expects performance to be "similar in terms of range and speed", but the developments in propulsion technology in the past 20 years have been dramatic, as have those in structures and, to a lesser degree, in aerodynamics. Guidance is today miniaturized, and may be expected to show advances over N-2, though N-11 has been widely exported, in one case as a substitute for N-7 Siren. N-11 has always been seen in a distinctive drum launcher, with sloping conical muzzle door. It was first deployed on the Osa II class missile boats, with four rounds each facing ahead. Four Kildin destroyers have been re-reconverted to have four N-11 missiles facing aft around the rear funnel, two twin gun turrets taking the place of the SS-N-1 SSM launcher. By 1967 Kashin class destroyers, advanced gas-turbine ships only about 8–11 years old, were appearing with a similar installation. Export customers include India, Finland and Iraq.

# UNITED KINGDOM

# USA

## USGW/Sub-Martel

Under-Sea Guided Weapon (CL.137) was a unilateral development by Britain to try to produce an effective submarine-launched missile to rival the Russian N-7. Collaboration with France was abandoned when Aérospatiale gave up the SM.38 Exocet, and though USGW was based heavily on Martel the French partner in this weapon,

Matra, did not participate. It would have had an extended Martel body, folding wings and fins, added boost motor and MSDS homing head. It began extremely promising development but was cancelled in 1975, after £16 million had been spent, in favour of buying Harpoon from the United States.

**Below:** *Artist's impression of USGW/Sub Martel breaking the surface and shedding its launch canister.*

## Loon

In March 1946 the Secretary of the Navy approved conversion of two submarines, SS-337 *Carbonero* and –348 *Cusk*, to carry and fire single navalized versions of the USAAF JB-2. Missile designation was KUW-1, later LTV-N-2, and the name Loon was bestowed. The missile was housed in a watertight drum behind the conning tower, the crew having to fit the wings and launch the weapon with four large rockets off a short aft-facing ramp. Many Loons were fired from Point Mugu, from the two submarines (first on 12 February 1947) and AVM-1 *Norton Sound*. Loon was never operational and terminated in 1950. Data as for JB-2 (p. 33).

## Standard SM-1 and ARM

Though originally a SAM (p. 202) or an air-launched anti-radiation missile (ARM) (p. 125) this weapon system was in the early

1970s also developed as the RGM-66D interim ship-to-ship missile for the US Navy. Compatibility was inherent because ARM itself grew out of the Standard ship-to-air missile, and RGM-66D can be fired from regular Standard launchers as well as from simple single launchers for small ships. It provides an over-the-horizon (OTH) capability against any source of radiation in the appropriate frequency bands, as discussed on p. 125, or an SARH anti-ship capability. As it needs little ship equipment it can be carried by small boats, and in 1970 demonstration of folding tail fins mated the RGM-66D to the Asroc launcher of a DDG (DE-1052 class). A single box launcher fitted ARM to the PG patrol gunboats. RGM-66D was first deployed aboard two PGs, *Douglas* and *Grand Rapids*; subsequently it has equipped two further PGs as well as six DDGs and six FFGs of the US Navy, and three destroyers of the Imperial Iranian Navy each of which has a quadruple box launcher.

**Left:** *Nice shot of LTV-N-2 Loon from USS* Carbonero *surfaced off the Naval Air Missile Test Center at Pt Mugu in May 1949.*

**Below:** *Standard ARM can be distinguished from the Standard SAM by its prominent ring of dark dielectric panels just behind the nose radome; inset, handling Standard ARM aboard carrier* **John F. Kennedy.**

# Harpoon

This potentially important weapon system began as an ASM (see p. 131) in 1968, but three years later was combined with a proposal for a ship- and submarine-launched missile. McDonnell Douglas Astronautics (MDAC) was selected as prime contractor in June 1971. The main development contract followed in July 1973, and of 40 prototype weapon systems 34 were launched in 1974–5, 15 being the RGM-84A fired from ships (including the PHM *High Point* whilst foilborne) and three from submarines, the other 16 being air-launched. At first almost wholly trouble-free, testing suffered random failures from late 1975, and the clearance for full-scale production was delayed temporarily. Production of all versions amounted to 315 in 1976, 538 in 1977 and 375 in 1978, with 400-plus scheduled for 1979.

Harpoon makes maximum use of existing hardware, such as ship fire control, submarine torpedo tubes (the missile being fired inside a buoyant capsule which remains until it breaks surface) and Tartar/Terrier/Standard/Asroc launchers. Unlike AGM-84, RGM-84 is initially

**Above: Unidentified underwater launch of complete Harpoon from submarine tube/capsule off San Clemente Island.**

**Inset above left: Harpoon launch from a DE of the Knox class (note just rear pair of Asroc/Harpoon boxes are elevated for firing).**

**Inset below right: On the first underwater launch on 24 September 1972 the missile had no wings. Black blob at left is the capsule nosecap.**

propelled by an Aerojet solid boost motor which accelerates the missile to Mach 0·75 in 2½ sec. Cruise propulsion is by a Teledyne CAE J402 turbojet, rated at 661 lb (300 kg) thrust, endurance at sea level being 15 min at Mach 0·85. Target data, which can be OTH if supplied from a suitable platform, are fed before launch to the Lear-Siegler or Northrop strapdown inertial platform which can steer the missile even if launched at up to 90° off the desired heading. Flight control is by cruciform rear fins. A radar altimeter holds the desired sea-skimming height, and no link with the parent ship is required. Nearing the target the Texas Instruments

PR-53/DSQ-58 active radar seeker searches, locks-on and finally commands a sudden pull-up and swoop on the target from above. The Naval Weapons Center 500 lb (227 kg) warhead is of the penetration blast type, with proximity and impact-delay fuzes. An EO-homing project is ISSM, described separately below. The Naval Weapons Center and MDAC are also studying possible versions with supersonic speed, torpedo-carrying payload, imaging IR homing, passive radiation homing, nuclear warhead, vertical launch, midcourse guidance updating and other features.

MDAC expect to make at least 5,000 systems by 1988 despite the delayed start. Of these well over 2,000 will be for the US Navy, for FF-1052 and FFG-7 frigates, DDG-37, DDG-47 and

DD-963 destroyers, CG missile cruisers, PHMs, all SSN attack submarines, and aircraft. Export orders were placed by Turkey, the Netherlands, Denmark, Iran, Australia, Israel, S Korea and Saudi Arabia (and other countries for AGM, p. 131). In 1978 the Royal Navy was expected to order the sub-launched version, having cancelled its own USGW/Sub-Martel, but encountered problems with industrial offsets involving making the non-standard RN launch capsule. Sweden, Japan and W Germany were in final negotiation for orders.

**Dimensions:** Length 15 ft 0¼ in (4·58 m); diameter 13½ in (343 mm); span 30 in (762 mm).
**Launch weight:** 1,470 lb (667 kg).
**Range:** Up to 68 miles (109 km).

NWC warhead

Midcourse guidance

Honeywell radar altimeter

Lear-Siegler/Nortronics strapdown inertial system

TI frequency-agile active radar

**Above:** *Famous picture of the first shot from PHM High Point. The fantail launch tubes are fixed.*

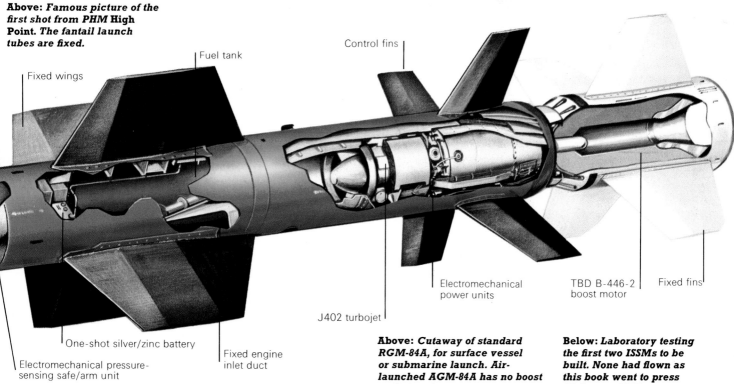

Fixed wings

Fuel tank

Control fins

Electromechanical power units

TBD B-446-2 boost motor

Fixed fins

J402 turbojet

One-shot silver/zinc battery

Fixed engine inlet duct

Electromechanical pressure-sensing safe/arm unit

**Above:** *Cutaway of standard RGM-84A, for surface vessel or submarine launch. Air-launched AGM-84A has no boost rocket motor.*

**Below:** *Laboratory testing the first two ISSMs to be built. None had flown as this book went to press (February 1979).*

# ISSM

The Imaging-Seeker Surface-to-surface Missile is a Naval Sea Systems Command project to explore the problems of detecting, identifying and hitting ship or other surface targets at or beyond the horizon. The basic airframe is RGM-84A Harpoon but, in place of active radar, the seeker head is the EO (electro-optical) seeker developed for the defunct Condor (p 128). The Walleye glide bomb (p 124) furnished a suitable data-link. Harpoon already has a digital autopilot capable of interfacing with different types of seeker head. MDAC was in 1978 building four ISSMs in a demonstration programme. One was to be used in captive tests, and the other three were to be launched from surface ships.

# SURFACE TO SURFACE MISSILES

In the years immediately following World War 2, when a true intercontinental (ie, strategic) missile appeared difficult to produce, it was logical to attempt to overcome the problem by fitting missiles to warships. In effect it added a further stage of propulsion, the first stage being the ship. For obvious reasons of stealth and vulnerability the favoured type of ship was the submarine, though this imposed especially severe constraints on the missile. It so happens that the submarine-launched strategic missile is still one of the most important weapons in the armouries of the great powers, but for quite different reasons. Today we can build missiles that could fly to other planets if we wished; what we find more difficult is to protect them from other missiles, and hiding them in the ocean is one of the few answers that appears to work with a fair degree of success.

There is no better way of studying the development of so-called strategic missiles than to examine the US Navy sequence: Loon, Triton, Rigel, Regulus, Polaris, Poseidon, Trident and Tomahawk. At first glance this appears to complete a circle of development from winged cruise missiles through ballistic weapons and back to wings. In fact today the ballistic missile and cruise missile are complementary, as the Soviet Navy appears to have known all along.

Loon, the submarine-launched version of the German "V-1", was by modern standards extremely crude and limited, but in historical perspective it was important. The German Navy left records showing only passing interest in the flying bomb programme, and few missiles of any kind were fired from any German ship in World War 2, despite the plethora of weapons developed for the Luftwaffe and army. Studies were carried out in 1943–4 for the flying bomb (and the "V-2") aboard submarines, but there was no way Germany could fire this missile from U-boats within a reasonable timescale. This was fortuitous; it would have been an annoying weapon, especially to New York and Washington. It is not surprising that the US Navy played with Loons, though how much of the experience was truly applicable to subsequent weapons is problematical.

Rigel and Triton, the little-publicised cruise missiles of the immediate post-Loon period, suffered from the fact that better answers emerged almost daily. It was hard to stick to one design, because by the time it was built it was vastly inferior to what could by then be achieved. The same problem afflicted the designers of manned aircraft, to a degree not encountered today. Coupled with the fact that it was all totally new, so that one had to rely entirely on one's own opinion to an extent unknown since the Wright brothers, it is easy to appreciate how difficult it was for either a customer service or an industrial prime contractor to decide at what point to stop drawing and start building. In the early 1950s such programmes as Rigel and Triton moved in a few action-packed years from the propeller and "buzz-bomb" era into the modern world of missiles able to carry a 3000 lb (1361 kg) warhead 1000 miles at Mach 2·5, and take evasive action if necessary. There is no doubt whatever that such things are at instant readiness in numbers in today's Soviet Navy.

These Soviet missiles are grouped in the preceding section, because it is assumed that they are for use primarily against ships. Thirty years ago the targets were mainly assumed to be cities, and this allowed the use of a wider range of navigation systems. One family of systems was based on radio methods, and the one picked for Rigel and Triton and later refined for other missiles was an area-coverage system of the familiar hyperbolic type in which either pulsed or CW emissions from two fixed stations (in this case two "radar picket" submarines) mutually interact to generate a fixed pattern of hyperbolic lines along which the missile could guide itself. A totally different method was astro-tracking in which a gyro-stabilized tracker in the missile locked-on to a star or other suitable heavenly body and navigated by a computerised version of traditional marine methods using a sextant. Astro was one of the methods which in theory could yield high accuracy over very long distances but which took years of patient toil before it could be relied upon.

By the mid-1950s the inertial system was beginning to emerge from the laboratory. The INS (inertial navigation system) was one of the bedrocks on which the submarine-launched strategic missile was eventually to rest, because it is not only wholly self-contained but it can also solve the problem of fixing the precise position of the submarine when it launches a missile. This was not so vital in the days of radio guidance, but for an inertially guided missile it is crucial.

An INS measures all the accelerations, in all three planes, experienced by a vehicle and then integrates these with respect to time to give a continuous record of its velocity; it then integrates the velocities with respect to time to give a continuous record of position. To do this it has to know exactly where the vehicle was at the start in order for the end of the flight to coincide with the target. Measuring the accelerations is done by sensitive accelerometers, which in principle are like small masses supported by springs. Three accelerometers could be arranged to measure up/down accelerations, left/right and fore/aft. They must be mounted on a stable platform, a frame held precisely level – not necessarily parallel to the land below, which may not be level, but so that the vertical axis of the platform passes through the centre of the Earth. If this precision were to be degraded some or all of the accelerometers would sense false accelerations due to Earth gravity. The platform is held level by gyros which are among the most accurate items ever made by humans. Depending on the way these are mounted on gimbals, to give two or three "degrees of freedom", the platform can be stabilised by two or three gyros; or for short-duration missions a simpler "strapdown" system can be used. The last fundamental requirement is to "Schuler-tune" the platform, in principal by fixing it to a pendulum with a period of 84 minutes, the same as a pendulum the same length as the Earth's radius, so that the platform does not stay stabilized with respect to true space but with respect to the Earth's centre. It can then be mounted in a submarine, or ballistic missile, and coupled to a computer and guidance system.

The INS was one of man's greatest technical achievements, and today it is the basic method of navigation of many ships, airliners, spacecraft and fighters as well as missiles. Its drawbacks are mainly its high price and need for highly skilled attention in the unlikely event of any servicing being needed. INS errors tend to be directly proportional to time, so with cruise-type vehicles, ships and spaceflight, intermittent updating is needed from astro, radio or other sources. For modern cruise missiles a good INS would suffice for nuclear attacks on soft targets, but in recent years much dramatic progress has been made in methods generally grouped under the name Tercom (terrain comparison). First studied 30 years ago, these no longer rely wholly or, in most cases, even partially on the two-dimensional appearance of the terrain around, or on the run up to, the target. Today the favoured method relies on a one-dimensional plot of the profile of the land surface. Selected areas of hostile territory are covered with a mosaic or grid to divide it up into a statistically significant number of squares, rectangles or hexagons. The mean height above sea level of each is then fed into the guidance computer which memorises the possible sequences. Over hostile territory the basic guidance is accurate enough to take the missile over the first selected

area, and an accurate radio altimeter tells the computer the profile actually passing beneath. The computer compares this with all possible profiles in its memory and, unless something is grossly wrong, one set must match. This answer is used to refine the INS or other guidance to hit the next selected area near the target, where the trajectory is further refined for accurate impact.

Tercom is used in the submarine-launched Tomahawk and several other existing or projected winged missiles. Obviously, if the position of the submarine at launch is not accurate, or if the missile fails for any reason to overfly the first selected Tercom grid, the final arrival will be wide of the mark. Likewise the method is hard to adapt to allow for twisting and turning to avoid defences, and a missile flying in a straight line and using a radio altimeter ought to be easy to shoot down. Again, any bright country ought to be able to instal a grid of transponders that could be tuned to match enemy radio altimeters to ensure that the missile received misleading height indications – perhaps in such a sequence that the missile could be persuaded to return whence it came. Such countermeasures are probably still in their infancy, but to every action, said Newton, there is an equal and opposite reaction, and this certainly applies to weapons.

This introduction has concentrated on cruise missiles and on guidance. The story of how the ballistic missile went to sea is relatively well documented, and is traced in this section for both the super-powers.

A final general point is that, compared with a land-based system using silos or even a nationwide system of railways or tunnels, the submarine-based strategic system has slightly poorer accuracy because of the reduced precision of the point of launch. A submarine on station might be expected to keep checking its position by all the means at its disposal, including INS, astro, navigation satellites and radio methods such as Omega. None of these require any emission by the submarine, nor anything bigger than a piece of wire to show above the water. The resulting fix might be accurate within, say, 50 metres, but this has a significant degrading effect on missile CEP, and for this reason submarine missiles are generally not used in a counterforce but in a countervalue role. Against cities it pays to have the maximum practical number of small warheads, rather than the one big one needed against a silo. This explains, for example, the seemingly trivial total yield of the Mirved warheads of Poseidon compared with Polaris.

# CHINA

In 1974 the American JCS chairman announced that the PRC was developing an SLBM, together with carrier submarines, for IOC not earlier than 1979–80. This opinion has been maintained since, the assumption being that the missile will be broadly similar to an early Polaris. It has been suggested that tests would be made using the three Serb launch tubes in the *Golf* class submarine built by the PRC and completed at Dairen in 1964.

# FRANCE

## MSBS

Mer-Sol Balistique Stratégique is a weapon system even more costly than the silo-launched SSBS, and in general it has been subjected to more relentless updating of a more advanced kind as the primary carrier of the French deterrent. The MSBS system was broadly based on Polaris but was achieved with little non-French help other than licensing of essential technology. Like the US weapon it is deployed in groups of 16 in SNLE (Sous-marin Nucléaire Lance-Engins) submarines which can fire all their missiles from deep under water in 15

**Left:** *Launch towards the Azores of an early MSBS M-1 from* **Gymnote,** *submerged off the CEL.*

**Right:** *MSBS M-1 missile shown "exploded".*

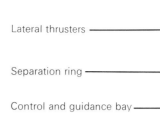

500 kT warhead in Aerospatiale RV

Lateral thrusters

Separation ring

Control and guidance bay

P4 Rita I second-stage motor

Inter-stage thrust frame

Fixed nozzle, liquid-injection TVC

Inter-stage fairing

Double-bolt separation ring

P10 Type 904 first-stage motor

Instrumentation conduit

Rolled and welded Vascojet casing

Four nozzles gimble by rotating on inclined bearings for TVC

Skirt

Heat-resistant shroud over nozzle actuation system

minutes. The DTE managed the programme for the state, SEREB acted as prime contractor for the missile, and original subcontractors included Direction des Poudres (propellants), Nord-Aviation (inter-stage structure and, with SNECMA, motors and cases), SEPR (gimballed 1st-stage nozzles) and Sud-Aviation (equipment bay and RV and, with SEPR, the 2nd stage). Production assembly and test was managed by Sud-Aviation, which was later merged with Nord and others to form Aérospatiale whose Division des Systèmes Balistiques et Spatiaux is today's prime for the whole system. SEPR is now SEP, part of G2P.

Following early tests of research vehicles at Hammaguir the M-011 vehicle (live 1st stage) flew in December 1967, the M-012A (live 2nd stage) in April 1968, the M-012B (with RV) in July 1968, and the M-013V (with guidance system) in November 1968. Most tests of early vehicles were from the CEM and then from the CEL, but the November 1968 shot was from a launch tube in the trials submarine *Gymnote*. The first SNLE, *Le Redoutable*, reached IOC in December 1971; *Le Terrible* followed in 1973, *Le Foudroyant* in 1974, *L'Indomptable* in 1977 and *Le Tonnant* was scheduled for early 1979. The SNLE base is at Ile Longue, near Brest.

The first MSBS missiles were of the M-1 type. These had a Type 904/P10 1st-stage with Vascojet case, four gimballed nozzles, 100,000 lb (45 360 kg) thrust for 50 sec, and the Rita I/P4 2nd-stage with glass-fibre case, single nozzle with Freon TVC and 39,682 lb (18 000 kg) thrust for 55 sec. Inertial guidance uses an EMD Sagittaire computer and with US platform technology licensed to Sagem, and the ablative RV contains a 500 kT warhead. The M-2 missile has a new Rita II/P6 2nd-stage, with six tonnes of Al/AP/Pu Isolane propellant instead of five, giving 70,547 lb (32 000 kg) thrust for 52 sec and extending the range. This equipped *Le Foudroyant* and was retrofitted into the two earlier submarines. The M-20 missile introduced a new RV with MR-60 1 MT warhead and penaids, with hardening against ABM explosions. This is now becoming standard on all SNLEs. The lighter MR-61 warhead, also of 1 MT, is to be fitted by about 1980.

For the second half of the 1980s a completely new M-4 missile is being developed. This has virtually nothing in common with earlier MSBS missiles, but like Poseidon – with which it is broadly comparable – it can be installed in the existing SNLE fleet after considerable alteration which includes new fire-control equipment, launch tubes and ejector systems. M-4 is a considerably larger missile, weighing almost twice as much as an M-20. It has near-perfect volumetric efficiency, in that it packs the maximum amount of propellant and payload into the new enlarged launch tube. It naturally offers greater maximum range, multiple warheads and enhanced protection against all forms of enemy defence.

Unlike all known previous SLBMs, but like Trident, it has three stages of propulsion. All are handled by Aérospatiale (cases) and SEP, with high-energy propellant produced by the G2P (Groupement pour les Gros propulseurs à Poudre) formed jointly by SEP and SNPE. Stage 1, called Type 401, has a metal case and a thrust of 154,320 lb (70 000 kg); stage 2, Type 402, has a glass-filament-wound case and gives 66,138 lb (30 000 kg); stage 3, Type 403, has a Kevlar case (no French Kevlar supply yet exists) and gives 15,432 lb (7000 kg). The inertial system is again by Sagem and EMD, but considerably lighter and more accurate than that of M-20. Other subcontractors, all French to the last nut and bolt, include Matra, Crouzet, SFENA, AMD, Air Equipement, Sintra, Wonder, Intertechnique, Séri, Ecan de Ruelle, Deutsch, Souriau, EFAB and CII-Honeywell Bull. The RV will house six or seven Mirvs, each with a yield of approximately 150 kT.

According to André Motet, Aérospatiale MSBS programme manager, engineering development of the numerous hardware items in the M4 system began around the spring of 1976. All system definition had been firmed up by the end of 1977, and extensive testing by mid-1978 included the static firing of at least two of the propulsion stages. Clearly, the need to begin again, rather than merely assign new work to an existing industrial team, caused extra work associated with RFPs and qualification of suppliers, and the list of names given is only a selection from the largest collective team ever applied to any national weapon system in Western Europe. France wishes to avoid external licensing in M-4 even more strenuously than in the earlier SLBMs, though the DTE and Aérospatiale have kept in close touch with the Poseidon and, where possible, the Trident programmes to incorporate the very latest concepts. Flight test of the M-4 is scheduled for "the early 1980s", with SNLE deployment proceeding in all five submarines from the middle of the decade.

**Dimensions:** Length (M-1, -2, -20) 34 ft 1½ in (10·4 m), (M-4) 36 ft 1 in (11·0 m); diameter (M-1, -2, -20) 59 in (1·50 m), (M-4) 75·6 in (1·92 m).
**Launch weight:** (M-1) 39,683 lb (18 000 kg), (M-2, -20) 44,091 lb (20 000 kg), (M-4) 79,365 lb (36 000 kg).
**Range:** (M-1) up to 1,491 miles (2400 km), (M-2, -20) 1,926 miles (3100 km), (M-4) over 2,485 miles (4000 km).

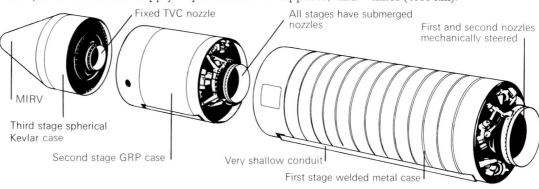

First and second nozzles mechanically steered

All stages have submerged nozzles

Fixed TVC nozzle

MIRV

Third stage spherical Kevlar case

Second stage GRP case

Very shallow conduit

First stage welded metal case

**Top:** *Main features of the MSBS M-4 SLBM, due to reach IOC around 1985. It will be compatible with today's SNLE force, after modification.*

**Right:** *Submarine launch of an MSBS M-20, externally very similar to earlier missiles despite greater performance.*

# USSR

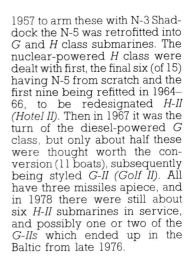

## SS-N-4 Sark

This was the first SLBM in the world to be built and declared operational. Its development began around 1953, possibly slightly earlier than the crystallization of the US Navy's interest in the concept and the studies for a seagoing Jupiter. It was probably the world's first large ballistic vehicle designed to be compatible with a ship, but the opportunity was not taken to try and produce a missile that would fit into the hull of a large submarine, vertically or horizontally. Instead N-4, called Sark by NATO, was allowed to be of a size that

Below: *Called SS-N-4 Sark by the West, this SLBM was first displayed in 1962. Three years earlier plans were passed to China.*

only just fitted between the keel of a submarine and the top of its conning-tower sail. This greatly diminished its value as a weapon, and the number that a submarine could carry. There is some evidence that this missile was in any case produced merely to explore the problems, and was never intended as a definitive operational weapon, but this suggestion is countered by the large number of submarines in which it was installed. N-4 appeared to have six solid charges at the base to blow it out of the launch tube, with the submarine at the surface. The base was then jettisoned and the two non-cryogenic liquid-propellant rocket stages fired in succession. RV yield is put at 1 MT. Following tests with Scud missiles launched from tubes on land and then in a rebuilt Z (Zulu) submarine, at

least seven Z class were rebuilt at Zhdanov yard in 1955–6 as the Z-V (the final patrol Zulus being Type IV), with a 36 ft (11 m) section spliced in amidships with two launch tubes. These were followed by the G (Golf) class, designed from scratch to carry three N-4 tubes in a more efficient installation. At least 22 G class were built at Severodvinsk and Komsomolsk in 1958–61. Almost simultaneously the big nuclear-powered H (Hotel) class were on the slipways, with the same three-missile bridge-fin. The first nine of this class also became operational with N-4, the last in October 1962, by which time a minimum of 38 submarines were operational with this cumbersome pioneer SLBM.

**Dimensions:** Length about 49 ft (15·0 m); diameter 71 in (1·8 m).
**Launch weight:** About 44,091 lb (20 000 kg).
**Range:** About 373 miles (600 km).

## SS-N-5 Serb

The second-generation Soviet SLBM, N-5 was developed in 1958–63, and probably was influenced by the decision of the US Navy to drop Jupiter and buy a much more compact missile. It is much the same size as the original Polaris, though it follows N-4 in having its own gas ejection system to pop it out of the launch tube. A cluster of 18 electrically fired cold gas nozzles form an ejector unit on the base of the missile, which is jettisoned as soon as ejection is complete and the 1st-stage motor can fire. Unlike N-4 this missile can be launched under water. Both motors have fabricated steel cases, and there is some evidence of solid propellant despite the recent belief of some Western observers that liquid propellants are used; if liquids are used they are storable and the missile travels on land at full weight, on a massive trailer towed by an AT-T tractor which, in public parades, also carries a handling crew of 16 Marines. Guidance is inertial and the warhead estimated at 1 MT. It is possible that N-5 was intended for multiple installation in the E (Echo) nuclear boats, but when the decision was taken around

Left: *This Hotel-II was photographed in 1972 limping home from its missile patrol area near Newfoundland with a major fault. Its missiles are the SS-N-5 Serb type seen below on display on 9 May 1965.*

1957 to arm these with N-3 Shaddock the N-5 was retrofitted into G and H class submarines. The nuclear-powered H class were dealt with first, the final six (of 15) having N-5 from scratch and the first nine being refitted in 1964–66, to be redesignated H-II (Hotel II). Then in 1967 it was the turn of the diesel-powered G class, but only about half these were thought worth the conversion (11 boats), subsequently being styled G-II (Golf II). All have three missiles apiece, and in 1978 there were still about six H-II submarines in service, and possibly one or two of the G-IIs which ended up in the Baltic from late 1976.

**Dimensions:** Length about 42 ft 4 in (12·9 m); diameter 56 in (1·42 m).
**Launch weight:** About 37,477 lb (17 000 kg).
**Range:** Estimated at up to 1,491 miles (2400 km), with the consensus closer to 994 miles (1600 km).

## SS-N-6 Sawfly

This third-generation SLBM again shows a totally fresh approach and when it was first seen in the November 1967 parade it posed several problems to Western observers. Geometrically superior to N-5 in that it has the optimum shape to fill a launch tube, N-6 was at first thought to have solid propulsion but has now come to be regarded as a storable liquid missile, almost certainly $N_2O_4$/UDMH. In its public appearances it has been towed by a Navy/Marines MAZ-537 tractor on a massive articulated trailer which appears to carry the missile with tanks full. The 1st stage appears to be very large, accounting for more than 75 per cent of the total launch weight, with four vectored nozzles. There is no cold expulsion device attached to the missile, and this undoubtedly is part of the launch installation in the Y (Yankee) class submarines which since 1967 have been the carriers of N-6 in service. These formidable nuclear-propelled vessels are considerably larger than any US Navy submarines yet in service, but their hull diameter is still well short of the length of the N-6 missile whose launch tube accordingly projects nine feet (2·74 m) into a large deck casing. Unlike earlier Soviet FBM submarines the Yankees at least avoid the gross projection of the missile into the sail (bridge-fin) and the standard vessel accommodates 16 launch tubes, the same number as the

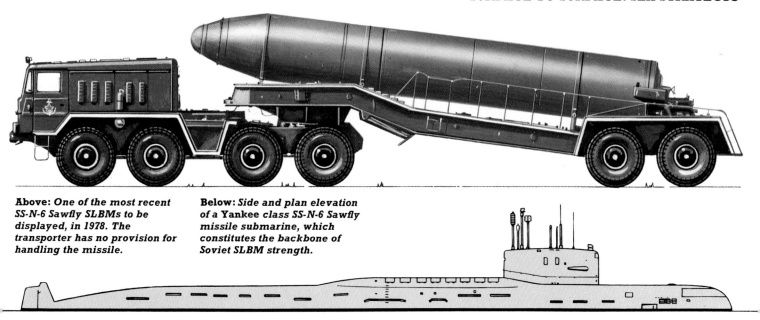

**Above:** *One of the most recent SS-N-6 Sawfly SLBMs to be displayed, in 1978. The transporter has no provision for handling the missile.*

**Below:** *Side and plan elevation of a Yankee class SS-N-6 Sawfly missile submarine, which constitutes the backbone of Soviet SLBM strength.*

**Right:** *The first clear view of a Delta-I running on the surface. These are larger than any Western submarine, but smaller than their Soviet successors.*

US Navy Poseidon and Polaris vessels. Clearly the N-6/*Yankee* combination was the first SLBM system the Soviet Union judged worthy of all-out effort, and from the mid-1960s most of the capacity at the gigantic yards at Severodvinsk and Komsomolsk, assisted by Severomorsk and Gorkii, was devoted to building *Yankees* at a rate that topped eight per year. A total of 34 were commissioned, representing 544 missiles in tubes, and total N-6 production is put by the MoD at about 1,000.

Three versions are known in the West, believed to be interchangeable. Mod 1, the original with bluff RV and full-length instrument conduit, has a warhead estimated at 1 to 2 MT. Mod 2, seen on test in 1972 and deployed from 1973, has "improved propulsion" giving a substantial increase in range (see data). The DoD states that Mod 2 could hit "any part of the United States" from the 100-fathom (600 ft, 183 m) contour offshore. Mod 3, which closely followed Mod 2, has three RVs, not independently targeted. According to the DoD Mod 3 still does not have sufficient combination of yield and accuracy to hit very hard targets, but it would be devastating against cities. It was thought in late 1978 that all N-6 at sea were then of Mod 3 type. Production of N-17 had then already begun as a replacement.

**Dimensions:** Length 42 ft 8 in (13·0 m); diameter about 71 in (1·8 m).
**Launch weight:** About 41,887 lb (19 000 kg).
**Range:** (Mod 1) 1,491 miles (2400 km), (Mods 2 and 3) 1,864 miles (3000 km).

## SS-N-8

In 1971 this missile began an apparently extremely successful flight test programme from a single rebuilt *Hotel* submarine, the so-called *H-III* vessel. The N-8 quickly demonstrated a range of 4,847 miles (7800 km), which the Chairman of the JCS, then Gen George S. Brown, said exceeded by at least 1864 miles (3000 km) the range of any SLBM existing elsewhere. It introduced "a totally new problem" into Western defence planning. The impact of subsequent testing, from October 1974, when N-8 demonstrated ranges exceeding 5,717 miles (9200 km), on full-range missions from the Barents Sea to a target area in the central Pacific, can thus be imagined. This missile, which at first was vainly hoped in the West to be merely an improved N-6, completely outperforms the Trident C-4 which will not reach the US Navy until 1980. So far no NATO name for N-8 has leaked out, and most details of its design are assumptions. It is believed to be a two-stage storable-liquid missile, and stellar-inertial guidance, unusual in a ballistic vehicle, is said to give CEP of about 1,312 ft (400 m). This, combined with estimated warhead yields (see below), puts N-8 at least in the class of pre-Mk 12 Minuteman, though the Soviet Union has such a mass of pinpoint high-yield ICBMs that it has no need to use N-8 as a counterforce weapon. Considerably larger even than N-6, this missile needed the largest submarines ever built to carry it, the *D (Delta)* class. Even with a hull diameter at least as large as the *Yankees* the missile length is such that the launch tubes project about 25 ft (7·5 m) into a giant box aft of the sail. In the *Delta I* class of about 18 boats the overall length is estimated at 450 ft (137 m) and the number of launch tubes 12. In 1976 *Delta II* submarines entered service, with an extra 50 ft (15 m) section increasing the number of tubes to 16; there are at least eight of these. In mid-1977 a *Delta III* was seen at sea, with a staggering further increase in length to about 600 ft (183 m) and 20 or 24 tubes (opinions differ on the number). Several *D-IIIs* were operational in mid-1978. The missile also exists in at least three forms: Mod 1 has a single 1–2 MT warhead; Mod 2 has three RVs of unknown yield; Mod 3 has three manoeuvrable independently-targeted RVs, the first to enter Soviet Navy service.

**Dimensions:** Length believed to be about 56 ft (17 m); diameter, variously reported as 79 in (2 m) and "same as N-6".
**Launch weight:** About 88,183 lb (40 000 kg)
**Range:** Observed up to 5,717 miles (9200 km).

# SS-NX-12

So far identified only on the foredeck of *Kiev*, the first of the *Kuril* class multi-role platforms, this long-range cruise missile is regarded as a successor to N-3 Shaddock and to be compatible with the shipboard magazines and handling systems of the earlier missile. On *Kiev* there are four twin launchers of a new type, associated with a railed deck handling system and with a crane on the right side of the deck apparently used to bring missiles aboard. Reloading the tubes from below-deck magazines appears to be completely mechanised. The new radar

*Below: Foredeck of Kiev, as the new ship emerged into the Mediterranean in July 1976. There are eight SS-NX-12 tubes.*

carried in a retractable mounting in the ship's bows, thought to operate in the E/F-band, is generally associated with this missile, which is expected to be a rocket-launched ramjet or turbojet cruise weapon with a range that could be as great as 1,864 miles (3000 km). Speed is generally put at "transonic"; it will probably be either Mach 0·9 or over Mach 2. The seemingly obvious propulsion would be a ram-rocket matched to a speed of Mach 2·5–3.

# SS-NX-13

This SLBM appears to be a clever way of evading SALT limitations on the number of strategic missiles that may be deployed. Though similar in size to SS-N-6 and deployed aboard *Yankee* class submarines, it is reported to be an anti-ship weapon and thus does not count for the purpose of totalling "strategic" missiles. It is almost certainly an N-6 with different guidance and warhead to give a depressed trajectory and range of 466–621 miles (750–1000 km). Initial target information is believed to be supplied by satellite, which puts the missile into a trajectory giving a near miss. At a range of some dozens of kilometres a terminal homing system with look-down capability (radar, IR or EO) locks-on and steers the RV to impact. The US Navy has suggested that Standard 2 with a nuclear warhead might be able to intercept the relatively slow (said to be Mach 4) RV.

# SS-NX-17

This is believed to be the first Soviet SLBM to use solid propellant. Prototypes were seen on flight test from land launch tubes in 1975, and testing at sea from submarines was expected to begin in 1977–78. It is reported as a two-stage missile with a PBPS, the first on a Soviet SLBM, though only a single RV was detected on early flight tests. Curiously, dimensions have been given as about 36 ft 3½ in (11·06 m) long and 65 in (1·65 m) diameter, which does not make NX-17 readily compatible with existing *Y* or *D* class launch tubes (though in 1978 the SecDef said one *Y* boat was testing NX-17

missiles). Several unofficial stories circulating in the West describe a new class of missile submarine under construction at Severomorsk, said to be called the *Typhoon* class by NATO; if this is so, it is a departure from the consistent use of phonetic-alphabet names, T being Tango. The DoD said in 1977 that no Soviet SLBM platform was known beyond the *D-III*, though other observers continue to insist on a completely new, even larger class. NX-17, however, has been positively identified and is expected to enter service, probably in rebuilt *Yankees*, in 1979.

# SS-NX-18

Yet another impressive new SLBM, first seen on flight test a few weeks later than NX-17 in 1975, this is reported as a storable-liquid weapon with a PBPS and, in most tests seen by late 1977, two Mirvs. Land launch-tubes were used many times in 1976, but in November of that year NX-18 first flew from a sub-marine, in the Beloye More (White Sea) to target off Kamchat-ka. All evidence to date suggests that NX-18 is the most formidable SLBM yet, with estimated length of 46 ft 3 in (14·1 m) and diameter of 71 in (1·8 m), similar to the projected Trident D5 but about a decade earlier in timing, and with a range of at least 5,903 miles (9500 km) with advanced Mirvs and penaids.

## USA

# Rigel

This programme was ahead of its time, for it produced a supersonic long-range cruise missile capable of being launched from a surfaced submarine from any point in the ocean and of carrying a nuclear or large conventional warhead to a distant target. The programme was initiated by the US Navy BuAer in 1946, and the prime contractor, Grumman, had by 1951 begun testing full-scale vehicles from the new missile range at Point Mugu. This was the first true weapon system to have supersonic ramjet propulsion, the contractor for which was Marquardt, and in many respects it is precisely the kind of strategic cruise-missile system looked on favourably today. Despite encouraging results Rigel was cancelled in 1952.

Data are for the final October 1952 TM (Tactical Missile):
**Dimensions:** Length 47 ft 2½ in (14·39 m); body diameter 45·0 in (1143 mm); span (over tip ramjets) 13 ft 3 in (4·04 m).
**Launch weight:** 25,000 lb (11 340 kg), 50% being four boost rockets.
**Range:** 576 miles (927 km) at Mach 2 with 3000 lb (1361 kg) warhead.

*Below: This illustrates the third Tactical Missile proposal of October 1952 with twin ramjet engines and four boost motors.*

*Bottom: Most of the Rigel test vehicles were of this configuration, with tandem booster and integral ramjet.*

*Below: Loading procedure for a Rigel test missile at Mare Island Naval Shipyard in 1952. Note the angle of the launch bin.*

# Triton

Largest fruit of the APL/JHU Bumblebee programme (p. 197), Triton was an SSM of extremely advanced concept. Features included integral ramjet propulsion giving a cruising speed exceeding Mach 2·5, folding airframe for submarine compatibility, and inertial guidance with radar monitoring and "map matching to refine the guidance and allow use of a low-yield warhead" – in 1951! XSSM-N-4 Triton was cancelled just before flight of the definitive missile in early 1955.

**Dimensions:** Length 45 ft (13·7 m); body diameter 60 in (1·52 m).
**Launch weight:** 19,600 lb (8891 kg).
**Range:** "several hundred miles"

# Regulus

This partner to Rigel was less advanced in concept, being a turbojet-propelled miniature aeroplane slower than some fighters of the day. It was started in parallel with Rigel in 1947, possibly to give the Navy something like the Air Force's Matador. Prime contract was awarded to Chance Vought, then located at Stratford, Connecticut, but about to move to a Naval Industrial Reserve plant at Dallas. The company patented Metalite construction in which large panels were made of a sandwich of light-alloy sheets bonded to a low-density balsa core. The layout could hardly have been simpler, to anyone used to carrier-based fighters. The engine was almost the same as the Matador's, the Allison J33-14, but fed from a nose inlet. The swept wing was mounted in the mid position and folded so that the missile could slide into a watertight cylindrical hangar on a submarine. There was no horizontal tail, the elevons on the wing and small rudder doing the whole job, as in the case of the much larger Snark. The wing was small but the body was large and, despite the straight-through air duct, there was plenty of room for kerosene, warhead (4,000 lb, 1814 kg, invariably nuclear) and autopilot/guidance bays. The latter could be opened from outside for ready servicing or replacement of the numerous faulty vacuum-tube modules. Designated SSM-N-8, Regulus (later styled Regulus I) was intended for use from submarines, surface ships and shore bases. Launched by two Aerojet JATO bottles, it navigated by radio command at over 30,000 ft (9144 m) until near its target, guided by radio signals from submarines at periscope depth whose position was known from Loran or other systems including astronavigation. It was to be used only against fixed targets, such as Peking.

Vought began flight testing in 1951, using recoverable vehicles with a tricycle landing gear and braking parachute. Though Vought was known to be testing a missile at Edwards AFB it was common practice to add a plywood cockpit canopy, and when an early Regulus crashed the project pilot, Roy Pearson, hurried to the scene and spread out his own parachute nearby for curious onlookers. Later Vought made a number of similar re-

coverable Regulus as training missiles, as well as 514 Regulus I in three series. These were deployed aboard the large Darter-class submarines Grayback and Growler, laid down in 1954, reclassified SSG and lengthened by 50 ft (15·24 m) with two side-by-side hangars above the bows, each housing two missiles, with launch rails leading aft, and commissioned in 1959. Two smaller SSGs, Tunny and Barbero, were each converted with a single hangar and two missiles. Halibut (see Regulus II) eventually carried five Regulus Is.

*Below: Launch of a definitive SSM-N-9 Regulus II from Edwards AFB on 30 January 1958. Previous test vehicles had had landing gear and braking parachute, for recovery.*

There was no other deployment, but all three sub-types of Regulus served in the inventory until 1964, redesignated RGM-6, 6A and 6B. The KDU-1 target and RPV became the BQM-6C.

**Dimensions:** Length 33 ft 3 in (10·13 m); diameter 51·0 in (1295 mm); span 21 ft 0 in (6·4 m).
**Launch weight:** 14,522 lb (6587 kg) for first sub-type.
**Range:** 400 miles (644 km).

# Regulus II

This totally different submarine-launched cruise missile may have been called Regulus to ease the problem of finding funds in the aftermath of the Korean war in late 1953. Designated SSM-N-9, it was a superb vehicle

with vastly greater capability. The General Electric J79-3A turbojet was rated at 15,000 lb (6804 kg) thrust with full afterburner, driving the missile at "beyond Mach 2". Launched by an Aerojet rocket of 115,000 lb (52 164 kg) thrust, Regulus II had a small canard for pitch control, and the vertical tail as well as the wings folded. Much larger than Regulus I, it not only carried a bigger warhead further but also had AC AChiever inertial guidance. The first of a series of recoverable test vehicles with J65 engines flew at Edwards on 29 May 1956, and after an excellent development an operational missile was fired from Grayback on 16 September 1958. SSGN Halibut was to be the first carrier, others being Grayback, Growler, Pollack, Permit and the CGN Long Beach. In retrospect it appears a major error to have abandoned this missile in 1959, thinking a cruise missile must be obsolete. Halibut was eventually completed in January 1960 carrying Regulus Is, and at least 100 Regulus II missiles were fired as RGM-15A training weapons or shot at as KD2U (MQM-15A) targets.

**Dimensions:** Length (excluding probe) 57 ft 6 in (17·5 m); diameter 50 in (1270 mm); span 20 ft 1 in (6·12 m).
**Launch weight:** 23,000 lb (10 433 kg), or about 30,000 lb (13 608 kg) with booster.
**Range:** Over 1,000 miles (1609 km).

*Right: Three photographs showing deployment of SSM-N-8 Regulus I aboard submarines of the US Navy. The main picture shows the spectacular launch of a scarlet RGM-6A training missile from the nuclear-powered USS Halibut (SSGN-587) in the early 1960s. Inset left is the big pre-nuclear Grayback (SSG-574) entering San Diego harbour with one of her missiles outside the hangar on the launcher. Inset right is pre-launch work on Barbero (SSG-317).*

# Polaris

No weapon system in history combined more dramatic new leaps in technology than this bold concept, driven through with immense energy in the late 1950s by Admiral William F. Raborn and a mighty team with industry headed by Lockheed Missiles & Space Co. Solid propulsion, lightweight ablative RVs, miniature inertial guidance, small nuclear and thermonuclear warheads, cold gas launch from a vertical tube deep underwater, submarine navigation, cavitation of high-speed underwater vehicles and countless other new areas of endeavour made Polaris require a greater R&D underpinning than any other single project. The Fleet

Ballistic Missile System (FBMS) would certainly have come about in any case in the 1960s, but it was made an accomplished fact by the US Navy with incredible rapidity in the 1950s.

Two vital decisions taken at the start of the FBMS project were to use solid propellant (PU/AP) and thus avoid the need to handle new and dangerous liquids aboard ship, and blow the missile from a vertical launch tube under gas pressure to remove the danger of rocket ignition inside the submarine and facilitate underwater launch. By 1957 this immense programme appeared to have a fair chance of success, and pressure to accelerate it turned it into a "crash" project. While Westinghouse explored five

main and two subsidiary launch techniques involving release of a buoyant capsule, air expulsion, gas from cold combustion and the submarine's own steam pressure, a large surface ship, *Compass Island*, was readied for missile launching at sea and a new class of submarine was hastily contrived by modifying the existing programme to build nuclear-powered attack submarines. The first of the class, SSN 589 *Scorpion*, was sliced in two, an extra 130 ft (39·6 m) section added amidships and completed as SSBN 598 *George Washington*, the most revolutionary warship in history. She was declared operational on 15 November 1960, having already fired missiles to target points down the AMR with complete success.

Subsequently the US Navy commissioned a total of 41 FBMS vessels, the original *Scorpion*-rebuilds SSBN 598–602, each 382 ft (116·4 m) long and with 16

launch tubes, being followed by the *Ethan Allen* class (SSBN 608–611 and 618) designed as FBMS submarines from the start, and 31 of the definitive design, the *Lafayette* class (SSBN 616–7, 619–636, 640–645 and 654–659). FBMS submarines each have two crews, a Blue and a Gold, which alternately train ashore and go on operational patrol to distant strategic locations for periods of 60–100 days. At any given time about half the 41-ship force is on patrol station, linked to the US command/control system and to VLF Omega and Loran, and to Transit and other satellites giving precise position and target updating. All 16 missiles in each submarine are ready to fire 95 per cent of the patrol time, and 14 for 100 per cent. Major FBMS bases are Charleston, SC; Holy Loch, Scotland; Rota, Spain; and Apra Harbor, Guam.

The original missile deployed in 598–602 was Polaris A-1, UGM-27A, with 1st and 2nd stages

**Below:** *Two consecutive photographs of a shot down the AMR by HMS* Revenge *(S27). The Royal Navy Polaris is similar to the US Navy A-3 apart from*

*having a British warhead system and RV. It will be seen in the main picture that the first-stage motor has ignited as the missile breaks surface.*

having steel cases and four nozzles with jetevator TVC. Warhead yield was 0·5 MT, and inflight guidance was by an MIT/GE/Hughes inertial system, linked with GE Mk 80 ship's fire control.

By 1959 Lockheed was developing an A-2 missile, UGM-27B, to fill the launch tube more completely by having a first stage 30 in (762 mm) longer. When this first flew, in November 1960, it had become a considerably more advanced weapon with a new 2nd stage with glass-filament-wound case and rotary-nozzle TVC. A-2 was fitted to the *Ethan Allen* class and first eight *Lafayettes*. On May 6, 1962, *Ethan Allen* fired a missile with live warhead to impact near Christmas Island, the only complete

test ever made of a US ballistic missile system; it was successful. By 1960 Lockheed was working on the third-generation Polaris A-3, UGM-27C. This has still better geometric efficiency, with full diameter and fat ogival RV, and is fractionally longer, but weight is little changed and most of the increased performance comes from high-energy Nc/Ng/AP propellant in the 2nd stage, which is by Hercules Inc instead of Aerojet which supplied all previous propulsion. Both stages have glass-filament-wound cases, and the 1st has four rotary nozzles and the 2nd Freon fluid-injection TVC. The Mk 2 guidance, associated with GE Mk 84 fire control, is about 60 per cent lighter than Mk 1, and though the Lockheed Mk 2 RV

originally had a single warhead it was modified in the early 1970s to carry three 200 kT MRVs.

Production of Polaris missiles ended with the last A-3 in June 1968, with 1,409 of all models delivered. The FBMS submarines were progressively converted to newer models of missile, A-1 being retired in October 1965 and A-2 in 1974, these versions subsequently being used in various programmes including serving as targets for Safeguard (p 172). Polaris A-3 is still operational aboard the ten FBMS boats of the 598 and 608 classes in the Pacific Strategic Force based on Guam, where they are expected to remain until 1985. The A-3 also arms four FBMS submarines of the Royal

Navy: S22 *Resolution*, S23 *Repulse*, S26 *Renown* and S27 *Revenge*. Supported by a base at Faslane, these British-designed and built vessels each have a 16-tube installation and much indigenous equipment. The US-supplied A-3 missiles carry British RVs, warheads, fuzing and arming systems. An extremely costly Polaris Improvement Programme, estimated at £450 million over 1974–79, is replacing the original three 200 kT MRVs by six Mirvs (Manoeuvrable independently-targeted RVs) each of 40 kT.

**Dimensions:** Length (A-1) 28 ft 0 in (8·53 m), (A-2) 30 ft 9 in (9·4 m), (A-3) 32 ft 3½ in (9·85 m); diameter (all) 54 in (1·37 m).
**Launch weight:** (A-1) 28,000 lb (12 700 kg), (A-2) 30,000 lb (13 608 kg), (A-3) 35,000 lb (15 876 kg).
**Range:** (A-1) 1,380 miles (2221 km), (A-2) 1,727 miles (2780 km), (A-3) 2,880 miles (4635 km).

**Below:** *Test shot 1749 on the Air Force Eastern Test Range was this Polaris, on 16 June 1965. Payload was a non-standard pointed low-drag RV.*

**Below right:** *The historic first submerged firing of Polaris A-1 from USS* George Washington *down the Atlantic Missile Range on 20 July 1960.*

**Foot of page:** *Apparently taken in a Royal Navy submarine, this illustration shows the Mk 84 fire-control computer which prepares missiles for launching.*

# Poseidon

Tests in 1960–62 showed that it was feasible to remove the glass-fibre liner in FBMS launch tubes, and the locating rings round the missile, to give a close fit between missile and tube. This opened the way to a dramatically enlarged missile, at first called Polaris B-3. Rechristened Poseidon C-3, UGM-73A, it made its first flight on August 16, 1968, and was fired under water from SSBN 627 *James Madison* on 3 August 1970. The new FBMS became operational on 31 March 1971.

Advantages in either range or payload of the tremendous increase (roughly 100 per cent) in volume are backed up by the improved accuracy of a completely new inertial system in which MIT managed development and GE, Hughes and Raytheon have collaborated for production, and which is linked to the GE Mk 88 submarine fire-control system. As in previous FBMS submarines the Mk 88 interfaces with the SINS (Ship's Inertial Navigation System, by Autonetics and Sperry) and Ulcer (which feeds in complete data on sea currents and other perturbation sources), to update the necessary trajectory for all 16 missiles on a continuous basis as the submarine's position changes. Missiles can be prepared for launch at one every 50 sec. In-flight guidance is all-digital and uses integrated-circuit microelectronics.

A vital feature of this system is that the missile closely fits the launch tube. In the Polaris FBMS the missile is located in the tube by "piston rings" of Teflon-coated polyurethane, which are blown out with the missile as it breaks through the Styrofoam sea-tight closure on the tube and rises to the surface. By eliminating the rings and tube liner the diameter of the missile has been increased by 20 in (508 mm), and Poseidon is ejected whilst sliding in close contact with the tube itself. Gas pressure is provided by steam generated by a water boiler heated violently by a small solid-fuel combustor, virtually a fixed rocket. (On the test of 3 August 1970 the Russian "oceanographic research ship" *Khariton Laptev* refused to leave the launch area and, as soon as the Poseidon broke surface, raced US vessels to recover floating debris. With Poseidon the only debris is the remains of the closure seal.) The 1st stage is produced jointly by Thiokol and Hercules, and the 2nd by Hercules alone (Aerojet having lost this programme). Nc/Ng/AP high-energy propellant is certainly used in the upper stage, and possibly in both. Both stages have filament-wound cases and submerged single nozzles which are gimballed with rotary seals, the actuators being pressurized by gas bleed from a small solid-fuel generator.

Poseidon's advanced RV was developed jointly by Lockheed and the AEC, and is still one of the

**Main picture:** *Liftoff from Pad 25C at Cape Canaveral Air Force Station of one of the last Poseidon development missiles in May 1970.*

**Left:** *An unusual shot of USS James Madison (SSBN-627) with all 16 missile tubes open. Some tubes are loaded, with white Styrofoam closures sealed.*

**Above:** *This Poseidon was shot down the Eastern Test Range on 25 September 1972 from USS George Bancroft (SSBN-643). It is already headed down-range.*

largest and most capable to have flown. From the start it was judged that, compared with Polaris A-3, the payload could be doubled and CEP (accuracy) halved, representing an eightfold increase in effectiveness against a hard target. No attempt was made to increase range over that of Polaris A-3. At maximum range ten Mk 3 Mirvs, each with a yield of 50 kT, can be flown together with a comprehensive kit of penaids in a manoeuvrable bus which ejects the warheads in timed sequence to give CEPs in the order of half a mile (0·8 km). Over a range of 2,485 miles (4000

km) 14 of these Mirvs can be carried, emphasizing the countervalue (anti-city) role.

Poseidon development testing was completed in June 1970, and plans were at once implemented to produce the UGM-73A system and retrofit it to the newest 31 of the US Navy's FBMS submarines. In 1973 Operational Test (OT) launches showed up deficiencies which required a major Poseidon Modification Program to eradicate. This resulted in a reliable missile which was fitted to the last ten submarines in the Poseidon programme; the first 20 in the

programme were subsequently refitted with the improved missile as they returned from patrol in 1976–78. Today the entire 616-class submarine force is at sea with Poseidon, based at Charleston, Holy Loch and Rota. In 1979 the FBMS squadron based at Rota was to be withdrawn to the United States for refit and installation of UGM-93A Trident I, as noted in the entry opposite.

**Dimensions:** Length 34 ft 0 in (10·36 m); diameter 74 in (1·88 m).
**Launch weight:** 65,000 lb (29 485 kg).
**Range:** 2,880 miles (4635 km).

# Trident I (C-4)

In the second half of the 1960s the US Navy, LMSC and others studied possible developments to, or successors to, the C-3 Poseidon system and these crystallized in 1971 as the Undersea Long-range Missile System (ULMS). In January 1972 President Nixon ordered development of this "far more effective missile", and the system was named Trident four months later. From the start it was compromised by the need to save money. Unlike the Soviet FBM forces, which have been allocated all the money needed to build a seemingly endless succession of completely new missiles and submarines, Trident has had to be developed in two main phases each linked to existing hardware, Trident II being described at the end of this entry. Even Trident I has progressed haltingly, been very severely hit by delays and cost-inflation, and postponed to such a degree that IOC has slipped from 1976 to 1979 or 1980, and the purpose-designed Trident-carrying submarines will not enter service until well into the 1980s. This is despite the fact, that, to enable Trident I to be retrofitted into Poseidon submarines, the missile is based on Poseidon itself and was originally Expo (Extended-range Poseidon).

The Trident I C-4, UGM-93A, missile is basically Poseidon C-3 with a 3rd-stage motor. Instead of being essentially spherical, as is the 2nd stage, this 3rd stage is an axially arranged cylinder, around which is disposed the RV and contents. After Poseidon-style launch by gas pressure the missile breaks surface and, as the 1st stage ignites, an aerospike – a long pointed probe – extends above the nose to form an inclined shockwave and improve aerodynamic performance. The two high-energy filament-cased motors burn in series, followed by the 3rd-stage burn; then the PBPS provides thrust and control to the Mk 4 RV and equipment section until the payload, initially eight Mk 4 Mirvs each of 100 kT, have been deployed. The Mk 5 flight guidance system, smaller and lighter than that of Poseidon, is integrated before launch with the Mk 98 fire-control system, and for the first time outside the Soviet Union incorporates a stellar sensor which, in the post-boost phase, takes at least one star sighting to refine the trajectory and reduce CEP. It has been said that CEP for Trident I will be the same as that for Poseidon, despite the range being increased by over 50 per cent.

It is natural that Trident should push the state-of-the-art, just as did the original Polaris. This is true in structure, propulsion, guidance and payload. Structure includes advanced composites, both filament-wound and fabricated by other means. All three propulsion stages use Class 7 propellant, with polyethylene glycol binder and energetic

**Above:** *Still one of the best Trident photographs, this was the very first launch at 14.03 local time on 18 January 1977 from Cape Canaveral AFS.*

plasticizer containing nitroglycerine. Lockheed co-ordinates the work of Thiokol (chiefly 1st-stage), Hercules (chiefly 2nd) and UTC-CSD (chiefly 3rd). In the early stages there was trouble. Partly owing to extreme difficulty in perfecting the thrust-termination system there were explosions at Bacchus (May 1974), NWC China Lake (July 1975 and May 1976, the latter demolishing the test stand), and 1st-stage nozzle destruction in September and October 1976. But the first test flight, in January 1977, was "a total success", and so were the next ten; No 12 had a

2nd-stage failure. There were also difficulties with the integrated-circuit guidance modules and with the challenging 1650°C hot-gas thrusters in the PBCS which caused leakage and valve-sticking. The existing Mirv bus may be replaced eventually by the General Electric Mk 500 MARV, should potential hostile defences warrant this. Named Evader, Mk 500 can perform pre-selected evasive manoeuvres during re-entry and is hoped to be qualified to fly on the C-4 missile.

To carry Trident the US Navy and Electric Boat Co designed a completely new class of gigantic submarine, the largest outside the Soviet Union, and markedly better than even the *Lafayettes*. Much quieter, with improved sonar and communications, these

great ships will each carry 24 missiles and have many secondary advantages over the existing FBMS vessels. But the entire programme has been plagued by technical delays, labour troubles and very severe cost escalation. The lead ship, SSBN-726 *Ohio*, was planned to reach IOC in 1978 at the same time as the missile. The missile itself has slipped more than a year; at the time of writing it is officially due for IOC in 1979, but as the first submerged firing is not due until the second half of that year even this is unrealistic. The IOC of *Ohio* has slipped until well into 1981, and the cost of this vessel was in 1977 put at $1193 million (not including any GFE), compared with the 1974 estimate of "$300 to 500 million". The planned force of 13 authorized *Ohio* class were in 1976 priced at $18,500 million, in 1977 at $22,200 million, and in 1978 at $27,140 million. This does not include $3160 million for backfitting Trident C-4 into the last ten *Lafayettes*, 16 per ship, in order to get this weapon into service from late 1979 or early 1980, the tenth reaching IOC in late 1984. These rearmed vessels will be based at a converted Army ordnance depot at King's Bay, Georgia, which replaces Rota, Spain, which the US Navy must vacate by July 1979. The *Ohio* class will have a new base, at Bangor, Washington, included in the above price. The cost escalations are the most severe experienced by any US weapon programme, and the Navy has had to emphasize the success of the flight test programme and express "greater confidence in Trident than in Polaris or Poseidon at this stage of development". In view of the frightening pace of Soviet SLBM development, which has already outranged Trident and demonstrated comparable accuracy, it would mean the collapse of the deterrent philosophy if the programme were to be significantly delayed further or reduced in scope.

# Trident II (D-5)

Few details have emerged regarding this longer-range missile, which is said to be compatible with the launch installations in Trident submarines. It would have greater range and/or payload than Trident I, and "improved accuracy, rivalling that of Minuteman". It is not clear whether D-5 is to be compatible with all Trident vessels or just the SSBN-726 *Ohio* class. It is intended for deployment in the second half of the 1980s, and is on the point of moving from the study phase to the costly hardware phase. Data below are for Trident I.

**Dimensions:** Length 34 ft 0 in (10·36 m); diameter 74 in (1·88 m).
**Launch weight:** About 32,000 lb (14 515 kg).
**Range:** About 4,350 miles (7000 km).

# Tomahawk

Begun in January 1974 as the US Navy's SLCM (Sea-Launched Cruise Missile), Tomahawk has since been developed into the most versatile missile in history. Land- and air-launched versions are described separately (respectively, on p. 41 and p. 142). The Navy began with a version fired from a standard submarine torpedo tube, and expects to buy Tomahawks to arm surface ships. All versions can have completely different guidance and warheads, the two main types of Tomahawk being the so-called land-attack version, with Tercom guidance and a nuclear warhead, and the anti-ship version with active homing and a conventional warhead. Except for the air-launched model all have a tandem rocket boost motor, and the main fuselage/wing/propulsion section is common to all.

In 1974 the Air Force and Navy were directed to collaborate on the ALCM (p. 140) and SLCM to the maximum degree practical, the former service being assigned responsibility for propulsion and the latter for guidance. General Dynamics won the SLCM programme over a Vought rival, and Teledyne CAE lost propulsion to Williams. In January 1977 both programmes were placed under a Joint-Service Cruise-Missile Program Office, at first headed by a Navy captain, which helped clarify roles and missions. SLCM has no rival, but as noted elsewhere ALCM and TALCM (Tomahawk ALCM) do tend to duplicate each other and one may be eliminated. As this book is written in 1978, the Navy has BGM-109 Tomahawk in full-scale development for submarine launch, and a contract option for the as-yet undesignated surface-ship version.

Both these variants are delivered in rigid capsules, by Rollmet, extruded from a billet. Steel is used for the 21 in (533 mm) calibre submarine capsule, while the proposed twin-tube surface launcher will take aluminium capsules. In a submarine launch the ship's tube is opened to the sea in the normal way to flood the tube, the missile automatically being air-pressurized to the hydrostatic level. The missile is checked out, with guidance aligned, and then fired out of the capsule by the hydraulic torpedo gear. About 33 ft (10 m) ahead of the submarine a lanyard runs taut between missile and capsule, and via quick interlocks this fires the Atlantic Research boost motor, in the 7,000 lb (3175 kg) class. This burns for about seven seconds, jet-tab TVC immediately commanding a 50° climb, at which attitude the missile climbs to the surface at about 56 mph (25 m/sec) whilst bleeding off its internal pressure. Breaking the surface, the shroud ring ahead of the booster is blown off, allowing the four tail fins to spring open and lock in place. Plugs blow off the slots in the sides from which the super-imposed wings emerge, one higher than the other, as the tail rolls the missile right-side up. The booster burns out as the cruise engine, a Williams F107-WR-400 turbofan of 600 lb (272 kg) thrust, is spun up by its starter cartridge while its ventral air inlet extends into the slipstream. As the booster drops off, the tail commands a zero-g pushover to minimise apogee on launch and avoid detection by hostile radar.

In the cruise mode the main guidance method is inertial, with Litton supplying the P-1000 platform and LC-4516 computer. Studies are in hand for linking the missile to a Navstar satellite, E-3A Awacs aircraft or other guidance source. Avionics are cooled in flight by a closed circuit using the cruise-engine's kerosene fuel. Tank capacity is much greater for the land-attack version, which normally has Tains guidance (Tercom-aided inertial navigation system). As explained elsewhere, Tercom (terrain-comparison) matches the ground beneath the missile with data stored in the missile on magnetic tape and fed from the submarine before launch. It is used when crossing the enemy coast or frontier, and thereafter when passing over selected small matrix areas of terrain, to update the inertial system which remains in command throughout. With a weapon of this type the approach to the target can be from any direction, and at altitudes closer to the ground than practical with manned aircraft. The land-attack warhead is the W-80, weighing 271 lb (123 kg) and having a yield of 200 kT.

The anti-ship Tomahawk has a front end based on that of the Harpoon missile. The nose is occupied by the Texas Instruments two-axis active radar seeker, which detects typical ship targets at a range of many miles even from wave-top height (maintained in this version by an accurate radar altimeter). The bay between the radar and the wings is occupied by a 1,000 lb (454 kg) conventional warhead derived from that of Bullpup, to ensure good lethality against ships. So far as is known, encapsulated rounds aboard a submarine are sealed and there is no provision for switching from anti-ship to land attack or vice versa.

Candidate platforms for BGM-

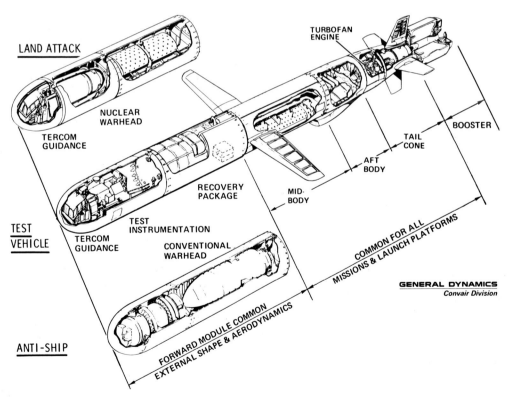

LAND ATTACK
NUCLEAR WARHEAD
TERCOM GUIDANCE
TURBOFAN ENGINE
BOOSTER
TAIL CONE
AFT BODY
MID-BODY
RECOVERY PACKAGE

TEST VEHICLE
TEST INSTRUMENTATION
TERCOM GUIDANCE
CONVENTIONAL WARHEAD

ANTI-SHIP

COMMON FOR ALL MISSIONS & LAUNCH PLATFORMS
FORWARD MODULE COMMON EXTERNAL SHAPE & AERODYNAMICS

GENERAL DYNAMICS
*Convair Division*

**Above:** *All Tomahawks have a common mid-section, shown here with wings, tail and inlet in the extended flight position. The booster is needed for all except the air-launched version. Land attack has more fuel.*

**Right:** *This land-attack Tomahawk is shown on 21 June 1978 updating its Tercom guidance prior to entering the target area at Dugway Proving Ground, Utah. Its unusual payload is shown at top right.*

**Above:** *Tomahawk releasing dispensed submunitions, each with parachute for slow fall.*

**Left:** *Sequence of a live launch from USS* **Barb** *(SSN-596), showing typical exit angle.*

109A include all the recent attack submarine classes, SSN-594, 637 and 688 classes, as well as the DD-963, CG-26, CGN-36/38, CGN-25/35 and CGN-9 class surface ships. Flight development has gone well, beginning with a fully guided anti-ship missile from Pt Mugu in March 1976 and a land-attack model at WSMR in June 1976. In 1977 there was a hiatus in underwater launching from April, due to a series of seemingly trivial faults, including random equipment failures, a missile damaged by being dropped, one that leaked water and another that left the torpedo tube too slowly for the lanyard to fire the booster. Not until 2 February 1978 did a submerged launch work, and then it was not from the San Clemente test rig but an actual submarine, USS *Barb;* but a second missile fired three hours later failed to achieve full cruise thrust and crashed. As noted in the AGM-109 story (p. 142) Tomahawks are now being tested against simulated Warsaw Pact defences.

**Dimensions:** Length 21 ft 0 in (6·40 m); diameter 20·87 in (530 mm); span 100 in (2·54 m).
**Launch weight:** 3,181 lb (1443 kg).
**Range:** Up to 2,300 miles (3701 km).

# AIR TO SURFACE MISSILES

Those who have not tried to do it might think that fitting guidance to an ASM – air-to-surface missile – the simplest of exercises. Surely, it might be thought, bombs fall by themselves, can readily be stabilised by fitting fins, and could just as easily be steered by making the fins move? It is natural that the earliest ASMs should have been based not on bombs but on aeroplanes, so, as far as the published record is concerned, the Siemens-Schuckert Werke did not encounter major unexpected problems. When other German companies began the history of what might be called modern ASMs 25 years later they almost came to believe that the notion of a guided bomb was contrary to natural laws. One team after another was to come to feel that the ASM, even more than most missile classes, was a temperamental species with a wicked nature. Completely fresh sets of difficulties were introduced as soon as attempts were made to make ASMs self-propelled. Further, and, in the long term, even greater difficulties attended the development of guidance systems. Eventually a special family of large missiles grew up for attack on strategic targets, and these are discussed in the next section. There is a clear distinction between Tactical and Strategic in the ASM category, one illustration of which is the fact that a strategic missile with a range that can handsomely exceed 100 miles (160 km) is officially named the Short-Range Attack Missile. In the tactical class such a long range would be almost unusable, and rather pointless because in war many tactical aircraft would operate against targets closer than that distance to their own airstrips. Again, of course, the tactical ASM seldom has a nuclear warhead, while the strategic kind seldom has any other.

Before considering guidance problems it is essential to decide why the missile is needed. With few exceptions all the earliest ASMs were developed in order to hit small targets that were beyond the capability of average free-fall bomb systems (by system I mean the sequence of bombsight, bombardier, human pilot, aircraft, atmosphere and bomb trajectories, all of which introduced errors) and which could not be destroyed except by a direct hit. One of the most important categories of such targets was bridges, but there were many others including warships. An important contributory factor was AA defence. Well-defended targets discouraged bombers or even fighter-bombers from trying any technique that brought them too close, such as dive attacks or bombing from low level. In a few cases early ASMs were developed whose accuracy was actually inferior to that of free-fall bombs but which could be released at a distance much greater than that of bombs and thus reduced exposure to the most intense defences.

Bearing in mind that the Luftwaffe had true precision-guided ASMs in action in the summer of 1943 the rest of the world put up an unimpressive performance. It was only the pressure of warfare that resulted in mass-production of several of the incredible galaxy of "glide bombs", "vertical bombs" and other guided ASMs studied in the United States in 1944–5. Nearly all suffered from basic shortcomings, often in turn stemming from inadequate underlying technology and experience. Guided ASMs reached USAAF bomb groups in England, Italy and Burma in the final 18 months of the war, but were generally viewed with disfavour, and most of the ASMs issued to European units lay unused.

The first really effective use of ASMs after World War 2 came in Korea, when the powerful Tarzon was dropped by B-29s on bridges, dams and similar difficult targets right up to the Manchurian frontier. The next systems to become operational were the US Navy's Bullpup and a growing family of French weapons developed by a team successively called SFECMAS, Nord and Aérospatiale in which steering was accomplished by deflecting the jet from the sustainer. Like almost all ASMs up to this time these missiles had to be commanded by a human operator to stay on the direct LOS (line of sight) to the target. In the past 25 years many thousands of such missiles have been produced, despite the obvious grave drawbacks. The worst fault is probably that, while accuracy may be better than that from a free-fall bomb, aircraft exposure to ground fire is not reduced and may be increased. What was needed, and spelt out in a Luftwaffe report in May 1943 and a USAAF report of January 1944, was a "fire and forget" missile.

Of course the proliferation of guidance systems in the years following World War 2 opened the way to plenty of self-contained missiles, but the ASM Tactical class in general has to be capable of use against transient or mobile targets. A transient target might be a concentration of armour; there is no point in hitting the spot five minutes after the force has departed. So guidance cranked into the missile before release, as can be done with an ICBM, is useless; the missile has to have the capability of being steered to hit a target whose position is not known in advance.

One of the most important classes of target comprises ships. Other targets are far more challenging and demand either guidance against a point in a background scene (as in firing a rifle) or self-homing. Either poses problems. The first method invariably still calls for a human operator who at some point in the mission has to acquire (see and identify) the target with his own eyes. In a direct attack he may be able to aim an EO or TV seeker in the nose of the missile at the target and, by his own action, lock it on that target. The missile can then be released and will home on the target. In an indirect attack the missile is released and either flown to the target by the operator, who sees a TV picture, transmitted from the missile on his cockpit monitor, or else uses inertial or DME as mid-course guidance to fly near the target whereupon it can be made to home by its own seeker. Anything calling for a missile to send back a TV picture, and an aircraft to send radio command signals, is wide open to ECM interference by the enemy. Using wire guidance is much more secure, but this method is possible only with relative slow, short-range missiles.

Wherever possible the best answer seems to be to turn the target into an emitter of radiation. Those that emit already are merely asking for trouble. Self-contained seekers tuned to radars or IR (heat) can make a missile home automatically from scores of miles away, and in this battle the missile appears to be on the winning side notwithstanding extensive ECM, IRCM, switching off the radar, and any other attempts by the enemy to make the missile break-lock and miss. The latest ASMs contain a memory so that they continue to home on the same spot even if the radiation suddenly ceases, but they may still be misguided by cunning decoy sources, and programming into a missile just how real targets are likely to behave is not easy.

Whenever possible an almost ideal method of turning the target into an emitter is to direct a laser at it. A laser designator can be aimed by forward troops at anything they can see in hostile territory, and any missile tuned to that laser's wavelength will home automatically on the light (which may not be in the visible band of wavelengths) scattered from the target. Though many lasers operate only on very exact wavelengths there are some lasers which are tunable, and this allows particular missiles to hit particular targets.

Just how do homing ASMs work? The basic principles fall into only two or three groups, no matter whether the EM (electromagnetic) radiation has long waves (IR), medium waves (radar) or short waves (laser light). Probably the simplest homing system of all was that developed by Texas Instruments for the Paveway "smart bombs". These were free-fall "iron bombs" to which a guidance unit was added on the nose. This unit had four fins driven by a control system fed with the output signals from four light-sensitive silicon detectors arranged in a quadrant. This quadrant array was mounted in a separate sensor bullet pivoted to the nose of the guidance unit by a universal joint and fitted with an annular ring tail. As the bomb fell, this sensor unit aligned itself with the airstream; in other words it always pointed where the bomb was going, no matter what the bomb's attitude might be. When the quad array detected light from the target it began to send signals to the control fins, which operated in a bang-bang mode to equalise the output of the four detectors. When the outputs were the same, the sensor was pointing directly at the target. As this was aligned with the direction of travel, it followed that the bomb would hit the target.

This is in many respects similar to other systems using IR and radar emissions. Unlike the latter emissions, laser light seldom originates at the target, and has to be aimed there by friendly designators. If the laser is aimed by forward troops or a mini-RPV the stage is set for the ideal "fire and forget" missile, able to hit precision targets from above cloud or smoke in any weather. An alternative, still standard procedure with all US services, is to carry a laser designator in one aircraft and launch missiles from another, and though this has some advantages (especially to the missile carrier) it could merely provide the enemy with two aircraft to shoot down instead of one. Doubtless in the course of time SAM systems will be delighted to home on to laser-equipped aircraft. For a single aircraft both to carry the missiles and the laser seems to be to assume unjustified inactivity or incapability on the part of the enemy.

Another of the wealth of factors influencing the ASM Tactical scene is man's increasing ability to see clearly in all battle conditions. Though both optical and radar wavelengths have been used to this end, the greatest progress has been made at the top end of the wavelength spectrum with IR, in what are called thermal-imaging systems (TIS). Most modern attack aircraft are, or will be, equipped with a TIS for "seeing" through camouflage, smoke, rain and snow, and darkness. This is an area where the Soviet Union appears to have considerable capability (though we know next to nothing about that country's ASMs). Many kinds of IR system are being used invariably with a visible display in the cockpit, in what are called FLIR systems. These are also now seen as desirable in anti-tank systems.

# ARGENTINA

The Scientific and Technical Research Centre of the Argentine Ministry of Defence is reported to have designed and built prototypes of a tactical ASM, probably with radio command guidance, weighing 254 lb (115 kg), with an 88 lb (40 kg) warhead and range of up to 4·35 miles (7 km). It is intended to arm aeroplanes and helicopters of the Argentine Navy, chiefly as a replacement for AS.12 on Alouette III helicopters. Production deliveries are expected by 1980.

# BRAZIL

Avibras Industria Aérospacial, which has produced large numbers of spin-stabilized rockets for military and research, has since 1973 been developing this guided missile for the Brazilian Army. Both TV and radio command and laser homing (with Rockwell laser) have been used. The missile weighs 100 lb (45 kg) and has a 20 lb (9 kg) warhead. No news since 1974.

# FRANCE

## Breguet 910

This inventor is widely reported to have built several radio-guided glide bombs with "payload up to 1000 kg (2,205 lb)" in 1938–39. Range is said to have reached 18 miles (29 km) for the largest, released from a Farman F.224 heavy bomber, which would have been unlikely to reach 20,000 ft (6000 m).

## De Rouméfort

This glide bomb was inspired by the wartime BV 246, and similarly had slender wings (aspect ratio 8) of reinforced concrete. The span was 157·5 in (4·00 m), and after release at 15,090 ft (4600 m) the steady speed was said to be 500 mph (805 km/h). Development took place in 1947–52.

## B.B. 10

Developed by SNCASE and other French partners, including SEPR for the small rocket motor, this guided bomb was intended as a weapon to be carried by the SNCASO 4050 Vautour IIB bomber. It utilised systems and even some components of previous German and American missiles, and after extensive testing was fitted with a nose vidicon (TV) camera and bang/bang radio command steering with powered nose fins and four fixed tail fins, which were surrounded by an annular fin. The warhead weighed about 441 lb (200 kg). In 1957, when the decision had been taken to abandon the programme, an unexpended test missile was displayed among the Vautour's armament. The IIB would have carried up to four on underwing pylons.

**Dimensions:** Length about 11 ft (3·35 m); rear-fin span 32 in (813 mm).
**Launch weight:** About 900 lb (408 kg).
**Range:** "Several miles" (say, 10 km).

## AS.11

Derived from the SS.11 army anti-tank missile, AS.11 is one of the oldest missiles still in production. Originally developed by Nord-Aviation in 1953–5 as Type 5210, it has been slightly improved over the years, notably by the introduction of the AS.11B1 with transistorized circuits and optional TCA semi-automatic IR-based guidance, in 1962, and will remain in production at Aérospatiale (into which Nord was merged) until at least 1980, with deliveries exceeding 179,000 of all versions. The first trials of an air-launched version were undertaken in France with Alouette IIs and in Britain using Twin Pioneers, in 1958. The weapon system is similar to that of the SS.11 but needs a stabilized sight and preferably an image intensifier or other magnifying all-weather vision system. Warheads include the Type 140AC hollow charge (perforation 24 in, 610 mm of armour), the Type 140AP02 which detonates a 5·72 lb (2·6 kg) explosive charge some 7 ft (2·1 m) behind a 0·4 in (10 mm) armour sheet at maximum missile range, and Type 140AP59 contact-fuzed fragmentation head. Carrier aircraft include most versions of Alouette and Gazelle, the British Army Scout, Navy/Marines Wessex and various STOL aeroplanes. In US service this missile is designated AGM-22A.

**Data:** see p. 239.

## AS.12

Developed in 1955–7 by Nord-Aviation, this missile was a natural extrapolation of the original SS.10 and 11 system to a bigger weapon, with a warhead weighing roughly four times as much and suitable for use against fortifications or ships. Trials began in 1958, and production of surface-launched SS.12 started in late 1959, with AS.12 following in 1960, the original planned carrier aircraft being the French Navy Etendard and Super Frelon. The usual OP.3C warhead weighs 62·6 lb (28·4 kg) and can explode on the far side of 1·57 in (40 mm) of armour plate. AS.12 can be used with the APX 260 (Bézu) or SFIM 334 gyrostabilized sight and with IR night vision equipment, but the wire-transmitted guidance system is the basic CLOS type with optical (flare) tracking; the TCA semiautomatic IR command guidance system is not available with AS.12. Maximum airspeed at launch is 230 mph (370 km/h). About 8,000 missiles had been produced by 1978, with deliveries continuing on a small scale. AS.12 has been carried by the Alizé, P-2 Neptune, Atlantic, Nimrod, Alouette, Wasp, Wessex, Gazelle and Lynx.

**Dimensions:** Length 73·9 in (1·87 m); diameter (max, warhead) 8¼ in (210 mm); span 25·6 in (650 mm).
**Launch weight:** 170 lb (77 kg).
**Range:** Launched at 230 mph (370 km/h) measured relative to surface, 26,250 ft (8000 m).

*Right: A bright-blue AS.12 used in the 1960s by Nord-Aviation for display purposes. It is mounted on the definitive launcher on an Alouette III, an unusual combination.*

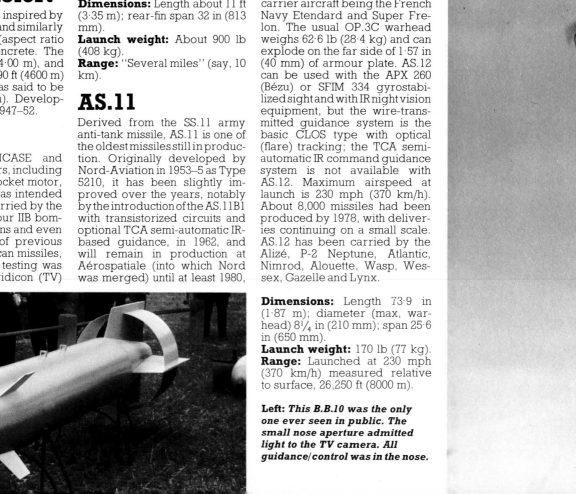

*Left: This B.B.10 was the only one ever seen in public. The small nose aperture admitted light to the TV camera. All guidance/control was in the nose.*

# AS.20

France's first really successful AAMs were the R.511 and AA.20 (Nord 5103), and the command guidance of the latter was such that the operator in the launch aircraft could, if he was able to hold the target in view all the way to impact, steer the missile just as well to a surface target as into a hostile aircraft. Trials at Cazaux in 1958 confirmed this hope, and Nord accordingly developed the Type 5110 missile, adopted as AS.20, specially configured for ASM use. One of the main changes was to remove the proximity fuze and fit a simple impact fuze and any of four larger warheads. Details of the rest of the system are generally as for the AA.20 (p. 209). Though a 73 lb (33 kg) warhead was originally available, the standard type weighs 66 lb (30 kg). Over 8,000 AS.20 missiles were delivered, especially to the French air force and navy, Luftwaffe and Italian air force, and this missile was the first ASM used by European NATO air forces in 1961. Many remain in use as training rounds integrated with the AS.30 system and, with an adapter, fired from aircraft normally armed with AS.30. The radar-guided AS.25 did not progress beyond the development phase.

**Data:** As for AA.20, p. 209.

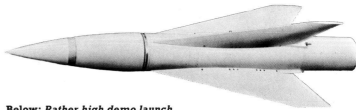

Below: *Rather high demo launch of AS.11 from Alouette III; inset, AS.11 on an Alouette III used by Aérospatiale, with roof-mounted sight.*

Above: *Standard production AS. 20. Many of these obsolescent ASMs remain in service, though chiefly in a training role.*

# AS.30

A logical scale-up of AS.20, this hard-hitting missile has a higher wing loading yet can be launched at Mach numbers down to 0·45 compared with the lower limit of 0·7 for the earlier missile. Originally the Nord 5401, it was developed in 1958 and was secret until disclosed on models of the Mirage III and Northrop N-156F in 1960. AS.30 was produced to meet a French DTE requirement for an ASM with range of at least 6·2 miles (10 km) without the launch aircraft having to come within 1·86 miles (3 km) of the target (a distance that today would be unacceptably close). CEP was to be 33 ft (10 m) or less, and all these demands were exceeded. Early AS.30 missiles, tested with excellent results from Canberras and Vautours at Colomb-Béchar and Cazaux, were aerodynamically similar to AS.20. The missile is not roll-stabilized and the sustainer of the dual-thrust motor is equipped with two nozzles, one on each side of the flat base of the missile. The operator watches tracking flares on the missile and keeps them aligned with the target by a radio link which sends signals to bias the behaviour of two vibrating trembler spoilers that intermittently interrupt the jets from the two nozzles. The missile autopilot interprets the guidance command to interrupt the correct jet to steer left/right or up/down. In 1964 an improved AS.30 was produced with four flip-out tail control fins indexed in line with the wings, and without spoilers on the sustainer nozzles. At the same time the TCA semi-automatic guidance system was introduced, with an SAT (Société Anonyme de Télécommunications) tracker in the aircraft continuously monitoring an IR flare on the missile and the pilot keeping the target centred in his attack sight, an on-board computer continuously trying to eliminate any difference between the two sightlines without the need to work a pitch/yaw joystick control. About 3,870 AS.30 missiles were delivered, most of them exported to the RAF (Canberra), South Africa (Mirage III and Canberra), Switzerland (Mirage IIIS) and Germany (F-104G); only the Armée de l'Air used the TCA semi-automatic guidance. The AS.30L is described separately.

**Dimensions:** Length (X12 warhead) 12 ft 7 in (3839 mm), (X35 warhead) 12 ft 9 in (3885 mm); diameter 13·5 in (340 mm); span 39·4 in (1·00 m).
**Launch weight:** 1,146 lb (520 kg).
**Range:** Typically 7 miles (11·25 km).

# AS.30L

As a company venture, Thomson-CSF and Aérospatiale began to work on a laser-guided AS.30 in 1974 (Ferranti in Britain proposed this with company hardware almost a decade earlier). Using Martin-Marietta licensed technology Thomson-CSF developed the Atlis (automatic tracking laser illumination system) target-designation pod and a complementary Ariel seeker head able to fit any missile of 3·94 in (100 mm) or greater diameter. Aérospatiale produced the AS.30L (AS.30 Laser) to make use of this more modern guidance system. Installation in the launch aircraft is simpler, because apart from the Atlis pod (or internal laser installation) all that is needed is a fire/jettison button, armament panel and launcher with suitable circuits; no command guidance is needed. In late 1977 an Armée de l'Air Jaguar A was testing an Atlis 1 pod at Cazaux, in the course of which unguided AS.30L prototype missiles were fired. These had roll-stabilization and were programmed to fly on a gyro reference in a pre-guidance phase, prior to picking up the radiation from the target. In mid-1978 Aérospatiale expected to produce AS.30L missiles "in the early 1980s" to arm various Armée de l'Air Jaguar and other units, and, the company hopes, other air forces.

**Data:** As for AS.30 except length 11 ft 11 in (3650 mm).

# AM.10 Lasso

This missile has been initiated by Aérospatiale to meet a requirement of the French Navy and capitalise on AS.12 experience in a more modern weapon having greater range. The name stems from Léger Air/Surface Semi-Automatique Optique, and the 65·5 lb (29·7 kg) warhead is derived from that of AS.12. TCA-type semi-automatic IR guidance is used, with a goniometer measuring angles from the launch platform to the target and to the missile IR flare, and a computer to try to reduce the difference to zero. Guidance commands are transmitted by wire, but with a range that can exceed 10 km there are problems with wire length and target vision. High-magnification IIR will be needed in the launch vehicle, which could be a helicopter or STOL aeroplane or various types of surface launcher. The present planning assumes two missiles on a Gazelle and four on a Puma, Dauphin or Lynx, with the APX 397 stabilized sight and Flir mounted in one unit. Lasso is to be generally compatible with existing AS.12 installations apart from the better sensing/optical systems giving longer range and darkfire capability. The programme was announced in 1977.

**Dimensions:** Length 82·7 in (2100 mm); diameter 8·67 in (220 mm); span 24·4 in (620 mm).
**Launch weight:** 152 lb (69 kg).
**Range:** Up to 6·8 miles (11 km).

# AS.15

Though AM.10 meets the requirements of the French Navy, it is right on the limits of what can be accomplished with wire guidance and could lose export sales to the British Sea Skua. To rival the British missile Aérospatiale is developing AS.15, in at least two versions, using the same warhead as AM.10 (65·5 lb, 29·7 kg) but with radio command guidance. The basic AS.15 appears to have much in common with AM.10 but the body is slimmer and there are flip-out rear fins. It can be launched from existing AS.12 installations provided they have been updated to AM.10 standard with a stabilized sight and, preferably, Flir or imaging IR. Like other Aérospatiale tactical missiles of this series the basic AS.15 has to be steered all the way to the target by the operator. AS.15TT (Tous Temps, all-weather), on the other hand, is a substantially different missile, though again carrying the standard warhead. It is not roll-stabilized and is guided semi-automatically. It is not known whether the TCA guidance using IR will be offered, but the basic system depends on Thomson-CSF Agrion radar (derived from the Iguane developed as a retrofit to the Alizé aircraft), with pulse-compression and frequency agility to improve behaviour in the presence of ECM. This radar continuously compares the sightlines to the target and missile, and a radio link, probably the same as for AS.15, drives the difference to zero. After a programmed descent to sea-skimming height on the radio altimeter the missile runs to within 1,000 ft (300 m) of the target and is then commanded to sink to immediately above the sea surface to be sure of hitting the target. Timing and export customers have not been disclosed.

**Dimensions:** Length (15) 85·63 in (2175 mm), (15TT) 102·75 in (2610 mm); diameter 7 in (180 mm); span (15) 23·6 in (600 mm), (15TT) 20·9 in (530 mm).
**Launch weight:** (15) 212 lb (96·2 kg), (15TT) 211·6 lb (96·0 kg).
**Range:** (both) 9·3 miles (15 km).

# Durandal

This missile is rocket-propelled and designed for attacking airfield runways. Developed by SA Engins Matra, it is believed to stem from the "concrete dibber" produced for Israel in 1969. This comprised a penetration/blast bomb fitted with four forward-facing twin rockets to slow the bomb after release at high speed and low level, and tilt it nosedown, and four aft-facing twin

*Above: Inert-warhead AS.30 on its special pylon adapter on an RAF Canberra B.6 in Cyprus. This is the improved version with tail controls.*

*Right: An A-type Jaguar of the Armée de l'Air with two AS.30L and centreline Atlis pod. The missiles have transparent noses to receive laser light from the target.*

rockets to drive it into the runway at high speed. Durandal has been many years in development.

**Dimensions:** Length 106·3 in (2700 mm); diameter 8·78 in (223 mm); span 16·9 in (430 mm).
**Launch weight:** 430 lb (195 kg).

# Smart Bombs

Both Matra and SAMP have since 1974 been developing laser-homing bombs matched to the Thomson-CSF Atlis 1 and 2 laser pods (see AS.30L). The main Matra effort has concerned the Ariel and Eblis seekers, while SAMP have used seekers by Rockwell. Various bomb sizes up to at least 2,205 lb (1000 kg) have been dropped, with Armée de l'Air collaboration and using military ranges such as Cazaux. The production weapons will also be matched to French army lasers to home on designators aimed by front-line troops.

# ASMP

It is difficult to know whether to class this weapon as tactical or strategic, and the French are not sure themselves. Though it has a short range, and the initials signify Air/Sol Moyenne Portée, it will have a nuclear warhead

*Right: Side and front elevations of AM.10 Lasso. This missile is actually shorter than AS.15TT depicted below right.*

with a yield of 500–600 kT. ASMP was initiated in 1971 to arm whatever emerged as the next-generation Armée de l'Air deep-penetration aircraft, successively the Mirage G, ACF (Avion de Combat Futur) and Super Mirage. Cancellation of the latter in 1976 reduced the pace of development, and no deep-penetration platform is now in prospect. Development was initially competitive between Matra, with turbojet propulsion, and Aérospatiale with a ram-rocket or ramjet. In March 1978 the go-ahead was given to Aérospatiale, reportedly with liquid-fuel ramjet propulsion. France has only limited experience with such propulsion, and may license technology from Vought, Marquardt, MBB or other company. Range specified for the original (January 1974) ASMP was 50–93 miles (80–150 km). Obviously inspired by SRAM, ASMP will have to be carried by aircraft lacking the range to launch it at strategic targets, and its purpose is therefore puzzling.

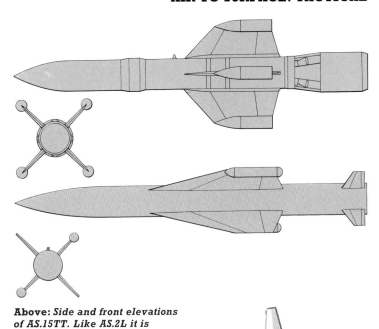

*Above: Side and front elevations of AS.15TT. Like AS.2L it is aerodynamically derived from Roland, though larger.*

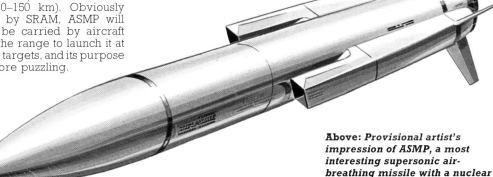

*Above: Provisional artist's impression of ASMP, a most interesting supersonic air-breathing missile with a nuclear warhead.*

*Below: A photo sequence of Durandal after release from a specially equipped trials Mirage IIIR (far right inset, Durandal on basic Mirage IIIC). No aircraft equipment is needed.*

# Exocet AS.39

Originally developed as a ship-launched missile (p. 72) Exocet was obviously a potential ASM and inert rounds were dropped by an Aéronavale Super Frelon in April 1973, followed by cut-grain powered launches in June of that year. In May 1974 the decision was taken to put the air-launched Exocet into production for the Aéronavale, and since then Aérospatiale has sold this missile to Pakistan and Iraq, with S Africa and other countries negotiating. Originally almost identical to MM.38, and designated AM.38, the ASM developed into AM.39 with a new propulsion system (SNPE Condor 2-sec boost after 1-sec delay, SNPE Hélios sustainer with 150-sec burn and steel case) and reduced overall missile length and weight giving increased performance. The wings and fins are reprofiled to facilitate carriage at supersonic speeds, and because of the greater range and flight-time the Adac seeker radar operates over a greater angular scan. AM.39 entered Aéronavale service in July 1977 carried aboard the Super Frelon (two missiles), followed by Pakistani Sea Kings. The Super Etendard followed in mid-1978 with either one or two on underwing racks, and the proposed Atlantic M4 patrol aircraft could

carry up to six internally and externally.

**Dimensions:** Length 15 ft 4¼ in (4680 mm); diameter 13·8 in (350 mm); span 39·37 in (1 m).

**Launch weight:** 1,433 lb (650 kg).
**Range:** Up to 32 miles (52 km) from low-level helicopter, or 47 miles (75 km) from high-level aircraft.

*Above: Launch of AM.39 Exocet from a Super Frelon 321 of the French Aéronavale. Targets are detected by the helicopter's search radar which assists initial missile guidance.*

# GERMANY

## SSW

Beyond doubt the most important programme of guided missiles prior to World War II was managed by the Siemens-Schuckert Werke (SSW) in World War I, chiefly for the Imperial German Navy. Dr Wilhelm von Siemens suggested a remotely controlled glide bomb as early as October 1914, and, as the company already had considerable experience of remotely controlled boats, progress was on a sound footing. Flight testing under Dipl-Ing Dorner began in January 1915, with gliders of increasing size. All were controlled by electrical command through fine copper wires unrolled from a spool. Servo controls, at first energised by a dry battery but by mid-1916 supplied by a windmill generator, operated a bang-bang rudder, self-centring after each command, and elevators which remained in the position last commanded. After many tests a method was perfected of making the left and right airframe halves – monoplane wings and half-fuselage – arranged to split open upon command to release a torpedo just above the water. Trials were flown from Siemens aircraft at Neumünster in the spring of 1915, and night testing began in August 1916. After 75 flights with larger biplane gliders the Navy made an airship available, and flights with 661-lb (300-kg) monoplanes and biplanes were made from

*Below left: One of the SSW biplane missiles launched from Zeppelin Z.XII. The airframe opened into left/right halves to drop a torpedo.*

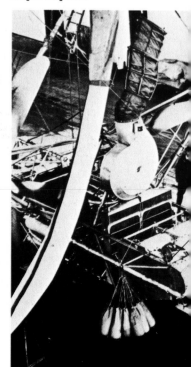

Zeppelin Z.XII near Hanover in April 1917. Then 661-lb (300 kg) gliders were flown from L.35 at Juterbog and Parseval PL.25 at Potsdam. L.35 carried numerous gliders of 1,102 lb (500 kg) size and a few of 2,205 lb (1000 kg), the last flight being by an SSW Torpedo-glider No 7 on 2 August 1918. It flew 4·7 miles (7·6 km) from release at 4,000 ft (1219 m) but the twin wires broke when the missile was just over the target at about 200 ft (61 m). At the Armistice SSW was starting more advanced trials at the airship base at Nordholz, using low-silhouette monoplanes of 13·7 to 16·4 ft (4·17–5·0 m) span. It was also hoped to release these pioneer ASMs from SSW bombers. There was inadequate ground clearance under the R.IV (R.4) but the R.VIII – the largest bomber of World War I – carried the impressive monoplane missiles beautifully. But they had not been released in flight when work was halted by the Allies in December 1918.

# Glide Torpedoes

In the late 1930s the RLM (German air ministry) sponsored development of improved torpedoes for aerial use, notably the 1,686 lb (765 kg) LT (Luft-torpedo) F5b with multiple tail surfaces and provision for adjusting the steering from the cockpit prior to release. Glide torpedoes by Blohm und Voss followed, leading to the L10 Friedensengel released from special outer-wing racks of a Ju 88A-4. This weapon, based on the F5b but with a large wing and tailplane with end-plate fins, could make a sustained glide prior to entering the water at the

*Above and right: L10 Friedensengel glide torpedoes slung from a crane and on the Luftwaffe heavy-store loader in front of an early Ju 88 trials aircraft.*

correct speed and attitude. About 450 were delivered, when production was transferred to the more advanced L11 Schneewittchen, few of which were completed. The BT (Bomber-torpedo) series were high-velocity weapons which separated from the carrier aircraft (usually an Fw 190F-8) automatically at the correct point in the dive towards the target, thereafter hitting the water and exploding immediately under the target ship. Standard models were BT 200, 400, 700 and 1400, the number being the mass in kg.

*Below: One of the 300-kg SSW monoplane missiles, apparently under Parseval airship PL.25. The final series of SSW glider missiles were much larger.*

**Data:** L10.
**Dimensions:** Length 153·3 in (3894 mm); diameter (of torpedo) 21·0 in (533 mm); span 110·3 in (2802 mm).
**Launch weight:** 1,686 lb (765 kg) torpedo plus 485 lb (220 kg) missile.
**Range:** Several miles (up to 10 km).

# BV 143

Seemingly an obvious weapon, this Blohm und Voss missile completely failed to work. Developed from 1942, it was a glide torpedo with large streamlined body (not a regular torpedo but a fuselage) and stubby wings and tail, with ailerons, rudder and elevators and autopilot to hold course towards the target ship. When about to dive into the water a hinged feeler arm 7 ft (2·1 m) long was knocked back by the waves, levelling out with elevators and igniting the T-stoff/petrol rocket motor with air-pressurized tanks which was to accelerate the sea-skimming

missile into the ship just above the waterline. Four BV 143s flown in 1943 all went into the sea, and in the absence of a radio altimeter (which could have worked) the feeler-arm idea was shelved.

**Dimensions:** Length 19 ft 7½ in (5·98 m); diameter 22·83 in (580 mm); span 10 ft 3¼ in (3·13 m).
**Launch weight:** 2,326 lb (1055 kg).
**Range:** 5 miles (8 km) at 258 mph (415 km/h).

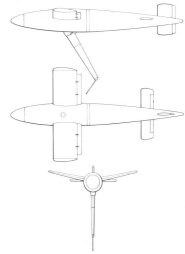

*Right: Three-view drawing of BV 143, showing the feeler arm extended. This device did not give enough time to pull out.*

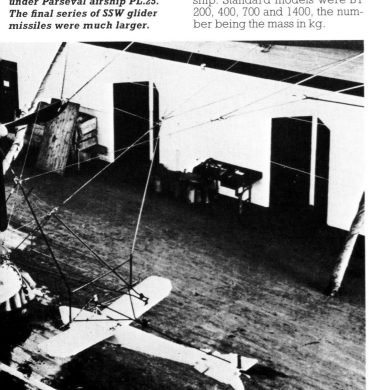

# BV 246

Originally designated BV 226, the Hagelkorn (hailstone) glide bomb was one of many German missiles of World War II made in large numbers but little used. The main effort was devoted to making a reliable stabilized glide-bomb, and devising a form of radio command link that could not be jammed or even countermanded by the British, whose ECM prowess had by 1942 become a cause for great argument among the Germans (some refused to believe it). The basic airframe comprised a beautifully streamlined fuselage, smaller than the BV 143, cruciform tail with most of the fin/rudder below the fuselage, and amazing high wings of 25·5:1 aspect ratio constructed of steel cores with aerofoils of die-cast concrete! Despite the high wing-loading of 102 lb/sq ft (515 kg/m ), the BV 246 flew well and had a gliding angle of 25:1. Thus, if a guidance system could be found, it could hit a target 130 miles (209 km) away if released at 34,450 ft (10 500 m). Extensive trials were flown from He 111H-6, Fw 190A and other platforms, using various crude radio-command, infra-red and other systems, including beams similar to ILS localizers. The best answer appeared to be to home on to Allied radars, but the Luftwaffe still showed only lukewarm interest. Production of the BV 246B-1 began at one of the Hamburg plants in late 1943, but in February 1944, when over 1,100 had been delivered in two months, the whole project was cancelled. Subsequently large numbers were launched by Fw 190F-8s flying from Karlshagen. These aircraft had struts pressing down the wings of the missile to make it spring cleanly away when released. Some of the last Hagelkorns to fly were fitted with the Radieschen (Radish) passive radar homer.

**Dimensions:** Length 139 in (3·53 m); diameter (max) 21¾ in (540 mm); span 21 ft 0 in (6·41 m).
**Launch weight:** 1,609 lb (730 kg).
**Range:** see text.

# GT 1200

Henschel developed the GT 1200 for underwater attacks on surface ships. Unlike the Hs 294 this was more a "clean sheet of paper" weapon, though the back-end, which separated on hitting the water, resembled a

twin-finned 294. It had a large wing and two rocket motors, one being internal for underwater use after tail-separation. There were underwater control surfaces.

# Zitteroschen

This was possibly the first winged supersonic guided missile, though data are scarce. It is credited to Henschel's Dr Voepl, who was supported by the RLM until October 1944 in developing this challenging weapon, whose name means torpedo-fish. It had small triangular wings with most taper on the trailing edge, a ventral fin and underslung tailplane. Two rocket motors were slung close under the wings alongside the large body. Roll control was by Wagner bars, a form of bang/bang spoiler behind the trailing edge of each wing which vibrated and was biassed by the command guidance. It is claimed that this missile was ready for production as an ASM when it was terminated in October 1944.

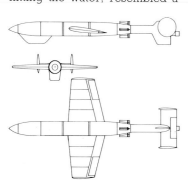

**Below left: GT 1200C was the final GT 1200, with under-nose target seeker. Length was 24 ft 1 in (7·35 m).**

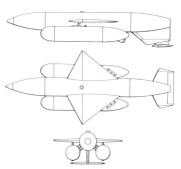

**Below: Zitteroschen was the first supersonic ASM. Most of the development was done in wind tunnels, to Mach 1·5.**

**Above: BV 246 Hagelkorns at Karlshagen in early 1944. The missile in the foreground has a non-standard nose (it might be Radieschen-equipped).**

# Fritz X

Also designated Fx (or FX) 1400, and called X-1 by the company that developed it and PC 1400X by the RLM, this was one of the great guided missiles of history and one of the very few to have achieved significant results in warfare. It was the king of the X-series of missiles conceived before the war by Dr Max Kramer at the DVL (Deutsche Versuchsanstalt für Luftfahrt, German aviation research institute), with steering in both axes (up/down, left/right) by means of spoilers

rather than conventional hinged surfaces. Kramer conducted extensive rig tests and tunnel experiments and in 1938–40, with RLM support, flew trials from Berlin-Adlershof using a command radio link to drive spoilers on completely new tails fitted to 551 lb (250 kg) bombs.

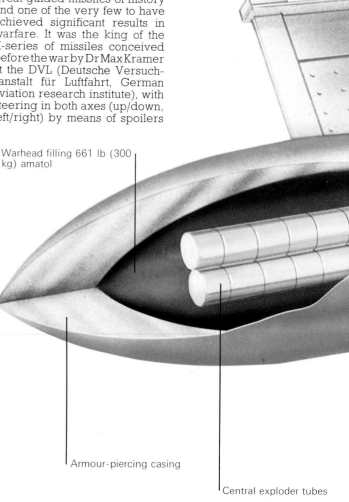

Warhead filling 661 lb (300 kg) amatol

Armour-piercing casing

Central exploder tubes

In 1940, despite the disinterest of the Luftwaffe High Command in anything of a long-term nature (because the war was thought to be already won), the DVL was allowed to expand its guided-missile work into several projects, and one, PC1400X, was selected for full development because it looked simple and fitted the offensive strategy of the time. It was a PC 1400 (1400 kg armour-piercing bomb) fitted with an enlarged version of the tail developed in the previous trials. A vertical-reference gyro drove tail spoilers to stabilize the weapon in roll, so that the

**Above: Production FX slung under a Do 217K-2 of III/KG 100. First mission came four days after II/KG 100 began operations with Hs 293.**

large tailplane and small fins could operate in the correct sense. In the thickest part of each surface was a solenoid driving four spoilers on the tailplane and two on the fins. Surrounding the tail was a 12-sided annular wing which restricted terminal velocity. Around the c.g. were four fixed wings. The RLM had in parallel sponsored an increasing number of radio communica-

tion and command links, and the one chosen was Kehl/Strassburg, comprising the Kehl transmitter in the launch aircraft and Strassburg superhet receiver in the tail of the missile. This was the basis of most command-guidance systems used by the Luftwaffe. The main contract for Fritz X was placed with Ruhrstahl AG, where PC1400X-0 pre-production deliveries began in February 1942. Trials from Karlshagen were held up by cloud, and in April 1942 the new E-Stelle Süd at Foggia, in the heel of Italy, took over and made better progress. DVL tunnel work solved a snag with sticking spoilers, and half the pre-production missiles hit within a 197-in (5 m) square. He 111H-6s were used as carriers, but without proving well-suited to the big missile, and the main operational carriers were the specially equipped Do 217K-2 and He 177A-5/R2.

After extensive service trials and indoctrination training, mainly over the Baltic by Lehrund-erprobungskommando 36, which also did the same for Hs 293, III/KG 100 with Do 217K-2s became operational at Istres in July 1943, under Maj Bernhard Jope. On 29 August 1943 Fritz X went into action, but the most famous exploit came on 9 September when the Italian fleet sailed from La Spezia to join the Allies, making an ideal target. Jope's geschwader caught the

line of ships in the Strait of Bonifacio, and concentrated on the two biggest battleships. *Roma* took two direct hits, blew up and sank; *Italia* shipped 800 tons of water but just reached Malta. Over the following week III/KG 100 paid attention to the Allied fleet off Salerno. Fritz X made the battleship *Warspite* limp to Malta with her decks almost awash (she was out of action a year); sank the cruiser *Spartan* and destroyer *Janus;* and severely damaged the cruisers *Savannah* and *Uganda,* caused a two-cruiser collision and sank numerous merchant ships. The only answer to Fritz X was better fighter cover, and this eventually drove III/KG 100 off.

When the programme was abandoned in December 1944 some 1,386 missiles had been delivered, well short of the planned output of 750 per month. Fritz X ended up being used over land, for example against bridges over the Oder in April 1945. There were numerous variations with different guidance, warhead and configuration.

**Dimensions:** Length 10 ft 8½ in (3262 mm); diameter 22·1 in (562 mm); span (horizontal tail) 53¼ in (1352 mm).
**Launch weight:** 3,461 lb (1570 kg).
**Range:** Horizontal travel about 3 miles (5 km).

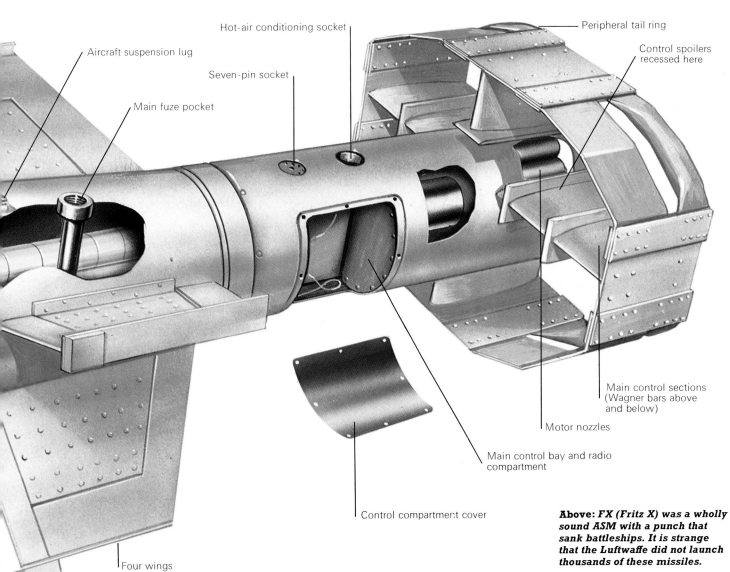

Hot-air conditioning socket

Aircraft suspension lug

Seven-pin socket

Main fuze pocket

Peripheral tail ring

Control spoilers recessed here

Main control sections (Wagner bars above and below)

Motor nozzles

Main control bay and radio compartment

Control compartment cover

Four wings

**Above: FX (Fritz X) was a wholly sound ASM with a punch that sank battleships. It is strange that the Luftwaffe did not launch thousands of these missiles.**

# Hs 293 family

Henschel Flugzeugwerke, formed in 1933 as the aircraft subsidiary of the great Kassel-based locomotive and truck company, was the first organization in the world to go into mass-production with guided missiles. The Hs 293 series was the most prolific and diverse in early guided-missile history, and large numbers made their mark on all kinds of enemy targets. The company got into the business in 1938, along with the Schwartz propeller firm and many other industrial concerns, with underpinning by the DVL.

In January 1940, Prof Dr Herbert A. Wagner left Junkers to head the Henschel missile teams. Work began on an air-launched sea-skimmer, probably the Hs 291, but this was dropped as too difficult. In its place the Hs 293 began in July 1940 as a glider bomb of aeroplane configuration, based on the SC 500 (1,102 lb, 500 kg) general-purpose bomb. Light-alloy wings and tail were added, with simple symmetric aerofoils, with solenoid-driven ailerons and an electric screwjack driving the elevator. A q-feel system, which measured dynamic pressure (varying with altitude and missile speed), altered the elevator gearing to minimise the effect of inaccuracy in applied angle. Early missiles of Hs 293 V2 type, dropped over Karlshagen about May 1940, were followed by V3 models in July with the definitive Kehl/Strassburg command link. By December 1940 the pre-production Hs 293A-0 was on test with an underslung pod containing a Walter 109-507B rocket burning T-stoff/Z-stoff fed by air pressure. This gave 1,323 lb (600 kg) thrust for ten seconds, to drive the missile rapidly ahead where the controller in the launch aircraft could see it. Though at least 100 missiles were tested with Dortmund/Duisburg wire guidance (over the remarkable distance of up to 19 miles [30 km] with wire fed from both the missile and aircraft) the radio link was standard, with a choice from 18 channels in the 48–50 MHz band, so that 18 aircraft could guide missiles simultaneously without mutual interference.

The first carrier was the Do 217E-5 (and, with Rüstsätze kits, other versions), which equipped Ekdo 36 for trials over the Baltic in July 1943, and II/KG 100 which became operational at Cognac in the summer of 1943. On 27 August the geschwader sank HMS *Egret*, a sloop, the first casualty in history to an aerial guided missile. Subsequently many vessels were sunk by hits from Hs 293A-1 missiles, including one Greek and four British

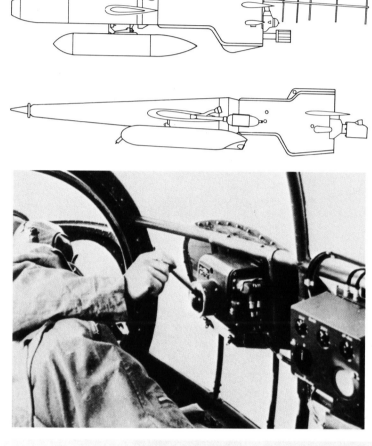

**Above left:** *Side elevations of two later members of the family, the TV-guided Hs 293D (top) and Hs 294B which was converted to wire guidance.*

**Left:** *Operator in an He 111H-12 steering an Hs 293A-1 by means of the joystick on the Kehl radio transmitter. Wire-guided versions had similar control.*

**Below:** *Features of a standard Hs 293A-1. This was quite effective when used against unarmoured targets.*

destroyers. Procedure was to keep the missile warm in flight with hot air piped from the launch aircraft (an He 111 or 177, Do 217, Fw 200 or, rarely, other types) before release. Day or night flares in the missile tail ignited, guidance became operative, the operator gave the motor ignition command, and thereafter steered in a series of arcs using a two-axis miniature joystick on the sidewall of the bombardier's nose compartment. As the missile closed on the target the control demands became excessive, depending on dive angle, missile speed varied from 270 to 559 mph (435–900 km/h). Most attacks took place in the Mediterranean/Italian theatre, though a special KG 100 geschwader was reformed in April 1945 to hit bridges across the Oder. Several thousand missiles were produced and at least 2,300 fired.

The Hs 293B had wire guidance on audio frequency. The 293C had a conical fuselage for underwater attack and led to the 294, a powerful missile with twin rockets of which some hundreds were made. The 293D was a bold attempt at TV guidance, and Wagner himself guided many of about 70 test firings, but TV/radio range limitation of some 2·5 miles (4 km) was prompting the use of wire signalling. Wingtip cones were drag bodies to restrict airspeed. The 293F was a delta with two motors, made of non-strategic materials. The 293G could be flown at very steep dive-angles. The 293H was to disrupt 8th Air Force bomber formations. The twin-motor 295 had an AP warhead, and the 296 mated this warhead to a 294 back-end and 293 guidance. Data are for the 293A-1.

**Dimensions:** Length 150 in (3·82 m); diameter 18½ in (470 mm); span 122 in (3·1 m).
**Launch weight:** 2,304 lb (1045 kg).
**Range:** Up to 11 miles (18 km).

# Mistel composite aircraft

The concept of launching an aeroplane from above, or below, another goes back to the earliest days of aviation. In 1941 a pick-a-back scheme was suggested – reputedly by Siegfried Holzbauer, Junkers test pilot – to the RLM as a way of making further use of operationally "tired" Ju 88 airframes. He believed that they could be converted into pilotless missiles, carrying enormous warheads with multiple fuze systems, which could be flown to their target by the pilot of a fighter riding on top. After release, the fighter pilot could then steer the missile into its target by radio command link.

The idea was initially rejected (as indeed any new idea would in the 1941 climate, which had a deep-seated belief the war was already won). In 1942 the DFS tested the practicality of flying a DFS 230 with a powered aircraft (Kl 35 or Fw 56) mounted above it. The bold experiment was then made of using a Bf 109E as upper component, and this made the RLM look at Holzbauer's idea again, and in 1943 an order for a Mistel (Mistletoe) conversion was received. The first conversion, flown in July 1943, comprised a Ju 88A-4 and Bf 109F, the latter having landing gear retracted and being supported on slim struts. The launch procedure was for the pilot of the upper component to release the rear strut which pivoted back to hit a yoke ahead of the Ju 88 fin. This triggered the elec-

trical release of the main fighter attachments. Demonstration that the scheme worked led to a further 15 conversions as weapons, code-named Beethoven. Tests with hollow-charge warheads of Ju 88 fuselage size against the French battleship *Océan* were encouraging and in further tests a thickness of 60 ft (18·3 m) of reinforced concrete was breached.

Junkers, DFS, Patin and Askania together developed a workable Mistel control system. On takeoff, and in emergencies (eg, if intercepted by hostile fighters) the fighter pilot could operate the flight controls of his own aircraft and the lower component in unison. Normally he could fly his own aircraft and merely use switches to re-trim the bomber's elevators or combined rudder/ailerons. The Ju 88 also had to have structural changes and a reskinned mid-fuselage. The first operational

version was Mistel 1 (rebuilt Ju 88A-4/Bf 109F) with the bomber's crew compartment replaced by a 7,716 lb (3500 kg) warhead with long contact fuze to give the correct stand-off distance.

Mistel 1 was first used by 2/KG 101, from St Dizier in France, it took off on night attacks on invasion shipping in Seine bay, scoring several hits but failing to sink any ships. But instructions were received urgently to convert 75 Ju 88G night fighters, to add a third Ju 88 wheel to avoid the burst tyres that had caused several takeoff accidents (which at full load exceeded Ju 88 overload limits), and to form II/KG 200 out of the short-lived III/KG 66 as the chief Mistel formation, with 100 composites on strength. This force built up in early 1945, nearly all being Mistel 2, but increasingly receiving the Mistel 3C, a complete change of policy in which the lower component was not a worn-out machine but one straight from the production line. The 3C lower

component was the long-fuselage Ju 88G-10 or H-4, the upper component being an Fw 190A-8 with doppelreiter overwing tanks and belly tank. On the outward trip the 190 drew 95-octane fuel from the Mistel, leaving it with its own 87-octane. Normally there was no radio command guidance, the Mistel merely being set up on line for its target and left to itself.

Over 250 Mistels were built or converted but the planned Eisenhammer (iron hammer) mission, that was really to smash the Allies, never took place. In the closing weeks of the war other Mistel combinations included the Ju 88G-7/Ta 152H, Ta 154/Fw 190, Ar 234/Fi 103, Do 217K/DFS 228 and many projects, such as the Ju 287/Me 262 and Ar 234C/Arado E.377 (small pilotless bomber).

Impracticable to give data in the usual way, since there were so many variations and combinations, many of which are numerically unrecorded.

**Right:** *The only Mistel to see active service was Mistel 1, the first mission being flown by Einsatz-staffel of IV/KG 101 on 24 June 1944.*

**Below:** *A Mistel S2 (Fw 190A-8 on Ju 88G-1), the widely used trainer for the operational Mistel 2 (Fw 190A-6 on Ju 88G-1 with warhead instead of crew compartment).*

# GERMANY

## Kormoran

The first major post-war missile programme in West Germany, this began life in 1964 to meet a Marineflieger (Navy Air) requirement. Based on a Nord project, the AS.34, using the Sfena inertial guidance planned for the stillborn AS.33, it became a major programme in the new consortium MBB, with Aérospatiale participation. The basic weapon exactly follows Nord/Aérospatiale principles, but incorporates more advanced guidance. After release from the F-104G or Tornado carrier aircraft the twin SNPE Prades boost motors give 6,063 lb (2750 kg) thrust each for almost 1 sec, when the SNPE Eole IV sustainer takes over and gives 628 lb (285 kg) for 100 sec, for cruise at Mach 0·9. Sfena/Bodenseewerk inertial mid-course guidance is used with a TRT radio altimeter to hold less than 98 ft (30 m) altitude. The missile then descends as it nears the pre-inserted target position, finally descending to wavetop height as the Thomson-CSF two-axis seeker (operating as either an active radar or passive receiver) searches and locks-on. Impact should be just above the water-line, and the 364 lb (165 kg) warhead contains 16 radial charges which project liner fragments with sufficient velocity to penetrate up to seven bulkheads. Flight trials from F-104Gs began on 19 March 1970. The first of an initial 350 Kormoran production missiles was delivered in December 1977, and by mid-1978 the Marineflieger MFG 2 at Eggbeck was fully equipped. The first Tornado-Kormoran unit will be MFG 1 at Schleswig-Jagel in 1981.

**Dimensions:** Length 173 in (4·4 m); diameter 13·54 in (344 mm); span 39·37 in (1·0 m).
**Launch weight:** 1,323 lb (600 kg).
**Range:** Up to 23 miles (37 km).

## Jumbo

In the late 1960s the expanding giant MBB decided it would be logical to use experience with Kormoran to develop a larger missile suitable for the hardest or most important surface targets. Initially to be carried by Luftwaffe F-4F Phantoms, it was intended primarily as a major weapon for the Luftwaffe and Marineflieger Tornado. Having a configuration similar to Kormoran, Jumbo was larger and had considerably greater body diameter. Bayern Chemie provided the single-charge motor, and guidance included strapdown inertial mid-course followed by either active radar homing (the seeker being in the nose) or command guidance with a TV camera in the front of

*Above: From this angle Jumbo reveals its TV seeker in the nose of the ventral fairing. This missile would have meant more punch per aircraft pylon.*

*Below: Launch of Kormoran from an F-104G Starfighter of Marineflieger Wing 2 based at Eggbeck. Two missiles can be carried by this aircraft.*

*Inset left: Kormoran firing from Italian Panavia Tornado over Decimomannu range, Sardinia, in July 1978. This aircraft carries eight.*

*Inset centre and right: Views by two different high-speed cameras of the same hit on a target destroyer. The sustainer is still burning.*

# INTERNATIONAL

an underbelly fairing between two of the wings. Four types of warhead were planned, weighing 1,102–1,764 lb (500–800 kg). In late 1975 the German government terminated development on the grounds that it would support only multinational collaborative projects.

**Dimensions:** Length 206·3 in (5·24 m); diameter 19·7 in (500 mm); span 49·25 in (1·25 m).
**Launch weight:** 2,535 lb (1150 kg).
**Range:** Up to 25 miles (40 km).

## Martel

This excellent weapon grew from studies by HSD in Britain and Nord-Aviation and Matra in France in 1960–3. In September 1964 the British and French governments agreed to develop the weapon system jointly, in one of the first examples of European weapon collaboration. In the event it was Engins Matra that became the French partner, responsible for the AS.37 anti-radar Martel. HSD developed the AJ.168 version with TV guidance. The name stems from Missile Anti-Radar TELevision.

Having a configuration similar to the AS.30, Martel has French propulsion, with boost/sustainer motors by Hotchkiss-Brandt, SNPE and Aérospatiale; AS.37 has a Basile boost and Cassandre sustainer and AJ.168 has slightly different motors tailored to the mission. Flight Mach number is typically about 0·9, though this depends on angle of dive. Several sources state that Martel is supersonic.

The operator of AJ.168 studies the target area as seen on his control screen in the cockpit of the launch aircraft, fed by the MSDS vidicon camera in the nose of the missile. When he acquires a target he manually drives a small graticule box over it to lock-on the TV seeker before launch. The weapon is then fired, holding height constant by a barometric lock, and steered by the operator's control stick via a streamlined underwing

pod which also receives the video signals from the missile. Special features assist the operator to steer the missile accurately to the target. AS.37 has an EMD AD.37 passive radiation seeker, with steerable inverse-Cassegrain aerial. If the rough location of a hostile emitter is known, but not its operating frequency, the seeker searches up and down a pre-set band of frequencies; when it detects the enemy radiation the aerial sweeps through 90° in azimuth to pinpoint the location. When it has locked-on the missile is launched, thereafter homing automatically. Alternatively, if the hostile radiation is known before takeoff the seeker can be fitted with a matched aerial and receiver module so all it need do is pinpoint the source. AS.37 continues to home no matter how the hostile radiation may change frequency so long as it remains within the preset band.

Both versions of Martel have a 330 lb (150 kg) warhead, AS.37 having a Thomson-CSF proximity fuze. AS.37 is carried by the Mirage III, Jaguar, Buccaneer and Atlantic; AJ.168 is used only by RAF/RN Buccaneers, but could be made compatible with the Phantom, Tornado and two-seat Jaguar or Harrier, and has been mentioned in a weapon list for Nimrod.

**Dimensions:** Length (AJ.168) 152·4 in (3·87 m), (AS.37) 162·2 in (4·12 m); diameter 15·75 in (400 mm); span 47·25 in (1·2 m).
**Launch weight:** (AJ) 1,213 lb (550 kg), (AS) 1,168 lb (530 kg).
**Range:** From treetop height, 18·6 miles (30 km); from greater height, 37·2 miles (60 km).

*Left: AJ.168 Martel on pylon of a Buccaneer of RAF Strike Command.*

*Below: AS.37 anti-radar Martel is carried by the Armée de l'Air Mirage IIIE, seen here, and several other types. Export sales: nil.*

# Otomat

Since early in the programme the partners responsible for this Italian/French weapon, Oto Melara and Engins Matra, have devised ASM versions suitable for specific launch platforms. In most studies the two rocket boost motors are not required, but reduced-size motors would be needed for the SH-3D Sea King, together with folding fins. Assisted by Fiat/Aeritalia a complete study was made for Otomat on the F-104 and G.91, and the Atlantic was taken to the point of compatibility tests though no missile was flown. No market had materialised by mid-1978.

# AS.2L

This proposed Franco/German missile is based on the Roland SAM, but may eventually diverge from Roland in many respects. Though the Roland is a product of Aérospatiale and MBB it is possible that AS.2L may embrace other partners. The designation, sometimes written AS.LL, comes from Air/Sol Léger Laser (air-to-surface lightweight laser), the guidance being closely similar to that of AS.30L and various French "smart bombs" with the Thomson-CSF Ariel seeker head. Compared with Roland, AS.2L would have a different airframe with fixed wings and fins, no boost motor,

and completely different guidance. Some reports have suggested AS.2L is not international but French; but MBB is unlikely not to participate, especially as AS.2L appears ideal for the Luftwaffe tactical Alpha Jets. By mid-1977 there was no commitment from either government.

# MDAC/MBB

Since 1976 McDonnell Douglas Astronautics Company and MBB have been jointly studying a range of possibilities for a guided missile to carry various payloads to heavily defended targets such as airfields. Rocket or airbreathing propulsion, fixed or variable-sweep wings, TV/EO/passive guidance and single/cluster/dispenser or even Mirved warheads are all matters for argument. So far as is known the studies are at the industrial level only, and no inter-government project had been agreed in mid-1978.

# JP-233

No industrial team had been announced for this Anglo-US airfield attack weapon by mid-1978. Also known by its AST number of 1217, it is reported to be unguided but to have various braking and propulsion systems to give maximum accuracy and cratering capability on paved runways.

# ISRAEL

# Luz-I

Since 1973 this tactical ASM has been intermittently reported in the media, without confirmation by the Heyl Ha'Avir (Israeli Air Force) or the alleged developer, Rafael Armament Development Authority. The general consensus of the reports is that Luz-1 is suitable for carriage by F-4E,

F-15 and Kfir aircraft, has TV guidance that is "impervious to jamming", a maximum range of about 50 miles (80 km) and is to destroy hostile SAMs, tactical SSMs and similar defence/offence-suppressive functions against point targets. The figure of 441 lb (200 kg) has been variously reported as the weight of the missile and of its warhead.

# ITALY

# Telebombe

During World War I the prolific inventor/scientist A. Crocco worked on a stabilized glide bomb which the post-war Italian Corpo Aeronautica Militare decided to evaluate. A dozen or more Telebombes were tested in 1920-2, apparently with inconclusive results as they lacked guidance. These miniature biplanes merely had a primitive autopilot, the gyro and servo-controls being fed from an air bottle. When dropped from 9,840 ft (3000 m) the range was about 6·2 miles (10 km). It is claimed that the 44 lb (20 kg) airframe carried a bomb of 176 lb (80 kg).

**Dimensions:** Span 26·4 in (670 mm) (impossibly small).
**Launch weight:** 220 lb (100 kg).
**Range:** See above.

# Marte

This ASM system was initiated by the Italian Navy in 1967 to give aircraft an all-weather attack capability against surface warships. After much study the Sea Killer 2 was selected as the missile part of the system, and Sistel was appointed prime contractor. Major associates are Agusta, who provide the helicopter platform, and SMA for the MM/APQ-706 fire-control radar. As described on p. 76 Sea Killer is a sea-skimming missile with various

**Top of page: *Launch of Sea Killer 2 missile in the Marte system from an Italian-built SH-3D Sea King.***

forms of azimuth and terminal guidance. The usual carrier is the Agusta-built Sikorsky SH-3D, though Marte has been studied for installation aboard smaller Agusta-built helicopters down to a gross weight of 6,600 lb (3000 kg). Smaller helicopters would carry only one missile and have no ASW capability. An SH-3D carries two missiles and the Marte system weighs a total of 2,568 lb (1165 kg), made up of 600 kg for the missiles, 400 kg for the launch equipment and control console,

143 kg for sonar and 22 kg for the optical sight. The standard operational technique is for the radar to acquire a target at maximum range, the helicopter then descending to wave-top height and flying towards the target, finally popping up to re-acquire the target and launch the missile, which takes just over a minute to reach the hostile ship.

**Data:** As for Sea Killer, p. 76.

# Airtos

In 1970-75 Sistel developed this short-range all-weather ASM for use by fixed-wing aircraft against rapidly manoeuvring ACVs and hydrofoils. It was unusual in

Above: *Sistel development missile based on Sea Indigo, lacking the active-radar seeker, used in the Airtos programme.*

having an active radar seeker locked-on before launch. Flying at Mach 1·9 it descended to 33 ft (10 m) from a typical launch height of 1,640 ft (500 m), finally sinking to 6·5–10 ft (2–3 m) just before impact. In the absence of home interest Airtos was abandoned in 1976.

**Dimensions:** Length 153·5 in (3·90 m); diameter 8·1 in (206 mm); span 33·75 in (857 mm).
**Launch weight:** 421 lb (191 kg).
**Range:** From 1·9–6·8 miles (3–11 km).

![Japan flag] **JAPAN**

## Funryu 1

In 1942 the Imperial Japanese Navy began to develop a Funryu (raging dragon) series of guided missiles at its Dai-Ichi Kaigun Koku Gijitsusho (1st Naval Air Technical Arsenal) at Yokosuka, its principal R&D centre. The first, Funryu 1, was an anti-ship ASM, with radio command guidance, an 882 lb (400 kg) warhead and an aeroplane-type configuration. Pre-production missiles were flight-tested from beneath the belly of a specially equipped G4M bomber, but development was abandoned prior to release for production. No other details appear to have survived.

## I-GO-1-A

This was the first of a series of ASMs developed for the Imperial Army at the Koku Hombu (Air Headquarters), which was responsible for managing Army Aviation R&D. Much of the actual fabrication and testing was almost certainly carried out at the Rikugun Kokugijutsu Kenkyujo (Air Technical Research Institute) at Tachikawa. Once basic research had been completed, in mid-1942, specific missile programmes were assigned to industry. I-Go 1-A was assigned to Mitsubishi, design being com-

**Right:** *Imperial Japanese Army I-Go-1A ready for test hung under a Ki-67-I bomber (Allied code name, "Peggy").*

**Below:** *I-Go-1B was the only Japanese missile to be built in quantity. This Army ASM had wooden aerodynamic surfaces, and the engine ran on HTP. Flight tests were mostly from the Ki-48-II "Lily".*

pleted in late 1943. A wooden miniature aeroplane, it had a rocket engine, believed to be produced by Nissan Jidosha KK, giving 529 lb (240 kg) thrust for 75 sec. The guidance was by radio command, and the 1,764 lb (800 kg) warhead had an impact fuze. Test drops of unguided missiles were made from the belly of a Ki-67-I in mid-1944. Guided flights are believed to have followed in October, but no production was undertaken.

**Dimensions:** Length 18 ft 11 in (5·77 m); span 11 ft 9¾ in (3·6 m).
**Launch weight:** 3,086 lb (1400 kg).
**Range:** Not known, would depend on launch height.

## I-GO-1-B

Assigned to Kawasaki Kokuki Kogyo, this promising ASM was smaller than 1-A but had the same radio command guidance. The HTP rocket motor was rated at 331 lb (150 kg) for 80 sec, and the 661 lb (300 kg) warhead had a direct-action fuze. Flight

trials began in late 1944 using a Ki-48-II, and by the end of the year more than 20 missiles were being launched each week from four of the bombers, each of which had a modified nose compartment equipped as the operator's station. The proposed operational carrier was the Ki-102b, but so far as is known no production missiles were delivered. Pre-production deliveries are reported to have numbered 180.

**Dimensions:** Length 13 ft 5 in (4·09 m); span 102·36 in (2·6 m).
**Launch weight:** 1,499 lb (680 kg).

## I-GO-1-C

Third and last of the I-Go ASM series, this missile was assigned to the Aeronautical Research Institute of the Imperial University in Tokyo. It was to have the extremely challenging homing guidance of sensing the direction of the shockwaves from gunfire, the targets being surface ships. Test results were described as promising, but were still at a relatively early stage when Japan surrendered.

**Dimensions:** Length 11 ft 5¾ in (3·5 m); diameter 19·7 in (500 mm).

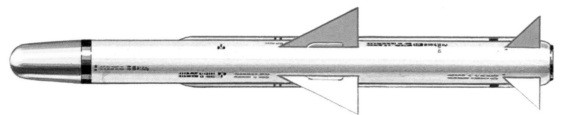

*Left: Drawn for this book, an up-to-date side elevation of Mitsubishi's ASM-1. This is a substantial missile for use against surface ships.*

## ASM-1

Mitsubishi Heavy Industries was selected as prime contractor for this transonic ASM in November 1973 by the Japan Defence Agency. The original studies assumed air-breathing propulsion, but a single-stage solid rocket motor, by Nissan Motors, has been used in prototype missiles. By 1980 it is expected that a suitable turbojet or turbofan will have been chosen to extend range. With a tandem boost motor ASM-1 could also be adapted to land or ship launching. The primary carriers are the Mitsubishi F-1 supersonic tactical aircraft and the P-3C Orion, and possibly P-2J, patrol aircraft. Mid-course guidance is by a Japan Aviation Electronics strapdown inertial system, with a TRT radio altimeter; Mitsubishi Electronics provide the active radar seeker for terminal homing. The guidance was tested in captive missiles flown on C-1 transports in 1977. The warhead has been reported to weigh both 309 and 441 lb (140 and 200 kg). Two unguided ASM-1s were launched from an F-1 over Wasaka Bay in December 1977, and guided flights from an F-1 followed in July 1978. Production at a unit price of $384,000 is planned for 1980. There has been no hint of a version for use against land targets.

**Dimensions:** Length 155·5 in (3·95 m); diameter 13·78 in (350 mm); span 47·24 in (1·20 m).
**Launch weight:** 1,345 lb (610 kg).
**Range:** Up to 28 miles (45 km).

# NORWAY

## Penguin

The characteristics of the Penguin ship-launched missile (p. 77) fit it admirably for air launch, and the Penguin 2 being developed jointly with Sweden forms the basis for the ASM version, for which no separate designation had been disclosed in mid-1978. Basic design study and simulation in 1973–5 led to carry-trials flights, mainly using an F-104G. The chief carrier in future operational use will be the F-16. In such fast aircraft no boost rocket is needed, the reduced missile weight allowing wing span to be reduced and allowing it to be fired from a standard Bullpup pylon. For slower launch platforms it is possible to adjust the booster charge needed for acceleration to Mach 0·8. Normal launch conditions for patrol aircraft are taken as 1,500 ft (457 m) and 200 kt (230 mph, 370 km/h). Kongsberg emphasize that, because of the simple launch-platform electronics needed, integration with most combat aircraft is relatively easy.

**Data:** As for ship-launched except for varying reduced weight and span (dependent on platform airspeed).

*Right: Air-launched Penguin carried by an RNorAF F-104G. Carry-trials are now in hand with the F-16A, to replace the F-104G from 1980.*

# SWEDEN

## RB 04

This hard-hitting ASM has enjoyed one of the longest active programmes of any guided missile, for the requirement was finalized in 1949, and missile hardware was being manufactured for 28 years (1950–78). Planned as a primary weapon to be carried by the Saab A32A Lansen, this missile was originally designed and developed by the Robotavdelningen (guided-weapons directorate) of the national defence ministry, whose first missile, RB 302, was flight-tested in 1948 from a T 18B bomber. The original RB (Robotbyran) 04 was made large enough to carry an active radar seeker, giving all-weather homing guidance earlier than for any other ASM apart from Bat. The configuration is of aeroplane type, with a rear delta wing with end fins and four control fins around the forebody. The two-stage solid cast-DB motor is by IMI Summerfield Research Station in Britain. The radar is by PEAB (Swedish Philips) and the autopilot, originally the XA82, is a Saab design with pneumatically driven gyros and surface servos. The first launch took place from a Saab J29 fighter on 11 February 1955, and following very successful development the first production version, RB 04C, entered service with the Swedish Air Force in 1958, equipping all A32A aircraft of attack wings F-6, -7, -14 and -17. In the early 1960s the Robotavdelningen developed a version with improved motor and guidance, RB 04D, which was in production in the second half of that decade. On 1 July 1968 the bureau became part of the Air Materiel department of the Försvarets Materielverk (Armed Forces Materiel Admin, FMV), and the ultimate development of this missile, RB 04E, was assigned to Saab (now Saab-Scania). Produced mainly to arm the AJ37 Viggen, which carries up to three, RB 04E has a reduced span, modernised structure and more advanced guidance. All versions have a 661 lb (300 kg) fragmentation warhead with prox and impact fuzes.

**Dimensions:** Length 14 ft 7 in (4·45 m); diameter 19·7 in (500 mm); span (C, D) 80·3 in (2·04 m), (E) 77·5 in (1·97 m).
**Launch weight:** (C, D) 1,323 lb (600 kg), (E) 1,358 lb (616 kg).
**Range:** Up to 20 miles (32 km) depending on launch height.

## RB 05

When the decision was taken to restrict what had been the Robotavdelningen to R&D only, Saab was the natural choice for this missile, prime responsibility for which was placed with the company in 1960. Originally known as Saab 305A, RB 05A is a simple command-guidance weapon readily adaptable to many types of launch aircraft. One unusual feature is supersonic flight performance, conferred by advanced aerodynamics and a Volvo Flygmotor VR-35 prepackaged liquid motor fed with Hidyne and RFNA, which are fed by a clever system of gas pressurization, a piston and collapsible aluminium bladder to burn rapidly in a boost phase giving around 5,511 lb (2500 kg), depending on temperature, and a sustain thrust of 1,102 lb (500 kg). Motor performance is independent of missile attitude or acceleration, and there is no visible smoke. The missile rapidly overtakes the launch aircraft and automatically centres itself dead ahead; it is then steered by a microwave link from the pilot's miniature control stick. The guidance is claimed to be highly resistant to jamming, able to control the missile at low altitudes over all kinds of terrain, and able to attack targets at large offset angles. The "very effective proximity-fuzed armament system" was developed at the research institute of national defence and is made by Førenade Fabriksverken.

In May 1975 it was announced that Saab was developing the

*Right: RB 05A, here with left body pylon adapter for an AJ37, can also be used against "certain airborne targets" (helicopters?). Its TV development was abandoned.*

Main picture: *RB 04E in service
with an AJ37 Viggen of the
Swedish Flygvapen wing F15 at
Soderhamn.*

Inset right: *Close-up of an
RB 04E on the centreline pylon
of an AJ37 Viggen retained by
Saab-Scania as a trials aircraft.
Black/white markings are for
position-fixing in cine
photographs.*

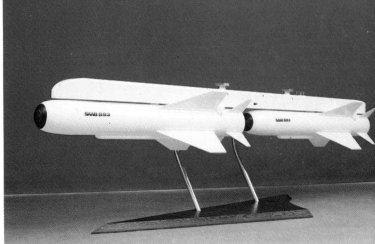

05B, a development of the 05A with a long parallel nose housing an EO seeker head derived from the Saab-Scania TVT-300 ground- or ship-based TV tracking system. This was locked-on before launch, leaving the carrier, again the AJ37A Viggen, free to take evasive action and depart. Compatibility trials were made, but the Swedish government chose to buy Maverick instead. Saab-Scania continued 05B development for a year but dropped the programme in late 1977. Data are for 05A.

**Dimensions:** Length 11 ft 10 in (3·6 m); diameter 11·8 in (300 mm); span 31·5 in (0·8 m).
**Launch weight:** 672 lb (305 kg).
**Range:** Up to 5·6 miles (9 km).

## RB 83

This light tactical ASM was in 1977 allocated SKr 400 million to develop it for use as the main guided missile of the proposed B3LA light attack and trainer aircraft. Looking like a small 05B, it incorporates the IR seeker from the shelved RB72 AAM, which has advanced signal processing and, working in the 7–14 micron band, has demonstrated its ability to distinguish between real surface targets and decoy

*Above: Desk-top model showing typical tandem installation of RB 83, a most attractive missile which could become a collaborative venture with British Aerospace in one form or another.*

flares. In May 1978 British Aerospace and Saab were discussing possible collaboration in this field, one solution being a joint ASM with airframe and motor of the Sabre and RB83 guidance. Data are not yet firm.

# USSR

## AS-7 Kerry

One of the more puzzling gaps in the immense array of Soviet airpower has been any type of tactical ASM. Even today this missile, about which little is known, is often reported as an interim type. It is said to have a solid rocket motor, radio command guidance, conventional warhead, range of about 6¼ miles (10 km) at Mach 0·6, launch weight of 2,645 lb (1200 kg) and to be launched at heights between 1,000 and 10,000 ft (300–3000 m). The chief carrier is said to be the Su-19, and certainly a weapon of this size would be a problem for some earlier FA (Frontovaya Aviatsiya) aircraft. There is no reason to doubt that tactical ASMs roughly equivalent to Bullpup and other early Western missiles have been tested in the Soviet Union for 25 years, but none has apparently entered service.

## AS-8

As yet not publicly associated with a NATO reporting name, this is said to be a "fire and forget" missile to be carried by all Soviet attack helicopters, such as the so-called Hind-D version of Mi-24 and the "A-10" gunship. Described as similar to the American Hellfire, it is reported to have a solid rocket motor, passive radiation seeker (Hellfire has a seeker that homes on

laser radiation) and range of 5–6¼ miles (8–10 km) at a flight Mach number of 0·5–0·8. IOC was apparently achieved in 1977 when AS-8 missiles began to appear on Mi-24 units in East Germany.

## AS-X-9

This is described as an ARM (anti-radiation missile), launched from Su-19 and other FA attack aircraft. Assumptions are that it has a solid rocket motor, large conventional warhead, passive radiation seeker of unknown sophistication, and a range of 50–56 miles (80–90 km). In early 1978 it was judged still to be under development.

## AS-X-10

This is reported to be an EO-homing ASM, with supposed solid rocket motor, conventional warhead, and range of about 6¼ miles (10 km) at Mach 0·6–0·8.

## ATASM

The Advanced Tactical ASM is believed to be a larger version of AS-X-10 with inertial or command mid-course guidance and EO-homing over the last part of its mission of up to 25 miles (40 km) at high-subsonic speed. Presumably it will become AS-X-11 to the DoD and receive a NATO name.

and BAe has privately financed studies matching Sea Skua to other aircraft (including fixed-wing) and in coast-defence installations. BAe expect that this missile, roughly one-tenth as heavy as Exocet but able to cripple the radars and weapon launchers of all known targets, will find very wide use.

**Dimensions:** Length 112·2 in (2·85 m); diameter 8·75 in (222 mm); span (control fins indexed 45° to fixed tail) 24·4 in (620 mm).
**Launch weight:** 325 lb (147 kg).
**Range:** Up to 9 miles (14·5 km).

## P3T

As yet unnamed, other than "active-radar Martel", this MoD-funded weapon system spent years being studied, partly because of doubt that it would be better than air-launched Harpoon, and finally progressed to the project-definition phase in the autumn of 1977. Based on Martel, it will have a longer body and Microturbo TRI-60 turbojet (772 lb, 350 kg, thrust at sea level)

**Above:** *Artist's impression of BAe Dynamics P3T, with a hint of the ventral engine inlet which seems well placed to ingest the odd wave-top.*

# UK

## Green Cheese

Though it suffered from indecision on guidance (TV, radio command, "H₂S" radar and SARH) this neat weapon was intended primarily for use against ships and there is no reason to doubt its eventual success. It was cancelled in 1958.

## Sea Skua

Originally known by its MoD project number of CL-834, this missile is significantly more advanced than the comparable French missiles being developed as successors to AS.12. Instead of having wire or radio command guidance Sea Skua is based on semi-active radar homing, and in its first application aboard the Lynx helicopter the target is illuminated by the specially developed Ferranti Seaspray overwater radar. The RN Lynx is equipped with this surveillance/tracking radar, as well as fire-control equipment and launchers for four missiles. The weapon system is intended

to confer upon helicopter-armed frigates and similar surface ships the capability to destroy missile-carrying FPBs, ACVs, PHMs and similar agile small craft at ranges greater than that at which they can launch their own missiles. This range is also said to be great enough to provide the launch helicopter with considerable stand-off protection from SAMs. The Decca Tans navigation system of the Lynx can combine with ESM cross-bearings to identify and fix the target, backing up the position on the Seaspray display. The Sea Skua, treated as a round of ammunition needing only quick GO/NO GO checks, is then launched and swoops down to one of four preselected sea-skimming heights, depending on wave state, using a BAe-manufactured TRT radio altimeter. Near the target a pre-programmed or command instruction lifts the missile to target-acquisition height for the MSDS homing head to lock-on. The warhead weighs 77 lb (35 kg). Guided trials began in 1978

*Four dummy Sea Skuas during early trials with a Lynx HAS.2. The entire weapon system is at instant readiness throughout the sortie, and can fire salvoes at a single target.*

giving very considerably extended range to well over 62 miles (100 km), to attack targets far beyond the visual horizon. This in turn means active homing, or passive homing on to the target's own emissions. In mid-1978 the expected choice of homing head was the MSDS programmable active-radar type exhibited at the 1976 SBAC show and described officially as "probably the most advanced seeker head in the world" (overwater use is implied, the comment does not reflect on such overland systems as Tercom which cannot be used at sea). The same head is proposed for

**Right:** *Mock-up of Sabre, a potentially extremely valuable missile which, if pressed at full speed, might sustain a gigantic programme.*

ASEM-ASSM, p. 74. In August 1977 the MoD surprisingly stated openly that P3T is "better than air-launched Harpoon", and BAe is now working towards a full development to qualify this extremely important long-range missile as the successor to AJ.168 on Buccaneers and a standard weapon for Tornadoes and Sea Harriers in the 1980s.

# AST.1227/Sabre

The British Air Staff Target 1227 calling for a precision-guided or cluster weapon for use against battlefield targets had by mid-1978 been narrowed to two con-

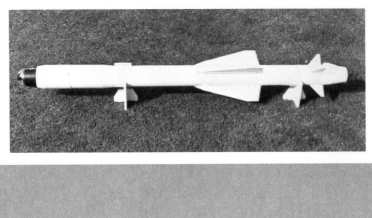

tenders. Hunting Engineering is promoting a cluster (dispenser) munition, either powered or free-fall and possibly fitted with flip-out wings. A free-fall cluster bomb, such as Hunting's established BL.755, is outside the scope of this book, but a winged, powered one becomes a missile. Its rival is indisputably a missile, and an exciting one: BAe's Sabre is based on a modified Rapier (p. 168) airframe fitted with a laser seeker in the nose. Almost certainly the seeker will be by Martin Marietta, related to that of Copperhead (p. 253) and compatible with advanced Ferranti designators and also with an expected NATO-standard Atlis 2 designator in which the US company is collaborating with Thomson-CSF. Sabre could be carried in large numbers, and would be compatible with tactical Hawk and similar aircraft. Each missile is calculated to have about 80 per cent kill probability against a battle tank, an important factor being the very short flight time resulting from the high-supersonic speed.

# USA

## BG Series

In World War 2 both the USAAF and Navy developed ASMs in the Bomb Glider category, the intention being that they should be towed to the target area and then guided by remote (radio or other) control to the point of impact. The three USAAF models were the Fletcher XBG-1 (PQ-11 conversion), Fletcher XBG-2 and tail-first Cornelius XBG-3. The Navy types were the LB series: Pratt-Read (Gould) LBE (three built, BuAer Nos 85290-2), Piper LBP, and Taylorcraft LBT (BuAer 85265-85289). Many of these simple ASMs were called Glombs (glider bombs) though this name was also applied to other weapons such as the GB series.

## GB Series

Several primitive ASM projects were started in the United States in 1940–1 but most suffered from official disinterest, by emphatic belief by the operational staff that such missiles had no value, and by the fact that developing organizations were skilled either in electronics or in aircraft, but never in both. The only project that, by its very simplicity, did continue in 1941–2 was the GB-1, first of the Guided Bomb series in which the bomb was a glider supported by wings. GB-1 research began in March 1941, partly in industry and partly at the Air Technical Service Command and Air Proving Ground. It was a standard 2,000 lb (907 kg) GP bomb fitted with 12 ft (3·66 m) wooden wings, and twin fins and tailplane carried on twin booms. At the rear of the bomb was the radio receiver and control servo, which biassed a simple Hammond autopilot to keep the bomb flying correctly and, in some versions, to impart course corrections. The original GB-1 had no guidance and was intended merely to be launched by the bombardier in the exact direction of the target at such a height and distance that it would reach the ground after travelling as far as the target – 20 miles (32 km) from 15,000 ft (4572 m). The advantage was that it kept the bombers out of the area of most intense flak. Production GB-1s were shipped to 8th Air Force bases in England in September 1943, but were not used. Then, as flak became more menacing, they were issued to the 41st Bomb Wing – the 303rd, 379th, and 384th Bomb Groups – each of whose B-17s was given two underwing GB racks. On 28 May 1944 Cologne Eifeltor marshalling yard was attacked by 109 bombs, with poor accuracy. Subsequently almost 1,000 were aimed at targets in Germany and Austria but accuracy was much worse than that of a free-fall bomb. GT-1 had a torpedo as payload. Later GB-2 to GB-15 versions incorporated improvements, and in some cases TV guidance. Only one saw combat service; in July 1944 the 388th BG set up a unit at Fersfield, called Project Batty, to operate the TV-guided GB-4. Potentially a pinpoint weapon, very successful in trials in California and Florida with AN/AXT-2 vidicon camera, GB-4 suffered severe difficulty in troops' hands in England and few found their targets. GB-4 weighed 2,500 lb (1134 kg) and glided at 240 mph (386 km/h), and achieved CEP averaging 200 ft (61 m). GB-6A was an excellent vehicle with the Offner IR seeker, flown many times before 1946. GB-8 was a direct visual-control glide bomb. GB-12 was an overwater light-contrast weapon. GB-13 homed on a bright flare. GB-14 was the first ASM to have active-homing radar guidance with BTL and NDRC radar equipment.

## VB Series

Unlike the GB family the VB (Vertical Bomb) weapons were free-fall missiles without wings, managed by Air Materiel Command at Wright Field. All the early models, at least up to VB-8, were based on existing bombs to which various types of guiding tail assembly was added. Some later models were ASMs with a complete airframe and separate warhead, with no vestige of bomb structure. Numerically the most numerous, and the only one to see widespread war service, VB-1 was called Azon, a contraction of AZimuth ONly. It had guidance in azimuth (direction) but not in range, ie in vertical trajectory. Thus the bombardier could do no more than try to ensure that the line of the trajectory appeared to pass through the target; he could do nothing if the bomb fell short or overshot. The basis was a 1,000 lb (454 kg) M-44 to which was added a new cruciform tail with a radio receiver, tracking flare, vertical gyro (to stabilize the bomb right-side-up) and left/right rudders. In good weather one bombardier, using one radio frequency, could guide five Azons at once. Field commanders were unenthusiastic, and a prevailing view was that, while azimuth steering had not been proved to increase accuracy, it could be proved that bomber casualties would be increased by prolonging the bombing run until impact. The US 8th Air Force rejected Azon in February 1944 and first batches went to the 15th AF in Italy. The 15th AF Bomb Groups learned fast and scored direct hits on the Danube locks at the Iron Gates and on the Avisio viaduct south of the Brenner Pass. But on 31 May 1944 the B-24 Liberators of the 458th BG from Horsham St Faith dropped 14 bombs against Seine bridges, scoring 14 near-misses. Previously, extensive US trials had shown Azon to be 29 times more accurate than free-fall bombs. Part of the trouble was lack of operator training, and the sheer difficulty of correctly sending left/right commands to the distant spot of light. Azon's greatest success came in Burma on 27 December 1944, when nine VBs sufficed to demolish a rail bridge at Pyinmana that had been missed

**Below left:** *Two of the 109 GB-1 glide bombs released some 20 miles from a Cologne target in May 1944 (inset, plan view showing tail booms).*

**Right:** *This photograph, taken at Eglin AFB in August 1950, shows the size of VB-13 Tarzon, large numbers of which were used in Korea, compared to a B-29.*

**Above:** *This member of the Roc family is said to be a VB-10 but lack of a TV vidicon camera suggests it was actually a command-guided VB-12.*

**Below:** *One of the original VB-1 Azons, hurriedly prepared as a public exhibit in 1946. Azon scored several vital hits in World War 2.*

by literally thousands of bombs in the two previous years. The 493rd BS and other 7th BG units later destroyed 27 difficult bridge targets, using 493 Azons of which 12–15 per cent scored direct hits. VB-2 was a 2,000 lb (907 kg) bomb with similar guidance.

More ambitious, the later VBs had range as well as azimuth guidance and thus VB-3 (1,000 lb) and -4 (2,000 lb) were called Razon. Developed mainly by ATSC and Division 5 of the NDRC, Razon had a tandem octagonal ring-tail, which was also used on VB-5 to -8. Using similar roll-stabilization, radio and flare, it eventually gave excellent results but saw no action in World War 2. Neither did the later and cleverer VBs, whose numbers multiplied the moment American staff heard of the Luftwaffe's use of ASMs in August 1943. VB-5 was a 1,000 lb (454 kg) bomb with image contrast light seeker. VB-6 Felix was a 1,000 lb (454 kg) bomb with the Bemis sensitive IR seeker cell in the nose which in 1945 demonstrated a CEP of 85 ft (26 m) in 12 drops. VB-7 and -8 were TV-equipped and radio guided. VB-9 to VB-12 used the NDRC ROC vehicle with an annular wing and fixed tail fins, "rocked" in pitch and yaw for control whilst keeping wing angle of attack virtually constant. Douglas built them, VB-9 having radar homing (useless, because of ground reflections), TV, IR and direct visual control respectively. The final VB, VB-13 Tarzon, was a monster 12,000 lb (5443 kg) missile 21 ft (6·4 m) long with a 54-in (1·37 m) annular wing. Built by Bell at Wheatfield, Tarzons destroyed such Korean targets as Hwach-On reservoir, Kanggye road bridge and Koindong railway bridge.

**Below:** *VB-3 Razon Mk IV, with diagonal aerial between the two octagon wings (rear set having twin rudders and elevators for control).*

# Bat

Undoubtedly the most sophisticated winged missile ever used in warfare prior to 1967, this miniature aircraft was a self-homing anti-ship missile and the first to have an Army/Navy missile designation. Its genesis lay in Dragon, begun in January 1941 by RCA who used their TV expertise to devise a TV-guided aerial torpedo for use against surface ships, with airframe by NBS (National Bureau of Standards). By late 1942, when the airframe had flown, the U-boat menace caused a change in direction. Dragon became Pelican and the payload a depth charge steered by semi-active radar homing, the radar being in the launch aircraft. By mid-1943 the U-boats had been defeated, and Pelican was again reorientated as an anti-ship missile, enlarged to carry a 2,000 lb (907 kg) GP bomb and with RHB radar homing. In 1944 the fourth and final fresh start resulted in Bat, so named because like a bat it sent out pulses and listened to the reflections. Using the same NBS airframe Bat carried a Western Electric pulsed radar in the nose and homed on the reflections from the target ship. Like Gorgon it had four small wind-mill-driven generators, and the autopilot servos drove the tail-plane (with fixed fins) and wing elevons. In the centre was a 1,000 lb (454 kg) GP bomb. Bat was developed at the Navy Bureau of Ordnance in close collaboration with MIT whose Hugh L. Dryden won the Presidential Certificate of Merit for it. The PB4Y-2 Privateer carried two Bats on outer-wing racks, and from May 1945 off Borneo took an increasing toll of Japanese ships, including a destroyer sunk at the extreme range of 20 miles (32 km) – range being a function of release altitude. With modified radar several Bats successfully homed on bridges in Burma and other Japanese-held areas.

**Dimensions:** Length 11 ft 11 in (3·63 m); span 10 ft 0 in (3·05 m).
**Launch weight:** 1,880 lb (852·7 kg).
**Range:** Depended on release height, flying at 300 mph (483 km/h).

# Glomb

These US Navy glide bombs were based on the successful Culver low-wing monoplanes, with TV guidance and 2,000 lb (907 kg) GP or 4,000 lb (1814 kg) light-case warhead in place of engine and occupants. Extensive manned flight testing took place in 1942–44 but the LBE-1 was terminated before a decision on operational use was settled.

# Gorgon

Under this name the US Navy flew a family of missiles and test vehicles of remarkable diversity in the eight years following

World War 2. The original members were all canard vehicles with the rear wing mounted shoulder-high. The first, Gorgon I KUM-1, was designed in 1946 at the Naval Air Modification Unit which occupied the former Brewster plant at Johnsville. NAMU became the Naval Air Development Station in August 1947, and two years later received its present title of NADC: Naval Air Development Center. Gorgon was one of its largest early projects, and though KUM-1 was intended as a SAM or SSM the later models were nearly all ASMs or AAMs, and increasingly served to provide the underlying basis of technology for later missiles. KUM-1 was designed for turbojet propulsion, but in late 1946 became KU2N-1 with a 350 lb (159 kg) acid/aniline rocket designed at the Naval Experiment station. By early 1947 work embraced Gorgon IIA (CTV-4), IIC with provision for surface launch, and IV (PTV-N-2), assigned to Martin, with the wing ahead of the tailplane and propelled by an underslung Marquardt ramjet. The final Gorgon was Mk V (XASM-N-5) also assigned to Martin, which was terminated in 1953.

*Left above: Production ASM-N-2 Bat in wartime service on a PB4Y-2 Privateer. The four small windmill turbogenerators are just visible.*

*Left: SWOD Mk 9 had a Pelican airframe but self-contained radar guidance. It was the prototype that led to the Bat series.*

*Below left: This air-to-air photograph of Gorgon IV was taken in 1946. Some Gorgons of this configuration were powered by the 9·5-inch Westinghouse turbojet.*

# Gargoyle

The first missile by McDonnell Aircraft, this ASM began life in November 1943 as an anti-ship glide bomb but at Navy BuOrd request was fitted with an acid/aniline rocket engine in March 1944. The compact airframe reflected sustained-cruise requirements, with fat fuselage, low wing and butterfly tail. A tracking flare surmounted the rocket nozzle, but, though many KSD-1 Gargoyles flew from December 1944, no definitive guidance system had been perfected when this vehicle was reduced to the status of a research project at the end of the war. It carried a 1,000 lb (454 kg) warhead

*Below: This Gargoyle is unusual in having no external markings. The dorsal blisters, which were standard, fair-in tandem suspension lugs above the bulkheads.*

at 690 mph (1,110 km/h) in typical ASM versions.

**Dimensions:** Length 10 ft 1 in (3·07 m); span 8 ft 6 in (2·59 m).
**Launch weight:** 1,517 lb (688 kg).
**Range:** Almost 5 miles (8 km) from 27,000 ft (8230 m) release.

# Kingfisher

In June 1948 McDonnell Aircraft established a Propulsion and Guided Missiles division, and one of its initial programmes was this impressive air-breathing cruise weapon developed for the Navy BuOrd. Test-flown from under the wings of a Douglas JD-1 Invader of the Naval Air

*Foot of page: Army Air Corps personnel at the McDonnell plant in St Louis study a Kingfisher, a Navy missile on an NAOTS Invader. The year was probably 1949.*

Ordnance Test Station, AQM-60A Kingfisher had small horizontal wings and butterfly tail and, usually, a McDonnell/Schmidt pulsejet. It was intended to home on ship or submarine targets and dive into the sea, the 1,000 lb (454 kg) warhead detonating under the surface. In two versions the payload was a torpedo.

# Dove

Developed under Navy BuOrd contract in 1945–53, this IR-homing bomb comprised a 1,000-lb (454-kg) GP bomb with added gyrostabilized nose seeker whose sensitive heat-seeking cells precessed the gyro until the target was in the centre of the field of view. Current from the precession motors drove four control fins behind the seeker head to steer the missile towards the target. The industry team was led by Eastman Kodak.

123

# Wagtail

The first retarded missile for release from low-level high-speed aircraft, Wagtail was a USAF programme of 1954–58. The internal rocket motor had vectored thrust for deceleration and steering. Prime contractor was Minneapolis–Honeywell.

*Left: Corvus was a supersonic liquid-rocket ASM first flown on 18 July 1959 from an A4D Skyhawk. It was intended to penetrate heavy defences.*

*Below: An XGAM-67A Crossbow on a DB-47E Stratojet at Holloman AFB on 9 April 1957. Crossbow was one of many terminated USAF missiles.*

# Corvus

Latin for Crow, this weapon was the progenitor of a family of ASMs and electronics platforms named after crow-like birds but was cancelled by the Navy after $80 million had been spent. Prime contractor was Temco Aircraft, of Dallas, whose first $16 million award was for design of ASM-N-8 in January 1957. A winged standoff weapon for such carrier-based types as the A3J (A-5) Vigilante and A2F (A-6) Intruder, it had a Reaction Motors (Thiokol) motor, Maxson/TI guidance and range of 50 miles (80 km). In one form the Corvus homed on hostile radars. The programme reached the stage of fully guided flights in March 1960 but was cancelled four months later.

# Crossbow

In 1956 the Radioplane (now Ventura) division of Northrop, a pioneer of radio-controlled target aircraft, became prime contractor for this long-range cruise missile, originally project MX-2013, with a multi-waveband passive seeker that homed it on to hostile radars. It cruised at 575 mph (925 km/h) on an air-breathing engine – usually the Westinghouse J81 or Fairchild J83 – but was later required to have supersonic dash capability, which would probably have eliminated its odd twin fins. In 1960 GAM-67 Crossbow was terminated and replaced by a more advanced, longer-ranged (200 miles, 322 km) missile named Longbow, part of Weapon System 121B. This in turn was cancelled in the early 1960s.

# Bullpup

During the Korean War the Navy urgently needed a precision ASM capable of being launched by carrier-based aircraft. Despite the vast heritage of prior effort not one tactical ASM was in use with any of the US forces, and RFPs were issued in 1953. The Martin Orlando Division's offering was chosen from 14 submissions in May 1954, and subsequently was developed as ASM-N-7 Bullpup. Similar in concept to the wartime German weapons, it comprised a standard 250 lb (113 kg) bomb inside a neat roll-stabilized airframe with Aerojet-General solid motor giving burnout speed of Mach 1·8, fixed rear wings, four pneumatically actuated nose control fins and twin rear tracking flares. The operator in the launch aircraft acquired the target visually, fired the missile and used a radio command joystick to impart left/right and up/down directions whilst keeping the flares lined up with the target as seen through his gunsight. N-7 became operational in April 1959, carried by the FJ-4B (AF-1E) Fury, A4D-2 and subsequent (A-4) Skyhawks and a rapidly growing range of other Navy and Marine Corps types including the HUS-1 helicopter.

The existence of this primitive weapon at a price near $5,000 resulted in very wide acceptance. In 1960 it was replaced in production by N-7A, with Thiokol prepackaged LR58 acid/amine motor, extended-range control and a new warhead. Restyled AGM-12B in 1962, it was put into second-source production by W. L. Maxson, which had participated in guidance and since 1963 has been US prime supplier for missiles, terminating at 22,100 rounds in 1970, and spares. Also called Bullpup A, AGM-12B was adopted by the Royal Navy and the forces of Denmark, Norway and Turkey, and from 1963 over 8,000 were built under licence by a European consortium headed by Kongsberg of Norway. Present carrier aircraft include the USN/USMC A-4, A-6, F-4, F-8 and P-3, and in Europe the F-4, F-5, F-100, F-104 and P-3.

Back in 1959 Martin Orlando, in Project White Lance, developed an improved version for the Air Force with radio guidance that freed the operator from the need to align the target with his sight, allowing guidance from an offset position. This was produced as GAM-83A, later styled AGM-12B (same as the Navy weapon) and used by TAC and other units with the

F-100, F-105 and F-4. At the same time Martin developed two new versions. For the Navy ASM-N-7B (AGM-12C), Bullpup B, was a larger missile with 1,000 lb (454 kg) warhead, wings greatly extended in chord and Thiokol LR62 liquid motor; 4,600 were delivered. The Air Force adopted GAM-83B (AGM-12D) using an airframe closer to the original but with an increased-diameter centre section able to house either a conventional or nuclear warhead. These were backed up by the TGAM-83 (ATM-12A/B/D) Bullpup Trainer developed by Martin's Baltimore Division around the standard 5 in rocket; this was later replaced by firing surplus AGM-12Bs with inert warheads. The final model was AGM-12E, briefly (840 rounds) built for the Air Force by Martin, with an anti-personnel fragmentation warhead.

There were several derived missiles intended to supplement or replace the established models. Texas Instruments

worked on Bulldog with EO (laser) guidance. Martin's AGM-79A Blue Eye competed with Chrysler's AGM-80A Viper, the former having a scene-correlation TV scanning system and Viper a strapdown inertial platform, both with warhead detonated by radio altimeter before impact.

**Dimensions:** Length (AGM-12B) 10 ft 6 in (3·2 m), (AGM-12C) 13 ft 7 in (4·14 m); diameter (B) 12 in (305 mm), (C) 18 in (457 mm); span (B) 37 in (940 mm), (C) 48 in (1·22 m).
**Launch weight:** (B) 571 lb (259 kg), (C) 1,785 lb (810 kg).
**Range:** (B) 7 miles (11·3 km), (C) 10 miles (16 km).

**Right:** *Some major variants of Bullpup include (front to rear) ATM-12A trainer, AGM-12D (note slight increase in warhead diameter), AGM-12B (Bullpup A) and AGM-12C (Bullpup B).*

**Below:** *Launch from a P-3B Orion of the US Navy of an unusual test Bullpup devoid of the usual lower pair of nose control fins.*

**Inset below:** *Laser-guided Bulldog was produced for the Marines. This example was launched from an A-4 at NWC in March 1971.*

**Left:** *Launch of GAM-83 Bullpup from an F-100D Super Sabre over the Eglin Gulf range soon after Bullpup had been adopted by the USAF.*

**Inset left:** *Assembling a GAM-83 for test from the F-84F seen in the rear at Edwards AFB on 8 September 1958 (prior to USAF adoption).*

# Walleye

An unpowered glide bomb with TV guidance, AGM-62 Walleye was developed from 1963 by the NOTS at China Lake, assisted from 1964 by the Naval Avionics Facility. Intended to overcome the aircraft-vulnerability hazard of visual radio-command ASMs, Walleye quickly proved successful, and in January 1966 Martin Orlando Division (the original supplier of Bullpup) was awarded the first production contract. This was later multiplied, and in November 1967 the need for Walleye in SE Asia resulted in Hughes Aircraft being brought in as second-source. In 1969 the Navy described this missile as "The most accurate and effective air-to-surface conventional weapon ever developed anywhere". The original Walleye I (Mk l Mod 0) has an 825 lb (374 kg) warhead, a cruciform of long-chord delta wings with elevons, a gyro stabilized TV vidicon camera in the nose, and ram-air windmill at the tail to drive the alter-

nator and hydraulic pump. The chief carrier platforms are the A-4, A-7 and F-4 of the US Navy, Marine Corps and Air Force, and the Israeli AF. The pilot or operating crew-member identifies the target, if necessary using aircraft radar, aims the missile camera at it, focusses it and locks it to the target using a monitor screen in the cockpit. The aircraft can then release the missile and turn away from the target, though it must keep the radio link with the missile. In theory the missile should glide straight to the target, but the launch operator has the ability to break into the control loop and, watching his monitor screen, guide it manually into the target. In 1968 the Navy funded several developments – Update Walleye, Walleye II, Fat Albert and Large-Scale Walleye among them – which led to the enlarged Walleye II (Mk 5 Mod 4) for use against bridges, larger ships and other worthwhile targets, with a 2,000 lb (907 kg) warhead derived from the Mk 84 bomb. In production by 1974,

Walleye II was deleted from the budget the following year and replaced by the first procurement of ER/DL (Extended-Range/Data-Link) Walleye II (Mk 13 Mod 0). The ER/DL system was originally planned in 1969 to allow a launch-and-leave technique at greater distance from the target, the missile having larger wings to improve the glide ratio, and the radio data-link allowing the operator to release the missile towards the target and then, when the missile was much closer, acquire the target on his monitor screen, focus the camera and lock it on. Operations in SE Asia showed that it would be preferable to use two aircraft, the first to release the Walleye (if possible already locked on the approximate target position) and then escape and the second, possibly miles to one side, to update the lock-on point and monitor the approach to the target. In 1978 about 1,400 Walleye I and 2,400 Walleye II missiles were being converted to ER/DL. Future plans include an improved data-link

and introduction of the AGM-65D IIR head for night attack.

**Dimensions:** Length (I) 135 in (3·44 m), (II) 159 in (4·04 m); diameter (I) 12½ in (317 mm), (II) 18·0 in (457 mm); span (I) 45½ in (1·16 m), (II) 51 in (1·3 m).
**Launch weight:** (I) 1,100 lb (499 kg), (II) 2,400 lb (1089 kg).
**Range:** (I) 16 miles (25·7 km), (II) 35 miles (56·3 km).

# Shrike

Based in part on the Sparrow AAM, this was the first anti-radar missile (ARM) in the US since World War 2. Originally called ARM and designated ASM-N-10, it was begun as a project at NOTS (later NWC) in 1961, and in 1962 became AGM-45A. Production by a consortium headed by Texas Instruments (TI) and Sperry Rand/Univac began in 1963 and Shrike was in use in SE Asia three years later with Wild Weasel F-105Gs and EA-6As. Early experience was disappointing and there have since been numerous models, identified by suffix numbers, to rectify faults or tailor the passive homing head to a new frequency band identified in the potential hostile inventory. Carried by the US Navy/Marines A-4, A-6, A-7

**Left:** *Here seen on an A-7E Corsair in December 1973, Mk 3 Mod 0 was the first of the ER (Extended-Range) models of Walleye.*

**Below:** *These Walleyes carried on a Skyhawk (probably an A-4M) of the Navy look blunt-nosed, but the shadow gives true shape. Note active-ECM pods.*

**Inset:** *Three frames from film taken by Walleye guidance camera showing attack on Ninh Binh railway bridge; fourth picture by an RF-4C.*

and F-4, the Air Force F-4, F-105 and EF-111 and the Israeli F-4 and Kfir, Shrike is switched on while flying towards the target and fired as soon as the TI radiation seeker has locked-on. Flight speed is Mach 2, on a Rocketdyne Mk 39 or Aerojet Mk 53 or 78 solid motor. The seeker continually updates the guidance by determining the direction of arrival of the hostile radiation, homing the missile into the enemy radar with its cruciform centre-body wings. The warhead is a 145 lb (66 kg) fragmentation type. There were at least 18 sub-types in the AGM-45-1 to -10 families, with over 13 different tailored seeker heads, of which 13,400 out of a planned total procurement of about 18,500 had been ordered by mid-1978. In the Yom Kippur war Israel used Shrike tuned to 2965/2990 MHz and 3025/3050 MHz to defeat SA-2 and SA-3 but was helpless against SA-6. Virtually all current procurement is of the -9 and -10 for the USAF to be carried by F-4G and EF-111A platforms, together with modification kits

*Below: Special test A-4C Skyhawk fires an early Shrike on 12 June 1964. Despite intensive testing Shrike was erratic in Vietnam.*

*Below inset: 3 January 1971 aboard the JFK (CVA-67), with four Shrikes tuned to SA-2 radars about to "go topside" and have wings fitted.*

to equip existing rounds to home on to later SAM and other radars.

**Dimensions:** Length 120 in (3·05 m); diameter 8 in (203 mm); span 36 in (914 mm).
**Launch weight:** Approximately 390 lb (177 kg) depending on sub-type.
**Range:** 18–25 miles (29–40 km).

# Standard ARM

In September 1966 the Naval Air Systems Command contracted with Pomona Division of General Dynamics for an ARM having higher performance, longer range and larger warhead than Shrike, which at that time was giving indifferent results. Unlike Shrike the whole programme was developed in industry, the basis being the Standard RIM-66A ship-to-air missile. Flight testing took place in 1967–8; production of AGM-78 Mod 0 began in late 1968 and ten years later had absorbed well over $300 million at a unit price initially in the neighbourhood of $128,000. AGM-78 Mod 0 was carried by the Air Force Wild Weasel F-105F and G and the Navy A-6B and E. The missile flies at Mach 2·5 on an Aerojet (Indian Head) Mk 27 dual-thrust solid motor, steering with tail

*Right: AGM-78B Standard ARM on Wild Weasel F-105F Thunderchief EW platform at Holloman AFB in 1967. Note centreline chaff dispenser.*

controls and very low aspect ratio fixed wings. A large conventional warhead is fitted. The Mod 0 AGM-78A of 1968 was fitted with the TI seeker used in Shrike. This was soon replaced by the Maxson broad-band seeker of the main (Mod 1) production version, AGM-78B. This has capability against search, GCI, SAM and other radar systems, and is intended to give the launch platform freedom to attack from any direction and turn away "outside the lethal radius of enemy SAMs". Carrier platforms preferably have a TIAS (Target Identification and Acquisition System) able to measure "specific target paramet-

ers" and supply these to the seeker head in the missile before launch. The Mod 1 missile is compatible with the APR-38 system carried by the USAF F-4G Wild Weasel which supplies this need. AGM-78C, D and D-2 have further-increased capability and reduced unit cost, but in 1978 production was not funded, while that of Shrike is continued. RGM-66D is a ship-launched version (p. 81).

**Dimensions:** Length 180 in (4·57 m); diameter 13·5 in (343 mm); fin span 43 in (1·09 m).
**Launch weight:** About 1,400 lb (635 kg).
**Range:** 35 miles (56·3 km).

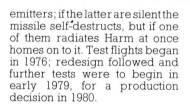

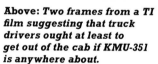

# Harm

Neither Shrike nor Standard ARM is an ideal air-launched ARM and in 1972 the Naval Weapons Center began R&D and also funded industry studies for a High-speed Anti-Radiation Missile (Harm). Among the objectives were much higher flight speed, to lock-on and hit targets before they could be switched off or take other action, and to combine the low cost and versatility of Shrike, the sensitivity and large launch envelope of Standard ARM, and completely new passive homing using the latest microelectronic digital techniques and interfacing with new aircraft systems. In 1974 TI was selected as system integration contractor, assisted by Hughes, Dalmo-Victor, Itek and SRI (Stanford Research Institute). The slim AGM-88A missile has double-delta moving wings and a small fixed tail. Thiokol provides the high-performance solid motor. The TI seeker has a simple fixed aerial (antenna), a low-cost autopilot is fitted, and Motorola supply an optical target detector forming part of the fuzing for the large advanced-design warhead. Carrier aircraft will include the Navy/

**Top:** *This A-7 Corsair parked by the control tower at China Lake has a Harm inboard and Shrike outboard. The difference in size is obvious.*

**Above:** *High-speed cine frame showing a Harm just before target impact. This missile was released on the NWC overland range in 1974.*

Marines A-6E, A-7E and A-18, and the Air Force APR-38 Wild Weasel F-4G and EF-111A, with Itek's ALR-45 radar warning receiver and Dalmo-Victor's DSA-20N signal analyser both interfaced. Harm can be used in three modes. The basic use is Self-protect, the ALR-45 detecting threats, the launch computer sorting the data to give priorities and pass to the missile a complete set of digital instructions in milliseconds, whereupon the missile can be fired. In the Target of Opportunity mode the very sensitive seeker locks on to "certain parameters of operation and also transmissions associated with other parts of a radar installation" which could not be detected by Shrike or Standard ARM. In the Pre-briefed mode Harm is fired blind in the direction of known

emitters; if the latter are silent the missile self-destructs, but if one of them radiates Harm at once homes on to it. Test flights began in 1976; redesign followed and further tests were to begin in early 1979, for a production decision in 1980.

**Dimensions:** Length 13 ft 8 in (4·17 m); diameter 9½ in (241 mm); span 44·5 in (1·13 m).
**Launch weight:** About 809 lb (367 kg).
**Range:** Over 11·5 miles (18·5 km).

# Paveway

This code-name identifies the largest and most diverse programme in history aimed at increasing the accuracy of tactical air-to-surface weapons. Begun with the establishment of a Paveway programme office at Wright-Patterson AFB in 1966, this USAF effort linked more than 30 separately named systems for airborne navigation, target identification and marking, all-weather/night vision, weapon guidance and many other functions, originally for the war in SE Asia. In the course of this work the "smart bombs" with laser guidance managed by the Arma-

**Above:** *Two frames from a TI film suggesting that truck drivers ought at least to get out of the cab if KMU-351 is anywhere about.*

ment Development and Test Center at Eglin AFB, from 1965, were developed in partnership with TI, using the latter's laser guidance kit, to form an integrated family of simple precision weapons. The first TI-guided LGB was dropped in April 1965. The following year the Paveway concept was drafted, and subsequently a demonstration of a smart version of the M117 bomb showed such remarkable accuracy, despite the release point being "out of range of ground fire" (small-arms fire is implied), that by 1968 this bomb was in use in SE Asia.

By 1971 the Paveway I family of guidance units had expanded to eight, in six main types: KMU-342/B, fitted to the M117 750 lb (340 kg) GP bomb; KMU-351A/B, fitted to the Mk 84 2,000 lb (907 fitted to the Mk 84 2,000 lb (907 kg) GP bomb, in high- and low-speed versions; KMU-370B/B, fitted to the M118 3,000 lb (1361 kg) demolition bomb; KMU-388A/B, fitted to the Mk 82 Snakeye 500 lb (227 kg) GP bomb,

**Above:** *This A-10A Thunderbolt II has Paveway munitions with high aspect ratio control fins. Note cannon firing.*

in high- and low-speed (high-drag) versions; KMU-420/B, fitted to the Rockeye Mk 20 Mod 2 500 lb (227 kg) cluster munition; and KMU-421/B (Pave Storm), fitted to the SUU-54/B 2,000 lb (907 kg) cluster munition. Subsequently the Paveway family was refined to exclude KMU-342 and -420, and -421/B was switched to the US Navy and Marine Corps Mk 83 1,000 lb (454 kg) GP bomb. In 1978 tests were still continuing on Pave Storm cluster munitions of the GBU-2 type.

All these bombs are extremely simple to carry, requiring no aircraft modification or electrical connection; they are treated as a round of ordnance and loaded like a free-fall bomb. Carrier aircraft have included the A-1, A-4, A-6, A-7, A-10, A-37, F-4, F-5, F-16, F-100, F-105, F-111, AV-8A, B-52 and B-57. Targets can be marked by an airborne laser, in the launch aircraft or another aircraft, or by forward troops. Like almost all Western military lasers the matched wavelength is 1·064 microns, the usual lasers (in Pave Knife, Pave Tack or various other airborne pods) being of the Nd/YAG type.

In all cases the guidance unit is the same, the differences being confined to attachments and the various enlarged tail fins.

**Left above:** *British 1,000 lb bomb with Paveway seeker head on XW986, one of the MoD (RAF) special carry-trials Buccaneer aircraft.*

**Left:** *One of the General Dynamics F-16A development prototypes with two Paveway bombs—probably KMU-351s.*

The silicon detector array is divided into four quadrants and is mounted on the nose of a free universal-jointed housing with an annular ring tail. As the bomb falls this aligns itself with the airstream, in other words the direction of the bomb's motion. The guidance computer receives signals from the quadrants and drives four control fins to equalize the four outputs. Thus, the sensor unit is kept pointing at the source of laser light, so that the bomb will impact at the same point. Electric power is provided by a thermal battery, energised at the moment of release, and power to drive the fins comes from a hot-gas generator.

Users include all US services, the Imperial Iranian Air Force, Saudi Arabia (chiefly KMU-370), and several other customers including the Royal Air Force for use on British 1,000 lb (454 kg) bombs carried by Buccaneers and Jaguars. Total production of Paveway guidance units has been very large; in the early 1970s output was at roughly 20,000 per year, at a unit price of some $2,500. Data are as for the original bombs plus about 6 in (152 mm) length and 30 lb (13·6 kg); the guidance package is 40 in (1·01 m) long but most of this is countered by reduced tail length on the other end of the bomb. Also in this series is KMU-353A/B, a Mk 84 with EO or IR guidance which looks slightly different and increases weight to 2,247 lb (1019 kg).

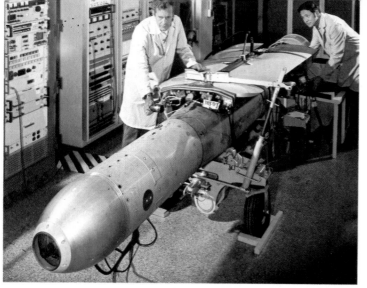

# Hobos

Even more versatile and diverse in form than the Paveway smart bombs, Hobos (HOming BOmb System) has since 1966 been the largest programme at Rockwell International's Missile Systems Division in Columbus, Ohio. Like Paveway it comprises a series of add-on modules attached to standard "iron bombs" of various kinds. At first these conferred only a precision-guidance capability, but today fur-

**Left: Hughes Aircraft engineers test a GBU-15(V), with wings aft, before it flew from a B-52 in November 1977 at WSMR.**

ther modules add extended stand-off range. The objective has been to achieve a direct hit with every bomb, whilst minimising exposure to enemy defences.

The original Hobos comprised either of two GP bombs, the Mk 84 of 2,000 lb (907 kg) or the M118 of 3,000 lb (1361 kg), with a guidance section on the nose, control section at the rear and an interconnect assembly tying the missile together. The guidance section was usually of the EO type, consisting of optics and an image-contrast tracker all mounted on a gyro-stabilized platform. For night and all-weather use TV and IR seekers were later developed, in 1969–72, in both cases with the unit on a stabilized platform, the IR seeker having a cryogenic re-

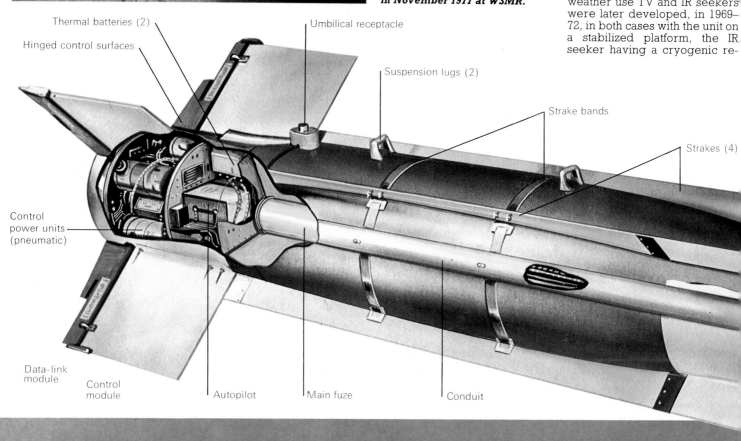

Thermal batteries (2)

Hinged control surfaces

Umbilical receptacle

Suspension lugs (2)

Strake bands

Strakes (4)

Control power units (pneumatic)

Data-link module

Control module

Autopilot

Main fuze

Conduit

frigeration system. The tail control section included four fins and pneumatically driven control flaps, autopilot to translate guidance signals into pitch/yaw steering commands, and an electric battery. Along the sides of the central bomb were four aerodynamic strakes, an electrical conduit on the right side and a top umbilical receptacle, all linked by two encircling strake bands. Total system cost is about $13,000.

This first Hobos generation went into action in SE Asia in 1969, and when properly used consistently demonstrated a CEP in the order of "a few feet". The basic EOGB (Electro-Optically Guided Bomb) required the pilot to acquire the target visually, align it in his gunsight (the carrier aircraft invariably being an F-4) and lock-on the chosen missile seeker by positioning the target precisely in the cross-

**Below: Cutaway of basic Hobos with Mk 84 bomb and EO nose package.**

hair gate of the monitor screen in the cockpit. After verifying the lock, the pilot released the missile and at once turned away to search for a fresh target. In theory there was no need to enter the AAA defence perimeter.

The next stage was to perfect the TV and IR all-weather guidance systems, and research further systems using DME radio navigation, anti-radiation homing, LLLTV, area correlation homing and various multi-mode systems, most of them as portions of the USAF Pave Strike defence-suppression programme. While this was being done, in 1972-8, quite different work by Rockwell increased the number of bomb payloads and added two new sets of wing modules to enable the missile to glide considerable distances more than matching the increased reach of potential hostile SAM systems. The winged missiles form a family of stand-off weapons all designated GBU-15(V).

The range of bomb payloads for GBU-15(V) will eventually number at least six, including FAE devices, an HSM (hard-structure munition) and the SUU-54 bomblet dispenser. The first stand-off modification kit, by Celesco Industries, comprises large cruciform rear wings and forward fins, indexed in line, to produce the Cruciform-Wing Weapon (CWW), designated GBU-15(V) EOGB II. This is a direct-attack missile, with modest increase in horizontal range; its main purpose is to increase manoeuvrability at low altitudes. When carrying an HSM the CWW can have four rocket motors on the tips of the rear wings to increase impact velocity. The longest-ranged EOGB, which in mid-1978 was still completing development, is the Planar-Wing Weapon (PWW), designated GBU-15(V) MGGB II (Modular Guided Glide Bomb). This has a smaller set of tail wings but a large dorsal fairing from which left and right long-span wings flip out after release. A ventral fin is also usually added under the nose. In most PWW flight testing in 1978 mid-course DME was used to bring the missile near enough to the target for EO homing to take over for the terminal phase. In 1978-9 further work is examining laser guidance (Rockwell tri-Service seeker), Loran guidance, homing-on-jamming, inertial guidance and radiometric area-correlation techniques. Carriers include the F-4E (two GBU-15 plus data-link pod, also used by Israel), F-111F (four plus pod and Pave Tack FLIR/laser pod) and B-52D (three plus pod). Data are for the original Hobos EOGBs, called SWW (Small-Wing Weapons).

**Dimensions:** Length (Mk 84) 149 in (3·78 m), (M118) 146 in (3·71 m); diameter (84) 18 in (457 mm), (118) 24 in (610 mm); span (84) 44 in (1·12 m), (118) 52 in (1·32 m).
**Launch weight:** (84) 2,240 lb (1016 kg), (118) 3,404 lb (1544 kg).
**Range:** A little further than free-fall.

**Inset left: Mk 84 Hobos with EO guidance on pylon of a fully swept F-111.**

**Left: Weapon of Hobos family, with larger wings, heads for a dummy radar target, apparently simulating Fan Song E.**

**Above: Life gets tough for the former DE-644 as it takes a direct hit from a Condor with live warhead on 4 February 1971. This was on the China Lake sea range.**

# Condor

This powerful ASM for Navy carrier-based aircraft resulted from a 1962 requirement, RFPs being issued in 1964 and Rockwell being selected in July 1966. Propelled to Mach 2·9 by an end-burning Rocketdyne Mk 70 solid motor, Condor had four delta wings and four rear control fins, and guidance involving mid-course command/computer and autopilot and terminal homing by TV, with dual-mode radar/EO as an alternative. Despite having a range of 68 miles (110 km) and a 630 lb (286 kg) 12-point linear shaped-charge warhead, the whole programme was cancelled in September 1976 after development had virtually been completed and a Turbo-Condor cruise missile was in prospect.

**Below: A China Lake A-6A Intruder trials aircraft pictured in 1971 with Rockwell's AGM-53B Condor aboard. Like Germany's Jumbo, this would have been a hard-hitting missile had its development been completed.**

# Maverick

Smallest of the fully guided or self-homing ASMs for US use, AGM-65 Maverick was approved in 1965 and, following competition with Rockwell, Hughes won the programme in June 1968. Since then an initial 17,000-missile package has been fulfilled, in 1975, and production has continued at reduced rate on later versions. The basic missile, usually carried in triple clusters under the wings of the F-4, F-15, F-16, A-7, A-10 and Swedish AJ37A Viggen, and singly by the F-5 and the BGM-34 RPV, has four delta wings of very low aspect ratio, four tail controls immediately behind the wings, and a Thiokol TX-481 dual-thrust solid motor.

In mid-1978 virtually all Mavericks in service were of the AGM-65A variety, of which 19,000 were delivered to the USAF and to the air forces of Greece, Iran, Israel, South Korea, Saudi Arabia, Sweden and Turkey. Many other countries have orders pending. The pilot selects a missile, causing its gyro to run up to speed and light a cockpit indicator. The pilot then visually acquires the target, depresses his uncage switch to remove the protective cover from the missile nose, and activates the video circuitry. The TV picture at once appears on a bright display in the cockpit, and the pilot then either slews the video seeker in the missile or else lines up the target in his own gunsight. He depresses the track switch, waits until the cross-hairs on the TV display are aligned on the target, releases the switch and fires the round. Homing is automatic, and the launch aircraft at once escapes from the area. Unguided flights began in September 1969, and on the first guided test three months later a direct hit was scored on a tank. Subsequently AGM-65A has been launched at all heights down to treetop level. In the 1973 Yom Kippur war it was used operationally, in favourable conditions. It requires good visibility, and even in mid-1978 the occasional $37,000 A-model breaks its TV lock and misses its target – for example, because of overwater glint.

AGM-65B, Scene-Magnification Maverick, has new optics, a stronger gimbal mount and revised electronics. The pilot need not see the target, but instead can search with the seeker and cockpit display which presents an enlarged and clearer picture. Thus he can identify the target, lock-on and fire much quicker and from a greater slant range. Approximately 7,000 B-series missiles were delivered, the last in April 1978. AGM-65C Laser Maverick is for close-air support against laser-designated targets, the lasers being the infantry ILS-NT200 or the airborne Pave Knife, Pave Penny, Pave Spike, Pave Tack or non-US systems. Flight testing began in January 1977, using the mass-produced Rockwell tri-Service seeker used in such other missiles as GBU-15(V) and Hellfire. Troop training has established the method of frequency and pulse coding to tie each missile to only one air or ground designator, so that many Mavericks can simultaneously be homed on many different sources of laser radiation. The USAF will probably buy AGM-65C in 1979 for use from Pave Tack F-4 and F-111F aircraft, while both the USAF and RAF may match this missile to Pave Spike in earlier F-4s and Buccaneers. Westinghouse is flight-testing Pave Spike with the Minneapolis-Honeywell helmet sight for single-seat aircraft such as the F-16 and Viggen.

In May 1977 engineering development began on AGM-65D IR-Maverick, with the Hughes IIR tri-Service seeker planned for GBU-15(V) and ER/DL Walleye II. Considerably more expensive than other versions, the IIR seeker – especially when slaved to an aircraft-mounted sensor such as FLIR, a laser pod or the APR-38 radar warning system – enables the Maverick to lock-on at least twice the range otherwise possible in north-west Europe in mist, rain or at night. Of course, it also distinguishes between "live targets" and

**Right upper:** *This pylon on a slatted F-4E was photographed in January 1978 with a regular AGM-65A and one of the new IIR (imaging infra-red) rounds.*

**Right:** *Standard AGM-65A on an A-7D Corsair II.*

"hulks". Using the centroid seeker in place of the original edge-lock optics, AGM-65D was tested from an F-4 in Germany in poor weather in January-March 1978. While Hughes continues to produce the common centre and aft missile sections, delay with the laser-seeker C-version means that possibly AGM-65D may get into pilot production first, in 1980.

All present Mavericks have the same 130 lb (59 kg) conical shaped-charge warhead, but different warheads are in prospect. The Mk 19 250 lb (113 kg) blast/fragmentation head is preferred by the Navy, giving capability against small ships as well as hard land targets, and may be fitted to C and D versions with new fuzing/arming and a 4 in (102 mm) increase in length. Another warhead weighs 300 lb (136 kg), while in December 1976 the Air Force expressed a need for a nuclear warhead. Data are for AGM-65A.

**Dimensions:** Length 97 in (2·46 m); diameter 12 in (305 mm); span 28 in (711 mm).
**Launch weight:** 462 lb (209·5 kg).
**Range:** 14 miles (22·5 km).

# Night Attack Missile

Not yet given a DoD designation, this is a US Navy study for a Maverick with a Raytheon non-imaging IR seeker. Much cheaper than AGM-65D, the seeker would be slaved to ships or other targets at long range by an air-craft FLIR. Trials from A-6 and A-7 aircraft began in 1977.

# Harpoon

As described on p. 82 most Harpoons ordered by 1978 are of the RGM-84 ship- and submarine-launched type, but the Navy and a growing number of foreign customers also intend to deploy an AGM-84A air-launched version. This is almost identical to the basic missile except for deletion of the tandem boost motor and launch capsule. Small differences are needed to interface mechanically and electrically to the aircraft, which will include the A-6, A-7, P-2, P-3, F-16 (Norway) and other aircraft for customers not announced by mid-1978. The first AGM-84A development round was dropped from a P-3C at 20,000 ft (6096 m) in May 1972, and powered flights began two months later. On 20 December 1972 an extremely successful test was made with a guided round ending in the pop-up terminal manoeuvre and a direct hit on USS *Ingersoll*. AGM-84A has been delayed like the other versions, but full-rate production has been started, and the weapon was cleared for service in the course in 1978. Meanwhile the NWC is working on an IIR seeker for the AGM version, captive flight trials being due to begin in 1979.

**Dimensions:** As for RGM-84A except length 12 ft 7 in (3·84 m).
**Launch weight:** 1,160 lb (526 kg).
**Range:** Approximately 68 miles (109 km).

**Left:** *AGM-84A Harpoon launch from a China Lake A-7 with three frames from high-speed film showing target impact of a different missile on the USS Ingersoll off Point Mugu.*

**Above and below:** *The first AGM-84A pictured on the wing pylon of a US Navy P-3 Orion and immediately after release in May 1972. Another launch platform is the S-3A Viking.*

**Main picture:** *Frame from high-speed cine film taken in March 1970 showing the first launch of AGM-65A Maverick from a special test F-4E. Inset, left, are two frames from another film taken by a remote-control camera near the target.*

# AIR TO SURFACE MISSILES

This important group of missiles has little in common with those of the preceding section. They were not developed to increase accuracy but to allow aircraft to hit targets that they otherwise could not reach at all. Of course, some of today's ASM Strategic missiles have such a long range that they offer a considerable extension to a carrier aircraft's radius of action; in fact it would be possible to hit many strategic targets with a missile released over the bomber's home airfield. The crux of the matter is what can be termed "penetrability". If this is lacking, the warhead never reaches the target, but is shot down en route.

It is not difficult to see how problematical was the penetrability of such propeller-driven bombers as the B-29 and B-36 in the decade following World War 2. While such aids as jet engines (to increase over-target speed and altitude) and even small piloted fighters released from the bomb bay (to fend off defending fighters) appeared to offer some improvement in ability to reach the target and return, a better answer appeared to be the development of ASMs that could cover the last and most dangerous part of the mission by themselves. This would allow the bomber to "stand off" at a safer distance, and so the missiles were sometimes called stand-off bombs.

The range required of these early weapons, such as Rascal and Blue Steel, was modest and related to the expected defences around major cities and similar strategic targets; but the sheer bulk and mass of the early nuclear weapons was so great that the missiles were correspondingly large, and not even the biggest bombers could carry more than one missile. By the mid-1950s the size of nuclear warheads was being reduced dramatically, and for several years concentration was focussed on the ALBM (air-launched ballistic missile). This offered two advantages. It enabled bombers to launch strategic missiles of unrivalled penetrability, apparently as "unstoppable" as the newly developed ICBMs and carrying similar re-entry vehicles and warheads, and – by looking at the problem from a different angle – promised to reduce the vulnerability of the ballistic missiles in time of crisis by lifting them away from fixed launch sites and repositioning them in unknown places within stratospheric regions covering some ten million square miles (26 m km²). Thus, no enemy could hope to knock out a nation's deterrent capability in a "pre-emptive first-strike" because he could not find the ALBMs, let alone hit them.

In the crisis-torn late 1950s and early 1960s USAF Strategic Air Command spent many millions of dollars in maintaining a large round-the-clock airborne alert which was extremely tough on crews and, especially, fatigue-prone airframes. Its only ASM was the winged Hound Dog, which apart from being much smaller did not offer much advance in penetrability over the monster B-52. The planned ALBM, Skybolt, went through all the phases of study, research, design, development and flight test, and was finally cancelled in an unprecedented political situation which knocked the whole British deterrent – based totally upon this US missile – into a cocked hat. President Kennedy described the ALBM as "in a sense the kind of engineering that is beyond us" which both then and today seemed sheer nonsense. The reason for abandoning this ALBM was simply because, at the time, the 1,000-missile Minuteman force appeared to be able to withstand any Soviet pre-emptive attack and still hit back with devastating force; President Kennedy also asked "How many times do you need to kill an enemy?" Today the situation has been overturned by the gigantic Soviet ICBM build-up, with accuracy high enough to hit individual Minuteman silos. So there is once more an urgent need for an air-launched strategic missile.

Today Hound Dog has been pensioned off, and there is only one Western missile in this category actually operational. This is SRAM, Short-Range Attack Missile, which demonstrates the amazing progress made in miniaturizing high-yield nuclear weapons. Said to have a radar signature "similar to that of a rifle bullet", and thus to be the most penetrable strategic weapon at present in use, SRAM was developed mainly to hit potential enemy SAM sites and other terminal-area defences. Small enough for a B-52 to carry 20, this missile is supposed to open the way for the penetration of manned bombers, which then use SRAMs or free-fall bombs on the relatively unprotected targets. On paper SRAM appears to be a most important and highly penetrable weapon, but it was designed to fit into a traditional "countervalue" scenario in which bombers attack cities. SRAM was not designed for use against hardened ICBM silos, which are the things causing most urgent concern to the United States. On the other hand this missile would almost certainly be effective against the Soviet Union's extensive ABM systems.

The present position of the United States, and thus the whole Western alliance, is unpredictably precarious. With the single exception of the SLBM (submarine-launched ballistic-missile) system, the whole deterrent has been degraded almost to the point where it ceases to deter. With the ICBMs vulnerable to a pre-emptive first-strike and the modern B-1 bomber cancelled, the absence of a long-range ASM becomes very serious indeed, because, even with SRAMs and numerous penaids to help it, the B-52 is almost Heaven's gift to modern defence systems. When he terminated B-1 as a production bomber President Carter said the main factor permitting this was "the recent evolution of the cruise missile". He explained that, armed with cruise missiles, the old B-52G and H would be able to continue in service "well into the 1980s".

This renewed interest in the cruise missile is one of the strangest and potentially most dangerous things ever to happen to the Western Alliance. Nobody would deny that it is today possible to build cruise missiles better than their predecessors, but the differences are only of degree, and the degrees are small. So one wonders what all the fuss is about. To claim that the cruise missile was "not envisaged" when the B-1 was designed is as ridiculous as the suggestion that the US could not build an ALBM. In the absence of an explanation, the hailing of the cruise missile as a wonder weapon must be suspect.

We have today a situation in which the entire air deterrence of the West is planned to devolve upon whichever of two cruise missiles wins a current 1979 series of competitive evaluations. These are being conducted with real AGM-109 and AGM-86B missiles flying real missions but only against simulated Soviet defences.

The USAF has talked of its "confidence" in a "4,000-round mass attack" with cruise missiles, and of thus overwhelming the Soviet defences, but with such talk it risks losing whatever credibility it has left; a 4,000-round attack would use up almost twice as many cruise missiles as the USAF plans to buy.

The nub of the matter is how well the cruise missile can penetrate. Essentially today's cruise missile is like a "V-1" but a little faster and cleverer. It does not have to fly straight and level, and it could carry extensive penaids, though of course only at the expense of fuel or payload. How well would it show up on ground or airborne radars? The answer, unless someone has found new laws of physics, is "very well indeed, from most aspects". Would it be difficult to shoot down? Again, the answer can only be "no". No matter whether it comes in at 30,000 ft (9144 m) or tree-top height, the cruise missile remains not a supernatural thing but just a small aeroplane, cruising at a modest Mach 0·7 or about 525 mph (845 km/h). Though I have no doubt the West would be hard-put to afford even a token force of B-1s, I think that would be preferable to

planned "mass attacks" by cruise missiles – unless the US Administration can find some enemies who lack air defence.

It is planned that both USAF cruise missiles will have the same guidance system, though with differences in packaging and interfacing. The basis will be inertial, with a drift of about 2,950 ft (900 m) per hour. Even on a full-range mission of some 2,000 miles (3200 km) this would only mean an error of some $2\frac{1}{2}$ miles ($3\frac{1}{2}$ km), which could be accepted in countervalue attacks. But for counterforce missions the accuracy must be of a totally different order, and both Tercom and scene-matching can be used to update and refine the inertial guidance to give a final CEP of considerably less than 330 ft (100 m). Tercom was explained in the introduction on page 85, and though fraught with difficulties appears to be working reliably in tests with manned aircraft and RPVs. Of course there is no way a Western observer without access to classified information can verify performance of Tercom in missions over virgin territory previously surveyed only by reconnaissance satellite, but the results must by now be fairly well understood. Scene-matching resembles the terminal radar area-correlation used in the tactical Pershing II to give pinpoint accuracy. The cruise missile would then compare the actual scene beneath with images stored in its computer memory, and in theory pick out the prescribed target.

This discussion ought not to be concluded without commenting on the way Western judgement may possibly be distorted by the fact that the Western democracies are an open society. We are free to discuss all manner of weapon programmes that are either still being developed or have not yet even been tested. Pershing II, for example, is not only not in use but had not, as these words are written in 1978, even been built. The much-vaunted cruise missiles barely exist, and no matter how well or how badly they show up in the 1979 tests against simulated defences – and one fervently hopes the defences will not have more than one hand tied behind their back – they will not get into operational service for several more years. In contrast, virtually all the Soviet weapon systems in this book are in full service, and the rest are either phased out as obsolete or are in advanced flight-test (which is how the West knows about them). Now that Americans plan an ASALM much more formidable than the slow, wing-lifted cruise missiles on which such immense responsibilities appear to rest, we ought not to forget that on the evidence available to us this is another area where the West is in second place.

# FRANCE

## ALCM

In a public address in March 1977 the former chief of the presidential defence staff, Gen Gau Méry, stated that France was developing both a strategic cruise missile and a military satellite whose functions would include missile guidance. Later the satellite was identified as Défense 1, for launch in 1985, and the cost of the cruise-missile programme was estimated at Fr $3 \times 10^9$ ($675 million). By mid-1978 there was no hint of any collaborative programme with friendly nations.

# USSR

## AS-1 Kennel

This was the first ASM to be seen in Soviet service, and from about 1957 large numbers were deployed by the AV-MF (Naval Air Force), the usual carrier being the Tu-16 Badger with one missile under each wing. The missile, whose true designation is not known despite its having been in service since 1960 in Egypt, Indonesia and possibly the PRC, has the appearance of a miniature fighter and may have been designed by Col-Gen Artem Mikoyan's aircraft collective. Features include a small turbojet with straight-through ducting (a likely engine is the RD-500, derived from the British R-R Derwent and rated at 3,527 lb, 1600 kg thrust), tailplane well up the large fin, swept wings with two fences on each side, and radomes pointing both fore and aft. Though the Tu-16 has two large radars under the nose in the anti-shipping missile-platform role, it is not thought able to identify and lock-on targets at the range quoted for this missile. The inference has been that the missile was launched in the general direction of a known target, flying on autopilot and possibly steered from time to time by radio command either from the launch platform or from another aircraft, possibly at lower level but closer to the target. At a distance of the order of 19 miles (30 km) the missile's own seeker, either an active radar or passive seeker, would lock-on to the target and home the weapon on to it. The carrier aircraft was designated Badger B by NATO; when the Kennel missile was judged no longer operational in 1971 this designation was eliminated. Indonesian Tu-16s and Kennels are in storage. A coast-defence version is Samlet (p. 28).

**Dimensions:** Length 27 ft (8·23 m); span 16 ft (4·9 m).
**Launch weight:** About 6,600 lb (3000 kg).
**Range:** Estimated at 62 to 93 miles (100–150 km).

## AS-2 Kipper

First seen at the 1961 Soviet Aviation Day display, this large ASM has a more advanced aeroplane configuration than AS-1 and is considerably larger, the Tu-16 Badger-C carrying one missile on the centreline recessed into the weapon bay. Propulsion is by a single turbojet, possibly a Lyulka AL-5 of 11,023 lb (5000 kg) thrust, in a short pod underslung at the rear. In appearance this missile faintly resembles Hound Dog, but is utterly different in mission, it being intended to attack moving targets with large radar signatures. Guidance probably duplicates that of AS-1, the new missile merely increasing flight performance and payload; the warhead is conventional and very large. Cruising speed has generally been estimated at Mach 1·2, at high altitude, with a final dive on target at over Mach 2.

**Dimensions:** Length 31 ft (9·4 m); span 16 ft (4·9 m).
**Launch weight:** In the region of 11,000 lb (5000 kg).
**Range:** Estimated at 132 miles (212 km).

## AS-3 Kangaroo

This missile was also disclosed at the 1961 Soviet Aviation Day display, when one was carried low overhead by a Tu-20 (Tu-95) Bear bomber. This particular installation was probably a full-scale model to prove aircraft compatibility; the vehicle lacked many features seen in the actual missile, and a streamlined white nose appeared to be a temporary fairing forming part of the aircraft. This fairing is absent from some of the so-called Bear B and C carrier aircraft, many, if not all, of which belong to the AV-MF, the Soviet Naval Air Force. The missile is aerodynamically similar to Mach 2 fighters of the mid-1950s, and could well have been based on the Ye-2A Faceplate by the Mikoyan bureau. This was powered by a Tumansky R-11 two-shaft afterburning turbojet rated at 11,244 lb (5100 kg), and this fits the missile perfectly. AS-3 has exactly the same wing, circular nose inlet, small conical centrebody, long instrument boom at the bottom of the nose, identical aerodynamic controls and the same fuselage structure, and the ventral fin at the rear resembles that of the earlier Mikoyan Ye-50 prototype. The tips of the tailplane have anti-flutter pods similar to those flown on the MiG-19 fighter but not fitted to Ye-2. AS-3 is commonly described as "operational since 1960" but was not seen in service until 1963. The main puzzle is how it steers itself to its target, because though it is easy to see how radio command/autopilot guidance could carry it up to 180 miles (290 km) from the launch aircraft, despite cruising at Mach 2 with full afterburner, the ultimate range is put by the DoD at 350 n.m., or 404 miles (650 km), far beyond the visual horizon and implying subsonic cruise. A nuclear warhead is assumed, and this suggests inertial or preprogrammed guidance against cities, ports and similar large fixed targets. In 1978 a few of these giant ASMs were thought still to be operational.

**Dimensions:** Length 49 ft 1 in (14·96 m); span 22 ft 6½ in (9·00 m).
**Launch weight:** About 22,045 lb (10 000 kg).
**Range:** Full payload to 404 miles (650 km).

*Below: Frame from Soviet propaganda film showing AS-1 dropping from right wing of Tu-16 "Badger B"; belly radar was not always present.*

*Below right: Excellent shot from the same film showing release of an AS-3, the world's largest-ever production ASM, from "Bear C".*

## AS-4 Kitchen

Yet another disclosure at the 1961 Soviet Aviation Day flypast was this much more advanced and highly supersonic ASM, carried recessed under the fuselage of one of the ten Tu-22 Blinder supersonic bomber/reconnaissance aircraft that took part. This aircraft, dubbed Blinder B by NATO, had a larger nose radome, and other changes, as have several other Tu-22s seen in released photographs. Most aircraft of this sub-type have the outline of the AS-4 missile visible on their multi-folding weapon-bay doors, but the missile appears seldom to be carried today and in any case most remaining Tu-22s are of other versions, serving with the ADD and AV-MF. The missile itself has slender-delta wings, a cruciform tail and, almost certainly, a liquid-propellant rocket. Prolonged discussion in the West has failed to arrive at any degree of certainty concerning the guidance, though the general consensus is that it must be inertial, possibly with mid-course updating by a Tu-95 or other platform. A homing system is obviously needed for moving targets such as ships. Both versions of the swing-wing Tu-26 Backfire multi-role platform are believed to have carried this missile, probably in AV-MF service.

**Dimensions:** Length about 37 ft (11·3 m); span about 8 ft (2·4 m).
**Launch weight:** About 15,432 lb (7000 kg).
**Range:** Probably about 186 miles (300 km), cruising at about Mach 2.

## AS-5 Kelt

First seen in a released photograph of September 1968, showing one of these missiles under the wing of a Tu-16, AS-5 is based on the airframe of AS-1 and some may even be rebuilds. In place of the turbojet and nose-to-tail duct there is a rocket with extensive liquid-propellant tankage. In the nose is a large radome. Superficially the nose and underbody fairing appear to be identical to those of SS-N-2 Styx (p. 79) and AS-5 thus is credited with the same choice of active radar or passive IR homing, having cruised to the vicinity of the target on autopilot, with initial radio-com-

mand corrections. By the early 1970s deliveries are thought to have exceeded 1,000, all of them carried by the so-called Badger G. This launch platform has the same pylons as the Badger B, and the broad nose radome of Badger C. In the early 1970s about 35 of these aircraft, plus missiles, were supplied to the Egyptian air force, possibly with Soviet crews and specialist tradesmen. In the Yom Kippur war in October 1973 about 25 missiles were launched against Israeli targets. According to the Israelis 20 were shot down en route, at least one by an F-4; five penetrated the defences. A supply dump was one of the targets hit, but at least two AS-5s homed automatically on to the emissions from Israeli radar stations. All the missiles were released at medium height of some 29,528 ft (9000 m), reaching a speed of about Mach 0·95; in the denser air at low level speed fell to about 0·85.

**Dimensions:** Length about 32 ft 1 in (9·78 m); span 15 ft 7 in (4·75 m).
**Launch weight:** About 10,580 lb (4800 kg).
**Range:** Widely reported to reach 200 miles (320 km).

## AS-6 Kingfish

At first thought to be a development of AS-4, this completely new missile gradually was reassessed as the first Soviet ASM publicly known that offers precision guidance over intercontinental ranges. It is still largely an enigma in the West, but is believed to have a very large fuselage with pointed nose, low-aspect-ratio delta wings and quite small aircraft-type tail controls. Propulsion is almost certainly by an advanced integral ram-rocket, and key features of AS-6 are much higher flight performance and dramatically better accuracy than any previous Soviet ASM. It clearly reflects vast advances in inertial guidance and nuclear-warhead design, and it is generally believed to possess terminal homing, either by active radar, area-correlation or some passive method. Development appears to have been protracted, and though reported prior to 1972 was still not in wide service in 1975, though by 1977 it was carried under the wings of both the Tu-16 (sub-type unknown) and Tu-26 Backfire. User services certainly include the AV-MF and possibly the ADD. Launched at about 36,000 ft (10,973 m) the missile climbs rapidly to about 59,000 ft (17 983 m) for cruise at about Mach 3. It finally dives on its target, the warhead yield being estimated at 200 kT.

**Dimensions:** Length in the region of 35 ft (10·7 m); span about 8 ft (2·4 m).
**Launch weight:** In the neighbourhood of 11,000 lb (5000 kg).
**Range:** Varies from about 404 miles (650 km) at high altitude to 155 miles (250 km) at sea level.

*Above: Though typically fuzzy, this Soviet photograph of a low-flying "Blinder B" appears to show a light on the left wing-tip of its AS-4 (three-view, right).*

*Below left: One of the few good photographs of AS-2 Kipper, as formerly carried by the Tu-16 version called "Badger C".*

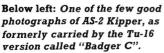

*Left above: Egyptian Tu-16 "Badger G" carrying AS-5 missiles with nose nadomes and tail-warning radar.*

*Left: Tu-16 version, probably to be dubbed "Badger H", with AS-6 under left wing. Note aileron deflection to fly level.*

*Below: Provisional AS-6 Kingfish.*

# UK

# Blue Boar

Though a free-fall bomb this was strategic in nature, because its largest size was for use by RAF Bomber Command against the most important targets. Again quoting the C-in-C of that command, Sir Hugh Lloyd said during a 1950 exercise "The sooner we get away from the free-falling bomb business the better". At that time the RAE was studying the problem at Farnborough and Vickers-Armstrongs (Aircraft) at Weybridge was working as a private venture on a guided bomb with a Smiths autopilot and EMI TV camera in its nose. In 1951 this was ordered to meet November 1947 Specification 1059, with codename Blue Boar. Unlike other strategic air to surface missiles, Blue Boar was designed for internal stowage, with flip-out cruciform wings of very low aspect ratio. By June 1954 Blue Boar had actually made fully guided trials at Woomera after release from a Valiant. The Vickers Guided Weapons Department had then become a mature organization with large facilities in England and at Salisbury, S Australia. In that month, after expenditure of £3·2 million and with the weapon almost ready for production in several sizes, the programme was abruptly cancelled.

# Blue Steel

Officially described as a "stand-off bomb", this large ASM was

*Below: Slow fly-past with airbrakes out by a Vulcan B.2 with Blue Steel in 1961. The anti-flash white gave way to low-level camouflage in 1964.*

started as a full engineering programme in 1954, in parallel with continuing studies on free-fall guided bombs and other weapons. Strongly influenced by the USAF Rascal (opposite), it was the principal project at the Weapons Research Division of A. V. Roe at Woodford and used the same technology as Avro's Type 730 supersonic bomber. Features of this technology included canard configuration, with delta foreplanes and ailerons on short-span rear wings (in the case of the missile also of delta shape and with down-swept tips), and a structure skinned in stainless-steel honeycomb sandwich. Propulsion was by an Armstrong Siddeley (later Bristol Siddeley and finally Rolls-Royce) Stentor rocket engine with superimposed thrust chambers of grossly dissimilar sizes burning HTP/kerosene. Guidance, with Elliott Brothers (later

Elliott-Automation and then Easams) as prime contractor, was ambitiously inertial and linked to the navigation system of the bomber for continual updating to the point of release. Subsequently Blue Steel could fly any desired trajectory or flight path at Mach 2 making doglegs or evasive manoeuvres and approaching the target at any flight level from 80,000 ft (24 384 m) down. The warhead was a thermonuclear device in the 1 MT range.

Launch of the programme was entirely a private venture by Avro, at first with Hawker Siddeley Group funding, though MoS cover was obtained in 1955 to specification. In this year the first two-fifths-scale aerodynamic models were flown, and in 1957 a full-scale vehicle was flown with control. A year later a Valiant released a Blue Steel test vehicle powered by a de Havilland Double Spectre, and several

*Below: Skilled RAF tradesmen service Blue Steels, festooned with ground power supplies, at Waddington (probably 83 Sqn) around 1963.*

of these flew with full tanks at the WRE at Woomera. Definitive missiles were tested in 1959, and in June 1962 IOC was achieved with Vulcan B.2 carriers of 617 Sqn, each aircraft carrying one missile recessed into the belly. Subsequently Blue Steel was operational with Vulcans of 27 and 83 Sqns and Victor B.2 aircraft of 139 Sqn (February 1964) and finally 100 Sqn. From 1965 some effort was expended in improving penetrability, providing for release at low level, and in increasing range or penaid payload. The missile was withdrawn progressively in 1973–5. A series of developed versions, including a turbojet low-level missile, the Mk 1* with doubled range, and the four-ramjet Mk 2 to specification 1159, were all abandoned.

**Dimensions:** (Mk 1 missile) Length 34 ft 9 in (10·59 m); diameter 67¾ in (1·72 m); span 12 ft 11 in (3·94 m).
**Launch weight:** 15,000 lb (6804 kg).
**Range:** 200 miles (322 km); much less with low-level release, and varied with engine programme.

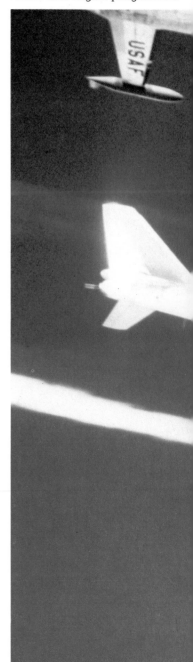

# USA

## Rascal

Despite the world lead of the USAAF with jet strategic bombers at the end of World War 2 there was doubt that such aircraft could unfailingly penetrate all defences. Accordingly in 1946 a contract was placed with Bell Aircraft Corporation at Buffalo, the builder of the XS-1 pioneer supersonic aircraft, for study of the world's first supersonic strategic ASM. In 1949–53 Bell flew several Shrike test vehicles, followed by the definitive XB-63 Rascal in 1953–7. Powered by a Bell motor with three superimposed equal-size chambers burning RFNA/JP-4, Rascal flew at Mach 1·6 and was controlled by upper and lower nose rudders, a fixed foreplane with elevators, rear wing with ailerons, and folding upper and lower rear fins. Three types of warhead, including two nuclear,

could be carried in the fuselage. Guidance was originally radio-inertial, by Federal Telecommunications and RCA, but the production GAM-63A had Bell inertial guidance. After about 40 test flights from DB-36 and DB-47 bombers, ending with four shots which achieved a 1,500 ft (457 m) CEP in 1957 at Holloman AFB, limited production was undertaken and the missile achieved IOC at Eglin on 30 October 1957. Rascal had a brief operational life, slung alongside the body of DB-47E carriers, being withdrawn in 1959 before entry to service of Hound Dog.

**Dimensions:** Length 31 ft 11½ in (9·74 m); diameter 48 in (1·22 m); span 16 ft 8¼ in (5·09 m).
**Launch weight:** 13,500 lb (6124 kg).
**Range:** 75 miles (121 km) on hi-lo profile.

*Above: Two views of Quail, in each case unfolded in the flight configuration. The B-52D was the trials aircraft.*

## Quail

First flown in 1958, McDonnell's Quail remains unique in that, though released from a bomber over hostile territory, it is not meant to hit a target. Though it has a missile designation, it is purely a carrier of ECM and its purpose is to confuse the enemy as to the strength and direction of the attacking force, its flight profile and its likely target. Powered by a 2,850 lb (1293 kg) thrust General Electric J85 turbojet, Quail has a glass-fibre airframe with wings that fold into a compact box shape to fit the rear bomb bay of a B-52. The missile, then designated GAM-72, went into service at Eglin AFB in February 1960, and the number in the SAC inventory peaked at 492 in 1962. Originally fitted to the B-52G, Quail, redesignated ADM-20A, B and C, was also issued to B-52D and H squadrons, each aircraft normally carrying two internally. In the late 1970s increasing sophistication of hostile defences, attrition and training launches gradually removed Quail from the active inventory. Plans to replace it with a more advanced missile, such as SCAD, have for 20 years failed to attract funds.

**Dimensions:** Length 12 ft 11 in (3·94 m); span (extended) 66 in (1·68 m).
**Launch weight:** 1,100 lb (499 kg).
**Range:** About 250 miles (400 km) in 30 minutes.

*Left: Rascal XGAM-63 drops from DB-47 in January 1957; inset, Bell MX-776A Shrike ignites below DB-50 in 1951.*

# Hound Dog

In the mid-1950s the USAF recognised that the B-52 heavy bomber would need help in penetrating hostile defences, and began two new programmes, Weapon System 131B for a supersonic stand-off missile carrying a thermonuclear warhead and WS-132B for one carrying ECM. In the event only WS-131 went ahead, and after a keen industry competition the programme was won in August 1957 by the Missile Development Division of North American Aviation at Downey, later to become Rockwell International whose Tulsa Division looked after the missile in its twilight years. The work helped fill the gap after cancellation of Navaho (p. 59), and the chosen configuration was derived from the Navaho test vehicle, the canard X-10. Originally designated GAM-77, the missile had small canard foreplanes, rear delta wings with ailerons, a small fin and rudder, very slim fuselage and a 7,500 lb (3402 kg) thrust Pratt & Whitney J52-6 turbojet in an underslung rear pod with variable inlet and nozzle systems to match behaviour of the non-afterburning engine to sharply contrasting Mach numbers (up to 2·1) and heights (tree-top level to 55,000 ft, 16 764 m). Carrying a 1 MT thermonuclear warhead, Hound Dog navigated by a North American Autonetics Division inertial system, linked to the aircraft navigation systems and continually updated by a Kollsman astro tracker (initially the KS-120) in the launch pylon. The first powered test vehicle flew from a converted B-52D down the Gulf Test Range on 23 April 1959, and IOC was reached at

**Main picture:** *The fifth B-52G Stratofortress was used as the compatibility trials aircraft in 1960-61.*

**Inset above:** *Another view of the same aircraft, showing two of the service-test GAM-77A Hound Dogs. Later, as AGM-28, they were camouflaged.*

Eglin in early 1961 with the first bomber designed for the missile, the B-52G. When deliveries ceased in 1963 SAC had 593 Hound Dogs. By this time GAM-77A had become AGM-28A, and the improved GAM-77B with KS-140 astro and other guidance refinements became -28B. All B-52G and H bombers were equipped with a Hound Dog pylon under each wing, the pylon staying with the missile when the latter was recycled through Tulsa for IRAN work. On takeoff the missile engines were at full power, making the bomber ten-engined; subsequently they were shut down and the missile tankage topped up from the B-52. The co-pilot started the selected missile engine a second time and other crewmembers checked updating of the guidance prior to launch. Flight profile could be high, low or any mix of dog-legs and diversions. Anti-radar and Tercom-guided models, modified from existing missiles, were dropped in 1975 and 1971 respectively, and Hound Dog was withdrawn from the SAC inventory in early 1976.

**Dimensions:** Length 42 ft 6 in (12·95 m); diameter 28 in (711 mm); span 12 ft 0 in (3·66 m).
**Launch weight:** 10,140 lb (4600 kg).
**Range:** On hi-hi profile 710 miles (1143 km).

# Skybolt

In 1958 several contractors demonstrated to the USAF, in funded study programmes, that large ballistic vehicles could be launched from strategic bombers at high altitude. The objective could be regarded either as a much faster stand-off weapon than the air-breathing winged Hound Dog or as a way to rescue a ballistic missile from the vulnerability of a fixed silo, no matter what its degree of hardening might be. In 1959 the USAF requested specific ALBM design proposals, and Douglas Aircraft, emerging from its panic on Thor, received a contract to study WS-138A, the missile being GAM-87. Douglas soon awarded subcontracts to Northrop Nortronics for guidance, Aerojet-General for propulsion and GE for the advanced RV. In February 1960 Douglas received the prime contract for full development, and drop tests of inert missiles were made over the Gulf Range in March 1961. The final model of B-52, the H, was designed to carry this dramatically new missile, with two twin pylons under the inner wings. While Boeing prepared to build

**Above:** *Eglin AFB in January 1962 and a live XGAM-87A Skybolt is about to be mated with the B-52F trials aircraft seen with Skybolt nose badge.*

102 of these fine carrier aircraft, Douglas and their team toiled to clear numerous snags. At an early stage, in March 1960, British Prime Minister Macmillan met President Eisenhower and agreed to buy Skybolt for the RAF. Blue Streak was promptly cancelled, and by July 1961 the Vulcan B.2 had completed compatibility testing with one Skybolt pylon under each wing and new avionics internally. Later in 1961 a B-52F from Eglin began dropping hot, guided missiles, with conspicuous lack of success. There is no reason to doubt that Skybolt could have been developed with complete success, but a new US administration headed by President Kennedy had reasons for eliminating it. The President's public explanation that Skybolt was "in a sense, the kind of engineering that is beyond us" just did not stand up. By sheer bad luck flight trials had scored nought out of five when McNamara got Britain to buy Polaris for sub-

in December 1967, live flights began in 1969, and IOC was reached in early 1972. Production of 1,500 AGM-69A missiles was completed in July 1975, the missile then equipping 18 SAC bases operating the B-52G and H and FB-111A.

Originally there were to be different guidance systems, Sylvania supplying a radar-homing version and an IR-homer also being required. These were not procured, and AGM-69A has only inertial guidance by Singer-Kearfott, with a Delco on-board computer to command very varied flight profiles. Four basic trajectories are: semi-ballistic; terrain-following; pull-up from "under the radar" followed by inertial dive; and combined inertial and terrain-following. The small, almost perfectly streamlined missile is said to have a radar cross-section "about as large as a bullet". The B-52 can carry eight on a rotary launcher reminiscent of a revolver cylinder in the aft bomb bay (exceptionally, and at the expense of other loads, it can carry three such launchers internally), plus two tandem triplets on each former Hound Dog pylon, modified for SRAM compatibility, a total of 20 missiles. The FB-111A can carry up to six, four on swivelling wing pylons and two internally. The bombardier selects each missile in turn, checks the updating of the KT-76 inertial guidance and lets it drop. The Lockheed Propulsion Co two-pulse solid motor accelerates it to about Mach 3, fast enough to fly and steer with body lift and three tail fins (there are no wings). Nearing the target the second propulsion stage is ignited. The W-69 warhead has a normal yield of 200 kT.

In mid-1978 about 1,300 missiles remained available to SAC's dwindling forces. AGM-69B, an improved missile with nuclear hardening throughout, the W-80 warhead, a completely new Thiokol HTPB-propellant motor and greatly increased computer memory, was almost ready for production for the B-1, which can carry 32; AGM-69B was cancelled in 1976 following discontinuance of the production programme for B-1. The remaining A-series missiles must, however, be fitted with the new Thiokol motor, because of ageing problems, and computer-memory and nuclear-hardening improvements are also projected. There is no money for production of new missiles, despite attractions of large carrier aircraft such as the 747-200F which could carry 72 internally and launch in rapid sequence.

**Dimensions:** Length with tail fairing for external carriage 190 in (4·83 m), (without fairing) 168 in (4·27 m); diameter 17½ in (444·5 mm); span, three fins at 120° each with tip 15 in (381 mm) from centreline.
**Launch weight:** 2,230 lb (1012 kg).
**Range:** 35–105 miles (56–169 km) depending on profile.

Above: *Looking up into the aft bomb bay of the aircraft pictured at left, showing loaded SRAM rotary launcher.*

Left: *USAF 60-0062 was the B-52H used for SRAM compatibility testing. Here the four external triplets are visible.*

marines instead, but on the very day the decision was taken (19 December 1961) an XGAM-87A made a full-range flight with perfect guidance. The B-52H went into service with single Hound Dog pylons and the RAF Vulcan, which with several other carriers had been sketched in forms carrying six Skybolts, bowed out to the Royal Navy.

**Dimensions:** Length with tail fairing 38 ft 3 in (11·66 m); diameter 35 in (889 mm); span (four fixed and four powered tail fins) 66 in (1·68 m).
**Launch weight:** 11,300 lb (5126 kg).
**Range:** 1,150 miles (1850 km).

# SRAM

Throughout the 1950s nuclear warheads became ever smaller, and by 1960 studies showed that a missile that could be carried by a fighter could deliver a large nuclear warhead from a range exceeding 100 miles (161 km). In the event the SRAM (Short-Range Attack Missile) has not been used by fighters, but by aircraft of SAC, primarily to neutralise potential hostile defences such as radars, SAMs and other AA systems. The adjective "short-range" has taken on a new meaning, while the compact lightweight design of this high-performance weapon multiplies in dramatic fashion the number of targets that one bomber can engage. Boeing, the final prime contractor, began SRAM studies in December 1963, ahead of the drafting of SOR-212 in 1964 which resulted in the establishment of WS-140A. A keen competition followed in 1965, with selection in November 1965 of Boeing and Martin and final choice of Boeing (now Boeing Aerospace Co) on 31 October 1966. A dummy SRAM was dropped from a B-52

# ALCM

Today potentially one of the most important weapons in the West's inventory, ALCM (Air-Launched Cruise Missile) was presented by President Carter as a new idea when he terminated B-1 as a bomber; he even said B-1 had been developed "in absence of the cruise missile factor", whose presence in 1976 made the bomber unnecessary. This is simply not true. The cruise missile never ceased to be studied from 1943, and – apart from such USAF examples as Mace and Snark – it was cruise-missile studies in 1963–66 that led to AGM-86 SCAD (Subsonic Cruise Armed Decoy) approved by DoD in July 1970. This was to be a miniature aircraft powered by a Williams WR19 turbofan, launched by a B-52 when some hundreds of miles short of major targets. Like Quail, SCAD was to confuse and dilute hostile defences; but the fact that some or all would carry nuclear warheads – by 1963 small enough to fit such vehicles – meant that SCAD could do far better than Quail. No longer could the enemy ignore the decoys and wait and see which were the bombers. Every SCAD had to be engaged, thus revealing the locations and operating frequencies of the defence sites, which could be hit by surviving SCADs, SRAMs or ARMs. SCAD was to be installationally interchangeable with SRAM, with a maximum range of around 750 miles (1207 km). SCAD ran into tough Congressional opposition, but the USAF knew what it was about and in 1972 recast the project as ALCM, retaining the designation AGM-86A. SCAD had had only a secondary attack function, but ALCM is totally a nuclear delivery vehicle, and like SRAM has the ability to multiply each bomber's targets and increase defence problems by approaching from any direction along any kind of profile. Compared with SRAM it is much easier to intercept, being larger and much slower, bit it has considerably greater range and allows the bomber to stand off at distances of at least 1,000 miles (1609 km).

The original AGM-86A ALCM was interchangeable with SRAM, so that a B-52G or H could carry eight on the internal rotary launcher plus 12 externally, and an FB-111A four externally plus two internally (though the latter aircraft has never been named as an ALCM carrier). This influenced the shape, though not to the missile's detriment, and necessitated folding or retracting wings, tail and engine air-inlet duct. Boeing, who won SCAD and carried across to ALCM without further competition, based ALCM very closely

*Right: Probably taken from the white B-52G, this AGM-86A is seen in perfect plan. Wings are about to deploy, and flame spurts from the impingement-start cartridge.*

on SCAD but increased the fuel capacity and the sophistication of the guidance, with a Litton inertial platform (finally chosen as the P-1000) and computer (4516C), updated progressively when over hostile territory by McDonnell Douglas Tercom (DPW-23). In 1976 the decision was taken to aim at maximum commonality with AGM-109 Tomahawk, but the guidance packages are not identical. The engine in both missiles is the Williams F107 of approximately 600 lb (272 kg) thrust, but in totally different versions; the ALCM engine is the F107-100, with accessories underneath and different starting system from the Dash-400 of AGM-109. The warhead is W-80, from SRAM-B.

AGM-86A first flew at WSMR on 5 March 1976. Many of the early flights failed – one undershot its target by a mile because its tankage had been under-

*Below: The very first flight of an AGM-86A, on 5 March 1976. The launch platform was a specially instrumented B-52G, since used for many further flights at WSMR.*

filled! – but by the sixth shot most objectives had been attained and 1977 was spent chiefly in improving commonality with Navy AGM-109, in preparation for something unforeseen until that year: a flyoff against AGM-109 in 1979 to decide which to buy for the B-52 force. It was commonly said Boeing were told to make AGM-86A short on range to avoid competing with the B-1. In fact no more fuel could be accommodated and still retain compatibility with SRAM launchers, and in 1976 Boeing proposed an underbelly auxiliary fuel tank for missiles carried externally.

Boeing also studied AGM-86B, ALCM-B, and with termination of B-1 this went into full development because it can be carried externally on a B-52 but could not fit inside a B-1. It also looks increasingly cost/effective to build a CMCA (Cruise-Missile Carrier Aircraft), which will probably be the Boeing YC-14, one of the defunct AMST (Advanced Medium STOL Transport) aircraft. For short ranges it could carry 40 missiles internally on rotary launchers, even if they were all

B-models. AGM-86B has a longer welded fuel tank, less wing sweep (25°), one-shot thermal batteries and many other changes. The B-52 must have structural modification to accomodate the longer AGM-86B launcher, which will preclude carriage of Mk 28 or other freefall nuclear weapons. A possible answer will be to retain the internal launcher for SRAMs and carry ALCM-B externally. The first AGM-86B was to fly in early 1979, and by July 1979 a total of ten (of 18 prototypes, all recoverable) was to have flown in competition against AGM-109A. If AGM-86 is adopted for the inventory it will be the B-model, and up to 2,300 missiles are in prospect, with IOC hoped for early 1980.

**Dimensions:** Length (AGM-86A) 14 ft 0 in (4·27 m), (B) 19 ft 6 in (5·94 m); diameter (both) 25 in (635 mm); span (A) 9 ft 6 in (2·90 m), (B) 12 ft 0 in (3·65 m).
**Launch weight:** (A) 1,900 lb (862 kg), (B) 2,800 lb (1270 kg).
**Range:** Depending on profile, up to (A) 745 miles (1199 km), (B) over 1,550 miles (2494 km).

**Above:** *Despite Boeing's instrumentation and test engineer this AGM-86B is only a mock-up, the first ALCM-B to be built. This doubled-range version is the one that will eventually go into the SAC inventory should this ALCM be selected over Tomahawk.*

**Above:** *One of the possible launch-platform options is this 747 with nine eight-round launchers. It appears to infringe SALT agreements, but seems a lot of deterrence.*

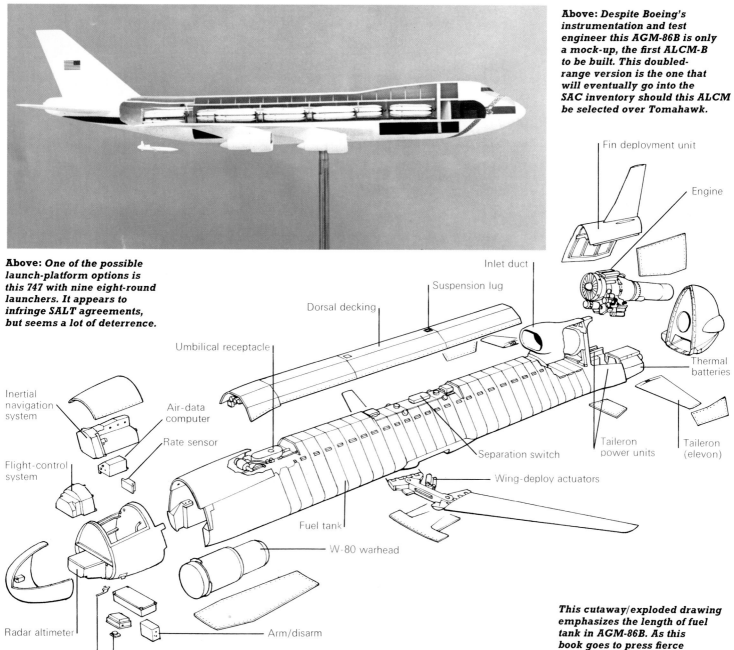

Fin deployment unit

Engine

Inlet duct

Suspension lug

Dorsal decking

Thermal batteries

Umbilical receptacle

Inertial navigation system

Air-data computer

Rate sensor

Flight-control system

Taileron power units

Taileron (elevon)

Separation switch

Wing-deploy actuators

Fuel tank

W-80 warhead

Radar altimeter

Arm/disarm

Pitot head

Radar altimeter aerial

*This cutaway/exploded drawing emphasizes the length of fuel tank in AGM-86B. As this book goes to press fierce arguments rage on ALCM value.*

Above: *Tomahawk development missile T4 heads inland from the PMR in the Tercom mode. In mid-course all Tomahawk versions look broadly alike.*

# Tomahawk

Also called TALCM (Tomahawk Air-Launched Cruise Missile), AGM-109 is the air-launched version of the Navy SLCM (p. 96) by General Dynamics, and arose as a result of successful air-drops of test vehicles in 1974–5. Not yet fully defined in mid-1978, AGM-109 has no launch capsule or tandem boost motor, and can have either of the two standard forward fuselages developed for BGM-109: Land Attack (W-80 warhead and Litton inertial/McDonnell Douglas Tercom guidance) or Anti-Ship (modified Harpoon warhead and TI DSQ-28 two-axis active-radar homing).

The first air-launch of an anti-ship Tomahawk was at PMR on 29 March 1976, before the emergence of AGM-109 as a missile in its own right. This unguided round was dropped from a wing pylon of an A-6 Intruder, as were subsequent test missiles which included the first fully guided flight on 5 June 1976 and the first free-fall launch and mid-air engine start on 15 November of the same year. In January 1977, when the whole concept of cruise missiles had appeared to leap ahead in strategic importance in US planning, both Tomahawk (Navy) and ALCM (Air Force) were placed under a Joint-Service Cruise-Missile Program Office under Capt Walter M. Locke, USN, with the Navy responsible for guidance and the Air Force for propulsion (AGM-109 uses the Williams F107-WR-401). Late in 1977 the

brilliant performance of all versions of Tomahawk forced the obvious conclusion: in February–July 1979 AGM-109 was to undertake a series of ten competitive flights against AGM-86B (ALCM-B), at least five of the flights being "all blue-suit", ie totally by Air Force personnel, with a winner-take-all outcome.

AGM-109 was not planned from the start for SAC missions and thus is being modified to achieve compatibility. It cannot be made compatible with the existing SRAM rotary launcher but does fit the new launcher under development for AGM-86B and the latter's wing pylon attachments on the B-52G and H. (The FB-111A has not been mentioned in connection with cruise missiles.) As soon as AGM-109 is released, its four tail fins spring open and the engine air inlet extends. When free fall has taken it a safe distance below the B-52, after about 1·5 sec, the fins are freed for control movements, the wings deploy laterally and the engine starts. Another version of Tomahawk for the Air Force is GLCM (p. 41).

**Dimensions:** Length 18 ft 3 in (5·56 m); diameter 21 in (533 mm); span 8 ft 4 in (2·54 m).
**Launch weight:** 2,550 lb (1157 kg).
**Range:** Over 1,550 miles (2494 km).

Centre: *First air-launch, from an A-6 Intruder of NWC, before the air-launched Tomahawk version had been defined as a weapon system.*

Above: *Contractor personnel make interface connections between an A-6E at NAS China Lake and an AGM-109, in mid-1978.*

## ASALM

The Air Force has for almost a decade recognised the size of the performance gap between existing strategic air-launched missiles and what is becoming possible, and in 1976 issued an RFP for the Advanced Strategic Air-Launched Missile. Generally written Asalm, pronounced as a word, all the submissions featured ram-rocket propulsion (integral rocket/ramjet) giving a cruising Mach number in the region of 3·5–4·5. This is fast enough for body lift to support the missile and give adequate manoeuvrability, so Asalm will probably have no aerodynamic surfaces except cruciform tail controls. Various arrangements of inlet and duct are proposed, a favoured inlet being in the chin position with a retractable or

*Above: Clean as a new pin, an AGM-109 test vehicle is readied for flight in the Convair plant at Kearney Mesa.*

blow-off fairing to streamline the missile during the rocket boost phase. In mid-1978 the industrial teams most likely to develop Asalm were Martin Marietta with Marquardt propulsion and McDonnell Douglas with CSD (UTC) propulsion. Rockwell and Raytheon are among probable guidance contractors. With a range of several hundred miles, flown in about 10 minutes, Asalm is to be effective against all forms of surface target including those of the highest degree of hardening; it is also to be able to destroy Awacs-type aircraft. Competitive flights could take place in 1981, with the winning missile reaching IOC in 1986.

*The sequence below shows how ASALM propulsion works. At launch a solid rocket fires for supersonic acceleration. This burns out, and charges separate the rocket nozzle and air-inlet fairing, so the case can become a ramjet.*

*Above: Artist's impression of a B-1 launching two ASALMs, one to destroy a hostile AWACS, the other as an ASM.*

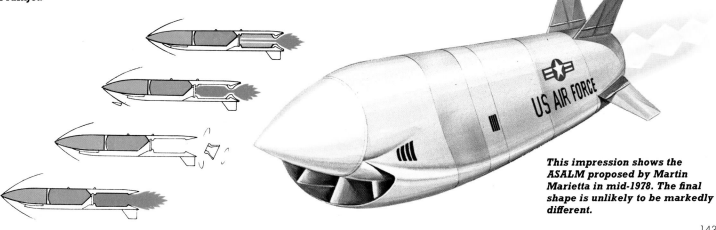

*This impression shows the ASALM proposed by Martin Marietta in mid-1978. The final shape is unlikely to be markedly different.*

# SURFACE TO AIR MISSILES

No category of missile includes greater diversity than this. It is a reflection on the history of World War 2 that, while the Germans devoted great and increasing attention to the SAM-Land category, the Allies ignored it. Today this section describes missiles weighing from a few pounds to several tons, and with a profusion of shapes and guidance methods.

Most of the early German army and Luftwaffe missiles used radio CLOS (command to line-of-sight). The operator(s) tracked the enemy aircraft in a steerable telescope, fired the missile and then sent steering commands by means of a radio link to keep the missile constantly aligned with the target. This was not very easy to do with the imperfect and often temperamental radio systems, missile control systems and extraneous disturbing influences such as suddenly changing aerodynamic forces as the missile accelerated through the local speed of sound. Bright flares were added to the missile to make it more visible, and electronics engineers were brought in to smooth out the guidance demands and prevent wild overcontrolling which in one or two cases resulted in the dangerous missile doing a high-speed stall and returning to the area of the launcher! Even today radio CLOS is very important, though all command systems using a radio link are vulnerable to countermeasures.

Chronologically the next method was radar command, used by several of the most widely deployed missiles in history. Here two pencil-beam radars are used, usually operating on different frequencies, one to lock-on and track the target and the other to lock-on and track the missile. When the target has been acquired, is being tracked and has failed to respond correctly to IFF (Interrogation Friend or Foe), the SAM is launched in a direction toward the target in such a way that it cannot fail to pass across the beam of the MTR (missile tracking radar). This second radar then feeds information on missile azimuth, elevation and range to a computer, where this is compared with the same data for the target. The computer's job is to reduce the difference between the two sets of data to zero, which it does by sending error signals which are either sent to the missile by a separate command radio link or coded into the MTR signals. The commands drive the missile control system to steer it towards the target. When the two sets of direction and range data are about to become identical a special signal is injected into the command link to detonate the missile warhead. Alternatively, the warhead can trigger itself by a proximity fuze.

Fuzes are obviously vital to a SAM. Unlike the missiles in the preceding sections, if a SAM misses by inches it might as well miss by miles if all it has is an impact fuze of the kind that would probably suffice for an SSM or ASM. Again, it was the Germans who did most of the groundwork in this extremely difficult field, though greater credit is due to the Americans who, in the infinitely more challenging field of radio proximity (VT) fuzes for gun-launched AA shells, achieved complete success and had the ammunition ready for use against the "V-1" in July 1944. By comparison, SAMs offer more room and suffer much milder launch acceleration, but still pose enough problems. By 1945 the German teams had actually fired SAMs with proximity fuzes based on optical methods (in effect they "saw" the target aircraft and triggered the warhead when it looked biggest), radar (when the missile/target distance passed through the minimum and began to increase), IR (like optical but using IR sightlines to the target exhaust pipes) and acoustic (triggered when target noise was a maximum). Some of the difficulties are obvious. How do you, for example, filter out the missile's own aerodynamic and motor noise and make the fuze listen for the dissimilar kinds of noise emanating from all kinds of hostile aircraft?

Of course, all these proximity fuzes operated on some emanation from the target that could be used to help steer the missile. The Germans were thus also the first to experiment with homing seekers, but in this case the problems were even greater and few reached the flight-test stage. The idea, of course, was to make the SAM home automatically on to the source of radar signals, heat or noise; the optical problem was compounded by the fact that a B-17 by day might look darker or lighter than the sky above, and might be followed by a brilliant white contrail which could attract the missile more than the aircraft, while a Lancaster in searchlights would be a brilliant light emitter against a dark sky.

After 1945 nobody could expect hostile aircraft to be so foolish as to pump out helpful radar signals, even at brief intervals. Britain, whose soldiers had enterprisingly done wonders in developing a beam-rider SAM which flew automatically up a single radar beam locked-on the target, abandoned all SAM work until the Korean war began in 1950. Then it developed two major systems which duplicated each other in most respects, one for the Army and the other for the RAF, choosing SARH (semi-active radar homing) guidance. In this the missile carries a passive receiver aerial on its nose which homes the missile on to radar signals scattered or reflected off the target, the latter being "illuminated" by a powerful radar on the ground. Of course the illumination is not in the range of wavelengths of visible light, though it is at a wavelength precisely matched to the seeker head in the missile. Like most SAM systems described so far, the result is what is called a "curve of pursuit". The SAM climbs along a curving trajectory which at any moment is directed towards the position of the target at that moment. With supersonic targets the curvature is considerable, adding greatly to the length of the trajectory; in other words the effective missile range is reduced. Today many SAMs use "proportional navigation" which yields a more efficient trajectory and increases the effective range. There are different laws for proportional navigation which can often be changed in flight, but in essence the missile does not continuously home on the target itself but on its predicted future position.

In the mid-1950s the US Army began development of a very small SAM which could be fired by infantry. It used a slim missile launched from a tube clipped to a hand-held guidance unit. The latter was aimed optically at the target, an IR seeker head on the nose of the missile locked-on, the missile fired, and a fresh tube clipped on ready for the next customer. The worst snag, apart from rather poor and unreliable performance, was that the seeker would not lock-on until the aircraft had made its attack and was going away, presenting its hot jetpipe(s). It took a decade to develop an all-aspect IR seeker on this small scale that could lock-on to an approaching aircraft. More recently Britain developed a more versatile infantry SAM with an IFF system (lacking in the original US weapon) which is automatically guided along the LOS for 1·5 sec and subsequently is steered to hit the target by a thumb-operated joystick. This of course works equally well against a head-on target or even a non-IR-emitting glider.

An extremely impressive Swedish infantry SAM uses laser guidance. The operator sights optically on the target (any aspect, any direction) and fires the missile. This switches on the laser, whose beam is sharpened by zoom optics as the range increases, and whose direction is governed by a servo-controlled gyrostabilized mirror to overcome effects of gusts of wind on the firing unit. The receiver aerials on the missile face rearwards, so jamming by the enemy is almost impossible. Trials in Sweden and Switzerland against modern supersonic attack aircraft making dummy runs against either the launcher or a point 0·6 mile (1 km) to one side

showed that, without the help of any warning radar and with the attacking pilot given complete freedom to plan his attack, seven kills would have been scored against each ten attackers. It is worth noting that this baby SAM has a laser proximity fuze set for a very short range to avoid premature detonation (possibly dangerous to friendly troops) on low-level trajectories over reflecting surfaces such as ice or water. When engaging anti-tank helicopters at near-zero altitude the prox fuze is deactivated, so a direct hit is then essential.

Britain's most important SAM, Rapier, is a "hittile" (direct-hitting missile) by design. Some industrial competitors have publicly doubted the feasibility of the hittile, but in ten years and some 1,500 live firings it has been amply demonstrated. One has only to compare Rapier with its nearest rivals, such as SA-6, Roland and Crotale, to see the advantages. Like an airliner, a missile's size is determined by its range and payload. A hittile needs a much smaller payload, and when the weight-saving is multiplied by the large scale-effect the result is truly startling. My belief is that the hittile will become universal for all low-level SAM systems within a decade, and that systems designed to explode a much larger warhead outside the target aircraft will be restricted to those few applications where for various reasons hittile accuracy is incapable of achievement.

One task for which this technique is probably inappropriate is the ABM (anti-ballistic missile) mission, which is always taken to mean an anti-ICBM. Such a task was judged beyond the state of the art 20 years ago, but today – despite the development of extremely sophisticated penaids to confuse and dilute the defences – the ABM can be designed with considerable assurance and can even function in any of a choice of ways. The first schemes grew out of the Nike systems in which separate radars tracked the target (an incoming RV) and missile, while a computer drove the two radar plots into 3-D coincidence. Subsequently the sheer scale of the operation and the need for great speed led to totally new kinds of radar, monster computers and, in the US Army, two kinds of missile for intercepting RVs either at a great distance or close at hand in a kind of last-ditch defence. For reasons which I never comprehended the US scientific fraternity led a powerful political lobby which killed the American ABM, leading to a tragi-comedy situation in which just one billion-dollar complex was built, readied for use, declared operational and then de-activated next day. The Russians do not have such problems and have powerful ABM installations.

# BRAZIL

General S.O.do Espiritu Santo announced in early 1978 that the Brazilian Army R&D Institute had "produced prototypes of two long-range surface-to-air missiles".

# CHINA

Prior to 1960 the Soviet Union supplied SA-2 Guideline (V750) systems and possibly concluded a licence agreement. Since 1970 the complete system has been manufactured on a large scale in the PRC and has not only been widely deployed around the Soviet frontier but also supplied to Albania where SAM sites have been equipped under Chinese supervision. It is certain that much later SAM systems must have been developed in the People's Republic of China but the Department of Defense has (mid-1978) not announced any evidence of deployment.

# FRANCE

*Below: SNCASE's Type 4300 had a massive tandem boost motor with a square-section casing carrying the enormous fins. The wings had either elevons or spoilers.*

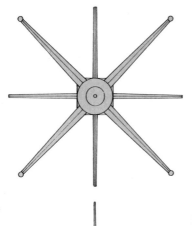

## SE.4300

The first guided missile in France to reach the flight-trials stage, this strange device had a tailless configuration once the large finned booster had departed. Propelled by an SEPR acid/aniline rocket, it had a cruciform of swept-back wings with elevons, and used simple radio command guidance by an operator who watched tracking flares on two wings. Developed by SNCASE, in 1954–56, it was a test vehicle for components and trained personnel of all three services in SAM operations.

**Dimensions:** Length (with booster) 18 ft 0 in (5·49 m); span 73 in (1·85 m).
**Launch weight:** 2,205 lb (1000 kg).
**Range:** About 5 miles (8 km).

## Matra R.422

First operational French SAM, and first weapon of this type to be developed in Western Europe, the R.422 was derived from R.042 (see M.04, p. 208) and test fired in November 1954. It reached IOC in late 1958, when Hawk (p. 175) was selected instead. It was intended for interception of bombers flying at between Mach 0·5 and 2·0 at heights from 10,000 to 66,000 ft (3048–20 117 m). The tandem boost had four SEPR motors in development missiles but the production weapon had one large motor. Guidance was based broadly on that of Nike Ajax, with CFTH (Thomson-Houston) radars tracking the target and the transponder-equipped missile, and SFENA providing radio command which, via an SEA computer, drove the missile into the target with cruciform foreplanes. A few R.422s had SFENA semi-active terminal homing. The continuous-rod warhead had a proximity fuze.

## Parca

Developed partly in-house by the French Army, with the assistance of a large industrial team, this was yet another early SAM using Nike Ajax style radio command guidance. It was in many ways a government counterpart of R.422, with almost identical body dimensions and some common guidance hardware. It was intended to fly rather faster, and the delta wings and control foreplanes were smaller. Boost motors were totally different, there being four wrap-round solid SEPR motors with large fins, making for a more compact missile. Over 120 Parcas were fired at Colomb-Béchar and other ranges in 1954–58, and a small number equipped an Armée de Terre AA regiment in 1958–62 prior to acquisition of Hawk. The name derived from Projectile Autoguidée par Radio Contre Avions.

**Dimensions:** Length 16 ft 5 in (5·0 m) (18 ft, 5·48 m with boosts); span 63 in (1·6 m).
**Launch weight:** 2,425 lb (1100 kg).
**Range:** 20 miles (32 km), with effective height to 65,600 ft (20 km).

*Right: One of several R.422s pictured in November 1956; probably at Colomb-Béchar, in north-west Algeria.*

*Below: DEFA was prime contractor for the impressive Parca, first fired in 1954.*

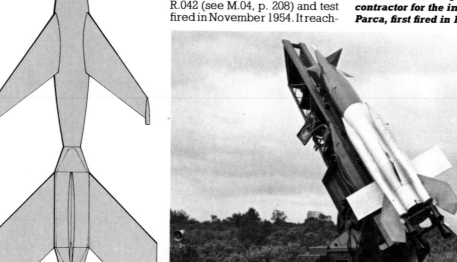

# Crotale/Cactus

On 2 May 1969 the South African Defence Minister announced that an all-weather SAM system was being developed for his country by France, with funding by the two governments. The system is Cactus, and it was developed by a team led by Engins Matra and Thomson-CSF to kill aircraft flying at up to Mach 1·2 at heights from 164–9,842 ft (50 to 3000 m) manoeuvring at 2 g. Work had begun at the two primes in 1964, field trials were held at the CEL and CEM, and series production began in 1968. By this time the system had also been adopted by France, as R.440 Crotale, and it has since attracted large additional export orders and been developed in a ship-to-air version (p. 183). A further variant is Shahine, described below.

In the standard Crotale system an E/F-band Thomson surveillance radar is mounted on a Hotchkiss-Brandt electrically driven vehicle, while quadruple launch tubes and a J-band Thomson pulse-doppler radar are mounted on the Fire Unit. Each surveillance vehicle, called the Acquisition Unit, can control up to three Fire Units. All are of under 33,069 lb (15 000 kg) weight, air-portable and have cross-country capability. The slim missile has cruciform control fins at each end, those at the

rear stabilizing roll and at the front effecting pitch/yaw guidance. On firing, the missile is accelerated to Mach 2·3 in 2·3 sec by an SNPE Lens single-stage motor with cast DB propellant. Thereafter the missile coasts, being gathered by an IR system with 5° vision, with stand-by TV and optical tracking if radar command is not possible, and slaved to the 1·1° J-band beam which is locked on the target. The warhead is a 33 lb (15 kg) device with directed (focalized) fragments lethal up to 26 ft (8 m), triggered by an IR proximity fuze.

There are many possible variations in the basic R.440 system. The standard is an SN-1050 real-time digital computer, landlines up to 1,312 ft (400 m) or radio links up to 3·1 miles (5 km). All 12 missiles in three Fire Units can be activated simultaneously whilst the digital circuits keep track of 18 additional targets. The 12 missiles can be fired at different targets, but usually would be directed in pairs to six targets all hit within 11 seconds. Reaction time from first detection to missile launch is 6 sec.

*Below: This illustration gives a perfect idea of a rather exposed deployment of a Land Crotale system, with one Acquisition Unit linked digitally to three Fire Units.*

The second export customer was the Lebanon, but this order could not be fulfilled due to civil war. The French Armée de l'Air has 20 Fire Units protecting Mirage IVA bomber bases. The largest user apart from South Africa is Libya, and other important customers include Saudi Arabia, Egypt, Abu Dhabi, Pakistan, Spain, Kuwait and other countries not announced in mid-1978.

**Dimensions:** Length 9 ft 7⅓ in (2·93 m); diameter 6·14 in (156 mm); span 21¼ in (540 mm).
**Launch weight:** 187·6 lb (85·1 kg).
**Range:** 1,640 ft to 5·3 miles (0·5–8·5 km).

## Shahine

This is an air-defence system, funded by Saudi Arabia, which entered the system-test phase in 1977 and should be in service by 1980. Based on Crotale, and with the same industrial team, it has important differences. The entire system is mounted on the AMX 30 tank chassis. The Acquisition/Designation vehicle has a different radar, a PD set with MTI and wide aerial giving beam-width of only 1·5° compared with 3·5° for Crotale. There is a TV turret concentric with this aerial but independent of it. The Fire Units have six launch tubes instead of four. The missile itself is the R.460, with a slightly longer motor giving higher burnout speed of Mach 2·5 and thus greater range (see data). The complete system also includes large numbers of Javelot rocket launchers and AMX 30SA

*Below: A realistically sand-smeared model of the Shahine system, of especial interest to users of the AMX 30 tracked chassis.*

twin-30mm guns, all tied digitally to the same automatic all-weather system. Egypt, and probably other countries, are negotiating to use the R.460 missile in the original Crotale system.

**Dimensions:** As Crotale, except length 9 ft 11¼ in (3·03 m).
**Launch weight:** About 198 lb (90 kg).
**Range:** 1,640 ft to 6¼ miles (0·5–10 km).

# Javelot

Though not guided, this system has extremely advanced pre-launch guidance and deserves inclusion. Prime contractor Thomson-CSF designed Javelot as an integrated SAM system with an acquisition radar, fire-control radar and digital fire-control computer, with options of optical fire-control and laser ranging. The missile is a spin-stabilized rocket carried in pre-loaded magazines which can be replaced within 30 sec. Each fresh magazine is positioned with its 64 missiles aligned with 64 launch tubes which diverge slightly to give dispersion patterns which depend on the tubes selected by the computer. Groups of 8, 16 or 32 can be fired at once, the total being an 8 × 8 matrix. Minimum delay between missile groups is 0·1 sec. Kill probability against any aircraft or missile target at 4,920 ft (1500 m) is put at 70%. The US Army is interested in this system, which in mid-1978 was at contract-feasibility stage. Catulle is the ship-based version.

**Dimensions:** Length 14·6 in (370 mm); diameter 1·57 in (40 mm).
**Launch weight:** 2·27 lb (1·03 kg).
**Range:** Effective to about 5,000 ft (over 1524 m).

# SATCP

Standing for Sol-Air Très Courte Portée (surface-to-air, very short range) this is a study programme involving Aérospatiale and Matra for an infantry weapon. It will not necessarily use single IR-homing rounds.

*Right: Another clever French model-picture, this time by Thomson-CSF and showing the proposed Javelot system. In this case the chassis is the familiar AMX 30.*

# GERMANY

# Hecht

Little is known about this early SAM by Rheinmetall-Borsig, except that its name means Pike and it had the specification given below. It may have been intended for R&D only, and around 1941 it was replaced by the F.55 version of Feuerlilie.

**Dimensions:** Length 8 ft 2½ in (2·5 m); diameter 15 in (381 mm); span 3 ft 1½ in (0·95 m).
**Launch weight:** 309 lb (140 kg).

# Feuerlilie

This vehicle began as a research project at the RLM under LFA aerodynamic principles, with use as a SAM increasingly in view. The name means Fire Lily, and the development progressed through three sizes, Feuerlilie 5 having a body diameter of 1·97 in (5 cm), and in late 1941 leading to F.25 (9.8 in, 25 cm) which was assigned to Rheinmetall in 1942. Following extensive testing with this high-subsonic (522 mph, 840 km/h) vehicle between May and September 1944 the much larger F.55 took its place, with autopilot and radio command guidance. Dr Konrad's R-Stoff/S-Stoff motor was not ready and the much less powerful Rheinmetall 109–515 diglycol motor was used. Surprisingly, F.55 survived almost to VE-Day, but never even approached operational service.

**Dimensions:** Length 15 ft 9 in (4·8 m); diameter 21·7 in (550 mm); span 8 ft 2½ in (2·5 m).
**Launch weight:** (With liquid motor) 1,036 lb (470 kg).
**Range:** 4·7 miles (7·5 km) at 932 mph (1500 km/h).

**Below: Three-view drawing of Feuerlilie F 55. Owing to lack of the intended engine, rated at 13,970 lb (6350 kg) for seven seconds, the full performance was not realised.**

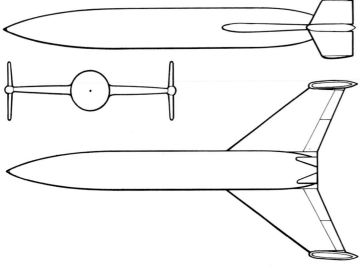

# Schmetterling Hs 117

This SAM came closer to operational use than any other for ten years. It began as one of Professor Wagner's SAM studies at Henschel Flugzeugwerke in 1941, called Hs 297. It took two years for the RLM to show interest; then, as the Allied bomber offensive began to hurt, a contract was placed and the designation changed to Hs 117. The name means Butterfly. Intended only for interception within visual range, the missile was initially mounted on a converted 37 mm Flak 18 gun mount. The target had to be visible, which in practice was a great handicap as the reaction time was too long for snap use against low-fliers. A standard Flak predictor was used to give future target position, and while an operator with a ×10 telescope sighted on this a second slaved the missile launcher to this sightline using a joystick. When fired, the missile accelerated to 680 mph (1100 km/h) in four seconds with upper and lower Schmidding 109–£53 diglycol boost

motors, which then separated. The sustainer, usually the BMW 109–558 rated at sea level at 827 lb (375 kg) on R- and SV-Stoff, kept speed at a constant IAS of 537 mph (864 km/h) by thrust-regulation as the ground operators used a Kehl/Strassburg command link to steer via solenoid Wagner bars on the wings. As no proximity fuze was ready the 55 lb (25 kg) warhead was detonated by command on a different frequency, which at great height was impossible to judge. The warhead was in the right nose prong, the left side being a windmill generator. Trials began at Karlshagen in May 1944 and, when production was authorised in December, 59 missiles had been fired from the ground and others dropped from He 111s, 34 failing to achieve objectives. Würzburg ground radars and Mannheim Riese displays were incorporated by late 1944 to give all-weather and night capability, but again with great difficulty, and the Fuchs (Fox) proximity fuze was tested on some of the final missiles flown. Production was intended to reach 150 per month in March 1945, rising to 3,000 per month by

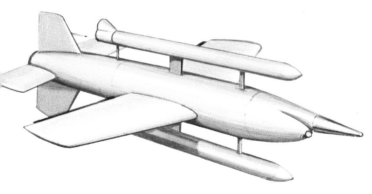

Left and below: *Schmetterling very nearly became operational during World War 2. In the photograph two missiles can be seen, the one in the background being elevated to about 30°.*

Above and right: *Big, crude and impressive, Rheintochter I is seen on its launcher with the original booster; the example in the London Science Museum in 1945 had strut-braced fins.*

November 1945, for firing from 60 sites initially. None went into action, though from September 1944 the Luftwaffe Flak R&D unit, LET 700, carried out trials and wrote the troop training handbook. A supersonic version was not completed. Hs 117H was an AAM tested from a Do 217.

**Dimensions:** Length (with fuze) 14 ft 0¾ in (4·29 m); diameter 13¾ in (350 mm); span 6 ft 6¾ in (2·0 m).
**Launch weight:** 924–981 lb (419–445 kg).
**Range:** 20 miles (32 km) against most targets, half as much for low-fliers; effective to 32,808 ft (10 000 m) altitude.

# Rheintochter

The Rhinemaiden (literally Rhine daughter) was a large and ambitious SAM developed in two forms, R I for the Army Ordnance Board from November 1942, and R III for the Luftwaffe (which was responsible for Flak defences) in the final year of war. The Rheintochter I was a remarkable creation for its day, with a large tandem boost motor giving 165,344 lb (75 000 kg) thrust for 0·6 sec, with four braced swept fins; six fixed wings similar to those of modern Mach 0·9 aircraft; four all-moving nose controls; and a sustainer rated at 8,818 lb (4000 kg) for 10 sec with

nozzles between each pair of wings. R I was blasted off a converted 88 mm gun mount at a steep angle and steered by radio CLOS, the operator having a joystick and watching flares on an opposite pair of wings. The first launch was at Libau (Ostsee) in August 1943. R I was abandoned in December 1944, when 82 had been flown, because it could not equal the altitude performance of Enzian or Schmetterling. Much better performance was achieved by R III, which had laterally mounted boost motors. It should have had Dr Konrad's Visol/SV-Stoff sustainer giving 43 sec burn time, but late delivery meant that five (possibly all) of the six

missiles flown at project termination in December 1944 were of the IIIp type with solid sustainer. Rheintochter's chief legacy, passed on to a later generations of weapons, was a wealth of practical experience and flight-proven guidhnce hhrdware.

**Dimensions:** Length overall (I) 20 ft 8 in (6·3 m), (III) 16 ft 3½ in (4·97 m); diameter 21¼ in (540 mm); span 87·4 in (2·22 m).
**Launch weight:** (I) 3,858 lb (1750 kg), (III) about 3,307 lb (1500 kg).
**Range:** 24·8 miles (40 km) but R I altitude limit 19,685 ft (6000 m) and R III effective to 49,213 ft (15 000 m).

# Wasserfall

Though Flak-Raketen (AA rockets) were entirely the province of the Luftwaffe, one of the most successful was developed at Peenemünde, an Army (Heereswaffenamt) establishment, because only there was the expertise available on Mach 3-plus vehicles. The Forschungslabor research department of the EMW (Elektromechanische Werke, the title of Peenemünde) began full-scale development of Wasserfall (Waterfall) in December 1942, basing the aerodynamics on the A-4 and that much larger missile's proposed winged derivative A-7. Like these, Wasserfall stood upright on a launch pad and took off under the relatively gentle thrust of its sustainer, with flight control by graphite vanes in the jet. Subsequently guidance was to be by radio command to the graphite vanes (terminating 15 sec after liftoff) and rudders on the cruciform tail, pulling up to 12 g in manoeuvres once speed exceeded 839 mph (1350 km/h). The ground guidance operator watched a complex display which indicated two sightlines, each two-dimensional, in the Rheinland system in which the target and missile were each tracked by a pencil-beam radar. Assuming the operator managed to steer the missile to keep the two sightlines coincident, he still had inadequate information on range to know when to press the warhead-detonation command button, so the 518 lb (235 kg) of explosive also had a proximity fuze. This large warload was made up of a 320 lb (145 kg) warhead and a 198 lb (90 kg) Nipolit-filament system to self-destruct the missile into harmless fragments in case it missed the target. Dr Thiel, head of Wasserfall motor design, was killed in the RAF attack on EMW on 17 August 1943 and M. Schilling took over the P.IX propulsion in which Visol and SV-Stoff (a great variety of different mixes were tried) were fed by nitrogen pressure through a system of burst-discs and starter valves to the SV-cooled chamber. Sea-level thrust was 17,637 lb (8000 kg) for 40 sec, a snag being shift of the c.g. as propellants were consumed. After terrible difficulties a Wasserfall reached the Greifswalder Oie pad in January 1944 but blew up. The second flew on 29 February 1944. When the programme was abandoned on 6 February 1945 at least 35 and almost certainly 51 full-scale missiles had been fired, plus many airdrops and scale-model launches. The programme was hindered by constant design-changes, by simple accidents (for example, explosive bolts were mistakenly thought to be needed to hold the missile down on the pad after possibly months in high winds, and these did not always all fire on launch) and the basic absence of underlying technology. The C2-8/45 production missile was fully defined at termination, and 900 a month

were to be built at a proposed underground factory at Bleichrode which was not even started.

**Dimensions:** Length 25 ft 8½ in (7·835 m); diameter 34·65 in (880 mm); span (tail rudders) 98·8 in (2·51 m).
**Launch weight:** 7,716 lb (3500 kg).
**Range:** Typically 22 miles (35 km), varying with target height and amount of manoeuvring needed; ceiling 58,071 ft (17 700 m).

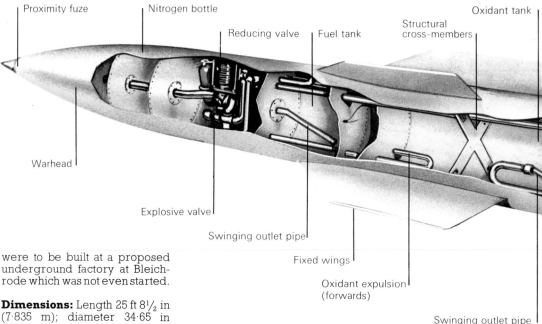

Proximity fuze — Nitrogen bottle — Reducing valve — Fuel tank — Structural cross-members — Oxidant tank — Warhead — Explosive valve — Swinging outlet pipe — Fixed wings — Oxidant expulsion (forwards) — Swinging outlet pipe

*Top: **Launch of a test Wasserfall at Greifswalder Oie in 1944. This was "learning the hard way" how to solve countless new and often dangerous problems. The gantry is A-4 size and unrelated to Wasserfall.***

*Above: **Cutaway of Wasserfall showing the proportion taken up by propellants and bulky radio equipment. The A-4 had much higher priority, and just how to deploy Wasserfall was never resolved.***

# Enzian

Preceded by a series of FR (Flak-Rakete) test vehicles, Enzian (Gentian Violet) was a large subsonic wooden SAM by Messerschmitt AG, initially designed by George Madelung and later led by Dr Hermann Würster at Oberammergau. Using Me 163 layout, with all control by elevons, Enzian was launched at a steep angle from a converted 88 mm gun mount under the thrust (15,432 lb, 7000 kg for 4 sec) of four Schmidding 109-553 diglycol boost motors. The E-1, -2 and -3 test vehicles had the Walter

*Above: **One of the first Enzians on its long rail launcher, probably in April or May 1944. About a dozen Enzians flew prior to the E-3B and E-4 versions, but none came near production.***

RI 210B sustainer fed by T-Stoff pumps with Br-Stoff and SV-Stoff, giving thrust falling over the 70-sec burn period to keep speed around Mach 0·85. At least ten of this series flew at Karlshagen from April 1944. Later vehicles had Kehl/Strassburg or Kogge/Brigg command guidance, but inaccurate thrust-axes often caused loss of control. The

operational E-4, a larger E-3B, was to have a warhead (661 lb, 300 kg, including self-destruct) with various proximity fuzes, and planned to have homing guidance systems including Madrid IR, Moritz radar and Archimedes acoustic. None of these guidance systems matured, nor at first did the planned Walter sustainer, so the 28-odd E-4 flights used a DVK (Konrad/

*Below: **Taifun F, of which some 600 were produced in the first weeks of 1945. How these rockets were aimed has not been explained.***

Beck) motor burning Visol and S-Stoff with performance similar to that of the E-3B motor. About 60 E-3B and E-4 Enzians were built, but though the original plan had been to avoid over-ambitious targets the programme kept being changed, and when it finally succumbed to the wholesale purge in January 1945 Enzian was still a long way from operational service. In February 1945 Messerschmitt tried to get support for E-5, a slim swept-wing supersonic version with a smaller warhead and improved sustainer. E-6 was a smaller wire-guided anti-tank version, probably not built. Data are for E-4.

**Dimensions:** Length 7 ft 10$\frac{1}{2}$ in (2·4 m); diameter 34·65 in (880 mm); span 13 ft 1$\frac{1}{2}$ in (4·0 m).
**Launch weight:** 3,968 lb (1800 kg).
**Range:** Maximum of 15$\frac{1}{4}$ miles (24·5 km) at target height of 8,202 ft (2500 m).

# Taifun

Though unguided, this AA rocket is interesting in that it was the last AA system actually worked on in Hitler's Germany, and represented a reaction against the uselessness of complex and immature guided SAMs. It stemmed from the obviously correct view of an EMW (Peenemünde) range officer, Dipl-Ing Scheufeln, that Wasserfall was not cost/effective, especially with no homing device. On his own initiative he began Taifun (Typhoon), a spin-stabilized rocket costing only DM 25 (about 62 pence or US cents), fired in salvo and carrying the optimum explosive weight needed to bring down a bomber (1·1 lb, 500 g) to a height of 49,213 ft (15 000 m). A neat Visol/SV-Stoff motor was used with features giving high directional accuracy and accelerating the rocket to 2,237 mph (3600 km/h) in 2·5 sec. The projector, a modified 88 mm gun mount, fired groups of 30 missiles at a time. There were many other ingenious features, and in January 1945 Taifun F (data below), the baseline production missile, was in mass-production at EMW. What remains a puzzle is how the projector was aimed to give accuracy at least as good as conventional AAA to extreme altitude.

**Dimensions:** Length 76·0 in (1·93 m); diameter 3·94 in (100 mm); span 8·66 in (220 mm) when fins deployed.
**Launch weight:** 46·3 lb (21·0 kg).
**Range:** Depended on target height, seldom over 5 miles (8 km).

# Mifla

Current (1972–8) studies by the MBB company for a SAM system having capability against tactical missiles and high-flying aircraft. International partners are sought. The name may derive from Mitleres FlugAbwehr.

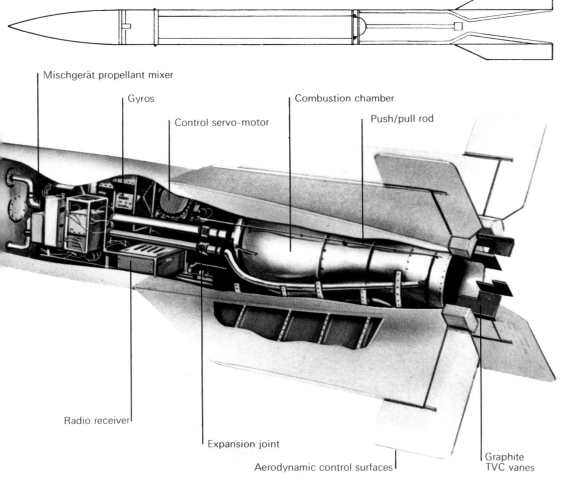

Mischgerät propellant mixer

Gyros

Control servo-motor

Combustion chamber

Push/pull rod

Radio receiver

Expansion joint

Aerodynamic control surfaces

Graphite TVC vanes

# INTERNATIONAL

## Roland

This SAM system for mobile battlefield use illustrates the manner in which modern weapon programmes can take longer and prove far more expensive than the original estimates. The original studies were made by Nord Aviation in France (under the acronym SABA, Sol-Air Basse Altitude) and Bölkow in Germany (designation P-250) in 1963. The two companies undertook joint development in 1964, and later, as Aérospatiale and MBB, formed Euromissile as a GIE to manage this and other weapon programmes. The first missile with full guidance destroyed a CT 20 target at the CEL in June 1968. IOC was predicted for January 1970 after extensive troop evaluations in 1969. In fact not one missile entered service until April 1977, and IOC of the version adopted by the US Army, originally scheduled for late 1977, is now predicted in "the early 1980s". Total Franco-German development cost has not been disclosed, but the cost of transferring the technology to the United States was put at $108 million in 1975 and $265 million two years later.

Despite this extremely long development Roland, whose name is that of a German folk-hero and also stems from a German acronym, is an extremely attractive weapon contained in a single vehicle which can travel with modern armoured forces. The original vehicle was the French AMX 30, followed by the German Marder SPz. The US vehicle is the M-109R. A further variation is the Berliet GBD wheeled (4 × 4) truck. All carry two missiles in their container tubes which also serve as the launch box, mounted on a trainable turret on top, plus two reload drums each containing four additional tubes, a total of ten rounds in all.

The basic missile was split in 1963 into a German front and French rear. Thus the propulsion is by SNPE, the boost charge (called Roubaix, cast-DB propellant) giving 3,527 lb (1600 kg) for 1·7 sec and the Lampyre sustainer 441 lb (200 kg) for 13·2 sec. This gives a Mach number of around 1·6 throughout most interceptions, which is considered enough for most purposes. There are front and rear cruciforms of fixed fins which flick open as the missile

leaves its tube. The forward fins are for destabilizing purposes, and all control movements are imparted by a typical Aérospatiale (Nord) jet-vane deflector operating across the motor nozzles which needs less control

power than aerodynamic surfaces. One of the cleverest and most costly features of Roland is its warhead, weighing only 14·3 lb (6·5 kg) but comprising 65 projectile charges lethal to a radius of 20 ft (6 m), detonated by a TRT proximity fuze of the radio-electric type.

The basic weapon system is Roland 1 (sometimes written I), which is a clear-air visual system adopted by the French Army. The AMX 30 carries the standard Siemens/Thomson-CSF pulse-doppler search and surveillance radar, with range of about 10

miles (16 km). This gives azimuth of a target, the operator being instructed how to manage his set in the presence of ECM and to notify the vehicle commander of a hostile. The vehicle is then stopped, the turret slewed to the threat azimuth, and the operator searches up and down on this bearing with his magnifying optical sight. When he acquires the target he waits until it is within range and then fires a missile by foot button. He holds his aim, and the missile is automatically gathered by the TCA (IR) system first used with Har-

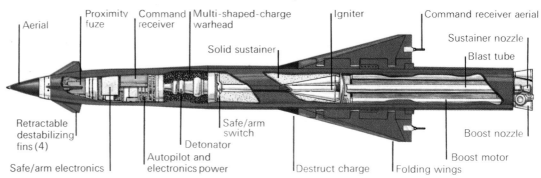

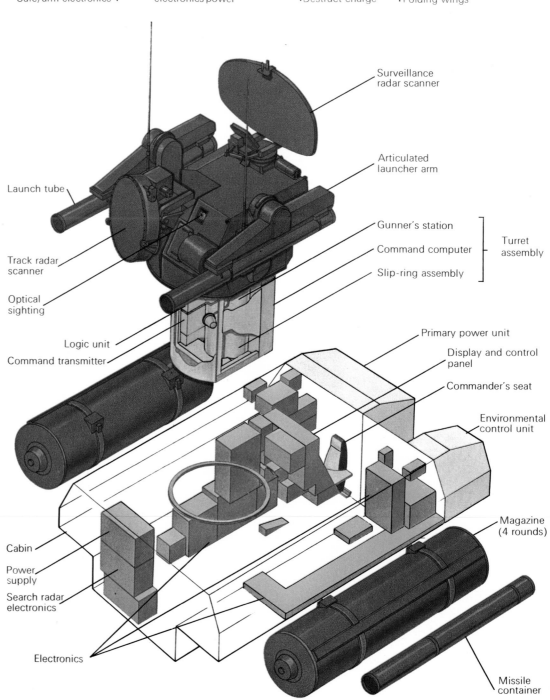

pon (p. 240) which zeroes the error on an IR goniometer and sends steering commands by centimetric radio link. The operator then continues to track the target until the warhead is detonated.

Aérospatiale is responsible for Roland 1, while MBB has charge of the all-weather Roland II carried on the Marder vehicle. This differs in that the engagement is controlled throughout by the vehicle commander. He studies the surveillance display, marks the azimuth of a hostile target, slews the turret and then

uses a tracking radar of Thomson-CSF Domino 30 type to detect and lock-on the target and continue the lock to warhead detonation. The missile is gathered in the usual way at a range of some 1,312 ft (400 m) – which is also the lower limit on "all-weather" visibility for this system – by an IR sensor and thereafter is kept in the radar beam centre automatically, using a CW beacon transmitting from the missile. The tracking radar is a monopulse set with a parabolic Cassegrain aerial gyrostabilized to allow targets to be

engaged while on the move – though this had not been demonstrated by mid-1978. France is buying 10,800 missiles to sustain 144 R 1 and 70 R 2 fire units in the field. German Army buy is 12,200, for 340 fire units. In the mid-1980s the Luftwaffe is expected to buy about 200 R 2 fire units for its air bases. Other R 2 buyers include Brazil, Norway and (in negotiation) Turkey, Israel, South Korea, Taiwan and one unannounced.

On 9 January 1975 the US Army announced selection of R 2 as its winner in a Shorads (SHOrt-

Range Air-Defense System) contest, to find a replacement for Chaparral. Hughes Aircraft was given US system responsibility, and today builds the EO sight, both radars, missile guidance section and fuze. Partner Boeing Aerospace builds the turret and launch arms, missile fins, propulsion section and warhead. Inevitably things did not run as planned, partly because the system had to some degree to be Americanised and partly because the system itself was still not final in 1975 and kept being refined. There were also more fundamental changes; for example the whole missile system is installed in the M-109 as a package which, in the event of chassis unserviceability, can be bodily transplanted to another. The tracking radar is also much more powerful than the European set, with greater ECCM capability. But the magnitude of the technology-transfer problems, combined with inevitable American resistance to "foreign" defence equipment, has caused giant efforts to be made to minimise changes and solve the difficulties, and Brig-Gen Frank Ragano, USA, the US Roland programme manager, has publicly emphasized the compatibility achieved which even extends to use of 50 Hz current.

In 1978 US Roland was in Extended Joint Tests at many locations, including tests with Franco-German missiles on the M-109 and US missiles on European vehicles. An initial production order for about 1,000 missiles was expected in October 1978, and when deployed at division level the USA will need up to 14,000 rounds costing some $4 billion.

Briefly mentioned earlier, the system mounted on the Berliet truck is designated Roland 2S and is compatible with existing Crotale hardware including the acquisition radar which has twice the lock-on range of the usual Roland radar. Since 1973 this has been studied by Belgium and later by six other countries. In 1970 Euromissile published details of a ship-based Roland, since often modified and usually with eight-round reload drums, but this has remained only a proposal. AS.2L is an ASM version (p. 112).

**Dimensions:** Length 94·5 in (2·40 m); diameter 6·3 in (160 mm); span (fins deployed) 19·7 in (500 mm).
**Launch weight:** 139 lb (63 kg).
**Range:** 1,600 ft to 3·85 miles (0·49–6·2 km).

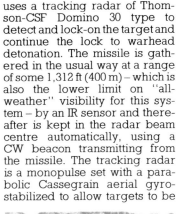

*Top: Hughes photo sequence showing a firing trial of the European-built system from a German Marder SPz at WSMR. Though the US system differs from the European, missiles are inter-operable.*

*Left: One of the first tests of the US-built missile from the US Army M-109 vehicle. Note fast deployment of wings as tube liner segments separate.*

# ITALY

## Indigo

This short-range SAM is a product of Sistel and Contraves Italiana. The latter, an associate of Swiss Contraves AG of Zurich, developed the original missile in the early 1960s and completed firing trials in May 1966. The missile itself has fixed tail fins, cruciform centrebody wings driven hydraulically, a British IMI single-stage motor giving 8,267 lb (3750 kg) thrust for 2½ sec, a 46·3 lb (21 kg) axi-symmetric fragmentation warhead, with IR proximity and impact fuzes, and choice of guidance systems. Originally triple or sextuple towed launchers were integrated with Contraves Italiana Lince (Lynx) acquisition radar and Contraves Zurich Super-Fledermaus (Bat) fire-control with IR tracker, guidance computer and command transmitter. After several changes, towed Indigo was adopted by the Italian Army as CT40 with LPD/20 pulse-doppler search radar but retaining the option of optical/IR tracking and command guidance in conditions of good visibility and severe ECM. In 1971 Sistel and Officine Galileo began development of MEI (Mirador-Eldorado-Indigo) as a self-contained mobile unit with Thomson-CSF radars. In 1978 this was, according to Sistel, adopted by the Italian Army, but with Sistel

radars substituted. A battery comprises a search/tracking unit, two launch units each with six missiles in trainable containers, and a support unit with 12 reloads. All are mounted on FMC M548 tracked vehicles.

**Dimensions:** Length 10 ft 10¾ in (3·32 m); diameter 7·68 in (195 mm); span 32·0 in (813 mm).
**Launch weight:** 267 lb (121 kg).
**Range:** Against low-level target to 6¼ miles (10 km).

## Spada

This short-range SAM system by Selenia, with Oto Melara as contractor for the launcher and mechanical integration, is the land-based system using the multi-role Aspide missile which also serves as an AAM (p. 214) and in the Albatros system (p. 186). These systems are compatible with the American Sparrow missile family. Spada exists in fixed and mobile forms, said to have "80% commonality", but in mid-1978 only the fixed form had been adopted (by the Aeronautica Militare Italiano, to defend its air bases). The system

*Right: Indigo is normally fired from a four-round box launcher, but this example was fired from Salto di Quirra range in Sardinia from an experimental single launcher with no container.*

# JAPAN

## Funryu 2

In 1943 this AA missile was studied at the Imperial Navy's Dai-Ichi Kaigun Koku Gijitsusho (1st Air Technical Arsenal) at Yokosuka, the chief Navy R&D centre. Along with several other SAM projects – all of which appear to have been intended for land rather than ship, installation – Funryu 2 proceeded to the flight-test stage but did not enter service. (The family name Funryu means Raging Dragon.)

Funryu 2 had a simple layout with cruciforms of fixed tail fins and elevon-equipped wings, propulsion off the 80° launch rail being by a solid motor giving 5,291 lb (2400 kg) thrust for 3½ sec. All-burnt speed is given as 525 mph (845 km/h), and the warhead weighed 110 lb (50 kg).

**Dimensions:** Length 86·6 in (2·2 m); diameter 11·8 in (300 mm); span 35·0 in (890 mm).
**Launch weight:** 816 lb (370 kg).
**Range:** Ceiling 16,404 ft (5000 m).

## Funryu 4

Whereas Funryu 2 guidance is not known (apart from the fact it had a simple autopilot), Funryu 4 was intended to become an operational weapon system and had radar command guidance with a computer (probably assisted by a human operator) to drive into coincidence the sightlines of two radars, one tracking the target and the other the transponder-equipped missile. It was better-looking than F 2,

*Below left: Approximate representation of Funryu 2, with the colour mere guesswork. No Japanese missile colour film is known to have survived into the 1950s.*

and appears to have had aeroplane configuration with fixed tailplanes and elevon-equipped wings. Propulsion was by a Toko Ro 2 (KR 10) pump-fed rocket burning C-Stoff and T-Stoff and rated at sea level at 3,307 lb (1500 kg) thrust (this was the Japanese copy of the Me 163 engine, built after an original Walter 109-509 had arrived by U-boat). Flight trials had not begun at VJ-Day.

**Dimensions:** Length 13 ft 1½ in

*Below: Funryu 4, which in fact was a much larger missile than Funryu 2. Like several SAM systems it had twist-and-steer configuration, but is believed never to have flown.*

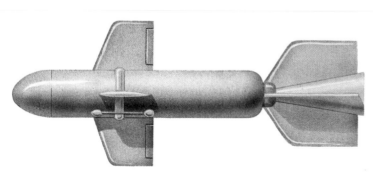

comprises a search and interrogation radar (SIR) able to control up to two fire units; a tracking and illuminating radar (TIR), also called the fire-control and guidance unit, of coherent-pulse type; and a missile launcher (ML) comprising four launch boxes in a trainable group with fixed 30° elevation. Selenia emphasize the system's fast digital processing, high resistance to ECM, and matching of missile performance to practical radar coverage. The system can be mounted on the M548, Fiat TM 69 truck or other 11,023 lb (5000 kg) carrier.

**Data:** As for Aspide, p. 214.

**Above:** *Inside the Spada tactical control centre, on top of which is the search/interrogation radar, feeding the display in the foreground.*

**Below:** *Splendid picture, again taken at Salto di Quirra, of Aspide launch in a test of the complete Spada SAM system. Note tracking flare.*

---

(4·0 m); diameter 23·62 in (600 mm); span, not known but about 30 in (762 mm).
**Launch weight:** 4,189 lb (1900 kg).
**Range:** Given as 18·6 miles (30 km).

# Tansam

Without announcing the fact, Toshiba (Tokyo Shibaura Electric) began the development of this low-altitude SAM system long enough ago for at least 17 missiles to have been fired by spring 1978. Intended to fill the gap between twin-35mm guns and the Hawk SAM, Tansam (an acronym) has IR guidance by the prime developer and reaches an all-burnt speed of Mach 2 on a Nissan Motor solid rocket. A new phased-array radar, an ambitious challenge, is used for target acquisition and tracking. The JMSDF is said to be interested.

**Dimensions:** Length 106 in (2·7 m); diameter 7·09 in (180 mm).
**Launch weight:** About 220 lb (100 kg).
**Range:** Up to 6¼ miles (10 km).

**Right:** *Illustration supplied by AB Bofors showing RBS 70 at the moment of firing. In the infantry role RBS 70 needs three men for transport.*

## SWEDEN

## RBS 70

AB Bofors, one of the world leaders in AAA, is promoting this extremely attractive man-portable SAM system as a replacement for guns. Unlike most infantry SAMs it can be integrated with a surveillance radar, IFF units and linked in other ways

with existing AA environments. The basic missile is fired from its transport container by a Bofors boost charge which separates at the mouth of the tube. Then the IMI solid sustainer takes over. The whole fire unit is carried in three packs: tripod stand, telescopic sight with gyrostabilized optics and laser, and missile tube. The whole assembly weighs about 176 lb (80 kg), and can be unpacked ready to fire in about 30 sec. The usual associated radar is the LM Ericsson Giraffe (previously designated PS-70/R), and this was expected to begin trials in late 1978 mounted on an Ikv 91 armoured vehicle. The operator rotates the sight housing for coarse aiming and uses a thumb-lever for tracking. The 2·2 lb (1 kg) pre-fragmented warhead has optical proximity and impact fuzes. Switzerland helped finance RBS 70 development. The system includes a simulator which eliminates the need for actual firings in troop training. The Swedish Army expects to deploy RBS 70 chiefly among armoured units.

**Dimensions:** Length 52·0 in (1·32 m); diameter 4·17 in (106 mm); span 12·6 in (320 mm).
**Launch weight:** 33 lb (15 kg) (with container, 48·5 lb, 22 kg).
**Range:** Up to 3 miles (5 km).

# SWITZERLAND

## RSC and RSD Family

These pioneer SAMs were developed as a normal commercial product by Contraves AG and the Armament Division of the Oerlikon Machine Tool Works (Bührle and Co) from 1947 onwards. Numerous test firings took place in Switzerland and France from 1950, by which time the RSC-50 was on offer as a fully developed system. The two-figure number denoted the year in which development was completed. In 1952 the US Air Force evaluated 25 RSC-51s at Holloman AFB under the designation MX-1868, the first sale involved the RSC-54, Italy (Contraves) made the MTG-CI-56, -57 and -58, testing them on the Salto di Quirra range in Sardinia, and from Switzerland RSC-57 and RSD-58 were delivered as training missiles to the forces of Switzerland, Italy and Japan. All had bodies Araldite-bonded from thin sheet, with rear control fins and sandwich-construction wings which could slide axially in slots to compensate for trim changes as the acid/kerosene propellants were consumed. Fired from twin elevating launchers, the missile was gathered in a wide radar beam and centred in a fine pencil beam, the 88 lb (40 kg) warhead having a radio proximity fuze. Training missiles had a parachute in place of the warhead. Data are for RSD-58.

**Dimensions:** Length 19 ft 8 in (6.0 m); diameter 15¾ in (400 mm); span 53 in (1.35 m).
**Launch weight:** 882 lb (400 kg).
**Range:** Max slant range 19 miles (30 km).

## Micon

In 1959 Contraves and Oerlikon decided the original RSC/RSD family had reached the end of its development and Contraves designed this weapon system as a private venture, the name being derived from MIssile CONtraves. The basic missile has a solid motor with a 9 sec boost phase and 16 sec sustain phase (holding speed between Mach 2 and 3, depending on altitude), large rear fins, a cruciform of hydraulically powered control fins near the pointed nose, and a 154 lb (70 kg) pre-fragmented warhead amidships triggered by nose impact and IR proximity fuzes. Micon is fired from a twin launcher, gathered by a D/F beam linked by computer with the launchers and main radar, and steered into the main radar beam. The monopulse differential radar tracks the target continuously and very accurately, and with range gates can steer three missiles simultaneously by command beam-riding. A

Micon battery comprises a computer unit, flanked by command-post vehicle and 55 kVA power vehicle, a fire-control radar and two D/F trailers plus two more power vehicles, and four twin launchers. No production was achieved.

**Dimensions:** Length 17 ft 8½ in (5.4 m); diameter 16.53 in (420 mm); span (control fins) 59 in (1.5 m), (fins) 78¾ in (2.0 m).
**Launch weight:** 1,764 lb (800 kg).
**Range:** 1.9–22 miles (3–35 km).

## Skyguard-Sparrow

As the successor to Super-Fledermaus Contraves has developed Skyguard, a more modern fire-control system with a digital computer linking two PD radars supplied by L. M. Ericsson of Sweden. Skyguard can control medium-calibre guns and SAMs in various combinations. The standard twin-35mm gun chassis can mount a Contraves Skyguard-Sparrow launcher with four boxes of RIM-7H Sparrow missiles. The system has been developed in partnership with Raytheon, and the missile launcher can be aimed by Skyguard or by a launch operator using a periscope. Skyguard is in production for several countries, including Switzerland, Austria and Spain, but no sale of Skyguard-Sparrow had been announced in mid-1978.

**Data:** As for Sparrow RIM-7H.

Above: *The chassis of the twin-Micon launcher bears a close family resemblance to that of the Indigo and other Italian systems.*

Below: *This photograph of the Contraves RSD-58 launcher was taken in Switzerland in the late 1950s. This was the first SAM offered for sale.*

Below: *Skyguard-Sparrow is being marketed mainly by the Swiss Contraves AG, unlike Micon which is chiefly Contraves Italiana.*

# USSR

## SA-1 Guild

First seen in the October Revolution parade through Red Square in November 1960, this SAM system has never excited much comment. In fact it was an incredible technical achievement, both in technology and in sheer scale. Development must have begun immediately after World War 2, because this system – called SA-1 by the DoD and given the NATO reporting name "Guild" – is estimated to have been in operational service in 1954, earlier than any other SAM apart from the Swiss RSC family. The main radar, called Yo-Yo by NATO, is a tour de force: it has six rotating aerials, covering an arc of 70° in both azimuth and elevation, and uses flapping-beam techniques to track more than 30 targets simultaneously. The peak power is estimated at at least 2 MW, on a frequency of some 3 GHz (E/F-band, the old S-band). For this and other reasons the DoD has always regarded this system as part of the Soviet Union's fixed strategic defences, though the missile itself has invariably been seen on the articulated transporter, with ZIL-157 type tug, which brings reloads to the (never seen) launcher. The missile is very large, yet has usually been credited with a rather poor flight performance, partly because (though until 1978 there was a large drum behind the tail see picture) it is thought to have no separate boost motor. Main propulsion is officially described as liquid-propellant. Control is by cruciforms of powered canard fins and cropped-delta rear wings each with an elevon or aileron. There appears to be a nose radar, and active homing would be entirely in keeping with this remarkable weapon. Guild has never been exported, and since the 1960s its numbers are assumed to have been dwindling from a peak of many hundred batteries.

**Dimensions:** Length about 39 ft 5 in (12 m); diameter 27·6 in (700 mm); span about 110 in (2·8 m).
**Launch weight:** About 7,055 lb (3200 kg).
**Range:** One British estimate is 20 miles (32 km).

## SA-3 Goa

The medium-altitude partner to SA-2, this equally aged system is widely used by the Soviet Ground Forces, Navy and many other countries. The missile is carried in pairs on ZIL-157 family tractors, mounted direct on the vehicle and not needing a trailer. The inclined ramps also serve as launchers. The same installation has been seen on three tracked chassis, and in Yugoslavia a quad installation is standard. When associated with the SA-2 this missile is fired from a power-rotated twin launcher elevated to 75°. Radars used in this system include P-15 Flat Face, a UHF acquisition set with superimposed parabolic aerials and range to about 155 miles (250 km), and Low Blow, a target-tracking and missile-guidance radar of up to 53 miles (85 km) range with mechanically scanned trough aerials at 45°. SA-3 and SA-2 batteries can also have early warning from P-12 Spoon Rest radars. SA-3 has a large tandem boost motor with giant rectangular fins which spread out through 90° at launch, a solid sustainer, fixed rear wings with ailerons on two opposite surfaces, and powered nose control fins. The warhead weighs 132 lb (60 kg). Details of guidance must be fully understood in the West, but have not been published. Terminal homing is provided, almost certainly by semi-active means, and Low Blow can steer up to two missiles simultaneously to the same target, with unspecified means of overcoming ECM. This missile is used by Cuba, Czechoslovakia, Egypt, East Germany, Hungary, India, Iraq, Libya, Peru, Poland, Soviet Union, Syria, Uganda, Vietnam, Yugoslavia and, in SA-N-1 form (p. 187) several navies.

**Dimensions:** Length about 22 ft (6·7 m); diameter (boost) 27·6 in (700 mm), (missile) 18·1 in (460 mm); span (boost) 59 in (1·5 m), (missile) 48 in (1·22 m).
**Launch weight:** About 882 lb (400 kg).
**Range:** Up to 18 miles (29 km).

*Below: SAM strength drawn up in perfect order before the Red Square parade of 7 November 1973. Behind the two "Galosh" tubes are SA-1 Guild and (beyond) SA-2 Guideline.*

*Left: SA-3 Goa vehicles on the march during a summer exercise. This missile can also be seen in the upper right corner of the photograph above.*

# SA-2 Guideline

For uniformity the Western designations of this system are given, though after capture of large numbers by Israel from 1967 onwards there are few secrets left and the Soviet designation is reported to be V75SM, the missile alone being (in one version) V750 VK. Unlike SA-1 this weapon system is quite normal in design, and it has for 20 years been perhaps the most widely used missile system of any kind in the world. Unlike SA-1 it was planned as a general-purpose land-mobile system, though the complete system is very bulky and weighs over 100 tons. First put into production in about 1956, this system has ever since been subjected to updating and improvement. The original basic missile comprised a shapely weapon with a cruciform of cropped-delta wings towards the rear, a cruciform of small fixed nose fins and a third cruciform of powered control fins at the tail, all indexed in line. In tandem was a solid boost motor with four very large delta fins, again indexed in line, one opposite pair of which had trailing-edge controls for initial roll-stabilization and gathering into the guidance beam. The missile rode on a ZIL-157 hauled

**Left above:** *Polish troops work on the guidance bay of an SA-2 (actually designated V750 series). Large numbers are fired in training.*

**Left:** *One of the scores of SA-2 vehicles captured by Israeli forces during the Yom Kippur war. There are many sub-variants.*

articulated trailer from which it was pulled backwards on to a large rotatable launcher incorporating many system-items and elevated to about 80° before firing, with blast deflector positioned at the rear. The boost burned for 4·5 sec, the acid/kerosene sustainer then burning for a further 22 sec. Apart from surveillance radars and Side Net heightfinders, the standard radar, called Fan Song by NATO, operates in A/B (E/F) or D/E (G) bands, locked-on to the target to feed data to the computer van. The latter set up the launcher and, after liftoff, used a UHF link to pass steering commands to the missile, which had to be centred in the guidance beam within 6 sec if it was not to fall out of control. The warhead was a 286·6 lb (130 kg) charge with an internally grooved heavy casing. Various impact, command and proximity fuzes were used. Subsequently there have been too many modifications to follow, involving radar, guidance, control, warhead, fuzing and, above all, ECCM. Very extensive combat experience in the Middle East and South East Asia forced numerous changes on top of an existing programme of new versions. The first externally evident change was introduction of cropped delta nose fins instead of rectangles. The latest family, first seen in 1967, have larger white-painted warheads (said to be nuclear), no nose fins and no boost control surfaces. Most effort has gone

**Below:** *This Soviet propaganda picture has a totally phoney appearance, yet is probably genuine. SA-2 really has been fired in salvoes.*

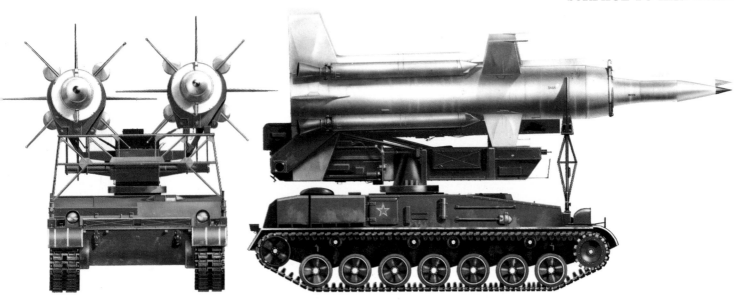

## SA-4 Ganef

into the radars, called Fan Song A to G in seven distinct types with track-while-scan elements and a sawtooth-profile flapping Lewis scanner backed up by various parabolic dishes. Once exceeding 4,000, SA-2 launchers in the Soviet Union are rapidly running down. Other users included Afghanistan, Albania, Algeria, Bulgaria, China, Cuba, Czechoslovakia, Egypt, East Germany, Hungary, India, Iraq, North Korea, Libya, Mongolia, Poland, Romania, Syria, Vietnam and Yugoslavia. A naval version is SA-N-2 (p. 187).

**Dimensions:** Length 35 ft 2 in (10·7 m) (varies with sub-type); diameter (boost) 27·5 in (700 mm), (missile) 21·6 in (500 mm); span (boost) 86·6 in (2·2 m), (missile) 66·9 in (1·7 m).
**Launch weight:** Typically 5,070 lb (2300 kg).
**Range:** Up to 31 miles (50 km).

First displayed in the Red Square parade on May Day 1964, this impressive long-range SAM is part of every Soviet Ground Forces combat army, to provide AA defence in great depth against targets at all speeds and altitudes. Fully mobile and amphibious, the SA-4 system moves with the advancing forces in nine batteries, each comprising three launch vehicles, one loading vehicle and one Pat Hand radar. Three of the batteries move forward about 6¼ miles (10 km) behind the most forward elements, and the other batteries follow some 9⅓ miles (15 km) further back. All are ready to fire at all times. The basic missile has four solid boost motors and a kerosene-fuelled ramjet sustainer giving great speed and manoeuvrability to the limits of its considerable range. Missiles

are put on targets initially by Long Track mobile surveillance radar (reported variously as operating in E-band and I-band and having very long range, most unlikely with I-band) and the widely used H-band Pat Hand provides command guidance and semi-active homing, the missile's receiver aerials being dipoles projecting ahead of the wings. It is persistently reported that this missile can also be used in the tactical surface-to-surface role, though how it is guided in this role has not been explained. It is typical of Soviet defence funding that a completely new tracked amphibious vehicle was developed to carry both the twin missiles ready for launch and the pair following close behind as reloads. Unlike previous Soviet SAMs this missile has its fixed fins indexed at 45° to the moving wings. There is a large conventional warhead. SA-4 was de-

*Above: This splendid artwork of SA-4 Ganef shows that the left missile is staggered above the right. A similar vehicle carries two reloads.*

ployed briefly in Egypt around 1970. It is standard with the Soviet Ground Forces and is gradually being issued to other Warsaw Pact armies beginning with East Germany and Czechoslovakia.

**Dimensions:** Length 29 ft 6 in (9·0 m); diameter 31½ in (800 mm); span 102 in (2·6 m).
**Launch weight:** About 3,968 lb (1800 kg).
**Range:** To about 47 miles (75 km).

*Below: 1974 Soviet picture showing two SA-4 Ganef launch units during manoeuvres. The caption claims that no other nation has such an "umbrella".*

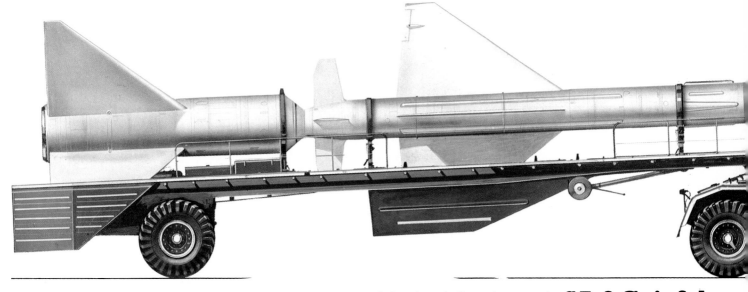

## SA-5 Gammon

One of the largest SAMs ever developed, this missile was first seen in the October Revolution parade through Red Square in November 1963, when the commentator called it an "anti-missile missile". At once dubbed "Griffon" by NATO, it has since become generally known as Gammon. Capability against an ICBM is clearly limited, but the exceptional speed and range of SA-5 certainly makes it useful against many other types of missile and all aircraft. It does not travel with the Soviet Ground Forces but instead is the longest-ranged anti-aircraft missile of the ZA-PVO, the "zenith rocket troops of the air defence of the homeland". This missile is launched singly from a trainable fixed launcher, but in parades it rides on a special articulated trailer, pulled by a Ural 357S tug, a separate crane being needed to transfer missiles to launchers. The target-tracking and missile-guidance radar is Square Pair, a large and powerful set believed to have been in use since 1964 but apparently still almost unknown by the West. Square Pair is said to be associated with Back Net or Barlock surveillance and Side Net heightfinder radars. These provide data on distant targets, allowing Square Pair to

**Top of page:** *The SA-5 Gammon is probably the largest conventional SAM system ever to have gone into service. Its launcher has not been seen.*

**Above:** *SA-5 Gammon vehicles seen in a Red Square parade in which they were described as "space interceptor missiles". Two are seen on p. 163.*

bring the missile to the correct block of airspace. Then the missile's own active radar, with a dish at least 24 in (600 mm) diameter, homes the missile to the target. SA-5 is believed to have third-stage propulsion for the separated warhead and terminal guidance system. Control for most of the trajectory is by cruciform rear fins, with ailerons for roll control. SA-5 was also known as the Tallinn system, because it was originally seen deployed near the Estonian capital. Today about 1,200 launchers are thought to be operational in many areas of the Soviet Union; no SA-5 installations have been reported from other countries. Warhead is thought to be nuclear, and it is certainly nuclear in supposed improved models – associated with a mobile phased-array ABM radar – observed on test from Sary Sagan in 1972.

**Dimensions:** Length about 54 ft 1½ in (16·5 m); diameter (boost) about 44 in (1·1 m), (missile) about 33½ in (850 mm); span (main wings) 156 in (3·96 m).
**Launch weight:** About 22,046 lb (10 000 kg).
**Range:** Estimated at 155 miles (250 km).

## SA-6 Gainful

Seen in Red Square on 7 November 1967, and many times since, this outstanding SAM system appeared to be misinterpreted by Western observers, even the ·ramjet inlet ducts merely being described as "prominent fairings". Suddenly in the Yom Kippur war in 1973 Israeli combat aircraft began to tumble out of the sky like ninepins, and SA-6 acquired an instant reputation for destroying its target no matter what the latter tried in the way of manoeuvres or ECM. The whole system is mobile, air-portable and amphibious, being mounted on modified PT-76 chassis. A fire unit comprises three vehicles each with triple launchers, a loading vehicle and a Straight Flush radar vehicle. Each Soviet Ground Force army

**Above right:** *6 October 1974, first anniversary of the Yom Kippur war, was marked by a military display in Egypt at which the SA-6 was revealed.*

**Below:** *After the parade the new SA-6 missiles were set up for firing and inspected by President Sadat. A feast for Western intelligence.*

deploys five such batteries, three keeping 3 miles (5 km) behind the front line and the other two filling the gaps 6 miles (10 km) further back. Various radars, notably Long Track, provide early warning and preliminary target data. In Egypt the van-mounted P-15 Flat Face has been deployed with SA-6 units, both in parades and in the field. But the key guidance radar is Straight Flush, which has two major turret-mounted aerials and provides several functions. The top dish tracks the chosen target with a 1° H-band (7·7–8 GHz) pencil beam, and guidance commands are transmitted to the missile in I-band (8·5–9 GHz), with frequency agility over a wide spread. Terminal semi-active homing is CW, to which Israel in 1973 had no antidote except generally useless chaff. The missile is a beautiful design, with integral ram/rocket pro-pulsion since urgently copied in the West. The solid boost motor accelerates the missile at about 20 g to Mach 1·5, burns out and the nozzle is jettisoned. The case then becomes a ramjet, with a larger nozzle, fed with ram air from the four ducts and with hot gas from a solid-fuel generator, which continues ac-celeration to a steady speed of about Mach 2·8. Control is by cruciform centrebody wings and fixed rear fins with ailerons for roll control and carrying com-mand/beacon aerials. The 176 lb (80 kg) warhead normally has impact and proximity fuzes, with IR fuzing a source of argument in the West. Users include Bul-garia, Czechoslovakia, Egypt, Iraq, Libya, Mozambique, Po-land, Soviet Union, Syria and Vietnam.

**Dimensions:** Length (with roc-ket nozzle) 20 ft 4 in (6·2 m); diameter 13·2 in (335 mm); span (wings) 49 in (1245 mm), (tail) 60 in (1524 mm).
**Launch weight:** 1,213 lb (550 kg).
**Range:** To 37 miles (60 km) against high-altitude target, half as much at low altitude.

*Left: **Here in the hands of a young Soviet artilleryman, the original SA-7 Grail is a very limited weapon, in the same class as Redeye.***

*Below: **The Grail missile is a slim grey tube with flick-out fins, here displayed alongside the launcher.***

# SA-7 Grail

Originally called Strela (arrow) in the West, this simple infantry weapon was originally very similar to the American Redeye, and suffered from all the latter's deficiencies. These included ina-bility of the uncooled PbS IR seeker to lock on to any heat source other than the nozzle of a departing attacker – with the single exception of most heli-copters which could be hit from the side or even ahead, if the jetpipe projected enough to give a target. The basic missile is a tube with dual-thrust solid motor, steered by canard fins. The operator merely aims the launch tube at the target with an open sight, takes the first pressure on the trigger, waits until the result-ing red light turns green (indi-cating the seeker has locked on) and applies the full trigger pres-sure. The boost charge fires and burns out before the missile clears the tube. At a safe distance the sustainer ignites and acceler-ates the missile to about Mach 1·5. The 5·5 lb (2·5 kg) warhead has a smooth fragmentation casing and both graze and impact fuzes. This is lethal only against small aircraft, and in the Yom Kippur war almost half the A-4s hit by SA-7s returned to base. Height limit is still widely given as 4,921 ft (1500 m) but in 1974 a Hunter over Oman was hit at 11,500 ft (3505 m) above ground level. An improved missile has been in production since 1972 with aug-mented propulsion, IR filter to screen out decoys, and much better guidance believed to house a cryogenic cooler in a prominent launcher nose ring. There are probably 50,000 mis-siles and nearly as many laun-chers, large numbers of them in the hands of terrorists all over the world. Users include Angola, Bulgaria, Cuba, Czechoslovakia, East Germany, Egypt (including American Motors Jeeps with four reload rounds surrounding the operator), Ethiopia, Hun-gary, Iraq, North Korea, Kuwait, Libya, Mozambique, Peru, Philippines (Muslim guerrillas), Poland, Romania, Soviet Union, Syria, Vietnam and PDR of the Yemen. A small-ship version is SA-N-7 (p. 181).

**Dimensions:** Length 53¼ in (1·35 m); diameter 2¾ in (70 mm).
**Launch weight:** (missile alone) 20·3 lb (9·2 kg).
**Range:** Up to 6¼ miles (10 km).

# SA-8 Gecko

A surprise in the 7 November 1975 Red Square parade was a dozen completely new vehicles each carrying quadruple launchers for this advanced and highly mobile system which was rather incorrectly called "the Soviet Roland", and it was almost certainly derived from SA-N-4 (p. 181). Despite its great size the 6 × 6 amphibious vehicle is air-portable in an An-22, and carries missiles ready to fire. Inside the body, or hull, are an estimated eight further missiles, enough for two reloads. Towards the rear of the vehicle is the rotatable and elevating quad launcher, surmounted by a folding surveillance radar probably operating in F-band at under 4 GHz. Between this installation and the cab is a large guidance group comprising a central target-tracking radar, two missile guidance-beam radars, two command-link horns for gathering, an optical tracker and an LLLTV and telescopic sight. All the radars have flat-fronted Cassegrain aerials, the main set being a J-band (13–15 GHz) tracker with a range of about 15½ miles (25 km). Each guidance aerial has a similar but smaller geometry, with limited azimuth movement; below each is the command link horn. After careful study semi-active radar homing has been judged unlikely and it is believed all SA-8 missiles have IR homing. The mis-

*This drawing shows the complete SA-8 system, which is accommodated in an apparently new amphibious vehicle.*

sile has small fixed tail fins, small nose canard controls, a radar beacon and external flare. The dual-thrust solid motor gives very high acceleration to a burn-out speed greater than Mach 2, the average speed in a typical interception being about Mach 1·5. It is believed missiles are fired in pairs, with very short time-interval, the left and right missile-tracking and command systems operating on different spreads with frequency-agility in the I-band to counter ECM and jamming by the target, with TV tracking as a back-up. The warhead weighs about 110 lb (50 kg) and has a proximity fuze. So far

*Below: Red Square on 7 November 1975 and disclosure of the impressive SA-8 Gecko SAM system. Third-rank vehicles have differences.*

as is known SA-8 is used only by the Soviet Ground Forces, in extreme forward areas.

**Dimensions:** Length 10 ft 6 in (3·2 m); diameter 8·25 in (210 mm); span 25·2 in (640 mm).
**Launch weight:** About 419 lb (190 kg).
**Range:** Probably up to about 8 miles (13 km).

# SA-9 Gaskin

First seen in the November 1975 Red Square parade, installed in BRDM-2A amphibious scout cars, this light SAM system was at once assumed to use a missile similar to a scaled-up SA-7. The missile itself had not (so far as is known) been seen in the West by mid-1978, but the complete

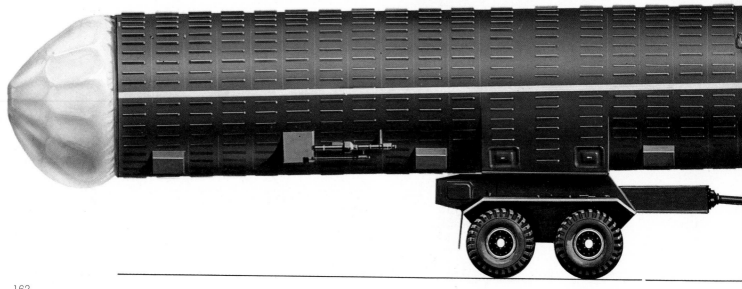

vehicle appears to be simple. In all examples so far seen it carries little but four launch boxes (sometimes only the outer pair are fitted) on an elevating and rotating mount which for travel-

**Below:** *One of the few SA-9 pictures, in this case with standard BRDM-2A carrying only the outboard missiles.*

ling can fold the boxes down on to the rear decking where protective grills can be clipped around the sides. There appears to be no radar, optical sight or other target acquisition or tracking system, though obviously one must be fitted. It is assumed that targets are acquired by radars in other vehicles which tell-off individual SA-9 operators by radio and may even slew the launcher automatically. Thereafter it is assumed that the operator sights visually and uses a small control panel with red/green lights to launch single, twin or all four missiles. In 1977 there were reports of BRDM-2A vehicles fitted with a new turret with a radar, almost certainly closely related to (or identical to) the Gun Dish used with the ZSU-23-4 Shilka AAA vehicle. Shilka has always been installed in the amphibious tracked PT-76 chassis, and this NBC-sealed vehicle would be ideal for SA-9 because it could carry missiles, radar and reload missile boxes whereas the four-wheeler is cramped. SA-9 is used by Warsaw Pact forces and Egypt, and is believed to be used by Syria, Iraq and possibly Iran. Data are approximate estimates.

**Dimensions:** Length 71 in (1·8 m); diameter 4·33 in (110 mm); span (fins are not retractable) 11·8 in (300 mm).
**Launch weight:** 66 lb (30 kg).
**Range:** Several miles/km.

# ABM-1B Galosh

Originally called SA-7 by the DoD, a designation later applied to the shoulder-fired Grail, this system is the only ABM in operational use in the world. It uses a large conical multi-stage missile first seen (or rather not seen) in its tubular container in the Red Square parade of November 1964. This was the first showing of the MAZ-543 eight-wheel tug, which has since become standard for towing many ICBMs on separate trailers, the tug accommodating numerous crew-members. With Galosh the missile travels in a ribbed tubular container pivoted above the rear wheels and with its own

powered truck further back. With this missile no attempt is made to carry extra crew in the tug. The missile travels base-first, the open front of the container revealing four first-stage nozzles. The other end of the container was covered by a fabric shroud attached over a light framework until 1969, when a light rigid convex end-closure apparently of plastic material was substituted. It is assumed that the travel container is mounted vertically in an underground silo and used as the launcher, the missile going through the top closure, with the tail fins unfolding beyond the tube. There are thought to be three propulsion stages and a thermonuclear warhead with a yield of several megatons (one report says 2–3 MT). The SALT I treaty allowed the Soviet Union to deploy 100 ABM launchers, and in the late 1960s eight extensive ABM complexes were started in areas around Moscow. These were to be fed with early-warning data by the first of the Hen series of gigantic ABM radars, Hen House. This was described by Dr John S. Foster, Director of DoD Research & Engineering in 1970, as "like three football fields lined up end-to-end and standing on their sides...to provide... the same radar coverage that the US will have some eight years from now if all of the Safeguard program is completed" (which, of course, it was not). Hen House installations are remote from

Galosh sites, for example near Irkutsk in Siberia, in Latvia and near the Barents Sea. The Galosh sites themselves each contain two large battle-management radars of the Dog House or Cat House phased-array type, four Triad (Try Add) engagement radars including Chekhov target/missile trackers, and 16 launch silos. Dog House became operational around 1968 and has a range of some 1,750 miles (2816 km). Each complex also has large computer installations and other supporting services. In the event only four complexes (16 launchers) have been completed, but ABM research continues "on a massive scale". Flight testing of an improved SH-4 Galosh missile was reported in 1976, with a manoeuvrable bus which can "loiter" while incoming warheads are separated from chaff and decoys, restarting its propulsion several times and then homing for the kill. Since 1976 the Soviet Union has also been building OTH radars said by DoD to be "on a scale much greater than anything we have ever considered deploying".

**Dimensions:** Length about 65 ft (19·8 m); diameter (fins folded) 101 in (2·57 m).
**Launch weight:** About 72,000 lb (32 700 kg).
**Range:** About 200 miles (322 km) reported, probably several times greater, but acurate figures have not been revealed.

**Below:** *The ABM-1 Galosh missile is transported tail-first in what appears to be its launch tube.*

**Above:** *The four first-stage nozzles of two ABM-1 Galosh missiles can be seen in their launch tubes.*

241504

# SA-10

As yet not associated with a public NATO name, and probably more correctly called SA-X-10, this new SAM system is still little understood in the West and has been the subject of conflicting and often silly reports. The few things that seem to be agreed are that it has exceptional flight performance, uses CW radar and is intended to kill cruise missiles. It therefore needs low-level capability and guidance against manoeuvring targets with extremely small radar signatures. The DoD announced the existence of SA-10 in October 1977, saying it might be in operational service in "seven to eight years". In 1978 two journalists claimed that the SecDef had privately told Congress it could be in service "by the end of 1978". This was hotly denied by the DoD, which nevertheless a few weeks later publicly stated that the first deployment could be in 1979. Range is given as "50 km" (31 miles) in some reports and as 2,000 n.m. (3700 km) in others. Some reports announce that the Soviet Union would need "500 to 1,000" of these missiles, while in others the figures are "5,000 to 10,000". In each case the cost of such deployment is put at "$30 billion". Most reports aver that a single-stage rocket gives 100 g acceleration, which is possible provided that the range is nothing like 2,000 n.m. Cruising speed is generally put at Mach 5, and the missile is said to have terminal homing by active radar; the CW set is presumably the airborne radar used for terminal guidance, though it could apply to both radars. Despite the nonsensical data, the DoD has been simulating SA-10 in cruise-missile tests and intends to use the information in the competitive AGM-86B/AGM-109 cruise-missile flights in the first half of 1979.

**Dimensions:** Length said to be 23 ft (7 m); diameter 17¾ in (450 mm).
**Launch weight:** Possibly 3,300 lb (1500 kg).
**Range:** Between the figures cited above.

# Anti-SRAM

As yet not associated with a public NATO or DoD designation, this system has been persistently reported since 1974. It is said to be mobile, despite incorporating a powerful C-band PAR (said to be called X-3 in the United States). The missile has launch acceleration of about 100 g to speed greater than Mach 5. No data.

# UNITED KINGDOM

## Brakemine

The only British SAM programme during World War 2, this pathetically funded weapon originated in a private paper written in 1942 by Capt H. B. Sedgefield, REME, which caused two members of A. C. Cossor Ltd – L. H. Bedford, director of research, and his assistant, L. Jofeh – to spend an overnight train journey working out how a missile could ride a radar beam locked-on to an aerial target. The GOC of AA Command held a meeting on 27 April 1943 and eventually Brakemine was authorised at AA Com-

**Foot of page:** *Few photographs survive from the Brakemine programme. This shows the whole launcher.*

**Below:** *One of the later Brakemines about to be launched. By this time (mid-1945) guidance was operative.*

mand's Research and Experimental Workshops at Park Royal, with Cossor handling guidance (and bearing all costs themselves). The first drawing was made on 7 February 1944 showing a weapon with cruciforms of wings and rear control fins, with four pairs of 3 in (76 mm) wrap-round boosts. Within 48 hr this was changed to six motors and single pairs of aerodynamic surfaces. Park Royal was eventually assisted by such contractors as Fairey Aviation, R. W. Crabtree, Hoffman Bearings, High Duty Alloys, Gillette and Sperry. The first missile was fired (unsatisfactorily) at Walton-on-the-Naze AA range in late September 1944. Thereafter trials continued for three years, most of the effort being devoted to providing a basis of underlying technology in such matters as how to trigger high-speed cameras and how to find and recover test vehicles from the sea. Differential expansion of the motor cases caused catastrophic break-ups, but missiles 11 to 20 made flights with radio guidance. From No 20 the airframe was cleaned up, wing chord was reduced, fin area almost doubled and the modified 3·7 in (94 mm) AA Gun launcher improved. Gradually Brakemine was turned into a usable weapon, but total lack of funding combined with the end of the war and dispersal of the small team to civilian life caused what had by 1947 become REME Experimental Establishment to cease work on this extremely promising programme.

**Dimensions:** Length 79·0 in (2·01 m); diameter 10·5 in (266·7 mm); span 33·0 in (838 mm).
**Launch weight:** 320 lb (145 kg).
**Range:** About 5 miles (8 km).

# Green Lizard

A SAM of unique character, this was the MoS code name for a programme at Vickers-Armstrongs (Aircraft) at Weybridge in 1952–4. Originally it was merely a contrivance to obtain Ministry funding for B.N. (later Sir Barnes) Wallis's variable-geometry research, the first ever to fly wings whose sweep was variable in flight. Green Lizard was a supersonic missile fired from a large gun. After clearing the barrel the wings flicked open and the missile flew to targets up to 100 miles (161 km) away on the integral turbojet sustainer. The warhead was a series of 100 spherical charges which scattered around the target. Guidance does not seem to have been explored. No data.

# Thunderbird

Though it was the logical successor to Brakemine, no attempt was made in this weapon system for the British Army to pick up where the earlier programme had left off. Instead the prime contract was placed with English Electric Aviation in 1949, which later formed a Guided Weapons

Division with headquarters at Stevenage and outstation at Salisbury, South Australia. The basic configuration was settled within weeks, and in 1950–54 numerous test firings took place from Aberporth of Red Shoes test vehicles, with cruciforms of fixed wings, rear control fins, four wrap-round boost motors and a liquid-propellant sustainer. Later Red Shoes incorporated semi-active radar guidance. Complete redesign then followed to turn Red Shoes into a robust Army weapon system with quick "repair by replacement" features, with the missile integrated into a large system operating autonomously or as part of a national or theatre air-defence network. The production Thunderbird 1 missile introduced a continuous-rod warhead, Bristol-Aerojet boosts, IMI solid sustainer, and a self-contained APU and hydraulic control system surrounding the sustainer tube. New missiles

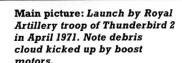

were received at a Field Assembly and Test Point for checkout and assembly. Each Army Battery had a Battery Command Post, Tactical Control Radar and Height-Finder Radar. It controlled up to six Firing Troops each with a Launch Control Post, Target-Illuminating Radar (TIR) and three launchers. The TIR was the BTH Sting Ray. The Royal Artillery trained at Ty Croes range and at the Thunderbird school at Manorbier, and the first regiment was operational in 1959.

Thunderbird 2 was designed in 1956–59 to offer greater performance and entered service in 1963. The missile had higher-impulse boost and sustainer motors, the TIR was the Ferranti Firelight X-band CW doppler

giving good homing against low-altitude targets or in the presence of ECM, and the whole system was made air-portable in Argosy aircraft. Thunderbird 2 was operated by 36 Heavy Regt RA based at Dortmund until 1976. In 1966 Saudi Arabia acquired Thunderbird 1 systems including 37 launchers withdrawn from the British Army, using these until replacement by Hawk in 1974. Libya ordered Thunderbird 2 in great strength in 1967 but the new regime cancelled the order.

**Dimensions:** Length (with or without boosts) 20 ft 10 in (6·35 m); diameter 20¾ in (527 mm); span 64 in (1·63 m).
**Launch weight:** not released.
**Range:** Up to 46¾ miles (75 km).

**Main picture:** *Launch by Royal Artillery troop of Thunderbird 2 in April 1971. Note debris cloud kicked up by boost motors.*

**Inset:** *A boosted Thunderbird 1 being used for troop indoctrination. The whole system was enormous, though each item was mobile.*

# Bloodhound

Developed by the Bristol Aeroplane Co and Ferranti as the RAF's SAM for home defence, under the code name Red Duster, this weapon system proved most successful and unlike most early British missiles achieved overseas sales. The missile had an unusual twist-and-steer configuration with aerodynamics similar to Brakemine. The tailplane was fixed, and semi-active radar homing drove the moving wings, which operated differentially or together. Launched at 45° elevation from a zero-length launcher by four Bristol-Aerojet solid boost motors linked to a common thrust-ring, Bloodhound cruised on upper and lower ramjet sustainers. The Thor ramjet was developed by Bristol Aero-Engines, using a test vehicle called the Bobbin with two smaller engines, and by 1956 had become one of the first Mach 2-plus ramjets to be available for use in the world. With a diameter of $15\frac{3}{4}$ in (400 mm), the first version had a centrifugal pump driven by ram-air turbine, pyrotechnic igniter and automatic controls, sea-level thrust at Mach 2 being 5,275 lb (2393 kg). Kerosene tankage was in the form of flexible cells collapsed by exterior gas pressure.

Production Bloodhound 1 missiles were first delivered from Bristol Aircraft's GW Divisional factory at Cardiff in late 1957 after very successful development at Aberporth and Woomera. Air Defence Missile Squadrons of RAF Fighter Command were deployed in 1958–61 to protect V-bomber bases. Though tied in to the existing Control and Reporting Network, each Bloodhound base needed an intermediate radar closer than the Type 80 surveillance stations, and the answer was a new Metropolitan-Vickers three-dimensional tactical radar linked to a high data-rate computer. This fed target data to the Fire Units usually comprising four sections of 16 launchers each. Each section's launchers were automatically linked in azimuth with a TIR, which in Bloodhound 1 was the BTH (later AEI) Sting Ray. Individual coding tied each section's missiles to its own TIR. At Woomera more than 12 targets were actually struck by Bloodhounds, but the operational missile had an exceptionally large continuous-rod warhead with EMI fuzing. In 1958 the Swedish Air Board purchased an evaluation quantity of Bloodhound 1 systems, and in 1959 the RAAF ordered the complete system which for 15 years equipped a squadron with detachments at Sydney, Darwin and NW Cape.

In 1958 development began of Bloodhound 2, with a missile of greater flight performance, CW guidance and improved lethality against low-level targets. Slightly longer, the missile had later Thor ramjets and larger boost motors. The whole system was upgraded and designed in either a portable or fixed-base form. The portable system used the Ferranti Firelight TIR (Ferranti had from the start been the largest subcontractor in the entire system) while the fixed-base set was the more powerful AEI Scorpion, likewise an I/J-band CW doppler but needing dismantling before being moved. Bloodhound 2 went into RAF service in 1964, and in the same

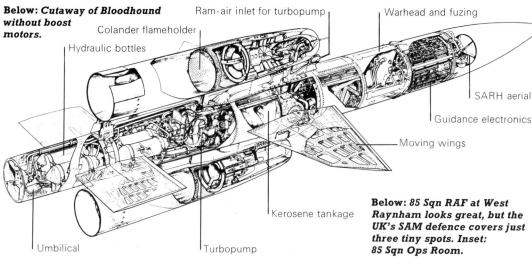

Below: *Cutaway of Bloodhound without boost motors.*

Ram-air inlet for turbopump

Colander flameholder

Hydraulic bottles

Warhead and fuzing

SARH aerial

Guidance electronics

Moving wings

Umbilical

Kerosene tankage

Turbopump

Below: *85 Sqn RAF at West Raynham looks great, but the UK's SAM defence covers just three tiny spots. Inset: 85 Sqn Ops Room.*

year was delivered to both Sweden and Switzerland. These two export orders were the largest then received for British missiles. The Swedish designation is RB 68; two squadrons remain operational. The Swiss designation is BL-84; two battalions have 64 launchers and a second training simulator was delivered from Ferranti in 1976. The RAF used Mk 2 in many theatres, and 28 launchers left by 65 Sqn in Singapore have since been operated by the Singapore Air Force. The remaining RAF deployment comprises only two squadrons: No 25 has one flight each at Brüggen, Laarbruch and Wildenrath, and No 85 has one flight each at Bawdsey, North Coates and West Raynham. No successor exists (but see Land Dart, p. 169). Data are for Mk 2.

**Dimensions:** Length 27 ft 9 in (8·46 m); diameter 21½ in (546 mm); span 9 ft 3½ in (2·83 m).
**Launch weight:** Not released.
**Range:** Over 50 miles (80 km).

# Blue Envoy

This was the code-name for the successor to Bloodhound with advanced SARH and passive homing, mentioned by Bristol Aircraft in 1961 as "Bloodhound 3" but cancelled a year later. Ferranti remained a major partner in the programme.

# Tigercat

This simple but timely SAM system was entirely a private venture by Short's Guided Weapons Division at Castlereagh, which had been one of the British pioneers of missiles and pilotless aircraft. It uses the same missile as the Seacat system, but mounts it in triplets on a neat trailer whose two wheels are removed before firing. Originally, in 1958–9, Tigercat was proposed for use against surface targets. A quad launcher on a Unimog chassis or LWB Land-Rover was one possibility, another was a launcher with radar in the centre, and a third was a Land-Rover carrying a larger radar and towing the launcher. In the event Tigercat was bought by a growing number of customers purely as a SAM, in a standard form with two tugs (usually Land-Rovers), a director trailer for the optical sight and operator, a launch trailer, the launch crew of five and power supplies. Most customers use the basic system, with Seacat-type thumb controller giving radio command guidance. Tigercat entered service with the RAF Regiment at Catterick in 1970, and has since been bought by Argentina (10 launchers), India, Iran, Jordan (since passed on to South Africa) and Qatar. At least one foreign customer uses the Radar Enhanced version with Marconi ST850 I/J-band radar giving blindfire/darkfire capability. Data: as for Seacat (p. 194).

# PT.428

This advanced SAM system was under development by BAC in 1962 but the MoD abandoned it as too difficult. Fully mobile and contained in one vehicle, it was to have had complete night and blindfire capability.

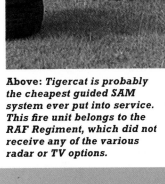

Above: *Tigercat is probably the cheapest guided SAM system ever put into service. This fire unit belongs to the RAF Regiment, which did not receive any of the various radar or TV options.*

Below: *Unlike those above, which are inert dummies for training, these are live Tigercats used for T/cat and S/cat training. Note the twin flares used to assist visual tracking.*

# Rapier

Originally designated ET.316, this weapon system was the first of the modern high-performance low-volume SAM systems to be developed. BAC announced the programme on 4 September 1964 and, after extremely successful work at Stevenage and Bristol, announced the start of production deliveries for the British Army and RAF Regiment in June 1967. By that time Rapier had acquired a reputation as a hittile – a missile that actually hits the target – and among the targets penetrated at that time was a Rushton towed target with a diameter of only $7^{1}/_{2}$ in (190 mm). This basic philosophy enabled the missile to be smaller, simpler and much cheaper than all rivals having remotely comparable performance. The missile has high launch acceleration conferred by an IMI Troy dual-thrust solid motor, the average flight speed on most engagements being about Mach 2. The four tail control fins are actuated by hot gas. At the front is a plastic nosecone covering the simple 1·1 lb (0·5 kg) semi-AP warhead, behind which is a crush fuze that detonates inside the hostile aircraft. In the 1960s several potential customers, in-

cluding the US Army, doubted the direct-hitting concept, but today the wealth of experience in the most adverse conditions has demonstrated SSKP over the entire field of coverage exceeding 60 per cent.

In its original form the system provides for visual engagement and comprises a two-crew Land-Rover or similar small vehicle which carries or tows the whole system loaded with four ready-fire rounds. A second vehicle with two more crew carries support gear and nine reload rounds. The launcher contains a Decca surveillance radar which operates without outside help. As soon as a target is detected it is automatically interrogated by the Cossor IFF. Absence of a correctly coded reply alerts the crew and slews the launcher to the target heading. The operator acquires the target through his Barr & Stroud optical sight, checks via the computer that the target is engageable and fires a round. Gathering is automatic, and flares on the missile are tracked by TV and any deviation from the sightline is corrected by the Decca J-band command link.

Most customers use this visual system, but there are many options including Blindfire radar and various self-contained vehicle systems. The MSDS Blindfire is the Type DN.181, an unmanned plug-in radar with extremely small beamwidth, pre-

**Below:** *Genuine photograph of Rapier launch from M548.*
**Note:** *Iran cancelled all Western arms deals in January 1979.*

**Below inset:** *An even later illustration showing the new low-profile VHF aerials (dark cylinders) which replace whip aerials on Tracked Rapier.*

**Right:** *Rapier shot against ultra-low-level target during British troop practice on the Hebrides range. Rapier has been operational since 1971.*

**Above:** *The RAF Regiment set up their visual-guidance Rapier system for the photo; normally the optical director would be further off, and the system less exposed.*

**Above right:** *The British Army is one of the customers for the extremely attractive Blowpipe, which is effective against aircraft (head-on), light armour and ships.*

**Right:** *Cossor provide the vital IFF, which is literally a "black box". It enables the operator of Blowpipe almost instantly to establish if an aircraft is hostile, before pressing the trigger.*

cise range-gates for target and missile and differential tracking of both simultaneously. It has many advanced features to minimise the effect of clutter, ECM and other influences such as heavy rain. This tracks the target automatically, but the operator always has the option of carrying out a visual engagement up to the moment of firing. Cable or microwave links can be used, or the whole system can be mounted on one vehicle. Yet another option is a cheaper blindfire tracker such as an LLLTV with or without a laser tracker. The DN.181 sent a Rapier straight into a Meteor target on the first Blindfire engagement in early 1972 and was fully operational with the system by 1975.

The first fully mobile Rapier system is carried on modified M548 vehicles, designated RC-748. Developed to meet a large £400 million order by the Imperial Iranian Ground Forces, this Tracked Rapier system installs the optical tracker in a retractable turret on the vehicle cab and carries all other system equipment on the same chassis. Eight ready-fire rounds are carried in two power-aimed quad boxes. The vehicle is air-portable in a C-130 but does not carry Blindfire radar (as used by the Imperial Iranian Air Force). This could be tied in from a second vehicle, and there is no technical objection to mounting the Blindfire system in one vehicle. By mid-1978 various types of Rapier system were operational in many parts of the world, and as well as Iran named customers for over 18,000 missiles include the British Army, RAF Regiment, Australian Army, Zambia, Oman, Abu Dhabi and Brunei.

**Dimensions:** Length 88·2 in (2·24 m); diameter 5·25 in (133 mm); span 15 in (381 mm).
**Launch weight:** 94 lb (42·6 kg).
**Range:** 0·3–4·5 miles (0·5–7·25 km).

# Blowpipe

Unlike such IR-homing SAMs as Redeye and, to a lesser degree, Stinger, this man-portable system can engage an oncoming target and has demonstrated extremely swift reaction and high performance. Blowpipe was a private venture by Short's GW Division in the mid-1960s, but eventually, in 1968, MoD funding was obtained because it was belatedly recognised that the system promised to meet a need of the British Army and Royal Marines. Subsequently 285 launchers were bought for the two services, and a further 100 have been ordered by Canada. These are pathetic quantities for what is demonstrably the best shoulder-fired SAM in the West, but one cannot expect swift acceptance of British weapons. The missile has cruciform nose control fins and fixed rear fins which before firing are positioned immediately behind the controls. This allows the storage tube to be only slightly larger in diameter than the missile body. To operate the missile a guidance unit is clipped to it, a target sighted visually, interrogated by IFF and, in the absence of a correct reply, the missile fired. The boost charge burns for 0·2 sec and pops the round from its tube, the rear fins locking into place at the tail and unfolding as they clear the tube. The Crake sustainer then takes the missile to Mach 1·5. An IR gatherer in the aiming unit senses missile flares to centre the round on the sightline; guidance is thereafter CLOS by thumb-controller, the 4·85 lb (2·2 kg) blast/shaped-charge warhead being triggered by an MSDS proximity fuze. The aimer

can be clipped to a fresh tube in seconds, the whole package weighing about 47 lb (21·3 kg) with IFF. Slam (p. 195) is a naval system incorporating this missile.

**Dimensions:** Length 55·1 in (1·4 m); diameter 3·0 in (76 mm); span (tail fins) 10·8 in (274 mm).
**Launch weight:** 24·5 lb (11·0 kg).
**Range:** Over 2 miles (3·2 km).

**Above:** *Many people, especially the British, would sleep more soundly if Land Dart was more* than *this artist's impression. It would be a natural successor to Bloodhound.*

# Land Dart

British Aerospace has designed a version of the Sea Dart system (p. 190) for fixed land applications. The same system elements could be used virtually without change, the twin launcher being above a hardened magazine. Land Dart could provide area defence over a very great range of altitudes with added capability against surface targets.

# USA

## Loki

This 3 in (76 mm) spin-stabilized rocket was used as a barrage weapon by the US Army briefly in 1949. Developers were Bendix and Grand Central Aircraft for propulsion.

## Nike Ajax

Though swiftly outdated as a weapon, this pioneer SAM was one of the great missiles of history, and in December 1953 the first Nike site near Washington DC became the first guided SAM system in the world to enter operational service. Developed as SAM-A-7 for the US Army, it was necessarily a large and cumbersome system by later standards, with large equipments installed in sites involving thousands of tons of concrete and steel. The system could later have been made mobile, but the original requirement was defence of the United States and friendly territory, with no thought of movement with a field army. Much of the storage, checkout and specialist accommodation was underground, though not specifically hardened against nuclear attack.

The guidance method was derived exactly from the radar-controlled AAA developed in World War 2, particularly including the M-9 fire control for 90 mm guns. The prime contractors for this had been Western Electric and its chief operating subsidiary BTL (Bell Telephone Laboratories), and they were again selected to mastermind the Army's first SAM. Targets were acquired by an acquisition radar, which in the United States was from 1956 tied into the SAGE network (Semi-Automatic Ground Environment) which used enormous computers to assign every intruder to a specific interceptor or SAM. The acquisition radar passed the target to a target-tracking radar (TTR) which continuously fed target data to a large computer using vacuum tubes (thermionic valves). This in turn selected one or more missiles and commanded the launch, simultaneously driving the missile into the beam of a missile tracking radar. The computer thereafter drove the two radar beams into coincidence at a predicted future target point, each beam being locked to either the target or missile. When the missile was just below the nose of the target aircraft the warhead detonation command was sent as a variation in the complex pulse coding of the beam transmissions.

The missile was a canard, with a large tandem boost motor. In early Nike 1 test vehicles the boost was by multiple short motors with four giant cropped-delta fins, but from 1949 the whole missile became extremely slender, the boost becoming a single Hercules charge giving 59,000 lb (26 762 kg) for 2½ sec and having three modest fins. Bell Aircraft produced the acid/aniline sustainer rated at 2,600 lb (1179 kg). Burnout speed was Mach 2·3. Control was by the cruciform foreplanes, and there were three warheads, weighing 12, 179 and 122 lb (5·44, 81·2 and 55·3 kg) respectively, each wrapped in ¼-in (6·35 mm) optimum cubic fragments. Airframe manufacture and missile assembly was handled by Douglas Aircraft at an Army Ordnance Missile Plant at Charlotte, North Carolina. By February 1958 approximately 16,000 rounds had been delivered. The Army had 40 battalions, each comprising four batteries of either nine or 12 launchers. The Army designated the system M-1, and in the new DoD system Ajax became MIM-3 and -3A. The name Nike is that of the Greek goddess of victory.

From 1957 Ajax installations were supplied to Belgium, Denmark, France, West Germany, Greece, Italy, Japan, the Netherlands, Norway, Taiwan and Turkey. None shared in original system manufacture, though a few, notably Japan, became involved in supporting the existing installations. By mid-1978 about 7,000 missiles had been fired in training, and a few sites remained on duty in Greece, Italy and Japan.

**Dimensions:** Length with booster 34 ft 10 in (10·62 m); diameter 12 in (305 mm); span 48 in (1·22 m).
**Launch weight:** (with booster) 2,455 lb (1114 kg), (without) 1,210 lb (550 kg).
**Range:** 25 miles (40 km).

**Right:** *No 31 Launcher Site of 740th AAA Missile Bn at Fort Winfield Scott, near San Francisco, March 1956.*

**Below:** *Three Northrop F-89D Scorpion all-weather, two-seater interceptors of the Air Defense Command make a low pass over an Ajax site near San Pedro, California.*

# Nike Hercules

The Nike system, like the world's railways, was so extensive and so widely used (there were over 3,000 launchers) that it was extremely costly to discard or alter. Consequently, though by 1951, long before Nike Ajax was in service, it was possible to criticise the system as cumbersome, complicated and inefficient, a successor system had to fit over the top of the existing system, and especially it had to be compatible with the existing radars, computers, auto-plotting boards and major ground installations. The same prime, Western Electric, did however transform the power and electronic performance of the system to match the dramatically increased flight performance of the Hercules missile. This missile succeeded Ajax on the Douglas-managed assembly line at Charlotte, and the new system became operational in January 1958. By June of that year all the Ajax batteries around New York City, Washington DC and Chicago had converted to Hercules, and funding for the gigantic task of conversion and new production was fluctuating at between $47·97 and $129·6 million per month, then an unprecedented rate.

A 1958 press release described Hercules, then designated SAM-N-25, as "fifteen times as effective" as Ajax. Typical prices for the Ajax and Hercules missiles, at peak production, were respectively $19,300 and $55,200, but if one accepts the "fifteen times" at face value the conversion was worth it. Certainly Hercules was a SAM of such performance that it swept away the notion that aircraft could evade defences by flying higher. Burn-out speed was typically Mach 3·35 in early production and 3·65 later, and except at extreme range it was possible to intercept accurately at altitudes to 150,000 ft (45 720 m). The boost motor was a four-barrel cluster by Radford Arsenal and Borg-Warner incorporating four Hercules solid motors each of Ajax

*Left: Launch of Hercules by USA field troop, probably at WSMR (undated).*

*Below: Hercules of 2 Bn, 562 Arty, is elevated during class in Alaska, 11 February 1969.*

performance. Thiokol's Longhorn Division at Marshall, Texas, cut its teeth on the high-performance sustainer with a solid charge centred on the CG and with a long tailpipe. AiResearch made the advanced APU which among other things drove the elevons on the trailing edges of the four extremely acutely swept delta wings. As in Ajax there were four small delta aerials to indicate the position of the guidance bay, behind which was the large conventional (fragmentation) or nuclear warhead.

At the peak of Hercules effort in 1957–60 Douglas was operating not only the Charlotte Ordnance Missile Plant but three other Nike Hercules facilities in the same state, at Winston-Salem, Burlington and Greensboro. Thiokol did not succeed with a self-consuming booster, but GE did provide not only fuzing for the nuclear warhead but also much of the enhanced guidance capability, notably with the Hipar (HI-Power Acquisition Radar) which despite having a 43 ft (13·1 m) aerial could fit into three trailers, compared with 20 or 21 in the original system, and thus opened the way to a semi-mobile system. Hipar was used in early 1960 when a Hercules at WSMR destroyed an oncoming Corporal ballistic missile. Later in that year a Hercules successfully intercepted another of its own kind at a closing speed of Mach 7 at a height of 19 miles (30·6 km). The system was less effective against really low-level aerial targets but did have capability in a surface-to-surface role.

By 1960 Hercules M6 and M6A1 was in operation with the US Army on Taiwan, Okinawa and in West Germany, and all the 73 battalions in the USA had been converted from Ajax. The US Army peak was 1963, when there were 134 Hercules batteries, and the system, by then designated MIM-14A and B, was also in use in Belgium, Denmark, West Germany, Greece, Italy, Japan (where missiles were made under licence by Mitsubishi Heavy Industries), the Netherlands, Norway, South Korea, Taiwan and Turkey. Total production exceeded 25,500. In 1978 Mitsubishi was still making the non-nuclear Hercules, despite its completely obsolescent character. The US Army planned to replace the whole system by Patriot (SAM-D) from 1975, and accordingly ran down its SAM strength. In 1974 the last 48 batteries were phased out, and since then there has been no SAM in the United States except for four batteries of Hercules retained for troop training in Florida and Alaska. Patriot (p. 178) is hoped to come into use in the 1980s.

**Dimensions:** Length with booster 41 ft 0 in or 41 ft 6 in (12·5 or 12·65 m); diameter 31·5 in (800 mm); span 74 in (1·88 m).
**Launch weight:** 10,405 or 10,710 lb (4720 or 4858 kg).
**Range:** More than 87 miles (140 km).

# Nike Zeus

By 1954 the ICBM was moving from science-fiction into the realm of imminent feasibility, and both the Army and Air Force managed studies into the Anti-ICBM (see Wizard, p. 174). Until 1955 these were lumped under the heading of "Antis" but in February of that year a study contract was placed with BTL for a new missile and radars within the general philosophy of the Nike system. In January 1958 SecDef McElroy selected Zeus over Wizard and ordered full development, to reach IOC in 1964. The missile was Zeus, XLIM-49A, and though at least as large a technical leap over Hercules as the latter was over Ajax it was a very small part of the overall system. The largest single item was the ZAR (Zeus acquisition radar) looking rather like the Great Pyramid and almost as large. One of its features was a Luneberg lens receiver aerial weighing about 1,000 tons. Even this could not distinguish between RVs and decoys, and the next link in the chain was a Discrimination Radar, the first ever built, with a mixture of mechanical and electronic scanning. These vast radars, to which RCA, Sperry and GE made major contributions, provided data for the target-track (TTR) and missile-track (MTR) radars which were more powerful versions of existing Nike equipment. No OTH capability was required, as the targets were all assumed to be on ICBM trajectories taking them several hundred miles above the Earth. The original Zeus missile was a large jagged beast aerodynamically derived from Hercules; the first was fired at WSMR on 16 December 1959. The fifth launch, on 28 April 1960, was of a different configuration with large canard controls and fixed tail fins. The tandem booster by Thiokol had a thrust of 450,000 lb (204 120 kg), then the highest ever attained through a single nozzle. The thermonuclear warhead had a spherical third-stage motor, the first-ever space bus to guide it to the point

*Above: Launch of the first flight Nike Zeus at WSMR on 16 December 1959. Data below are for the later version.*

of interception. TTR tests at Ascension Island against Atlas RVs in 1960 were followed by interceptions from KMR (Kwajalein Atoll) against similar targets on the PMR. This system developed into Safeguard.

**Dimensions:** Length with booster 63 ft 3 in (19·28 m); diameter 60 in (1·52 m); span (both) 98·0 in (2489 mm).
**Launch weight:** With booster, approximately 40,000 lb (18 144 kg).
**Range:** More than 250 miles (402 km).

# Safeguard

After 1960 the problems of Ballistic-Missile Defense (BMD) so proliferated that the Nike Zeus system was no longer adequate. The Air Force and Navy took an increasing interest, though by that time these services had abandoned their own ABM (Anti-Ballistic Missile) programmes. Surveillance systems, the largest single R&D effort in BMD, expanded as outlined in an accompanying map. One of the most difficult problems was that of discrimination between the hostile RVs and decoys or chaff in a mass attack. The cost of deploying any kind of ABM system appeared to start at a very high level in 1956 and rose each year to unacceptable levels. As time brought fresh problems to the surface the concept of an ABM defence for the United States was quietly abandoned. It was replaced first by defence for the major metropolitan areas and finally, after the 1972 SALT talks, by a mere single site defending part of the Minuteman ICBM force.

President Eisenhower decided against Zeus deployment in May 1959. He was advised that mechanical scanning was too slow for any radar in the system, that computer memory, processing speed and programming had to be re-thought, and that a new high-acceleration missile should be developed for last-ditch defence against the RVs that would inevitably pass through the main defences. A new system was authorised in January 1963, called Nike X, and

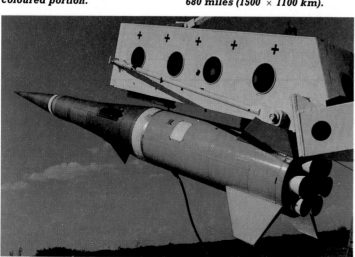

*Below: Squirt, here seen just before firing at WSMR on 14 July 1964, was a test vehicle for the airframe of Sprint, the dark-coloured portion.*

*Right: Launch of Spartan from KMR silo (believed to have been a late R&D firing). Spartan defended an elliptical area 930 × 680 miles (1500 × 1100 km).*

Martin Marietta was selected to build the Sprint high-acceleration missile. Complete hardening of the system was accepted wherever possible, but the vital radars could barely be afforded in any case and hardening them was out of the question. Moreover the problems were by this time compounded by the need to defend against depressed-trajectory attacks by SLBMs and FOBS, demanding even faster speed of reaction and the completion of an interception within five minutes in the worst case. This eliminated the possibility of using hard (thermal) X-rays

as the kill mechanism, because these are strongly attenuated within the atmosphere. Yet another problem was that low-altitude (say 10 miles, 16 m) detonation of the largest hostile warheads would be almost as catastrophic on the ground as detonation at optimum height (with the single exception of attacks on hardened targets in very remote areas).

By October 1965 the complete Nike X system was designed, with Spartan and Sprint missiles and two major radars, the PAR (Perimeter Acquisition Radar) and MAR (Multi-function Array Radar). Cost of each was put at $1·5 million, $1·1 million, $130 or $160 million (depending whether the PAR had one or two faces) and $165 million, respectively. Though quantum jumps in technology were needed by both missiles, the biggest effort was needed on the radars, and on the missile warheads. The MAR went on test at WSMR in July 1964, but was superseded by Raytheon's MSR (Missile Site Radar) which first operated on Meck Island (KMR) in September 1968. This radar had four faces each with 5,001 phase shifters in E/F-band giving great speed and discrimination to over 700 miles (1126 km). The first Bendix PAR, FPS-85, was mysteriously destroyed by fire at Eglin AFB in 1965 and did not operate until 1969.

The exo-atmospheric (outside the atmosphere) defence of Nike X was to be provided by XLIM-49A Spartan, a direct outgrowth of Zeus. Prime contractor (under Western Electric) was McDonnell Douglas Astronautics which, with three stages of propulsion by Thiokol, created a missile that could take a thermonuclear warhead at an average speed exceeding Mach 10 to within lethal range of an oncoming RV, ignoring decoys, and detonate it by ground computer command. It killed by X-ray flux. Spartan first flew from a concrete cell at WSMR in March 1968 and after 15 shots, only 11 of which were fully successful, R&D firings were completed in April 1970. Sprint, which apparently had no other designation, was developed by Martin's Orlando Division. It was a conical, hypersonic vehicle, which accelerated faster than any other missile known in order to convey a warhead in the low-kiloton range – killing chiefly by neutron flux – to an incoming RV about 25 miles (40 km) distant in a few seconds. Sprint was popped from its hardened cell by an expulsion

charge; above ground it was immediately tilted towards its target and the two stages of Hercules solid propulsion fired. Control was by body lift and TVC by Vought liquid-injection into the motor nozzles. Sprint first flew at WSMR in November 1965. By 1971 both missiles were giving encouragingly reliable performance in actual interceptions from KMR of Minuteman and even Polaris RVs. The warheads, the most challenging single components, had both been completely developed in underground testing.

On 18 September 1967 SecDef McNamara announced that, instead of a national ABM scheme, a "thin" system named Sentinel would be deployed, chiefly to guard against possible Chinese attack. On 14 March 1969 this was replaced by a different scheme named Safeguard, with roughly the same strength and cost (some $6,000 million) but moved from cities to SAC bases to protect the US deterrent. In 1972 the SALT I agreement limited the USA to one ICBM site and the capital, Washington DC. Work went ahead on installations to protect the Minuteman ICBM wing at Grand Forks AFB, North Dakota, including a PAR, MSR and Spartan and Sprint silos. This first Safeguard installation was declared operational on 1 October 1975. On the following day Congress ordered the system deactivated. Since that date ABM activity has been confined to research.

**Data for Spartan:**
**Dimensions:** Length with booster 55 ft 2½ in (16·83 m); diameter 42 in (1067 mm); span 118 in (3·0 m).
**Launch weight:** 28,700 lb (13 018 kg).
**Range:** About 465 miles (748 km).

**Data for Sprint:**
**Dimensions:** Length 27 ft 1 in (8·25 m); diameter at base 55·0 in (1397 mm).
**Launch weight:** 7,500 lb (3402 kg).
**Range:** 25 miles (40 km).

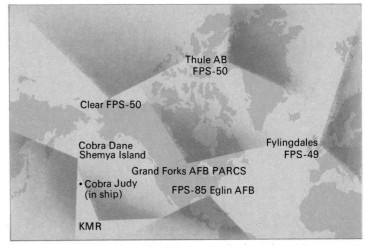

# USA

## Wizard

The original Anti-ICBM programme of the US Air Force of 1954–58 was two competing studies, one by Convair-Astronautics and RCA and the other by Lockheed Missiles & Space Co and Raytheon. In each case the objective was to intercept 1,000 miles (1600 km) from the hostile ICBM's target. Important features such as multi-function array radars, area defence and capability against SLBMs or FOBS, were all present in Wizard and later incorporated into the Army Nike X system.

## Bomarc

This unique SAM was a pilotless interceptor for area defence, identical in concept to a Bloodhound scaled up to US territorial needs. The long range prohibited use of semi-active homing, and Bomarc was from the start the world's first active-homing SAM system. The involvement of Boeing with SAM systems began in 1945 with the GAPA (Ground-to-Air Pilotless Aircraft) programme which after the end of the war embraced ramjet as well as rocket propulsion. The early GAPAs had been short-range wingless devices launched from clumsy lattice towers, but by 1949 the concept had changed to an instant-readiness supersonic cruise vehicle with range of several hundred miles. Studies were made by Boeing Airplane Co (as it then was) and the University of Michigan, and the name was coined from BOeing and Michigan Aeronautical Research Center. In 1951 the Air Force placed a full development contract, with designation XF-99. This was changed to IM-99A and after 1962 to CIM-10A.

The missile had aeroplane configuration, with an advanced airframe tailored to vertical (tailstanding) launch and a cruise Mach number of 3 (with peaks approaching 4). The high-mounted wing had tips cropped at the Mach angle and arranged to pivot to serve as ailerons. The top of the fin was a rudder and the tailplanes were powered slabs acting as elevators. Body pylons carried the two Marquardt ramjets of 28 in (711 mm) diameter, each giving sea-level thrust of 10,000 lb (4536 kg) in the initial IM-99A version. This was housed in large shelters, the first design being split into left/right halves opening apart to allow the missile to be raised to the vertical position, superseded by a cheaper shelter with sliding roofs. Interceptions were controlled by the SAGE and, after 1958, by the SAGE/BUIC system covering the United States. Bomarc was not intended for overseas deployment or for mobile use, but was the fixed-base area-defence weapon of Air Defense Command (later Aerospace Defense Command, ADCOM). A missile could be launched within two minutes of SAGE acquiring a suitable

**Above:** *Though an official USAF drawing, it is doubtful that Wizard would have looked exactly like this. Stages are shown separating.*

target; later this time was cut to 30 sec. There was no pre-programmed guidance. Vertical launch was effected by an Aerojet-General acid/JP-4 rocket motor with a gimballed chamber for control. After a few seconds the RJ43-3 ramjets, burning 80-octane gasoline, were lit and the aerodynamic controls became effective. The missile was rolled so that its upper surface pointed at the target. As cruising height of about 65,000 ft (19 812 m) was reached it was pulled over in a positive-g trajectory, finally half-rolling to cruise the right way up. At a target distance of about 10 miles (16 km) the Westinghouse DPN-34 radar in the missile's nose locked-on to the target, cutting out SAGE control and homing the missile by itself. Either a conventional or nuclear

warhead was fitted.

The first XF-99 propulsion test vehicle flew at Cocoa Beach on 10 September 1952, and the first IM-99A with all propulsion systems operating followed in February 1955. On 2 October 1957 an IM-99A was fired from Patrick AFB under control from the SAGE centre at Kingston NY and passed within lethal distance of an X-10 flying at Mach 1·6 at 48,000 ft (14 630 m). Subsequently Boeing's Pilotless Aircraft Division delivered 366 A-series missiles which in 1957–60 completed every possible kind of interception against QF-80, QB-47 and KD2U (Regulus II) drones. The first bases were Dow AFB, Maine; Otis AFB, Mass; McGuire AFB, NJ; and Suffolk County AFB, NY; with one or two 28-missile squadrons.

In January 1959 the Canadian government cancelled its Arrow interceptor and bought IM-99B Bomarc B for the RCAF, Canadair receiving offset subcontracts for the manufacture of wings and ailerons. Flight-testing this improved missile began in May 1959, but snags with the propulsion and other systems preventing any of the first seven Bomarc Bs accomplishing their missions. Bomarc B had a Thiokol M51 solid booster giving 50,000 lb (22 680 kg) for 30 sec and then jettisoned. There was extra tankage for JP-4 fed to RJ43-7 ramjets each with a sea-level rating of 14,000 lb (6350 kg). This greatly extended range, and in the nose was the Westinghouse DPN-53, the first production PD radar in the world. In 1961–65 Boeing delivered 349 production CIM-10B missiles for service at the existing IM-99A (CIM-10A) bases, plus Kincheloe AFB, Mich; Duluth Municipal Airport, Minn; Niagara Falls Municipal Airport, NY; and two RCAF bases, North Bay, Ontario, and La Macaza, Quebec. The last CIM-10B squadrons were deactivated in 1972.

**Dimensions:** Length (A) 45 ft 3 in (13·8 m), (B) 43 ft 9 in (13·3 m); diameter 35 in (890 mm); span 18 ft 2 in (5·54 m).
**Launch weight:** (A) about 15,000 lb (6804 kg), (B) 16,000 lb (7258 kg).
**Range:** (A) 230 miles (370 km), (B) 440 miles (708 km).

**Left:** *Lift-off of an IM-99A from AFMTC; note dense fuel vapour from ramjets.*

**Below:** *CIM-10B elevated at Hurlburt Field (near Eglin AFB) in 1967.*

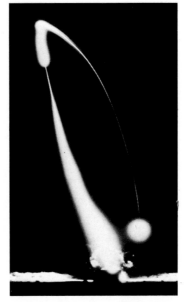

*Far left: A USA Improved Hawk battery emplaced in West Germany (late 1970s).*

*Left: Hawk shot at WSMR on 9 January 1975; F16 camera aperture for 15 seconds caught both stages plus warhead.*

*Left below: Hawk launcher and (on right) loader on display in 1965 at Peterson Field, Colorado Springs.*

# Hawk

The Hawk (Homing All-the-Way Killer) system was begun in 1954, the prime Army Ordnance Missile Command contract being placed with Raytheon Co, of Lexington, whose facilities at Andover, Bedford, Wayland and Waltham were all heavily committed. Unlike almost all other 1954 missile systems, Hawk is still in production in 1979, and it is the most widely used SAM in the world in terms of number of customers.

The original requirement was for a SAM system capable of hitting low-altitude aircraft and of travelling with a field army. By today's standards the whole system is overlarge, cumbersome and costly in money and manpower, but it happened to be available at a time when nothing else was, and cumbersome hardware is better than paper studies. In any case the original concept was correct in all the main choices, notably in the use of CW and PD radars and in dual-thrust solid propulsion. The main weakness of the system lies in its sheer size, needing large numbers of heavy vehicles; but this confers some degree of redundancy and targets can be engaged with certain supporting vehicles out of action.

Originally designated SAM-A-18, and with the Ordnance number M3E1, the MIM-23A missile comprises a homing head, warhead, four wings and a motor. The latter, by Aerojet-General, was originally the M22E8, the first dual-grain solid motor to be produced in quantity. At launch the fast-burning central grain fires to accelerate the missile to about Mach 2·5; when it burns out the slow-burning outer grain provides sustainer propulsion. Propellant mix is AP/PU. The highly swept aluminium-honeycomb delta wings and hydraulic trailing-edge elevons have always been made by Northrop. The 120 lb (54·4 kg) continuous-rod warhead with impact and proximity fuzes is provided by Iowa Ordnance Depot. Missiles were assembled at the Red River Arsenal at Texarkana.

In the original weapon system triple launchers were mounted on a light single-axle trailer, as were most of the other system elements to make each item air-portable in aircraft smaller than the C-130, or as slung loads under helicopters. The whole system, however, is not normally airportable, because it includes the five-man BCC (Battery Control Centre) where threats are assessed and assigned to Fire Control Operators (FCO). The BCC also includes two radars slaved together in azimuth, the volume-coverage Pulse Acquisition Radar and the CW Acquisition Radar which can see low-flying targets. In special circumstances a third Range-Only Radar can be used, slaved to either of the target illuminators, to provide rapid range and range-rate information. The CW guidance group comprises the twin-dish illuminator and the seeker aerial in the nose of the missile. The illuminator searches in the designated target direction and locks-on as long as the target is present. The three-round launcher is slaved to the illuminator in azimuth and elevation, and can be rapidly reloaded by an M727 tracked loader.

Hawk became operational in 1959, and the Army initially deployed 13 battalions, each with six or 12 triple launchers, in Germany, Okinawa and the Canal Zone. The Marine Corps followed in 1960. In 1960 a Hawk intercepted an Honest John rocket, and subsequently successfully engaged a Little John and a Corporal. In 1958 five NATO nations – France, West Germany, the Netherlands, Belgium and Italy – decided to adopt Hawk and build the system. SETEL was formed in Paris to co-ordinate the work of CFTH (later Thomson-CSF) of France, Telefunken of Germany, Philips of the Netherlands, ACEC of Belgium and Finmeccanica of Italy. In 1968 Mitsubishi Electric was awarded a JGSDF contract to build most of the system under licence. SETEL manufacture was completed in 1971, but Japanese production continued until 1978. Other foreign customers include Brazil, Britain, Denmark, Greece, Iran, Israel, Jordan, Kuwait, the Philippines, Saudi Arabia, South Korea, Spain, Sweden, Taiwan and Thailand.

Throughout the 1960s Raytheon and the Army worked on Improved Hawk, MIM-23B, and this was finally defined in 1968 and put into production, the first battalion of the 7th Army in Germany being converted by November 1972. I-Hawk has a new CW acquisition radar, a new guidance group with high-power illuminator giving greater range and capability, especially against manoeuvring targets of small cross-section; increased ECCM; increased system automaticity; solid-state circuitry; reduced reaction time; and an improved missile with Aerojet M112 dual-thrust motor, larger warhead, and "certified round" status eliminating need for any field maintenance or testing. By 1978 all customers other than Belgium, Japan, Morocco, Sweden, Taiwan and Thailand had ordered I-Hawk, sales of which exceeded 11,300 out of a Hawk total of over 38,300. Raytheon has also offered, but in mid-1978 had not sold, completely SP Improved Hawk systems, one carried on M727 tracked amphibious prime movers of the M113 family and the other mounted on the Lockheed Missiles & Space Co's Dragon Wagon all-terrain wheeled vehicle.

**Dimensions:** Length (MIM-23A) 198 in (5·03 m), (MIM-23B, Improved) 201·6 in (5·12 m); diameter 14 in (356 mm); span 47·5 in (1·206 m).
**Launch weight:** (A) 1,295 lb (587 kg), (B) 1,380 lb (626 kg).
**Range:** (A) 22 miles (35 km), (B) 25 miles (40 km).

# Mauler

This was perhaps the greatest-ever example of biting off more than the technology could chew, so that a potentially outstanding system ground to a halt and was replaced by a much less-advanced one that happened to be capable of attainment. The ARG-MA assigned Mauler to Convair-Pomona in 1959, and in 1960 the first illustration appeared showing a slim high-acceleration missile carried in a box of 12 on an XM546 tracked chassis (the same as in today's Tracked Rapier) together with gyro-stabilized dishes for Raytheon acquisition and tracking radars. The whole system, with crew of two, Burroughes computer and power supplies, fitted into the one vehicle weighing 25,000 lb (11 340 kg) which could spearhead amphibious or airborne assaults and offer instant-reaction capability against low-flying aircraft and tactical missiles. Designation became XMIM-46A in the 1962 scheme, while the stillborn Sea Mauler – which could have been very useful – was XRIM-46A. The system was replaced by Chaparral in 1965.

**Dimensions:** Length 72·0 in (1829 mm); diameter 5·0 in (127 mm); span 13·0 in (330 mm).
**Launch weight:** 120 lb (54·4 kg).
**Range:** 5 miles (8 km).

*Right: This photograph, almost certainly taken at WSMR, shows that Mauler was very much into the hardware stage.*

Main picture above: *Launch of test Chaparral by C Btry, 6th Bn, 67 Air Defense Arty, 1st Inf Div, at Fort Bliss on 20 October 1970; inset, standard M730 vehicles on the march.*

# Chaparral

In the spring of 1965 Philco-Ford (today the Aeronutronic Division of Ford Aerospace) received an Army Missile Command contract for this land-mobile SAM system using the existing Sidewinder 1C AAM (p. 226). The Navy procured the original inventory of missiles, which were closely similar to the AIM-9D but with small modifications for surface launch. Test firings began in July 1965 from prototype fire units, and production has continued at Aeronutronic's Anaheim plant since April 1966. Four rounds are carried on a rail launcher mounted on the M730 vehicle, one of the tracked amphibious M113 family.

The launcher is retracted for travelling but if hostile air activity is expected the vehicle is stopped, the launcher raised and, if FAAR (Forward-Area Alert Radar) is available, this is used to provide some warning and IFF identification. The M730 carries eight reload rounds as well as five launch crew and rations for three days. The vehicle is designated M48, which could be confused with the M48 tank, a totally different vehicle. It has no radar or other aid to aiming except an optical sight, with which the gunner in the launch turret aims at the target. As soon as the selected IR seeker has locked-on the missile is fired, thereafter homing automatically.

In 1970–74 the Army managed an improvement programme which resulted in MIM-72C, first delivered to field troops in July 1977. This has an improved missile with M-250 warhead developed at Picatinny Arsenal triggered by the M-817 Dido (directional doppler) fuze developed at Harry Diamond Labs, and the DAW-1 all-aspect IR seeker. Further improvements, still being incorporated, include the Stinger IFF package, smokeless Rocketdyne motor, antiglint canopy for the launcher, and all-weather radar. For the latter the British DN-181 Blindfire (Rapier) radar appears most suitable, but studies have also included radars by Raytheon and ITT/Gilfillan. Chaparral has been sold to Israel (where the first combat kill was a Syrian MiG-17 in October 1973), Morocco, Taiwan and Tunisia. Total production is about 9,000 rounds, two-thirds being the A-version. In the US Army Roland was to have replaced Chaparral from the mid-1970s but extra MIM-72C fire units have been bought in each of the last four fiscal years to make up the deficiency.

**Data:** as for Sidewinder AIM-9D (see page 226).

# Redeye

In the mid-1950s the demon-strated effectiveness of small IR homing missiles such as Side-winder suggested the possibility of a SAM for use by infantry. There had been an earlier study of wire guidance for such a mis-sile, but the only part dangerous to aircraft was found to be the wires! The US Army carried out a feasibility study in 1958 and the following year assigned full de-velopment to Convair (later GD) Pomona Division. Most of the slim missile comprises the At-lantic Research M115 dual-thrust motor. The round is packaged in its launch tube which is then attached to the operator's sight. The complete package weighs 29 lb (13 kg) and is not too tiring to carry through difficult terrain. If hostile aircraft are sighted the operator must identify them visually (there is no IFF), acquire a target through the optical sight and activate the IR seeker head which looks through the missile's glass nose. The sensitive cell is gas-cooled by three battery-energised units in the launch tube. As soon as it acquires and locks-on the target the seeker triggers a buzzer in the sight unit gripstock. The operator at once squeezes the trigger. The boos-ter pops the missile from the tube, its efflux blowing through a nozzle at the rear to cancel out axial thrust on the tube. About 20 ft (6 m) in front of the tube the main propulsion charge fires, accelerating the missile to super-sonic speed. The seeker homes by proportional navigation, steering with two flip-out nose controls and four folding tail fins. The fragmentation head has a contact fuze. Redeye, XMIM-43A and now FIM-43A, had a troubled development and it was almost ten years before Army and Marine Corps units became fully operational. By this time (1968) production reached 1,000 per month, US procurement being completed in 1970 at about 85,000. Each combat battalion normally has a Redeye section with four to six two-man firing teams each with one sight. Other users include Sweden (designation RB 69), West German Army (FLF-1 Flie-gerfaust), Denmark (improved model named Hamlet), Austra-lian Army, Greece, Israel and Jordan.

**Dimensions:** Length 48 in (1·22 m); diameter 2·75 in (70 mm); span 5·5 in (140 mm).
**Launch weight:** 18 lb (8·2 kg).
**Range:** 2·1 miles (3·4 km).

# Stinger

From the late 1950s it has been self-evident that Redeye is far from being an ideal SAM for infantry. It cannot fire until the attacker has done its work and is departing, presenting its jet-pipe as a target. Throughout the 1960s Army and GD Pomona testing sought to define a guid-ance system for Redeye II, with all-aspect capability. In the early

1970s this work was directed to the achievement of the ideal Manpads (MAN-Portable Air-Defense System) and Redeye II was restyled XFIM-92A Stinger in 1972, though no public an-nouncement was made. Since then development has been as prolonged as that of Redeye, and when the first guided tests took place at WSMR in 1974 they were discouraging. Ford Aerospace Aeronutronic Division was ur-gently commissioned to develop Alternate Stinger with laser beam-riding guidance, which continued as a back-up until late 1977. Stinger achieved some success in 1975 and in February 1976 DoD said "early guidance problems have been solved", but the expected production decision has been continually deferred and in mid-1978 all that could be said was that Stinger was "ready for produc-tion". The missile has integral IFF and some ECCM and anti-IRCM. It has a seeker cell more sensitive than Redeye's, work-ing on 4·1–4·4 microns and thus able to lock-on to the exhaust plume of the target so long as the latter is not absolutely head-on. Guidance circuitry then cor-rects the steering demand to make the missile hit the aircraft, not the plume. Atlantic Research provides the dual-thrust motor which, despite the heavier mis-sile, gives higher speed and longer range than Redeye. The Picatinny Arsenal fragmenta-tion head is much larger (6·6 lb, 3 kg) and has a Motorola proxi-mity fuze. The 1977 DoD budget included an initial $6·5 million for an alternative seeker (not to be confused with Alternate Stin-ger) of an electro-optical (EO) type using cells sensitive either to IR or UV. This POST (Proposed Optical STinger) could form three-quarters of production.

**Dimensions:** Length 60·0 in (1·52 m); diameter 2·75 in (70 mm); span 3·6 in (91·4 mm).
**Launch weight:** 22·3 lb (10·1 kg); with launcher 30 lb (13·6 kg).
**Range:** 3 miles (4·8 km).

**Above:** *USA infantryman firing Redeye (no details of place, time or unit). Missile coasts until well clear of user.*

**Below:** *Boost, coast and then first-stage ignition of the first Stinger fired in July 1975 at WSMR (launch area 34).*

**Foot of page:** *1978 picture of USA soldier about to fire a Stinger. This is the proposed production system.*

# Patriot

One of the most important SAM systems in the West, this programme has, like several others, suffered serious delays and cost escalation. It was carefully studied, as the FABMDS (Field Army Ballistic-Missile Defense System) and AADS-70 (Army Air Defense System for 1970) from 1961 onward. By January 1965 the system design had been specified, called SAM-D, subsequently designated MIM-104. A hardware programme began at once to verify component design, detailed Concept Formulation Studies were completed in mid-1965 and in August 1965 SAM-D went ahead under the Army Missile Command as a system with capability against aircraft at all levels and short-range missiles despite the most adverse use of ECM and other hostile conditions. RFPs were issued in April 1966, Contract Definition awards followed in August 1966 to Raytheon, Hughes and RCA, and Raytheon received the full contract in May 1967. Subsequently a further twelve years of work have yet to put one missile in the hands of combat troops.

Reading between the lines, the demands made on the system have increased over the years, and in 1974 the TVM (track via missile) guidance was first publicly mentioned at a time when production should have been

Left: *Any Patriot firing is dramatic, especially when the action is arrested; almost certainly WSMR in 1977.*

already starting. The ability to engage multiple targets simultaneously is new. The missile itself, together with its shipping/launching canister, is the responsibility of Martin Orlando. Thiokol provides the TX-486 advanced single-stage solid motor, of which no details have been released. Raytheon has handled the extremely ambitious guidance which, when it matures, will still probably be ahead of anything else in the world despite the long delays.

In a system of this performance and scale it is not possible to mount everything on one vehicle. The Army issued artist's sketches in 1967 showing the system installed on just two M548 tracked amphibious vehicles, but in mid-1978 this had been replaced by a less ambitious Firing Platoon comprising three truck-mounted units and up to eight launching stations, with poor cross-country performance, no amphibious capability and air-portable only in the largest aircraft. Possibly the system may eventually be repackaged into lighter and more versatile prime movers. What has been achieved is to create a single phased-array radar serving all functions of the system,

**Right:** *Patriot launch from one of the earlier experimental tubular boxes at WSMR on 15 March 1976. Different twin launcher on ground at right.*

**Below:** *Another shot from the proposed production launcher with four box-type canisters, probably in 1978.*

which in Nike Hercules and I-Hawk require nine radars. This outstanding multi-function radar is MPQ-53, and it provides early warning, target lock-on, tracking, ranging and range-rate, missile tracking, command guidance and SARH. It has a circular planar aerial and rides on a two-axle trailer which is unhitched and levelled on jacks before use. Electric power is supplied by a 6 ×6 truck carrying the MJQ-20 power plant with four 60 kW gas-turbine generators. Each XM-901 launch station has its own 15 kW diesel generator, a remotely aimed launcher able to carry four missile canisters and a radio command link, the whole riding on a two-axle trailer which again is unhitched and jacked before use. The platoon's hub is the MSQ-104 Engagement Control Station, the only manned equipment. This 6 × 6 truck carries the weapon control computer which provides the man/machine interface, monitors the hardware and

provides immediate fault-detection, location and isolation, and sequences each interception.

The Patriot missile is delivered as a certified round, the canister being loaded direct on the launcher by the reload vehicle. Missiles on launchers are subject to periodic lot sampling. At the appropriate point in an interception the computer fires the missile straight through the front closure. The radar continuously tracks both target and missile, and a unique feature is the TVM (track via missile) downlink and the combination of ground command plus homing. The seeker receiver in the missile is aimed at the target by the ground radar and locked-on in flight. The flight speed of Mach 3·9 is high enough for body lift and four powered rear control fins to outmanoeuvre any target. The warhead is conventional fragmentation or nuclear.

Firing Platoon 2, the first representative mobile tactical unit, began firing missiles at WSMR

in late 1977. The first year was encouraging, and culminated in a test at WSMR in June 1978 in which three missiles were fired seconds apart from the same launcher at manoeuvring ECM-equipped targets (two Firebees and a PQM-102); one Patriot failed to receive guidance and was destructed but the others both passed within lethal range of their targets. A production decision is hoped earlier than the predicted date of between May and September 1980.

**Dimensions:** Length 204 in (5·18 m); diameter 16 in (406 mm); span 36 in (914 mm).
**Launch weight:** About 2,200 lb (998 kg).
**Range:** Not released.

# Safesam

This US Army proposal envisaged a mix of Safeguard sites and SAM-D (later Patriot) bases to protect American cities against all forms of attack. It was an active concept in 1969–72.

# SDM

Site Defense of Minuteman was originally known as Hardsite, and was studied in 1971–74 as an add-on and possibly successor to Safeguard to protect the Minuteman sites against growing threats with which Safeguard could not cope. McDonnell Douglas Astronautics was prime contractor and SDM consumed large sums, Martin Orlando alone receiving a May 1972 contract award in the amount of $186,360,000 for Sprint II missile development, and a roughly similar sum being spent over the four years on new facilities at KMR. SDM was progressively downgraded to a technology-demonstration project, which in turn appears to have continued (if at all) with modest funds and in a low key since 1976.

# ASAT

The study of Anti-SATellite weapons has naturally been a minor preoccupation of all US services since 4 October 1957, but interest has hardened in recent years and in September 1977 Vought was named winner of an industry competition for an ASAT for Norad (North American Air Defense Command). The USAF Samso (Space And Missile Systems Organization) is managing the programme, and Vought's first $58·7 million contract is for engineering development to last until 15 April 1980. It is believed to involve clusters of small-projectile warheads launched by SAMs, fighters in zoom climbs or satellites. FY79 money is being split three ways. Improved space surveillance accounts for $36·1 million, improved survivability of US military satellites about $19·2 million, and the ASAT weapon system about $17·7 million. No flight testing is planned at present, and the US hopes to agree a ban on such weapons with the Soviet Union.

# SURFACE TO AIR MISSILES

In September 1939 the Royal Navy not unnaturally asked for something with which to deter dive bombers. Later ships were to carry so many rapid-fire guns of 20 to 40 mm calibre as to deter any low-level aircraft – even a modern jet – but the only answer the British came up with was a succession of devices based on UPs (Unrotated Projectiles, the name "rocket" being secret). Ingenious systems fired salvoes of UPs into the sky, often with dispersion taking the place of aiming, while others shot tubular vehicles much taller than a man which disgorged a string of cables, parachutes and contact-fuzed mines. Though very preliminary studies were made of projectiles guided by radio, nothing was done to build a guided missile when Allied ships were really having a hard time in 1939–42. Then the pressure eased, until in the summer of 1944 the Japanese Kamikaze menace suddenly spurred renewed activity which this time centred around the first ship-based SAMs.

Britain's single effort, the Stooge, could hardly have been more primitive. Predictably the United States attacked the problem on a much broader front, and the various Navy units and industrial contractors who began to research the SAM problem were soon firing into the sky large numbers of missiles of contrasting and generally unconventional shape. It is a reflection on the difficulties that, whereas the logical sequence is to solve the problems with test vehicles and then build a missile, these anti-Kamikaze weapons began with optimistic attempts at missiles and gradually petered out in a prolonged succession of test vehicles. This is in no sense meant as criticism. It merely reflects the lack of underlying technology, which might have been provided by steady progress in missile aerodynamics, propulsion and guidance throughout the war.

After 1945 the magnitude of the problem was as well appreciated as the possibilities, and vast research establishments, special trials ships and powerful groups of industrial contractors collaborated to furnish major surface ships with SAM defence. Without exception the menace was envisaged as a jet bomber flying at high altitude at about Mach 0·8, and the shipboard SAM is inevitably likely to be such a large system that it cannot easily be redesigned to meet fresh demands. Some of the illustrations in this section show just how large the early systems were – or are, for most are still in use. The missile and launcher are merely the tip of the iceberg that shows on the surface. Inside the ship are large magazines, ready rooms, mechanical handling systems, workshops, stores, training systems,

power supplies, computers, operating centres with displays and complicated consoles, loading systems and, by no means least, a whole array of radars with the electronics and power units below decks and the giant aerials on the masts or stacks. Several important classes of ship have been unable to accommodate SAM systems through lack of available space, while others cannot accept the mass of aerials at the required height without becoming dangerously unstable in roll.

Most first-generation SAMs had to be fitted with boost motors to impart very high thrust for a brief period to accelerate them off the launcher at a high angle of elevation so that they could be gathered into the guidance radar with their control fins and wings fully operative. Usually the speed at boost burnout was supersonic. It was then the duty of the internal sustainer motor to hold this speed for most of the rest of the flight, the actual speed usually gently increasing or decreasing during the sustainer burn period of 15–45 sec. Once the sustainer had burned out speed fell rapidly, especially if violent manoeuvres were being called for. Most shipboard SAMs have rocket sustainers, but a few have ramjets and these generally offer a much longer sustainer burn. This not only greatly extends the range but also maintains the full power of manoeuvre out to the extreme limits of range, in a way that the burned-out coasting rocket missile cannot approach.

In the United States, Soviet Union and France the decision was taken to use tandem boost motors. This resulted in missiles that were neat but of unwieldy length, necessitating separate storage of missiles and boost motors which were joined together only on the way up to the launcher. With ramjet missiles, such as Talos, means had to be found to enable the airflow to build up through the sustainer while the boost rocket was still in place. Britain, on the other hand, appeared to have a fixation for wrap-round multiple boost motors for all its early SAMs, and with the Seaslug the mounting of these around the forebody of the missile enabled boost stabilizing fins to be dispensed with, thereby reducing the overall bulk of the boosted weapon.

These first-generation SAMs became operational in 1956–9, and though cumbersome, costly, temperamental and so large that they greatly detracted from other ship capabilities – so that, for example, the British *County* class ships have the armament of a small destroyer in a hull like an ocean liner – they did at least offer proven capability against high-flying jets. But the size of these SAM systems limited them to a very small number of ships in any fleet. To help the other vessels a British company, Shorts, developed a simple command-guidance system, with small missiles that could be loaded on a multiple launcher by hand, which quickly became one of the best-selling SAMs of all time. Significantly, a proposed supersonic version of this missile, which appeared when the basic system was quite new in 1960, was not proceeded with. For close-in defence the instantly available, reliable and cheap command-guidance SAM has proved to be adequate against all known manned aircraft, and is updated by darkfire or blindfire add-ons.

By the early 1960s it was clear that shipboard SAMs were becoming divided into two distinct classes. The big-ship systems offered area defence capability, out to a range of possibly 50 miles (80 km) and thus able to kill most attacking aircraft before they could release many types of anti-ship ASM. With modifications it was possible to make most of these first-generation big-ship systems effective against low-level aircraft and even against other ships, though in most cases they were grossly inefficient in the anti-ship role compared with a purpose-designed weapon. A very few shipboard SAMs have the option of a nuclear warhead which obviously would be effective against a ship, but the remainder have warheads designed for use against aircraft, with continuous-rod or preformed fragments that would prove deadly to aircraft but much less so to ships. So far as is known no SAMs have the option of a purpose-designed anti-ship warhead.

The need for point defence has increasingly been accorded greater emphasis until today the big-ship systems are taking a back seat. This is partly because the anti-ship aeroplane can now stand off so far that it cannot be reached by shipboard SAMs at all, which have yet to demonstrate an OTH (over the horizon) capability to match that of such ASMs as Harpoon and Tomahawk, and thus must be downed by sea-based air power, and partly because of the rapid emergence of the anti-ship missile and its deployment from aircraft, surface ships and submarines. Even more than the front-line soldier, today's sailor needs short-range SAMs in order to survive. Fortunately the requirements are such that the resulting systems can be accommodated in almost all warships likely to be attacked; in fact some of the best SAM systems can even be installed in a small FPB.

For obvious reasons work began around 1957 to try to make different missiles fit into the same shipboard system elements. With first-generation weapons this was often impossible, but modern US Navy vessels often use common launchers for various combinations of Standard and Sea Sparrow SAMs, Asroc ASW missiles and ARM anti-radar missiles. Obviously this commonality extends where possible to the associated radars, data processing, displays and command/control systems. Aegis is the outstanding example of an integrated system despite the fact it is at present configured only for SAM use with Standard missiles. Several industrial companies have developed simpler but more versatile systems able to control SAMs, guns and, in some cases, ASW weapons. One drawback to at least some of these otherwise attractive systems is that small localised damage in the wrong place could incapacitate virtually all the armament and thus knock out the ship (this is not a shortcoming of Aegis). Attention is now being focused on local back-up systems.

By 1978 there had arisen a wealth of point-defence systems for ships which attempted to answer a challenging range of requirements. Warships will always attract missiles, and the bigger the ship the more powerful the attraction and the more diverse the weapons likely to be used against it. Unlike the modern mobile army, whose limitations are generally imposed by logistic considerations, the ship has a strictly limited amount of real estate and carrying capacity. Most major surface vessels now in use could have their radars replaced by more modern systems that would offer twice the capability for half the weight.

Today the activity triggered off by the sinking of the *Eilat* in 1967 has borne fruit in (1) multi-barrel SAMs, (2) rapid-fire cannon, (3) batteries of unguided rockets, and (4) unconventional weapons still in the laboratory. The two middle items in this list, examples of which are the US Navy Phalanx CIWS (Close-In Weapon System) and the French Catulle and British Seafox, show that the SAM is by no means the only answer to a problem where speed of reaction is one of the most vital factors. To a considerable degree the need to defend against the anti-ship missile is like the old Kamikaze problem, in that the oncoming enemy has intelligence, seems to be aimed at you personally and cares nothing about saving its own skin. In such a situation a sailor needs to have absolute confidence in his defence and so far nobody has produced a SAM that does not have to be ripple-fired in multiple to guarantee a kill against each missile. But the British Seawolf can practically guarantee a kill for each round, and has even demonstrated its ability to intercept shells from conventional naval guns. If it were American it would by now be standard throughout the Western Alliance.

# CANADA

*Canadian Sea Sparrow launch from HMCNS* **Iroquois,** *leadship of the chief Canadian warship class.*

## Canadian Sea Sparrow

This system was developed jointly for the Canadian Armed Forces by Raytheon Canada and NV Hollandse Signaalapparaten of the Netherlands. Key elements are Signaal's M22/6 fire-control system and the AIM-7E2 Sparrow missile (p. 228). The M22/6 is one of the widely-used M20 series of I/J-band radars which can track air and surface targets simultaneously. It features monopulse TWS, MTI search, PD tracking, extensive ECCM capability and CW missile guidance. The M22/6 system also includes a back-up optical sight which, like the radar aerial, is fully stabilized. The fire-control system aims a four-missile launcher which can be installed either in a forwards 190° arc or in dual left/right arcs with duplicated cross-linked control systems giving all-round arc of fire. Canadian Sea Sparrow can be used against air or surface targets. A dual installation, weighing 81,500 lb (36 968 kg) and needing four operators, completed testing in 1972. The four DDH-280 *Iroquois* destroyers each have two dual installations (ie, four quad launchers) and support ships *Preserver* and *Protecteur* have singles.

**Data:** as for Sparrow AIM-7E2.

# FRANCE

## Masurca

This wholly French SAM system has a history as long as that of Terrier/Standard. Work began at DEFA, at the Ruelle Naval Arsenal and the DTCN in 1945, and its first major fruit was a test and training vehicle named Maruca (MArine RUelle Contra Avions). Though of aeroplane configuration, launched by four wrap-round boosters, it provided assistance in perfecting guidance and launch techniques and critical hardware items. From it stemmed Masurca (MArine SUpersonique Ruelle Contre Avions) first fired in 1955 and with guidance in 1958. This had a totally different configuration, with tandem booster with four large fins, four fixed rear fins with ailerons for roll-control and four hydraulically driven canard nose controls. The sustainer was a unique end-burning motor whose 882 lb (400 kg) charge was progressively pushed towards the nozzle by hydraulic pressure to minimise c.g. problems. Guidance was by radio command using CFTH radars, and with command detonation of the warhead. Launch weight with booster was 3,198 lb (1450 kg) and maximum slant range 15·5 miles (25 km). Testing from the R&D ship *Ile d'Oléron* took place in 1960. The expected production did not come about, and instead the system was redesigned with a completely different missile identical in aerodynamics and control to the contemporary Advanced Terrier (p. 200). Masurca Mk 2, in whose manufacture Matra shared, has tail controls and fixed wings of very low aspect ratio. Mk 2 Mod 2 has CLOS beam-riding guidance, while in 1970 Mk 2 Mod 3 introduced SARH

**Right:** *Twin Masurca launcher aboard* **Colbert,** *with one side only loaded.*

**Right below:** *Brightly painted Masurca training round on a totally non-standard single (underneath rail) launcher.*

using the Thomson-CSF DRBR-51 radar. Only Mod 3 is in service, though a proportion of Mod 2s lasted through to 1975. Mod 3 has a receiver aerial at the front whose signals are compared with signals received direct from the ship at two horns at the rear. This gives a doppler velocity which enables proportional navigation to be used in the interception. The SNPE Polka booster gives average thrust of 76,675 lb (34 780 kg) for 4·6 sec, and the SNPE Jacée sustainer 5,342 lb (2423 kg) for 26 sec, flight speed being about Mach 3. The 265 lb (120 kg) continuous-rod warhead has a Thomson-CSF proximity fuze. Mod 3 equips the frigates *Suffren* and *Duquesne* and AA cruiser *Colbert*, each of which has duplicated DRBR-51s and one twin launcher fed with 48 missiles.

**Dimensions:** Length with booster 338 in (8·6 m); diameter 16·14 in (410 mm); span 30·3 in (770 mm).
**Launch weight:** 4,585 lb (2080 kg); without booster 2,359 lb (1070 kg).
**Range:** 31 miles (50 km).

## Catulle

This name identifies the shipboard version of Javelot (p. 148). Thomson-CSF state that after lengthy study – originally under the name Mureca – the system is to be further developed for the French Navy.

Top: *Naval Crotale installation aboard a French warship (from height of deck, probably the Jeanne d'Arc).*

Above: *Thomson-CSF model of the Catulle system being developed for the French Navy.*

Above right: *Model of FPB of La Combattante II type showing proposed Hirondelle launcher at stern.*

# Naval Crotale

Originally proposed by Thomson-CSF in 1970 in a system called Murène, and in 1972 combined with naval Javelot in a combined system Murène-Mureca, this system progressed through several stages of expansion and refinement, was adopted by the French Navy, funded by DTCN and by 1978 had begun to notch up a succession of foreign sales. Though the missile is the standard R.460 Crotale, the system is totally different. Low-flying aircraft or missiles are detected by Thomson-CSF DRBV-26 D-band surveillance radar, acquired by G/H-band DRBV-51C with MTI, and interrogated by LMT IFF. The fire control room has Senit data processing and display. Engagement can be automatic or manual. The launcher carries two quad groups of ready-fire rounds in tubes whose nosecaps are of a lightweight design to prevent damage to ship helicopters. Each launcher also carries the guidance radar dish, radio command aerial, IR gathering and TV camera. There is much more auto checkout equipment than in land-based systems, and such add-ons as auto hold-back of a missile whose motor ignites prematurely, and a brake on launcher slewing if two on the same side should ignite accidentally. Two rounds can be fired within 8½ seconds of target designation and SSKP is 0·75.

Naval Crotale has been engineered swiftly since 1976, with the magazine and loading system manufactured by Navy yards. In mid-1978 the French Navy was buying systems for the 16 C70 corvettes, three F67 frigates and helicopter carriers *Jeanne d'Arc* and PH75. Tests have shown the entire system can be installed and checked out in a suitably prepared ship in eight days. Foreign customers had not been identified in mid-1978.

**Data** as for R.460 Crotale.

# Hirondelle

In 1973–76 Electronique Marcel Dassault proposed a close-range shipboard weapon system using the Matra Super 530 missile (p. 210). These were to be integrated with the ship's radar(s) and fired from a quad launcher. At one time it was even announced that Hirondelle would be operational in 1977, in *La Combattante II* patrol boats, but since 1976 nothing has been heard of this system and no order has been announced.

# Flash

This last-ditch weapon is designed to kill sea-skimming missiles, and takes the form of IR/TV tracking, laser ranging and a rapid-reload launcher firing salvos of 16 or more spin-stabilized 167·6 lb (76 kg) rockets. Promoters are SEP (propulsion), Creusot-Loire (launcher and loader) and CSEE (Compagnie des Signaux d'Enterprises Electriques). International partners were being sought in mid-1978.

# GERMANY

During World War 2 several types of spin-stabilized rocket were fired from experimental launch tubes built into *Type VIIC* and *Type IX* U-boats, in trials to determine their value in surface-to-surface and surface-to-air roles. No guided missile was fired from any vessel of the Kriegsmarine.

## Kumar

Study for a close-range ship-to-air missile system by VFW-Fokker, which ran from 1975 but was terminated in 1977 because no international consortium could be constructed around it. Its features included vertical launch from a simple fixed eggbox, thereafter swiftly turning towards the target under TVC. IMI and Sperry, both of Britain, were in 1977 collaborating in a Kumar motor of 8,000 lb (3629 kg) thrust with two spherical-joint nozzles giving fast-reaction TVC in any direction within arcs of ± 8° for 30 g manoeuvres. See Sesta.

## Sesta

With a name derived from SEnkrecht STArt (vertical launch), this VFW-Fokker naval SAM appears to be a candidate around which an international consortium could be constructed to meet the NATO 6S requirement (see opposite). The Bundesmarine staff envisage Sesta as popping up to a peak of about 100 ft (30 m) and immediately homing on its target (aircraft or sea-skimming missile) with active radar. In 1978 international partners were being sought, an American (Raytheon) homing head being preferred.

## FlaM 80

Yet another German close-range ship-to-air system, Flugabwehr Marine 80 is a study by AEG-Telefunken to replace ASMD (see opposite).

**Right:** *Underwater launch of solid-propellant missile from Type IXC U-boat in summer 1942.*

# INTERNATIONAL

## Jason

Since 1969 Roland (p. 144) has been studied by Euromissile in ship systems. One, originally called Roland MX, was later named Jason, and was current in 1974–77. Like previous studies it featured a twin-launcher backed up by an eight-round reloader on each side, and the reaction time was short enough to permit engagement of anti-ship missiles. The studies have been overtaken by vertical-launch concepts.

## Ram

This programme was succinctly outlined by GD Pomona in 1977: "The Anti-Ship Missile Defense (ASMD) system for the point defense of ships is being developed under a joint program between the US Navy and the Federal Republic of Germany. ASMD will provide both navies' smaller ships with increased defense and survivability, and high-value ships with complementary defense in depth against anti-ship missile threats. It will use both existing and advanced shipboard sensors and tactical-data systems for threat extraction, command and control. The missile, with all-weather dual-mode RF and IR terminal guidance and 5-inch (127 mm) rolling

**Below:** *The final arrangement proposed for Jason featured two eight-round reloaders, larger than could reasonably be accommodated by army AFVs.*

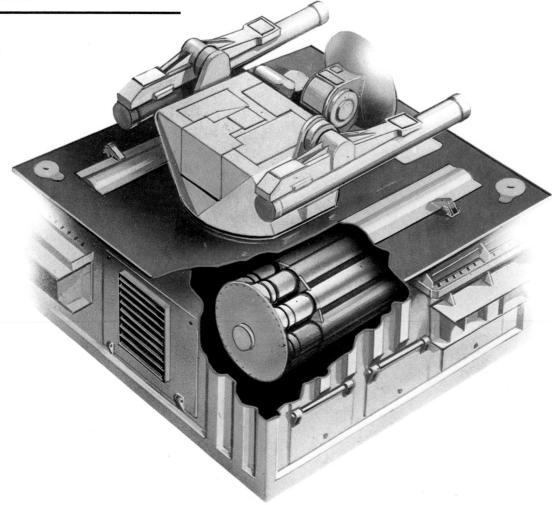

airframe, has been flight tested. It uses available components to provide a low-cost, lightweight missile with high engagement kill probability. The rolling airframe makes it possible to launch a large number of rounds from the Sea Sparrow launcher or from a stand-alone lightweight launcher. Advanced development is to be completed in early 1978". The ASMD as in flight test in mid-1978 has an improved Rocketdyne Mk 36 (Chaparral) motor, Stinger IR seeker combined with a passive RF sensor, and Sidewinder (large size WDU-17B) warhead. When Sea Sparrow is fitted to a ship, ASMD can use its launcher, even if other

rounds on the same quad are Sea Sparrows. ASMD, which was designated XRIM-116A and named Ram, is being studied in various comprehensive ship-defence systems integrated with BPDS Sea Sparrow, Chaffroc ECM launchers and CIWS Phalanx gun systems, as well as longer-range SAMs. In the simplest systems ASMD could be fitted to the smallest vessels such as FPBs, though some means of detecting an anti-ship missile must be provided. ASMD flies at about Mach 3, fast enough to manoeuvre by body lift and tail controls only. Rods projecting from the forebody are receiver aerials for the passive RF guid-

ance, and one obvious problem is how to cover the entire range of possible anti-ship missile frequencies in so small a guidance receiver (it has been suggested that in large ships the oncoming missile's emissions would be analysed and used to tune the ASMD homing circuits in the last split second before launch). RF homing is regarded as a reliable method for countering all anticipated anti-ship missiles of the next decade. The glass nose over the IR seeker is available as a back-up should the target cease to radiate RF, but is chiefly for terminal homing. No industrial contractor has been named in West Germany, but the F122

frigate class has been named as the first German recipient. Germany has been described as a "more than equal partner". Other nations may enter the programme before this book is published.

**Dimensions:** Length 110·0 inches (2·79 m); diameter 5·0 in (127 mm).
**Launch weight:** About 156 lb (70·7 kg).
**Range:** Probably within 3 miles (5 km).

Below: *Bits of Chaparral, Stinger and Sidewinder are all helping the Ram (XRIM-116A) (probably China Lake, 1977).*

# ITALY

## Albatros

This comprehensive system was developed by Selenia in Mk 1 form in 1968–71 to provide fire-control for ships down to the size of small escorts, using both guns and the RIM-7H Sparrow SAM. This system underwent trials from land sites and in Italian ships in 1973 but has been superseded by Albatros Mk 2 in which the missile is Selenia's own Aspide, claimed to be superior to RIM-7H in important respects (see p. 214). The basic system comprises a dual-channel radar, separate gun and missile control systems, an operator's console and an eight-cell SAM launcher whose mechanical and electrical parts were produced by Oto Melara. The dual radars comprise Selenia's Orion RTN 10X PD tracking radar and Sirio RTN 12X CW target-illumination radar. Aspide, like Sparrow, has SARH guidance using CW illumination of the target. In this system Aspide is claimed to have capability against all anti-ship aircraft or missiles including those descending from above or skimming the waves. Selenia offers a choice of fire-control for guns, by Ferranti or Elsag, and the Aspide SAM portion can be retrofitted into ships with other (gun) fire-control already installed. Reaction time to missile launch is said to be 8 seconds. A lightweight version, with four-box launcher, is offered for small vessels down to 200 tons. By mid-1978 customers included the Italian Navy (starting with four *Lupo* and six *Maestrale* frigates), Egypt (two *Lupos)*, Greece (four *Themistokles* destroyers), Peru (four *Lupos)* and Venezuela (six *Lupos)*. The missile is identical with the Aspide AAM except for cropping of the wings and fins.

**Data:** As Aspide except span (moving wings) 31·5 in (800 mm), (fixed fins) 25·2 in (640 mm).

## Sea Indigo

Sistel began the development of this shipboard SAM version of Indigo (p. 154) in 1963 and made over 80 trial launches using the Sea Hunter fire-control system. Development was abandoned.

## Vanessa

Oto Melara was in 1978 reported to be studying, with other companies, a shipboard SAM system using a relatively large subsonic missile in order to gain the advantage of a larger warhead than can be carried in small highly supersonic missiles. It is said to have radar CLOS guidance, very large boost propulsion and advanced proximity fuzing. Partners in Vanessa have not been identified.

**Above:** *Albatros octuple launch box aboard Aviere, the Italian navy trials ship (a former wartime USN destroyer).*

**Below:** *Albatros system fires Sparrow III from Aviere in late 1972. Without missiles the launcher weighs seven tons; max elevation is 65°.*

# USSR

## SA-N-1 Goa

So far as one can tell from poor-quality photographs this SAM system for large ships uses a missile identical to the land-based SA-3 (p. 157), but almost every other part of the system is completely different. So far as Western observers can tell the basic installation is standardized, with a two-deck magazine for 20 reload missiles, assembled with tandem boosters and stored vertically, which progress on railed trolleys to the vertical hoist which loads them on to the launcher set to 90° elevation. The launcher has twin rails on a stabilized mounting and can be driven by powerful servos to the azimuth and elevation of the associated radar. The latter is known to NATO as the Peel Group, and like most Soviet shipboard radars is of instantly distinctive appearance with four solid-reflector ellipsoidal dishes, a large pair with axes vertical and horizontal and a small pair with axes vertical and horizontal. It is thought the large aerials, probably G/H-band, are for searching the sky in the direction indicated by the surveillance radar (usually Head Net) and locking-on to the target, thereafter commanding the small pair, thought to be I-band, which provide precision tracking and missile guidance. The installation of magazine, loader, launcher and radars is fitted both fore and aft in the four *Kresta I* cruisers and 19 *Kashin/Kashin-Mod* destroyers. The four *Kynda* cruisers have one system forward, while the eight *Kotlin-SAM* and seven *Kanin* destroyers each have one system aft. A further *Kotlin-SAM*, *Warsawa*, serves with the Polish Navy, and in 1978 SA-N-1 was identified on a new Indian frigate design.

**Data:** As for SA-3 Goa.

## SA-N-2

A single ship, the ageing cruiser *Dzerzhinski*, was around 1969 rebuilt with X turret replaced by a major installation for what appears to be a unique ship installation using the SA-2 Guideline (V750VK) SAM. The installation appears to occupy most of the considerable space between the aft funnel and Y turret. The stabilized twin launcher is quite unlike land launchers for this missile and has the launch rail above the missile. Ahead of the launcher is a hangar-like building which probably encloses the reload system. Ahead of this is the Fan Song E radar group, which almost certainly posed problems on a ship (especially in rough weather) and may have been the main reason for abandoning further SA-N-2 installations. Between the funnels is the only known installation on a ship of the High Lune nodding HFR (height-finder radar), thought to be related to the land-based Cake series HFRs, which provides necessary height information. The performance of this missile is thought to be comparable to the land based version.

**Data:** As for SA-2.

*Top: Frame from a Soviet propaganda film showing SA-N-1 Goa missiles aboard an unidentified warship.*

*Right: Boost fins not quite fully deployed as an SA-N-1 leaves a Kashin destroyer. Photo issued February 1975.*

*Below: Outstanding photograph of SA-N-1 Goa, apparently the forward installation in a Kashin-Mod destroyer.*

*Below right: Poor retouched photograph of the SA-N-2 installation in Dzerzhinski.*

# SA-N-3 Goblet

When the ASW cruisers (helicopter carriers) *Moskva* and *Leningrad* were first seen in 1967 their SAM launchers were described as "similar to Goa". A little later they were described as "of an improved Goa type" but by the mid-1970s, when SA-N-3 was widely used in cruisers, it was belatedly recognised that the SAM system of these ships bears virtually no resemblance to SA-N-1 Goa at all. In all ships so far seen with this weapon system the installation appears to be the same, and to comprise: below-decks magazine for about 24 reload rounds; vertical reload mechanism with two pairs of lifts to four hatches so that by swivelling 180° between each reload the launcher can double its rate of fire (compared with SA-N-1, for example); modern twin-rail launcher which, as it appears to have no gyro-stabilization, suggests highly positive missile gathering and guidance; the extremely large and powerful Top Sail 3-D surveillance

radar; and the intensely interesting Head Light Group of SAM radars. Like SA-N-1's Peel Group this installation comprises two large (G/H-band?) aerials and two small (probably I-band), but Head Light dishes are circular open mesh, and larger. There seems to be little similarity to the Straight Flush radars of the SA-6 Gainful SAM, apart from one possible equality in wavelength, but since 1973 there has been prolonged speculation in the West that SA-N-3 Goblet uses the SA-6 Gainful missile, or a near-relative. In mid-1978 no Soviet captain had been unlucky enough to be caught by Western aircraft with his Goblets showing. This obviously successful and formidable area-defence weapon is fitted to the two ships mentioned (two installations forward), the big *Kiev* and other *Kuril* class multi-role carriers (one forward), the five (or six) new *Kara* class cruisers (one forward, one aft) and the ten *Kresta II* cruisers (one forward, one aft).

**Data:** not yet known in West.

# SA-N-4

As yet not publicly associated with a NATO reporting name, this is the standard short-range shipboard SAM system of the Soviet Navy. It has been installed in over 100 vessels of all sizes and sold to foreign customers, though details are still tantalisingly sparse in the West. Not until the appearance of the land-mobile SA-8 Gecko (p. 162) with its near-identical radar group could some definite form be added to the bare externals of ship-radar bin and launch bin. N-4 was first seen in the late 1960s installed in the foredeck of the *Grisha* corvettes, and soon afterwards in the new *Krivak* destroyers and two converted *Sverdlov* cruisers: *Admiral Senyavin* appeared in 1972 with an N4 installation built into the top of a helicopter hangar (which with the landing pad replaced X and Y turrets) and *Zhdanov* had just an N4 installation above a large deckhouse in place of X turret. The handsome *Krivaks* have one installation forward

*Right: Superstructure of Moskva showing SA-N-3 launcher and the two groups of associated twin Head Light guidance radars. Higher up are Head Net 3D and Top Sail air surveillance.*

*Below: Excellent picture (by Lt Paul Parrack, HMS Daedalus) of a Krivak class ship passing through the English Channel. A is the bin housing SA-N-4; B is the associated Pop Group radar and optical sight head.*

---

# UNITED KINGDOM

## Stooge

The reluctance of Britain to develop even simple guided missiles in World War 2 was remarkable, and evidence of immense German efforts merely branded such weapons as undesirable. Only one project was started, and this was the most primitive SAM that could be imagined (Brakemine, p. 164, never received proper funding at all). A specification was written in early 1944 for a radio guided vehicle to be fired from ship launchers to defeat Kamikaze attacks, but the guidance system was never properly thought out and in practice would have needed modification. Known as the Stooge, the airframe was assigned to Fairey Aviation at Hayes, and it had an aeroplane configuration with aluminium structure, simple autopilot driving ailerons and elevators, and a command receiver for steering and for detonating the 220 lb (100 kg) warhead. Launch was by four 3 in (76 mm) solid motors of the type then made by the million, giving 5,600 lb (2540 kg) thrust for 1·6 sec to blast Stooge off a 10 ft (3·3 m) elevating and trainable ramp. When the boosts were jettisoned a weight was also released from the nose to preserve c.g. position (!). Sustainer propulsion was by four 5 in (127 mm) Swallow motors each giving either 40 lb (18 kg) or 75 lb (34 kg) for 40 sec, resulting in speed in a typical climb of either 350 or 500 mph (563 or 804 km/h). Urgent work by many groups got the first Stooges into the air by February 1945, but at

VJ-Day the whole programme was abandoned, and no attempt was made to put the work to use. In 1947–53 Fairey conducted experiments into slow-acceleration near-vertical launch of delta vehicles, but this was aimed at manned interceptors.

**Dimensions:** Length 90·5 in (2·3 m), (with boosters) 126 in (3·2 m); diameter 12·6 in (320 mm); span 82·0 in (2·08 m).
**Launch weight:** 738 lb (335 kg).
**Range:** 8 miles (12·9 km).

## Seaslug

With this ship-to-air system Britain at last embarked on an effective weapon, and though its development took an unimpressive 13 years (1949–62) Seaslug nevertheless remained an outstanding weapon throughout the 1960s and can still deter manned aircraft, though the system is naturally much larger than modern counterparts. The three chief contractors were Armstrong Whitworth (subsequently Whitworth Gloster, HSD and BAe Dynamics Group) for the missile airframe and system integration, Sperry for flight control and GEC for radar beam-riding guidance. From the start Seaslug had an airframe entirely of aluminium alloy, with machined wings and tail controls indexed in line. Test vehicles had rectangular wings, four conical-nose boosters (mounted on the forebody to obviate the need for fins and thus reduce the overall bulk) and an acid/methanol sustainer. The production missile had wings cropped at the rear corners, flat-fronted boosts by

*Above: Launch of Fairey Stooge of late series with warhead and endplates on wings. This picture was probably taken at Aberporth.*

Bristol-Aerojet and an ICI solid sustainer. Guidance boxes were redesigned with printed circuits and arranged in pressurized 120° segments, Sperry introduced a refined hydraulic control package surrounding the motor blast tube, and the missile was given surface-to-surface capability. The 297 lb (135 kg) warhead had DA and proximity fuzes.

Seaslug Mk 1 was installed in the first four *County* class GW destroyers, *Devonshire*, *Hampshire*, *Kent* and *London*. Vickers Engineering contributed the magazine and launcher and interconnecting handling gear, which was the first in any European ships. It had been planned to use a triple launcher, and many of the 250-plus R&D firings, from Aberporth, and the trials ship *Girdle Ness*, used a triple system. On several trials two rounds were fired with about 1 sec interval, and on each occasion the first struck the target and the second the largest piece of

wreckage. Overal SSKP was put at 92 per cent by 1961, the Royal Navy calling the Mk 1 weapon "the best we have ever had".

All *County* class ships have essentially the same basic system. RN Type 965 surveillance radar is used for long-range air search, with a single AKE-1 aerial in the first four ships and double AKE-2 in the second four, in each case with on-mounted Cossor IFF. Aft of the mainmast is the Type 277 HFR, while approximately in X position is the large searchlight-shape of the Type 901, with a stabilized aerial thought to operate in G/H-band. In each case Marconi Radar Systems is main contractor. Targets are tracked by the 965 and 277 and designated to the 901 in three Cartesian co-ordinates. The missile installation is not triple but twin. The Type 901 locks-on to the target, aims the lattice launcher and fires a missile as soon as the range is correct. The missile is gathered and locked to the centre of the coded pencil beam. In the surface-target role the same beam is used though there are small differences in technique. It is assumed that most such targets are surface ships.

and one aft, while in 1973 the *Nikolayev*, first of the almost futuristic *Kara* class cruisers, showed an N4 installation on each side amidships. With this system not even the launcher or radar need be visible; in each case the whole assembly is normally retracted inside a circular bin closed by a lid. All that was seen by Western observers until 1976 was the Pop Group radar and sight system, and even this was often hidden inside its deckhouse bin under two sliding lids. Pop Group was first noticed on a *Nanuchka* small missile boat, and after further sightings was recognised as a high-speed target- and missile-tracking radar group, almost certainly supplemented by optical and TV sight systems, able to guide the N4 missile and the twin 30 mm gun turret(s) usually mounted close by. In 1976, when the *Kiev* (and, presumably other *Kuril* carriers) was seen to have three N-4 installations, a photograph became available showing the launcher of a corvette in the raised position. It is des-

cribed as a twin launcher, but in fact could carry four Gecko-size boxes. The first overseas user is India, whose *Nanuchkas* have the system installed.

**Data:** assumed similar to SA-8 Gecko.

## SA-N-7

This is the DoD designation of the version of SA-7 Grail used aboard all the chief classes of missile boat and MTB (motor torpedo boat) for close-range AA protection. So far as is known the missile and launch tube/sight are identical with the improved form of SA-7 (p. 161), and it is strange that the SA-9 Gaskin vehicle-mounted system should not be used. In most installations the tube is pivoted to the superstructure at a convenient place and aimed by hand in the usual way. N-7 has been seen on all recent *Osa I* and *II* missile boats and *Shershen* torpedo boats, which are also used by certain Arab countries.

**Data:** Presumed as for SA-7.

In the 1961 Navy Estimates first public mention was made of Seaslug 2. As in the case of all British SAM programmes of the 1950s it soon became apparent that far higher performance – greater speed and range, and improved guidance accuracy and resistance to ECM – could readily be introduced without altering the basic ship system. Seaslug 2 is externally similar to Mk 1 and though slightly longer and heavier is interchangeable in the magazine and loading system. The main changes are in the propulsion total impulse, which is significantly greater, and in the guidance electronics, which in ways not made public offer much greater capability against low-flying or surface targets and hostile ECM. The Mk 2 missile again suffered most protracted development which was not completed until a series of firings from HMS *Fife* at Barking Sands range, Hawaii. Seaslug Mk 2 arms the second group of four County ships, *Fife*, *Glamorgan*, *Antrim* and *Norfolk*. It had always been intended that Seaslug 2 should be retrofitted to the earlier four ships, but the modest sum needed to do this was never made available.

**Dimensions:** Length (Mk 1) 19 ft 8 in (5·99 m), (Mk 2) 20 ft 0 in (6·10 m); diameter 16·1 in (409 mm); span 56·6 in (1437 mm).
**Launch weight:** Never disclosed.
**Range:** (Mk 1) 28 miles (45 km), (Mk 2) 36 miles (58 km).

## Orange Nell

This extremely advanced system was intended to give small ships defence against both aircraft and anti-ship missiles. Guided by CW SARH, it met Staff Requirement G.02769/53 but was cancelled in 1957.

**Above:** *Launch of Seaslug from a County class cruiser in June 1975. Blast on the launcher is considerable.*

**Below:** *Another shallow-angle Seaslug launch, this time from HMS* Hampshire. *Note Type 965 surveillance radar.*

**Right:** *Seaslug has a unique configuration, here drawn in side elevation with wings and controls at 45°.*

**Right:** *Front view of Seaslug twin launcher showing lattice construction. Both sides are loaded (note flat-nosed boosts).*

# Sea Dart

This outstanding area-defence system was created by the team that developed Seaslug, and though the missile is more compact, and the system can fit into much smaller ships, the performance against all kinds of target has been dramatically multiplied. The main new member of the team was Bristol Siddeley (today Rolls-Royce) whose ramjet propulsion gives sustained thrust throughout the flight and thus enables the maximum power of manoeuvre to be maintained to the furthest limits of range. A further change compared with Seaslug is that guidance is by SARH, with proportional navigation (to laws varied during the interception to achieve optimum efficiency) giving either a direct hit or an extremely small miss-distance. As CF.299 the system was placed under contract in August 1962, and test firings began in 1965. The system quickly showed its ability to meet all requirements, including high rate of fire, the ability to hit targets at all altitudes (including small ships and other surface targets) and extremely high SSKP against air- and surface-launched anti-ship missiles.

Most Sea Dart (GWS.30) ships have the Type 965 air-search radar, with AKE-2 double aerial and on-mounted Cossor IFF. This designates targets in three dimensions, as in Seaslug, and points the Type 909 missile radar(s) and twin launcher. Marconi's Type 909 is thought to operate in G/H-band and to incorporate its own IFF. Its aerial is enclosed under a weatherproof radome. In the first Sea Dart ship, HMS *Bristol*, there is one Type 909; all others have two. This radar locks-on to the target and illuminates it for the missile's receiver and homing system. Missiles are stored vertically, ready to fire, hoisted through an intermediate stage and then rammed up the rails of

the launcher elevated to 90°. The launcher is aimed electrically at the target, the selected round launched by automatic signal and accelerated to Mach 2 in 2½ sec by the IMI composite DB tandem boost motor which gives 35,000 lb (15 876 kg) thrust. As the missile leaves the launcher the boost fins pivot open 90°. Before boost burnout the integral ramjet has completed its starting sequence, initially exhausting through inter-stage vents. The Rolls-Royce Odin is one of the most advanced ramjet engines in service anywhere, and the other portions of the missile either form the double wall of its duct or are built around it. It probably burns kerosene and can be precisely controlled in flight to give any desired speed/range profile up to Mach 3·5. The latter speed is normally maintained all the way to interception, thus giving much reduced flight time and increased accuracy at all ranges. The Type 909 radar illuminates the target throughout, and Sea Dart homes by proportional navigation using four interferometer receiver aerials around the double-shock nose inlet. A dish aerial could have been installed in the inlet centrebody but these interferometer probes are of a new type overcoming previous difficulties with this type of aerial system. Combined with extreme accuracy by the radar and exceptionally fast control response by the missile, which manoeuvres with four tail fins (the four narrow-span wings are almost superfluous except at reduced

**Right:** *Sea Dart launcher fully operational aboard HMS* **Bristol** *in July 1973.*

**Below:** *Close-up of Sea Dart on unidentified ship. Existing missiles may be updated by improvements, including a new guidance package and a high-performance boost motor with TVC.*

Mach numbers) Sea Dart probably has smaller miss-distances than any other SARH missile with comparable range. The warhead is powerful and has an externally grooved casing and EMI proximity fuze.

The first production order was placed in November 1967 and the system has since gone into service in HMS *Bristol* (Type 82), ten Type 42 destroyers (not all commissioned by mid-1978) and two Type 42 of the Argentine

*Below: BAe artist's impression of LWSD (Light Weight Sea Dart) aboard typical 50 m FPB for the 1980s; Marconi 800-series radars would be standard.*

*Foot of page: Launch of Sea Dart from a Type 42 destroyer; the twin mount is in B-position on these ships, but at the stern in Bristol.*

Navy, and is also being installed in HMS *Invincible* and two further through-deck cruisers. Total system development cost was about £300 million. There is no doubt Sea Dart has better all-round performance over a larger flight envelope than any other SAM system, sea or land-based, available in the West or likely to be available within the next eight years. So outstanding is its performance that, despite extreme financial parsimony, the whole system and especially the missile itself are being improved into Sea Dart 2, for use until at least 2000. One of the chief improvements will be a new airborne guidance system with advanced solid-state logic and LSI circuits to reduce mass and bulk despite having an extra duty in steering the initial flight off the launcher by means of a more powerful booster with TVC (in theory the missile could make a

180° turn straight off the launcher). More room will be available for ramjet fuel, giving increased speed and/or range. Considerably enhanced ECCM will be incorporated. Like Sea Dart 1 the improved missile will have LOS capability against surface targets.

BAe Dynamics Group has for some time offered this immensely powerful system in a Light Weight Sea Dart (LWSD) form for installation in vessels as small as 50 m FPBs. Missiles will be stored in sealed containers which also serve as the launcher. There is also a proposed land based version (p. 169).

**Dimensions:** Length 14 ft 5·25 in (4·40 m); diameter 16·5 in (420 mm); span 36 in (910 mm).
**Launch weight:** 1,210 lb (549 kg).
**Range:** Exceeds 50 miles (80 km).

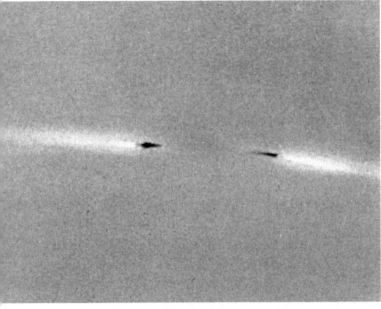

Left: *Two frames from high-speed film showing the unique ability of Seawolf to destroy extremely small supersonic targets (Petrel, Mach 2.4).*

# Seawolf

The only anti-missile system actually in service with any navy – in the Western world, at least – Seawolf is of immense potential importance, and if it had been American would by now be standard in almost all Western navies. In recent years MoD(PE) has adopted a more positive attitude in ''selling'' British systems, and by the time this book is published Seawolf may belatedly have been recognised as doing today what many paper projects hope to do at some time in a more costly future. Until now it has been short-sightedly criticised as too costly or too heavy, but as it works, is available, and fits ships down to little over 500 tons displacement, such comments are no more than excuses for doing no more than trying to copy it.

Work was triggered by an RN Staff Target of 1964 for an anti-missile system for fitting in frigate hulls. Studies by MoD and industry (code-named Confessor) showed that the system should have PD air-surveillance radar, PD radar differential tracker and CLOS missile guidance. The project was defined in an RN Requirement of February 1967; this was approved in 1968 and full development was authorised, with system designation PX.430. The prime contract was placed with BAC GW Division at Stevenage (now BAe Dynamics Group). Subsequently the system was named Seawolf. Firing trials took place at Aberporth

and Woomera in 1970–76, and in 1976 full system firing trials commenced in HMS *Penelope*, the *Leander* class trials frigate. Seawolf was first selected for the Type 22 frigates (*Sheffield* et seq) and will also be retrofitted into the last ten *Leander* class in place of Seacat. Plans to do the same with the Type 21 (*Amazon* et seq) were shelved in 1976 because it was said the system weight required keel ballast that would cut ship speed, but these ships have so few weapons (compared with Soviet counterparts) there must be something wrong with their design if this is true. In any case lightweight installations could not possibly require ballast.

The basic RN system is GWS. 25. Incoming targets are detected by the Marconi Type 965 L-band PD radar. The entire sequence is automatic and operations take milliseconds. Range, bearing and velocity are fed to the Ferranti FM.1600D computer which forms an unambiguous track, initiates threat evaluation and IFF interrogation. If these processes, taking about 5 sec in all, result in an immediate-threat designation, an appropriate launcher/tracker is selected and aimed in azimuth. The Type 910 tracker group has one main and two side auxiliary dishes, all circular and operating in I/J-band, and uses EAT to give precise and smooth tracking. It searches up and down on the designated azimuth and the accuracy of surveillance computer data is such that this seldom takes more than a fraction of a second. The tracker computer calculates the aim-off necessary to direct the selected missile into the gathering beam. If the target is extremely low, so that radar tracking is degraded in elevation, the system may automatically switch to a TV mode. The Marconi-Elliott TV is mounted on the Type 910 group and bore-sighted to the radar axis.

CLOS guidance resulted in a small missile, with delta wings and tail control fins. The missile is launched at high acceleration by the Bristol Aerojet/RPE Black-cap motor which burns for about 2 sec to give a peak speed of about Mach 2. The control actuators surrounding the motor blast pipe are driven by hot gas. The missile slides from its Vickers six-box launcher on a small locating frame which keeps the command-link aerials on the wingtips clear of the box. All six launch boxes can be trained and elevated together at high rates. The missile is light enough for manual reloading, using a rail conveyor system with the laun-

Left: *Launch crew aboard HMS Penelope reload No 1 box in October 1977. The GWS.25 system is now operational, and light-weight variations are likely soon to mature.*

Right: *Frame from high-speed film showing launch of Seawolf from No 4 box aboard Type 22b frigate.*

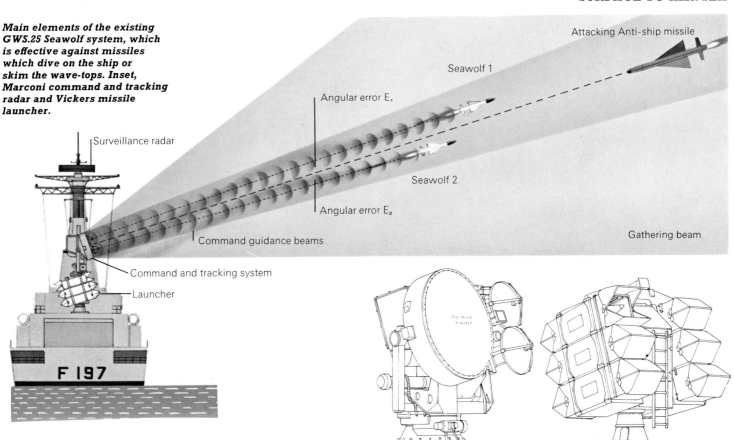

*Main elements of the existing GWS.25 Seawolf system, which is effective against missiles which dive on the ship or skim the wave-tops. Inset, Marconi command and tracking radar and Vickers missile launcher.*

Attacking Anti-ship missile

Seawolf 1

Angular error E₁

Surveillance radar

Command guidance beams

Command and tracking system

Launcher

F 197

Seawolf 2

Angular error E₂

Gathering beam

cher at a low elevation. Clamshell doors at each end seal each box so that each "barrel" can remain loaded for long periods. Testing and maintenance are eliminated.

The system can fire up to three barrels in rapid succession and steer all to the same target simultaneously. Firing is as automatic as the rest of the system, the first barrel being fired the moment the target is in a position such that the interception point is within range. Missiles are gathered in the wide-angle beam and then held precisely on the axis of the target beam, with EAT allowing small excursions from the centreline to be measured without mechanically moving the radar on the ship. With TV guidance the target is tracked manually, holding crosshairs on a monitor screen, and the missile gathered and steered automatically as before. EMI proximity or contact fuzes detonate the 31 lb (14 kg) warhead. In development firings

Seawolf has actually struck a 4.5 in Mk 8 shell.

There are numerous alternatives to GWS.25. Seawolf Psi uses two new Marconi air-search and surveillance radars and light twin or triple launchers. Delta is a darkfire version with two lightweight launchers and one tracker radar and a TV. VM.40 is an extremely important system with the Signaal STIR-derived dual-frequency radar which automatically adopts higher-frequency tracking for

very low targets or in the presence of clutter affecting the lower frequency. No TV is needed and total system weight with light power-loaded twin launcher is reduced to about 13,225 lb (6000 kg). Another alternative is to use Rapier DN.181 Blindfire instead of TV.

**Dimensions:** Length 75.0 in (1.9 m); diameter 7.1 in (180 mm); span 22.0 in (559 mm).
**Launch weight:** 180 lb (82 kg).
**Range:** 4 miles (6.4 km).

# Seacat

Short Brothers (then Short Bros & Harland) were one of the leaders of British GW development, and the company's GW division at Castlereagh also pioneered RPV conversions of piston and jet fighters and bombers. In 1956 the SX-A5 research SAM was based on the Malkara anti-tank weapon (p. 238), using essentially the same airframe. From it was derived Seacat, with long swept wings. The initial Seacat contract was dated April 1958. It was the first shipboard system designed for close-range defence as a replacement for rapid-fire guns. Guided trials took place in 1960, shipboard trials from HMS *Decoy* (a *Daring* class destroyer) in 1961 and full evaluation at sea in 1962. The simple system was subsequently purchased by 16 navies, making it the most widely used ship-to-air guided missile. Most customers expect to retain it in

service until the late 1980s, making this probably the most cost-effective weapon in its class.

The missile has an IMI dual-thrust solid motor, four fixed tail fins, hydraulically driven wings clipped around the square-section forebody, potted guidance packs, and a relatively large blast and continuous-rod warhead with DA and proximity fuzes. Seacat is delivered and stored in glass-fibre containers which fit closely around the wings, and is small enough for loading to be manual if necessary. It has radio command guidance of the most basic kind and can thus be integrated with almost any form of sighting and fire control system. The simplest, introduced as standard and styled GWS. 20 by the Royal Navy, slaves a quad launcher to a director bin manned by two operators. One rotates the director, and thus the launcher, to the target azimuth while the other searches with powerful binocu-

lars whose elevation is followed by the missiles. As soon as the target is acquired within range a missile is fired, coming into view of the optics in about 7 sec at 1,000 ft (300 m). The operator keeps the tracking flares on two fins lined up with the target by a command joystick, GWS 21 and 22 use different RN radars to give darkfire capability. Seacat has also been linked with Signaal M40 and M4-1, Contraves Sea Hunter and San Giorgio NA9 and Marconi-Elliott 323 series CCTV which reduces gathering time and allows the operator to be armoured and more efficient. Further options are a lightweight triple launcher and one-man sight/director suitable for inshore minesweepers and 30 m FPBs, and a retrofit avionics package which enables the missile to hold 20 ft (6 m) above the sea to attack small ships or intercept sea-skimming missiles.

Operators of Seacat, in various forms, include the Royal Navy

and Argentina, Australia, Brazil, Chile, West Germany, India, Iran, Libya, Malaysia, Netherlands, New Zealand, Nigeria, Sweden, Thailand, and Venezuela. The land-mobile system is Tigercat (p. 167); Hellcat is a proposed ASM version. In 1961 Short exhibited Seacat 2, a supersonic missile fitting the same basic system, but this was not proceeded with.

**Dimensions:** Length 58·3 in (1·48 m); diameter 7·5 in (190·5 mm); span 25·6 in (650 mm).
**Launch weight:** 143 lb (65 kg).
**Range:** Up to 4 miles (6·5 km).

# SLAM

Mystery surrounding this simple system and its customers even extends to the meaning of its name, rendered variously as Surface-Launched Air Missile and Submarine-Launched Airflight Missile. The system was developed by Vickers Ship-

Left: *Launch of Seacat from the basic GWS.20 quad launcher. The missile has already begun to roll to the right. At this stage it is unguided.*

Below inset: *The standard GWS.20 launcher, with three production missiles ready for firing. The missile is light enough for reloading to be manual.*

Below: *Launch from the lightweight three-round launcher used to defend FPBs and minesweepers. The other two rounds are still in containers.*

building Group to give submarines capability against aircraft, ACVs (SESs) and ships. It comprises a GRP pressure vessel inside the bridge fin (sail) housing a hydraulically extended stabilized launcher for six Blowpipe missiles (p. 169) together with a TV sight system and guidance electronics. The single operator searches for a target in his attack periscope, to which the launcher is slaved, acquires it, tracks it on the TV screen, and fires a missile. This disconnects the launcher (which continues tracking on a rate-memory circuit) and transfers the operator's thumb-button to steering the missile to impact. Sea trials on HMS *Aeneas* were successfully concluded in November 1972. Since then Vickers has included Slam as part of the weapons fit on 500- and 1,000-ton submarines, and in mid-1978 the system was in service with several navies, on both new construction and as retrofits.

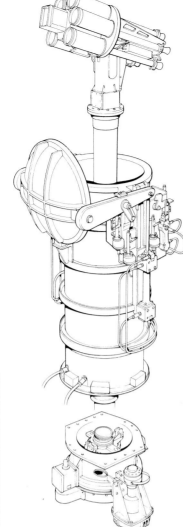

**Above:** *SLAM as evaluated in HMS* Aeneas, *with launcher retracting into watertight bin. System includes built-in test gear and plug-in simulator.*

**Below:** *BAe Dynamics Group art showing Sea Flash in action from FPB. Markedly superior to the Sea Sparrow systems, it would benefit further from cross-fertilization with AIM-7F.*

The only known operator is Israel. Several European shipbuilders have designs for submarines, FPBs and other vessels incorporating Slam, but a low profile is being maintained.

**Data:** As for Blowpipe.

# Shield

HSD (Now BAe Dynamics Group) completed a study in 1976 under MoD contract for a derivative of SRAAM (p. 221) installed as the primary SAM on FPBs and other small vessels or as a CIWS in larger ships. The missile was to be identical to that of the AAM except that the IR seeker would have greater sensitivity. The system would clearly have fast reaction and use a multiple launcher, but in mid-1978 there had been no news of further progress towards hardware.

**Below:** *BAe Dynamics Group art showing Shield in action from FPB. With government funding this system could mature very fast, the missile being already largely developed.*

# Sea Flash

British Aerospace has studied a ship-launched SAM system using the Sky Flash missile (p. 229). The target-tracking and CW illuminating radar would be one of the new Marconi 800-series, such as specified in some Seawolf Psi systems. A lightweight multi-box launcher would be used.

**Data:** As for Sky Flash.

# Seafox

Though unguided, this advanced weapons system is being developed as "a new concept in naval point defence weapons". It will fire salvoes of highly accurate rockets, specifically described as "large", at future anti-ship missiles, with secondary capability against aircraft and helicopters. MSDS provide the surveillance/tracking radar and proximity fuze, both able to pick out small sea-skimmers at extremely low levels. Seafox will be compatible with ships as small as FPB.

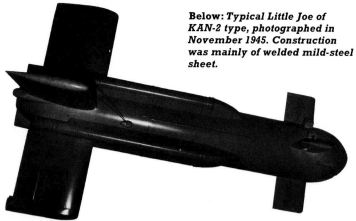

**Below: Typical Little Joe of KAN-2 type, photographed in November 1945. Construction was mainly of welded mild-steel sheet.**

## USA

## Little Joe

Development of this and other pioneer ship-launched SAMs was triggered in the summer of 1944 by the start of Kamikaze suicide attacks on US Navy and other Allied ships in the Pacific. There existed in the United States considerable expertise in solid rocket motors and a little in high-speed airframe technology; and the proximity fuze matured at precisely the right time. The first SAM to be designed and built was Little Joe, in two versions designated KAN-1 and -2, in a programme managed directly by the Navy Air Materiel Unit. This was probably the earliest SAM of any kind in the United States, and it had a bluff unstreamlined form, with a cruciform of nose fins and rear wings.

**Left: One of the last Lark launches, from the new trials vessel AVM-1 Norton Sound Photo dated 5 June 1953, but event probably pre-1951.**

The latter carried two ailerons for roll-stabilization, but the pitch/yaw steering to intercept the target was by radio command operating trailing-edge controls on the four nose fins. Launch was from a rail launcher by four wrap-round 3-in (76·2 mm) cordite motors, and a 1,000 lb (454 kg)-thrust Aerojet JATO (Jet-Assisted Take-Off, meaning rocket-assisted) motor served as the sustainer. In early trials rocket smoke made optical sighting difficult. Flight speed did not exceed 400 mph (644 km/h). The 100 lb (45 kg) warhead had a proximity fuze. A considerable number of missiles were fired, especially of the improved KAN-2 type with flare, ground optics and radio command link, but by February 1945 it was clear there was a long way to go and that there were better alternatives and this project was cancelled.

**Dimensions:** Length 11 ft 4 in (3·45 m); diameter 22·7 in (577 mm).
**Launch weight:** (KAN-2) 1,210 lb (549 kg).
**Range:** 2 miles (3·2 km).

## Little Lark

Though begun at roughly the same time as Little Joe, Little Lark (later the prefix "Little" was dropped) was a more advanced missile with a configuration still acceptable today. There were at least a dozen different sub-types of Lark but all had a cruciform of rectangular wings and a cruciform of fixed tail fins indexed at 45°. Another feature common to all was sustainer propulsion by a Reaction Motors acid/aniline rocket, with the propellants fed by the compressed-gas inflation of plastic bags inside the integral tanks. Most early Larks, of 1945 vintage, were developed and built in-house at the Navy Jet-Propelled Missile Board, with flight testing at the NOTS at Inyokern. Like Little Joe the weapon was not ready for production at VJ-Day, but its potential was much greater and work continued, with the prime contract passed to Fairchild, which started a Guided Missile Division on the strength of it. Lark flight control was complicated and variable but usually the tail fins carried ailerons for roll-stabilization (and sometimes for use as trimmers) and the four wings all had trailing-edge elevons for pitch/yaw steering. In some models roll-control was by bang/bang spoilers or ailerons in the vertical pair of wings. Guidance was always by radio command, most

**Left: This sequence taken in 1945 of Little Joe in action against an F4F Wildcat target shows what may have been the first guided shipboard SAM shot.**

later Larks having receiver aerials moulded into GRP tail fins. The wings were aluminium extrusions. Later versions were among the first missiles in the world to have SARH, with a receiver aerial in the nose under a GRP radome specially designed for high-speed flight. A lot of work went into perfecting not only the functioning of the guidance but also its packaging into 90° or 180° body segments with single multi-pin connectors for quick repair by replacement. Early rounds had two lateral boost motors but post-war launching was by tandem twin Aerojet boosters linked to a large stabilizing box-like fin assembly. Testing at NOTS and at Pt Mugu continued until at least 1950, by which time the designation CTV-N-9 had been bestowed.

**Dimensions:** Length 13 ft 11 in (4·24 m), (with final boost unit) 18 ft 6 in (5·64 m); diameter 18·0 in (457 mm); span (wings) 6 ft 3 in (1·9 m).
**Launch weight:** (late model, with booster) 2,070 lb (939 kg).
**Range:** 4 miles (6·4 km).

# Bumblebee

This was not a missile but the name of an important R&D programme deserving brief mention. The inauspicious results obtained with Little Joe and Lark quickly convinced the US Navy it needed to buy a vastly greater fund of advanced technology to underpin its SAM effort, which was suddenly a top priority. In late 1944 the Navy Department authorised the Applied Physics Laboratory of the Johns Hopkins University (APL/JHU) at Baltimore to study the feasibility of using guided missiles in the anti-Kamikaze role, and in January 1945 the BuOrd assigned to APL/JHU a considerably larger programme which involved not mere study but full research and development including hardware. This programme became known as Bumblebee and it was probably the most useful in all GW history where finding the answers to basic problems is concerned. The specific objective was to develop missile technology in order to supply the Navy with a supersonic SAM system meeting all tactical requirements. The work soon separated into two major divisions: propulsion and guidance. One of the first major end-products of Bumblebee was the selection of industrial, scientific and academic contractors, who became known as Section T. The resulting missiles initially all were assigned names starting with this letter: Terrier, Talos, Triton Tartar and Typhon. Among the industrial primes were Convair and McDonnell for airframes and Bendix (ramjet) and several rocket firms for propulsion. (Note: Triton is on page 90.)

# Talos

In March 1945 Bendix was asked by APL/JHU to develop the fuel metering system for a supersonic missile ramjet. Three months later the first ramjet "fashioned from the exhaust piping of a P-47" flew from a windy New Jersey beach; though it had a diameter of only 6 in (152 mm) it soon generated more power than the engine of the P-47. This was the start of the mighty programme that yielded Talos, a long-range area-defence missile that broke as much

**Top:** *RIM-8G Talos on CLG-4 Little Rock before firing at Salto di Quirra on 23 April 1975. Note "RDX", non-nuclear warhead.*

**Above:** *Configuration of early Talos versions (probably an RIM-8F) is shown by this launch picture (no date or ship name).*

new ground as any missile apart from A-4. It entered service in 1958, was an active development programme until 1977 and will remain in service until 1985. Few other missiles have enjoyed such longevity.

Most Talos missiles are beam riders with terminal homing. Most Talos ships have SPS-43 very high-power search radar, with on-mounted IFF, information from which is passed to the SPS-30 long-range 3-D radar which gives target parameters in full detail to the Talos radars. The latter are the Sperry SPG-56 and -49. Working in G/H-band, SPG-56 is the target-tracking set into whose beam the large missile is gathered. Talos is fired from a twin stabilized launcher under the thrust of a tandem solid booster, by M. W. Kellogg or Allegany Ballistics, which in the early 1950s set new records

for solid-motor size and performance. As the missile leaves the launch rail the mating clamp is released, and at boost burnout in 2·2 sec the motor separates by air drag. The integral ramjet burns kerosene (in some models with naphtha added) expelled by nitrogen bladders to the air-turbine pump and combustion section. Above the nose is a pitot head which, with a temperature sensor, modulates fuel flow to maintain constant airspeed at Mach 2·5 in the face of rapid variation in drag and guidance demands. The missile is gathered in the beam and steered by four independent hydraulically powered wing servos which first stabilize roll and then move in pairs to zero the error signal from the beam-riding receiver.

This mid-course phase may last from 2 up to over 65 miles

(3·2–105 km). When the target is acquired by the range gate SARH guidance takes over, the ship's SPG-49 illuminating the target and the missile homing on the signals of the four interferometer aerials disposed around the nose. Finally the large continuous-rod or nuclear warhead (which can be selected separately from the magazine for automatic loading on a missile on the launcher) is detonated by a proximity fuze.

Talos was at first designated SAM-N-6, but it became RIM-8 in 1962. By that time RIM-8A (N-6B) to -8D (N-6BW1) were no longer in use. The system reached IOC in CLG-3 Galveston in 1958 and subsequently was installed in six further ships of which four are left (three with two twin installations, one with a single twin). Talos systems were subjected to prolonged evaluation by the US Army, as a mobile area-defence system, and the USAF to protect SAC bases. Until well into the 1960s the standard missile was the RIM-8F (N-6B1-CW) with pulse homing, but subsequently in the same missile the receiver was changed to CW operation and a new series of CW-interferometer missiles was introduced: RIM-8E (N-6C1), RIM-8G and -8J. In 1968 small batches of the 2,200-odd Talos (out of 2,825 produced) were converted into RGM-8H anti-radar missiles and used in the SSM role in Vietnam,

where the RIM-8E hit two MiGs at extreme range. Since 1974 older models have progressively been rebuilt as MQM-8G Vandal targets used at PMR to simulate anti-ship missiles.

**Dimensions:** Length (missile) 21 ft 0 in or 22 ft 3 in (6·4 or 6·78 m); diameter (basic external) 30·0 in (762 mm); span 9 ft 6 in (2·9 m).
**Launch weight:** (J) 3,505 lb (1590 kg), (with booster) 7,805 lb (3540 kg).
**Range:** Typical limit 75 miles (120 km).

*Below: Launch of the first SAM-N-8 Typhon LR at Naval Ordnance Test Facility, WSMR, on 23 March 1961.*

*Below: Secretary of the Navy W. Graham Claytor plugs his ears as a current Talos (probably 8G) leaves CG-10 Albany in September 1977.*

# Typhon

The ultimate missile system to evolve from the Bumblebee programme was given this curious name, took many years to reach the hardware stage (in 1960) and was finally abandoned in 1963 in favour of steady plodding with the Terrier/Tartar/Standard family. From the start Typhon was seen as a Fleet area-defence weapon, and though based on tandem-boost integral-ramjet propulsion like Talos, with the same Bendix/McDonnell team, it had completely different aerodynamics with long-chord wings carrying long-chord moving tip extensions for control. Westinghouse was res-

ponsible for an advanced phased-array multi-function ship radar, and the missile had its own active seeker. SAM-N-8 Typhon LR was placed under contract in June 1961, and, deployed in medium-range and long-range forms – respectively given 1962-designations of RIM-55A and RIM-50A – would have given the US Navy a defence capability it has never had. One of the difficulties was the weight of the high-mounted ship radars.

**Dimensions:** Length 28 ft (8·5 m), (with booster) 46 ft (14 m).
**Launch weight:** Typhon LR, about 20,000 lb (9072 kg).
**Range:** 200 miles (322 km) at Mach 5.

# Terrier/Tartar

Occasionally a weapon system enjoys such a combination of early (but not too early) timing, professional management and sound basic principles that it proliferates into a great diversity of more or less contrasting weapons over a long period. In missiles the outstanding example is this family of ship-to-air weapons which not only became so different they received different names but they also later included missiles for SSM and ASM use (featured elsewhere in this book, as noted below). None of the members of the family was especially outstanding; they just happened to be part of a pro-gramme which began early and by relentless effort has been kept abreast of growing threats for 30 years.

The whole family stemmed from the Bumblebee Program (p. 197). One of the largest industrial participants was Consolidated Vultee (Convair) which at its Vultee Field Division in Downey carried out most of the development of the Gnat (CTV) in 1945–46, which in parallel with rival Little Lark explored steering with moving wings and fixed fins. In 1946 this begat Snoot (STV), fired in April 1948 a few months after Vultee had closed and Convair San Diego had taken over. In February 1949 BuOrd awarded a contract to Convair for a tactical proto-type of a full ship-based SAM with tandem rocket boost, internal rocket sustainer and beam-riding guidance. This was SAM-N-7 Terrier. The first round was delivered on 31 January 1950 and fired at NOTS China Lake on 16 February. In parallel Sperry and Reeves developed a target-tracking and missile-guidance radar which matured around 1954 as SPQ-5. Ford Instrument and Western Electric assisted with guidance, and Northern Ordnance handled the stabilized twin launcher.

Outbreak of war in Korea in June 1950 suddenly injected urgency into the programme, and it was decided to produce a production ship system quickly, despite deficiencies. Two cruisers, *Boston* and *Canberra*, were withdrawn for conversion and this work established a space envelope and general system design that has of necessity been adhered to ever since. Convair (later General Dynamics) took over a large new BuOrd production facility at Pomona, near Riverside, California, and this became GD Pomona Division and the centre of design and development of this and other weapon systems. The first-generation tactical missile flew in 1951. Designated BW-0, for Beam-riding, Wing control, Zero version, it had a solid sustainer by MW Kellogg Co, tandem booster by Allegany Ballistics, compressed-air control power and proximity-fuzed conventional warhead. The first sea firing took place from the newly rebuilt AVM-1 *Norton Sound* in late 1951, and in 1953 BW-0 destroyed its first target drone. The predicted deficiencies were progressively corrected by serial introduction of revised production blocks until 1953 when BW-1 introduced major internal repackaging and other changes to improve ease of manufacture and reliability. Out-

Left: *A lot of defence went up in smoke on 1 February 1963 when CG-10* Albany *fired Talos missiles from bow and stern and a Tartar amidships.*

Below: *Two Advanced Terriers (probably RIM-2Ds) aboard DLG-27* Josephus Daniels, *under way off Chile on 13 September 1968.*

put rose sharply, delivery dates were met and price was reduced. BW-1 was effective against sub-sonic, passive, non-manoeuvring targets, and achieved IOC aboard CAG-2 *Canberra* on 15 June 1956, followed by CAG-1 *Boston* on 1 November 1956. Each ship had two installations at X and Y positions, the twin launchers each being served by a 72-round rotating magazine with vertical storage and hydraulic loading to the launcher set at 90° elevation. Both ships introduced the SPS-43 search radar, SPS-30 3-D radar and twin SPQ-5 missile-guidance radars. Other ship installations followed, beginning with destroyer *Gyatt*, and the Marine Corps rather briefly deployed two battalions with a mobile land system engineered mainly by Vitro and Universal Match. In the 1962 DoD scheme SAM-N-7 became RIM-2A.

In the late 1950s news filtered through of Terrier 2, or Advanced Terrier. This was in fact BT-3 (Beam-rider, Tail control, 3rd version), and it was totally redesigned aerodynamically with the moving-wing cruciform moved to the tail and long strakes – they could hardly be called wings – along the body. The strake-wings and tail controls were indexed in line, a further change. The reason was to increase manoeuvrability to meet the emerging threat of supersonic aircraft. Further major changes included higher-impulse motor propellant to increase speed and range, a solid-propellant APU to provide increased control power on a longer flight, and an improved autopilot. Though it had to be wholly compatible with the ship system, the new BT-3 increased the performance envelope by 50 per cent. Designated RIM-2C in the revised scheme, this missile was built at a high rate and eventually armed three carriers, six cruisers and 30

frigates of the US Navy (some DLG frigates have two twin installations and most were later converted so that the magazine/launcher can also fire Asroc, p. 258), three cruisers of the Italian Navy and one of the Royal Netherlands Navy.

Studies in 1956 showed that, with minor modification to the ship's direction system, missile propulsion and warhead, a longer-range Terrier could be produced that would be effective against surface targets, and ships in particular. In 1958 BT-3A (RIM-2D) replaced -3 on the Pomona assembly line, with capability as an SSM as well as unimpaired performance in the original role. Range was approximately doubled by a new end-burning Allegany sustainer motor, control power being assured by a longer-burning charge supplying the APU and power system. The beacon/receiver which provides the two-way interface with the guidance radar was made transistorised. A proportion of the 3,000-odd BW/BT missiles were of the -3A(N) type with a nuclear warhead specifically for the SSM role.

In the early 1950s there was naturally pressure for a SAM that could be fired from smaller ships than the 5,000-odd ton limit of Terrier. Prolonged studies showed that major advances in guidance and propulsion would make this possible, and by 1956 the BuWeps had schemed Tartar, later designated RIM-24, and production engineering was in hand at the extended Pomona plant. This was the only change in the shipboard space envelope, and it allowed the system to be installed in destroyers. Tartar incorporates an Aerojet Mk 1

**Right:** *Scale side elevations of all missiles in the Terrier, Tartar, Advanced Terrier, Standard and Standard ARM families. This is the largest missile family.*

**Below:** *A Marine ordnanceman activates the launcher after loading a BW-1 Terrier in the short-lived Land Terrier (China Lake, 1957).*

**Inset right:** *Tartar on Mk 22 launcher on DEG-4 Talbot. The Mk 22 is lighter (92,395 lb, 41,910 kg) than the Mk 11 or 13 of DDGs.*

Mod 0 dual-thrust PU/AP motor (burnout, Mach 2·8), weighing 760 lb (345 kg), obviating the need for a separate booster. Raytheon was prime for the new SARH guidance, the SPG-51 radar also serving as a major element in the Mk 73 gun/missile director and initially pointed by the ship's search radar (typically SPS-52). Believed to operate in I-band, SPG-51 illuminates the target for the homing seeker in the dielectric nose of the missile. From the start, Tartar Basic RIM-24A and Tartar Improved RIM-24B have had a performance envelope generally greater than that of Terrier BW. Tartar production proceeded in parallel with Terrier, and at the close in 1968 this system was installed or being installed in approximately 50 ships of the US, Australian, French, German, Iranian, Italian, Japanese, Netherlands and Spanish navies. Over 6,500 Tartar missiles were delivered.

By 1957 Tartar's demonstration of SARH guidance had resulted in a new Terrier, HT-3 (Homing Terrier). This not only made maximum use of Tartar guidance hardware, including SPG-51 family radars, but introduced many new production techniques to boost output and further reduce costs. Reliability was dramatically increased, and at extreme range HT-3 achieves an SSKP roughly 30 per cent higher because of increased accuracy. This missile, RIM-2F, was the last basic Terrier to be built, remaining in production until 1966. Throughout the 1960s both Terrier and Tartar missiles were continually improved in a Retrofit programme in which they have been recycled back through Pomona, some two or three times, for improvements mainly of an electronic nature. Among the changes incorporated are solid-state devices, ECCM capability, multiple-target capa-

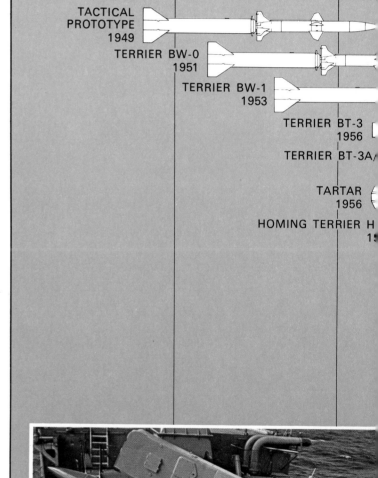

TACTICAL PROTOTYPE 1949

TERRIER BW-0 1951

TERRIER BW-1 1953

TERRIER BT-3 1956

TERRIER BT-3A/

TARTAR 1956

HOMING TERRIER H

1950          1955

bility and reliable guidance in SSM attack. By this time Terrier/Tartar had become Standard (overleaf).

**Dimensions:** Length (Terrier RIM-2A) 14 ft 10 in (4·52 m), (with booster) 27 ft 1 in (8·25 m), (RIM-2F) 14 ft 9 in (4·5 m), (with booster) 26 ft 2 in (7·98 m), (Tartar, typical) 15 ft 0 in (4·57 m); diameter (all) 13·5 in (343 mm); span (RIM-2A) 46 in (1·17 m), (others) 42·0 in (1·07 m).

**Launch weight:** (RIM-2A) 2,900 lb (1315 kg), (RIM-2F) 3,090 lb (1402 kg), (Tartar, typical) 1,425 lb (646 kg).

**Range:** (RIM-2A) 12 miles (19·3 km), (RIM-2F) 21·5 miles (35 km), (Tartar, typical) 11 miles (17·7 km).

**Right:** *Tartar launch from the US guided missile destroyer DDG-10 Sampson during an exercise in the Mediterranean on 24 April 1975.*

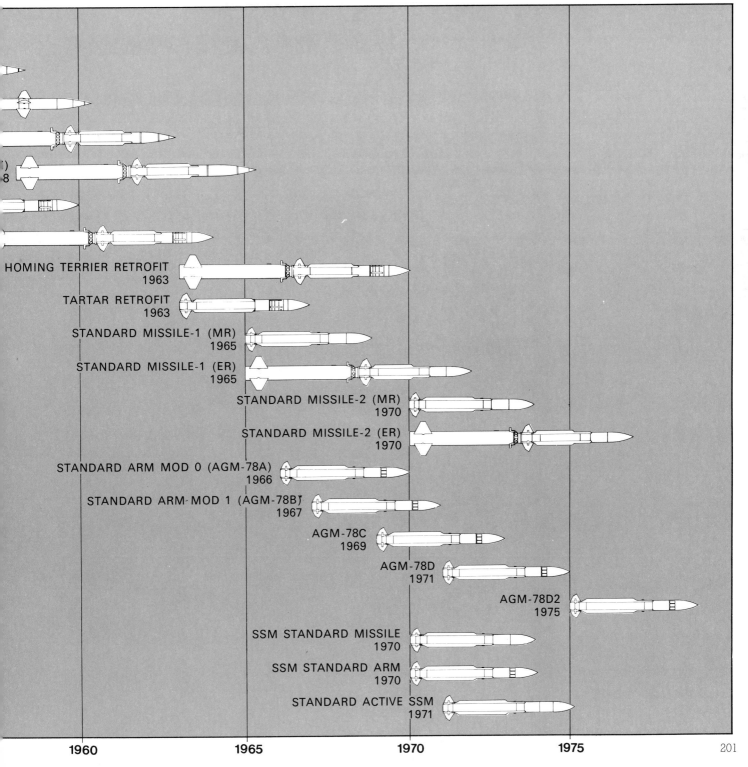

HOMING TERRIER RETROFIT
1963

TARTAR RETROFIT
1963

STANDARD MISSILE-1 (MR)
1965

STANDARD MISSILE-1 (ER)
1965

STANDARD MISSILE-2 (MR)
1970

STANDARD MISSILE-2 (ER)
1970

STANDARD ARM MOD 0 (AGM-78A)
1966

STANDARD ARM MOD 1 (AGM-78B)
1967

AGM-78C
1969

AGM-78D
1971

AGM-78D2
1975

SSM STANDARD MISSILE
1970

SSM STANDARD ARM
1970

STANDARD ACTIVE SSM
1971

1960          1965          1970          1975

# Standard

In the early 1960s the US Navy BuWeps authorised GD Pomona to incorporate in a new family of weapons a range of alterations and improvements sufficient to warrant a new name: Standard Missile. This family began as two missiles, Standard MR (Medium Range) RIM-66 to replace Tartar and Standard ER (Extended Range) RIM-67 to replace Terrier. Each missile was installationally interchangeable with its predecessor, and required no change whatever to magazines, handling gear and launchers on ships and at Naval weapon stations, and existing shipboard direction systems could be used with minor changes, mainly to software. But, though similar externally, the new missiles were quite dissimilar inside.

One of the largest changes was elimination of fluid power systems and use of a dry battery as power source for an all-electric missile (believed to be the first in history). The storage battery does not deteriorate after years of inactivity but is activated just prior to launch and among other services drives the actuators for the four independent tail controls. All electronic circuits are solid-state which improves reliability, eliminates need for shipboard checkout and reduces warmup time and power consumption. ECCM capability began better than Terrier/Tartar and has since 1970 been upgraded in successive production blocks. Standard MR has a further major advance in the Aerojet/Hercules Mk 56 motor, weighing 907 lb (411·5 kg), which considerably extends the performance envelope.

While studies went ahead with SSM and ASM versions, as outlined below, the basic development of Standard MR and ER was completed by GD Pomona in 1963–66, and a production contract worth $120,651,191 was signed in March 1967. Ship fitting began in 1968, IOC was reached in 1969 and by 1971 over 70 ships had Standard missiles, divided roughly equally between the two versions. Meanwhile, several things happened to diversify the programme. The first was the urgent need in South East Asia for an ASM offering better defence against hostile SAM installations than the early Shrike versions, and in a matter of weeks GD had evolved from Standard MR an ARM (Anti-Radiation Missile) incorporating as a stop-gap the existing Shrike seeker. This missile, Standard ARM (AGM-78A) and its developments are dealt with on p. 125. The second external event was the sinking of the *Eilat* by Soviet-supplied SSMs in 1967, which prompted the Navy to rethink its entire shipboard defence against anti-ship missiles. The third was the need to give ships a stop-gap SSM capability while Harpoon (p. 82) was being developed.

The most far-reaching effort was directed to countering potential anti-ship missile threats,

which by the late 1960s had still sparked hardly any US response. The first studies and stop-gap modifications were called SAMID (Ship Anti-Missile Integrated Defense), but this was superseded by an extremely complex and costly system at first called ASMS (Advanced Surface Missile System) and finally named Aegis. Surprisingly, the Navy did not develop small-ship anti-missile systems but chose to base the ordnance on

the Standard MR, in a modified form, and construct around this an electronic system of unparalleled scope and diversity. This book cannot go deeply into Aegis other than to note that the prime contractor is RCA, though the Mk 99 fire control (with SPG-62 target-illuminating radar), and SPY-1 high-power multifunction phased-array radar, which can simultaneously detect and track multiple targets, are all by Raytheon, and the

multiple UYK-7 digital computers are by Remington Rand Univac. The Mk 26 twin electric launcher can fire Standard Missiles, Harpoons or Asrocs. A typical system might have four SPY-1 planar arrays, four SPG-62 illumination channels and one or two twin launchers with 24, 44 or 64 missiles.

This comprehensive system for large surface platforms called for changes in the Standard Missile, principally in the in-

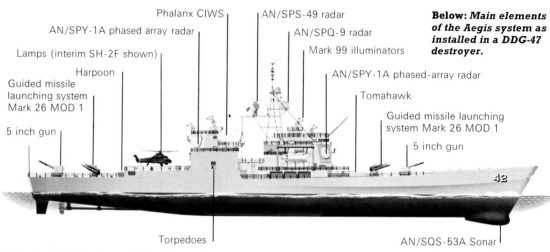

**Below: *Main elements of the Aegis system as installed in a DDG-47 destroyer.***

Phalanx CIWS — AN/SPS-49 radar — AN/SPY-1A phased array radar — AN/SPQ-9 radar — Lamps (interim SH-2F shown) — Mark 99 illuminators — Harpoon — AN/SPY-1A phased-array radar — Guided missile launching system Mark 26 MOD 1 — Tomahawk — 5 inch gun — Guided missile launching system Mark 26 MOD 1 — 5 inch gun — Torpedoes — AN/SQS-53A Sonar

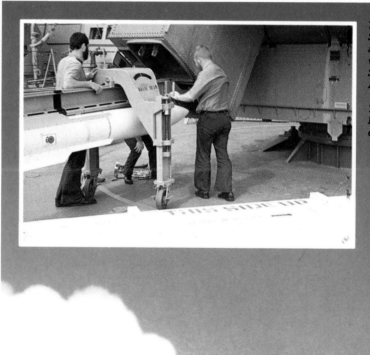

**Inset left: *Offering-up an SM-2 missile to the fully automatic Mk 26 launcher with superimposed boxes for Standard (MR or ER), Tartar, Asroc or Harpoon missiles.***

**Main picture: *Launch at Point Mugu of Standard MR from an overhead rail launcher.***

corporation of midcourse guidance. The result is Standard Missile 2 (SM-2), which will eventually replace SM-1 in production in both MR and ER forms. The main changes are: replacement of the conical-scan SARH receiver by a monopulse receiver; provision of an inertial reference unit for midcourse guidance; a two-way telemetry link for missile-position reporting and updating the target position and guidance correction; and a digital instead of analog computer. The inertial reference unit enables the missile to navigate itself to the vicinity of the target when SARH takes over. This results in a far more energy-efficient trajectory, giving a stag-

gering increase in range of 60 per cent for MR and over 100 per cent for ER, with no change in propulsion. SM-2 also incorporates further ECCM refinements and by firing more rapidly can make full use of the multiple-target capability of the Aegis system. In April 1977 the trials ship *Norton Sound* simultaneously used one illuminator against two targets.

The final part of the story begins in 1970 when feasibility demonstration firings in the SSM role took place with both Standard MR and ARM from surface vessels much smaller than those able to carry Aegis and the SAM versions. The SSMC (SSM Conversion) programme subsequently led to the deployment aboard DE, DDG, FFG and PG classes as described on p. 81.

**Left:** *RCA picture of the AN/SPY-1 multi-function phased-array radar (large flat panels on ship's superstructure at left and right). It simultaneously handles search, multi-target tracking, SM-2 midcourse guidance, illuminator pointing and kill evaluation.*

**Below:** *SM-2 ER on the original overhead rail launcher.*

**Dimensions:** Length (MR) 176 in (4·47 m), (ER) 314 in (7·98 m); diameter (both) 13·5 in (343 mm); span 36·0 in (914 mm).
**Launch weight:** (MR) 1,280 lb (581 kg), (ER) 2,350 lb (1066 kg).
**Range:** SM-1 MR 19 miles (30·6 km), SM-1 ER 35 miles (56·3 km), SM-2 MR 30 miles (48·3 km), SM-2 ER 75 miles (121 km).

# PDMS/Sea Sparrow

The use of the Sparrow AAM (p. 228) in a ship-to-air role was considered in the 1950s, but it was not until 1964 that a need for a short-range rapid-reaction weapon was suddenly identified. The US Navy urgently planned a close-in system called PDMS (Point-Defense Missile System) or BPDMS (Basic PDMS), using existing hardware almost exclusively. Intended for installation not only in small craft but also as the close-in defence of large vessels, PDMS was assembled from the Frequency Engineering Labs Mk 115 fire-control system, operated manually, and Mk 51 CW radar director/illuminator steered by handlebar controls. The missile was the AIM-7E or -7E2, slid manually along rails to a modified eight-cell Asroc launcher on a converted gun mount. Total system weight is 39,000 lb

(17,690 kg). When a target is acquired it is tracked manually, while the launcher follows automatically. Frangible doors over the selected cell(s) can be left in place if time is short. The missile homes as in the AAM, and follows a downhill trajectory against sea-skimmers above the LOS from the director to the target. The first ships to reach IOC with the PDMS were attack carriers, led by a single installation on Forrestal in 1967. Several CVA and CVAN now have triple installations. By 1975 the BPDMS was installed in 43 ships (58 installations) and by mid-1978 all 79 planned installations were operational.

In 1968 the amazing crudity of BPDMS was recognised by the development of an improved system, Mk 57, which was launched as a co-operative effort with various NATO countries (though, as it is so directly based on BPDMS, it is dealt with here in the US section). Belgium, Denmark, Italy and Norway signed

with the United States at the start, the Netherlands joined in 1970 and West Germany in 1976. Each participant contributes to the cost of development in proportion to the number of systems purchased, but there has been little co-production and in September 1969 Raytheon received the $23·1 million contract for engineering development. Three systems were then built, one remaining at Raytheon, one supplied to the US Navy (first used on 3 March 1972 when a target was engaged by the escort Downes) and the third installed on KNM Bergen of the Royal Norwegian Navy in 1973. The main changes in what has become known as NATO Sea Sparrow Missile System (NSSMS) are the use of the RIM-7H folding-fin missile, a much smaller lightweight eight-cell launcher, and far superior automatic fire control with a powered director/illuminator and digital computer. The last of about 110 single and dual systems was delivered in

1978, 75 of them going to the US Navy (four being for an undisclosed foreign customer) and the rest to frigates and destroyers of the NATO partners plus an F-80 frigate of Spain. A further 16 systems are being supplied to the JMSDF by Mitsubishi Electric.

A further development is IPDSMS (Improved Point-Defense Surface Missile System) with the new Hughes D-band TAS (Target-Acquisition System). It was not known in 1978 how many of the US Navy BPDMS were being upgraded to NSSMS or IPDSMS standard. RIM-7H was also used in Italy's Albatros (p. 186). Canada has a separate Sea Sparrow system (p. 182).

**Data:** See Sparrow (p. 229).

# Sea Phoenix

In the early 1970s the Navy BuWeps not unnaturally studied the powerful Phoenix AAM (p. 232) in the surface-launched

**Main picture below:** *BPDMS launch from CVA-67* John F. Kennedy. *Launch box can be refurbished. Tail belongs to EKA-3B Skywarrior of VAH-10.*

**Inset left:** *Raytheon photo showing high-angle launch of NATO Sea Sparrow. Missile has folding fins, which have deployed quickly.*

**Inset below right:** *Operator on BPDMS refresher training holds his ears as missile departs from* LCC-19 Blue Ridge *amphibious command ship.*

**Right:** *Another photo taken on* JFK *showing BPDMS launcher in January 1975. Note doors under flight deck for the eight reloading channels.*

role, and by 1975 this interest had hardened to the point where preliminary studies were in hand for Sea Phoenix as a replacement for the limited and primitive PDMS Sea Sparrow, especially as close-range defence of the largest carriers. In 1976 a virtually unmodified Phoenix was successfully fired at NWC China Lake, travelling more than 13½ miles (22 km) downrange in 90 sec, more than twice the limit for Sea Sparrow. The existing F-14A Tomcat radar and fire-control, the Hughes AWG-9, could be transferred almost bodily to a ship, 27 of the 29 boxes being compatible. In late-1978 interest waned; Phoenix is unhelpful to Aegis.

# SIRCS

Standing for Shipboard Intermediate-Range Combat System, this is planned as the fourth major ship missile system for the next 20 years, the others being ASMD, Aegis/Standard and Harpoon/Tomahawk. Most of the requirement could be met by variations already available of the Seawolf system (p. 192) but for various reasons the US Navy has chosen to start from scratch and in 1976–78 funded three competing studies by RCA/ Martin Marietta, McDonnell Douglas/Sperry and Raytheon/ Lockheed/RemRandUnivac. Details of the requirement include ability to engage air attacks at intermediate range (including mass or stream onslaught by up to four missiles for small 1,000-ton ships and 14 missiles for large), attack surface ships, and provide fire support against hostile shores. In 1977 it was stated that the three studies had resulted in "truly alternative systems". The FY78 budget for SIRCS was increased by Congress to $13 million on condition that it uses the AMRAAM missile (p. 235). A production decision for the chosen team may be taken in 1984, but a stumbling block appears to be that the SIRCS teams are not the same as the AMRAAM teams.

**Data:** None yet meaningful.

# LRDMM

First announced in 1978, the Long-Range Dual-Mission Missile is a project of immense importance for use in the late 1980s. Probably to be powered by a ram-rocket, it will be vertically launched from large surface ships against anti-ship missiles, aircraft and surface targets. It will have OTH capability out to 461 miles (742 km), and though no decision on guidance had been taken as this book went to press the USA (which has responsibility for multi-mode guidance in a joint programme with the Navy) expects to use information from E-2C Hawkeyes and satellites. Flight speed will probably be about Mach 5 and the warhead conventional. Read-across, in both directions, with ASALM (p. 143) is expected.

# AIR TO AIR MISSILES

The Luftwaffe pioneered the guided AAM, and though no type actually reached a combat unit it was a close-run thing and both radio command and wire-guided AAMs completed their development and were ready for production. Yet in the immediate post-war years the German weapon that most influenced the Allies was the R4/M unguided spin-stabilized rocket that formed the basis for the armament of the first generation of USAF jet interceptors and have also been used by the million in the air/surface role. Useful AAMs took a surprisingly long time to create.

Amidst a profusion of other systems from many countries the Sidewinder stands out as having modest design goals which, via an exceptional number of rounds produced for many customers, have yet again shown that the fairly good can often do better than the best. It has scored unprecedented worldwide success largely by being available cheaply and hung on any aircraft, whereas better missiles would not have been purchased at all, except in very much smaller numbers by the few customers able to use them. It so happens that virtually all Sidewinders have had IR (heat homing) guidance. One US company produced a radar version, with SARH guidance matched to the US Navy Crusader fighter, but it was not wholly successful. Only now, in 1979, is a really good radar Sidewinder becoming available as a result of a new homing head by a British company. Updating old missiles is going to be as important as updating old fighters.

The only other US missile produced in numbers similar to Sidewinder is the USAF Falcon family, which began in the late 1940s and is still in use. Successive models have been made available with a choice of homing heads, either IR or SARH. The same philosophy has been followed by the Soviet Union, whose PVO interceptors appear always to have at least one AAM of each type on board. It is unwise to lay down dogmatic rules about which guidance is preferable to the other, because radar performance depends strongly on wavelength. Especially in the early days 20 and more years ago all AAM guidance systems tended to be extremely unreliable and erratic in performance. IR seekers locked-on to the Sun or its reflection in a lake or friendly greenhouse, and were almost useless in cloud or even a light shower of rain. Radar guidance pierced the atmosphere better but had other drawbacks in demanding a compatible radar in the launch aircraft and requiring it to illuminate the target right up to missile impact. Of course, it was always theoretically possible to instal a radar in the

missile. One of the first programmes for an active-radar AAM was the British Vickers/GEC missile developed with a choice of radars, pulse-doppler or CW. Typically, this was abandoned.

In the late 1950s both the US Navy and Soviet Union became interested in active-radar monsters. Eagle died and was replaced by Phoenix, while the giant "Acrid" is probably only one of several Soviet active-radar AAMs. Obviously there are considerable advantages in having a radar seeker riding in the nose of the missile. Not least is that the AAM becomes a "fire and forget" weapon. Another is that it can be used at any range to which its propulsion system can take it.

There is now abundant experience with the two chief kinds of AAM guidance, IR and SARH, to discuss their performance on a broad basis. The advantage of IR is that the seeker head is self-contained, needs no connection or equipment in the launch aircraft (except possibly to a cryogenic refrigeration system) and probably results in the lowest total missile cost. In particular types of AAM there are other advantages, but the drawbacks are if anything such as to outweigh these. In general an IR missile cannot be used in bad weather or at low altitude (where most targets are now likely to be found) and in many cases was limited to attack from the rear in order that the seeker should see and lock-on to the hot jetpipes. Today IR seekers of new types offer vastly improved sensitivity, better ability to distinguish between real and false targets, and in the latest designs with Cassegrain optics focusing the radiation on either one or a whole matrix of detectors overcoming virtually all the previous problems. The technology is closely related to the FLIR and IIR systems used in land battles.

Despite this the future AAM appears most likely to have an SARH seeker, if not an active one. AMRAAM, the USAF/USN programme for a future advanced AAM, is strongly biased towards radar guidance, though SARH requires that the target be illuminated by the launch aircraft throughout the interception. The first radar AAMs in the 1950s were totally based on analog data-processing by circuits of the traditional type using discrete components and thermionic valves (vacuum tubes). By the early 1960s vacuum tubes were fast being eliminated, and digital processing was more gradually replacing analog. Only in quite recent years has the obvious move to silicon planar technology, microelectronics, large-scale integration and similar techniques, all pioneered in the laboratory well before 1970, actually reached the weapons on the production line.

The changes have had a marked beneficial effect. Accuracy has been improved, reliability has been utterly transformed, and the reduced weight and bulk of the guidance systems has allowed the propulsion motor to be enlarged, if extra speed and range were desirable and compatible with the guidance, or else the fitment of a larger warhead. In at least one case miniaturised guidance has allowed the airframe to be made heavier in order to eliminate very costly honeycomb and replace it by thick sheet. Even without reduction in guidance size some important AAMs have had their range more than doubled by the introduction of improved motors either with storable liquid or, more often, advanced solid propellant, to give either greater thrust to put more kinetic energy into a faster-acceleration weapon or else to burn for a longer period.

Perhaps the most instructive analysis of modern air combat yet to be made public is the Aimval (air-intercept missile evaluation)/Aceval (air-combat evaluation) programme mounted at Nellis AFB jointly by the USAF and Navy. One could write a large book on what emerged from these missions, which were at one time reported to have been intended to compare the Navy F-14 with the Air Force F-15 but in fact had the two expensive super-fighters operating side-by-side against little F-5s acting the part of MiG-21s. Several factors dramatically drove home the importance of long-range target identification and engagement. Of course, the F-14 with its AWG-9 radar and Phoenix AAMs has a unique capability, created by Hughes, with radar seeing over 125 miles (201 km) and able to track 24 targets simultaneously and fire at ranges only slightly less at six targets going in different directions at grossly different heights. For this reason the AWG-9/Phoenix was (the Navy might judge unfairly) barred from the evaluation. Instead the defenders had to rely on their medium-range AIM-7F Sparrows. On many missions the fighters were able to use a TVSU (TV sighting unit) slaved to the radar so that as soon as the back-seater locked-on to a target he was immediately presented with a TV picture of it. The picture was magnified greatly, and unaffected by bad weather, night or any other environmental condition. At 10 miles (16 km) an F-5 could be positively identified; even at 15 miles (24 km) it could be identified in good conditions and in most aspects seen to have tip tanks or Sidewinders or other underwing load. At 50 to 70 miles a B-52 or 747 could be positively identified. This is a marvellous advance over

anonymous blips on a cockpit display, even with IFF to decide who is friendly. Everyone who has used TVSU, or other similar equipment derived from Northrop's Tiseo (target-identification system electro-optical), has become excited and convinced that being able to "see" aircraft many times more distant than the limits of the unaided eye is bound to revolutionise air combat.

Another important factor that was not new but had not previously been so clearly demonstrated as in the Nellis evaluations was the handicap of any missile using fighter nose radar to give SARH guidance. When the F-14 or F-15 identified and locked-on to an F-5 it did so well before the smaller aircraft had even acquired the larger fighter. A Sparrow would then be launched (not "for real", but in electronic simulation), and for the next 30 seconds the two fighters would speed towards each other – the F-5 to acquire, identify and fire at the big fighter, and the big fighter because it had to keep pointing its radar at the enemy. The result was invariably that, at the last moment just before it was "killed" by the big fighter's Sparrow, the F-5 would let go a close-range Sidewinder that would "kill" the big fighter. Like all IR-homers Sidewinder is a "launch and leave" weapon, and goes on homing on its quarry even after the fighter that launched it has ceased to exist. One answer that seems to me obvious is that, if we must have AAMs with SARH, the fighter ought to have the CW illumination aerial facing to the rear.

At present, as in so many missile fields, AAM development is centred on two basic classes. The medium-range missile is if possible smaller than Sparrow, has a range of about 20 miles (32 km) and if possible more, and extremely advanced radar guidance which in my view ought to include active terminal homing. How the missile flies the mid-course section is anybody's guess; with a bit of luck it may need nothing but the simplest-ever autopilot to keep flying the way it is pointing, and at Mach 5 it should reach the active-homing phase in about ten seconds. Several companies, including MSDS, Hughes and Raytheon, would be delighted to produce seeker heads. Unfortunately SARH is much more likely, so we need an aft-facing illuminator. The other kind of AAM is the close-range weapon which must be able to be fired at a moment's notice and have such instant response and unprecedented manoeuvrability as to kill a fighter crossing the bows of the launch aircraft. Both kinds of missile are bound to rely on body lift rather than wings, and to use TVC steering. The seeker head for the dogfight missile could be either SARH or IR; or perhaps both.

# CANADA

## Velvet Glove

In 1949, the Canadian Air Staff in Ottawa issued a requirement for two sizes of AAM, for use by the CF-100 interceptor then being built by Avro Aircraft. Studies were made by the NRC (National Research Council) under the direction of Gerry Bull, and by 1950 engineering development was in hand at CARDE (Canadian Armament Research and Development Establishment) at Valcartier, Quebec, under Johnny Green. The configuration selected was cruciforms of rectangular moving wings and fixed fins indexed in line, and the guidance was by IR homing. Little work was done on the larger missile, Meteor, weighing about 600 lb (272 kg), but Velvet Glove gradually became a major weapon pro-gramme involving more than 100 companies led by Canadair. After extensive component testing complete missiles began static flight test in December 1952, with launches from August 1953, the usual carrier being an F-86 or CF-100 Mk 2. Prolonged difficulties were encountered in making the PbS seeker respond only to aircraft jetpipes and not the Sun, or its reflection in lakes. Development lagged until the CF-100 programme had been virtually completed without the missile being incorporated. Velvet Glove was terminated in 1954, though by this time good results were being obtained and the missile would have matured in ample time for the Avro CF-105 Arrow. According to Dr O. M. Solandt of the Defense Research Board the expenditure was $23·8 million.

**Dimensions:** Length 10 ft 5 in (3·17 m); span (wings) 38 in (965 mm); span (tail) 24 in (610 mm).
**Launch weight:** 310 lb (141 kg).
**Range:** 5 miles (8 km).

*Above: Avro Canada CF-100 Mk 2 of Central Experimental and Proving Establishment, Namao, with two Velvet Gloves on pylons under engines.*

# FRANCE

## Matra M.04

This finely streamlined weapon was probably the first AAM to fly in Western Europe after 1945. Work began at Société Matra in 1948, and the first flight, without guidance, took place at Colomb-Béchar from a Halifax in May 1950. The M.04 was extremely large, with cruciforms of swept wings and smaller tail fins, the latter being used for control with pneumatic actuation. Propulsion was by an SEPR acid/aniline rocket giving 2,756 lb (1250 kg) thrust for 14 sec, the propellant weight being 242 lb (110 kg). The guidance system was never developed, but with a large tandem booster an enlarged canard derivative, the R.042, was worked on until 1955 in the SAM role.

**Dimensions:** Length 15 ft 1 in (4·6 m); diameter 16·0 in (406 mm); span (wings) 70·8 in (1·8 m).
**Launch weight:** 1,014 lb (460 kg).
**Range:** Not known.

## AA.20

This simple missile was undoubtedly the first guided AAM actually to reach IOC in Western Europe. This is the more remarkable in view of its relatively late start: 1953, well behind de Havilland Propellers with Blue Jay. The contract was placed by the French Air Ministry with SFECMAS, which had just been formed from l'Arsenal de l'Aéronautique and in November 1954 was absorbed into the SNCA du Nord. This air-to-air programme, conducted in parallel with the pioneer anti-tank weapon (SS.10, p. 238), was designated SFECMAS 5103, later becoming the Nord 5103 and receiving the type designation AA.20. To speed development the objectives were simple, and this weapon was always regarded as an interim or training missile. Like all the early SFECMAS projects it had no aerodynamic surfaces other than cruciform fixed wings which imparted a steady roll. Guidance was by visual command, which greatly restricted operational value. Wire guidance was studied and tested but radio command was adopted. AA.20 was launched by the outer twin-nozzle booster charge of the Hotchkiss-Brandt or SNPE solid motor, while a small cordite capsule spun-up the autopilot gyro. The sustainer, again a solid motor, exhausted through a small central nozzle around which were four solenoid-biassed interrupter blades. The operator in the launch aircraft kept the missile's tracking flare aligned on the enemy air-

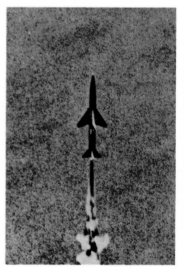

*Above: Light-up of Matra M.04 seen from Halifax launch aircraft vertically above, with Algerian desert below.*

*Below: This photograph, dated 10 April 1953, gives the length of Matra M.04 as "14 ft" and launch weight as "920 lb".*

craft by means of a small joystick which, via the microwave link, deflected the sustainer jet to steer the missile. When 50 ft (15 m) from its target the proximity fuze detonated the 50 lb (23 kg) warhead which was pre-fragmented and contained 11 lb (5kg) of a mixture of Hexogen and Tolite. Nord AA.20 Type M2RT missiles went into production at Chatillon in 1956, some 6,000 being delivered. Most Armée de l'Air and Aéronavale fighter squadrons used them until after 1960, carrier aircraft including the Mystère 4A, SMB.2, Mirage IIIC, Etendard IVM, Aquilon and Vautour IIN. The SS.11 was used for training from the Magister.

**Dimensions:** Length 102·4 in (2·6 m); diameter 9·84 in (250 mm); span 31·5 in (800 mm).
**Launch weight:** 295 lb (134 kg).
**Range:** 2·5 miles (4 km).

# AA.25

After SFECMAS became part of Nord the limitations of the AA.20 system were partly removed by replacing visual sighting and manual command by automatic radar command guidance. The Nord 5104 used the same airframe and propulsion as 5103, with the same jet-deflection steering, but the guidance receiver was made compatible with the target-tracking beam of the CSF Cyrano Ibis radar of the Mirage IIIC. Thus the intercepting pilot had merely to acquire the target by radar and lock-on, and the missile could then be made to ride the coded beam to the target. It still tended to mean a curve-of-pursuit chase, but the target no longer had to be visible, and thus Nord 5104 missiles could be used at night or in cloud or other adverse circumstances. Called AA.25 in service, many were modified from AA.20 missiles.

**Data:** As Nord AA.20 except launch weight 298 lb (135 kg) and range 3 miles (5 km).

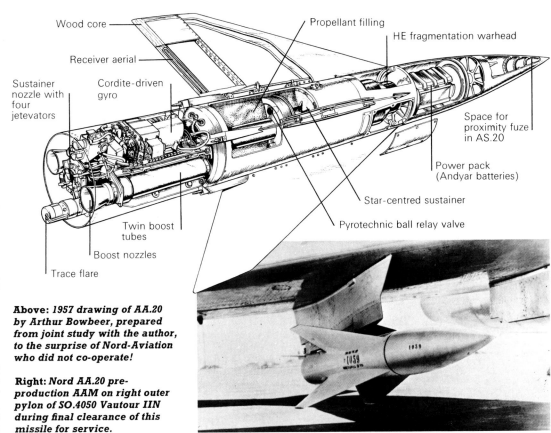

Wood core — Receiver aerial — Sustainer nozzle with four jetevators — Cordite-driven gyro — Propellant filling — HE fragmentation warhead — Space for proximity fuze in AS.20 — Power pack (Andyar batteries) — Star-centred sustainer — Pyrotechnic ball relay valve — Twin boost tubes — Boost nozzles — Trace flare

**Above:** *1957 drawing of AA.20 by Arthur Bowbeer, prepared from joint study with the author, to the surprise of Nord-Aviation who did not co-operate!*

**Right:** *Nord AA.20 pre-production AAM on right outer pylon of SO.4050 Vautour IIN during final clearance of this missile for service.*

# R.511

While SFECMAS was designing the interim Type 5103 missile, Société Matra was at work on what was expected to be the definitive "advanced" AAM for the Armée de l'Air. Derived from the R.042 and R.05, this first matured in 1956 as the R.510. The light-alloy airframe was notable in being of the twist-and-steer type, with nearly all the weight taken by a delta wing at the rear, with ailerons to control roll. At the nose were hydraulically powered foreplanes. Directional stability was improved by small fins on the wing tips and a rudder under the rear body. Propulsion was by a two-stage Hotchkiss-Brandt solid cast-DB motor. The chosen guidance for R.510 was an optical

*autodirecteur* comprising a photocell with 20° field of view directly ahead through a small glass lens in the nose. The same optical system triggered the 66 lb (30 kg) blast/fragmentation warhead in the mid-fuselage. Extensive testing from Meteor NF.11s began at Hammaguir in October 1952 and led to a limited production series of about 100 rounds, but by 1957 the 510 had been replaced by the R.511 with SARH guidance. By 1960 this had been greatly refined, with slightly different controls, large motor, and a new Thomson-CSF homing head. During development the target-illuminating radar had been that of the Vautour IIN, and some 500 production missiles were delivered to units equipped with this all-weather fighter which could

carry four missiles on separate under-wing pylons. At least a further 1,000 rounds were matched to the Cyrano Ibis radar of the Mirage IIIC and these remained in use with Armée de l'Air Mirage squadrons as training missiles until at least 1976. Owing to limitations of this early Cyrano radar the R.511 could not be used below about 10,000 ft (3000 m). Data are for R.511.

**Dimensions:** Length 10 ft 1·6 in (3·09 m); diameter 10·2 in (260 mm); span 39·37 in (1·0 m).
**Launch weight:** 406 lb (184 kg).
**Range:** 4·3 miles (7 km).

**Below:** *Matra R.511 production rounds on left pylons of Vautour IIN. Photo probably taken during final trials at Colomb-Béchar range.*

# R.530

By 1957 Matra had become the most experienced AAM company in Europe, and work began on this completely new weapon which has enjoyed a long and successful life. Abandoning twist-and-steer, the company reverted to cruciform delta wings and tail controls, two of the wings having ailerons for roll control. Having experience of various guidance systems, the Air Ministry and Matra still could not make up their minds and at first conducted trial firings with either SARH or IR homing. Both types became established in production and to this day R.530 is normally carried in pairs, one missile being a heat-homer and the other a radar-homer.

Propulsion is by Hotchkiss-Brandt/SNPE Antoinette dual-thrust solid (Plastargol) motor, with 2·7 sec of boost at 18,740 lb (8500 kg) thrust and then $6\frac{1}{2}$ sec sustain. The two homing heads, which can if necessary be exchanged by a user squadron to suit circumstances on operations, are the SAT type AD.3501 IR seeker, claimed to have all-aspect capability including head-on, and the EMD type AD.26 matched to the Cyrano Ibis or II of Mirage III interceptors or the Cyrano IV of the Mirage F1. A slightly different receiver is used by the Aéronavale for missiles carried by the F-8E(FN) Crusader, with APQ-94 radar. The warhead is again interchangeable, Hotchkiss-Brandt supplying either a continuous-rod or a pre-fragmented type both with a total weight of 60 lb (27 kg) and combined proximity and DA fuzing. No other West European AAM has rivalled this missile in its timescale, and sales amounted to just over 4,000, to 14 countries which are known to include Argentina, Australia, Brazil, Colombia, Iraq, Lebanon, Pakistan, South Africa, Spain and Venezuela. At one time the R.530 was also used by Israel. A typical price per round was $44,000.

**Dimensions:** Length (IR) 125·9 in (3198 mm), (radar) 129·3 in (3284 mm); diameter 10·35 in (263 mm); span 43·43 in (1103 mm).
**Launch weight:** (IR) 426·6 lb (193·5 kg), (radar) 423·3 lb (192 kg).
**Range:** 11 miles (18 km).

*Above: Matra R.530 on centreline pylon of the 91st Mirage IIIC, formerly in service with* **Les Cicognes** *Groupe de Chasse at Dijon.*

*Right: Launch of Super 530 test round from a Mirage F1 trials platform (note wing camera pod); inset, Super 530 on wing pylon of the Canberra trials platform at the CEV.*

# Super 530

By January 1971, when development of this missile started, Matra was a mature AAM producer able to take a studied look at the requirements and secure in the knowledge that R.530 would probably remain in production almost a further decade. Though to a slight degree based on the R.530, as reflected in the designation, this is in fact a totally new missile marking very large advances in flight performance and offering doubled acquisition distance and effective range and also introducing snap-up and -down capability of 25,000 ft (7600 m), believed to exceed that of any other AAM other than Phoenix. From the start only one method of guidance has been associated with Super 530, SARH. This uses the EMD Super AD-26, matched with the Cyrano IV radar of the Mirage F1; later a different receiver will be fitted to suit the PD radar of the Mirage 2000. To match the performance of these guidance systems Thomson-Brandt have developed the Angèle propulsion motor, with Butalane composite propellant of much higher specific impulse than that of earlier French motors. This is reported to accelerate the missile rapidly to Mach 4·5, thereafter sustaining approximately this speed for a further 4 sec to sustainer burn-out. Wings are not necessary at this speed, but Super 530 does have four wings of very low aspect ratio, manoeuvring by the cruciform of tail fins which have an unusual shape. The homing head was test-flown in September 1972, and an inert missile airframe was air-launched in July 1973. Firing trials from a Canberra of the CEV began in 1974, progressing to trials with guidance in 1975. Firing trials from a Mirage F1.C

began at Cazaux in 1976, and evaluation firing at CEAM has been in progress since 1975, targets in 1978 including the supersonic Beech AQM-37A for which Matra has concluded a licensing/marketing agreement. IOC of Super 530 is predicted for 1980.

**Dimensions:** Length 11 ft 7·3 in (3·54 m); diameter 10·2 in (260 mm); span (wing) 25·2 in (640 mm), (tail) 35·4 in (900 mm).
**Launch weight:** 529 lb (240 kg).
**Range:** 22 miles (35 km).

# R.550 Magic

Alone among European companies Matra took on the Sidewinder (p. 226) in head-on competition and has not merely achieved technical success but has also established 11 export customers and an output rate exceeding that of any other AAM ever produced in Western Europe. Wisely the weapon was made installationally interchangeable with Sidewinder, but the design requirements were greater than those of pre-

sently available versions of the US missile, including launch anywhere within a 140° forward hemisphere at all heights up to 59,000 ft (18 000 m) and with limitations at higher altitudes; ability to engage from almost any target aspect (head-on will shortly be achieved); ability to snap-fire at ranges down to 984 ft (300 m); ability to fire from a launch platform flying at any speed (no minimum) up to over 808 mph (1300 km/h) whilst pulling up to 6 g; and ability to pull 3·5 g and cross in front of the launch aircraft only 164 ft (50 m) ahead. The IR guidance uses the SAT type AD.3601, the PbS seeker being cooled prior to launch by a liquid-nitrogen bottle in the launch rail. Its output drives the electric control section with four canard fins (almost the reverse shape of those of Super 530) stationed immediately downstream of four fixed fins with the same span as the tips of the controls. The tail fins are free to rotate around the nozzle. Propulsion is by an SNPE Roméo single-stage composite-DB motor which gives high acceleration for 1·9 sec. The warhead weighs 27·6 lb (12·5 kg) of which half is the explosive charge detonated by IR proximity and DA fuzes. Matra began development as a company venture in 1968, receiving an Air Ministry contract in 1969. After various simpler air trials a missile with guidance was fired from a Meteor of the CEL against a CT-20 target in a tight turn on 11 January 1972. On 30 November 1973 a Magic was fired from a Mirage III in an extreme test of manoeuvrability. IOC was reached in 1975, since when production at Salbris has continued at the rate of 100 per month for the Armée de l'Air, Aéronavale, Abu Dhabi, Ecuador, Egypt, India, Iraq, Oman, Pakistan, Saudi Arabia, South Africa, Syria and at least one other customer. Unit price is in the order of $15,000.

**Dimensions:** Length 109 in (2·77 m); diameter 6·2 in (157 mm); span 26 in (660 mm).
**Launch weight:** 198 lb (89·8 kg).
**Range:** Up to more than 6·2 miles (10 km).

*Left: Firing a Magic dogfight AAM from the British Aerospace Jaguar International development prototype (Adour 804 engines and overwing weapon pylons).*

*Inset left: Posing with a genuine R.550 Magic on the second Mirage F1 prototype. The seeker head is covered by a protective metal cap.*

*Inset right: Magic guidance and control sections on the production line in the Matra plant at Salbris.*

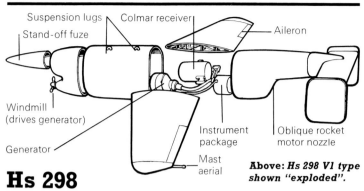

# GERMANY

Suspension lugs — Colmar receiver
Stand-off fuze — — Aileron
Windmill (drives generator)
Generator — Instrument package — Oblique rocket motor nozzle
Mast aerial

## Hs 298

This was the first AAM in the world to be built and developed, though like most German weapons it was abandoned in December 1944. Unlike other Henschel missiles it had an oval-section fuselage, with a mid-mounted swept wing with Wagner-bar ailerons. The tail had Wagner-bar elevators but the twin fins were fixed, control being by twist-and-steer. The command link was usually Kehl/Colmar, with a coded pulse for warhead detonation. It was hoped that a proximity fuze would become available, and one report claims that the 298 actually flew with both the Fox and Kranich fuzes. The fuze occupied the conical

*Right: Cutaway of typical X-4, developed just too late to be effective in World War 2.*

upper nose, the warhead containing 55 lb (25 kg) of explosive. The lower nose carried a windmill generator supplying guidance and control current. In the enlarged Hs 298 V2 series, of which a few were built at the end of the programme, these posi-

*Above: Hs 298 V1 type shown "exploded".*

tions were reversed. There was also to be a wire-guided version with a much larger warhead (105·8 lb, 48 kg) which may also have been intended for the V-2 series. More than 300 Hs 298 missiles were actually fired, mainly at Karlshagen from Ju 88G, Ju 388L and Fw 190A or G carriers. It was established that the attack had to be within a cone of about 30° semi-angle astern of the target, the axis of the cone being inclined about 15° upwards.

**Data:** Hs 298 V-1.
**Dimensions:** Length 78·9 in (2003 mm); depth of fuselage 16·34 in (415 mm); span 50·79 in (1·29 m).
**Launch weight:** 209·5 lb (95 kg).
**Range:** 1·5 miles (2·5 km).

## X-4

This AAM was one of the great missiles of history, for it not only established the AAM as a practical concept but it also proved the reliability and immunity to countermeasures of wire guidance, subsequently to dominate the field of anti-tank and many other tactical weapons. It was started under Dr Max Kramer at Ruhrstahl in early 1943, and received the RLM "8-series" aircraft type number of RK 344. Dispensing with aeroplane configuration, it followed Kramer's FX arrangement with a cruciform of wings around the c.g. and with control by rudders on cruciform tail fins indexed diagonally relative to the wings. The wings were of low aspect ratio and swept back, giving reduced

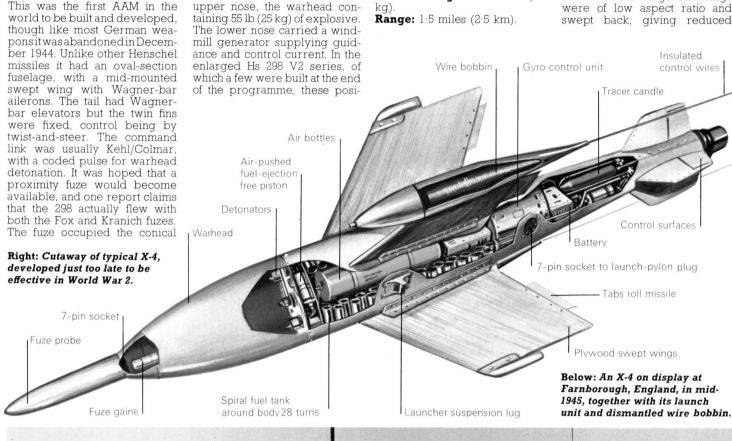

Wire bobbin — Gyro control unit — Insulated control wires
Tracer candle
Air bottles
Air-pushed fuel-ejection free piston
Detonators
Warhead
Control surfaces
Battery
7-pin socket to launch-pylon plug
Tabs roll missile
7-pin socket
Fuze probe
Fuze gaine
Spiral fuel tank around body 28 turns
Launcher suspension lug
Plywood swept wings

*Below: An X-4 on display at Farnborough, England, in mid-1945, together with its launch unit and dismantled wire bobbin.*

drag when slung under a jet fighter and allowing speed briefly to exceed that of sound at burnout of the BMW 548 motor. The latter ran on Salbei and Tonka hypergolic propellants each fed by air-bottle pressure applied to a free piston sliding along a unique spiral-tube tank. This complex feed was intended to ensure even consumption to the last drop, despite violent manoeuvres. X-4 was launched at about the same level as the target, preferably from astern, at a distance greater than 0·93 miles (1·5 km). The pilot sighted on the target and kept the missile aligned with it by the small joystick of the Düsseldorf/Detmold command link which used current variation for yaw and bang/bang polarity reversal for pitch. Small tabs on the wings rolled the

missile slowly, and an autopilot fed demands to the appropriate tail controls, signals being transmitted via duplicate wires unrolled from bobbins on two of the wings. The big warhead, with 44 lb (20 kg) of explosive, was to have a Kranich or Meise acoustic proximity fuze (by 1945 the Pudel programme was seeking to make X-4 home acoustically on its target). By late 1944 about 1,300 missiles had been produced, and many hundreds – most with Schmidding solid motors – tested. The first firing

at Karlshagen was from an Fw 190 on 11 August 1944, and the Ju 88G and 388L were also used. In the second half of 1944 over 1,000 pre-production X-4s were made, but their motors were destroyed by bombing of BMW's Stargard plant. As far as is known, no X-4s reached combat units, though some were "fired in anger".

**Dimensions:** Length 78·78 in (2001 mm); diameter 8·74 in (222 mm); span 22·64 in (575 mm).
**Launch weight:** 132 lb (60 kg).
**Range:** 2·17 miles (3·5 km).

# Viper

In 1969 the Federal German government authorised Bodenseewerk-Gerätetechnik (BGT) and Dornier to begin studies of a new AAM to replace Sidewinder, the early 9B version of which had been made under licence by a BGT/Perkin Elmer-led consortium. After prolonged study, and drawing upon BGT's detailed knowledge of IR guidance in AAM scenarios, Viper emerged as a much more formidable weapon with a radically new seeker head in which the entire sensitive cell, cooling system and Cassegrain optics were gimballed. This gave much greater look angle, higher target tracking speed and other advantages compared with the head of IR-homing Sidewinders. By 1972 extensive hardware testing was in hand, and Kongsberg of Norway came in as associate contractor responsible for propulsion (again with Sidewinder experience). Viper had large slender-delta wings not far behind the c.g., and an extremely advanced passive-IR proximity fuze amidships. There was every indication it would become an outstanding weapon, but in 1974 the programme was terminated because of the existence of a rival American project (AIM-9L). It is to be hoped that in the future NATO can and will use its design talent properly.

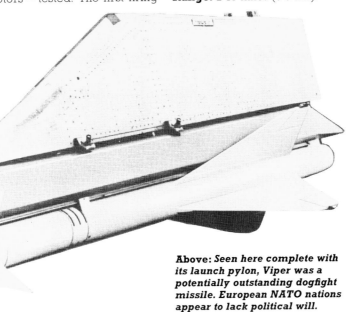

**Above:** *Seen here complete with its launch pylon, Viper was a potentially outstanding dogfight missile. European NATO nations appear to lack political will.*

# ISRAEL

## Shafrir

Development of this wholly Israeli AAM, derived by Rafael Armament Development Authority from early Sidewinders, was started in 1961, and by 1965 Shafrir had in many respects overtaken the US missile. Many details are still classified but it is clear that all models have a Cassegrain optical system behind a large hemispherical nose, pneumatic control fins, and fixed wings indexed in line and containing recessed rollerons similar to those of Sidewinder. The most fundamental difference introduced with the Israeli weapon is a substantial increase in body diameter, which must greatly improve many aspects of design and lethality. Simplicity was the keynote throughout, and a price of $20,000 has been quoted. Mk 1

did not complete development, but Mk 2 entered Heyl Ha'Avir service in 1969, and in subsequent fighting is credited with the destruction of over 200 aircraft. Of these more than half were destroyed during the brief Yom Kippur war in October 1973, claimed to indicate an SSKP of 60 per cent. Mk 2 is carried on a pylon adapter which can also carry alternative weapons. When the seeker locks-on, the pilot is informed both visually and aurally. The Mk 2 homes by lead-collision using proportional navigation. The 24·3 lb (11 kg) warhead, containing 8·8 lb (4 kg) of explosive, is detonated by DA or proximity fuzes, there being a ring of small circular fuze windows around the nose. This model is used by the Heyl Ha'Avir on Mirages and Kfirs, and also by Taiwan and Chile; there are probably other customers not yet disclosed. Mk 3 has been under test for several years and has a later guidance and control section, and possibly different aerodynamics, to give all-aspect capability and greater power of manoeuvre.

**Dimensions:** Length 8 ft 1 in (2470 mm); diameter 6·3 in (160 mm); span 20·5 in (520 mm).
**Launch weight:** 205 lb (93 kg).
**Range:** 3·1 miles (5 km).

**Left:** *Production Shafrir on right wing of Kfir fighter. Note diameter larger than very constricted Sidewinder, and also the hard-over repose position of two pairs of control canards.*

# ITALY

## Sispre C-7

Italy's first guided missile was a simple AAM originally designed by Contraves Italiana and tested at the government Centro Razzi, reaching the stage of flight trials with an F-86 in 1957. It was basically similar to Sidewinder, and owed much to the latter's seeker head, but manoeuvred by twist-and-steer using left and right rectangular wings of double-wedge section which were driven in unison for pitch and differentially for roll. The cruciform tail fins were fixed. In 1957 the programme was taken over by Sispre – Società Italiana Sviluppo Propulsione a Reazione, a subsidiary of Fiat and Finmeccanica – and a small production series was made in 1961–2 for use as a training and indoctrination missile by units equipped with the F-86 and G91.

**Dimensions:** Length 77·0 in (1956 mm); diameter 6·3 in (160 mm); span 25·0 in (635 mm).
**Launch weight:** 143 lb (65 kg).
**Range:** Claimed 7 miles (11·5 km).

## Aspide

Though a wholly Italian development, and the largest single missile programme in the country, this impressive weapon was

*Above: This is one of only very few pictures available of the C-7, and it shows a display model without pylon lugs or electrical socket.*

designed to be compatible with systems using Sparrow (p. 228). This extends to AAM applications, for which the immediate prospect is the Italian Air Force F-104S Starfighter originally tailored to AIM-7E, and several surface-launched applications. The Italian SAM system using this missile is named Spada (p. 154) in its mobile land form; a different ship-to-air system is named Albatros (p. 186). Similar to Sparrow in basic configuration, Aspide is powered by an advanced single-stage motor by SNIA-Viscosa (which made the motors for Italian Sparrows) giving higher thrust and a speed of Mach 4 at burnout. The all-round performance is claimed to exceed that of even AIM-7F, and the guidance is likewise claimed to have significant advantages over that of the American missile. Matched with an I-band monopulse fighter radar, it is said to have greater ECCM capability, to offer increased snapdown performance and to be markedly superior at very low altitudes. The seeker aerial system is driven hydraulically. The radome and forebody are described as redesigned for more efficient operation at hypersonic speeds, and in the AAM role the moving wings have extended tips with greater span. The SNIA-Viscosa fragmentation warhead weighs 77·2 lb (35·0 kg) and, as in the -7F Sparrow, is ahead of the wings. Following carry-trials in 1974 and prolonged static testing of the seeker, firing trials at Salto di Quirra, Sardinia, began in May 1975. By 1977 fully representative Aspide missiles, including the AAM version, had completed qualification firings and production began in 1978. The AAM is to

replace Sparrow in the Italian Air Force and will also be a possible missile for Italian Tornados.

**Dimensions:** Length 12 ft 1·7 in (3·7 m); diameter 8·0 in (203 mm); span (AAM) 39·37 in (1·0 m).
**Launch weight:** 485 lb (220 kg).
**Range:** Claimed up to 62 miles (100 km).

**Main picture, right:** *Launch of Aspide from a ground box at Salto di Quirra range. This missile is interchangeable with Sparrow and fits into AAM and land and sea SAM systems.*

**Inset right:** *Four frames of film record of impact by Aspide (with telemetry in place of warhead) on CT-20 target drone.*

# JAPAN

## AAM-1

Almost a direct copy of Sidewinder AIM-9E, this AAM was developed in 1960–9 by Mitsubishi Heavy Industries for use by F-86F, F-104J and F-1 fighters of the JASDF. In 1969–71 a total of 330 rounds were delivered and these have subsequently been in the JASDF inventory alongside larger numbers of Sidewinders. AAM-1 is unofficially reported to be slightly smaller (102 in, 2·6 m) and lighter (154 lb, 70 kg) than

most Sidewinders, and to have the modest range of 4·3 miles (7 km).

## AAM-2

Under development at Mitsubishi Heavy Industries from 1972 until termination in 1977, this more advanced AAM was intended to succeed AAM-1 with all-aspect collision-course guidance using an IR seeker head by Nihon Electric. More than 60 development missiles were fired but the JASDF decided to adopt an advanced Sidewinder as its next AAM. Mitsubishi Heavy Industries is reported now to be studying advanced close-range dogfight missiles.

*Below: AAM-1 hung on the two fuselage pylons of a Mitsubishi-built F-104J. No good picture or data are available on this missile.*

# SOUTH AFRICA

## Whiplash

In 1969 the then Minister of Defence – now Prime Minister – P. W. Botha, announced that an "all South African" AAM had been under development since 1966 and was nearing production after a firing trials programme at the St Lucia range. In September 1971 the SAAF announced the successful engagement of a Mach 2 target three seconds after launch from a Mirage IIICZ. Subsequently unofficial reports have stated this missile uses IR homing.
No data.

# SWEDEN

## RB 72

The Swedish government authorised Saab to begin full engineering development of this missile, also designated Saab 372, in July 1975. Intended as primary AAM for the JA37 fighter version of the Viggen, RB 72 was planned to meet the requirements of both long-range all-weather interception and close dogfighting, and had a configuration with large delta wings and relatively large cropped-tip tail control fins. Saab-Scania's Electronics Division produced

the nitrogen-cooled IR sensor feeding a modern all-solid-state digital guidance system. After testing the seeker on another missile the company announced it could be "launched from any point in the JA37 operational envelope, and against a target from any aspect". Solid-propulsion contractor had not been decided, nor had several other major choices, when the programme was halted in April 1978. The British Sky Flash was ordered instead, but the work completed on the RB 72 seeker is likely to read across to B 83 (p. 115).

**Dimensions:** Length 103·6 in (2631 mm); diameter 6·89 in (175 mm); span 23·9 in (607 mm).
**Launch weight:** About 243 lb (110 kg).
**Range:** Not disclosed (figure of 2·3 miles widely reported is an underestimate).

*Left: A Saab "372" mounted for carry-trials purposes on a Viggen in 1977.*

*Right: A side view of the same missile. Sweden was almost certainly wise to terminate this programme and instead study future applications of its excellent guidance system, produced mainly by Saab Electronics Division.*

# USSR

## AA-1 Alkali

So far as is known, this was the first AAM to go into operational use in the Soviet Union. Like all other known Soviet AAMs the original user was the PVO air-defence force. Development must have started around 1950, tailored closely to the parallel development of the somewhat crude interceptor radars grouped under the Soviet name of Izumrud. The earliest models of this radar known in the West are codenamed Scan Fix, and are said to have "fixed scan". This contradiction in terms is thought to mean that they are boresighted to point directly ahead, for ranging and target illumination for semi-active missile guidance. This primitive set was installed in the MiG-17P in the early 1950s, entering service by 1958. A few months later the gunless MiG-17PFU entered service with underwing racks for four of these early missiles. The associated radars are thought to operate in E/F-band. In contrast the missile next appeared on the MiG-19PM interceptor, associated with the later Scan Odd radar with alleged complex scanning patterns and operating in I-band at 9300–9400 Hz. Like most Soviet AI radars this has two PRFs, around 900 pps for search and doubled frequency for tracking. This aircraft again carried four launch rails, apparently identical to those of MiG-17PFU and hung on prominent pylons. The third installation was the Su-9 all-weather interceptor, which again has the same four clumsy rails. This aircraft has yet another radar, called Spin Scan by NATO but believed actually to be designated R1L, and of a later family than the Izumruds. They operate in I-band, one version having over 100 kW peak and PRFs of 825/895 for search and 1750/1795 for track, with spiral scan. The missile is thus highly adaptable. It is widely said to be radar homing and to manoeuvre by trailing-edge controls on the rear wings.

This is strange, because everything points to the following: beam-riding guidance, with coding to give automatic error-correction; control by the cruciform of nose fins; roll-stabilization by wing ailerons; and twin (lateral) motor nozzles well ahead of the streamlined boat-tail. There are at least six models of AA-1, some having cone/cylinder projections on the nose and all having fairings on the wingtips. The warhead is behind the canard controls. By 1978 all were thought to be withdrawn.

**Dimensions:** Length 74·0 in (1·88 m); diameter 7·5 in (190 mm); span 22·75 in (578 mm).
**Launch weight:** About 200 lb (91 kg).
**Range:** About 5 miles (8 km).

## AA-2 Atoll

Unlike most Russian weapons this AAM is beyond doubt a copy of a Western original, the early AIM-9B Sidewinder. When first seen on 9 June 1961, carried by various fighters in an air display, it was almost identical to the US weapon. Since then it has followed its own path of development, and like Sidewinder has diversified into IR and SARH versions. Body diameter is even less than that of Sidewinder, and so far as is known all models have the nose-to-tail sequence of AIM-9B (see p. 226). The 13·2 lb (6·0 kg) warhead is a BF type with smooth exterior. Believed to be designated K-13A or SB-06 in the Soviet Union, several early versions have been built in very large numbers as standard AAM for most models of MiG-21, which carry two on large adapter shoes (which house the seeker cooling system in later models) on the underwing pylons. Licence production by the MiG complex of Hindustan Aeronautics has been

in progress since the early 1970s, and it is generally believed there is also a Chinese version. Other users include all Warsaw Pact air forces, Afghanistan, Algeria, Angola, Cuba, Egypt, Finland, Iraq, North Korea, Syria and Vietnam. Since 1967 there have been later sub-types called AA-2-2 or Advanced Atoll by NATO. Some reports ascribe these designations to the SARH versions, but the consensus of opinion is that there are IR and radar versions of the first-generation missiles, in various sub-types, and IR and radar versions of the Advanced model. Several photographs indicate that later models have quite different control fins. These fins are driven in opposite pairs through 30°, and the later fin is unswept, has a cropped tip and greater area and is fitted after loading on the launcher. Like AIM-9 versions, IR missiles have hemispherical noses transparent to heat, and radar versions slightly tapered noses that appear opaque. Current carriers include all later fighter MiG-21s, with four missile shoes instead of two, and the MiG-23S swing-wing fighter which also carries later AAMs. Various versions have also been seen on MiG-17PFU fighter-trainers, in place of AA-1. All AA-2 models have plenty of combat experience in the Middle East, SE Asia and over India/Pakistan. Early results were not impressive. The pilot's aural buzz, which changes to an increasingly urgent warbling as the missile

seeker locks-on and range closes, could not be relied upon as proof of subsequent homing. Today's missiles are probably more reliable, and it is assumed an all-aspect IR seeker is now also in service.

**Dimensions:** Length (IR) 9 ft 2 in (2·8 m), (SARH) about 9 ft 6 in (2·9 m); diameter 4·72 in (120 mm); span (early canard) 17·7 in (450 mm), (tail and later canard) 20·9 in (530 mm).
**Launch weight:** Typically 154 lb (70 kg).
**Range:** About 4 miles (6·4 km).

## AA-3 Anab

This second-generation AAM was the first large long-range all-weather missile to reach the PVO, which it did at about the time dummy examples were displayed carried by an early Yak-28P interceptor at Tushino at the 1961 Soviet Aviation Day display. At that time it was at first thought by the West to be an ASM, but gradually it was identified as a straightforward AAM carried in both IR and SARH versions, usually one of each. The carriers are the Yak-28P in all versions except trainers, Su-11 and Su-15. All these aircraft have the radar called Skip Spin by NATO, a much more capable installation than those associated with the earlier AAMs and probably derived from the Scan Three fitted to the Yak-25. Believed to be designated RP-11, it operates in I-band between

*Right: Su-11 interceptor of PVO, usually armed with AA-3 Anab but in this case carrying only a pair of AA-2 Atolls.*

*Below: Launch of AA-1 Alkali from No 3 position on Su-9 interceptor of PVO. Compare with later Su-11 above right.*

*Below: AA-3 Anabs (probably of the co-called "advanced" type) on Flagon-F, the latest version of Su-15 interceptor.*

8690/8995 MHz at peak power of 200 kW, with a PRF of 2700/3000 pps and pulse-width of about 0·5 microsec. It is assumed that CW illumination is provided for missile homing. AA-3 has large rear wings indexed in line with cruciform canard controls, and solid propulsion is assumed. Aerodynamics may be derived from AA-1, though as there appear to be no wing control surfaces it is probable that the canards can be driven as four independent units for roll control. There is no information on either type of homing head; the motor has a single central nozzle, and may have boost/sustainer portions, and the warhead is amidships, with a proximity fuze. An AA-3-2 Advanced Anab has been identified since 1972, but how it is "advanced" has not become public. Anab has been used by several WP air forces but was not exported, and since 1975 has been progressively replaced by AA-7.

**Dimensions:** Length (IR) 157 in (4·0 m), (SARH) 142 in (3·6 m); diameter 11·0 in (280 mm); span 51·0 in (1·3 m).
**Launch weight:** About 606 lb (275 kg).
**Range:** Probably at least 20 miles (32 km).

## AA-4 Awl

In the mid-1950s the Soviet Union took great interest in the British and American attempts to develop a fully active AAM, and

by about 1958 had begun work itself, using unknown radar homing guidance. Virtually no information is available on the weapon beyond what can be deduced from the inert test vehicles carried at the 1961 Aviation Day display at Tushino under the wings of the large twin-engined Mikoyan prototype codenamed Flipper. (This aircraft sired the I-75F swept-wing interceptor with AA-3 Anabs and the single-engined world-speed-record breaker Ye-166.) Codenamed Awl by NATO's ASCC, the missiles were exceedingly large and superficially rather crude vehicles, with cruciforms of wings and fins of almost rectangular shape indexed in line on a large tubular body with a conical nose. There has been speculation that this missile, designated AA-4 by the DoD, was a two-stage device, the rear fins separating with the boost motor to leave a shorter missile that manoeuvred at hypersonic speed by body lift. Data are very approximate.

**Dimensions:** Length 17 ft (5·2 m); diameter 12 in (305 mm); span 6 ft (1·8 m).
**Launch weight:** About 880 lb (400 kg).
**Range:** Possibly 62 miles (100 km).

## AA-5 Ash

This large AAM was developed in 1954–59 specifically to arm the Tu-28P long-range all-weather

interceptor, and genuine missiles were seen carried by a development aircraft of this family at the 1961 Aviation Day display at Tushino. (This aircraft had a very large ventral bathtub believed to house side-looking or early-warning radar, not seen subsequently.) Early versions of Tu-28, at first mistakenly reported as Blinder but corrected to Fiddler, carried two of these missiles on underwing pylons. So far as one can tell, they were SARH guided, associated with the Big Nose radar of the carrier aircraft, a very large and powerful I-band radar which had no counterpart operational in the West until the AWG-9 of 1974. The missile is matched to the radar in scale, being larger than any Western AAM. For many years Western estimates of AA-5 range were ludicrously low, but they are creeping up and may now be about half the true value for the radar version. Early Tu-28s are thought to have entered PVO service soon after 1961, filling in gaps around the Soviet Union's immense frontier. By 1965 the Tu-28P was being armed with the newly introduced IR version of this missile. This aircraft has four underwing pylons carrying the IR version, with Cassegrain optics behind a small nose window, on the inners and the SARH model, with opaque (usually red-painted) conical nose on the outers. Early versions of MiG-25 Foxbat interceptor were also armed with this missile, usually one of each type. It is not known whether these aircraft also had Big Nose or an early model of Fox Fire radar. Ash has been reported to have been served with most other WP air forces, but as no nation except the Soviet Union has used either of this missile's carrier aircraft the report appears to be false. This large weapon remains in the inventory.

**Dimensions:** Length (SARH) about 217 in (5·51 m), (IR) 205 in (5·21 m); diameter 12 in (305 mm); span 51 in (1·3 m).
**Launch weight:** both about 860 lb (390 kg).
**Range:** (SARH, author's estimate) about 40 miles (64 km), (IR) about 13 miles (21 km).

*Left: AA-5 Ash missiles about to be mounted on Tu-28P long-range interceptors. The three in front are of the IR-homing type; others probably SARH.*

## AA-6 Acrid

Largest AAM in the world, this awesome weapon family was designed around 1959–61 originally to kill the B-70 Valkyrie (which instead was killed by the US Congress) and entered PVO service as definitive armament of the Mach 3·2 MiG-25 "Foxbat A" interceptor. With four missiles, two IR-homers on the inner pylons and two SARH on the outers, this aircraft is limited to Mach 2·8. (It is, of course, totally a straight-line aircraft at such speeds, and in its original form was not intended for any kind of close encounter with hostile aircraft. Since 1975 developed versions with many changes have emerged able to withstand about +6g at Mach 2 and armed with AA-6 and AA-7 missiles.) Like the Tu-28, the MiG-25 was intended to detect targets at long range, using the Markham ground-air data link to give a cockpit display based on ground surveillance radars, switching to its own Fox Fire radar at about 100 miles' (160 km) range. This equipment, likened to an F-4 AWG-10 in character but greater in power, includes CW aerials in slim wingtip pods to illuminate the target for the SARH missiles, which could probably lock-on and be fired at ranges exceeding 65 miles (100 km); both peak-pulse/CW power and receiver-aerial size are considerably greater than for any Sparrow and closely similar to AWG-9/Phoenix. The IR version has much shorter range, though there is no reason to doubt that current Soviet technology is increasing IR fidelity as is being done elsewhere. Acrid has a large long-burning motor, giving a speed generally put at Mach 4·5 (the figure of 2·2 in one report is nonsense) and manoeuvres by canard controls, with supplementary ailerons (possibly elevons) on all four wings. The latter have the great area needed for extreme-altitude interception, for the B-70 cruised at well over 70,000 ft (21 km); but early Acrid missiles did not have look-down capability. Soviet films suggest that, when the range is close enough, it is usual to follow national standard practice and ripple missiles in pairs, IR closely followed by SARH. The two homing heads are different in shape, as in the case of AA-5 which AA-6 probably replaces. No missile of this family has been seen on any carrier aircraft except the PVO MiG-25.

**Dimensions:** Length (SARH) 248 in (6·3 m), (IR) 232 in (5·9 m); diameter 15·7 in (400 mm); span 88·6 in (2·25 m).
**Launch weight:** (SARH) about 1,874 lb (850 kg), (IR) 1,433 lb (650 kg).
**Range:** (SARH) 62 miles (100 km), (IR) 15·5 miles (25 km).

*Left: MiG-25 Foxbat-A with four AA-6 Acrids, SARH outboard and IR inboard. Alternatives are ECM or twin AA-7 Apex.*

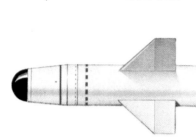

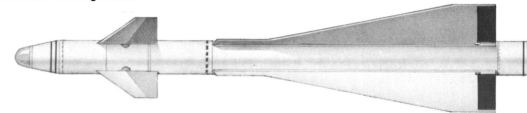

**Above:** *Provisional drawing of the IR-homing version of AA-7 Apex, based on even scantier evidence than the equally provisional drawing below.*

# AA-7 Apex

Standard medium-range AAM of the MiG-23S in all except export versions, this intensely interesting missile is large and apparently formidable. It has a unique configuration with three sets of aerodynamic cruciform surfaces, all indexed in line. It appears to be roll-stabilized by tail controls and to manoeuvre by the canards, but it is possible that in extreme manoeuvres both front and rear sets work together. Combined with a flight Mach number of 3·5 this could give unprecedented manoeuvrability. The central wings do not appear to carry movable surfaces. Predictably, Apex is issued in equal numbers of both SARH and IR versions, the homing heads having the usual distinctive forms. Most MiG-23S carry one of each type on their wing-glove pylons, leaving the body pylons for other stores. Twin Apex are also sometimes carried on each outer pylon of the MiG-25, though it is not known what overall mix of SARH/IR missiles is preferred. One report states that this family of missiles can be carried by the "MiG-21" but no version of

this aircraft appears to be compatible with the SARH Apex which is matched with High Lark radar. It is assumed that this missile replaces AA-3. It became known in the West in 1976 but by mid-1978 no good illustration had been published. It is assumed that this missile is for use mainly at low/medium altitudes and has look-down/look-up capability. One report suggests a warhead of 88 lb (40 kg). Data are, of course, estimates.

**Length:** (SARH) 177 in (4·5 m), (IR) 166 in (4·22 m); diameter 10·2 in (260 mm); span 55·1 in (1·4 m).
**Launch weight:** (SARH) 705 lb (320 kg), (IR) slightly less.
**Range:** (SARH) 30 miles (48 km), (IR) 12 miles (20 km).

# AA-8 Aphid

In contrast to its wealth of formidable large long-range AAMs, the PVO never had a good dogfight weapon until this neat missile entered service after 1975 with the MiG-23S. Aerodynamically it appears to be a baby Acrid, though vastly different in scale. The canard controls are of very low aspect ratio and apparently rectangular (though some representations show a curved leading edge/tip). These surfaces are very close to the nose, and are driven by control impulses from either of the two usual types of homing seeker. It is suggested by Western drawings that there are the usual differences in head geometry. MiG-23S can carry one of each type on the body pylons, re-

**Above:** *This drawing of the (probably IR-homing) version of AA-8 Aphid is known to be accurate only in basic shape. Disclosure of Soviet AAMs of this generation has been slow.*

placing Atoll. It is not yet known if AA-8 can be carried by the MiG-21, the VTOL Yak-36 or by attack aircraft such as the MiG-27, Su-19 or Hind-D helicopter. One report gives warhead weight as 13·2 lb (6 kg).

**Dimensions:** Length (SARH) 84·6 in (2·15 m), (IR) 78·7 in (2·0 m); diameter 5·1 in (130 mm); span 20·5 in (520 mm).
**Launch weight:** 121 lb (55·0 kg) (possibly SARH heavier, IR lighter).
**Range:** (SARH) 9·3 miles (15 km), (IR) possibly slightly less.

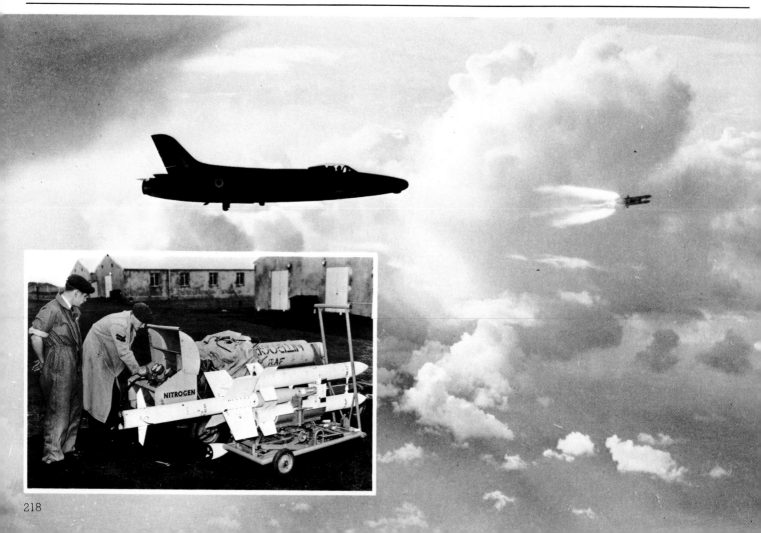

# UNITED KINGDOM

## Fireflash

The first AAM to enter hardware development in Britain, under the 1949 codename Blue Sky, this missile had a strange configuration that remains unique. The basic missile was merely an unpowered dart, with large almost rectangular wings indexed at 45° to the very small cropped-tip tail controls. This was accelerated to Mach 2 by a pair of solid boost motors arranged in a clumsy manner one above the other. This odd arrangement was adopted to leave a clear line of sight to the guidance receiver aerials on the flat base of the missile, without interference from flame, ionised gas and soot. The motors had oblique nozzles, losing part of the thrust for geometric reasons, and their high-drag linking struts and clamps, and two sets of cruciform fins, nullified the fine shape of the central dart. Another snag was that 1·5 sec after launch the missile was coasting at rapidly falling velocity, and the more it had to manoeuvre the slower it went (but its drag was less than if it had an internal motor). Plessey and Ekco provided the pencil-beam radar guidance. The radar fitted the nose of a Hunter trials aircraft based at Llanbedr for firing over Cardigan Bay, though the first unguided firings took place from a Meteor NF.11 in 1954. Prime was Fairey Aviation's Weapons Division at Heston. By 1955 it had been decided not to procure this weapon for the inventory, but the fact that it actually existed and worked did result in over 300 being issued to No 1 Guided Weapon Development Squadron at Valley, equipped with the Swift F.7. This had the airframe of the FR.5 but with the long-span wing of the stillborn PR.6 and a long nose housing the radar. The black/white Fireflashes – as Blue Sky was renamed – contained telemetry to gather 24 statistical parameters. What these figures accomplished, or what the pilots learned, is obscure.

**Dimensions:** Length 111·75 in (2·84 m); diameter (basic missile) 6·0 in (152 mm); span (wings) 28·1 in (713 mm).
**Launch weight:** 300 lb (136 kg).
**Range:** 3 miles (4·8 km).

*Left: Pleasing study taken over Cardigan Bay in 1957 of a Swift F.7 firing its second and last Fireflash. The pylon rear sockets can be seen projecting below the wings.*

*Left, inset: Tradesmen at RAF Valley topping up the gas bottle of a Fireflash (with telemetry instead of warhead) prior to firing it into Cardigan Bay from a Swift.*

## Firestreak

Originally codenamed Blue Jay, this was the first guided missile of British origin to reach TOC, in 1958. Development began seven years previously, the prime contractor de Havilland Propellers being assisted by the RAE, RRE and RARDE, and with Mullard playing a central role in the IR guidance. Guided rounds were fired from 1954, a unique result being such an unbroken string of total successes that the team at first learned nothing (later the programme became more normal!). In 1955 a Venom launched a pre-production Blue Jay against a Firefly U.9, and about 100 rounds were then fired at the WRE from Avon-Sabres against Jindiviks. In 1958 the missile was named Firestreak, and in Mk I form entered service with the Sea Venoms of 893 Sqn RN (two missiles), followed by the Javelin FAW.7 (four) with 33 Sqn RAF in August 1958. Subsequently various sub-types served with the Sea Vixen FAW.1 and 2 of the RN (four) and all marks of Lightning (two) of the RAF, Saudi Arabia and Kuwait. Several thousand rounds were produced, ending in 1969, and a few remain operational with Lightning users. The layout was very back-to-front. The aircraft equipment varied considerably, and in the Venom and Sabre was in an external bulge. Operational interceptors had a slaving unit which pointed the IR seeker head's Cassegrain telescope to look at the target held by the fighter's radar. Another unique feature was the eight-sided glass nose, like a sharp pencil. Error signals commanded proportional navigation by very small tail controls driven by long push/pull rods from actuators in the forebody fed with air from a toroidal bottle near the motor nozzle! The air also drove a turbo-alternator. The seeker cell and potted electronics were cooled by nitrogen from the fighter. Nearing the target, two rings of IR sensors located behind glass windows ahead of the wings locked-on to the target to form a two-beam proximity fuze feeding target bearing and range and, at the correct point, detonating the 50 lb (22·7 kg) warhead surrounding the motor tube just ahead of the fins. Firestreak eventually achieved an SSKP of 85 per cent when fired within a 10,000 ft (3050 m) radius hemisphere to the rear of the target.

**Dimensions:** Length 125·5 in (3188 mm); diameter 8·75 in (222·5 mm); span 29·4 in (746·8 mm).
**Launch weight:** Close to 300 lb (137 kg).
**Range:** 5 miles (8 km).

**Right:** *The glass nose and two rings of fuze windows on a Firestreak hung on a Lightning of 92 Sqn RAF in Germany in 1973.*

**Below:** *Four Firestreaks on a Javelin FAW.9 flying without visible unit markings. The IR fuze windows look from this distance like black bands.*

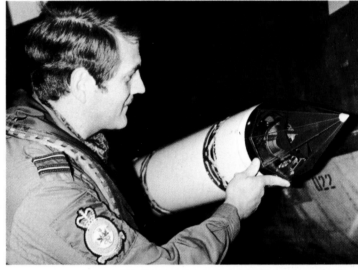

# Red Dean/ Red Hebe

It is a scarcely credible fact that, while Britain developed an IR-guided AAM and a very large weapon with fully active radar homing, it did no more than paper studies on SARH weapons in this category, though the latter might have been thought the natural complement to the IR variety and could have used the same airframes. Obviously the problems with fully active AAMs are much greater, and so far as is known none entered service until 1974 (Phoenix). To attempt such a missile in October 1952 was biting off as much as the technology could chew. Indeed, the team at Vickers-Armstrongs (Aircraft) at Weybridge, to whom the prime contract was awarded, soon encountered severe difficulties that were never fully solved. The choice of guidance radar was likewise a thorny one, as was the question of whether the missile had to be locked-on to the target prior to launch. The basic missile was the Vickers Type 888, but there were two quite different guidance systems with different codenames: Red Dean had PD guidance in J-band and Red Hebe was to use a CW radar with different characteristics. The relevant specifications were 1105 and 1131. Although nothing was ever disclosed, the decision had to be taken to use SARH for most of the missile's long flight, then accomplishing the difficult task of automatically switching to the weapon's own seeker much closer to the target (probably within 3 miles, 4·8 km). The Type 888 was a conventional vehicle with cruciforms of large wings and high aspect ratio tail controls indexed in line, with a large long-burning solid motor. Carry trials began from a Canberra at Wisley in late 1955, and other Canberras were prepared for guided firings at Aberporth and Woomera in 1956. Several large all-weather interceptors were planned to carry whichever weapon resulted (Red Hebe finally became favoured), notably the Gloster G.50 "thin-wing Javelin" and various contenders to F.155/T specification. All these were cancelled in 1956–7 and the missile pro-gramme itself followed in June 1957, in the belief that there would be no need for future manned interceptors.

**Dimensions:** Length 16 ft 1 in (4·9 m); diameter 12·5 in (317·5 mm); span 45·0 in (1143 mm).
**Launch weight:** 1,330 lb (603 kg).
**Range:** Exceeded 40 miles (64 km).

# Red Top

Originally called Firestreak Mk IV, this was a rationalised Fire-streak with the components re-assembled in a more logical arrangement, and with a completely new seeker head, motor and warhead to give very much greater lethality. The basic requirement, of late 1956, was to produce a missile not confined to the ± 15° squint angle of first-generation IR seekers, and, by developing a seeker able to home on the target's jet itself, or other hot parts, attack successfully from any direction. As early as 1958 an American publication reported that "Red Top . . . has a 68 lb conventional warhead and a range of 14,000 yards, with . . . a cooled lead telluride cell receiving in a 4 to 5 micro range". Though slightly garbled, this disclosed valuable information which at the time was highly classified, and even today no details of the seeker may be given. In the course of development the missile was redesigned with an untapered forebody to accommodate a larger warhead. The improved motor gave a speed of just over Mach 3 at burnout, while the nose was redesigned as a full-diameter glass hemisphere. Wings and tail controls were completely redesigned with greater area, and with planform and section profile matched to Mach 3, greater altitudes and much greater lateral acceleration. The powerful warhead, of a new type, had a later IR fuzing system in advance of any other AAM system of the late 1950s. It was positioned as a single package ahead of the wings, while the control group was relocated next to the control fins. Development was rapid and successful, and by late 1964 a few Red Tops were being issued to 74 Sqn, whose Lightnings were being upgraded to F.3 (later F.6) standard with a larger vertical tail to counter the slightly larger side area of the new missile. At the same

*Below: When Red Dean was cancelled Britain also threw away this transporter/loader.*

Left: *Early production Red Tops on a Lightning F.3 of 29 Sqn, RAF. The larger Red Top necessitated an increase in the fighter's fin area.*

time Red Top was issued to the first RN squadron equipped with the Sea Vixen FAW.2, No 899, replacing Firestreak on four wing pylons. Red Top was subsequently improved in small details and remains in service with Lightnings of the RAF, Saudi Arabia and Kuwait.

**Dimensions:** Length 130·6 in (3·32 m); diameter 8·75 in (222·25 mm); span 35·75 in (908 mm).
**Launch weight:** About 330 lb (150 kg).
**Range:** 7·5 miles (12 km).

# SRAAM

Experience in Vietnam, to some degree brought about by the insistence of the US government on positive visual identification of all hostile air targets (which ruled out long-range AAM shots on the basis of IFF interrogation), rammed home the urgent need

Left: *Remarkable high-speed film frame showing launch of SRAAM from Hunter trials aircraft in 1977. Note fins unfolding from body.*

for close-range air-combat weapons. Guns were put back in fighters, and at Hatfield HSD (now BAe Dynamics Group) put company money into a study of close-range AAMs. Obviously it was possible to do very much better than any conceivable development of Sidewinder, and by 1970 the missile, named Taildog, had been completely designed other than details of the solid motor and IR seeker. Later in that year a small MoD contract was received and engineering development proceeded under the name SRAAM-100, later changed to SRAAM (Short-Range AAM). Extremely shortsightedly the contract was terminated in 1974, and replaced by a low-key technology-demonstration programme to be undertaken without urgency and involving merely eight firings, from ground launchers and a Hunter fighter. The first shot with guidance in April 1977 passed within lethal range of a difficult target, triggering the novel BAe fuze. Subsequent firings proved SRAAM's unparalleled manoeuvrability, which can include a 90° turn immediately on leaving the launcher. The objective of the designers, abundantly achieved, was to produce a simple AAM system, of low cost,

that could be attached to any aircraft without needing modification of either the aircraft or launcher; to give the pilot unprecedented SSKP in a dogfight, while greatly reducing his workload; and to offer high snap-shot lethality against targets in previously impossible situations such as crossing at minimum range. SRAAM is instantly available and fired automatically as soon as the seeker acquires a target coming into view ahead. It is carried in a lightweight twin-tube launcher whose adapter shoe houses the fire-control system (and, in development firings, a camera). The chosen missile tube flicks open its nose doors, fires the round, and closes the doors to reduce drag. The six small tailfins flip open and the passive IR seeker commands the missile by four jetevators in the solid-motor efflux. In August 1977, when AIM-9L (p. 226) was chosen for British use, it was stated that SRAAM would be "kept alive" to provide a coherent design base for possible collaboration on a future weapon in this class. Had SRAAM been a priority programme from the start it could today be the standard throughout the West, offering capability the AIM-9L cannot approach. Shield is a proposed ship-based version (p. 197).

**Dimensions:** Length 107·25 in (2724 mm); diameter 6·5 in (165 mm).

![USA flag] **USA**

# Meteor

MIT began the development of this missile under Navy BuOrd contract in September 1945. Federal Telecommunications Laboratory handled SARH guidance and Bell Aircraft was assigned the airframe, which had cruciforms of rear wings and canard controls indexed in line. Firing trials at Pt Mugu began in July 1948, using a JD-1 Invader, and progressed to F3D Skyknights in 1951. Meteor was the first missile designed for carrier-based aircraft, and it reached Mach 3 at burnout of the liquid motor. Launch weight was 500 lb (227 kg), of which 25 lb (11·34 kg) was the fragmentation warhead.

Meteor received the designation XAAM-N-2, but was cancelled in 1953.

# Oriole

A large and ambitious missile for USN carrier-based interceptors, AAM-N-4 Oriole was developed under BuOrd contract by Glenn L. Martin Company in 1947–55. Guided by an active radar, it had cruciform wings and tail controls, weighed 1,500 lb (680 kg) and reached Mach 2·5 on a solid motor. The intended range was 20 miles (32 km).

Below: *Reserve Officers Training Corps cadets study cutaway Oriole at Pt Mugu.*

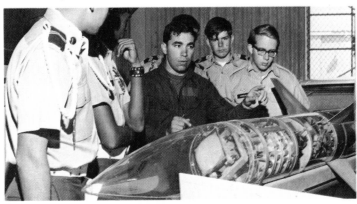

# Gorgon

Two of the members of this cruise-type missile family were intended to become AAMs, as related on p. 120. In fact the original Gorgon project dated from an AAM proposal of 1937, which after various paper modifications became a firm design with Westinghouse 9·5 turbojet propulsion in 1941. During 1942 such propulsion was criticised as unnecessarily costly and for one Gorgon family a derivative of a simple liquid rocket was substituted (the engine was that being developed at Annapolis by Robert C. Truax, former midshipman, as a JATO unit). In October 1943 semi-production began, 25 of each of two designs (one a canard) being built. Subsequent work was directed chiefly towards a SAM.

# Firebird

The first post-war AAM to reach the flight-test stage outside Germany, this attractive-looking weapon was designated XAAM-A-1 and resulted from a USAAF contract placed with Ryan Aeronautical in 1947. Ryan had already begun development of the XQ-2 radio-controlled target from which stemmed the Firebee series, today the most diverse and important family of drones and RPVs in the world. Firebird likewise had radio guidance, with a microwave command link which was intended to take it close to the target. It was hoped to develop it for night and all-weather use, using radar beam-riding, but this was not introduced until well after 1950. The difficult part was terminal homing, and SARH was attempted for the first time. Some hundreds of Firebees were built, and their testing from DF-82C and DB-26B aircraft at Holloman AFB in 1950–55 provided a solid underpinning of technology for later AAMs, and for the SARH Falcons in particular. Firebird was launched (one, two or four at a time) by a 30 in (762 mm) solid motor which was then jettisoned by a small explosive charge. The Ryan acid/aniline sustainer then burned for 15 sec, the trajectory being controlled by the cruciform of moving wings indexed at 45° to the swept tail fins. The warhead had DA, proximity and self-destruct fuzes.

**Dimensions:** Length with booster 120·0 in (3048 mm), without booster 90·0 in (2286 mm); diameter 6·0 in (152 mm); span 36·0 in (914 mm).
**Launch weight:** 600 lb (272 kg).
**Range:** 5 to 8 miles (8–12·8 km).

# MX-904

This Hughes AAM was intended as a BDM to protect the B-36 heavy bomber. To weigh 75 lb (34 kg) with a 10 lb (4·5 kg) warhead, it was to fly at Mach 2·5 on a solid motor and be aimed by radio command against interceptors still out of range of guns.

**Top:** *Take-off of P-61 bailed to the Navy carrying Gorgon 4, PTV-N-2, ramjet-driven final member of the Gorgon family to reach flight test stage.*

**Above:** *Ryan MX-799 Firebird on left wing of DB-26B Invader at Holloman in August 1949. Note visual coding of four wings for camera record.*

**Top right:** *One of the first F-4C Phantoms built for the USAF loaded with two Genies (just inboard of tanks) as well as its four recessed Sparrows.*

**Centre right:** *Excellent portrait of AIR-2A Genie, with fins folded, in front of F-106A Delta Dart of Adcom; unlike the Phantom, photographed during trials, this uses the Genie.*

# Genie

Though it is an unguided rocket, which flies a near-ballistic trajectory, this can certainly be classed as an AAM and the most powerful in the world because it has a nuclear warhead. Developed was begun by Douglas Aircraft in 1955, as soon as LASL (Los Alamos Scientific Laboratory) could predict complete success with the special 1·5 kT warhead. The first live missile was fired from an F-89J at 15,000 ft (4572 m) over Yucca Flat, Nevada, on 19 July 1957. The rocket was detonated by ground command, and USAF observers standing unprotected at ground zero (ie directly under the burst) suffered no ill effects. During development this pro-gramme was called Ding Dong and subsequently High Card; its original designation was MB-1, changed in 1962 to AIR-2A. A training missile, with a white-cloud spotting charge instead of a warhead, was called Ting-a-Ling and is now ATR-2A. Genie is carried externally by the CF-101B and internally by the F-106, having earlier also armed the F-89J and F-101B. The Hughes MA-1, MG-10 or MG-13 fire-control tracks the target, assigns the missile, commands the pilot to arm the warhead, fires the missile, pulls the interceptor into a tight turn to escape the detonation, and finally triggers the warhead at the correct moment. Lethal radius is several hundred metres (over 1,000 ft). Missile propulsion is by a Thio-kol TU-289 (SR49) motor of 36,600 lb (16 602 kg) thrust. Flick-out fin-tips give the missile stability, and correct roll and gravity-drop. Several thousand Genies had been built when production ceased in 1962; the improved TU-289 motor remains in production.

**Dimensions:** Length 116·0 in (2946 mm); diameter 17·5 in (445 mm) (warhead larger); span (fins out) 40·0 in (1016 mm).
**Launch weight:** 822 lb (373 kg).
**Range:** 6·2 miles (10 km).

# Eagle

In the summer of 1957 the US Navy took the decision to ask for RFPs on a radically new kind of fleet air defence system. It was to involve a radar-equipped interceptor carrying AAMs which were to bear "the entire burden of effecting the interception". The carrier platform might

have been a propeller-driven transport, for its sole purpose was to lift six missiles to a suitable vantage point at 35,000 ft (10 668 m) about 150 miles (241 km) from the fleet. There it would search with its own radar and, finding a target, turn the active homing radars of its own missiles in that direction. The missile selected would then have

to acquire the target or fly a long mid-course section and finally home on the target with its own radar. This was novel only in that it had not before been done with an AAM; Bomarc could fly the same mission, but this missile was too large for reasonable "fighter" aircraft to carry. Despite the problems, industry participated enthusiastically. After

a prolonged competition Douglas won the carrier platform in early 1960 with the F6D-1 Missileer, powered by two TF30 turbofans and strictly subsonic, carrying three of the giant AAMs under each wing. The missile was awarded to Bendix Systems Division at Ann Arbor, beating 15 other companies, with Grumman responsible for the airframe, propulsion integration and ground equipment. Eagle grew swiftly, despite being the largest AAM of its day. Westinghouse played the central role in the vital matter of radar: APQ-81, the first fighter TWS radar, was developed for the Missileer, and a novel PD active seeker for the missile was derived from the DPN-53 of Bomarc B. Goodyear made the missile radome, still the largest on any missile intended to fly through heavy rain or hail at Mach 4 for the range given in the data. Aerojet provided the long-burning solid motor, AiResearch the APU, Litton the tactical computer, and Sanders the target seeker equipment. The Missileer/Eagle promised much, and was potentially a very large programme: $3,400 million, at a time when this was real money. But after suffering months of doubt about the concept of a "slow fighter" (which was irrelevant) the outgoing SecDef, Thomas S. Gates, cancelled Missileer in December 1960. He let Eagle temporarily trickle on, and its technology helped Hughes with the AWG-9/Phoenix (p. 230).

**Dimensions:** Length 16 ft 1½ in (4·91 m), (without booster) 11 ft 7 in (3·53 m); diameter (missile, max) 14·0 in (356 mm), booster) 16·1 in (409 mm); span (missile) 34·0 in (864 mm), (booster, fins extended) 50·2 in (1275 mm).
**Launch weight:** 1284 lb (582 kg), (without booster) 652 lb (296 kg).
**Range:** Varying with target data to 127 miles (204 km).

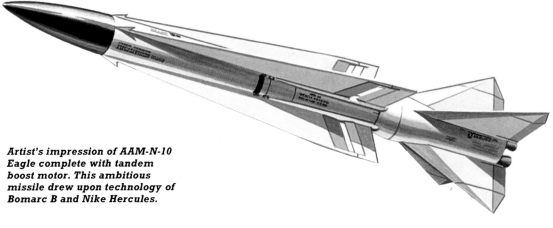

*Artist's impression of AAM-N-10 Eagle complete with tandem boost motor. This ambitious missile drew upon technology of Bomarc B and Nike Hercules.*

# Falcon

First guided AAM in the world to enter operational service, Falcon was created with impressive assurance by a new team. In 1947 the newly created USAF asked for bids on a completely new radar-based fire-control system for manned interceptors, and a guided AAM for the following interceptor generation. To the surprise of most bidders both packages were won by Hughes Aircraft, lately diversified into advanced technologies and at that time of daily concern to Howard Hughes himself. By 1955 the family of fire-control systems had included the E-9, fitted to the F-89H, with a new computer and software for guns, FFARs or guided missiles. Subsequently the more advanced MG-10 followed for the supersonic F-102, the MG-13 for the F-101 and the semi-automated MA-1 for the F-106. All were matched to the missile Hughes created, at Culver City, and put into production at a new plant at Tucson in 1954. Called Project Dragonfly, and at first classed as an experimental fighter (XF-98, see table), it matured as GAR-1 Falcon, but was later re-styled AIM-4, and for clarity the 1962 designations will be used throughout.

AIM-4 was an amazing exercise in packaging. The air-

**Below:** *One of the challenging installations was the retractable triple launcher on the wing tips of the F-89H (photo at Holloman AFB in 1959).*

frame, about the size of a man, contained a large proportion of GRP construction. Accelerated at about 50 g by a single-charge Thiokol solid motor, it had a hemispherical nose radome flanked by receiver aerials like small nose fins, giving SARH proportional navigation and steering by elevons on the trailing edges of the slender-delta wings. Most early installations were internal, three being housed in the tip pod on each wing of the F-89H and J and six fitting the weapon bay of the F-102A. Both reached IOC with Air Defense Command in mid-1956. Later that year the first IR Falcon, AIM-4B, entered service with a

**Right:** *The first members of the family were (from left): AIM-4G, -4A, -4F, -4C, -26A and (foreground) -4D.*

**Below:** *1957 picture of GAR-1D (black nose) and -2A (white) lined up for weapon bay of F-102 Delta Dart of ADC.*

distinctive glass nose, followed by AIM-4A (radar) with improved manoeuvrability from larger controls carried well behind the wings. AIM-4C had a better IR seeker able to lock-on against a wider range of ambient (background) temperatures. The IR missiles were especially popular in permitting the interceptor to break away as soon as the missile(s) had been launched (though, as in the Soviet Union, it was common doctrine to fire one missile with each type of guidance to ensure a kill). These early Falcons accounted for three-quarters of the total production.

In 1958 deliveries began of

AIM-4E, the first so-called Super Falcon, to meet the greater demands of the F-106A. It introduced a longer-burning motor, advanced SARH guidance with a new receiver behind a pointed radome of new material, long wing-root fillets and a more powerful warhead. In May 1959 the Tucson plant switched to the -4F with a new motor having boost/sustainer charges, improved SARH guidance with greater accuracy and specific ECCM provision, and airframe modifications including a white moistureproof sleeve over the forebody and a 4 in (102 mm) metal probe on the nose to form a weak oblique shock and im-

## THE FALCON FAMILY

| 1947 | 1950 | 1962 | Export | Sweden | Guidance | Length | Diameter | Span | Launch wt | Speed | Range | Production |
|------|------|------|--------|--------|----------|--------|----------|------|-----------|-------|-------|------------|
| XF-98 | GAR-1 | AIM-4 | — | — | SARH | 77·8 in (1·98 m) | 6·4 in (163 mm) | 20·0 in (508 mm) | 110 lb (50 kg) | M2·8 | 5 miles (8 km) | 4,080 |
| — | GAR-1D | AIM-4A | — | — | SARH | 78·0 in (1·98 m) | 6·4 in (163 mm) | 20·0 in (508 mm) | 120 lb 54 kg) | M3 | 6 miles (9·7 km) | 12,100 |
| — | GAR-2 | AIM-4B | — | — | IR | 79·5 in (2·02 m) | 6·4 in (163 mm) | 20·0 in (508 mm) | 130 lb (59 kg) | M3 | 6 miles (9·7 km) | 16,000 |
| — | GAR-2A | AIM-4C | HM-58 | RB 28 | IR | 79·5 in (2·02 m) | 6·4 in (163 mm) | 20·0 in (508 mm) | 134 lb (61 kg) | M3 | 6 miles (9·7 km) | 13,500 (inc. 1,000 HM and 3,000 RB) |
| — | GAR-2B | AIM-4D | — | — | IR | 79·5 in (2·02 m) | 6·4 in (163 mm) | 20·0 in (508 mm) | 134 lb (61 kg) | M4 | 6 miles (9·7 km) | 4,000 |
| — | GAR-3 | AIM-4E | — | — | SARH | 86·0 in (2·18 m) | 6·6 in (168 mm) | 24·0 in (610 mm) | 150 lb (68 kg) | M4 | 7 miles (11·3 km) | 300 |
| — | GAR-3A | AIM-4F | — | — | SARH | 86·0 in (2·18 m) | 6·6 in (168 mm) | 24·0 in (610 mm) | 150 lb (68 kg) | M4 | 7 miles (11·3 km) | 3,400 |
| — | GAR-4A | AIM-4G | — | — | IR | 81·0 in (2·06 m) | 6·6 in (168 mm) | 24·0 in (610 mm) | 145 lb (66 kg) | M4 | 7 miles (11·3 km) | 2,700 |
| — | XGAR-11 | XAIM-26 | — | — | SARH | 84·0 in (2·13 m) | 11·0 in (279 mm) | 24·4 in (620 mm) | 200 lb (91 kg) | M2 | 5 miles (8 km) | c100 |
| — | GAR-11 | AIM-26A | — | — | SARH | 84·25 in (2·14 m) | 11·0 in (279 mm) | 24·4 in (620 mm) | 203 lb (92 kg) | M2 | 5 miles (8 km) | 1,900 |
| — | GAR-11A | AIM-26B | HM-55 | RB 27 | SARH | 81·5 in (2·07 m) | 11·4 in (290 mm) | 24·4 in (620 mm) | 262 lb (119 kg) | M2 | 6 miles (9·7 km) | 2,000 (inc. 400 HM and 800 RB) |
| — | GAR-9 | AIM-47A | — | — | SARH/IRTH | 126·0 in (3·2 m) | 13·2 in (335 mm) | 33·0 in (838 mm) | 800 lb (363 kg) | M6 | 115 miles (213 km) | c80 |
| — | — | XAIM-4H | — | — | ALH | c80 in (2·03 m) | 6·6 in (168 mm) | 24·0 (610 mm) | 160 lb (73 kg) | M4 | 7 miles (11·3 km) | c25 |

**Left: This picture of a QB-17M Fortress being hit by an early Falcon was the first ever released of an AAM in action. Impact angle unexplained.**

prove aerodynamics. A few weeks later came AIM-4G with the -4F airframe and a new IR seeker able to lock-on to smaller targets at considerably greater ranges.

In 1960 came a dramatic development. AIM-26 was developed to give high SSKP in head-on attacks. IR was judged inadequate in such engagements, and because of the reduced precision of SARH it was decided to use a much more powerful warhead. AIM-26A was fitted with almost the same nuclear warhead as Genie, triggered by four active-radar proximity-fuze aerials almost flush with the body ahead of the wings. The body naturally had to be of greater diameter, and a larger motor

was necessary to achieve the required flight performance. AIM-26B followed, with large conventional warhead, and this was exported as HM-55 and licence-built by Saab-Scania as RB 27. Today about 800 of the -26B model are the only Falcons left in USAF Aerospace Defense Command service. The Swiss Flugwaffe uses the HM-55 on the Mirage III-S, matched with Hughes Taran radar.

In 1958 Hughes began work on a challenging fourth-generation fire-control and AAM system to arm the Mach 3·2 "Zip-fuel" North American F-108 Rapier interceptor. The ASG-18 radar was used for mid-course guidance and target illumination over ranges exceeding 100 miles (161 km), and the missile, then called GAR-9, was also given IR terminal homing. Propulsion was by a Lockheed Propulsion Co storable liquid rocket giving hypersonic speed, so that the

wings became mere strakes along the body. In 1959 this very large AAM, still called Falcon, was transferred to the proposed YF-12A "Blackbird" research interceptor with which it conducted much basic fact-finding in advanced interception techniques.

The final production Falcon was the AIM-4D of 1963. The only Falcon tailored for anti-fighter combat, it was a cross-breed combining the small airframe of early models with the powerful motor and advanced IR seeker head of the large -4G. The result is a very fast and effective short-range missile. More than 8,000 -4A and -4C have been remanufactured to this standard. In 1969 the AIM-4H was funded to improve the -4D by fitting an AOPF (Active Optical Proximity Fuze) with four laser pancake beams at 90° to the major axis. It was abandoned for budgetary reasons in 1971.

USA

# Sidewinder

One of the most influential missiles in history, this slim AAM was almost un-American in development for it was created out of nothing by a very small team at NOTS China Lake, operating on the proverbial shoe-string budget. Led by Doctor McLean, this team was the first in the world to attack the problem of passive IR homing guidance, in 1949, and the often intractable difficulties were compounded by the choice of an airframe of only 5 in (127 mm) diameter, which in the days of vacuum-tube electronics was a major challenge. In 1951 Philco was awarded a contract for a homing head based on the NOTS research and today, 28 years later, the guidance team at Newport Beach, now called Ford Aerospace and Communications, is still in production with homing heads for later Sidewinders. The first XAAM-N-7 guided round was successfully fired on 11 September 1953. The first production missiles, called N-7 by the Navy, GAR-8 by the USAF and SW-1 by the development team, reached IOC in May 1956.

These early Sidewinders were made of sections of aluminium tube, with the seeker head and control fins at the front and four fixed tail fins containing patented Rollerons at the back. The Rolleron is similar to an air-driven gyro wheel, and one is mounted in the tip of each fin so that it is spun at high speed by the slip-stream. The original solid motor was made by Hunter-Douglas, Hercules and Norris-Thermador, to Naval Propellant Plant design, and it accelerated the missile to Mach 2·5 in 2·2 sec.

The beauty of this missile was its simplicity, which meant low cost, easy compatibility with many aircraft and, in theory, high reliability in harsh environments. It was said to have "less than 24 moving parts" and "fewer electronic components than the average radio". At the same time, though the guidance method meant that Sidewinder could be carried by any fighter, with or without radar, it was erratic in use and restricted to close stern engagements at high altitude in good visibility. The uncooled PbS seeker gave an

## THE SIDEWINDER FAMILY

| Model | Guidance | Length | Control fin span | Launch wt | Mission time | Range | Production |
|---|---|---|---|---|---|---|---|
| AIM-9B | Uncooled PbS, 25° look, 70 Hz reticle, 11°/sec tracking | 111·4 in (2830 mm) | 22·0 in (559 mm) | 155 lb (70·4 kg) | 20 sec | 2 miles (3·2 km) | 80,900 |
| 9B FGW.2 | CO$_2$-cooling, solar dead zone reduced to 5° | 114·5 in (2908 mm) | 22·0 in (559 mm) | 167 lb (75·8 kg) | 20 sec | 2·3 miles (3·7 km) | 15,000 |
| AIM-9C | Motorola SARH | 113·0 in (2870 mm) | 24·8 in (630 mm) | 185 lb (84·0 kg) | 60 sec | 11 miles (17·7 km) | 1,000 |
| AIM-9D | N$_2$-cooled PbS, 40° look, 125 Hz reticle, 12°/sec tracking | 113·0 in (2870 mm) | 24·8 in (630 mm) | 195 lb (88·5 kg) | 60 sec | 11 miles (17·7 km) | 1,000 |
| AIM-9E | Peltier-cooled PbS, 40° look, 100 Hz reticle, 16·5°/sec tracking | 118·1 in (3000 mm) | 22·0 in (559 mm) | 164 lb (74·5 kg) | 20 sec | 2·6 miles (4·2 km) | 5,000 (ex-9B) |
| AIM-9G | As -9D plus SEAM | 113·0 in (2870 mm) | 24·8 in (630 mm) | 191 lb (86·6 kg) | 60 sec | 11 miles (17·7 km) | 2,120 |
| AIM-9H | As -9G plus solid-state, 20°/sec tracking | 113·0 in (2870 mm) | 24·8 in (630 mm) | 186 lb (84·5 kg) | 60 sec | 11 miles (17·7 km) | 7,720 |
| AIM-9J1 | As -9E plus part-solid-state | 120·9 in (3070 mm) | 22·0 in (559 mm) | 172 lb (78·0 kg) | 40 sec | 9 miles (14·5 km) | 10,000 (ex -9B) |
| AIM-9L | Argon-cooled InSb, fixed reticle, tilted mirror system | 112·2 in (2850 mm) | 24·8 in (630 mm) | 188 lb (85·3 kg) | 60 sec | 11 miles (17·7 km) | 8,360 |

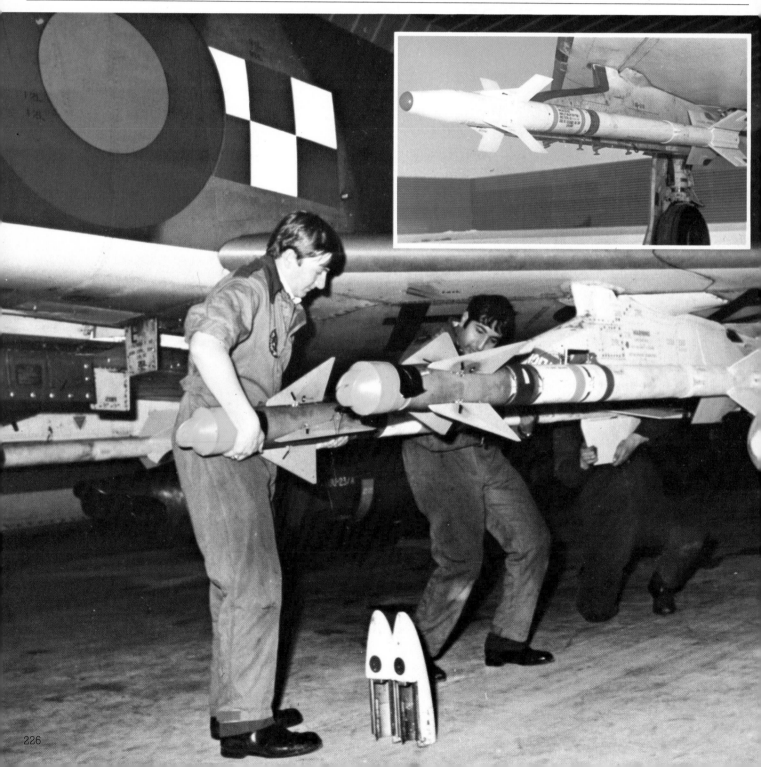

SSKP of about 70 per cent in ideal conditions, but extremely poor results in bad visibility, cloud or rain, or at low levels, and showed a tendency to lock-on to the Sun, or bright sky, or reflections from surface lakes or rivers.

The pilot energised his missile homing head and listened for its signals in his headset. It would give a growl when it acquired a target, and if it was nicely positioned astern of a hot jetpipe the growl would become a fierce strident singing that would rise in intensity until the pilot let the missile go. There were plenty of QF-80, Firebee and other targets that had early Sidewinders up their jetpipe in the 1950s, but unfortunately real-life engagements tended to have the wrong target, or the wrong aspect, or the wrong IR-emitting background. In October 1958, however, large numbers of Sidewinders were fired by Nationalist Chinese F-86s against Chinese MiG-17s and 14 of the latter

were claimed in one day. This was the first known use of AAMs in warfare.

The staggering total of nearly 81,000 of the original missile were built in three almost identical versions which in the new 1962 scheme were designated AIM-9, 9A and 9B. Nearly all were of the 9B form, roughly half produced by Philco (Ford) and half by Raytheon. A further 15,000 were delivered by a European consortium headed by BGT, which in the late 1960s gave each European missile a new seeker head of BGT design known as FGW Mod 2. This has a nose dome of silicon instead of glass, a cooled seeker and semiconductor electronics, and transformed the missile's reliability and ability to lock-on in adverse conditions.

By 1962 SW-1C was in use in two versions, AIM-9C by Motorola and -9D by Ford. This series introduced the Rocketdyne Mk 36 solid motor giving much greater range, a new airframe with tapered nose, long-chord controls and more swept leading edges on the tail fins, and completely new guidance. Motorola

produced the 9C for the F-8 Crusader, giving it SARH guidance matched to the Magnavox APQ-94 radar, but for various reasons this odd man out was unreliable in performance and was withdrawn. In contrast, 9D was so successful it formed the basis of many subsequent versions, as well as MIM-72C Chaparral (p. 176). The new guidance section introduced a dome of magnesium fluoride, a nitrogen-cooled seeker, smaller field of view, and increased reticle speed and tracking speed. The control section introduced larger fins, which were detachable, and high-power actuators fed by a longer-burning gas generator. The old 10 lb (4·54 kg) warhead with passive-IR fuze was replaced by a 22·4 lb (10·2 kg) annular blast fragmentation head of the continuous-rod type, fired by either an IR or HF proximity fuze.

AIM-9E was fitted with a greatly improved Ford seeker head with Peltier (thermoelectric) cooling, further-increased tracking speed and new electronics and wiring harnesses, giving increased engagement boundaries especially at low level. AIM-9G has so-called SEAM (Sidewinder Expanded Acquisition Mode), an improved 9D seeker head, but was overtaken by 9H. The latter introduced solid-state electronics, even faster tracking speed, and double-delta controls with increased actuator power, giving

greater manoeuvrability than any previous Sidewinder as well as limited all-weather capability. AIM-9J is a rebuilt 9B or 9E with part-solid-state electronics, detachable double-delta controls with greater power, and long-burning gas generator. Range is sacrificed for high acceleration to catch fast targets. There are J-1 and J-3 improved or "all-new" variants. The latest, and almost certainly last, Sidewinder is 9L, with which NWC (as NOTS now is) has at last responded to the prolonged demands of customers and the proven accomplishments of BGT. The latter's outstanding seeker head developed for Viper was first fitted to AIM-9L to give Alasca (AL1-ASpect CApability), a great missile that was merely used by Germany as a possible fall-back in case 9L failed to mature. AIM-9L itself, now in full production, has pointed delta fins, a totally new guidance system (see table), and an annular blast fragmentation warhead sheathed in a skin of performed rods, triggered by a new proximity fuze in which a ring of eight GaAs laser diodes emit and a ring of silicon photodiodes receive.

About 16,000 of the 9L series are expected to be made by 1983, and at least a further 9,000 are likely to be made by a new BGT-led European consortium which this time includes Britain and, probably, Sweden. Customers for earlier versions were Argentina, Australia, Brazil, Britain, Canada, Chile, Denmark, West Germany, Greece, Iran, Israel, Japan, South Korea, Kuwait, Malaysia, Netherlands, Norway, Pakistan, Philippines, Portugal, Saudi Arabia, Singapore, Spain, Sweden, Taiwan, Tunisia and Turkey.

*Left: Armament tradesmen of 19 Sqn RAF slide ancient AIM-9B (FGW.2) Sidewinders on to a Phantom FGR.2. Note yellow plastic protective nose caps.*

*Left, inset: AIM-9J (now modified to J1 standard) on USAF Phantom F-4E.*

*Left: Deck crew aboard CVA-19 Hancock in 1967 load radar-guided -9C on F-8E Crusader.*

*Below: March 1975 at NWC and a target (apparently an F-1 Fury) suffers the annular blast/frag warhead of the new AIM-9L (inset).*

227

# Sparrow

Considerably larger than other contemporary American AAMs, this missile not only progressed through three fundamentally different families, each with a different prime contractor, but late in life mushroomed into totally new versions for quite new missions as an ASM (Shrike, p. 125) and a SAM (two types of Sea Sparrow, p. 182 and 204). Though it cannot rival the production totals of Falcon and Sidewinder, the 40,000-plus Sparrows represent a larger monetary total than either, and one of the largest programmes of any missile in history.

Speery Gyroscope began the programme as Project Hot Shot in 1946, under US Navy BuAer contract. By 1951 Sperry had a contract for full engineering development of XAAM-N-2 Sparrow I, and the suffix I was added because by that time there was already a Sparrow II. The first representative guided flight tests took place in 1953, using various carrier aircraft such as the F3D Skyknight and even a DB-26, at Pt Mugu. This missile was a beam rider, with flush dipole aerials around the body which picked up the signals from the fighter radar beam (assumed to be locked-on to the target) and drove the cruciform delta wings to keep the missile aligned in the centre of the beam. At the tail were four fixed fins indexed in line with the wings. Propulsion was by an Aerojet solid motor, and missile assembly took place at the Sperry-Farragut Division which operated a Naval Industrial Reserve plant at Bristol, Tennessee. The whole forebody was tapered

**Below: Launch of AIM-7D by F-4B (No 149455) off Point Mugu on 13 August 1964. Frame from high-speed film by an accompanying RF-8A Crusader reconnaissance aircraft.**

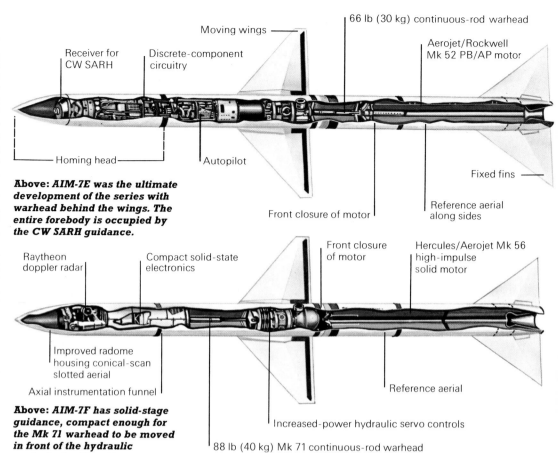

*Above: AIM-7E was the ultimate development of the series with warhead behind the wings. The entire forebody is occupied by the CW SARH guidance.*

Receiver for CW SARH — Discrete-component circuitry — Moving wings — 66 lb (30 kg) continuous-rod warhead — Aerojet/Rockwell Mk 52 PB/AP motor

Homing head — Autopilot — Front closure of motor — Reference aerial along sides — Fixed fins

*Above: AIM-7F has solid-stage guidance, compact enough for the Mk 71 warhead to be moved in front of the hydraulic controls, doubling the range.*

Raytheon doppler radar — Compact solid-state electronics — Front closure of motor — Hercules/Aerojet Mk 56 high-impulse solid motor

Improved radome housing conical-scan slotted aerial — Axial instrumentation funnel — Increased-power hydraulic servo controls — Reference aerial — 88 lb (40 kg) Mk 71 continuous-rod warhead

to a fine point and contained a 52 lb (23.6 kg) blast/fragmentation warhead with proximity fuze. Carrier aircraft included the Vought F7U-3M Cutlass, Douglas F3D-2M Skyknight and McDonnell F3H-2M Demon, all of which could carry four missiles on underwing racks. IOC was reached in July 1956, and Sparrow I was soon serving in the Atlantic and Pacific Fleets, and with the Marine Corps from shore bases.

In 1955 Douglas Aircraft managed to obtain limited BuAer funding for Sparrow II, as main armament for the proposed F5D-1 Skylancer Mach 2 interceptor. Sparrow I was potentially a powerful weapon but its roots went back a long way and it suffered from basic shortcomings which Douglas knew could be rectified. Amazingly, however, the company did not switch to SARH guidance but to fully active radar, and this was tough in a missile of 8 in (203 mm) diameter, a figure common to all Sparrows. Bendix-Pacific was given the job of managing this guidance system, Westinghouse providing Aero X-24A radar for the aircraft. The missile airframe had much greater volume, especially in the forebody, and larger square-tipped aerody-

namic surfaces. But in mid-1956 the Navy decided to terminate both the F5D Skylancer and the Sparrow II missile, partly because by this time there was a Sparrow III and various more advanced fighters such as the XF4H Phantom II and XF8U-3 Crusader III. Instantly the defunct programme was snapped up by the Royal Canadian Air Force as armament for the Arrow supersonic interceptor, which could carry up to eight in its weapon bay, but would normally have carried three plus eight mixed radar/IR Falcons. Under intense pressure a large US/Canadian Sparrow II programme

**Above:** *Checkout of the first two AIM-7F Sparrows produced by the new second-source supplier, GD Pomona, in late 1977. Combined rate with Raytheon, 2,000 rounds a year.*

was constructed with Douglas Aircraft remaining prime contractor but assisted by Canadair, Honeywell Controls and Computing Devices of Canada, and with RCA-Victor handling the exceedingly ambitious and costly Astra I radar fire-control system. Extreme technical difficulty was compounded by a cutback in US funding of contractors working for foreign customers and a ridiculous system of non-communications which prohibited direct contact between the major partners in the two countries. Premier Diefenbaker cancelled Astra and Sparrow II on 23 September 1958, and the Arrow itself the following February.

Three years previously Raytheon had begun to work on Sparrow III, taking over the plant in Bristol on completion of Sparrow I production in 1956. Sparrow III used almost the same airframe as Sparrow II but with more sensible SARH guidance. By the mid-1950s Raytheon had become one of the most capable missile companies, possibly because its background was electronics rather than mere airframes. It built up a missile engineering centre at Bedford, Massachusetts, with a test base at Oxnard (not far from Pt Mugu), California; production of Sparrows was finally shared between Bristol and a plant at South Lowell, near Bedford.

Most of the airframe is precision-cast light alloy. Early Sparrow III missiles had an Aerojet solid motor, not cast integral with the case, and introduced CW guidance. AIM-7C, as it became, reached IOC in 1958 with Demons of the Atlantic and Pacific fleets. AIM-7D introduced the Thiokol (previously Reaction Motors) prepackaged liquid motor, and was also adopted by the Air Force in 1960 as AIM-101 to arm the F-110 (later F-4C) Phantom. All fighter Phantoms can carry four Sparrows recessed into the underside of the fuselage, with target illumination by the APQ-72, APQ-100, APQ-109, APQ-120, or APG-59 (part of AWG-10 or -11) radar. In the Italian F-104S Starfighter the radar is the Rockwell R-21G/H, and in the F-14 Tomcat the powerful Hughes AWG-9. The AIM-7D was also the basis for PDMS Sea Sparrow.

AIM-7E, the next version (also used in the NATO Sea Sparrow system), uses the Rocketdyne free-standing solid motor with Flexadyne propellant (Mk 38), which gives a slightly increased burnout speed of Mach 3·7. The 66 lb (30 kg) warhead is of the continuous-rod type, the explosive charge being wrapped in a tight drum made from a continuous rod of stainless steel which shatters into about 2,600 lethal fragments. DA and proximity fuzes are fitted. Many thousands of 7E missiles were used in Vietnam by F-4s, but, owing to the political constraints imposed on the American fighters, were seldom able to be fired. Accordingly AIM-7E2 was developed with shorter minimum range, increased power of manoeuvre and plug-in aerodynamic surfaces requiring no tools. The

**Left:** *Test launch of AIM-7F from F-16 prototype at China Lake in November 1977 (Mach 1·05, 0·6 sec from first to last frame). F-16 is not yet able to use Sparrow.*

**Above: *Phantom FGR.2 of 41 Sqn, RAF, over Scarborough with seven BL 755 cluster bombs, four AIM-7D and four AIM-9D.***

# Sky Flash

While the US industry develops its own monopulse seeker for Sparrow, the UK industry began such work in 1969, leading to a brilliant series of test firings in November 1975 and production delivery to the RAF by BAe Dynamics in 1978. Originally XJ.521, and later named Sky Flash, this missile is a 7E2 with a completely new MSDS homing head operating in I-band with inverse processing by all-solid-state microelectronics. The warm-up time has been reduced from about 15 sec to less than 2 sec. The short range of the basic 7E2 is considered acceptable for European conditions, though the 7F motor could be fitted if needed. The trials programme from Pt Mugu is judged the most successful of any AAM in history; more than half actually struck the target, often in extremely difficult conditions of glint or evasive manoeuvres, while the miss-distance of the remainder averaged "about one-tenth that of most radar-guided AAMs". Moreover, the warhead is triggered by a deadly EMI active-radar fuze

**Above: *First firing of Sky Flash, from US Navy F-4J at Point Mugu in November 1975. In production for RAF and Swedish AF.***

AIM-7C, D and E accounted for over 34,000 missiles.

Introduced in 1977, AIM-7F has all-solid-state guidance, making room for a more powerful motor, the Hercules Mk 58, giving further-enhanced flight speed and range, as well as a larger (88 lb, 40 kg) warhead. Claimed to lock-on reasonably well against clutter up to 10 db, -7F is compatible with CW PD radars (and thus with the F-15 and F-18), and has a conical-scan seeker head. In 1977 GD Pomona was brought in as second-source

supplier, and with Raytheon is expected to deliver about 19,000 missiles by 1985, split roughly equally between the Navy and Air Force, plus a hoped-for large number of exports. Well before that time Raytheon is expected to introduce a new model of Sparrow with an AMS (Advanced Monopulse Seeker), selected over a GD head derived from Standard Missile 2, to improve look-down lock-on and resistance to hostile ECM and help Sparrow compete with Sky Flash. From 1985 AMRAAM

(p. 235) is expected to replace all Sparrow versions.

Total production of Sparrows exceeds 40,000, the accompanying table being for AAM versions only. Selenia and others have built the 7E in Italy, and Mitsubishi the 7E in Japan. Other users include West Germany, Greece, Iran, Israel, South Korea and Turkey.

## THE SPARROW FAMILY

| 1950 designation | 1962 | Guidance | Length | Span | Launch wt | Range | Production |
|---|---|---|---|---|---|---|---|
| AAM-N-2 Sparrow I | AIM-7A | Radar beam riding | 140 in (3·56 m) | 39 in (0·99 m) | 310 lb (141 kg) | 5 miles (8 km) | c2,000 |
| AAM-N-3 Sparrow II | AIM-7B | Active radar homing | 144 in (3·66 m) | 39 in (0·99 m) | 420 lb (191 kg) | ? | c100 |
| AAM-N-6 Sparrow III | AIM-7C | SARH CW | 144 in (3·66 m) | 40 in (1·02 m) | 380 lb (172 kg) | 25 miles (40 km) | 2,000 |
| AAM-N-6A/AIM-101 | AIM-7D | SARH CW | 144 in (3·66 m) | 40 in (1·02 m) | 440 lb (200 kg) | 25 miles (40 km) | 7,500 |
| AAM-N-6B | AIM-7E | SARH CW | 144 in (3·66 m) | 40 in (1·02 m) | 452 lb (205 kg) | 28 miles (44 km) | 25,000 |
| — | AIM-7F | SARH CW solid-state | 144 in (3·66 m) | 40 in (1·02 m) | 503 lb (228 kg) | 62 miles (100 km) | 3,500* |
| | Sky Flash | I-band monopulse solid-state | 145 in (3·68 m) | 40 in (1·02 m) | 425 lb (193 kg) | 31 miles (50 km) | c400† |

* about 19,000 planned; † 1,350 planned, plus exports.

placed behind the seeker, the warhead being behind the wings. Sweden has adopted Sky Flash as RB 71 for the JA 37 Viggen. Sky Flash, possibly with a planar aerial and modified radome, will be matched with Foxhunter radar on the RAF's Tornado F.2 interceptor.

## AIM-82A

This short-range dogfight AAM was studied by the USAF in 1969 to arm the FX (later F-15). In February 1970 RFPs were sent to 12 companies, asking for a missile that could acquire and lock-on to its target from any angle and home on it while the parent aircraft turned away. It was announced that AIM-82A would be compatible with the A-6, A-7, F-4, F-14 and FB-111. In July 1970 definition contracts at $1·5 million each were awarded to Hughes, Aeronutronic (Ford) and GD Pomona, but the system was cancelled two months later.

## Agile

This advanced close-range weapon, AIM-95, was an active project at NWC in 1971–75, chiefly to arm the F-14 and F-18. Features included IR homing and TVC solid-motor steering. Unrelated to the Sidewinder, and intended to replace AIM-9L, it was abandoned in favour of a common USN/USAF Asraam, mentioned later.

## Claw

Studies for this CLose-range Attack Weapon to succeed AIM-9 versions were abandoned by the USAF in 1976 in favour of a joint-user Asraam.

## Brazo

This passive ARM-type AAM was studied by Hughes and the Navy in 1972 to determine the lethality of a missile that homed on the emissions of hostile aircraft. In 1973 it was linked with the USAF Pave Arm to become a joint-service investigation, and in 1974 firing trials at PMTC began with Sparrow airframes fitted with a broad-band passive homing seeker developed at the Naval Electronics Center. Head-on and tail-on look-down attacks were made against BQM-34A targets. The project was abandoned in 1978.

**Main picture above right:** *One of the few photographs taken of Agile testing at NWC. Date of this land-box launching was April 1974.*

**Inset, top:** *Testing the stack of printed-circuit guidance boards of an experimental Agile AAM at an NWC laboratory in April 1971.*

**Right:** *Hughes checks out the first air-fired Brazo in April 1974, after loading on USAF F-4D but before clipping on wings and tail fins.*

# Phoenix

By far the most sophisticated and costly AAM in the world, this missile provides air defence over an area exceeding 12,000 square miles (31 000 km²) from near sea level to the limits of altitude attained by aircraft or tactical missiles. But it can be fired only from the F-14A Tomcat and costs nearly half a million dollars.

Following the classic aerodynamics of the Falcon family, Phoenix was originally AAM-N-11 and Hughes Aircraft began development in 1960 to replace the AIM-47A and Eagle as partner to the AWG-9 for the F-111B. This advanced fire-control system was the most capable ever attempted, and includes a very advanced radar (derived from the ASG-18 carried in the YF-12A) of high-power PD type with the largest circular aerial (of planar type) ever carried by a fighter. It has look-down capability out to ranges exceeding 150 miles (241 km), and is backed up by an IR tracker to assist positive target identification and discrimination. AWG-9 has TWS capability, and an F-111B with the maximum load of six Phoenix missiles could engage and attack six aircraft at maximum range simultaneously, weather conditions and target aspect being of little consequence; indeed the basic interception mode assumed is head-on, which is one of the most difficult at extreme range.

Propulsion is by a long-burning Rocketdyne (Flexadyne) Mk 47 or Aerojet Mk 60 motor, giving a speed to burnout of Mach 3·8. Combined with low induced drag and the power of the large hydraulically driven tail controls this gives sustained manoeuvrability over a range not even approached by any other AAM, despite the large load of electrical battery, electrical conversion unit, autopilot, electronics unit, transmitter/receiver and planar-array seeker head (all part of the DSQ-26 onboard guidance) as well as the 132 lb (60 kg) annular blast fragmentation warhead with Downey Mk 334 proximity fuze, Bendix IR fuze and DA fuze.

Hughes began flight test at PMTC in 1965, using a DA-3B Skywarrior, achieving an interception in September 1966. In March 1969 an F-111B successfully engaged two drones, and subsequently Phoenix broke virtually all AAM records including four kills in one pass (out of a six-on-six test, there being one no-test and one miss), a kill on a BQM-34A simulating a cruise missile at 50 ft (15 m); and a kill on a BQM-34E flying at Mach 1·5 tracked from 153 miles (246 km), the Phoenix launched at 127 miles (204 km) and impacting 83·5 miles (134 km) from the launch point. The first AWG-9 system for the F-14A Tomcat, which replaced the F-111B, was delivered in February 1970. Production of Phoenix AIM-54A at Tucson began in 1973, since when output has averaged about 40 per month. By the third quarter of 1978 output had passed 2,500 out of a planned total exceeding 3,000, with manufacture due to continue to 1983. Customers comprise the US Navy (including Marine Corps) and 484 for the Imperial Iranian Air Force.

Since late 1977 production missiles have been of the AIM-54B type with many improvements including sheet-metal wings and fins instead of honeycomb structure, all-digital guidance with some microminiature circuits, non-liquid hydraulic and thermal-conditioning systems, and simplified engineering. In January 1982 production is due to switch to AIM-54C with much enhanced ECCM capability and reliability, incorporating a new target-detecting device being developed at the NWC.

**Dimensions:** Length: 157·8 in (4·01 m); diameter 15·0 in (381 mm); span 36·4 in (925 mm).
**Launch weight:** 985 lb (447 kg).
**Range:** 130 miles (209 km).

*Below: **About half the cost of the extremely expensive F-14A Tomcat is accounted for by the Hughes AWG-9 radar and Phoenix missiles.***

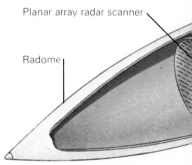

Above: *Early days, a photograph taken in June 1967 showing an XAIM-54A Phoenix with prototype handling gear going aboard an F-111B.*

Planar array radar scanner

Radome

**Above:** *An F-14A of the Point Mugu Test Center carrying the maximum long-range interception load of six Phoenix, two on wing pylons. All can be fired near-simultaneously against different targets.*

**Inset above:** *Phoenix launch by F-14A on detachment to PMTC.*

**Below:** *Cutaway showing main features of production AIM-54A Phoenix. Current production has cheaper wings without honeycomb construction.*

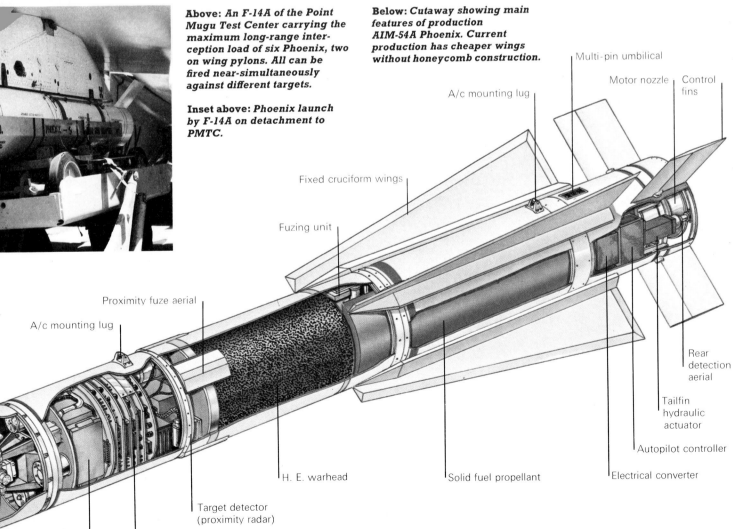

A/c mounting lug

Multi-pin umbilical

Motor nozzle

Control fins

Fixed cruciform wings

Fuzing unit

Proximity fuze aerial

A/c mounting lug

Rear detection aerial

Tailfin hydraulic actuator

Autopilot controller

H. E. warhead

Solid fuel propellant

Electrical converter

Target detector (proximity radar)

Radar avionics

Transceiver

# Seekbat

Designated XAIM-97A, this AAM was a General Dynamics project intended to intercept MiG-25 Foxbats flying at extreme altitude. It comprised a Standard ARM airframe fitted with a larger motor and passive IR seeker.

# BDM

Studies of a Bomber Defense Missile in 1968–73 did not involve any specific hardware programme. Current BDM studies are noted under the heading Asalm.

# ASALM

The Advanced Strategic Air-Launched Missile concept is one of the larger research programmes of USAF Systems Command, and the eventual vehicle could become not only a BDM (Bomber Defense Missile) but also an offensive delivery vehicle capable of flying many kinds of mission. In its primary role ASALM would be carried in multiple by a strategic bomber and would be compatible with SRAM and cruise-missile pylons or rotary launchers. Triggered and launched automatically by the bomber's defence system, with radar and IR coverage at least over the entire rear hemisphere, the missile would quickly "air slew" (ie change course) to the desired heading to intercept the detected threat. Propulsion would be by an advanced ram-rocket giving high launch acceleration at all altitudes and sustained propulsion for a flight of more than 100 miles (161 km). Cruising speed would probably be about Mach 4, rendering wings unnecessary. There would naturally be "a sophisticated guidance system, low radar and IR signatures and sustained high-g maneuver capability". The warhead would be nuclear. McDonnell Douglas and Martin Marietta are engaged in technology integration and flight-dynamics studies, while CSD and Marquardt work on the propulsion system. Obviously the main carrier will be the B-52 but ASALM is also to be compatible with the FB-111A. This means it must be shorter than ALCM AGM-86B.

# LCLM

The Low-Cost Lightweight Missile is a proposal by Aeronutronic (Ford Aerospace) to arm the F-16 and other fighters in the mid-1980s. It is a candidate in the Asraam programme described below.

# ASRAAM

Also known as WVR (Within Visual Range) missile, the Advanced Short-Range AAM is a joint USAF/Navy programme to find the best dogfight missile for the period after 1985 when AIM-9L is expected no longer to be adequate (it is barely adequate in 1979). The two services found some of the fundamental answers in the Aceval/Aimval (Air-Combat EVALuation and Air Intercept Missile EVALuation) studies flown by large numbers of tactical aircraft at the ACMR in 1976–78. These carefully quantified simulated air combats and situations were intended to define seeker parameters such as look angle and tracking rate, and the required missile manoeuvrability. By 1978 a broad programme of hardware research was investigating IR seeker cooling systems, dual-mode seekers, TVC and other propulsion systems, and various warhead and fuzing systems.

# AMRAAM

Also called BVR (Beyond Visual Range) missile, the Advanced Medium-Range AAM is the highest-priority AAM programme in the United States, because AIM-7F is becoming long in the tooth and is judged urgently in need of replacement in the 1980s by a completely new missile. Amraam is a joint USAF/USN programme aimed at producing a missile having higher performance and lethality than any conceivable advanced version of Sparrow, within a package that is smaller, lighter, more reliable and cheaper. Amraam will obviously be matched with later versions of F-14, -15, -16 and -18 equipped with programmable signal processors for doppler beam-sharpening and with advanced IR sensors able to acquire individual targets at extreme range. The missile would then be launched automatically on inertial mid-course guidance, without the need for the fighter to illuminate the target, the final terminal homing being by a small active seeker. The task clearly needs a very broad programme to investigate not only traditional sensing and guidance methods but also new ones such as target aerodynamic noise, engine harmonics and laser scanning to verify the external shape and thus confirm aircraft type. Multiple-target and TWS will be needed, and Amraam will have a high-impulse motor giving rapid acceleration to a Mach number higher than 4, with subsequent manoeuvre by TVC and/or tail controls combined with body lift, wings not being needed. Before this book appears, two rival teams will have been chosen (from Ford Aerospace/MSDS/EMI, Hughes, Raytheon, GD Pomona and Northrop/Motorola) to build missiles for a competitive shoot-off in 1981.

Above: *This BDM test vehicle was part of an earlier Cornell Aeronautical Lab programme.*

Above right: *The contractor's model of Seekbat on show at Eglin Armament Lab in 1972.*

*Right: Northrop photo of test firing in the Amraam programme. By 1979 test vehicles were exploring guidance and TVC.*

*Inset: Hughes engineer at Canoga Park adjusts Amraam SARH guidance gimbal. This company is a finalist.*

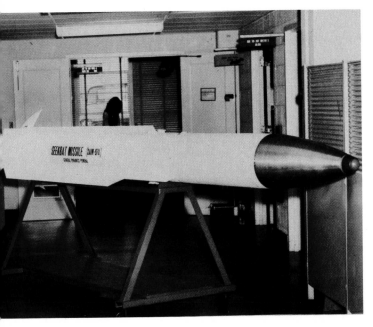

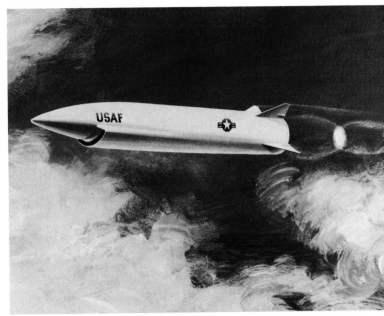

**Above:** *Typical proposed configuration for ASALM flying in the cruise (ramjet) mode.*

**Left:** *Typical proposed configuration for Amraam, probably not an air-breather.*

# ANTI-TANK MISSILES

In most respects this is by far the simplest of all missile classes. Hostile armour has traditionally been engaged at close range, after direct visual sighting. It offers targets which are large masses of metal, relatively slow moving and unable to dodge. Compared with ships and aircraft their ECM and IRCM capability has been at best low and usually non-existent. There is no special problem in carrying a warhead able to pierce their armour and cause havoc inside. Until shortly before World War 2 nearly all anti-tank weapons relied upon kinetic energy to carry a small but very hard (often tungsten carbide) core of a larger shell through the armour. Then, in addition to various infantry weapons such as "sticky bombs" and "Molotov cocktails", researchers produced the hollow-charge or shaped-charge warhead in which the explosive has a forward face in the form of an inverse cone with a thin metal liner. When the head detonates, the explosion is focused radially inwards and projects a jet – formed from extremely hot gas, liquid and vaporised metal – directly forwards at so great a velocity that its own kinetic energy exceeds the strength of armour, and it punches straight through a remarkable thickness. To be effective the warhead has to be at the correct stand-off distance from the armour. Obviously the more oblique the angle at which it hits, the greater the apparent thickness through which it must pierce; $90°$ is the optimum.

Though there are still many other kinds of anti-armour technique the hollow charge is by far the most important in missiles. A few anti-tank missiles have used the HESH (high-explosive squash head) type which does not pierce the armour but explodes with great violence on its outer surface. The shockwaves transmitted through the armour impart such high (but small-amplitude) acceleration to the armour that chunks are spalled off the interior. In the case of the HESH head it is these flying fragments that do the damage. In the case of the hollow-charge head it is the intense high-temperature jet. Existence of these warheads opened the way to new types of anti-armour weapon that did not need high impact velocity. One was the British Piat (projector, infantry, anti-tank) of World War 2, and another the American Bazooka. The German army introduced a wide range of rocket weapons generally called Panzerfaust. It also worked on the first of the modern family of anti-tank guided missiles. Red Riding Hood was a curious little weapon, but absolutely right in all essentials, and had it been developed a few years earlier – as it might have been, because no

part of it was completely new – it would have given the German army such an advantage that the campaign in the Soviet Union might actually have gone according to Hitler's plan and been over in 1941, with a possible different outcome to World War 2.

The truly significant feature of this pioneer German weapon was its use of wire guidance. This had a few months earlier been adopted for the X-4 AAM, but anti-tank scenarios are different. The whole idea is to keep the operator at the launch point continuously able to command the missile by transmitting command signals in the form of varying voltages through extremely fine wires. In most modern wire systems there are two wires to complete the circuit, and the wire is insulated and not much thicker than human hair (the amperage is trivial). Small anti-tank missiles can carry several miles of it, the twin wires being left behind as the missile flies. Usually it is uncoiled from a large drum in a way that minimises drag on the missile. In some cases it is important to cut off the spent wires at the launcher before firing the next missile.

After 1945 there was an amazing and inexplicable lack of interest by the victors in anti-tank missiles. The German missile was not only known but actually available to be tested. Yet it was left to the enthusiasts at SFECMAS, in the heart of France, to come up with a weapon that carried on where the German missile left off. In 1954 SFECMAS became Nord, and soon armies all over the world began to buy the little missile, which had four wings with Wagner-bar vibrating spoilers biased by wire guidance.

While Nord improved their guidance system, the US Army naturally developed their own missile. Having tested all the French missiles they wished, the Army and its contractors produced the cumbersome Dart missile. In Britain, things ran true to form. Vickers began a beautiful little missile with their own money. The Ministry of Supply instead showed interest in a giant Australian missile with a HESH head (which at least had a modest wing span) and also commissioned a large and expensive weapon from Fairey. Having announced the Fairey programme to the public it was promptly cancelled and, after playing with the giant Malkara, the eventual choice fell on the privately produced Vickers Vigilant. This was not only smaller, neater, faster and harder-hitting than contemporary missiles from other countries in the late 1950s but it also had the velocity-type control system which was markedly easier to use than the old acceleration control. Displacement of the thumb controller merely displaced the missile any desired amount from its original path. Restoration of the control to neutral restored the original heading but along the new path. Keeping the bright tracking flare aligned with any tank target was positively simple, and the wing span was so extremely small that catching on trees or other obstructions was rare indeed.

Soon it was common to offer extra capabilities. A single operator could lay out a row of missiles (though he could not carry them all by himself) and then, having settled himself into a snug and obscure vantage point, fire each in turn, gather it into his line of sight and steer it into an enemy tank. Some missiles could jump straight off the ground, with a tray underneath to stop a tell-tale cloud of loose debris, but most were fired from a launcher or from their carrier box. Most had magnifying optical sights, and all could be lethal in the hands of a skilled and determined operator. But perhaps not all operators had quite the required skill and determination, and their task had to be made easier.

It was Nord, later Aérospatiale, who again led all the rest in finding a standard answer. They produced TCA, which asked the operator to do no more than keep his optical sight exactly on target. This optical system was boresighted parallel to a second set of optics, sharing the same input mirror, which served an IR localizer. On the rear of the missile was an IR source, such as a ring of small flares, and the position of this source was continuously measured by the localizer. Any deviation from the desired flight path – which was also the centreline of the optical system and the LOS to the target – resulted in a command signal being generated in a computer and sent through the launcher along the trailing wires to the missile control system. The latter could have been moving aerodynamic surfaces, but in all the French weapons from SS.11 onwards control was effected by TVC of the sustainer motor. Of course, this meant that the sustainer had to continue burning all the way to the target. TCA automatic command guidance was a major landmark in anti-tank missiles, and many weapons in use today have it in one form or another.

Today the majority of anti-tank missiles are too heavy for true infantry use, and are instead really tailored to use by small vehicles, one's own armour or helicopters. Most have advanced sight systems, and for any sophisticated platform it is only common sense to give the operator the best sight that optical and IR technology can buy. IIR is vital for battlefield use, and not only in bad weather or at night. Combined with powerful magnifying optics it enables the operator to see the enemy at a distance where, with luck, he may not have seen you, and to guide small missiles with the necessary accuracy over ranges up to LOS limits.

I do not know how many "generations" of anti-tank missiles there have been, but the current crop have again introduced important improvements. Though the IR-slaved optical sighting and wire guidance has been retained, the missiles are now launched from tubes and fly much faster. Tube launch and high speed resembles a gun, so in extremis the missile can be fired at very close range without doing more than aim the tube. High flight speed, which in the case of the most important missile of all – Tow – is about that of a typical jet aeroplane, has the great advantage of cutting time of flight. On the other hand it means that the operator must be on the ball; he has only to cough or sneeze to miss the target.

Today some of the most attractive anti-tank missiles are semi-active laser homers. It does not matter whether the target is illuminated by laser light from near the launcher or from a quite different source. One system uses a laser somewhere in the front line, either aimed by an infantryman or by a mini-RPV, while the warhead is delivered in a missile fired by artillery from a great distance. Making a true artillery shell into a precision guided missile is even more of a feat than was the proximity fuze 35 years ago.

In conclusion, there is no reason why anti-tank missiles should be an exception to the rule of action and counter-action that characterises all weapons. Obviously one of the counter-actions is better armour, and already publicity has been given to multi-laminate spaced armour, to detonate the warhead too far from the innermost layer to have much effect, and Britain's Chobham armour which is at once secret and exported. Other countermeasures have been difficult to contrive. No modern anti-tank missile can be detected by an enemy tank commander either at launch or, except by chance and at a time far too late to do anything about it, in flight; and even if the missile was seen early in its approach there is not very much the tank can do except dart into a handy depression in the ground that takes it out of the enemy LOS. Wire guidance is popularly said to be "immune to countermeasures" – though cartoons have shown soldiers equipped with scissors! It is surprising that no AFV manufacturer appears to think a simple wire-mesh box, larger than the tank and offering just enough resistance to operate the warhead fuze, worth the slight extra inconvenience.

# AUSTRALIA

## Malkara

After World War II no attempt was made by Britain to develop an anti-tank missile or even follow up the wartime German work with basic research, but in 1951 the Australian government launched a project for a wire-guided anti-tank missile handled by the Government Aircraft Factories at Fishermen's Bend, Melbourne, with assistance by other groups including the Aeronautical Research Laboratories of the Department of Supply and the RAE in Britain. From the start the British MoS collaborated closely, and insisted that the missile should be extremely large. The body was larger than a man necessitating vehicular deployment. Propelled by a dual-thrust solid motor, Malkara had wire guidance, tracking flares on the tips of the large moving wings on the square-section centre body, fixed rear fins indexed at 45° and a 57·5 lb (26·1 kg) HESH head containing 35 lb (15·9 kg) of explosive. Design was completed in 1954 and guided flight trials began in November 1955 at Woomera, followed by troop firings at Puckapunyal and in Britain at Kirkudbright and near Lulworth. Small numbers were deployed by the British Royal Armoured Corps on the Hornet (Humber 4 × 4) scout car carrying two on a zero-length overhead launcher and two stowed.

**Dimensions:** Length 76·0 in (1·93 m); diameter 8·0 in (203 mm); span 31·0 in (787 mm).
**Launch weight:** 206 lb (93·4 kg).
**Range:** 7,000 ft (2134 m).

Above: *Malkara was a sound weapon, but overlarge and cumbersome in relation to its mission. It had a large "squash-head" instead of a shaped charge.*

Below: *Malkara of the Royal Armoured Corps being used up in a training shot as recently as 1975. Hornet AFV at right.*

# BRAZIL

In 1968 the Ministry of Defence stated that the Army's Central Missile Commission was developing a wire-guided anti-tank missile with a range of 1·86 miles (3 km). Nothing more has been heard of it, and it may have been abandoned.

# FRANCE

## SS.10

This missile is at once one of the smallest, cheapest, earliest and most significant in history. In the years after 1945 the German development of a wire-guided anti-tank missile was ignored by every country except France, where in 1948 the Arsenal de l'Aéronautique began to study the problems of developing a new weapon in this category. In late 1952 the team at Chatillon sous Bagneux, with other Arsenal facilities, was reorganised into a group called SFECMAS, and this in turn was merged into Nord-Aviation in November 1954. The missile thus became the Nord 5200 series, and though it used German techniques was wholly French in design. Eminently logical, it comprised a short dual-thrust solid motor surrounded by four wings each fitted with a vibrating spoiler, based on the classic Wagner bar, at the inner end of the trailing edge. On the front was attached an 11 lb (5 kg) hollow-charge warhead, able to penetrate 16 in (406 mm) of armour, or an inert head for training. Associated equipment was at first merely a command box and a light carrying box which served as the launcher. By eliminating an autopilot and using a crude missile which rolled throughout its flight, with acceleration control by a small joystick, the price of the missile was initially kept to only £340, and the control box to £1,750, the latter reused as often as necessary. Development was complete in 1955, and in November 1956 this missile was instrumental in enabling the Israeli army to defeat Egyptian armour in the first Middle East war. Produced as the Nord 5203, SS.10 (sol/sol, surface-to-surface) was in production until January 1962, when 29,849 had been delivered. In 1954 prototypes were the first guided missiles to be tested by US Army Ordnance. Of the total output, 61 per cent was exported to 11 countries.

**Dimensions:** Length 33·9 in (861 mm); diameter 6·5 in (165 mm); span 29·5 in (750 mm).
**Launch weight:** 33·0 lb (15·0 kg).
**Range:** 5,250 ft (1600 m) at 180 mph (290 km/h).

Below: *Probably taken at Mailly in the early 1960s, this row of 19 SS.10s was fired in a matter of minutes.*

Foot of page: *This USA soldier gives an excellent idea of the size of SS.10, the first guided missile of its kind to go into service. Use in such terrain was tricky.*

# SS.11

Started by SFECMAS in 1953 as Type 5210, this missile carried the same principle further in range and hitting power, at the expense of a missile too heavy for infantry to carry. Its chief feature was a much higher performance obtained by a new motor using the TVC system already proven in the 5100-series AAM (AA.20). The eventual propulsion system comprised the SNPE Simplet cast-DB charge burning for 1·2 sec, followed by the Sophie sustainer burning for 20 sec, with the jet intermittently deflected by four solenoid-biassed vibrating spoilers pivoted around the base. The missile rolls slowly, like SS.10, because of slight off-setting of the four swept wings. The quickly attached head can be an inert one for training, or Type 125 (later Type 140) AC for penetrating 24 in (609 mm) of armour, or 140CCN for naval use, or 140AP02 for penetrating thin armour and exploding on the far side, or 140AP59 fragmentation with DA fuze. SS.11 has been launched from many kinds of vehicles and ships, and AS.11 (p. 107) is an air-launched version. An infantry system was eventually devised with transistorised "waist-belt fire control" and with one man carrying three warheads and three more carrying the missiles. SS.11 entered service in 1956, and production at Chatillon was soon augmented by a new missile factory built at Bourges in 1957–8 where total production reached 1,500 per month. In 1962 SS.11B1

entered production with transistorised electronics and other improvements. Small numbers were still being made in 1978, with the total standing at 168,450, almost a record for any missile. A typical price is $1·900, and customers include Abu Dhabi, Argentina, Belgium, Brazil, Britain, Brunei, Canada, Denmark, Finland, West Germany*, Greece, India*, Iran, Iraq, Israel, Italy, Kuwait, Lebanon, Libya, Malaysia, Netherlands, Norway, Peru, Portugal, Saudi Arabia, South Africa, Spain, Sweden, Switzerland, Tunisia, Uganda, United States* and Venezuela. Missiles were produced under licence in the countries asterisked. US designation is M22.

**Dimensions:** Length 47·0 in (1·19 m); diameter 6·46 in (164 mm); span 19·7 in (500 mm).
**Launch weight:** 66·0 lb (29·9 kg).
**Range:** 9,842 ft (3000 m) at 360 mph (579 km/h).

# Entac

Developed in competition with private-industry's SS.10 by the government DTAT, this very similar missile took much longer to mature but emerged distinctly superior. Though it car-

ries a smaller warhead than SS.10 it can penetrate a greater thickness of armour, and the missile is lighter, has smaller span, flies rather faster and has longer range. A great advantage to the operator is that the control is partly of the velocity-type, and whereas in the early days it needed a crew of two to fire Entac at all, eventually a way was found to make this a one-man missile with the operator up to 360 ft (110 m) from a battery of up to ten missiles all under his control. The name derives from ENgin Téléguidé Anti-Char. This missile was developed at DTAT Puteaux and adopted by the French Army in 1957 in Model 58 form, with sheet-metal construction, mid-span wing spoiler control and an SNPE Entac motor with 0·7 sec boost charge and 18

sec sustainer. Normal head is a 9·0 lb (4·1 kg) hollow charge able to penetrate 25·6 in (650 mm) of armour at up to 78° incidence. Missiles are supplied in polyester waterproof containers and are normally fired from quad boxes on Jeep-like vehicles. In US Army service the designation is MGM-32. Other users include Australia, Belgium, Canada, France, India, Indonesia, Morocco, Netherlands, Norway, South Africa, and Switzerland. Production was completed at 139,417 rounds in 1974.

**Dimensions:** Length 32·3 in (820 mm); diameter 6·0 in (152 mm); span 14·76 in (375 mm).
**Launch weight:** 26·9 lb (12·2 kg).
**Range:** 6,562 ft (2000 m) at 190 mph (305 km/h).

# Harpon

This name was given the SS.11 when fitted with TCA semi-automatic guidance developed by SAT. The latter developed this IR-based system in 1959–66, and Harpon was introduced to the Bourges production line in 1967. By this time Nord had become part of Aérospatiale, and since then the French missile producer has been known as the Division Engins Tactiques of this giant nationalised aerospace company. The Harpon operator aims his optical sight at the target and the missile is automatically captured and held within 40 in (1 m) of the centreline of the IR beam aligned parallel to the sight. Apart from increased accuracy and virtual elimination of missiles lost through errors, such guidance reduces minimum range (to about 1,200 ft, 400 m, with Harpon) by greatly shortening the time needed to acquire and guide the missile after launch. Command signals are, of course, still passed along twin wires. Harpon users include France, West Germany and Saudi Arabia. Production total is included in that for SS.11. Data: as for SS.11B1 except length 47·8 in (1215 mm) and launch weight 67·0 lb (30·4 kg).

# Acra

One of the most advanced and attractive anti-tank systems, ACRA (Anti-Char Rapide Autopropulsée) was a gun-launched projectile system developed at Puteaux by DTAT, now part of GIAT. The operator had a choice of two projectiles, both fired from a 5·59 in (142 mm) gun and boosted to higher speed by a rocket. The unguided projectile had a choice of warheads for soft-

**Above: Harpon was at one time deployed in this quad launcher carried on the AMX-13 chassis. The TCA sight can be seen projecting above the turret.**

skinned targets or troops, while the guided projectile, considerably longer and heavier, had a shaped charge. On leaving the muzzle four small anti-roll fins and four larger control fins flicked open and the missile was gathered into a laser beam held on the target by the operator's optical sight. A distance of 1·86 miles (3 km) could be covered in only 7 sec. Development involved over 500 firings in 1968–74, but plans for production were abandoned for budgetary reasons. Data for guided ACRA.

**Dimensions:** Length 47·24 in (1·20 m); diameter 5·59 in (142 mm); span (fins deployed) 16·0 in (406 mm).
**Launch weight:** 57·3 lb (26·0 kg).
**Range:** 9,843 ft (3000 m) at over Mach 1.

**Below: The two types of ACRA ammunition, showing the contrast in size between the unguided round (left) and the missile with laser guidance.**

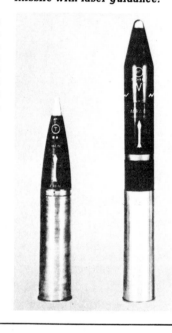

stick whose correction signals were transmitted along the duplicate wires and passed by a multiplexer gyro to drive the spoiler in the correct sense. A substantial number of X-7s were made at the Brackwede plant and it is believed that some hundreds reached front-line troops, though in an evaluation and development status.

There were various developments and more advanced missiles, though it is difficult to ascertain which were derivatives. Steinbock (Capricorn) was an X-7 with automatic IR homing. Peifenkopf (Pipe Bowl) and Pinsel (Paint-brush) were EO-guided missiles, one or both of which had a spiral-scan vidicon head able to detect the optical contrast of the target against the background. One of these was probably a BMW missile, because it was tested at that company's Stargard works in December 1944. BMW was brought in at the end of 1944 and quickly produced its own anti-tank missile resembling the X-4 AAM, with a derivative intended for air launch against hard targets. Data are for standard X-7 as produced in September 1944.

**Dimensions:** Length 37·4 in (950 mm); diameter 5·9 in (150 mm); span 23·6 in (600 mm).
**Launch weight:** 19·84 lb (9·0 kg).
**Range:** 3,937 ft (1·2 km).

# Cobra

The first post-war German missile, this neat weapon was originally designed in Switzerland by Contraves-Oerlikon and subsequently marketed and further developed by Bölkow GmbH from 1957. After most successful trials it went into production and reached IOC in 1960. The four plastic wings have swept-forward leading edges, and steer via Wagner-type spoilers. The missile is light enough for an infantryman to carry two, plus the control unit and cabling, and fire both by himself. Each missile can be simply placed on the ground, pointing towards the enemy. The boost motor, attached externally on the underside, has an angled nozzle so that, when

---

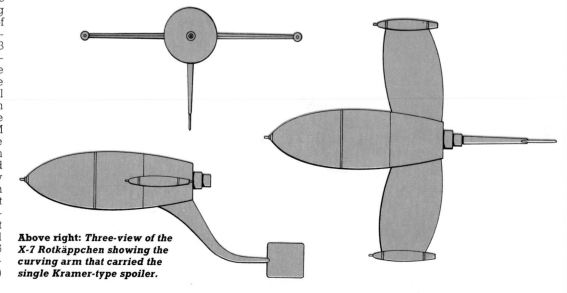

# GERMANY

# X-7

This odd little missile was the true ancestor of all today's family of anti-tank missiles using wire guidance. It was one of several crash programmes begun in early 1944 (prior to 3 February) by order of the Heereswaffenamt to try to stem the tide of Soviet armour. Of these projects only that of Ruhrstahl made rapid progress, underlain as it was by prior experience with the wire-guided X-4 AAM (p. 212). Though it looked strange at rest, and even stranger in operation, Rotkäppchen (Red Riding Hood) was a thoroughly sound concept that after ten months of effort was almost ready for production and proving deadly to even the heaviest tanks. The fat but streamlined body housed a Wasag 109–506 diglycol dual-thrust motor giving a boost thrust of 150 lb (68 kg)

for 2·5 sec and a sustainer thrust of 12·1 lb (5·5 kg) for 8 sec. In the nose was a shaped-charge head

containing 5·5 lb (2·5 kg) of explosive, with DA fuze. On each side was a curved-edge wing, with a wire bobbin on each tip. At the rear was a long curving arm carrying a single Kramer-type spoiler. The missile rolled slowly as it flew, and the operator tried to line up the motor flame with the target with a small joy-

**Above right: Three-view of the X-7 Rotkäppchen showing the curving arm that carried the single Kramer-type spoiler.**

it is fired, it projects the missile diagonally up and along, giving it ample height for the operator to catch it with coarse control demands and then steer it to the target. A plate can be placed under the booster on surfaces where firing could throw up dust or other matter that would betray the position. A single operator can be cable-linked to up to eight Cobras up to 230 ft (70 m) away. In 1968 Bölkow merged with Messerschmitt and in 1969 became part of MBB. By that time the production missile was the Cobra 2000, with longer range (the original limit was 5,250 ft, 1600 m) and choice of either a 5·95 lb (2·7 kg) hollow-charge head, with penetration of 19·7 in (500 mm), or an anti-tank fragmentation head of the same weight. Customers for Cobra include Argentina, Brazil*, Denmark, West Germany, Greece, Israel, Italy*, Pakistan*, Spain and Turkey*. Countries asterisked made the system under licence. The total number produced exceeded 170,000.

**Dimensions:** Length: 37·5 in (953 mm); diameter 3·94 in (100 mm); span 18·9 in (480 mm).
**Launch weight:** 22·71 lb (10·3 kg).
**Range:** 6,562 ft (2000 m) at 186 mph (300 km/h).

# Mamba

The interim successor to Cobra, MBB produced Mamba by small but helpful modifications, the most important of which was the introduction of a new dual-thrust combined boost/sustainer motor which not only offers the jump-start capability but also automatically corrects for gravity-drop throughout flight so that the operator does not have to maintain back-pressure on the stick. Second, the launch acceleration is lower, giving the operator more time to gather and start controlling, while in the later stages the speed is much faster than for Cobra, so that smaller wings can be used. A new controller is used, with ×7 optical sight and a clockwork-driven electric generator, and up to 12 rounds can be fired from one station. Mamba is compatible with Cobra warheads and vehicle launchers. Production will be much smaller than for Cobra, and no exports have been announced.

**Dimensions:** Length 37·6 in (955 mm); diameter 4·72 in (120 mm); span 15·75 in (400 mm).
**Launch weight:** 24·7 lb (11·2 kg).
**Range:** 6,562 ft (2000 m) at 311 mph (500 km/h).

Main picture above: *Jump take-off of Cobra from the quad cross-country wheeled launcher adopted by Germany and possibly other users.*

Above inset left: *1962 USA picture showing the complete Cobra system set out for tests at Aberdeen Proving Ground. Cobra was not adopted.*

Above inset right: *MBB photo showing two Cobras resting on the ground ready to fire close to the operator. This would be hazardous in war.*

Below: *A Mamba photographed with its completely different controller incorporating a monocular sight and clockwork generator.*

# INTERNATIONAL

## Hot

The larger vehicle/helicopter-mounted partner to Milan, this missile should really be Hott (the name is often written all in capitals), because it is Haut-subsonique Optiquement Télé-guidé Tire d'un Tube – high-subsonic optical remote-guided fired from a tube. Like Milan, work began with joint Franco-German army requirements, studies by Nord and Bölkow in 1964, engineering development and prolonged firing trials by Aérospatiale/MBB (which jointly formed Euromissile) and the start of mass production in 1977. Each missile is delivered as a round of ammunition in a sealed GRP tube. This can be attached to a vehicle or helicopter in many ways, and in most AFV mounts is clipped to a trainable casemate or turret with any of six manual or powered reload systems, combined with the optical sight and SAT/Eltro IR tracker for the TCA guidance. Unlike Milan there is no need to pop the missile out and ignite the motor after a delay. The ignition signal fires the thermal battery, gyro and flares, gas pressure blowing the end-caps off the tube. The SNPE Bugéat booster then fires inside the tube, burning for 0·9 sec and accelerating the missile to the speed given in the data; the SNPE Infra sustainer then takes over and maintains this speed over a further 17·4 sec burn, giving times of 8·7 sec to 6,562 ft (2000 m), 12·5 sec to 9,842 ft (3000 m) and 16·3 sec to 13,123 ft (4000 m). The boost motor has four oblique nozzles near the roots of the spring-out wings, but the sustainer exhausts centrally where a single TVC spoiler can steer the missile in the usual way. About 100–165 ft (30–50 m) from the launcher the safety system is deactivated to allow the sensitive fuze to detonate the 13·2 lb (6 kg) hollow-charge head as soon as the streamlined nose skin is distorted. Penetration is 24 in (600 mm) at 0° and 11 in (280 mm) at 65°. It is probable that Hot will later be offered with anti-personnel and anti-ship heads. Of course, Hot is ideal for anti-tank helicopters, and has been tested from the PAH-1 (BO 105) with six tubes, Gazelle with six (but to be used by France with four), Dauphin with eight (for export from 1981) and Lynx (eight). Conversely, Hot has potential as an anti-helicopter or even anti-fixed-wing weapon by virtue of its fast gathering and high speed. As with Milan, while production of dawn-to-dusk systems proceeds at 800 rounds and 35 firing posts per month, development and integration of night FLIR sights is a matter of urgency. Germany has adopted a TI system made under licence, while France will use a derivative of the SAT/TRT Thermidor. The main carriers with the two sponsoring armies are the German RJPz-3 tank-destroyer with one tube and eight rounds inside, and the Saviem VAB armoured car, with the Méphisto system of retractable four-tube launcher and a further eight rounds inside the vehicle. Other customers include Egypt, Iraq, Kuwait, Saudi Arabia and Syria, plus four unnamed export customers.

**Below, upper:** *Demonstration firing, probably at Camp de Mailly, of Hot from Gazelle helicopter of ALAT (French army light aviation). Note sight (red) above cabin.*

**Foot of page:** *Departure of Hot from RJPz-3 (Rakete Jagdpanzer) on test in 1974. All 316 of these vehicles were originally armed with the SS.11.*

**Dimensions:** Length 50·2 in (1275 mm); diameter (maximum, warhead and guidance section) 6·5 in (165 mm); span 12·3 in (312 mm).
**Launch weight:** 55·1 lb (25·0 kg).
**Range:** Well over 13,123 ft (4000 m) at 560 mph (900 km/h).

# Milan

The Missile d'Infanterie Léger ANti-char is the successor to the mass-produced first-generation systems by Nord in France and Bölkow in Germany. Following an agreement between the two governments in 1961 the two companies jointly studied Milan in 1962 and completed the design in 1963. The basic system comprises a missile in a sealed launch tube, two of which can be carried by one man, and a firing post comprising an optical sight, IR tracker and (for infantry) a tripod mount, carried by a second man. The guidance is the familiar TCA system, but the missile is wholly new. The operator removes the rear cap from the tube, gets the target in his

**Main picture below:** *Milan ready to fire, with rear cap removed. The operator is on the far side, looking through the optical sight.*

**Below, inset:** *Photograph of Milan firing taken from the operator's side. Launch tube departing to the rear, but missile boost motor not yet fired.*

optical cross-hairs and squeezes the firing button. A stack of thin DB discs in the tube impart 75 g for 0·01 sec to pop the missile from the tube, simultaneously blowing through the nozzle (previously covered by the rear cap) and also ejecting the tube backwards off the firing post. At a safe distance ahead, the SNPE Artus motor fires, this 1·5 sec boost phase being followed by an 11-sec sustainer burn which gives steady acceleration to burnout, at a distance of some 6,562 ft (2000 m). Thus, average speed increases with range, giving times of 7·1 sec to 3,280 ft (1000 m) and 12·5 sec to double this distance. Four small fins spring open as the missile leaves its tube, rolling the missile for stability and holding a level about 20 in (0·5 m) above the line of sight. Steering is by motor TVC. Since 1975 two rival Franco-German teams, SAT/Eltro and TRT/Siemens, have developed IR imagers for night use, and British industry has also studied night and all-weather operation. The original Nord/Bölkow team became Aérospatiale (which handles missile assembly) and MBB, which provides firing post,

tubes and 6·6 lb (3 kg) hollow-charge heads which trigger at incident angles as high as 80° and penetrate 13·9 in (352 mm) at 65°. The two partners formed Euromissile, which in turn licensed manufacture to British Aerospace to supply the British Army. Milan is widely used on vehicles as well as by infantry, but there is no air-launched version. Customers include Belgium, Britain, France, Germany, Greece, South Africa, Spain, Syria and Turkey. Orders by April 1978 were 66,900 of a planned 200,000, with production at about 2,000 rounds and 130 firing posts per month.

**Dimensions:** Length 30·3 in (770 mm); diameter (body) 4·6 in (117 mm); span 10·5 in (267 mm).
**Launch weight:** 14·8 lb (6·7 kg).
**Range:** 6,562 ft (2000 m).

# Atlas

With a name coined from Anti-Tank Laser-Assisted System, this extremely attractive semi-automatic weapon was a joint proposal by BAC and FN of Belgium in 1967–73. Over ranges of the order of 656 ft (200 m) the folding-

wing projectile could be fired as an unguided Bazooka, but for longer ranges a second man with a laser aligned on the target could provide an automatic guidance beam.

# ATEM

The Euromissile partners in France and Germany have for eight years informally discussed collaboration with Britain, and though the latter's adoption of the American Tow missile has not helped this objective the decision was taken in 1977 to form ATEM or Atem (Anti-Tank EuroMissile) as a formal consortium embracing Aérospatiale, MBB and BAe Dynamics Group. This is now jointly studying the design of a new-generation missile to replace existing infantry and light vehicle weapons in the period after 1985. It is too early to predict whether the missile that results will meet a single multinational requirement, have supersonic speed, fire-and-forget guidance or be suitable for air launch. At the time of writing there was no formal collaboration with the USA Ahams studies.

# ITALY

## Mosquito

Though originally designed (as Cobra 4) by Contraves-Oerlikon in Switzerland, and manufactured by Contraves Italiana, this is not exactly an international programme because the partners are all employed by the same parent company. Designed in 1954–7, Mosquito is a typical light first-generation missile with GRP airframe with spoilers on its four folding sandwich-construction wings. A rigid box carries the missile, less its 8·8 lb (4 kg) hollow-charge or fragmentation warhead, and serves as the launcher. Penetration of the anti-tank head is claimed to be 26 in (660 mm). Production took place in the 1960s for the Italian Army, but Switzerland, the original design country, chose the Swedish Bantam.

**Dimensions:** Length 43·7 in (1110 mm); diameter 4·7 in (119 mm); span 23·6 in (600 mm).
**Launch weight:** 31·1 lb (14·1 kg).
**Range:** 7,546 ft (2300 m) claimed, at 205 mph (330 km/h).

**Right:** *Photograph taken during Italian army troop training with Mosquito, which has also been fired from the Agusta-Bell 47 and light army vehicles.*

**Below:** *Only photograph available of Sparviero in late 1978, presumably showing the heavy tripod-mounted launcher/sight system. Enemy tanks might notice launch.*

## Sparviero

Described as a "third-generation" system, for use in the mid-1980s, Sparviero (Hawk) dispenses with guidance wires and instead rides an IR beam aimed optically at the target. The missile has a long tubular body, dual-thrust SNIA-Viscosa solid motor, and is launched by the firing of the boost charge from a tube clipped to the top of the firing post. The latter, with loaded tube, weighs over 152 lb (69 kg), which is a severe handicap, because this missile is being developed chiefly for infantry use. On leaving the launcher the cruciforms of nose controls and tail fins spring open, and the missile's flush IR receiver aerials steer the weapon to equalise the reception from each, which occurs when the missile is centred in the beam. Prime contractor is Breda Meccanica Bresciana, and the guidance subcontractor is Officine Galileo. It would be logical to assume that the beam will eventually come from a laser. The hollow-charge warhead weighs 8·8 lb (4 kg).

**Dimensions:** Length 54·3 in (1380 mm); diameter 5·1 in (130 mm); span 20·9 in (530 mm).
**Launch weight:** 36·4 lb (16·5 kg).
**Range:** 9,843 ft (3000 m) at speed rising to 648 mph (1043 km/h).

# JAPAN

## KAM-3D

Another typical first-generation weapon, this system was studied in 1956 and placed in full development the following year by Kawasaki Heavy Industries, working under contract to the JDA's Technical R&D Institute. Nippon Electric provided the velocity-type guidance, Daicel/Nippon Oils & Fats the dual-thrust solid motor, and Daikin Kogyo the hollow-charge warhead. Many features, including the guidance and the trailing-edge spoilers, were based on Swiss prototypes of Mosquito imported for study in 1956. KAM-3D was adopted by the JGSDF in 1964 as Type 64 ATM (Anti-Tank Missile), despite the fact that it needs a firing team of two men, and if possible three. Most are carried in pairs on Jeep-type vehicles and light helicopters.

**Dimensions:** Length 39·0 in (991 mm); diameter 4·7 in (120 mm); span 23·6 in (600 mm).
**Launch weight:** 34·6 lb (15·7 kg).
**Range:** 5,905 ft (1800 m) at 190 mph (306 km/h).

## KAM-9

Also called TAN-SSM, this is a natural second-generation system featuring tube launch, optical sighting and SACLOS guidance. Details of the latter have not been disclosed but it is likely to be based on the TCA method with IR tracking and computer-generated error-correction commands transmitted along twin guidance wires. The missile has a long cylindrical body containing a Nippon Oils & Fats booster, which ejects the missile from the sealed storage tube, Daicel solid sustainer, fired when well ahead of the tube, four high-aspect-ratio flip-out control fins, and 4·2 lb (1·9 kg) hollow-charge warhead which can penetrate up to 19·7 in (500 mm) at angles up to 80° (obviously at oblique angles penetration would be much less than the claimed figure). Loaded tubes are placed on a tripod launcher for firing, and several can be interconnected by cable to one launcher fitted with the optical sight and guidance tracker. Pre-series production began in 1974, and the prime contractor, Kawasaki Heavy Industries, has commented on KAM-9's deployment against ''armoured vehicles on ...water'', construed as meaning AFVs engaged in amphibious assault.

**Dimensions:** Length 59·0 in (1·5 m); diameter 5·9 in (150 mm); span 13·0 in (330 mm).
**Launch weight:** not disclosed but about 53 lb (24 kg).
**Range:** Not disclosed but should be up to 13,123 ft (4000 m) at high-subsonic speed.

**Right top:** *KAM-3D (ATM-1 Type 64) ready for firing.*

**Centre:** *KAM-9 system: three launchers (one with tracker), electronics box and cable.*

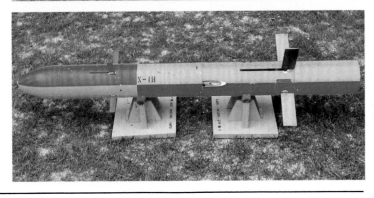

**Right:** *KAM-9 missile.*

# SWEDEN

## Bantam

Developed almost entirely by AB Bofors as a private venture from 1956, this is one of the smallest and lightest first-generation anti-tank missiles, and was notable for introducing a GRP airframe with folding wings to fit a slim container/launcher. In its simplest form for infantry the whole system, with one missile, weighs 44·0 lb (20 kg), with 66 ft (20 m) of cable to link the operator and launcher. If necessary the operator can add another 328 ft (100 m) of cable. Bantam has been fired from light aircraft such as the SK61 Bulldog and Saab Supporter and Agusta-Bell 204 helicopter, and the Puch-Häflinger light 4 × 4 vehicle carries a battery of six ready to fire and six more at the rear. On leaving the launch box the wings flip open, their curved trailing-edge tips rolling the missile so that it can be steered by the trailing-edge spoilers sequenced by a pellet-spun gyro. The solid dual-thrust motor is a Bofors product, and the 4·2 lb (1·9 kg) hollow-charge warhead has electrical double-skin fuzing and can penetrate up to 19·7 in (500 mm). Sweden adopted Bantam as missile RB 53 in 1963, and – despite having their indigenous Mosquito – Switzerland followed in 1967. Production continued until about 1978.

**Dimensions:** Length 33·4 in (848 mm); diameter 4·3 in (110 mm); span 15·75 in (400 mm).
**Launch weight:** 16·75 lb (7·6 kg).
**Range:** 6,562 ft (2000 m) at 188 mph (303 km/h).

**Right:** *Bantam launch from Gnome-powered Agusta-Bell 204B of Swedish Army Aviation.*

**Below:** *Bantam with its GRP wings deployed into the flight position.*

# USSR

## AT-1 Snapper

The first-generation Soviet anti-tank missile was not only much in evidence in the July 1967 Middle East war but numerous examples were captured by the Israeli army and so it soon became well known in the West. At that time it was carried in a quad mount on the GAZ-69 4 × 4 car, the missiles travelling nose-up and the whole launcher being cranked down for use, with a further crank to train it in the required direction, facing to the rear. Oddly, each missile was fired from an overhead guide rail, and two bent tubes at the rear contained sockets to which the guidance wires for that missile had to be screwed prior to

**Right: Standard triple installation of AT-1 Snapper on BTR-40P (BRDM-1) as used by most WP armies.**

**Below: Photograph taken on manoeuvres by Soviet Ground Forces in 1973 showing BRDM-1 with AT-2 Swatter installation. Behind, AT-1 Snapper BRDM.**

launch. If necessary the launcher could be fired by an operator up to 164 ft (50 m) distant. The missile, actually believed to be 3M6 and dubbed Shmell (Bumblebee), was called AT-1 in the West and codenamed Snapper. It has four large wings, a single-charge

solid motor and 11·5 lb (5·25 kg) hollow-charge warhead with penetration of at least 13·8 in (350 mm). The missile is spin-stabilized, the operator sighting optically on the tracking flares on the tips of the horizontal wings and steering with plastic-insert spoilers on all four wings, the vertical wings having additional outboard spoilers for roll control. By 1970 the usual carrier in WP armies was the BRDM amphibious scout car which can have a retractable triple mount-

ing. Users have included Afghanistan, Bulgaria, Cuba, Czechoslovakia, East Germany, Egypt, Hungary, Jugoslavia, Mongolia, Poland, Romania, Soviet Union and Syria.

**Dimensions:** Length 44·5 in (1130 mm); diameter 5·51 in (140 mm); span 30·7 in (780 mm).
**Launch weight:** 49·05 lb (22·25 kg).
**Range:** 7,546 ft (2300 m) at 199 mph (320 km/h).

## AT-2 Swatter

This much more advanced missile has also seen action in the Middle East and been captured by Israel, yet as far as published information is concerned Western observers cannot make up their minds on the most basic features. Things which are not in dispute are that it is carried on a quad launcher on the BRDM, and has a cruciform of rear wings, all fitted with control surfaces which are probably elevons and two carrying what look like tracking flares, an internal solid motor with oblique nozzles between the wings which fires it off a launch rail of surprising size (so there is no high-thrust booster), and a hemispherical nose, behind which are two small fin-like projections. Most observers flatly state that

wire guidance is not used, and in the author's opinion it never was used with this weapon. Others insist the opposite, while another source describes "Swatter A" with wires and "Swatter B" without. There seems little doubt it is command guided by radio, which facilitates deployment from the various versions of Mi-24 tactical helicopter, and, it is believed, the AV-MF Ka-25. Air applications are thought to be of an interim nature, pending availability of AS-8 (p. 116).

The remaining puzzle is the nose, which suggests IR terminal homing, possibly in conjunction with the two small "foreplanes". In mid-1978 this is pure speculation, though an IR seeker head is not impossible with a hollow-charge weapon. The warhead in this case has never been described in the West, but is said to penetrate 19·7 in (500 mm). Users include WP countries, Egypt and Syria.

**Dimensions:** Length 35·5 in (902 mm); diameter 5·9 in (150 mm); span 26·0 in (660 mm).
**Launch weight:** 55 lb (25 kg).
**Range:** 7,218 ft (2200 m) at 335 mph (540 km/h).

**Below:** *BMP-1 APCs on parade, showing AT-3 Sagger on its launch rail above the low-pressure 73 mm main gun.*

# AT-3 Sagger

During the Middle East war in October 1973 two-man teams of Egyptian infantry opened what looked like small suitcases and inflicted casualties on Israeli battle tanks the like of which had seldom been seen on any battlefield. Ever since, the little missile codenamed Sagger by NATO has been treated with great respect, though it is still a simple device with no tube launcher or any guidance other than optical sighting and wire command. Called Miliutka in the Soviet

**Below:** *Israeli photograph of a captured AT-3 Sagger being test-fired. So much Russian material was captured in 1973 that the Israelis produced their own training documents.*

**Bottom:** *First public appearance of BRDM-2 armed with quintuple AT-5 Spandrel tubes*

Union, it was first seen in a Moscow parade in May 1965. Since then it has been seen on BRDMs (six-round retractable launcher topped by armoured roof), BMP and BMD (single reloadable launcher above the main gun) and Czech SKOT (twin reloadable rear launcher). The Mi-24 Hind A helicopter can also carry this missile on its four outboard launchers, presumably firing from the hover or at low forward speeds. The missile is accelerated by a boost motor just behind the warhead with four oblique nozzles, and flies on a solid sustainer with jetevator TVC for steering. There are no aerodynamic controls, but the small wings can fold for infantry packaging. A tracking flare is attached beside the body, and it is claimed that an operator can steer to 3,281 ft (1000 m) with unaided eyesight, and to three times this distance with the magnifying optical sight. The Western estimated penetration of 15·75 in (400 mm) for the 6 lb (2·72 kg) warhead is almost certainly a considerable underestimate. Users include the WP armies and Afghanistan, Algeria, Angola, Egypt, Ethiopia, Iraq, Jugoslavia, Libya, Mozambique, Syria, Uganda and Vietnam, and probably at least five further countries.

# AT-4 Spigot

Code-named Spigot by NATO, this is a high-performance infantry missile fired from a tube and generally similar to Hot. In early 1979 available evidence suggested that it is a man-portable version of AT-5. It probably needs a team of at least three to operate.

# AT-5 Spandrel

Allotted the NATO reporting name of Spandrel, this is the tube-launched system first seen on BRDM-2 armoured cars in the Red Square parade of 7 November 1977. Each vehicle has five tubes in a row, on a trainable mount admidships. The tube resembles that of Hot and has a blow-out front closure and flared tail through which passes the efflux from the boost charge. This blows the missile out prior to ignition of its own motor. Folding wings, SACLOS guidance via trailing wires and general size similar to Hot seem reasonable, but the suggested range of 4km appears optimistic. The Group of Soviet Forces in Germany is thought in 1979 to have replaced all its Swatter and Sagger missiles with Spandrel.

# AT-6 Spiral

This missile, code-named Spiral by NATO, is believed to be a large laser-guided weapon able to demolish any AFV. It is believed to be standard on the Hind-D helicopter and may also be fitted to the laser-equipped Soviet battle tanks. The suggestion that it is based on the SA-8 SAM appears unlikely.

# UNITED KINGDOM

## Python

In 1955 the British electronics company Pye Ltd studied the problem of anti-tank missile guidance, with little encouragement from the War Office or MoS, and in 1957 began testing a complete missile. Too large for infantry, but well matched to many light vehicles, its unique feature was roll-stabilization not of the whole missile but just of the Bristol-Aerojet dual-thrust motor, behind the fixed wings, with TVC trajectory control. The warhead was of 30 lb (13.6 kg). Official disinterest prevented production.

**Dimensions:** Length 60.0 in (1.52 m); diameter 6.0 in (152 mm); span 24.0 in (610 mm).
**Launch weight:** 81 lb (36.75 kg).
**Range:** 9,000 ft (2743 m) at 250 mph (402 km/h).

## Vigilant

Again reflecting apparent British official disinterest in anti-tank missiles, except the grossly oversized Malkara, this neat and, for its day, extremely advanced missile had to grow up as a private venture by industry. In this case the determined creator was Vickers-Armstrongs (Aircraft) whose guided-weapon team at Weybridge was thrown out of a job by cancellation of the missiles that the government had thought to order (Blue Boar, Red Rapier and Red Dean) so, to keep the team together, V.891 was designed in a very short time in 1956. Later named Vigilant, it was fired in 1958 and by sheer merit managed to reach production for Britain, and subsequently Finland and Kuwait (1963), Saudi Arabia (1964), Libya (1968) and Abu Dhabi (1971). Had Britain enjoyed the kind of government/industry partnership of France this missile would probably have equalled the sales of SS.10 and Entac combined, because it offers much higher lethality and several other advantages. The airframe is largely of GRP, and has extremely short-span long-chord wings with trailing-edge elevons driven by cordite gas. Launched by a dual-thrust IMI solid motor from its carrying box, Vigilant flies on a twin-gyro autopilot and was the first missile to have velocity control to ease the operator's task. The warhead, weighing 13.2 lb (6 kg), a remarkable proportion of the total weight, is triggered by a stand-off contact probe and can penetrate more than 22 in (559 mm). Vigilants have been used by infantry, with whom it has proved very popular, and in twin installations on the Ferret

**Right: *The REME sergeant is actually larger than his Python missile; demonstration picture, 1957.***

**Below: *Launch of Vigilant (production missile) from a Ferret 2/6; two reloads are carried instead of a spare wheel. (Inset, Airborne infantry with two Vigilants ready to launch.)***

2/6 and Shorland armoured cars and the Soviet GAZ used by Finland.

**Dimensions:** Length 42.2 in (1072 mm); diameter (warhead) 5.1 in (130 mm); span 11.0 in (279 mm).
**Launch weight:** 31.0 lb (14.0 kg).
**Range:** 5,250 ft (1600 m) at 348 mph (560 km/h).

## Orange William

Once Vickers really got started with an anti-tank missile the British government woke up and ordered one from someone else. The unlucky contractor was Fairey Engineering, at Heston. In late 1958 the Secretary of State for War announced "We have under development an anti-tank guided weapon which will . . . remove the heavy tank from the battlefield". Soon afterwards the whole programme was cancelled. Vickers picked up some of the pieces.

## Swingfire

Following the extremely rapid development of Vigilant, Vickers-Armstrongs (Aircraft) studied a larger missile in 1958 using TVC steering, and when Orange William was cancelled in 1959 took over Fairey's experimental work and produced Swingfire by 1961. The name stemmed from the fact that, thanks to relatively low launch acceleration and TVC control, the missile can be turned 45° early in its flight and also up or down 20° in elevation. This hard-hitting missile can be set to Direct Fire when controlled from the launch vehicle, which must then see the target; alternatively the vehicle can be tucked away and the missile fired and guided by a remote operator. Swingfire has an IMI motor with 6 sec boost

phase, giving gently increasing speed, and a long sustainer burn for TVC control. The four wings spring open as the missile clears the launch box, and the 15·4 lb (7 kg) hollow-charge warhead is one of the most powerful fitted to any anti-tank weapon (penetration said to "defeat all known combinations of armour"). Swingfire entered British Army service in 1969 in the FV.438 APC, with two rounds ready to fire and 12 reloads. The FV.712 Ferret Mk 5 has two ready and two reloads. CVR(T) Striker, used also by Belgium, has five ready and five stowed. Hawkswing was an air-launched version, tested from the Lynx. Infantry Swingfire, formerly called Beeswing, has three pairs of demountable boxes on a Land-Rover. Infantry-transportable Swingfire, formerly called Golfswing, is a neat system for open terrain in which up to six boxes, each on a small two-wheel trolley, can be fired by one man.

Light Air-transportable Swingfire puts a new four-round pallet on an Argocat all-terrain vehicle for para-dropping or slinging under a Puma helicopter. All systems are active except Hawkswing, and Egypt is using Infantry Swingfire and will build several thousand additional rounds under licence. The original developer became BAC(AT) Ltd and is now British Aerospace Dynamics Group.

**Dimensions:** Length 42·1 in (1·07 m); diameter 6·7 in (170 mm); span 15·35 in (390 mm).
**Launch weight:** 59·5 lb (27·0 kg).
**Range:** 13,125 ft (4000 m) at 415 mph (667 km/h).

*Below: Launch of Swingfire from Striker CVR(T) of the Belgian Army. (Inset, launch from Land-Rover of Infantry Swingfire.) In both pictures it is possible to see guidance wires from previous shots.*

*Hawkswing under evaluation with Lynx helicopter; the British government instead chose to buy Tow.*

# USA

## Dart

The first anti-tank missile to reach full-scale trials in the United States, SSM-A-23 Dart was extremely large and made the SFECMAS 5200-series missile, then being played with by the US Army, look puny and insignificant. Development began at ARGMA under the Los Angeles Army Ordnance District in late 1951, and the industrial prime was Aerophysics Development Corporation of Santa Barbara, a subsidiary of Curtiss-Wright. The dual-thrust solid motor came from Grand Central Rocket Co, and the optical sight by H. A. Wagner Co. Dart was launched from a zero-length launcher on an M59 truck, and was gathered by the operator into his binocular vision and steered by wires and a complex control system with powder-driven gyros. The missile was roll-stabilized by large ailerons on the four wings and then steered by spoilers near the tips. Under the fixed tail fins, indexed at 45°, was a sodium flare. The warhead weighed nearly 30 lb (13·6 kg). In August 1956 another Curtiss-Wright subsidiary, Utica-Bend, was awarded a production contract for $16,565,000, in those days a large order. It was then the Army discovered that, except in the desert, the long-span wings caught on trees and that the sys-

tem was too cumbersome to be useful. Dart was terminated in early 1958.

**Dimensions:** Length 60·0 in (1524 mm); diameter 8·0 in (203 mm); span 40·0 in (1016 mm).
**Launch weight:** 98·9 lb (44·86 kg).
**Range:** Intended to be 10,000 ft (3048 m) at a claimed 600 mph (966 km/h).

## Shillelagh

This was probably the first gun-launched guided projectile. The system was begun as XM13 in 1959 under USAMICOM (Army Missile Command) at Redstone Arsenal. Prime contractor was Aeronutronic Division of Ford. The missile was a considerable challenge, partly because of the dense packaging, the complex guidance and fierce acceleration, and also from protracted

**Below left:** *Launch at WSMR of a Dart with black/white camera targets. Note particles in jet from boost motor.*

**Below right:** *Dart set up for firing from early launcher at WSMR on 28 October 1955.*

**Foot of page:** *Round 3 leaves the Sheridan barrel during test of the Shillelagh system at Yuma Proving Ground on 31 July 1966. Difficulties were not yet over.*

problems with the original vehicle. The 152 mm gun accelerates the missile to high-subsonic speed, and can also fire conventional ammunition of a special type (M409 HEAT, with combustible case). Velocity is then increased to the extraordinary figure given below by a 1·18-sec burn of an Amoco Chemicals single-stage solid motor. The missile is subsequently steered by four spring-out fins. The operator sights his optical crosshairs on the target and the missile is automatically gathered into the parallel IR beam. The missile at first sinks below the LOS and cannot be guided; at 3,750 ft (1143 m) it rises into view of the tracker and responds to the latter's command signals. The warhead is an octol shaped-charge weighing 15 lb (6·8 kg). Limited production began in 1964 and IOC was reached in 1967. Subsequently 36,000 MGM-51A and inert trainer MTM-51A missiles were delivered at a unit price of about $13,890. The carriers are the M551 General Sheridan airborne assault/armoured-reconnaissance vehicle and the M60A2 battle tank, which has a slightly different gun-launcher. Shillelagh has been air-fired from a UH-1B helicopter, and since 1975 there has been evaluation of laser-guided versions. Though costly, and until 1973 troublesome, this system has proved very potent.

**Dimensions:** Length 45·0 in (1143 mm); diameter 5·98 in (152 mm); span 11·5 in (292 mm).
**Launch weight:** 59 lb (26·8 kg).
**Range:** 17,060 ft (5200 m) at peak speed of 2,630 mph (4233 km/h).

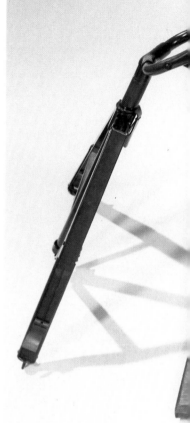

**Main picture:** *Informative cutaway of the complete Dragon system, with the launcher and, on the wooden baseplate, the optical sight unit.*

## Dragon

Developed originally by McDonnell Aircraft at St Louis as MAW (Medium Anti-tank/assault Weapon) to replace the 90 mm recoilless rifle, this unique missile was designed in 1966 and soon afterwards was moved to McDonnell Douglas Astronautics following the merger with Douglas. MDAC readied the system for service use at Titusville, Florida, and reached IOC in 1973. It has the designation FGM-77A and Army Ordnance number M47. Its unique feature is that the missile is shot from its sealed tube by a solid charge which blows through the rear port to cancel recoil, and then navigates to the target by 30 pairs of miniature thrusters arranged around the sides of the body. Three flip-out fins stabilise and roll the missile, and the operator keeps his cross-hairs on the target to make the missile centre itself on the LOS. The usual method is followed of having an IR tracker sense the position of the missile relative to the LOS, sending corrective signals via wires. These signals steer the missile by firing successive pairs of thrusters, each giving 265 lb (120 kg) thrust for 0·7 sec. The linear shaped-charge HEAT warhead weighs 5·4 lb (2·45 kg) and has penetra-

**Inset:** *MDAC photograph showing one of the Dragon troop evaluation firings. Some of the equipment and instrumentation is not part of the production M47.*

tion of up to 23·6 in (600 mm). To fire Dragon a loaded tube is clipped to the Kollsman SU-36/P optical/IR tracker. MDAC delivered over 50,000 rounds before Raytheon won second-source production; subsequently Raytheon won the whole production, and Kollsman all trackers, but MDAC remains prime, and producer of support equipment. The USA will buy about 250,000 rounds, of which 129,000 had been produced by September 1978. Other customers include the Marine Corps and Denmark, Iran, Israel, Jordan, Morocco, Netherlands, Saudi Arabia and Switzerland, and Spain and Sweden have been named as probable purchasers. A night sight having maximum commonality with that for Tow is under development.

**Dimensions:** Length 29·3 in (745 mm); diameter 5·0 in (127 mm); span 13·0 in (330 mm).
**Launch weight:** 13·5 lb (6·1 kg).
**Range:** 3,281 ft (1000 m) at 560 mph (901 km/h) final velocity.

# Hornet

This precision air-launched missile was first developed as ZAGM-64A for the USAF by North American Rockwell in 1963–66. Its purpose was to determine the feasibility of homing

systems, especially TV and EO guidance, against armour on a typical battlefield. Fitted with a short-burn solid motor and cruciform wings with trailing-edge controls, Hornet was normally guided by a stabilised vidicon which, locked-on prior to launch, resulted in homing by proportional navigation without further attention from the launch aircraft. A derived guidance was used for Hobos ASMs (p. 128). In 1970 Hornet was reactivated by the USA as Terminal Homing Flight Test Vehicle for development of seekers for the next generation of anti-tank missiles. A direct result is Hellfire.

# Hellfire

A direct descendent of Hornet, this Rockwell International missile could be included in the air/surface tactical section, because it has applications against hard point targets of all kinds, though it is officially described as "the USA's next-generation anti-armor weapon system". Numerous development firings took place from 1971 before full engineering go-ahead was received in October 1976. The missile resembles Hornet in configuration but has semi-active laser homing, with several other seeker heads also being tested in the ED (Engineering Development) phase in 1978. Among the seekers are the Iris (formerly Irish) IIR from TI and the ATVS (Advanced TV Seeker) from Martin Marietta. Current flight tests use Rockwell's own tri-Service laser seeker also used on Maverick, GBU-15V and other "smart" devices. Among carriers of Hellfire are the Cobra and AH-64 families of helicopters (these have flown with six and 16 missiles, respectively) and the A-10A Thunderbolt II fixed-wing platform. The standard head is a Firestone shaped-charge weighing about 20 lb (9 kg). Numerous Hellfires have been launched without prior lock-on, some of them from ground launchers; the missile notices the laser radiation in flight, locks-on and homes at once. IOC will not be before 1981, by which time this missile will probably have many air and ground applications.

**Dimensions:** Length about 70 in (1·78 m); diameter 7·0 in (178 mm); span 13·0 in (330 mm).
**Launch weight:** not over 95 lb (43 kg).
**Range:** Up to several miles/km, depending on launch height.

*Upper picture left: **ADSM (air-defense suppression missile) was a Rockwell derivative of Hornet with dual ARM and IR homing. Here mounted on a UH-1 helicopter, it was intended to home on AA vehicles.***

*Left: **Hellfire test from AH-1 HueyCobra at very flat angle. Hellfires have been tested in rapid or ripple firings, direct or indirect, and may later have various alternative guidance systems.***

# Tow

Often written TOW (Tube-launched, Optically tracked, Wire-guided), this effective weapon is likely to set an all-time record for guided-missile production. Like the Boeing 727 civil airliner, it has for a long period enjoyed the situation in which new customers keep buying it because it has been made on so large a scale it beats all rivals on the important score of price, despite the fact that, instead of following a falling "learning curve", the price has climbed through inflation from $3,500 in 1973 to a current $8,600.

Prime contractor Hughes Aircraft began work in 1965 to replace the 106 mm recoilless rifle. The missile developed swiftly. Its basic infantry form is supplied in a sealed tube which is clipped to the launcher. The latter, developed and produced by Emerson, weighs 172 lb (78 kg) and comprises a tripod, GRP launch tube, sight, smooth-motion traversing unit and guidance computer. The missile tube is attached to the rear of the launch tube, the target sighted and the round fired. The Hercules K41 boost charge burns for 0.05 sec to pop the missile from the tube, firing through lateral nozzles amidships. The four wings indexed at 45° spring open forwards, and the four tail controls flip open rearwards. Guidance commands are generated by the optical sensor in the sight, which continuously measures the position of a light source in the missile relative to the LOS and sends steering commands along twin wires. These drive the helium-pressure actuators working the four tail controls in pairs for pitch and yaw. The smokeless sustainer burns for 1 sec, giving speed near Mach 1; at extreme range speed is still 250 mph (402 km/h) so Tow can pull well over 1 g laterally. In 1976 production progressively switched to ER (Extended-Range) Tow with the guidance wires lengthened from 9,842 ft (3000 m) to the figure given below. Sight field of view reduces from 6° for gathering to 1.5° for smoothing and 0.25° for tracking. The missile electronics pack is between the motor and the Picatinny Arsenal 8.6 lb (3.9 kg) shaped-charge warhead, containing 5.3 lb (2.4 kg) of explosive. A major advance introduced from 1977 is a TI TAS-4 thermal-imaging night sight, compatible with many Tow installations.

Tow reached IOC in 1970, was used in Vietnam and the 1973 Middle East war, and has since been produced at a higher rate than any other known missile. In the USA and Marines it is deployed to company level, originally on Jeeps and the M113 APC with single launcher manually reloaded with ten additional rounds. The M65 airborne Tow system equips the standard American attack helicopter, the AH-1S TowCobra and the Marines' twin-engine AH-1J and -1T Improved SeaCobra, each with a TSU (Telescopic Sight Unit) and two quad launchers. Other countries will use Tow systems on the BO 105, Lynx, A109, 500M-D and other helicopters, while it will be a basic fit on the forthcoming USA's AH-64A. In 1978 the USA in Germany introduced the ITV (Improved Tow Vehicle), the M901, with an armoured weapon station containing two launchers, day sight, night sight and wide-field target-acquisition sight, with powered elevation, 360° rotation and auto reloading. The equally new Infantry Fighting Vehicle (previously MICV) has the Tow/Bushmaster turret with 25 mm gun and single reloadable launcher.

By September 1978 deliveries from Tucson totalled approximately 190,000 BGM-71A missiles for the USA and Marines, and about 53,000 exports to Britain, Canada, Denmark, West Germany, Greece, Iran, Israel, Italy, Jordan, Jugoslavia, South Korea, Kuwait, Lebanon, Luxemburg, Morocco, Netherlands, Norway, Oman, Pakistan, Saudi Arabia, Spain, Sweden, Turkey and Vietnam.

**Dimensions:** Length 45.75 in (1162 mm); diameter 6.0 in (152 mm); span 13.5 in (343 mm).
**Launch weight:** 46.1 lb (20.9 kg).
**Range:** 12,300 ft (3750 m) at peak of 623 mph (1003 km/h).

# Copperhead

Conceived by the USA's Rodman Labs in 1970 as CLGP (Cannon-Launched Guided Projectile) this is another "smart" weapon that promises to revolutionise the land battle. Carried aboard an M109A1 SP 155 mm gun or the towed XM198 gun of the same calibre, M712 Copperhead is fired by a regular artillery crew with no special training to an impact point anywhere within

Below: *Cutaway showing major elements of Tow. When packed in its launcher each round is of 8 in (203 mm) diameter, 50 in (1·27 m) long and weighs 53 lb (24 kg).*

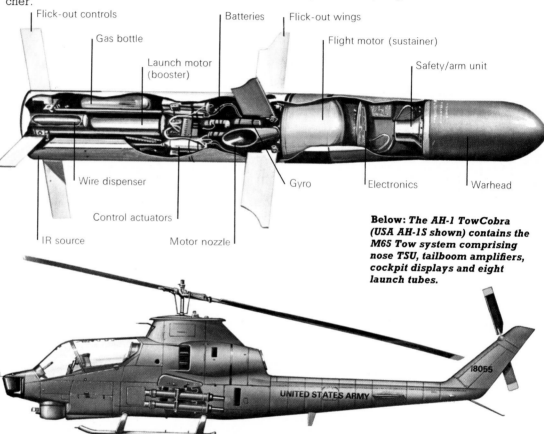

Flick-out controls — Gas bottle — Launch motor (booster) — Batteries — Flick-out wings — Flight motor (sustainer) — Safety/arm unit — Wire dispenser — Control actuators — Gyro — Electronics — Warhead — IR source — Motor nozzle

Below: *The AH-1 TowCobra (USA AH-1S shown) contains the M65 Tow system comprising nose TSU, tailboom amplifiers, cockpit displays and eight launch tubes.*

UNITED STATES ARMY          18055

Below: *Post-storage reliability testing of 26 Tow missiles by M113 of 1st Bn, 61st Inf, 5th Inf Div, at Fort Polk, La, on 4 August 1977.*

about 0·62 mile (1 km) radius of the target. The extreme acceleration of the launch activates the missile, causing the thermal battery to energise, the rear fins to spring open, the gyro to spin up on a spring (thereafter being torqued electrically) and the seeker head to search for laser radiation. The target can be illuminated by a laser on the ground, in a manned aircraft or an expendable mini-RPV, the precise coding of the laser emission being programmed into the missile before firing. When the seeker detects a target the mid-body wings open, steering the projectile home on the radiation from the target, giving pinpoint accuracy by day or night even in marginal weather or with low cloud. Martin Marietta, prime contractor, eventually demonstrated outstanding success, reliably killing tanks even after deliberate mis-aiming by the gun. The usual warhead is a heavy 50 lb (22·7 kg) HESH, but Martin is developing a new head and also an ARM version. Nearly all active NATO nations and other 155 mm gun users have signified intention to use and participate in a large co-production programme, which will probably begin around 1980.

**Dimensions:** Length 54·0 in (1372 mm); diameter 6·1 in (155 mm); span 20·0 in (508 mm).
**Launch weight:** 140 lb (63·5 kg).
**Range:** up to 12·4 miles (20 km) at artillery speeds.

## Ahams

The Advanced Heavy Anti-tank Missile System will probably replace Tow after 1985. It cannot be gun-launched because it must be compatible with infantry, and the highly supersonic speed and 3·73 miles (6 km) range will eliminate wire guidance. Aeronutronic (Ford), Hughes, McDonnell Douglas, Martin and Northrop were in 1978 well advanced in system definition, later to be thinned out.

## CLBRP

The Cannon-Launched Beam-Rider Projectile would be fired from a standard British (US) 105 mm gun and ride a laser beam to the target. Aeronutronic (Ford) and Northrop are studying how best this can be accomplished.

## TGSM

Developed by Vought's Michigan Division, the Terminally Guided Sub-Missile is carried in multiple as the payload of a larger artillery missile (notably Lance, p. 39). Nearing a target area the main missile payload compartment ejects the six to nine TGSMs, each of which slows itself with an airbrake, opens cruciforms of wings and tail controls, and searches for a target with its own seeker head. The latter may be passive, selective IR or MRCH (millimetre radiometric correlation homing). The dispensing technique was demonstrated in 1974.

**Dimensions:** Length 35·0 in (889 mm); diameter 5·9 in (150 mm); span 12·75 in (324 mm).
**Unit weight:** about 35 lb (16 kg).
**Range:** up to about 100 miles (160 km) with Lance carrier.

**Above:** *High-speed sequence showing impact on M47 battle tank of inert Copperhead (Baseline 8 missile) at 4K range WSMR on 9 December 1977. Impact angle suggests very short range.*

**Below:** *Film sequence showing Lance missile dispensing unspecified number of TGSMs in test at WSMR on 29 April 1974. Today TGSM has grown a second (forward) set of wings (bottom picture).*

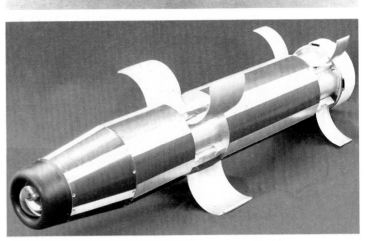

# ANTI-SUBMARINE MISSILES

Though there is no dictionary definition to exclude vehicles moving through water from the "missile" family, the traditional torpedo is rather loosely considered not to be a member of it. Until World War 2 torpedoes were unguided; they were merely aimed, and held on course by a marine autopilot. Then came torpedoes able to home on a ship or submarine by a variety of methods, and there is even one group with wire command guidance. Apart from unconventional methods the way to destroy a submarine, which is the purpose of ASW (anti-submarine warfare), is to detonate a large explosive or nuclear charge close enough to it to crush the hull. This is done either by a free-fall device with a hydrostatic fuze, the so-called depth charge or depth bomb, or by using a guided torpedo that will actually strike the submarine. The problem has naturally been to deliver either weapon to the right place.

In the past 30 years a vast amount of money and man-hours has been expended in learning about the oceans and even sea-water itself, most of it with ASW objectives in mind. We have learned much, but the characteristics of sea-water are such that most types of man-made signal peter out within a short distance. Optical frequencies are sometimes fairly good but usually very bad, and not much can be done in the visible-light band of frequencies. (For this reason sunlight penetrates only a few hundred feet down, the bulk of the deep ocean being pitch dark.) Some specific wavelengths can penetrate much better than others, such as the 10·6-micron wavelength, and the invention of the laser has enabled these precise spots in the electromagnetic spectrum to be exploited at high power. One of the best tools is the neodymium-glass laser, whose second harmonic – a greenish-yellow light at 5305 Angstroms – falls near the centre of one of the transmission "windows" in the ocean, and ASW teams have for years been trying to use it in order to see deeply submerged submarines at useful distances.

It is an uphill struggle. There is no doubt the Soviet Union is No 1 in this field, because they have built immense lasers with power eclipsing anything even attempted in the West, but even they are probably a long way from piercing the impenetrability of the ocean by optical means. Today we are still stuck with only two methods where existing weapon systems are concerned. The chief kind of signal is the intense sound wave. It is backed up by MAD, magnetic-anomaly detection, which rests on the fact that any large metal body, such as a submerged submarine, distorts the Earth's magnetic field slightly by attracting the field (which can be represented as lines of force) to pass through it. MAD systems use a sensitive magnetometer, such as a single-oriented caesium cell, or a large battery of cells, often gyro-stabilized. Modern systems are sensitive enough to detect changes in field intensity of some 0·005 gamma, several orders of magnitude better than a few years ago; but it is difficult to see how such a system could be built into a missile homing seeker head. So far as the author knows, it has never been done, and one must bear in mind that nuclear submarines are able to store extremely large amounts of energy in their fuel and, especially if they were motionless "on station", could probably protect themselves by powerful decoy electromagnets.

Virtually all the ASW missiles at present in use derive their guidance information mainly or wholly from sonars. The name comes from SOund Navigation And Ranging, and the acronym's similarity with "radar" is not misleading. Modern sonar can be thought of as radar that operates in the ocean, and it both offers all the opportunities of all-round coverage or directionality, doppler velocity measurement, range measurement and interference by countermeasures as does radar, and it also suffers from the same problems of unwanted reflections (especially in shallow water) and misleading indications.

Again like radar, sonar can be active or passive. The latter simply comprises a listening device, sensitive enough to detect the propeller or hull noises of a submerged submarine under way at a range of many kilometres. But modern submarines are designed to be extremely quiet, to the extent that dropping a metal spoon so that it hit the metal structure of the hull would be serious (so it cannot happen). A modern submarine lying doggo is hard to detect by passive means, and even harder as a target for an ASW missile. So most sonars are of the active type. Intense "pings" of sound are emitted, in various controlled ways, by piezoelectric ceramics such as barium titanate which convert large electromagnetic oscillator power into intense sound. Frequency may be fixed, at levels around 9 to 10 kHz (10 kHz is 10,000 cycles per second) or variable up to these levels. The echoes from a submerged object may be heard by loudspeaker and will certainly be displayed on a CRT (cathode-ray tube) as in a radar. Skilled operators can thus detect, track (bearing and range known throughout) and identify (classify) each echo, positively identifying a hostile submarine as a "contact".

Extremely powerful sonars are built into the underside of the hull of ASW surface ships, and into the bows of most submarines. In most warships sonar systems can also be used as an underwater or secure means of short-range communication, the range being similar to that of ASW sonar at distances up to 15–20 miles (24–32 km). The signal may be a replica of the original voice or other waveform or it may be a modulated ultrasonic output. Sonar communication is also used to transmit digital data in ASW systems, and for example can transmit target position information from a sensor platform to a ship equipped with ASW missiles. In the same way, US Navy submarines equipped with the Subroc missile must be able to use sonar communications to keep the missile heading for the updated target position throughout the airborne phase of its trajectory. In recent years the variable-depth sonar (VDS) has become important, packaged into a streamlined body towed behind the parent ship at depths from about 25 to 1,000 ft (say, 8–300 m). VDS and many other sonars can have a scanning capability, like surveillance radars. Another type of sonic sensor is the sonobuoy, a self-contained package either strewn into the sea by ship or aircraft or "dunked" on a cable by a helicopter. All these sources can provide target information for ASW missiles. The world is still waiting for the ASW missile intelligent enough to home on its quarry by itself.

Nearly all today's ASW missiles that can be included in this book comprise torpedoes or depth bombs that can be launched from a surface vessel to enter the ocean at the optimum point above the enemy submarine. Some are plain rockets, flying a ballistic trajectory that makes up in speedy delivery for lack of in-flight guidance. Some are miniature aeroplanes, carrying a torpedo as payload, which can be kept under radio command as they wing their way across the sea, finally being commanded to tip up and let the torpedo dive into the water. One "missile" not included in this book was the QH-50C DASH (Drone Anti-Submarine Helicopter), which was a small radio-controlled helicopter launched from frigates or destroyers and guided like the winged ASW missiles to the correct dropping point. It is no longer in service, and caused a few US Navy hairs to turn white, but certainly falls into the grey area where the question "Is it a missile?" is hard to answer.

Of course, virtually all navies use simple ASW bombs which are thrown by a mortar-like projector or rocket propulsion on a ballistic trajectory to impact somewhere above the target. These are no more "missiles" than are mortar bombs on land. So why include the widely used Asroc? The answer is the weak one that Asroc is a degree more sophisticated, and important enough not to omit, even though it has no in-flight guidance. Terne is even more marginal. With the winged delivery systems there is no argument, and the point must be made that in ASW the delivery system is likely to be just one link in a closely forged chain where one weak link may mean a miss. With submarines able to outpace almost all surface ships – other than ACVs and hydrofoils – there is little room for guesswork, and a few seconds "aiming at the last-known predicted point" can prove to be too long.

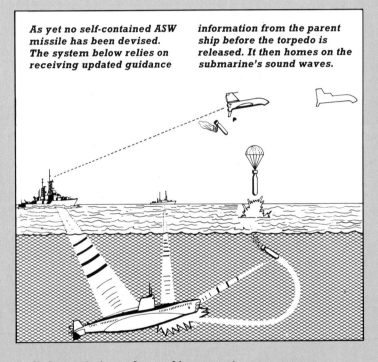

As yet no self-contained ASW missile has been devised. The system below relies on receiving updated guidance information from the parent ship before the torpedo is released. It then homes on the submarine's sound waves.

Subroc is in a class of its own (except, one assumes, its unknown Soviet counterpart). This remarkable missile is fired like a torpedo from the regular 21 in (533 mm) tubes of an attack submarine. Its rocket engine starts, thrusting it up to the surface and along a long arching trajectory – but, unlike so many simpler weapons, under full guidance using the input from various sensors which need not all be located in the parent ship. After its rocket burns out or is cut off and separates, guidance still continues, this time using aerodynamic fins. At supersonic speed the nuclear warhead plunges into the sea, sinks, and detonates close to the target. This is one of the most remarkable missiles in this book, and any engineer will find entertainment in pondering on the multitude of problems that had to be solved to make it work. Though last in these pages, it is certainly a case of "by no means least".

# AUSTRALIA

## Ikara

This missile was designed as a rapid-reaction ASW torpedo carrier capable of all-weather operation. The original, and usual, payload is the lightweight Mk 44 ASW torpedo, weighing 1,157 lb (525 kg) and with acoustic homing. It is attached to a deep fuselage with a dual-thrust rocket motor, carried in the ship's magazine, automatically loaded on to a trainable and elevating launcher (where the delta wings and tail fins are attached) and aimed by data from the ship's sonar and other ASW sensors. The Ikara is launched at an angle usually greater than 45° on the correct heading, is stabilised by its autopilot and radio altimeter, and steered by radio command signals to its wing elevons. It is gathered by the ship's broad-beam radar and subsequently tracked by a narrow-beam radar throughout its flight, a transponder on the missile giving a clear position indication. The system was developed by the Australian Departments of Supply and Navy, the Government Aircraft Factories and WRE. An integral part of the original system is the shipboard computer. The RN adopted a system, called RN Ikara, taking data from the ADAS (Action Data Automation System). Further information can be supplied by a second ship or helicopter; in fact, the parent ship may not itself be in contact with the target, but its computer and radar/command system is used to instruct the missile throughout flight. At the correct location the torpedo is released and descends by parachute, thereafter homing in the usual way. Ikara is fitted to *Perth* and *River* destroyers of the RAN, HMS *Bristol* and eight *Leander* frigates of the RN, and four *Niteroi* Mk 10 frigates of Brazil, the latter having a modified system called Branik. British defence cuts in 1977 killed an extended range version, and in 1978 Britain decided not to participate in a new Ikara carrying a later lightweight torpedo.

**Dimensions:** Length 135 in (3·43 m); span 60·0 in (1·52 m).
**Launch weight:** not disclosed.
**Range:** about 11 miles (18 km).

*Right: BAe Dynamics photo of Ikara launch at sea; the ship is unidentified but appears to be one of the Vosper Thorneycroft Mk 10S frigates of the Brazilian Navy. If so, this is the Branik system.*

*Inset far right: RN Ikara specialists have already clipped the wings and fin on this round before it has reached the launcher; there are several handling systems.*

# FRANCE

## Malafon

Developed from 1956 by Société Industrielle d'Aviation Latécoere, this is a command-guided glider carrying an ASW homing torpedo and boosted to high speed (516 mph, 830 km/h) by two SNPE Vénus solid rocket motors. By 1959 there had been 15 test flights from ground launchers at the Ile du Lévant and the trials vessel *Ile d'Oléron*, and six drops from aircraft. In 1962 guided flights began from the ASW escort *La Galissonnière* and the system has been further refined since. Early missiles had three fins, but production Lat-233 Malafon Mq 2 has two larger fins. The launch is towards the updated submarine contact, the missile thereafter coasting on radar altimeter at a height of 328 ft (100 m), steered by radio command via the two variable-incidence wings, while tracked optically (the wing tips contain flares). At a position 2,625 ft (800 m) short of the latest predicted target position a command signal streams a braking parachute. The torpedo, usually the Alcatel L4 of 1,190 lb (540 kg), separates forwards by its own inertia and falls into the water, thereafter homing acoustically. At least 18 ships have this system, and with some 370 updated missiles in use a further batch is being built.

**Dimensions:** Length 20 ft 2 in (6·15 m); diameter 25·6 in (650 mm); span 10 ft 10 in (3·3 m).
**Launch weight:** 3,197 lb (1450 kg).
**Range:** 8 miles (13 km).

*Main picture below: Excellent launch view of Malafon Mq 2; no information on ship platform or date. Installed aboard two Suffren, three Tourville, three Georges Leygues and five Surcouf class destroyers and frigate Aconit.*

*Inset below: Malafon Mq 2 on unidentified destroyer.*

# NORWAY

## Terne

Unguided in flight, this rocket-assisted depth charge is often given the status of a missile. Terne III can fire six rounds in 5 sec to a range of about 1·9 miles (3 km).

**Below: *Terne III is normally part of a sonar/computer ship system with a magazine housing* six six-missile salvoes. With a good crew it takes 40 sec to load a fresh salvo.**

# USSR

## Soviet systems

Though the Soviet Union has a vast array of torpedoes and ASW rocket launchers, little is known (in December 1978) of its ASW missile systems. The *Moskva* and *Leningrad* ASW cruisers each have a large twin launcher on the foredeck whose projectiles had not, at the time of writing, been seen in the West. The main ASW missile, thought to be fired from this launcher and possibly also from the "SS-N-10" tubes of all the latest cruisers, is called SS-N-14 by the DoD. It is believed to be a winged drone carrying an ASW torpedo or nuclear depth charge to a range of about 23 miles (37 km). An even blinder guess is an ASW rocket, called FRAS-1, said to have a range with nuclear warhead of 18·6 miles (30 km). Yet another ASW weapon that appears to be little more than supposition is SS-N-15, a high-speed missile fired from Victor-class nuclear attack submarines and credited with a range against hostile submarines of 24·8 miles (40 km).

**Below: Krivak *destroyer seen by RAF in 1974 showing SS-N-10 tubes and 12-barrel ASW units.***

# USA

## RAT

This Rocket-Assisted Torpedo (RAT) was an early member of the ballistic delivery systems with very limited range. In fact, when NOTS were developing it, they had to build in a new safety system to ensure that, in the event of the Mk 41 homing torpedo entering the water facing toward the parent vessel, it would not home on the latter. Rat comprised a shipboard ASW sensing and launcher aiming system, a launcher modified from a 5 in gun mount, and a simple propulsion system comprising an Allegany Ballistics Lab solid rocket and associated structure and stabilizing aerodynamic surfaces. Flight was unguided after launch, and at a programmed or radio-commanded point a braking parachute was deployed, followed by a second larger canopy. The airframe was jettisoned and the torpedo entered the water almost vertically. The system was cancelled at the production stage in January 1959.

**Dimensions:** Length (with torpedo) 13 ft 6 in (4·1 m); diameter 15·0 in (381 mm).
**Launch weight:** not including 1,250 lb (567 kg) torpedo, 480 lb (218 kg).
**Range:** 5 miles (8 km).

**Below: *RAT firing from large surface ship, apparently cruiser of* Baltimore *class. RAT was smaller than its successor Asroc (see page 258).***

(see page 258)

# Petrel

The prolonged research accomplished with such vehicles as Kingfisher and the Martin KDM Plover had by 1952 resulted in a firm basis of knowledge for the design of an air-launched ASW system able to put a homing torpedo into the water with fair accuracy at the very limits of radar range. The NBS designed this system as XAUM-N-2 in 1952–54 and passed it to the Fairchild Guided Missile Division at Wyandanch at the end of 1954. It was a rather large and cumbersome twin-finned vehicle, though the Fairchild J44 axial turbojet, rated at 1,000 lb (454 kg) thrust and fed by a ventral inlet, offered ample range. Petrel was carried on a large underwing pylon on the P2V Neptune, P5M Marlin, S2F Tracker and CL-28 Argus. The APA-80 radar gave semi-active homing guidance to the projecting parts of a submarine, or to a ship, and at the appropriate point the airframe was jettisoned and the payload, a Mk 13 or Mk 21 torpedo, entered the water for its own homing run on the target. In theory Petrel allowed vulnerable aircraft to attack any ship or submarine out of range of the latter's defences, but in practice it was difficult to find targets and guide the missile without coming much closer to the target than the missile's potential flight range. Petrel was deployed in some dozens in 1958, but was cancelled early in that year.

**Dimensions:** Length 24 ft 0 in (7·3 m); diameter 24·5 in (622 mm); span 13 ft 2 in (4·01 m).
**Launch weight:** 3,800 lb (1724 kg), including 2,000 lb (907 kg) torpedo.
**Range:** 20 miles (32 km) at 380 mph (612 km/h).

Above: *Petrels on P2V-6B from Naval Air Ordnance Test Stn, Chincoteague, Virginia, on 8 September 1954.*

# Grebe

This simple system was the last adopted by the US Navy in which no target-position information was furnished to a winged missile after launch. The device, prime contractor for which was Goodyear Aerospace, comprised a Mk 41 Mod 0 acoustic homing ASW torpedo carried in a rocket-propelled airframe with twin fins, elevators, ailerons on folding wings and an autopilot. Grebe was carried in a magazine of an ASW destroyer, rammed on a launcher installed on a twin 5 in 38-cal gun mount, fired at 25° on the correct azimuth and allowed to glide for a preset distance before pushing over into a dive to release the torpedo. A single ship could sustain a rate of fire of one per minute, and one minute was also the flight time from launch to maximum range. Grebe was terminated in 1956.

**Right:** *Manufacturer's three-view of Grebe, showing kinship to German air-launched missiles of World War 2.*

**Dimensions:** Length 16 ft 4½ in (5 m); diameter 21 in (533 mm); span 14 ft 0 in (4·267 m).
**Launch weight:** 2,450 lb (1111 kg), including 1,250 lb (567 kg) torpedo.
**Range:** 1,650–15,000 ft (503–4572 m) at burnout peak speed of 357 mph (574 km/h).

# Asroc

Today bearing the designation RUR-5A, this was the system which finally made sense and remained in the USN inventory, because it is an exact match between shipboard capabilities and flight-vehicle capability. The flight vehicle comprises little more than a Naval Propellant Plant tandem boost solid rocket, of 11,000 lb (4990 kg) thrust, and a parachute to lower the payload into the water at the correct point after a long ballistic trajectory. The original payload in 1955–65

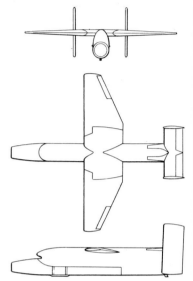

**Main picture below:** *Asroc detonation; the carrier appears to be CVS-20 Bennington, which did not carry Asroc and decommissioned in 1970.*

**Inset:** *Asroc leaves Aegis launcher.*

was the Mk 44 lightweight 12·75 in (324 mm) acoustic homing torpedo. Since 1965 it has been the deep-diving high-speed Mk 46 of the same calibre. From the start the prime contractor has been Honeywell. IOC was reached aboard the large destroyer *Norfolk* in 1960, using SQS-23 sonar. Today improved Asroc systems, using eight-box launchers for Asroc or Standard missiles in the Aegis system, are operational aboard many ships of the US Navy. In some Asroc missiles the payload is a nuclear depth charge. Foreign customer navies include Brazil, Canada, West Germany, Greece, Indonesia, Iran, Italy, Japan, Spain, Taiwan and Turkey.

**Dimensions:** Length 181 in (4·6 m); diameter 12·6 in (320 mm); span 33·25 in (845 mm).
**Launch weight:** 959 lb (435 kg).
**Range:** with Mk 46, 6·1 miles (9·9 km).

# Subroc

In 1965, when it became operational, the Chief of BuWeps described this system as "a more difficult technical problem than Polaris". Morris B. Jobe, president of Goodyear Aerospace, prime contractor, said "As the first . . . system capable of underwater launch and rocket motor ignition, guided airborne trajectory, and underwater detonation, Subroc's development called for major advances in the state of the art – and for strong management capabilities". These statements have real meaning, and reflect an extraordinary story that began in 1955 with an idea, progressing to full system development in June 1958 followed by eight years of solving problems.

Subroc (submarine rocket) was made possible by the de-velopment of submarine detection systems – in theory if not yet in practice – in the mid-1950s. The chief realization of these advances is today's Raytheon BQQ-2 integrated sonar system fitted to attack submarines (SSN). Together with radar, optical and other devices this provides the input on target future position to the Mk 113 fire-control system by Librascope division of Singer-General Precision. This has "capabilities far greater than any other fire control for undersea use" and uses a network of analog and digital computers, working in real-time, to ready a UUM-44A Subroc missile for launch on a precise trajectory. The SSN can be moving, and heading in any direction.

The chosen missile, which may have been in its launch tube for months, is fired in the normal way from a regular tube by the fire control system, which handles multiple targets and can command Subrocs and torpe-does simultaneously. Within one second of tube exit the TE-260G solid motor, by Elkton division of Thiokol, fires with the missile still horizontal. Its four jetevator nozzles then guide the missile upward to the surface; great difficulties were met with underwater hydrostatic pressure, the chilling of the water and the formation of a giant cavitation bubble which either snuffed out the rocket or interfered with trajectory control. Garrett Ai-Research provides the unique APU which feeds the missile with

hydraulic and electric power throughout its mission. Kearfott, another Singer-General Precision division, supplies the world's only inertial platform able to streak through water, sky and re-enter the water.

Even the transition from ocean to atmosphere posed problems of a kind not previously encountered. Exit angle is usually in the neighbourhood of 30°, unlike the submarine-fired ballistic missiles which are substantially vertical, and severe shock and vibrations as well as trajectory disturbances took years to overcome. Clear of the water, the Subroc quickly accelerates to supersonic speed, whilst continuously guided by the SD-510 inertial system and jetevator nozzles. At the required cutoff speed to give the correct range the propulsion is arrested; in 60 milliseconds explosive bolts release the warhead, forward-facing ports reverse the thrust of the rocket motor, and the inertial system begins to control the trajectory of the warhead by means of small aerodynamic fins. Unlike ballistic missiles, the guidance continues on the downward trajectory, which again posed new problems. Yet another new

hurdle to be overcome was re-entry to the water at supersonic speed, still under guidance and without affecting the complex safe/arm system for the nuclear warhead. The device sinks to optimum depth and is there triggered, with lethal radius of 3–5 miles (5–8 km).

Subroc was to have reached IOC with SSN 593 *Thresher*, lead ship of a new class of attack submarine tailored to the BQQ-2/ Subroc system. On 10 April 1963 *Thresher* was lost with all hands, and the first vessel to deploy Subroc was accordingly SSN 594 *Permit*, since followed by 12 further SSNs of this class, the 37 of the SSN 637 *Sturgeon* class, the new SSN 688 *Los Angeles* class and several non-standard attack submarines, the planned force numbering 75 with the Atlantic and Pacific Fleets. Each normally has six or seven missiles. Production of Subroc probably ended in 1978, but the system has been updated to meet each new threat.

**Dimensions:** Length 20 ft 6 in (6·25 m); diameter 21·0 in (533 mm).
**Launch weight:** 4,085 lb (1853 kg).
**Range:** Up to 35 miles (56·3 km).

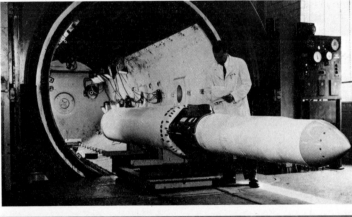

# GLOSSARY

**This glossary is intended to include all technical terms, acronyms and organizational initials (including companies) the average reader might be expected not to know nor be able readily to look up in a dictionary. It does not include national designations, such as DDG for a US Navy missile-armed destroyer, nor EM frequency bands.**

## A

**AA** Anti-aircraft.
**AAA** Anti-aircraft artillery.
**AAM** Air-to-air missile.
**AB** Airbase.
**Aberporth** The chief missile-testing and development centre of the United Kingdom, administered by the RAE, located on Cardigan Bay.
**ablative** Capable of being smoothly and slowly worn away in a hypersonic air or gas flow, as in re-entry, whilst vaporising surface material to reject waste heat energy.
**ABM** Anti-ballistic missile.
**ABMA** Army Ballistic Missile Agency (US).
**ABRV** Advanced ballistic re-entry vehicle.
**acid** Invariably means concentrated nitric acid or RFNA.
**ACMR** Air Combat Maneuvering Range of the USAF, at Yuma and other areas near Nellis AFB.
**active** Emitting its own signals, which are reflected from the target and thus enable the missile to home on a passive target by its own efforts.
**ACV** Air-cushion vehicle, often called a hovercraft or surface-effect vehicle.
**Adcom** Aerospace Defense Command (USAF).
**ADC** Air Defense Command (later Adcom).
**AEC** Atomic Energy Commission (US).
**AEG** Allgemeine Elektrizitäts Gesellschaft (German company).
**AEI** Associated Electrical Industries.
**Aerozine** Trade name for a family of rocket fuels based on hydrazine (MMH and UDMH).
**AFB** Air Force Base (US).
**AFBMD** Air Force Ballistic Missile Division (US).
**AFV** Armoured fighting vehicle (tanks, armoured cars etc).
**AI** Airborne interception, ie installed in a night or all-weather interceptor aircraft.
**AIRS** Advanced inertial reference system.
**ALBM** Air-launched ballistic missile.
**ALCM** Air-launched cruise missile.
**ALH** Active laser homing.
**AMD** Avions Marcel Dassault.
**AMF** American Machine and Foundry (US company).
**AMR** Atlantic Missile Range (US)
**AMTE** Adjusted megaton equivalent, the unit of soft-target capability.
**aneroid** Thin-walled airtight capsule whose size varies with external gas pressure (inside a barometer, altimeter or airspeed indicator).
**ANG** Air National Guard (US).
**AP** 1 Armour-piercing.
2 Ammonium perchlorate.
**APL** Applied Physics Laboratory of JHU.
**apogee** The highest point in a trajectory or orbit.
**APU** Auxiliary power unit, to provide on-board electrical/hydraulic/pneumatic power.
**ARH** 1 Anti-radiation homing (or anti-radar homing).
2 Active radar homing.
**ARM** Anti-radiation missile (or anti-radar missile).
**ASCC** Allied Standards Co-ordinating Committee, a NATO body to agree terminology and other language problems and which assigns code-names to all major Warsaw Pact hardware.
**ASM** Air-to-surface missile.
**aspect ratio** Slenderness of a wing (square of wing-span divided by area).
**A-stoff** Liquid oxygen (German).
**ASW** Anti-submarine warfare.
**ATGW** Anti-tank guided weapon.
**ATSC** Air Technical Service Command (USAAF).
**AV-MF** Soviet naval air force (for further information on WP air forces see companion volume "Soviet Air Power").
**azimuth** Bearing or direction in the horizontal plane; rotation about a vertical axis.

## B

**BAC** British Aircraft Corporation.
**BAe** British Aerospace.
**bang/bang** Control system which has only two states, on and off; thus a bang/bang control fin is either in the neutral central position or driven quickly to the limit of its travel, unlike the smoothly modulated control exerted by a pilot.
**beam rider** A vehicle equipped with a radio receiver and control system which automatically tends to keep it travelling along the centre of a coded radar beam.
**blast/fragmentation** A warhead which relies on both blast and the fragments of a thick-walled casing or rod.
**BGT** Bodenseewerk Gerätetechnik GmbH (Germany).
**blindfire** Able to operate without visually acquiring the target.
**body lift** At high supersonic speeds aerodynamic lift from a vehicle body can easily exceed the weight with enough margin for rapid manoeuvre, thus making wings unnecessary.
**booster** Propulsion imparting large thrust for a short time, to give high acceleration at the start of flight.
**Br-stoff** Aviation gasoline (petrol) or benzole (German).
**B-stoff** Hydrazine hydrate (German).
**BTH** British Thompson-Houston Co.
**BTL** Bell Telephone Laboratories (US).
**BUIC** Back-Up Interceptor Control (SAGE).
**BuOrd** Bureau of Ordnance (US Navy).
**burnout** Point at which all a rocket's propellants are consumed.
**BuWeps** Bureau of Weapons (US Navy).

## C

**canard** Air vehicle in which the auxiliary horizontal surface is ahead of the wing, ie a foreplane instead of a tailplane.
**CARDE** Canadian Armament Research and Development Establishment.
**carry trials** Flight testing of an aircraft whilst carrying a new load externally (such as a missile).
**Cassegrain optics** Use of two parabolic mirrors to magnify (concentrate) IR or optical radiation
**CEAM** Centre d'Expériences Aériennes Militaires, Mont de Marsan (France).
**CEL** Centre d'Essais des Landes (France).
**CEM** Centre d'Essais de la Méditerranée (France).
**CEP** A measure of the accuracy of missiles or other projectiles, usually rendered as "circular error probable" but better put as "circle of equal probabilities" because it is the radius of the circle in which half the shots are statistically likely to fall.
**CEV** Centre d'Essais en Vol (France).
**c.g.** Centre of gravity.
**CLOS** Command to line of sight.
**conventional** Not nuclear, ie high explosive.
**counterforce** Directed against enemy weapons, especially strategic weapons.
**countervalue** Directed against enemy society, eg cities.
**cropped-tip** Aerodynamic surface, such as a wing or fin, whose tip is cut off at the Mach angle (the angle of shockwaves at the supersonic vehicle's Mach number).
**cruise missile** One that flies for long distances whilst supported by a wing or body lift (see ASM Strategic introduction).
**cryogenic** Kept at very low temperature, eg liquefied gases.
**CS** Cassegrain system.
**CSD** Chemical Systems Division (US).
**C-stoff** A prepared fuel consisting mainly of methanol, with 30% hydrazine hydrate, 13% water and a little additive (Germany).
**CTPB** Carboxy-terminated polybutadiene, a rocket propellant.
**cutoff** Point at which a rocket is shut down, with some propellant remaining unburned.
**CW** Continuous-wave, as distinct from pulse radiation.

## D

**DA** Direct-action fuze, ie triggered by impact.
**darkfire** Capable of operating at night, but not necessarily in bad weather.
**DARPA** Defense Advanced Research Projects Agency (DoD).
**DB** Double-base rocket propellant.
**DEFA** Direction des Etudes et Fabrications d'Armement (France).
**depressed trajectory** Ballistic-missile trajectory modified to minimise detection by defending radar, at expense of reduced range.
**designator** An illuminator, usually a laser, that makes a target a source of radiation.
**D/F** Direction-finding by radio.
**DFS** Deutsche Forschungsanstalt für Segelflugzeug (German sailplane research).
**differential tracker** A radar that can simultaneously measure the angular difference between two targets (eg a missile and its intended target) and thus provide information for a guidance system that eliminates this difference.
**differential controls** Some control surfaces can move in unison, to steer a missile, or differentially (in opposite directions on opposite sides of the body) to roll it, or to check a tendency to roll.
**dihedral** Angle at which wings or other surfaces slope up from root to tip.
**DMA** Délégation Ministérielle pour l'Armement (France).
**DME** Distance measuring equipment, a radio navaid.
**DoD** Department of Defense (US).
**doppler radar** Radar whose operation depends on the apparent change of frequency caused by relative velocity between the radar and the target.
**DTCN** Direction Technique de Constructions Navales (France).
**DTE** Direction Technique des Engins (France).
**dual-thrust** Rocket which starts operating at high (boost) thrust and then operates for prolonged period at low (sustain) thrust.
**DVK** Deutsche Versuchsanstalt für Kraftfahrtzeug und Fahrtzeugmotoren (Germany).

## E

**EAT** Electronic-angle tracking.
**ECCM** Electronic counter-counter measures.
**ECM** Electronic countermeasures.
**EM** Electromagnetic; EM radiation includes (in order of increasing wavelength) light, microwaves for radars and communications, longer wavelengths for radio, and IR (heat).
**engin** French for missile or other pilotless vehicle.
**EO** Electro-optical, guidance involving visible light and usually of a TV nature.
**error signal** An electrical signal whose characteristic, such as voltage, amplitude, frequency, coding or other quality, varies directly with departure of the missile from a desired trajectory.
**ESM** Electronic support (or surveillance) measures.

## F

**FA** Frontal aviation; ie tactical air force (USSR).
**FAE** Fuel/air explosive.
**FAMG** Field Artillery Missile Group (US Army).
**FBM** Fleet Ballistic Missile, thus FBMS is Fleet Ballistic Missile System (US Navy).
**FFAR** Folding-fin aircraft rocket; sometimes rendered as free-flight air-to-air rocket.
**FLIR** Forward-looking infra-red.
**FOBS** Fractional-orbit bombardment system, warhead delivered from partial satellite orbit and thus approaching from any direction.
**FPB** Fast patrol boat.
**frequency-agile** Radio or radar whose operating frequency automatically hops and jumps in seemingly random manner to confuse the enemy, or which can be positively controlled according to a prior programme.
**fully active** Active.

## G

**g** Acceleration due to gravity, multiplied in manoeuvres.
**GaAs** Gallium arsenide, a light-emitting semiconductor.
**GAPA** Ground-to-air pilotless aircraft.
**gathering** The phase just after launch of a beam-rider or other missile which has to be gathered into a narrow radar beam or optical LOS.
**GCI** Ground control of interception.
**GD** General Dynamics Corporation (US).
**GE** General Electric Company (US).
**GFE** Government-furnished equipment (US).
**GIAT** Groupement Industriel des Armements Terrestres (France).
**GIE** Groupement d'Interêt Economique, an industrial consortium formed from several companies with a common interest.
**gimballed** Mounted on pivots so that it can tilt in any direction.
**GLCM** Ground-launched cruise missile.
**glint** Continual erratic changes in the apparent radar centre of a target, fluctuating between the major reflective areas and often momentarily going off the target altogether.
**GMS** Groupement des Missiles Stratégiques.
**GO** Gaseous oxygen (sometimes gox).
**goniometer** An instrument for measuring angles, used in direction-finding.
**GP** General-purpose (bomb).
**GRP** Glass-reinforced plastics.
**GSE** Ground-support equipment, ie the hardware needed to keep a weapon system functioning.
**GW** Guided weapon.
**GWS** Guided Weapon System (Royal Navy).

## H

**hardness** The ability of a target to resist explosions (usually nuclear), and their effects of overpressure, heat, radiation, EM pulse and ground shock. The loose expression "hard" merely means armoured or buried behind concrete.
**HE** High explosive.
**HEAT** High-explosive anti-tank.
**HESH** High-explosive squash head, anti-armour warhead which instead of penetrating the armour detonates on the outside with such violence that pieces of armour are "spalled" off the inner face.
**HFR** Height-finder radar.
**Hi** High, ie at around 30,000 ft (9100 m) or above, for fuel economy.
**Hidyne** Fuel more powerful than alcohol/water comprising 60% UDMH and 40% diethylene-triamine.
**hollow-charge** See shaped-charge.
**homing** Automatically flying towards a target.
**HSD** Hawker Siddeley Dynamics.
**HSM** Hard-structure munition.
**HTP** High-test peroxide, hydrogen peroxide undiluted by water.
**HTPB** Hydroxy-terminated polybutadiene, rocket propellant.
**hypergolic** Igniting spontaneously when two products are brought into contact.
**hypersonic** Speed much higher than that of sound, ie Mach 4 or above.
**Hz** Hertz, cycles per second.

## I

**IAS** Indicated airspeed, which for any given speed falls off as height is increased.
**ICBM** Intercontinental ballistic missile.
**IFF** Identification friend or foe.
**IIR** Imaging infra-red
**ILS** Instrument landing system, radio aid for winged aircraft.
**impulse** Total propulsion energy imparted by a rocket, average thrust multiplied by operating time in seconds.
**InSb** Indium antimonide, a sensitive IR detector.
**interferometer** Device for measuring with individual wavelengths, thus a radar can be constructed with receiver aerials sensitive to successive pulses or CW peaks.
**IOC** Initial operational capability, agreed date when a weapon system can be considered capable of being used by troops even though still not fully developed and troops not fully trained.
**IR** Infra-red, ie heat.
**IRAN** Inspect and repair as necessary.
**IRBM** Intermediate-range ballistic missile (range in the order of 1,500 nautical miles, 1,727 miles, 2780 km).
**IRCM** Infra-red countermeasures.
**IRTH** Infra-red terminal homing, ie IR homing only when close to the target.
**ITT** International Telephone and Telegraph Corporation (US).

## J

**JASDF** Japan Air Self-Defence Force.
**JATO** Jet-assisted take-off (actually means boost by rocket).
**JCS** Joint Chiefs of Staff (US).
**JDA** Japan Defence Agency.
**jetevator** Mechanical device for deflecting jet from a rocket or other jet engine.
**JGSDF** Japan Ground Self-Defence Force.
**JHU** Johns Hopkins University.
**JMSDF** Japan Maritime Self-Defence Force.
**JP-4** Common military aviation turbine fuel, a wide-range distillate.
**JPL** Jet Propulsion Laboratory of Caltech (US).

## K

**kinetheodolite** Tracking instrument comprising special high-speed camera whose angular position (in azimuth and elevation) is always precisely known.
**KMR** Kwajalein Missile Range, in mid-Pacific.
**KSC** Kennedy Space Center, NASA, (USA).
**kT** Kiloton, ie explosive yield equivalent to 1000 tonnes of TNT.

## L

**LCC** Launch control centre.
**LCP** Launch control post.
**LFA** Luftfahrtforschungsanstalt, flight research institute (Germany).
**LGB** Laser-guided bomb.
**Llanbedr** Airfield associated with Aberporth.
**LLLTV** Low-light-level television.
**LMSC** Lockheed Missiles & Space Company (US).
**lo** Low, ie flight at minimum safe height to avoid the ground.
**lock-on** Ability of certain tracking systems, either radar, IR or optical, to search for a target and, having found one, to cease search and instead continuously track that target.
**look-down** Ability of certain radars to detect and track targets flying at lo level despite the fact the ground is so close behind them when seen from hi.
**LOS** Line of sight.
**lox** Liquid oxygen.
**LRBM** Long-range ballistic missile.
**LSI** Large-scale integration (microelectronics technique).

## M

**MAP** Ministry of Aircraft Production (UK).
**MAR** Multi-function array radar.
**maraging** Family of high-strength steels.
**Marv** Programme for manoeuvrable re-entry vehicles (US).
**MDAC** McDonnell Douglas Astronautics Company (US).
**$MgF_2$** Magnesium fluoride, thermally transparent material.
**mid-course** Over most of a missile's flight, ie all except the launch (including gathering if applicable) and terminal phases.
**MIRV** Manoeuvrable independently targeted re-entry vehicle.
**MIT** Massachusetts Institute of Technology.
**MMH** Monomethylhydrazine, rocket fuel.
**MoD** Ministry of Defence.
**monocoque** Single-shell construction, as a lobster claw.
**monopulse** Radar technique in which four overlapping beams (two azimuth, two elevation) give zero output voltage for a target exactly in the centre.
**MoS** Ministry of Supply (UK).
**moving wings** Left and right wings pivoted independently so that they can be driven in unison to command the vehicle in pitch and differentially to command in roll.
**MRBM** Medium-range ballistic missile.
**MRV** Multiple re-entry vehicles.
**MSDS** Marconi Space & Defence Systems (UK).
**M-stoff** Methanol (Germany).
**MT** Megaton, ie explosive yield equivalent to 1,000,000 tonnes TNT.
**MTE** Unit of area destruction, defined as that caused by a 1 MT weapon.
**MTI** Moving-target indication, ie radar can make moving targets stand out and can erase the fixed background.
**MTR** Missile-tracking radar.
**MW** Megawatts (millions of watts).

## N

**$N_2O_4$** Nitrogen tetroxide, rocket propellant.
**NBS** National Bureau of Standards (US).
**Nc** Nitrocellulose.
**Nd** Neodymium, element used in certain solid-state lasers.
**NDRC** National Defense Research Committee (US).
**Ng** Nitroglycerine.
**n.m.** Nautical mile, about 1·15 miles, 1·85 km.
**NOTS** Naval Ordnance Test Station (US).
**NWC** Naval Weapons Center (US).

## O

**Oboe** An area-coverage radio navaid.
**offset** 1 Built-in inaccuracy in missile testing to achieve results with reduced expenditure on targets.
2 Industrial work offered as inducement to a country to buy particular defence hardware (need not be on the programme bought).
**on-mounted** Mounted on a surveillance radar and rotating with its aerial.
**orthicon** Various forms of TV camera.
**OTH** Over the horizon, ie not subject to LOS limitations as are all other radars and optical systems.
**overpressure** Peak positive and negative pressures experienced at a particular place from a particular nuclear explosion.
**oxidant** Constituent of rocket propellant, or in liquid rockets supplied as separate fluid, to provide oxygen for combustion of the fuel.

## P

**passive** Not itself emitting, eg the human eye sees but is passive.
**Patrick AFB** US Air Force Base at head of the AMR, geographically same as Cape Canaveral/KSC.
**payload** Total mass of warhead and associated arming, fuzing and safety systems, penaids and other devices to be transported to target.
**PBAA** Polybutadiene acrylic acid, rocket propellant.
**PBCS** Post-boost control system.
**PBPS** Post-boost propulsion system.
**PbS** Lead sulphide, a compound sensitive to IR.
**PD** Pulse-doppler.
**penaid** Penetration aid, anything to confuse, decoy or dilute the enemy defences, to assist delivery of a warhead to its target.
**performance envelope** Limiting boundaries of air-vehicle flight performance, in terms of Mach number (plotted horizontally) and altitude (vertically).
**pitch** In this book usual meaning is rotation nose-up or -down about the transverse axis, ie to climb or dive.
**pitot** Ram pressure sensed by an open-ended tube pointing forwards.
**PMR** Pacific Missile Range
**PMTC** Point Mugu Test Center.
**Point Mugu, California,** US Navy missile test centre.
**pps** Pulses per second.
**PRC** Peoples Republic of China.
**PRF** Pulse repetition frequency.
**prime** The industrial contractor charged with development of a complete weapon system, with power to subcontract to others.
**profile** Trajectory of a flight vehicle in the vertical plane
**propellants** Substances which burn to provide rocket thrust; in a liquid rocket there are usually two, kept separate until the moment of combustion.
**PU** Polyurethane, rocket propellant.
**pulsejet** Air-breathing jet engine in which combustion is a succession of discrete explosions.
**pulse radiation** Not CW, but a succession of very brief bursts of RF energy.
**PVO** Air defence of the homeland (USSR).

## R

**radio command** Human steering via a radio link.
**RAE** Royal Aircraft Establishment (UK).
**RAF** Royal Air Force.
The PRC (Peoples Republic of China) has not disclosed the designations of its weapons.
**ramjet** Air-breathing jet engine in which compression is effected entirely by the profile of the interior of the air duct and the high speed of the vehicle, combustion being continuous.
**ram-rocket** Propulsion system which at launch is a solid rocket but which, when the propellant has been consumed, transforms itself into a ramjet, drawing on a different fuel supply.
**range** 1 Maximum distance a vehicle can fly with full payload.
2 Designated area where missiles can be safely flight-tested.
**RARDE** Royal Armament Research & Development Establishment, Fort Halstead.
**rate** Rate of change of a variable rather than the variable itself.
**RCA** Radio Corporation of America.
**RCAF** Royal Canadian Air Force.
**R&D** Research and development.
**RDT&E** Research, development, test and engineering.
**reaction time** Minimum time taken for a system to fire, measured from first detecting a target or receiving a launch instruction.
**re-entry** ICBM RVs have to rise into the space beyond the atmosphere and then plunge back into the atmosphere at hypersonic speed, without burning up through friction and kinetic heating.
**refractory** Designed to retain strength at very high temperatures.
**REME** Royal Electrical and Mechanical Engineers (British Army).
**RF** Radio frequencies.
**RFC** Royal Flying Corps.
**RFNA** Red fuming nitric acid, concentrated acid plus about 13% $N_2O_4$ to suppress decomposition (some rockets burn IRFNA, the I signifying "inhibited", a trace of hydrogen fluoride being added to form a skin on the tankage to protect it against corrosion).
**RFP** Request for proposals.
**RHB** Radio homing beacon.
**RLM** Reichsluftfahrtministerium, air ministry (Germany).
**RN** Royal Navy
**roll** Rotation about the longitudinal axis (in an ICBM at launch this axis is vertical, in a cruise missile horizontal).
**roll-stabilized** Prevented from rolling, except to bank in a turn.
**RP-1** Rocket Propellant No 1, kerosene-type fuel.
**RPE** Rocket Propulsion Establishment (UK).
**RPV** Remotely piloted vehicle, ie the human pilot does not ride on board but is in another aircraft or on the ground.
**RRE** Royal Radar Establishment (UK).
**R-stoff** Rocket fuel comprising mixture of xylidine and triethylamine.
**RV** Re-entry vehicle.
**RVSN** Strategic rocket forces (USSR).

## S

**sabot** Attachment, usually arranged to come apart into sections, to guide a projectile along the bore of a gun launcher.
**SAC** Strategic Air Command (USAF).
**Saclos** Semi-automatic command to LOS.
**SAGE** Semi-automatic ground environment (US defence system for alerting and controlling SAMs and interceptors).
**SAGEM** Société d'Applications Générales d'Electricité et de Mécanique.
**SAGW** Surface-to-air guided weapon.
**SAH** Semi-active homing.
**Salbei** SV-stoff.
**SALT** Strategic Arms Limitation Talks.
**SAM** Surface-to-air missile.
**SAMSO** Space and Missile Systems Organization (USAF).
**SAR** Semi-active radar.
**SARH** SAR homing.
**SAT** Société Anonyme de Télécommunications (France).
**semi-active** Homing on radiation reflected or scattered off the target but originally sent out by an illuminator not flying with the missile.
**SEP** Société Européenne de Propulsion (France), formerly SEPR, Société Européenne de Propulsion par Réaction.
**SEREB** Société pour l'Etude et la Réalisation d'Engins Balistiques (France).
**SFECMAS** Société Francaise d'Etudes et de Constructions de Matériels Aéronautique Spéciaux.
**SFENA** Société Francaise d'Equipements pour la Navigation Aérienne.
**shaped charge** Warhead whose forward face has the form of a deep re-entrant cone; upon exploding, this directs a jet of gas and vaporized metal forwards at such speed that it penetrates thick armour
**shaping** Electronically processing guidance signals to ease the problem of accurate human guidance without overcontrol.
**signature** The characteristic fine detail of any emitter—a hostile radar, aircraft, RV or surface target—analysed into precise frequencies, PRFs, amplitude modulation and other variables, to give a result that positively identifies the emitter and which is needed to design effective ECM or detection systems.
**SLBM** Submarine-launched ballistic missile.
**SLCM** Surface-launched cruise missile.
**smart** Possessed of precision guidance, especially of tactical ASMs when contrasted with "iron bombs" (colloquial term for unguided GP bombs).
**SMS** Strategic Missile Squadron (USAF).
**SNECMA** Société Nationale d'Etude et de Construction de Moteurs d'Aviation.
**SNLE** Sous-marin Nucléaire Lance-Engins (French for missile-firing nuclear submarine).
**SNPE** Société Nationale des Poudres et Explosifs.
**soft** Not hard, ie a normal surface target unprotected against attack.
**solid** Rocket propellant cast or extruded in a solid or semi-plastic form which is burned in situ inside its case, contrasted with a liquid rocket whose propellants are fed through pipes to a combustion chamber.
**solid-state** Electronics based wholly upon semiconductor technology, eliminating vacuum tubes (thermionic valves).
**specific impulse** A measure of rocket performance, defined as the thrust obtained per unit consumption of total propellants (eg thrust in kilograms for consumption of 1 kg/sec).
**spin-stabilized** Unguided but kept pointing towards the target by spinning at high speed.
**spoiler** Aerodynamic control surface in the form of a small plate presented more or less square-on to the airstream, causing high drag and possibly loss of lift (in missiles usually bang-bang controls which are retracted out of the airstream when in the neutral position).
**squint angle** Maximum angle from the missile central axis at which a homing head can acquire and lock-on to a target.
**SRBM** Short-range ballistic missile.
**SSKP** Single-shot kill probability.
**SSM** Surface-to-surface missile.
**S-stoff** Nitric acid (Germany).
**stand-off** 1 The distance from a target at which an aircraft can release an ASM.
2 The distance from the surface of the armour at which a shaped charge should ideally be detonated, which anti-tank missiles seek to achieve by their nose and fuze design.
**STOL** Short take-off and landing.
**strapdown** Simplified inertial guidance dispensing with the triple-gimbal stable platform necessary for the longer-time flights of manned aircraft.
**sustainer** Propulsion for a protracted period, operative after the boost or launch phase.
**SV-stoff** So-called "mixed acids", typically 95% RFNA and 5% sulphuric.

## T

**TAS** True airspeed.
**TCA** Télécommand automatique, Saclos.
**telemetry** Sending measured data from a vehicle by radio or other means.
**Tercom** Terrain comparison.
**terminal** The final near-target phase of flight.
**TGSM** Terminally guided sub-munition.
**thermionic valve** Traditional radio valve whose electrons move in free space (called a vacuum tube in North America).
**throw-weight** Aggregate payload of a ballistic missile.
**TI** In this book, refers to Texas Instruments Inc.
**TIR** Target-illuminating radar.
**TIS** Thermal-imaging system.
**Tonka** R-stoff.
**tracking** Automatically or manually following a target or missile by optical, radar or other means.
**T-stoff** HTP with a little oxyquinoline (Germany).
**TT** Tous-temps (all-weather).
**TTR** Target tracking radar.
**TV** Television.
**TVC** Thrust-vector control, deflecting or orientating thrust to control vehicle trajectory.
**twist and steer** Using no controls other than left/right moving wings which first roll to the desired bank angle and then pull in unison to change heading.
**two-pulse** Rocket comprised of boost and sustainer or, more often, two sustainer charges fired individually in succession.
**TWS** Track while scan (radar).

## U

**UDMH** Unsymmetrical dimethylhydrazine.
**UHF** Ultra-high frequency.
**USA** In this book, United States Army.
**USAAF** US Army Air Force.
**USAF** US Air Force.
**USMC** US Marine Corps.
**USN** US Navy.

## V

**vernier** Final fine adjustment, eg a small rocket used to trim final cutoff velocity of an ICBM to achieve correct range.
**VfR** Verein für Raumschiffahrt, society for spaceship travel (Germany).
**VHF** Very high frequency.
**video** TV, especially the transmitted signal.
**vidicon** TV camera.
**visol** Butyl ether with about 15% aniline, used with Salbei (Germany).
**VVS** Air force (USSR).

## W

**Wagner bar** Patented spoiler-type control with bang-bang operation.
**WDD** Western Development Division (USAF).
**wire guided** Guided by electrical signals transmitted through (usually two) extremely fine insulated wires connecting vehicle and source of guidance commands.
**Woomera** Main place-name associated with WRE (Aboriginal, spear-thrower).
**WP** Warsaw Pact.
**WRE** Weapons Research Establishment (Australia).
**WS** Weapon System.
**WSMR** White Sands Missile Range, New Mexico.

## Y

**YAG** Yttrium-aluminium garnet.
**yaw** Rotation of vehicle about vertical axis, ie to different azimuth.
**yield** Explosive power, especially of nuclear device, expressed in kT or MT.

## Z

**Z-stoff** Aqueous solution of calcium (rarely sodium) permanganate.
**ZAR** Zeus acquisition radar.

# MISSILE DESIGNATIONS

## CHINA

The PRC (People s Republic of China) has not disclosed the designations of its weapons. NATO and the DoD assign "reporting numbers" similar to those for Russian weapons but prefaced by a C. Thus, CSS-1 is the first identified Chinese land-based SSM.

## GERMANY

Most of the Luftwaffe missiles were given RLM "8-series" numbers as were piloted aircraft. There were many exceptions, such as the FX 1400 and the Hs 117 (117 already being assigned to a Heinkel aircraft). Army missiles had no designation scheme.

## USSR

The Union of Soviet Socialist Republics assigns complex designations to all its military hardware, as well as occasional popular names. All evidence indicates that the designations fit into large and detailed patterns, but few of the true designations are publicly known. Accordingly the DoD assigns "reporting numbers" which are pure invention; thus, SS-N-3 means the third identified Russian naval SSM. Likewise NATO's ASCC assigns "reporting names" whose initial letter gives a clue to the mission; thus, names beginning with A are AAMs, G are SAMs, K are ASMs and S are SSMs.

## UK

The United Kingdom began in World War 2 by assigning simple names, such as Stooge and Brakemine. In 1949 the colour code was started, in which all new missiles, radars and certain other classified defence items were assigned code names with a colour followed by a (more or less appropriate) name. Though many have sought a system in this the choices were in fact random, and often had "in" jokes concealed in a harmless exterior. Missile colours included Red, Blue, Green, Orange and Pink, with test vehicles and radars adding Black, White, Purple, Indigo and several other hues.

In 1962 this system was replaced by letter/number codes generated by a random-number programme. There are two letters followed by three numerals. Weapons selected for production are usually then given a single popular name.

## USA

The United States assigned more than 70 missiles and test vehicles to its wartime scheme in which designations for the Army and Navy were totally dissimilar. Uniquely, the Navy letter code included one letter to identify the manufacturer or design authority. Air Force designations, from 1948, treated missiles as "fighters" or "bombers" depending on whether they were for use against aircraft or surface targets. Thus the Matador pilotless bomber was designated XB-61, and the Falcon AAM XF-98.

In 1949 an attempt at uniformity was made by the Army/Navy staff who promulgated a system in which all missiles were assigned letter/number codes indicating the mission. Thus SSM-A-3 meant the third type of Army surface-to-surface missile, while XAUM-N-2 meant the second type of Navy air-to-underwater missile, still in experimental status. As well as X (experimental), Y was assigned as a prefix for service-test and Z for obsolete, but seldom used. In addition, Army weapons authorised for service were assigned Ordnance numbers, such as M8 or XM9. Almost always a name was assigned as well, by all services.

In February 1955 the Air Force introduced its own nomenclature for missiles, henceforth reserving aircraft-type designations for manned vehicles. Surface launched missiles were given designations TM (tactical missile), SM (strategic) or IM (interceptor), sometimes prefaced by X or Y or two new prefixes, U (training) or H (hardened). Air-launched missiles became AGM (air-to-ground missile), AGR (air-to-ground unguided rocket), GAM (air-to-air missile) and GAR (air-to-air unguided rocket), the training prefix in this case being T.

In 1962 the DoD at last introduced a completely uniform system for all US armed services. Missiles normally have three-letter codes with the following meaning: first letter, A air-launched, B launched from more than one environment, C "coffin", F fired by infantry, H silo stored but launched at ground level, L silo launched, M mobile, P soft pad, R ship, and U underwater-launched; middle letter, D decoy, E special electronic, G surface attack, I aerial intercept, Q drone RPV, T training, U underwater attack, and W weather; third letter, M guided missile, N probe, and R unguided rocket. This system is still in use.

# INDEX